Annual Index

to

POPULAR MUSIC RECORD REVIEWS 1976

by
Dean Tudor
Linda Biesenthal
Nancy Tudor

The Scarecrow Press, Inc.
Metuchen, N.J. & London
1977

Library of Congress Catalog Card No. 73-8909

ISBN 0-8108-1070-0

TABLE OF CONTENTS

INTRODUCTION

We continue to believe that the modern library has a major responsibility in preserving the American and international musical tradition in popular music. We likewise believe that popular recorded music should be widely available in all types of libraries. This reference work, then, is to aid in the selection of records for these collections.

This book is primarily an index to record reviews. It can be used to find particular reviews and/or be used as a record selection tool based on the evaluations given by the reviews themselves. We have not listed certain data because of a lack of space and time. This year's index offers citations to 5586 individual records; in the 1975 volume, 5084 were cited. The total number of reviews indexed for 1976 decreased to 12,346 from last year's 12,678. We hope to offer a comprehensive index to popular recorded music by continually reevaluating our sources and the popular music media.

The responsibilities for the general preparation, editorial work, and comments have been shared by the co-compilers.

Dean Tudor
Linda Biesenthal
Nancy Tudor

March 17, 1977

v

EXPLANATION OF THE FORMAT

This index to record reviews has 11 sections arranged according to musical form: rock; mood--pop; country; old time music and bluegrass; folk; jazz; blues; soul, reggae and salsa; popular religious; show; and "anthologies and concerts." Within each section the arrangement is alphabetical by artist. Each record is numbered for easy reference and for retrieval by use of the Artist Index.

The discographic information is displayed as follows:

Number. ARTIST [surname inverted]. Album Title. Label and Serial Number (number of discs per set). Reel-to-Reel Tape Serial Number. Four Track Cartridge Serial Number. Eight Track Cassette Serial Number. (Country of Origin [if not U.S.]). (Reissued Release).

The review information is displayed as follows:

Periodical abbreviation. Month or number of issue numerically expressed as "month-day" or "month/month." Page citation. Number of words in review [rounded to nearest 25]. Reviewer's evaluation.

Anthologies and concerts are entered in the last section under their common name or titles.

Notes

Evaluation: A scale of 0 to 5 has been used to rate the opinions of each record reviewer. This is a simple numerical translation. This should indicate to the user the general evaluation of any single review or group of reviews. Bear in mind the importance of the specialist magazines. "0" means a completely poor production. (In some cases the reviewer so thoroughly rejected an album that the compilers of this Index could have assigned a -5 to several reviews.) "$2\frac{1}{2}$" is either a review that is non-critical and descriptive, or a review where the pros and cons of a release appear to balance out. And "5" is a superb recording--an ultimate release. There were very few of these awarded. These numerical evaluation translations were based on both the compilers' experiences and the terms of reference under which the reviewer works. By the latter is meant the non-musical concern of the reviewer. For instance, the music may be worthwhile, but a particular album may be downgraded in the eyes of reviewers for any number of reasons: poor pressing, poor recording qualities, derivative stylings, excessive duplication among previous reissues, poor packaging, lack of liner notes, and so forth--all non-musical. It is important to bear in mind that only the reviews are numerically translated, not the record nor the music itself. In certain cases, the compilers have strongly disagreed with the reviewer, but that has not affected their numerical evaluation of the review itself. No review of less than 25 words is included here.

Tapes: Tape numbers for Reel-to-Reel, Cartridges, and Cassettes were given only where known or available to Schwann or Harrison. The absence of a tape number does not mean that a tape is not available for a particular release since often record companies issue the tape versions somewhat later than the discs. The compilers have not listed tape information for foreign records, nor for quadraphonic sound as this latter is still in flux. Note that most tapes bear the same serial number as the phonodisc.

Country of Origin: This is not given when there is also an American release; the comparable initial foreign release is not given as the disc will be available in the United States. The exception has been made for deleted domestic offerings or reissued material. "(E)" stands for a release from the British Isles; all other countries have their names spelled out. Prices in foreign currency are not given for foreign releases because of the changeable international monetary situation and differences in tax and excise applicability (both domestic and foreign) for libraries.

Show Music: Immediately following the entry by title, the

user is informed of the composer, the lyricist, and the arranger, where such information is known. After the basic discographical information but before the review citations, the source of the performance is given (e.g., Original Film Soundtrack, or Original London Cast).

More Than One Artist: The compilers have not analyzed each record to pull out the major artists. Apart from the evaluative nature of such an effort (calling for judgment) the sheer numbers cannot be coped with. However, two aspects were noted:

ARTIST and ARTIST: This means that the two perform together on the release, and have been given equal billing by the record company.

ARTIST/ARTIST: This means that there are two artists who are not performing together. Usually, one side is devoted to one artist, and the flip side is devoted to the other.

These secondary artist entries have been indexed in the Artist Index (along with prominent performers from the Show category).

Abbreviation List

ARG	American Record Guide	DB	Down Beat
AU	Audio	EDS	English Dance and Song
BGU	Bluegrass Unlimited	ETH	Ethnomusicology
BM	Black Music	FO	Footnote
BS	Black Stars	FR	Folk Review
BU	Blues Unlimited	GP	Guitar Player
CAC	Cassettes and Cartridges	GR/GRA	Gramophone
CAD	Cadence	HF	High Fidelity
CC	Canadian Composer	JEMF	John Edwards Memorial
CIR	Circus		Foundation Quarterly
CK	Contemporary Keyboard	JF	Jazz Forum
CM	Country Music	JJ	Jazz Journal
CMP	Country Music People	JM	Jazz Magazine
CMR	Country Music Review	JR	Jazz Report
CO	Coda	LB	Living Blues
CR	Consumer Reports	LP	Listening Post
CRA	Crawdaddy	MH	Modern Hi-Fi and Music
CRE	Creem	MJ	Music Journal
CS	Country Style	MM	Melody Maker
CYR	Country Rambler	MN	Muleskinner News
CZM	Crazy Music	MR	Mississippi Rag

OLR	Ontario Library Review	RR	Records and Recording
OTM	Old Time Music	RRE	Record Review
PIC	Pickin'	RS	Rolling Stone
PMS	Popular Music and Society	SO	Sing Out
PRM	Phonograph Record Maga-zine	SOU	Sound
		SR	Stereo Review
RA	Ragtimer	ST	Storyville
RFJ	Radio Free Jazz	TB	Talking Blues
RM	Record Month	TM	Traditional Music
RO	Rock	WHO	Who Put the Bomp

THE PERIODICALS INDEXED

The totals of reviews refer to popular music records only. The addresses are mainly for placing subscriptions; in many cases, the Editorial Offices are located elsewhere. In all, 12,346 reviews were indexed from 60 magazines. Prices quoted are in American dollars, and are the prices for overseas subscriptions in the case of British publications. The magazines added for this year are:

American Record Guide
Cadence
Country Style
Crazy Music
Footnote
Jazz Forum
Jazz Magazine
John Edwards Memorial
   Foundation Quarterly

Phonograph Record Magazine
Radio Free Jazz
Record Month
Record Review
Rock
Talking Blues
Traditional Music
Who Put the Bomp

Dropped for a variety of reasons (cessations, mergers, slowness in arrival, change of policy, etc.) are: Beetle, Blues Is..., Blues Link, Circus Raves, Different Drummer, Flipside, Folk Music Journal, Jazz New England, Journal of American Folklore, New York Times (Sunday Edition), Previews, Record Exchanger, Rock, Hi-Fi News and Record Review, Modern Recording, Music Canada Quarterly, New Musical Express, Pop Top, Shout, Stereo Guide, Whiskey, Women and..., Zoo World.

AMERICAN RECORD GUIDE. [new series] 1976-   monthly $7.50
   p.a.
   One Windsor Place, Mellville, N.Y. 11746
   For almost 40 years, ARG was a leading journal of music criticism (mainly classical). After its suspension in 1973, it returned in November of 1976. Popular music relates to folk and jazz.
   Indexed: Music Index
   No. of 1976 reviews: 11

AUDIO. 1917-   monthly $10 p.a.
   North American Pub. Co., 134 N. 13th St., Phila., Pa. 19107
   Contains articles on audio equipment. Record reviews tend to emphasize sound dynamics. Lengthy reviews of jazz records.
   Indexed: Music Index

No. of 1976 reviews: 220

BLACK MUSIC. 1974-   monthly $18 p.a.
   IPC Business Press (sales and distribution) Ltd.; Subscription
   Dept., Oakfield House, Perrymount Road, Haywards Heath,
   Sussex RH16 3DH, England
   A glossy but expertly edited magazine concerned with blues,
   rhythm 'n' blues, soul, gospel, reggae, and jazz. Good re-
   views of records, and various current awareness services.
   A major cut above black fanzines.
   Indexed: Popular Music Periodicals Index
   No. of 1976 reviews: 416

BLACK STARS. 1974-   monthly $10 p.a.
   Johnson Pub. Co., 820 S. Michigan Ave., Chicago, Ill. 60605
   Incorporating Tan Magazine, this glossy features soul music.
   Indexed: Popular Music Periodicals Index
   No. of 1976 reviews: 67

BLUEGRASS UNLIMITED. 1966-   monthly $7 p.a.
   Broad Run, Va. 22014
   Popular approach to the growing field of bluegrass. Excellent
   articles on current scene and expert reviews. Oldest of blue-
   grass specialty magazines.
   Indexed: Popular Music Periodicals Index
   No. of 1976 reviews: 178

BLUES UNLIMITED. 1963-   bimonthly $10 p.a.
   8 Brandram Road, Lewisham, London SE13 5EA, England.
   The leading blues magazine, with exceptional photographs and good
   record reviews. Music covered includes: Cajun, old timey,
   and gospel, plus rhythm 'n' blues.
   Indexed: Music Index; Popular Music Periodicals Index
   No. of 1976 reviews: 101

CADENCE. 1976-   monthly $8 p.a.
   Rt. 1, Box 345, Redwood, N.Y. 13679
   An exceptionally well-developed jazz and blues magazine, pocket-
   sized, with superb coverage of virtually every jazz record re-
   leased in North America, Japan, France, Sweden, etc. In-
   depth interviews also cover artists' relations with the industry.
   Indexed: Popular Music Periodicals Index
   No. of 1976 reviews: 1175

CANADIAN COMPOSER. 1967-   10 nos./yr $2.50 p.a.
   Suite 904, 40 St-Clair Ave. W., Toronto M4V 1M2, Canada
   The organ of the Composers, Authors and Publishers Association
   of Canada (CAPAC), an agency similar to BMI and ASCAP.
   Articles and record reviews deal with Canadian classical and
   popular artists and composers.
   Indexed: Popular Music Periodicals Index
   No. of 1976 reviews: 86

CASSETTES AND CARTRIDGES. 1973-   monthly $10 p.a.

General Gramophone Publications, Inc., 177-179 Kenton Rd.,
Kenton, Harrow, Middlesex, England
A spinoff from the Gramophone, this monthly deals solely with
tapes. It does equipment reviews, reviews new tapes avail-
able, and does feature articles on many different types of
artists, some historical material, and lists of tapes available.
Indexed: Popular Music Periodicals Index
No. of 1976 reviews: 671

CIRCUS. 1969-   bi-weekly $12 p.a.
797 Third Avenue, New York, N.Y.   10017
A rock fan magazine with many photos and biographies of current
stars. Intended for a younger audience. Reviews are sur-
prisingly critical for a "puff" mag.
Indexed: Popular Music Periodicals Index
No. of 1976 reviews: 467

CODA. 1958-   bi-monthly $10 for 10 issues
P.O. Box 87, Postal Station J, Toronto, Ont. M4J 4X8, Canada
World coverage. Leads the field of jazz magazines with in-depth
articles and thorough jazz and blues record reviews.
Indexed: Popular Music Periodicals Index; Music Index
No. of 1976 reviews: 354

CONSUMER REPORTS. monthly $11 p.a.
P.O. Box 1000, Orangeburg, N.Y.   10962
Began to review a few popular music records in 1975.
No. of 1976 reviews: 3

CONTEMPORARY KEYBOARD. 1975-   monthly $12 p.a.
P.O. Box 907, Saratoga, Cal.   95070
A spinoff from Guitar Player, emphasizing all aspects of key-
boards (piano, organ, electronic music synthesizer, etc.).
Record reviews, book reviews, equipment reviews, articles
on personalities, music, instructions, tips. Became monthly
in 1977.
Indexed: Popular Music Periodicals Index
No. of 1976 reviews: 46

COUNTRY MUSIC. 1972-   monthly $8.95 p.a.; $14.95/2yrs
475 Park Avenue South, New York, N.Y.   10016
This glossy magazine for C & W fans has popular articles and
non-critical record reviews.
Indexed: Popular Music Periodicals Index
No. of 1976 reviews: 107

COUNTRY MUSIC PEOPLE. 1970-   monthly $4 p.a.
Powerscroft Rd., Footscray, Sidcup, Kent, England
British C & W fan magazine with an emphasis on the country
music scene in England. Some historical articles.
Indexed: Popular Music Periodicals Index
No. of 1976 reviews: 279

COUNTRY MUSIC REVIEW. monthly $9 p.a.

19 Westbourne Rd., London N7 8AN   England
British C & W music magazine with excellent articles on per-
    formers and current country scene.   Good evaluative reviews.
Indexed: Popular Music Periodicals Index
No. of 1976 reviews: 265

COUNTRY RAMBLER.   1976.   Ceased publication, 1976.

COUNTRY STYLE.   1976-   biweekly $17 p. a.
11058 W. Addison St., Franklin Park, Ill.   60131
Tabloid newspaper style, reminiscent of early Rolling Stone
    magazine.   Short pithy articles on the current stars, as
    well as some coverage of country music history.
Indexed: Popular Music Periodicals Index
No. of 1976 reviews: 26 (began Sept. 1976)

CRAWDADDY.   1966-   monthly $7.95 p. a.; $14/2yrs; $19/3yrs
72 Fifth Ave., New York, N.Y.   10011
American rock music and youth culture brought together in this
    pioneer magazine.   Like Rolling Stone this is not just about
    rock.   Contains book and record reviews.
Indexed: Popular Music Periodicals Index
No. of 1976 reviews: 199

CRAZY MUSIC; the journal of the Australian Blues Society.   1974-
    quarterly $2 Australian
P.O. Box 1029, Canberra City, ACT 2601, Australia
Well-written blues magazine, devoted to the local Australian
    scene as well as interesting recordings from the Oceania area.
Indexed: Popular Music Periodicals Index
No. of 1976 reviews: 80

CREEM.   1969-   monthly $10 p. a.
187 S. Woodward, Birmingham, Mich.   48011
Calls itself "America's only rock 'n' roll magazine."   A hip
    counterculture mag with a format much like Crawdaddy.   Prob-
    ably the most entertaining record reviews in the business.
Indexed: Popular Music Periodicals Index
No. of 1976 reviews: 562

DOWN BEAT.   1934-   biweekly (21 nos./yr) $11 p. a.; $18/2yrs
Maher Publications, Inc., 222 W. Adams St., Chicago, Ill.   60606
Contains jazz news, interviews, transcriptions of improvised jazz
    solos.   Its self-rated reviews tend to be overrated.
Indexed: Popular Music Periodicals Index; Music Index
No. of 1976 reviews: 417

ENGLISH DANCE AND SONG.   1936-   quarterly $4 p. a.
English Folk Dance and Song Society, Cecil Sharp House, 2 Re-
    gents Park Rd., London NW1 7AY, England
Covers dance, song, folklore and crafts, with thoughtful, though
    brief, record and book reviews.   Includes subscription to
    Folk Music Journal (an annual).

Indexed: Popular Music Periodicals Index
No. of 1976 reviews: 39

ETHNOMUSICOLOGY. 1953-   3 nos./yr $18 p.a.
Society for Ethnomusicology, c/o William P. Malm, School of
    Music, University of Michigan, Ann Arbor, Mich.   48104
Scholarly articles and extensive record and book reviews. Each
    issue has an extensive "Current Bibliography and Discography
    Section."
Indexed: Popular Music Periodicals Index; Music Index
No. of 1976 reviews: 44

FOLK REVIEW. 1971-   monthly $8 p.a.
Austin House, Hospital St., Nantwich, Cheshire, England
Monthly journal of British folksingers with profiles, articles, and
    reviews. Positive proof of the booming British folk scene.
Indexed: Popular Music Periodicals Index
No. of 1976 reviews: 121

FOOTNOTE. 1970-   bimonthly   £1.75
44 High Street, Meldreth, Royston, Herfordshire SG8 6JU, England
Pocket-sized format, devoted to the history of New Orleans music.
Indexed: Popular Music Periodicals Index
No. of 1976 reviews: 58

GRAMOPHONE. 1923-   monthly $14 p.a.
General Gramophone Publications, Ltd., 177-179 Kenton Rd.,
    Harrow, Middlesex, HA3 OHA, England
Solid journal on record collecting and audio equipment. Attempts
    to be comprehensive in coverage in all fields of music.
No. of 1976 reviews: 601

GUITAR PLAYER. 1967-   monthly $12 p.a.
Box 615, Saratoga, Cal.   95070
The magazine for material on guitars, guitar playing, and guitar
    players. Record reviews are oriented toward guitars. Col-
    umns of instructions, tips, and equipment reviews.
Indexed: Popular Music Periodicals Index
No. of 1976 reviews: 151

HIGH FIDELITY. 1951-   monthly $7.95 p.a.
1 Sound Ave., Marion, Ohio   43302
Articles on audio equipment. Record reviews are chiefly classical.
Indexed: Readers' Guide to Periodical Literature; Music Index;
    Popular Music Periodicals Index
No. of 1976 reviews: 227

JAZZ FORUM. 1967-   bimonthly $12 p.a.
Grand Central Station, P.O. Box 2805, New York, N.Y.   10017
Printed in Poland but distributed through Austria, this magazine
    speaks for the International Jazz Federation (formerly, Euro-
    pean Jazz Federation) with articles, concert reports, and rec-
    ord reviews of mainly modern jazz (and European jazzmen)

Indexed: Popular Music Periodicals Index
No. of 1976 reviews: 148

JAZZ JOURNAL. 1948-   monthly $12.80 p.a.
1/3 Upper James St., London WIR 4BP, England
Excellent detailed articles, with thorough descriptive and disco-
   graphic information for all reviews and articles.
Indexed: Popular Music Periodicals Index; Music Index
No. of 1976 reviews: 521

JAZZ MAGAZINE. 1976-   quarterly $10 p.a.
30 Makamah Beach Road, Northport, New York 11768
An attractive package emphasizing good layout and graphics,
   printed on quality paper. Articles concentrate on living
   and modern performers; record reviews.
Indexed: Popular Music Periodicals Index
No. of 1976 reviews: 70

JAZZ REPORT. 1958-   irregular 6 nos./$3
Box 476, Ventura, Cal. 93001
"The record collector's magazine" (subtitle), this is an informal
   mimeographed publication with record reviews and book re-
   views concentrating on the "trad" period. Only published two
   issues in 1975; none in 1976.
Indexed: Popular Music Periodicals Index
No. of 1976 reviews: none

JOHN EDWARDS MEMORIAL FOUNDATION QUARTERLY
   [J.E.M.F.Q.] 1963-   quarterly $10 p.a.
Folklore and Mythology Center, University of California at Los
   Angeles, Los Angeles, Cal. 90024
A scholarly journal-type presentation of articles dealing with
   American folklore and old time music plus country music in
   particular. Sections deal with discographies, commercial
   graphics, histories of songs. Record reviews (beginning in
   1976) and in-depth reviews of books.
Indexed: Popular Music Periodicals Index
No. of 1976 reviews: 27

LISTENING POST. 1971-1976. Ceased with June issue
No. of 1976 reviews: 302

LIVING BLUES. 1970-   bimonthly $6 p.a.
P.O. Box 11303, Chicago, Ill. 60611
Good American coverage of modern blues through news and ar-
   ticles. Record and book reviews tend to be slim. Became
   bimonthly in 1975.
Indexed: Popular Music Periodicals Index
No. of 1976 reviews: 114

MELODY MAKER. weekly $39 p.a.
IPC Business Press (Sales & Distribution) Oakfield House, Per-
   mount Rd., Haywards Heath, Sussex RH16 3DH, England

This is probably the best of the five British weeklies devoted to
popular music. It devotes a great deal of space to non-rock
items, such as jazz, folk, blues, soul, reggae, country, and
so forth, both in its reviews and in its articles. There is
also much material here on audio equipment and problems.
Indexed: Popular Music Periodicals Index
No. of 1976 reviews: 914

MISSISSIPPI RAG; the voice of traditional jazz and ragtime.   1974-
monthly $5 p.a.
P.O. Box 19068, Minneapolis, Minn. 55419
Tabloid format on newsprint. Good, in-depth reviews. Histor-
ical articles; excellent coverage of concerts and festivals (with
photos).
Indexed: Popular Music Periodicals Index
No. of 1976 reviews: 28

MODERN HI-FI AND MUSIC. 1973-   quarterly $10 p.a.
699 Madison Ave., New York, N.Y. 10021
Articles on stereo equipment. Record reviews are popular and
evaluative. Formerly, MODERN HI-FI AND STEREO GUIDE.
Indexed: Popular Music Periodicals Index
No. of 1976 reviews: 89

MULESKINNER NEWS. 1970-   monthly $10 p.a.
Rt. 2, Box 304, Elon College, N.C. 27244
Articles on bluegrass performers, playing bluegrass instruments,
schedules of festivals and performances. Good reviews of
bluegrass and old time music.
Indexed: Popular Music Periodicals Index
No. of 1976 reviews: 51

MUSIC JOURNAL. 1943-   monthly (exc June & Aug) $11 p.a.
370 Lexington Ave., New York, N.Y. 10017
A general interest magazine for music educators, covering classical and popular music. Most reviews are for mood-pop or
jazz items (e.g., Stanley Dance).
Indexed: Music Index; Popular Music Periodicals Index
No. of 1976 reviews: 89

OLD TIME MUSIC. 1971-   quarterly $4 p.a.
33 Brunswick Gardens, London W8 4AW, England
American country old time music. Transcriptions and discographic essays. Record reviews of old time string band music.
Indexed: Popular Music Periodicals Index
No. of 1976 reviews: 152

ONTARIO LIBRARY REVIEW. 1916-   quarterly $3/3yrs
Ontario Provincial Library Service, 14th Floor, Mowat Block,
Queen's Park, Toronto M7A 1B9, Canada
Includes a regular record review column, concerned with "Cana-
dian Content." No music book reviews.

Indexed: Canadian Periodical Index; Library Literature; Library
and Information Science Abstracts
No. of 1976 reviews: 67

PICKIN'.   1974-   monthly $9 p.a.
Universal Graphics Corporation, 46 Ford Road, Denville, N.J.
07834
Similar to Bluegrass Unlimited this new and handsome magazine
is devoted to bluegrass and old-time music.   Good historical
articles, interviews and excellent material on string instruments used in bluegrass bands.
Indexed: Popular Music Periodicals Index
No. of 1976 reviews: 82

PHONOGRAPH RECORD MAGAZINE.   1969-   monthly $6 p.a.
6922 Sunset Blvd., Hollywood, California   90028
Once supported by United Artists, this tabloid concentrates on
recordings with a touch of humor (e.g. "Blindfold tests" sa-
tires).   Good coverage of soul and jazz.
Indexed: Popular Music Periodicals Index
No. of 1976 reviews. 164

POPULAR MUSIC AND SOCIETY.   1971-   quarterly $6 p.a.;
$15/3yrs
318 South Grove Street, Bowling Green, Ohio   43402
An interdisciplinary journal "concerned with music in the broad-
est sense of the term" (editorial policy).   Scholarly articles,
books are reviewed.   Record reviews usually not signed.
Indexed: Popular Music Periodicals Index
No. of 1976 reviews: 62

RADIO FREE JAZZ.   1974-   monthly $10 p.a.
6737 Annapolis Road, P.O. Box 2417, Landolver Hills, Mary-
land   20784
Mainly intended for jazz radio programmers, this tabloid has
good coverage of current records plus assorted articles of
varying quality.   The jazz news is quite excellent, as are the
playlists.
Indexed: Popular Music Periodicals Index
No. of 1976 reviews: 138

RAGTIMER.   1962-   bimonthly $8 by mbrship only
Ragtime Society, Inc., P.O. Box 520, Weston, Ont. M9N 3N3
Articles, news, book and record reviews.   Reproduction of sheet
music.   Loose-leaf format.   Record reviews tend to go out-
side ragtime music per se.
Indexed: Popular Music Periodicals Index; Music Index
No. of 1976 reviews: 27

RECORD MONTH.   1975-   monthly $12 p.a.
216 Carlton Street, Toronto M5A 2L1, Canada
While there is a distinct emphasis here on Canadian music, this
periodical is valuable for its "international" outlook from a

Canadian perspective.
Indexed: Popular Music Periodicals Index
No. of 1976 reviews: 131

RECORD REVIEW. 1976-   bimonthly $6 p. a.
    P.O. Box 91878, Los Angeles, California 90009
    "In-depth articles blending review, interview, biography, and
        discussion of a cross-section of the latest record releases"--
        all put in perspective with an artist's or group's previous
        recordings. Unlike most record review media, much space
        is given to individual track analyses. Began in November,
        1976.
    Indexed: Popular Music Periodicals Index
    No. of 1976 reviews: 9

RECORDS AND RECORDING. 1957-   monthly $14.90 p. a.
    Hanson Books, Artillery Mansions, 75 Victoria St. , London SW1,
        England
    Record news and reviews, chiefly classical. Popular music
        stress strong "rock" and "jazz" and "blues" reviews.
    No. of 1976 reviews: 476

ROCK. 1976-   bimonthly $12 p. a.
    257 Park Avenue South, New York, New York 10010
    A typical rock magazine, with articles and pictures and record
        reviews. Printed in Time-size format, with newspaper stock.
    Indexed: Popular Music Periodicals Index
    No. of 1976 reviews: 68

ROLLING STONE. 1968-   biweekly $20 p. a.
    Straight Arrow Publishers, 625 Third St. , San Francisco, Cal.
        94107
    America's strongest youth culture magazine, now moving away
        from just music to a description of a life style in general.
        Very opinionated book and record reviews.
    Indexed: Music Index; Popular Music Periodicals Index
    No. of 1976 reviews: 652

SING OUT. 1950-   bimonthly $7.50 p. a.
    595 Broadway, N. Y. , N. Y. 10012
    News on the folk, blues, and bluegrass scene, plus book and
        record reviews.
    Indexed: Popular Music Periodicals Index
    No. of 1976 reviews: 48

SOUND. 1970-   10 nos./yr $5 p. a.
    62 Shaftesbury Ave. , Toronto M4T 1A4, Canada
    Articles on audio equipment and the Canadian music scene.
    Indexed: Popular Music Periodicals Index
    No. of 1976 reviews: 113

STEREO REVIEW. 1958-   monthly $7.98 p. a.
    P.O. Box 2771, Boulder, Colo. 80302

Audio equipment news, articles on performers and composers.
Heavier emphasis on popular music than High Fidelity.
Indexed: Music Index; Popular Music Periodicals Index
No. of 1976 reviews: 613

STORYVILLE. 1965-   bimonthly $5 p.a.
   66 Fairview Dr., Chigwell, Essex, England IG7 6HS
   This magazine tends to concentrate on "trad" or "classic" jazz,
      blues, and subsequent re-interpretations or revivals. Articles
      are devoted to exploring minor figures or minor facts about
      major performers in this genre, as well as copious discogra-
      phies of the period. A good research-oriented magazine.
   Indexed: Popular Music Periodicals Index
   No. of 1976 reviews: 73

TALKING BLUES. 1976-   quarterly   £2 p.a.
   Record Information Services, P.O. Box 226, London SW4 OEH,
      England
   At present in mimeographed form, this replacement for Blues
      Link and Blues World promises to further explore the aspects
      of the pre-war blues and gospel music.
   Indexed: Popular Music Periodicals Index
   No. of 1976 reviews: 89

TRADITIONAL MUSIC. 1975-   3 x year   £1.20
   90 St. Julian's Farm Road, London SE27 ORS, England
   Examines all aspects of folk music in Great Britain, especially
      with long in-depth articles on the older countryside singers.
      Many songs and texts; first-rate long record reviews.
   Indexed: Popular Music Periodicals Index
   No. of 1976 reviews: 18

WHO PUT THE BOMP. 1974-   quarterly [but irregular] $8 for
      eight issues
   P.O. Box 7112, Burbank, Cal.   91510
   The leading "oldies" magazine, the only one on glossy paper and
      with color photographs. Good articles on rock 'n' roll revivals
      and on the early rock period of the 1960s.
   Indexed: Popular Music Periodicals Index
   No. of 1976 reviews: 40

ROCK

Rock music developed from Britain with the English "beat" and "blues" groups. These bands re-exported to America the styles and songs created by black American music, primarily the gospel-infused rhythm'n'blues. But rock had other roots too. It borrowed its form and feeling from the blues, the call and response riffs plus the driving repetitive rhythms from r'n'b, improvisation from jazz, melismatic singing from gospel, and social consciousness from folk music. By so doing, rock music became almost parasitic, absorbing and transmuting all aspects of popular music (with deleterious results) as well as the main influences in these other forms of music. This synthesis is augmented by its pragmatic but diverse nature, for rock music tends to re-emphasize styles of music in reinforcement patterns. Whatever works is usually good, and stylists tend to stay in one mode of performing with little variation or exploration. The audience works in a similar but fickle fashion, and there is a common expression: "You are as big as your last record." For this reason, many performers do not switch styles.

Rock music is essentially studio-oriented. The recording studio and electronics are its primary instruments, unlike the vocals in the blues, the instruments of jazz, or the microphones of the pop singer. Songs were created and written in the studio; there they are also mixed and edited from 32 tracks down to two or four, and the music electronically altered for dynamics, textures, volume, echo, and so forth. Technology gave rock musicians new instruments such as the electric piano, the electronic synthesizer, the devices of fuzz tone, reverberation, and wah-wah. The amplifier enabled the speaker systems (and hence the musician) to possess raw, swinging power. Tapes and albums gave the musician time to lay out all his ideas, enough room for suites, operas, extended songs, variations, experimentation with unstructured music, etc.

Rock music also advanced 1950s rock and roll. During that decade, smart operators uncovered post-war black music and re-cast the mold to fit young, urbane white singers. The beat was still there, but the voice was silky instead of rough, the accompanying rhythms were simple instead of complex, and the lyrics were changed to prevent misunderstandings in words out of context. But the British blues bands, by side-stepping rock and roll and emulating the source of rock and roll, dramatically reversed the sequence. And, as is common in every popular music field, once the traditional elements or the borrowed songs run out, then the performers

21

have to create their own materials. Given the existing technology and format, several streams opened up. The established 32-bar song with a bridge was the first to give way to such innovations borrowed from jazz as changing time signatures and shifting meters, and from r'n'b came blunt lyrics and screaming vocals. In time this led to the performer creating all of his own material. This was a true singer-performer-songwriter, for the groups now play their own instruments and sing their own songs. Many of the finer soloists and groups even had complete control over their product, down through the editing, album design, and liner notes. Their instrumental prowess expanded so that both guitar licks (configurations within a chord) and guitar runs (configurations bridging notes between chords in a progression), as borrowed from jazz and country music, could easily be performed. They borrowed the mobile electric bass from soul music to pin down the rhythm, thus freeing the drummer from merely keeping the beat. While the 1950s rock and roll scene projected an alienation against parental control of teenagers, and defined the society of the rock and roll admirer, it took rock music to crystallize and fuse this feeling of frustration into an ideology and a youth culture of peer control. This, of course, relates to the post-World War II baby boom, for in the era of rock and roll the large young audience was growing up from 10 to 15 years of age; with rock in 1964, they were at least eight years older (18-23) and now in a position to solidify any fragmented alienation.

But rock music is fragmented when it comes to fans that support the music. Not only are there different formats, but also there are diversified themes that might not appeal to all persons interested in rock music. Some of the handles given to these formats include country-rock, jazz-rock, blues-rock, folk-rock (and a subgenre, good-time-rock), punk-rock (or pop-rock), soft-rock (usually equated with modern rock and roll), acid-rock, and hard-rock (better known now as "heavy metal music").

Blues-rock came first. The blues revival in the United States was a culmination of the urban folk music and urban blues craze, the developing British rock music based on black music, and accented by the proliferation of skiffle or jug bands in England. Rock musicians in England further extended the country blues-folk-jug band idiom into Chicago blues. They tried to approximate the unintentional distortion of electric blues recordings (unintentional, because the Chicago blues men used old equipment that was falling apart and malfunctioning). They experimented with fuzz-tone and sustained notes. The leaders were Jimmy Page, Eric Clapton, and Jeff Beck (all ex-Yardbirds), plus Jimi Hendrix from the United States, who both traveled to England for his success and picked up an English bassist and drummer. He was profoundly influenced by Clapton. Vocalists, however, simply did not exist. For some reason, none was ever found that was better than mediocre. The two vocal leaders--Robert Plant of Led Zeppelin, and Rod Stewart--had to spend a decade in developing. On the other hand, American groups such as Electric Flag, Paul Butterfield's Blue Band, and the

Rock   23

Blues Project had several good vocalists. But their recordings
were strictly in the Chicago mold, changing only with added ampli-
fication--and cleaning up the distortion. Unfortunately, this made
the blues as interpreted seem monotonous and lacking in excitement.

Blues-rock was most of the "British invasion" of the mid-
sixties when rock and roll was given a big shot in the arm by amplification. After the Beatles came several similar pop groups, followed by a whole alphabet of British musicians working in the blues
mode. American imitators of British imitators of Chicago blues
quickly followed, and by the end of the 1960s, folk-rock, acid-rock
and blues-rock co-existed in neat categories. But then folk-rock
transmuted into troubador music, and blues-rock adopted some of
the technical devices of the fading acid-rock. The results of this
latter subgenre was heavy metal music.

Acid Rock, also known as psychedelic rock, had several in-
tents. One was to reproduce the distorted hearing of an individual
under the influence of LSD or other hallucinogens. Another was to
recreate for a drugless individual the illusion of psychedelia through
the music and an on-stage visual light show. A third was to create
music while under the influence of drugs. Unfortunately, this third
intent does not work, as drugs severely restrict one's technical abil-
ities (as was the case with John Fahey). All of this should not be
construed as to condone the use of drugs, but merely to reproduce
or recreate its musical effects. Acid rock was originally for those
not on drugs, but not all acid rock was suitable for those who took
drugs and went on trips. Psychedelic rock was intended for listening, and not for dancing. This abrupt shift in a form of music that
previously had rhythmic capabilities to produce happiness dramatically changed the whole concept of rock music. To reproduce disturbed music, the musicians needed electronic technology for advanced amplification and weird sounds.

The music was developed mainly in San Francisco in 1965
by the Jefferson Airplane and the Grateful Dead; however, the style
was developed earlier by the Beatles, who showed the paths through
structural complexities, rhythmic intricacies, and other experimentation. They composed "Norwegian Wood" and "Day in the Life," employing Indian raga music styles and the sitar (this Oriental association followed drugs around, even if the hallucinogen was marijuana).
Some of the music even reflected social themes found in folk music,
especially the stream of consciousness ideas of Bob Dylan. Progression in acid rock embraces sustained and languid melodies, complex instrumentation, variety and imaginative stylings, and imagery
in lyrics. The musical phrases came in lurches of surging power,
a sort of tripping and uncertain movement. As with art, acid rock
dealt with tone, coloration, texture, and density. Most live concerts,
which went on for hours (such as those of the Grateful Dead), added
improvisation for spontaneous effects. On record, the long timings
of each track allow for some development of the many themes, and
the variations on a chord. The one drawback to the intellectual

music of acid rock (but one of its attractions to the folk element) is that "finesse replaces visceral excitement." It is "head" music that needs no surging energy nor buoyancy as was happening in regular rock music of the time. The period of acid rock extended to 1970, and included such material as Van Dyke Parks' Song Cycle, the Beach Boys' "Good Vibrations," the Rolling Stones' "Paint It Black," and the Byrds "Eight Miles High." Since 1970, acid rock returned infrequently because of the expense of touring light shows and the limited scope of experimentation.

Heavy metal music seemed to take the worst offerings of acid-rock and blues-rock. The music played by groups here demanded an extraordinary volume, distortion and mechanical riffing. Keyboards and electric basses were added to the music of lead guitarists and some rather pedestrian drummers. Much of the music deliberately disregarded the dancing and rhythmic aspects, sticking with the propensity of acid-rock towards "non-swing" music (e.g. Led Zeppelin's "Dazed and Confused"). Much of the singing and the lyrics were subordinated to the instrumental sound, which preferred "chaos over coherence." Thus, within a relatively easy blues progression there appears to be a jackhammer approach for solos rather than a developed set of thematic variations. This was called "blitzkrieg obbligatos," and a typical example can be found by Eric Clapton on Cream's "Spoonful." The basic elements of this music were very monotonous, but to be successful heavy metal relied on imaginative performers to project a unique sound, and thereby become "stylists" through technical tricks. When innovations ceased to exist (or when they were never there), then the lack of imagination quickly forced the band to become an exponent of punk rock.

This term described the "trash with flash." Everything was thrown at an audience except good music. Punk rock was mainly done by those who wanted to play the blues--an easy medium--but couldn't. They evolved a style which didn't require virtuosity. The guitar solo was dropped, as the guitarist was deficient, in favor of the insistent riff being played by all instruments at once. The lyrical quality changed to reflect weird violence, madness, drugs, disease and pestilence. Not only are some of these groups dull, but they are also short on ideas. They all begin to sound alike, and were appreciated by an audience which largely couldn't keep pace with musical development. Their few redeeming values lie in the stageshow of themes, lights, and stories, such as contributed by Alice Cooper, David Bowie, and Lou Reed. These are enjoyable in themselves, but fall flat on discs which transmit only the aural passages. Older groups from the past included MC5, Iggy Pop and the Stooges, Blue Cheer, Iron Butterfly, Velvet Underground, and Grand Funk Railroad. Influences back and forth across the Atlantic follow the route of, for example, the Chicago blues to British blues to Grand Funk Railroad to Black Sabbath to the Blue Oyster Cult, with each emulating the sound of the immediate predecessor.

Experimentation has not always been successful, but in the rock music world it did help to pave the way for derivative and pop groups. As rock music is pragmatic, then whatever sells must be good, and the whole industry begins emulation. Most rock experiments are done by reasonably proficient groups who can convince recording companies that their work should be made available to the masses who so rarely buy this type of music anyway. Much of it is contrived and self-conscious; most of it is simple, derived in turn from the classics or from jazz. Some strength does come from underground or counter-culture fans (usually a loyal cult), but usually they go through the mainstream of records unnoticed until some other musician tries his hand with a simple modification and succeeds. Their sources are mainly acid-rock and the new electronic instrumentation. Heavy metal groups did contribute "theater rock," where the music is presented as a whole conception of light, sound, story and performance. But they are a failure on disc because the albums are very incomplete, containing aural information only. Jim Morrison of the Doors started it all with his long, improvised live concert renditions of his ten-minute album songs. The latest extension of the show tunes has been such groups as Queen, Kiss, and the New York Dolls.

Country-folk-rock is the fusion of material and traditions derived from the folk-music idiom with the instrumentation and beat of rock. It is an amorphous combination of blues, rock and roll, country music, popular music and protest songs. Its greatest impact was in the mid-1960s when protest songs merged with rock rhythms, and this type of music found a new audience. Its next manifestation was as country-rock, which meant going through the folk process from traditional sources to written materials. Country-rock was favored by those who could sing; folk-rock was left to those who couldn't sing, but simply growled in the time-honored folk tradition. The last permutation after country-rock became the troubador or singer-songwriter, who was essentially first a folk-type and then a rock musician. At this level the merger was not as complete because the folk-derived lyrics dominated.

The singer-song writer developed out of the folk and country tradition. Now called troubadors (and troubettes for some), they bring personal visions through their unique place and role in popular music. A popular song is a 50-50 relationship between the words and the music. The words were not meant to be read as poetry. In the troubadour's song, the records can stand alone as poetry, or be poetry put to music. This is a crucial distinction, and it marks a dramatic shift in popular music history. Some of the strongest troubadors have been displaced poets (Richard Farina, Bob Dylan, Leonard Cohen, Paul Simon, Tim Hardin).

To understand the troubador phenomenon one must first understand the conditions of the late 1950s and 1960s folk revival. The folk purists either preferred "authentic" singers from the past (forgetting that these singers themselves were interpreters) or memorizations of every phrase and nuance lifted off Library of Congress or old-time music commercial recordings. Audiences recognized both as "roots," with the memorizers standing in for the originals.

A clear fossilization of performing styles emerged. At the same time, Alan Lomax's philosophy of "to be folk, you live folk" found acceptance with other singers and audiences. The dichotomy of "purism" vs. "life experiences" split the folk music world. The pattern (which, incidentally, was established during the 1920s with old-time music) was to listen to early records and to do imitations, with some singers eventually adapting the material creatively to develop their own musical styles. Such a process was common to blues, jazz, rock, etc. But it took Bob Dylan to put it all together. He made it possible for the acceptance of folk-singers to emerge from their fossilized self-made traps to be "living experience" singers with original words, music, styles and variations.

The existence of the troubador actually began with the folk revival of the Depression. In this earlier period, the stress was on anonymity. But in the 1960s, with alienation from society and singing protest songs of persuasion, the stress became focussed. The lyrical ballads of troubadors look back to older British forms in themes:

1. Life and Nature, which stresses that all natural phenomena are interdependent and sympathetic. This "pathetic fallacy" resulted in landscape and scenery songs, plus idyllic viewpoints. Three specific manifestations here include:
    (a) the erotic songs of similes and images, concentrating on sexual euphemisms such as germination or fruitfulness.
    (b) the ritualistic manner of life form cycles, concentrating on dances, ceremonies, and "good times" generally,
    (c) metaphorically extending the pleasures of love between partners to that of the whole natural environment (and vice versa), quite often as an echo of reinforcement.

2. Pure Love, dealing with stories of success, non-success, and bitter frustrations, quite often presented in the first person.

3. Psycho-analytic Autobiographies, in which a selection of self-conscious expressions and subconscious ideas are presented in the manner of the bluesman "to talk it out."

4. Commentaries, presenting some criticism but offering few or no solutions. Most songs here are rhetorical in nature, indicating the condition and merely describing it. As most people have jobs and/or the basic necessities of life, then it is mainly the imperfections of society that are pointed out rather than the root evils. Alienation and outrage makes this an individual discontent rather than the anonymous cohesion found in the 1930s. Three specific types here include:
    (a) a social commentary on the manner of urban life, in which the singer tries to define social reality,
    (b) a political commentary,
    (c) a labor commentary about jobs, industries, capitalism, working conditions, etc.

Troubadors can promote many superficialities. In attempting to jump on the band wagon, many have produced puzzling responses. One critic called them the "quack minstrels of a non-existent America." Something does appear to be out of sequence when the children of well-to-do parents start singing about "hard times" that they have never experienced. Other material falls into a too-common pattern: there is slight biographical material, meaning that the singers remain closed to their private lives; the Dylan "stream of consciousness" has been overdone by lesser mortals; much material concerns drugs, lost love, or country music influences; and the general pattern of many songs has been characterized as being "landscapes" or scenery songs.

By analyzing rock lyrics, these can be grouped together into eight distinct themes (in no particular order):

1. Summertime Paeans--Odes to the good life of celebration and surfing. These can also be instrumentals, and because of their good-time nature and relation to soft-rock, most love ballads fall within this category.

2. Dance Music--This is happy music, with no social commentary. Throughout the last 25 years it had limited popularity, but it was unpretentious and honest, stressing the dance rhythms. In 1976 it resurged as "disco" music.

3. Sexual Themes--Either implied or explicit, sexual adventures also included sadism, masochism, and perversions. Originally, this was the derivation of the term "rock and roll," as physical emulation of sexual intercourse. Sexuality was the one dominant theme of 1950s r'n'b.

4. Rebellion--Either non-violent (the self-consciousness of growing up and the loss of innocence, coupled with the need for group or peer unity) or violent (the protest against the establishment of law, police, complacency, war efforts in Viet Nam). This music was best handled in the form of a satire or of a parable. If it was too explicit, then, as with early sexual songs, the record was banned from the airwaves.

5. Civil Rights--Social causes espoused by whites in the 1960s, and then by blacks in the 1970s. Strange as it may seem, white rock music in the 1970s has been silent on the matter of civil rights.

6. Social Concerns--Problems, but few solutions, are discussed in rock music. Material here concerns pride, interracial relationships, slums, ghettos, "messages," "lessons," and "advice."

7. Drugs--Either implied or explicit, along with psychedelic trips, acid music, similes and metaphorical expressions.

8. Lifestyles--The world of the rock super star, usually a male
    macho world, concerning his musical roots and life on the
    road.

        Nearly every magazine has an article now and then on rock
music or a rock personality. General magazines with adequate reviews and occasional articles include High Fidelity and Stereo Review. Specific periodicals geared to the rock fan come and go depending upon finances. The ones that have remained include Circus,
Creem, and Melody Maker. Crawdaddy and Rolling Stone are less
than half music, and have been since 1972.

        Specific periodicals examine one aspect of rock music. Con-
temporary Keyboard and Guitar Player provide guidance and instruc-
tion for performing on those respective instruments. Popular Music
and Society will examine sociological impact, while Down Beat will in-
vestigate jazz-rock.

        According to the reviews for 1976, the following appear to
be the best ROCK records:

        BISHOP, Elvin. Hometown Boy Makes Good. Capricorn CP
            0176
        BLUE Oyster Cult. Agents of Fortune. Columbia PC 34164
        BROWNE, Jackson. The Pretender. Asylum 7E-1079
        COODER, Ry. Chicken Skin Music. Reprise MS 2254
        DYLAN, Bob. Desire. Columbia PC 33893
        FRAMPTON, Peter. Frampton Comes Alive. A & M SP
            3703
        GALLAGHER, Rory. Calling Card. Chrysalis CHR 1124
        GENESIS. A Trick of the Tail. Atco SD 36-129
        GOODMAN, Steve. Words We Can Dance To. Asylum 7E-
            1061
        KISS. Rock 'n' Rollover. Casablanca NBLP 7037
        LYNYRD Skynyrd. Gimme Back My Bullets. MCA 2170
        McGARRIGLE, Anna and Kate McGarrigle. Warner Brothers
            BS 2862
        MITCHELL, Joni. Hejira. Asylum 7E-1087
        PALMER, Robert. Pressure Drop. Island ILPS 9372
        PARKER, Graham. Howlin' Wind. Mercury SRM 1-1095
        PINK Floyd. Wish You Were Here. Columbia PC 33453
        RAITT, Bonnie. Home Plate. Warner Brothers BS 2864
        REDBONE, Leon. On the Track. Warner Brothers BS 2888
        ROLLING Stones. Black and Blue. Rolling Stones COC 59106
        RONSTADT, Linda. Hasten Down the Wind. Asylum 7E-1072
        SEGER, Bob. Night Moves. Capitol ST 11557
        SOUTHSIDE Johnny and the Asbury Jukes. I Don't Want to
            Go Home. Epic PE 34180
        SPARKS. Big Beat. Columbia PC 34359
        STEELY Dan. Royal Scan. ABC ABCD 931
        STEWART, Rod. A Night on the Town. Warner Brothers BS
            2938
        10 CC. 100cc. UK UKS 53110

THE WHO. By Numbers. MCA 2161
WINGS. At the Speed of Sound. Capitol SW 11525.

1   ABBA. Atlantic SD-18146. Cass. CS-18146
    CRA Jan. p78. 100w. 3
    CRE Jan. p66. 400w. 4
    LP Jan. p5. 200w. 1

2   ABBA. Arrival. Atlantic SD 18207. Cass. CS 18207
    MM Dec. 4 p21. 625w. $3\frac{1}{2}$

3   ABBA. Greatest Hits. Atlantic SD 18199. Cass. CS 18199
    (reissue)
    MM April 3 p31. 100w. 2
    RR June p82. 75w. $3\frac{1}{2}$

4   AC/DC. High Voltage. Atco SD 36-142. Cass. CS 36-142
    MG Dec. p63. 50w. 4
    MM July 3 p23. 150w. $2\frac{1}{2}$
    RS Dec. 16 p81. 125w. 0
    WHO Winter p42. 250w. 4

5   ACE. Time for Another. Anchor ANCL-2013. Cart. 8308-
    2013H. Cass. 5308-2013H
    CRA May p70. 425w. $1\frac{1}{2}$
    GR March p1518. 25w. 3
    HF May p105. 100w. 3
    LP April p5. 100w. 2
    RS Feb. 12 p90. 300w. $2\frac{1}{2}$
    SR April p82. 150w. 5

6   AEROSMITH. Rocks. Columbia PC-34165. Cart. PCA-34165.
    Cass. PCT-34165
    AU Oct. p138-9. 500w. 1
    CIR Aug. 24 p10, 12. 500w. 1
    CRE Dec. p14. 75w. 4
    GR Aug. p351. 25w. 2
    HF Sept. p109. 150w. $3\frac{1}{2}$
    MM July 10 p22. 250w. $3\frac{1}{2}$
    RR Sept. p88. 50w. 3
    RS July 29 p49. 300w. $2\frac{1}{2}$
    SR Nov. p94. 125w. $2\frac{1}{2}$

7   ALBERT, Morris. Feelings. RCA APL1-1018
    SR June p76. 100w. 4

8   ALICE Cooper. Goes to Hell. Warner BS-2896. Cart.
    M82896. Cass. M52896
    CIR Oct. 26 p9-10. 300w. 2
    CRE Sept. p60. 350w. $2\frac{1}{2}$
    GR Sept. p493. 50w. 3

MG Oct. p65. 25w. $3\frac{1}{2}$
MM Aug. 14 p27. 400w. 3
RS Aug. 26 p58. 225w. 2
SR Nov. p94. 125w. 2

9   ALLEN, David. Good Morning. Virgin V2054 (E)
MM July 3 p22. 175w. $3\frac{1}{2}$

10 ALLEN, Peter. Taught by Experts. A&M SP-4584. Tape
4584. Cass. 4584
SR Oct. p90. 200w. 4

11 ALLMAN Brothers. At the Fillmore East. Capricorn SD2-802.
(2 discs)
CRA March p81. 150w. 4

12 ALLMAN Brothers. The Road Goes on Forever. Capricorn
CPO164 (2 discs). Cass. J5-0164
CAC April p13. 315w. 4
CRE Feb. p63. 50w. 4
LP April p5. 200w. $2\frac{1}{2}$
MG Feb. p36. 50w. $2\frac{1}{2}$

13 ALLMAN Brothers. Win, Lose, or Draw. Capricorn CPO156.
Tape M80156. Cass. M50156
CRE Jan. p12. 25w. $2\frac{1}{2}$
CRE Jan. p64-65. 1000w. 2
LP Jan. p5. 250w. 4
SR Jan. p78. 325w. 2

14 ALLMAN Brothers. Wipe the Windows.... Capricorn 2CX-
0177 (2 discs)
MM Nov. 27 p26. 800w. $1\frac{1}{2}$

15 ALPHA Band. Arista AL4102.
PRM Nov. p34. 375w. $2\frac{1}{2}$
RS Dec. 2 p100. 125w. 3

16 AMAZING Blondel. Bad Dreams. DJM DJLPS 472 (E)
CAC Oct. p256. 150w. $1\frac{1}{2}$

17 AMAZING Rhythm Aces. Stacked Deck. ABC ABCD-913.
Tape 8022-913H
CRA Jan. p79. 75w. $1\frac{1}{2}$
CRE Feb. p12. 50w. $4\frac{1}{2}$
LP March p5. 150w. 4
SR Feb. p78. 250w. 3

18 AMAZING Rhythm Aces. Too Stuffed to Jump. ABC 940
CIR Sept. 13 p14. 275w. $3\frac{1}{2}$
CRE Aug. p14. 25w. 3
GR Sept. p493. 75w. 3

MM Sept. 11 p29. 425w. 3
RS July 1 p75. 325w. $3\frac{1}{2}$

19 AMBROSIA. 20th Century Records T-434
CK Jan. p46-7. 200w. 4

20 AMBROSIA. Somewhere I've Never Travelled. 20th Century
510
MM Nov. 27 p28. 100w. $\frac{1}{2}$

21 AMEN Corner. The Return of the Magnificent Seven Immediate
1ML 1004 (E)
MM May 1 p30. 75w. 2

22 AMERICA. Greatest Hits. Warner BS-2893 (Reissue)
CAC May p58. 100w. $3\frac{1}{2}$
GR March p1518. 125w. $3\frac{1}{2}$
HF Feb. p119. 100w. $3\frac{1}{2}$
MG Feb. p38. 50w. 5

23 AMERICA. Hideaway. Warner BS-2932. Tape M8-2932.
Cass. M5-2932
MM May 8 p24. 400w. 3
PRM May p31. 50w. 1
RS June 17 p60. 250w. 3
SR Aug. p72. 200w. 3

24 AMERICAN Flyer. United Artists LA-650-G. Cart. EA650-H.
Cass. CA650-H
AU Dec. p82-3. 300w. 0
CRA Oct. p78. 150w. 2
CRE Nov. p62. 350w. $2\frac{1}{2}$
MM Nov. 20 p28. 375w. $2\frac{1}{2}$
RS Sept. 23 p117. 325w. $3\frac{1}{2}$
SR Dec. p102. 150w. $3\frac{1}{2}$

25 AMERICAN Tears. Tear Gas. Columbia PC 33857
MG April p39. 50w. $2\frac{1}{2}$
MG Jan. p44. 50w. 3
RS April 22 p67. 225w. 3

26 AMON Duul II. Made in Germany. ATCO SD36-119. Cart.
TP36-119. Cass. CS36-119
CRE Jan. p69. 400w. $3\frac{1}{2}$
LP March p5. 75w. $1\frac{1}{2}$
SR Jan. p78. 150w. 2

27 ANDERSON, Eric. Sweet Surprise. Arista AL 4075.
Cart. 8301-4075
CIR Aug. 10 p12. 100w. $2\frac{1}{2}$
HF Sept. p110. 200w. 1
RS July 29 p47. 300w. 3
SR Sept. p90. 250w. 3

28 ANDERSON, Jon. Olias of Sunhillow. Atlantic SD-18180
       CRE Nov. p61. 100w. 2
       CK   Oct. p47. 50w. 4
       GR   Sept. p493. 50w. $1\frac{1}{2}$
       MM   July 3 p21. 975w. $3\frac{1}{2}$
       RS   Oct. 7 p81. 150w. 2
       SR   Nov. p94. 150w. 2

29 ANGEL. Casablanca 7021
       CRE March p61-2. 325w. 3
       MM   March 13 p23. 50w. $2\frac{1}{2}$

30 ANGEL. Helluva Band. Casablanca 7028
       CRE Sept. p62. 175w. 1

31 APRIL Wine. The Whole World's Gone Crazy. London PS
    675
       CRA Dec. p72-3. 300w. 3
       RS Dec. 16 p100. 100w. $2\frac{1}{2}$

32 ARDLEY, Neil. Kaleidoscope of Rainbows. Decca Gull GULP-
    1018 (E)
       CAC Oct. p252. 225w. 3
       GR   Oct. p669. 75w. 3
       MM   Aug. 14 p29. 1000w. 5

33 ARGENT. Anthology. Epic PE 33955 (Reissue)
       CAC June p94. 275w. $3\frac{1}{2}$
       HF   June p105. 75w. $2\frac{1}{2}$
       MM   May 1 p30. 250w. 3

34 ARGENT, Rod. Counterpoints. United Artists, UA-LA 560-g
       CK   Oct. p47. 125w. $4\frac{1}{2}$

35 ARIZONA. RCA LPL1-5123
       CAC May p58. 200w. $3\frac{1}{2}$

36 ARMSTRONG, Frankie. ...Out of Love, Hope and Suffering.
    Bay 206
       AU Nov. p94. 200w. $3\frac{1}{2}$

37 ARROWS. First Hit. RAK SRAK 521 (f)
       MM May 15 p26. 350w. 1

38 ARTFUL Dodger. Columbia PC33811
       CIR March 23 p14. 150w. 4
       CRE Sept. p14. 50w. 4

39 ARTFUL Dodger. Honor Among Thieves. Columbia PC34273
       CRE Dec. p14. 50w. 4
       CRE Dec. p60-1. 450w. $2\frac{1}{2}$
       MG Nov. p56. 50w. $3\frac{1}{2}$

RS Oct. 21 p107, 109.   225w. $3\frac{1}{2}$

40   ATLANTA Rhythm Section.   Dog Days.   Polydor PD 6041
CAC   Feb.   p443.   175w. $3\frac{1}{2}$

41   ATLANTA Rhythm Section.   Red Tape.   Polydor PD 6060
CRA   Aug.   p77.   100w.   3
GP   Aug.   p81.   25w.   3
GR   Sept.   p493.   75w.   3
MM   Sept. 11   p29.   450w.   4
RS   July 1   p76.   375w. $3\frac{1}{2}$

42   AUGER, Brian and Oblivion Express.   Reinforcements.   RCA
APL1-1210.   Cart. APS1-1210.   Cass. APK1-1210
CRA   Jan.   p77.   75w.   3
LP   Nov.   p5.   50w.   1
RS   Jan. 1   p59.   175w.   3
SR   Feb.   p78.   100w.   2

43   AUTOMATIC Fine Tuning.   Charisma (E)
MM   Nov. 20   p25.   250w. $1\frac{1}{2}$

44   AUTOMATIC Man.   Island ILPS-9397
CR   Dec.   p49.   50w.   3
RS   Nov. 4   p76.   200w.   3

45   AVERAGE White Band.   Soul Searching.   Atlantic SD-18179
BM   Sept.   p44-5.   150w.   4
CAC   Sept.   p216.   100w.   2
CIR   Oct. 26   p14.   150w.   1
CRA   Sept.   p81.   200w. $2\frac{1}{2}$
MG   Sept.   p55.   300w.   3
MM   Aug. 7   p18.   225w.   2
RS   Sept. 9   p55.   225w.   2

46   AXELROD, David.   Seriously Deep.   Polydor PD-6050
LP   Jan.   p5.   225w.   3

47   AXTON, Hoyt.   Fearless.   A&M 4571
CMP   Sept.   p22.   400w.   3
CMR   Nov.   p29.   150w. $1\frac{1}{2}$
HF   Sept.   p107.   200w. $3\frac{1}{2}$
MM   May 15   p25.   300w.   3
SR   Aug.   p72.   150w.   3

47a   AXTON, Hoyt.   Southbound.   A&M SP 4510
CMR   Feb.   p29.   200w. $2\frac{1}{2}$

48   AYERS, Kevin.   Harvest Heritage SHDW-407 (E) (Reissue)
GR   Feb.   p1389.   100w.   3

49   AYERS, Kevin.   Odd Ditties.   Harvest SHSM 2005 (E)
CAC   April   p13.   125w.   3

MM   June 19 p21.   525w.   3
RR   April p78.   50w.   3

50 AYERS, Kevin. Yes We Have No Mananas.   Harvest SHSP4057
(E)
     CAC   Nov. p294.   225w. $2\frac{1}{2}$
     GR   Sept. p493.   100w. $2\frac{1}{2}$
     MM   Aug. 14 p29.   550w. $3\frac{1}{2}$
     RR   Sept. p88-9.   75w.   3

51 AZTEC Two Step. Second Step. RCA APL1-1161.   Cart.
APS1-1161
     LP   Jan. p5.   150w. $2\frac{1}{2}$
     MM   April 3 p29.   50w.   1
     RS   Feb. 12 p92.   250w.   0
     SR   Feb. p78.   100w.   4

52 AZTEC Two Step. Two's Company. RCA APL1-1497
     RS   Dec. 16 p94.   200w.   3

53 BABE Ruth. Kids Stuff. Capitol ST 11515
     MM   Sept. 25 p24.   50w. $1\frac{1}{2}$

54 BABE Ruth. Stealin' Home. Capitol ST-11451
     LP   March p5.   100w. $2\frac{1}{2}$
     RS   Feb. 12 p93.   175w.   2

55 BACHMAN-TURNER Overdrive. Best of.   Mercury SRM1-1101
(Reissue)
     CRA   Dec. p72-3.   300w.   3
     CIR   Nov. 10 p13, 16.   475w. $2\frac{1}{2}$

56 BACHMAN-TURNER Overdrive. Head On. Mercury SRM
1-1067.   Cart. MC8-1-1067.   Cass. MCR-4-1-1067
     CAC   April p13.   150w.   4
     CIR   April 8 p14, 16.   50w.   1
     CRA   April p72.   550w.   1
     GR   May p1812.   25w.   1
     LP   April p5.   175w. $1\frac{1}{2}$
     MG   March p43.   50w.   2
     MM   April 3 p33.   275w.   2
     RS   March 11 p63-4.   250w. $2\frac{1}{2}$
     SOU   Feb. p44.   225w.   2
     SR   May p82.   25w. $2\frac{1}{2}$

57 BACKSTREET Crawler. The Band Plays On. ATCO SD 36-125.
Cart. TP 36-125. Cass. CS 36-125
     LP   April p5.   50w.   3
     MG   Jan. p34.   50w.   1
     SR   March p82.   150w.   3

58 BACKSTREET Crawler. Second Street. ATCO SD 36-138
     CRA   Oct. p70.   250w.   5

MM   Jan. 19   p21.   475w. $4\frac{1}{2}$
RS   Sept. 9   p60.   300w. $3\frac{1}{2}$

59   BAD Company.   Run with the Pack.   Swan Song SS-8415.   Cart.
T P-8415
AU   Nov.   p95-6.   350w. $3\frac{1}{2}$
CIR   June 1   p14.   350w. $2\frac{1}{2}$
CRA   May   p77.   150w.   3
CRE   June   p12.   50w. $3\frac{1}{2}$
GR   April   p1670.   75w.   3
MM   Jan. 17   p30.   600w. $3\frac{1}{2}$
PRM   March   p37-8.   150w.   2
RS   April 8   p63-4.   1500w.   4
SR   June   p76.   150w.   3

59a   BAEZ, Joan.   From Every Stage.   A&M AM SP3704 (2 discs)
CAC   May   p58, 60.   225w.   3
CIR   May 13   p18.   150w.   2
CMR   Aug.   p31-2.   225w. $2\frac{1}{2}$
CRE   June   p57.   325w.   2
GR   May   p1812.   125w.   3
MM   Feb. 21   p28.   700w. $2\frac{1}{2}$

59b   BAEZ, Joan.   Gulf Winds.   A&M SP 4603
PRM   Oct.   p35-6.   900w. $3\frac{1}{2}$

60   BAKER-Gurvitz Army.   Elysian Encounter.   Atco SD36-123
CRA   Jan.   p75.   225w. $3\frac{1}{2}$
LP   Jan.   p5-6.   150w.   3

61   BALLARD, Russ.   Winning.   Epic PE-34093
MH   Oct./Nov.   p69.   150w. $3\frac{1}{2}$
MM   April 3   p32.   300w.   3
RS   July 1   p73.   125w. $2\frac{1}{2}$
SR   Sept.   p90.   175w.   4

62   BANCO.   Manticore MA505VI
CRA   April   p76.   50w. $2\frac{1}{2}$

63   THE BAND.   Best of.   Capitol ST-11553.   Cart. 8XT-11553.
Cass. 4XT-11553 (Reissue)
CRA   Dec.   p82.   500w.   3
CIR   Nov. 25   p18-9.   300w. $3\frac{1}{2}$
SR   Dec.   p98.   150w.   4

64   THE BAND.   Northern Lights--Southern Cross.   Capitol
ST-11440.   Cart. 8XT-11440.   Cass. 4XT-11440
CIR   April 27   p14.   50w.   3
CMR   April   p41.   75w.   3
CRE   March   p12.   175w. $4\frac{1}{2}$
CRE   March   p58-60.   1100w.   3
DB   May 6   p26.   350w.   4
GR   March   p1518.   25w.   4

    HF   March p104. 250w. $4\frac{1}{2}$
    LP   March p6.   300w. $4\frac{1}{2}$
    OLR June   p105. 50w.   5
    PMS V4/#3 p193. 25w.   3
    RR   March p73.   75w.   4
    RS   Jan. 29 p44-5. 1400w. $3\frac{1}{2}$
    SOU Jan.   p35.   300w. $2\frac{1}{2}$
    SR   April p82.   175w. $4\frac{1}{2}$

65 BARCLAY James Harvest. Octoberon. MCA 2234
    MM Nov. 20 p28. 300w. 1

66 BARCLAY James Harvest.   Time Honoured Ghosts.   Polydor
    PD-6517
    CAC March p488. 75w.   2
    LP   April p5-6. 225w. 3
    SOU Jan.   p33-4. 325w. $2\frac{1}{2}$

67 BARCLAY, Nickey. Diamond in a Junkyard. Ariola ST 50006
    MM July 10 p22. 25w. $2\frac{1}{2}$

68 BAREFOOT Jerry. Grocery. Monument PZG33909 (2 discs)
    MG March p43. 50w. $1\frac{1}{2}$

69 BAY City Rollers. Arista 4049. Cart. 8301-4049-H. Cass.
    5301-4049-H
    CRE March p12. 25w. $2\frac{1}{2}$
    LP   March p6.   100w. $1\frac{1}{2}$
    SR   Jan. p78. 2

70 BAY City Rollers. Dedication. Arista AL-4093. Cart.
    8301-4093H. Cass. 5301-4093H
    CRA Nov. p81.   200w. $2\frac{1}{2}$
    RS   Nov. 18 p77. 300w. 2
    SR   Dec. p102. 150w. 2
    WHO Winter p43. 450w. $2\frac{1}{2}$

71 BAY City Rollers. Rock n' Roll Love Letter. Arista AL 4071.
    Cart. 8301-4071-H
    CIR July 6 p15. 75w.   2
    CRE Sept. p14. 25w.   3
    PRM April p24. 50w.   4
    SR   June p76. 250w. 0

72 BEACH Boys. Christmas Album. Capitol Sm 502164
    RS Dec. 30 p63. 75w. $2\frac{1}{2}$

73 BEACH Boys. Fifteen Big Ones. Brother/Reprise MS 2251
    (Reissue)
    AU   Oct. p137-8. 500w. 3
    AU   Nov. p95.   400w. 3
    CIR Sept. 28 p12. 600w. 2
    CRE Sept. p14. 100w. 4

        CRA   Sept.   p69-70.   1700w. $2\frac{1}{2}$
        MM   July 10   p21.   275w. $3\frac{1}{2}$
        RS   Aug. 12   p52.   2000w. $3\frac{1}{2}$

74 BEACH Boys.   Twenty Golden Hits.   Capitol EMTV 1 (E)
    (Reissue)
        CAC   Sept.   p216.   150w.   4
        MM   July 3   p21.   25w. $3\frac{1}{2}$
        MM   July 10   p21.   275w. $3\frac{1}{2}$

75 BEATLES.   Abbey Road.   Apple SO 383
        CRA   March   p80.   250w.   5

76 THE BEATLES.   Rock 'n' Roll Music.   Capitol SKBO-11537
    (two discs).   Cart. 8X2K-11537.   Cass.   4X2K-11537 (Reissue)
        AU   Oct.   p139.   150w. $3\frac{1}{2}$
        CIR   Oct. 12   p12-3.   825w.   3
        GR   Aug.   p350-1.   100w. $2\frac{1}{2}$
        MF   Oct./Nov.   p64.   300w.   3
        MM   June 26   p22.   375w.   4
        SR   Oct.   p90.   375w.   3

77 BEAU Dommage.   Capitol ST 70-134 (Canada)
        OLR   Sept.   p189.   25w.   3

78 BEAUREGARD, Violetti.   En plein orgasme.   Columbia FS
    90306 (Canada)
        OLR   Sept.   p189.   25w.   4

79 BE BOP Deluxe.   Modern Music.   Harvest ST-11575
        CRE   Dec.   p61.   325w.   2
        GR   Nov.   p899.   75w. $2\frac{1}{2}$
        MM   Sept. 11   p28.   650w.   3
        PRM   Oct.   p36.   550w.   2
        RR   Dec.   p99.   100w.   4
        RS   Dec. 2   p102.   175w.   4

80 BE BOP Deluxe.   Sunburst Finish.   Harvest ST 11478
        AU   Aug.   p67-8.   550w. $3\frac{1}{2}$
        CAC   April   p13.   200w.   4
        GR   April   p1670.   100w. $4\frac{1}{2}$
        MM   Jan. 31   p23.   350w.   4
        RS   April 8   p77.   200w. $3\frac{1}{2}$

81 BECK, Jeff.   Blow by Blow.   Epic PE-33409
        RRV   Jan.   p8-9.   1200w. $4\frac{1}{2}$

82 BECK, Jeff.   Truth.   Epic BN 26413
        CRA   March   p76.   475w. $2\frac{1}{2}$

83 BECK, Jeff.   Wired.   Epic PE-33849.   Cart. PES-33849.
    Cass. PET-33849
        CAC   Sept.   p214.   225w.   3

CIR   Sept. 28 p13. 375w.   2
CRA   Oct. p69. 550w.   4
CRE   Sept. p60. 425w. $2\frac{1}{2}$
DB   Sept. 9 p22. 350w. $3\frac{1}{2}$
GP   Sept. p86. 225w.   2
GR   Sept. p493. 100w.   4
RR   Sept. p88. 175w. $3\frac{1}{2}$
RS   July 29 p44. 850w.   4
SR   Oct. p90. 200w.   2

84   THE BECKIES. Sire SASD-7519
CIR   Sept. 28 p14-5. 550w. $2\frac{1}{2}$
CRE   Dec. p14. 100w. $3\frac{1}{2}$
SR   Oct. p90. 150w.   2

85   BEE Gees. Children of the Future.   RSO 3003
CRA   Nov. p77. 200w.   3
MM Dec. 25 p17. 500w.   3
PRM   Oct. p22. 50w.   1
RM   Nov. p31. 100w. $2\frac{1}{2}$
RS   Nov. 4 p67-8. 250w. $3\frac{1}{2}$

86   BEE Gees. Odessa. RSO 3007
SOU   March p40-1. 625w. $4\frac{1}{2}$

87   BELLAMY Brothers. Flow. Warner Brothers BS 2941
RS   July 15 p67. 200w. $2\frac{1}{2}$

87a BELLAMY Brothers. Let Your Love Flow. Warner Brothers
BS 2941
MM June 19 p21. 400w.   2

88   BIM. Kid Full of Dreams. Casino CA 1007 (Canada)
OLR   June p106. 25w. $1\frac{1}{2}$
SOU   March p44-5. 450w. $2\frac{1}{2}$

89   BIRD, Tony. Columbia PC 34324
CRA   Dec. p77. 375w.   4
MM May 22 p25. 75w. $1\frac{1}{2}$

90   BISHOP, Elvin. Best of/Crabshaw Rising. Epic PE-33693
(2 discs) (Reissue)
MG   Jan. p34. 50w. $3\frac{1}{2}$

91   BISHOP, Elvin. Struttin' My Stuff. Capricorn CP-0165. Cart.
M8-0165. Cass. M5-0165
CAC   Oct. p261. 50w.   2
CMP   Aug. p31. 275w.   2
CRA   April p69-70. 550w.   3
CRE   April p12. 50w.   4
CRE   April p61-2. 300w. $3\frac{1}{2}$
MG   April p39. 50w. $3\frac{1}{2}$
MM May 8 p22. 175w.   3
SR   May p82. 100w.   5

92 BLACK Oak Arkansas. Balls of Fire. MCA 2199
    MM   Sept. 4 p18. 175w. 0

93 BLACK Oak Arkansas. Live, Mutha! Atco SD36-128. Cart.
    TP-SD36-128. Cass. CS-SD36-128
    CRE   April p62. 50w. $2\frac{1}{2}$
    MM   April 3 p32. 200w. 3
    SR   May p82. 25w. 0

94 BLACK Oak Arkansas. X-rated. MCA 2155. Cass. MCAC2155
    LP   Jan. p6. 200w. 2

95 BLACK Sabbath. Sabotage. Warner BS2822. Cart. M82822.
    Cass. M52822
    SR   Jan. p78. 75w. 0

96 BLACK Sabbath. Technical Ecstasy. Warner Brothers BS
    2969
    CIR   Nov. 25 p17-8. 350w. 2
    MM   Oct. 16 p25. 375w. 4

97 BLACK Sabbath. We Sold Our Soul for Rock 'n' Roll. Warner
    Brothers 2BS 2923 (2 discs) (Reissue)
    MM   March 6 p28. 300w. 4

98 BLACKMORE'S Rainbow. Rainbow Rising. Oyster 1601
    CAC   Aug. p176. 275w. $3\frac{1}{2}$
    CRE   Aug. p67-8. 675w. 1
    GP   Aug. p80. 100w. $3\frac{1}{2}$
    GR   Aug. p351. 25w. 3
    MM   July 31 p21. 150w. $2\frac{1}{2}$
    RS   July 15 p67. 225w. 3

99 BLOOD, Sweat and Tears. Child Is the Father of the Man.
    Columbia CS 9619
    CRA   March p77. 125w. 4

100 BLOOD, Sweat and Tears. More than Ever. (E) Columbia
     PC 34233
     CAC   Oct. p256, 258. 275w. $3\frac{1}{2}$
     MM   Aug. 14 p29 450w. 3

101 BLOODSTONE. Lullaby of Broadway. Decca (E) SKL 5238
     CAC   Oct. p258. 200w. $2\frac{1}{2}$

102 BLUE, David. Comin' Back for More. Asylum 7E1043
     HF   March p108. 150w. 1

103 BLUE, David. Cupid's Arrow. Asylum 7E 1077
     CRA   Dec. p78. 225w. 3

104 BLUE Jug. Capricorn CP 0158. Cass. M5 0158
     LP   March p6. 100w. $1\frac{1}{2}$

RS   Jan. 1   p56.   300w. $4\frac{1}{2}$

105   BLUE Oyster Cult.   Agents of Fortune.   Columbia PC 34164
      AU   Dec.   p84.   150w.   1
      CIR   Aug. 24 p14.   325w. $4\frac{1}{2}$
      CRA Sept. p81.   375w.   3
      CRE Aug. p68.   500w.   3
      HF   Sept. p107.   200w. $2\frac{1}{2}$
      MM   June 19 p20.   575w.   4
      RR   Sept. p88.   150w.   2
      RS   July 15 p63, 65.   325w.   4

106   BLUES Project.   Live at Town Hall.   Verve FT/FTS 3025
      CRA March p77.   125w. $1\frac{1}{2}$

107   BOBB B. Soxx and the Blue Jeans.   Phil Spector Wall of
      Sound, vol. 3.   Polydor (E) (Reissue)
      CAC March p493.   75w. $2\frac{1}{2}$

108   BOLIN, Tommy.   Private Eyes.   Columbia PC 34329
      CRA Dec.   p70.   325w. $4\frac{1}{2}$
      MM   Nov. 6 p20.   200w.   2
      RS   Nov. 18 p76.   175w. $2\frac{1}{2}$

109   BOLIN, Tommy.   Teaser.   Nemperor NE-436.   Cass. CS-436
      CIR   March 23 p13-4.   575w.   3
      CRA Feb.   p74.   200w. $3\frac{1}{2}$
      CRE March p60-1.   175w.   2
      GP   April p79.   100w. $3\frac{1}{2}$
      LP   April p6.   200w. $3\frac{1}{2}$
      RS   Feb. 12 p92.   200w.   3

110   BOND.   Columbia ES90301 (Canada)
      OLR   June p105.   25w. $3\frac{1}{2}$

111   BONZO Dog Band.   I'm the Urban Spaceman.   Sunset SUS
      50350 (E) (Reissue)
      CAC Feb.   p446.   150w. $3\frac{1}{2}$

112   BONZO Dog Band.   Keynsham.   Sunset SUS 50375 (E) (Reissue)
      CAC Feb.   p446.   150w. $3\frac{1}{2}$

113   BOSTON.   Epic PG 34188
      CIR   Dec. 14 p14-5.   250w.   3
      CRA Dec.   p78-9.   200w. $3\frac{1}{2}$
      CRE Nov.   p59.   325w.   3
      GP   Dec.   p105.   25w. $2\frac{1}{2}$
      MM   Nov. 20 p25.   275w. $1\frac{1}{2}$
      PRM Oct.   p22.   50w.   3
      RS   Oct. 7 p84.   125w. $3\frac{1}{2}$

114   BOTTOM Line.   Crazy Dancin'.   Polydor GTMC009 (E)
      CAC Aug.   p176.   25w.   3

115 BOWIE, David. Changesonebowie. RCA APL1-1732. Cart.
APL1-1732. Cass. APK1-1732
SR Nov. p95-6. 125w. 2

116 BOWIE, David. Station to Station. RCA APL1-1327. Cart.
APS1-1327. Cass. APK1-1327
AU Dec. p84-5. 400w. 0
CIR April 8 p12, 14. 350w. $2\frac{1}{2}$
CRE April p12. 50w. $4\frac{1}{2}$
CRE April p58. 1225w. $4\frac{1}{2}$
CRA May p77. 175w. 4
GR April p1670. 50w. $2\frac{1}{2}$
MG May p46. 100w. $2\frac{1}{2}$
MM Jan. 24 p26. 2050w. 5
RR May p74. 200w. 1
RS March 25 p60, 62. 250w. $2\frac{1}{2}$
SR May p82. 250w. 3

117 BOXER. Below the Belt. Virgin PZ-34115. Cart. PZA-
34115
AU Nov. p96. 300w. 3
CRE Sept. p14. 50w. $3\frac{1}{2}$
CRE Sept. p65. 100w. 1
MHF May p60. 175w. 3
MM Feb. 14 p30. 400w. 4
RS July 1 p71. 75w. $3\frac{1}{2}$
SR Sept. p90. 125w. 2

118 BRAMBLETT, Randall. Light of the Night. Polydor PD 6064
CRE Aug. p14. 50w. 4
RS May 20 p72. 225w. 3

119 BRAMBLETT, Randall. That Other Mile. Polydor PD 6045
AU Jan. p65. 450w. 4

120 BRAMLETT, Bonnie. Lady's Choice. Capricorn CPO169
MG Nov. p56. 50w. $4\frac{1}{2}$
RM Nov. p31. 125w. $3\frac{1}{2}$
RR Dec. p100. 50w. $1\frac{1}{2}$
RS Nov. 7 p76. 250w. $3\frac{1}{2}$

121 BRAMLETT, Delaney and Blue Diamond. Giving Birth to a
Song. MGM SE-5011
SOU Feb. p42-3. 400w. $2\frac{1}{2}$

122 BRAND X. Unorthodox Behavior. Passport 98019
MM July 3 p23. 350w. $3\frac{1}{2}$

123 BRASS Construction. United Artists LA 545 G
CRE June p12. 50w. 3

124 BRIGATI. Lost in the Wilderness. Elektra 7E-1074
RS Oct. 7 p175. 100w. 3

SR Dec. p103. 300w. $4\frac{1}{2}$

125 BROMBERG, David. How Late'll Ya Play 'Til. Fantasy
F-79007 (2 discs)
GP Dec. p104-5. 200w. 4
RS Nov. 4 p80, 82. 200w. $3\frac{1}{2}$

126 BROOKS, Elkie. Rich Man's Woman. A&M SP4554 (E)
CAC May p56. 175w. $3\frac{1}{2}$
CRA Feb. p76. 150w. 3
GR Jan. p1258. 25w. 2
RS Feb. 26 p80. 225w. $2\frac{1}{2}$

126a BROWN, Arthur. Dance with.... Gull 405
CRE Jan. p71. 25w. 1

126b BROWN, Arthur. The Lost Ears. Gull GUD 2003/4 (2 discs)
(E)
CAC Oct. p252. 175w. 4
MM Nov. 13 p28. 75w. $2\frac{1}{2}$

127 BROWN, Charity. Rock Me. A&M SP 9019 (Canada)
OLR March p39. 25w. $3\frac{1}{2}$

128 BROWNE, Jackson. The Pretender. Asylum 7E-1079
PRM Nov. p19. 1400w. 4
MM Nov. 13 p22. 400w. 4

129 BRUSSEL Sprout. MCA 2211 (Canada)
CC Sept. p31. 50w. 3

130 BRUTUS. For the People. GRT (Canada)
RM Dec. p34. 75w. 3

131 BRYARS, Gavin. The Sinking of the Titanic. Obscure (E)
MM Feb. 21 p28. 250w. 3

132 BUCHANAN, Roy. Polydor 2482275 (E) (Reissue)
CAC June p94. 250w. 4
MM May 15 p25. 50w. $2\frac{1}{2}$
GR July p226. 50w. 3

133 BUCHANAN, Roy. Live Stock. Polydor PD 6048
LP Jan. p6. 175w. $4\frac{1}{2}$

134 BUCHANAN, Roy. A Street Called Straight. Atlantic SD-
18170. Cart. TP-18170. Cass. CS-18170
MG June p44. 50w. $2\frac{1}{2}$
SR Sept. p90. 250w. 3

135 BUCKACRE. Morning Comes. MCA 2218
AU Dec. p82-3. 300w. 0
MM Nov. 27 p28. 100w. 2

136 BUDGIE. Best of. MCA MCF2766 (E) (Reissue)
     CAC Nov. p294. 250w. 3
     MM Oct. 2 p30. 75w. 3

137 BUDGIE. If I Were Brittania I'd Waive the Rules. A&M
    SP 4593
     CAC Aug. p176. 225w. 3
     GP Oct. p97. 25w. $2\frac{1}{2}$
     RS Nov. 18 p80. 125w. 2

138 BUFFALO Springfield. Atco 5033 200A (Reissue)
     CRA March p74. 1000w. $3\frac{1}{2}$

139 BUFFETT, Jimmy. Havaña Daydreamin. ABC 914
     CMP May p18. 325w. 3
     CRE June p12. 75w. 4
     SR July p89. 475w. $4\frac{1}{2}$

140 BURDON, Eric. Stop. Capital SMAS-11426. Cart. 8XT-
    11426. Cass. 4XT-11426
     SR Jan. p78. 50w. 0

141 BYRD, Joseph. Yankee Trancendoodle. Takoma C 1051
     RS Dec. 2 p102. 275w. 4

142 BYRDS. Sweetheart of the Rodeo/The Notorious Byrd Brothers.
    CBS 22040 (2 discs) (E) (Reissue)
     CAC Sept. p216. 425w. $3\frac{1}{2}$
     CMP Dec. p13. 300w. 3
     MM July 31 p21. 400w. 4
     RR Sept. p89. 125w. $3\frac{1}{2}$

143 BYRDS. Turn, Turn, Turn/Tambourine Man. Columbia
    CG 33645 (2 discs) (Reissue)
     MM June 26 p22. 50w. 2

144 BYRON, David. Take No Prisoner. Mercury SRM 1-1074
     CIR June 1 p17. 75w. $2\frac{1}{2}$

145 CADDICK, Bill. Rough Music. Park SHP 102 (E)
     MM Aug. 7 p19. 275w. 3

146 CAJUN Moon. Chrysalis (E)
     MM June 26 p21. 275w. 3

147 CALDERÓN, Jorge. City Music. Warner Bros. BS 2904
     MG June p44. 50w. $3\frac{1}{2}$

148 CALE, J. J. Troubadour. Shelter SRL-52002
     CRA Nov. p77. 100w. 2
     GP Dec. p105. 50w. 3
     GR Nov. p899. 125w. 3
     PRM Oct. p22. 75w. 1
     MM Sept. 4 p18. 450w. $3\frac{1}{2}$

RS   Nov. 4   p67.   150w. $2\frac{1}{2}$

149   CALE, John.   Helen of Troy.   Island
        CRA   May   p71.   950w.   3
        MG   July   p46.   50w.   3

150   CALE, John.   Slow Dazzle.   Island ILPS9317
        CRE   April   p12.   25w.   4
        LP   Jan.   p6.   275w.   3

151   CALICO.   United Artists UA-LA-454-G
        PMS   V4/#4   p255.   350w.   4

152   CAMEL.   Moonmadness.   Janus 7024
        CAC   June   p94   150w. $4\frac{1}{2}$
        CK   Aug.   p46.   50w. $3\frac{1}{2}$
        CRA   Aug.   p76.   125w.   3
        GR   June   p98.   50w. $3\frac{1}{2}$
        MM   April 3   p32.   450w. $4\frac{1}{2}$

153   CAMPBELL, Alex.   No Regret.   Look LKLP 6043 (E)
        MM   Aug. 28   p21.   450w. $2\frac{1}{2}$

154   CAN.   Unlimited Edition.   Caroline CAD 3001 (2 discs) (E)
        MM   June 26   p22.   50w. $2\frac{1}{2}$

155   CANNED Heat.   Cookbook.   Sunset SUS 50377 (E) (Reissue)
        CAC   Feb.   p442.   175w.   3

156   CANNED Heat.   Live at the Topanga Corral.   DJM DJSL 072
        (E)
        CAC   Oct.   p258.   325w.   4
        MM   June 5   p20.   450w.   3

157   CANNED Heat.   Memphis Heat.   Blue Star L39058 (France)
        (Reissue)
        CZM   June   p41-2.   25w. $2\frac{1}{2}$

158   CAPALDI, Jim.   Short Cut Draw Blood.   Island ILPS9336
        AU   July   p70.   250w.   3
        CAC   Jan.   p402.   125w.   2
        RS   May 11   p63.   350w.   3
        SR   Aug.   p72.   200w.   2

159   CAPTAIN Beefheart.   Trout Mask Replica.   Straight STS 1053
        CRA   March   p78.   200w. $3\frac{1}{2}$

160   CARAVAN.   Blind Dog at St. Dunstan's.   Arista AL 4088
        CAC   July   p137.   150w.   3
        GR   July   p226.   75w. $3\frac{1}{2}$
        MM   May 22   p23.   450w. $3\frac{1}{2}$

161   CARDIER, Glenn.   EMI EMC 3115

MM   July 10   p21.   50w.   2

162 CARMEN, Eric.   Arista AL 4057
    AU   Feb.   p87.   500w.   4
    CIR   Feb.   10   p48.   300w.   3
    CRA   Jan.   p77.   25w. $2\frac{1}{2}$
    CRE   March   p12.   50w.   3
    HF   Feb.   p120.   200w.   2
    LP   April   p6.   150w.   2
    MG   Jan.   p33.   75w.   3
    SR   Jan.   p78-9.   475w.   3

163 CARMEN.   The Gypsies.   Mercury SRM1-1047.   Cart. MC8-
    1047.   Cass.   MCR4-1047
    MG   March   p43.   50w.   1
    SR   May   p82-3.   100w.   1

164 CARR, Peter.   Not a Word on It.   Big Tree BT 89518
    GP   Dec.   p104.   75w.   4
    RS   Nov.   4   p75.   175w.   3

165 CATE Brothers.   Asylum 7E-1050
    MM   Jan.   24   p26.   225w.   3
    RS   Jan.   29   p45-6.   300w. $3\frac{1}{2}$

166 CATE Brothers.   In One Eye and Out the Other.   Asylum
    7E-1080
    MM   Nov.   13   p29.   350w.   3
    RR   Dec.   p90.   100w. $3\frac{1}{2}$
    RR   Dec.   p100.   50w. $2\frac{1}{2}$

167 CAYENNE.   Bucksnort BRO1
    HF   March   p106.   50w. $3\frac{1}{2}$

168 CHALKITIS, Harris.   Barclay 80-565 (E)
    MM   July 24   p25.   75w.   3

169 CHANDLER, Gene.   Duke of Earl.   DJM (E) (Reissue)
    MM   Nov.   27   p24.   175w. $2\frac{1}{2}$

170 CHAPIN, Harry.   Greatest Stories Live.   Elektra 7E-2009
    (2 discs).   Cart. ET-82009.   Cass.   TC-52009
    MM   July 3   p21.   25w. $2\frac{1}{2}$
    SR   Sept.   p91-2.   324w.   2

171 CHAPIN, Harry.   On the Road to Kingdom Come.   Elektra
    7E-1082
    MM   Dec.   11   p22.   375w. $1\frac{1}{2}$

172 CHAPIN, Harry.   Portrait Gallery.   Elektra 7E-1041.   Cart.
    ET-81041
    CRE   Jan.   p66.   300w.   1
    HF   Jan.   p104.   200w. $3\frac{1}{2}$

```
              LP   Jan.   p7.   250w.   1
              SR   Feb.   p78-9.   100w.   1
```

173 CHAPMAN, Michael. Savage Amusement. Decca Gama 5242
     (E)
```
              CAC   Oct.   p252.   125w.   2
              MM   Aug.   7  p18.   325w.   4
```

174 CHARLEBOIS, Robert. Londue Distance.   Solution SN 905
     (Canada)
```
              CC   June   p31.   50w.   3
```

175 CHARLES, Ronnie. Prestidigitation. 20th Century T-491
```
              MM   Feb.   7  p25.   375w.   0
```

176 CHARLIE. Fantasy Girls. Columbia PC 34081 (E)
```
              CAC   April   p19.   25w.   3
              MM   April   17   p23.   150w.   2
              RR   April   p78.   50w.   3
```

177 CHARLIE and the Pep Boys. Daddy's Girl.   A&M SP 4563
```
              CIR   Sept.   13  p16.   125w.   2½
              CRE   Nov.   p63.   50w.   1½
              RS   July   29   p50.   250w.   3
```

178 CHICAGO. X. Columbia PC-34200. Cart. PCA 34200.
     Cass. PCT 34200
```
              CAC   Sept.   p218.   150w.   2
              MG   Oct.   p65.   25w.   1
              MM   Aug.   14   p29.   50w.   3
              RS   Aug.   12   p58.   350w.   3
              SR   Nov.   p96.   50w.   1
```

179 CHICAGO. Greatest Hits. Columbia PC33900 (Reissue)
```
              CAC   Feb.   p442.   150w.   2
              HF   April   p135.   100w.   1
              MG   Feb.   p36.   50w.   4
```

180 CHILLIWACK. Rockerbox. Sire 7511
```
              OLR   June   p105.   50w.   2½
```

181 CITY Boy. Mercury SRM 1-1098
```
              AU   Oct.   p132, 134.   400w.   4
              CAC   April   p13-4.   275w.   3
              CRA   Oct.   p81.   150w.   3½
              MM   April   3   p32.   250w.   3
              RS   Aug.   26   p66.   175w.   4
```

182 CITY Lights. Silent Dancing. Sire SASD 7512
```
              MG   Feb.   p38.   50w.   3½
```

183 CLANCY. Every Day. Warner Brothers K56206 (E)
```
              MM   March   6   p27.   325w.   4
```

184 CLAPTON, Eric. No Reason to Cry. RSO 3004. Cart.
8T1-3004. Cass. CT1-3004
    CAC Nov. p295. 275w. $3\frac{1}{2}$
    CIR Dec. 30 p14. 275w. $2\frac{1}{2}$
    CRA Nov. p68-9. 725w. 5
    MM Aug. 28 p20. 600w. $3\frac{1}{2}$
    PRM Oct. p35. 650w. $3\frac{1}{2}$
    PRM Nov. p22. 100w. 1
    RR Dec. p99. 50w. 3
    RM Dec. p33. 100w. 3
    RS Nov. 18 p71-2. 1150w. 2

185 CLARKE, Allan. I've Got Time. Asylum 7e-1056
    CIR Aug. 10 p14. 200w. $2\frac{1}{2}$
    RS May-June p62, 65. 250w. 2
    SR May p90-1. 350w. 3

186 CLEARLIGHT. Forever Blowing Bubbles. Virgin V2039 (E)
    MM Jan. 17 p32. 200w. $2\frac{1}{2}$

187 COCHRAN, Eddie. C'Mon Everybody. Sunset 50155 (E) (Reissue)
    CAC Feb. p447. 275w. 4

188 COCKBURN, Bruce. Joy Will Find a Way. True North TN
23 (Canada)
    OLR March p39. 25w. 4

189 COCKER, Joe. Stingray. A&M SP14574 (E)
    CAC Aug. p176. 200w. $2\frac{1}{2}$
    CIR July 22 p14. 200w. 2
    CRA July p73. 300w. 3
    GR Aug. p351. 100w. 4
    HF Sept. p109. 200w. 3
    MM June 5 p20. 750w. 3
    RR Aug. p78-9. 200w. $1\frac{1}{2}$
    RS July 1 p65. 775w. 2

190 CODY, Phil. One. Reprise MS 2232
    CRA July p81. 100w. 2
    RS May 6 p69, 71. 350w. 3

191 COHEN, Leonard. Best of. Columbia PC 34077
    AU June p81. 150w. 4
    CAC Jan. p403. 50w. 3
    CIR July 6 p14. 100w. $4\frac{1}{2}$
    OLR Sept. p188. 50w. 4

192 COLLINS, Judy. Bread and Roses. Elektra 7E-1076. Cart.
ET8-1076. Cass. TC5-1076
    CIR Dec. 14 p16-7. 250w. 2
    MM Sept. 11 p27. 800w. 2
    SR Dec. p104. 125w. 4

192a COLLINS, Judy. Wildflowers. Elektra EKS 74012
      CRA   March p78.   75w. $3\frac{1}{2}$

193   COLOSSEUM II. Strange New Flesh. Bronze (E)
      MM   June 5 p19.   675w.   4

194   COMANOR, Jeffrey. Rumor in Time. Epic PE 34080
      RS   June 3 p80.   100w.   2

195   COMMANDER Cody and His Lost Planet Airmen. Hot Licks,
      Cold Steel and Truckers' Favourites. Warner (E)
      MM   Aug. 21 p19.   125w.   3

196   COMMANDER Cody and His Lost Planet Airmen. Tales from
      the Ozone. Warner BS 2883. Cart. B8 2883
      CM   Feb. p51-2.   650w.   1
      CMP March p19.   200w.   3
      CRE Jan. p71.   50w.   1
      SR   Feb. p79.   100w.   2

197   COMMANDER Cody and His Lost Planet Airmen. We've Got
      a Live One Here. Warner 2LS2939 (2 discs). Cart. L5 2939.
      Cass. L5 2939
      CIR Nov. 25 p17.   650w. $2\frac{1}{2}$
      CM   Nov. p64.   250w.   2
      GR   Oct. p669.   100w. $3\frac{1}{2}$
      MG   Oct. p65.   25w. $1\frac{1}{2}$
      MM   Aug. 21 p19.   125w.   3
      SR   Nov. p96.   75w.   1

198   CONRAD, Tony. Outside the Dream Syndicate. Virgin
      CRE June p60.   25w. $1\frac{1}{2}$

199   COODER, Ry. Chicken Skin Music. Reprise MS 2254
      AU   Dec. p80.   450w.   4
      CIR Dec. 14 p12-3.   350w.   4
      CRA Nov. p79.   250w.   5
      CRE Nov. p59.   275w. $3\frac{1}{2}$
      RR   Dec. p99-100.   100w. $3\frac{1}{2}$
      RS   Sept. 23 p112, 115.   225w. $3\frac{1}{2}$

200   COOLIDGE, Rita. It's Only Love. A&M SP-4531
      CAC April p10.   175w. $2\frac{1}{2}$
      CM   April p47.   550w. $4\frac{1}{2}$
      CMP March p20.   200w.   3
      HF   March p106.   150w.   2
      RS   Feb. 26 p80.   100w.   3
      SR   April p82.   200w.   3

201   CORMAN, Gene. Thimble TLP 7
      LP   Jan. p7.   125w.   2

202   COUGAR, Johnny. Chestnut Street Incident. MCA 2225

RS Dec. 16 p94. 250w. 0

203 COURTNEY, David. First Day. United Artists UALA
     553G
          AU Aug. p69. 350w. $2\frac{1}{2}$
          CRA April p76. 50w. 1

204 COYNE, Kevin. Heartburn. Virgin V2047
          CRA July p80-1. 200w. 1
          MM June 5 p19. 500w. 3

205 COYNE, Kevin. Matching Head and Feet. Virgin V2047
          CRE July p68. 25w. $2\frac{1}{2}$

206 CRACK the Sky. Lifesong LS6000
          CRE April p12. 25w. 3
          MG Feb. p36. 50w. $1\frac{1}{2}$
          RS Jan. 1 p56. 350w. 4
          RS Dec. 26 p82. 250w. 3
          SOU Feb. p44-5. 250w. 4

207 CRACKIN'. Makings of. Warner Bros. BS 2989
          CRE Jan. p12. 25w. 2

208 CRAZY Cavan and the Rhythm Rockers. Rockability. Charly
     (E) (Reissue)
          MM Oct. 2 p30. 50w. $2\frac{1}{2}$

209 CREEDENCE Clearwater Revival. Chronicle. Fantasy CCR2
     (2 discs) (Reissue)
          CAC Aug. p176-7. 275w. $3\frac{1}{2}$
          CRA May p77. 250w. $4\frac{1}{2}$
          MM July 24 p25. 50w. 3

210 CROCE, Jim. The Faces I've Seen. Lifesong LS-900 (2
     discs)
          LP March p7. 250w. 3
          SR Feb. p79. 225w. $4\frac{1}{2}$

211 CROSBY and Nash. Whistling Down the Wire. ABC ABCD-956
          AU Nov. p97. 250w. $3\frac{1}{2}$
          CAC Sept. p218. 175w. 2
          CIR Nov. 10 p18. 100w. 1
          CRA Sept. p80. 200w. 1
          GR Nov. p899. 50w. 1
          MG Oct. p65. 50w. 2
          MM Aug. 28 p20. 450w. 3
          RS Sept. 9 p58. 150w. $1\frac{1}{2}$

212 CROSBY and Nash. Wind on the Water. ABC 902
          AU Feb. p86. 100w. 0

213 CROWN Heights Affair. Dreaming a Dream. De Lite 2017

CAC   March   p493.   75w. $2\frac{1}{2}$

214   CRYER and Ford.   RCA APL1-1235
MG   Jan.   p33.   75w.   3

215   CRYSTALS.   Phil Spector Wall of Sound, vol. 2.   Polydor (E)
CAC   March   p493.   75w. $3\frac{1}{2}$

216   CUMMINGS, Burton.   Portrait PR 34261
RM   Dec.   p30.   125w.   3
RS   Dec. 16   p86.   225w. $2\frac{1}{2}$

217   CURVED Air.   Midnight Wire.   RCA BTM 1005 (E)
GR   March   p1518.   25w. $2\frac{1}{2}$

218   DANIELS, Charlie.   Nightrider.   Kama Sutra KSBS-2607
LP   Jan.   p7.   250w. $4\frac{1}{2}$

219   DANIELS, Charles.   Saddle Tramp.   Epic PE-34150.   Cart.
PEA-34150.   Cass. PET-34150
CM   Sept.   p57.   75w.   3
MM   Sept. 18   p21.   300w.   3
RS   July 29   p52.   125w.   4
SR   Oct.   p92.   150w.   2

220   DAVIS, Betty.   Nasty Gal.   Island ILPS 9329
CRA   Jan.   p72.   150w.   0
MG   Feb.   p36.   50w. $2\frac{1}{2}$

221   DEAF School.   Second Honeymoon.   Warner K56280 (E)
MM   Aug. 21   p18.   500w. $3\frac{1}{2}$
RR   Oct.   p102.   75w.   1

222-3 DECAMERON.   Third Light.   Transatlantic TRA 304 (E)
CAC   April   p14.   200w.   3

224   DEEP Purple.   Come Taste the Band.   Warner PR-2895.
Cart. M8P 2895
CAC   Feb.   p443.   75w.   3
CIR   March 23   p13-4.   575w. $3\frac{1}{2}$
CRA   Feb.   p77.   300w. $2\frac{1}{2}$
CRE   March   p60-1.   175w.   2
LP   April   p6.   225w.   3
MG   Feb.   p38.   50w. $3\frac{1}{2}$
RS   Feb. 12   p90.   200w. $2\frac{1}{2}$
SR   April   p82.   125w.   3

225   DENVER, John.   Live in London.   RCA RS 1050 (E)
CMR   Nov.   p29.   200w.   4
MM   May 1   p30.   375w. $2\frac{1}{2}$

226   DENVER, John.   Rocky Mountain High.   RCA APL1-1201
MG   Jan.   p33.   50w.   3

227 DENVER, John. Spirit. RCA APL1-1694
    CAC Nov. p310. 125w. $2\frac{1}{2}$
    CMP Dec. p13. 125w. 2
    CRE Nov. p60. 300w. 2
    CS Dec. p42. 300w. 2
    CYR Nov. 4 p36. 200w. 3
    MM Sept. 18 p24. 600w. $2\frac{1}{2}$
    RS Oct. 7 p75-6. 225w. 2

228 DENVER, John. Windsong. RCA APL1-1183. Cart. APS1-1183
    CMR April p42. 250w. $3\frac{1}{2}$
    CRA April p75. 75w. $2\frac{1}{2}$
    CRE March p12. 50w. 2
    HF March p109. 100w. $2\frac{1}{2}$
    PMS V4/#4 p190. 50w. 2
    SR Jan. p80. 225w. 2

228a DE PAUL, Lynsey. Love Bomb. Mercury SRM 1-1055
    PRM Jan. p29. 150w. 4
    SR June p78-9. 100w. 0

229 DERRINGER, Rick. Blue Sky PZ-34181. Cart. PZA-34181.
Cass. PZT-34181
    CIR Oct. 12 p15. 300w. $2\frac{1}{2}$
    GP Sept. p87. 25w. $2\frac{1}{2}$
    GR Oct. p669. 125w. 4
    MM Sept. 11 p26. 25w. 3
    RR Dec. p99. 25w. 2
    RS Aug. 12 p67. 250w. $3\frac{1}{2}$
    SR Nov. p96. 100w. 3

230 DICKSON, Barbara. Answer Me. RSO 2394 167(E)
    CAC May p60. 50w. $2\frac{1}{2}$
    MM April 17 p22. 350w. 2

231 DIESEL Hydraulics. Westerns. Argo (E)
    MM May 15 p24. 250w. 3

232 DIGA Rhythm Band. Round RX LA600
    CRA Sept. p81. 100w. $2\frac{1}{2}$

233 DILLINGER. Don't Lie to the Band. Daffodil 9216-10055
(Canada)
    CC Sept. p30. 50w. 3

234 DINNER, Michael. Tom Thumb the Dreamer. Fantasy F-9512.
Cart. 8160-9512. Cass. 5160-9512H
    MG Nov. p56. 75w. 4
    SR Dec. p104. 175w. 1

235 DION. Born to Be with You. Phil Spector International 2307
002 (E)
    RS Sept. p54-5. 375w. 4

236 DION. Pick Hits of the Radio Good Guys, vol. 2. Phono-
     gram SON 004 (E) (Reissue)
     CAC Oct. p258. 75w. 2

237 DION. Streetheart. Warner BS-2954. Cart. M8-2954. Cass.
     M5-2954
     CIR Nov. 26 p14. 200w. $1\frac{1}{2}$
     CRA Sept. p32-4. 625w. $2\frac{1}{2}$
     GR Oct. p669. 75w. $2\frac{1}{2}$
     MM Sept. 11 p28. 300w. $3\frac{1}{2}$
     RS Sept. 9 p54-5. 400w. 2
     SR Nov. p96, 98. 175w. $2\frac{1}{2}$

238 DIONYSOS. Deram XDEF 125 (Canada)
     CC Sept. p29. 50w. $2\frac{1}{2}$

239 DR. FEELGOOD. Malpractice. Columbia PC-34098. Cart.
     PCA-34098
     CIR June 1 p15. 175w. $3\frac{1}{2}$
     CRA May p70. 225w. 3
     CRE June p12. 75w. 4
     CRE July p64. 200w. 3
     MHF May (vol. 6 no. 2) p60. 175w. $3\frac{1}{2}$
     PRM Jan. p229. 200w. 4
     PRM April p24. 50w. $4\frac{1}{2}$
     SR June p79. 150w. 3

240 DR. FEELGOOD. Stupidity. United Artists UAS-29990
     (E)
     MM Oct. 2 p28. 575w. $3\frac{1}{2}$

241 DR. HOOK. A Little Bit More. Capitol ST-11522. Cart.
     8XT-11522. Cass. 4XT-11522
     CAC Aug. p181. 150w. 3
     CYR Oct. 21 p28. 200w. 3
     GR Aug. p351. 75w. $3\frac{1}{2}$
     MM May 29 p26. 500w. 4
     SR Oct. p94. 250w. 3

242 DR. JOHN. Cut Me While I'm Hot. DJM 22019 (E)
     MM March 13. p25. 125w. 3

243 DR. JOHN. Hollywood Be Thy Name. United Artists UALA-
     552-G. Cart. EA-552-H. Cass. CA-552-H
     CRA Feb. p76. 175w. $2\frac{1}{2}$
     CRE Feb. p12. 25w. 2
     GR April p1670. 100w. 2
     MG Feb. p38. 50w. 3
     SR March p82-3. 400w. 2

244 DOCTORS of Madness. Figments of Emancipation. Polydor
     2383 403 (E)
     CAC Nov. p294. 200w. $2\frac{1}{2}$

MM   Nov. 20   p29.   75w.   3

245   DOCTORS of Madness.   Late Night Movies, All Night Brain-
      storms.   Polydor 2383 378 (E)
         CAC   May   p56.   200w. $2\frac{1}{2}$
         MM   May 22   p25.   50w.   1

246   DOHENY, Ned.   Hard Candy.   Columbia PC 34259
         RS   Dec. 16   p97.   175w.   3

247   DOLENZ, Jones, Boyce and Hart.   Capitol ST 11513
         RS   July 29   p51.   225w. $2\frac{1}{2}$
         SR   Dec.   p104.   200w. $1\frac{1}{2}$

248   DOLLARHIDE, Roger.   The Righteous Rock of.   Tom Cat
      BYL-11127
         LP   Jan.   p8.   225w.   2

249   DONATO.   Capitol ST 6423 (Canada)
         OLR   March   p40.   25w.   4

250   DONOVAN.   Pye (Reissue)
         HF   Feb.   p119.   100w. $2\frac{1}{2}$
         LP   March   p7.   175w. $3\frac{1}{2}$

251   DONOVAN.   Slow Down World.   Epic PE-33945.   Cart. PEA-
      33945.   Cass. PET-33945
         CRE   Aug.   p14.   75w.   2
         RS   July   p52.   275w.   3
         SR   Sept.   p92.   175w.   2

252   DOOBIE Brothers.   Best of.   Warners BS 2978 (Reissue)
         MM   Dec. 11   p21.   325w.   3

253   DOOBIE Brothers.   Takin' It to the Streets.   Warner Brothers
      BS 2894
         CIR   Aug. 10   p14.   225w.   3
         CRA   July   p76.   225w.   3
         GP   Aug.   p81.   25w.   3
         GR   July   p226.   50w.   4
         MG   July   p46.   50w. $3\frac{1}{2}$
         PRM   May   p31.   75w.   1
         RS   June 3   p80.   200w. $2\frac{1}{2}$
         SOU   May   p40.   400w.   3

254   THE DOORS.   Best of.   Elektra K 42143 (E) (Reissue)
         RR   Dec.   p101.   25w.   1

255   DOWNCHILD.   Dancing.   Special Records 9230-1049
      (Canada)
         Coda   June   p18.   175w.   3

256   DOWNCHILD.   Ready to Go.   GRT 9230-1060 (Canada)

54   Record Reviews, 1976

        CC Jan. p38. 50w. 3

257 DRANSFIELDS. The Fiddler's Dream. Transatlantic TRA 322
     (E)
        MM Sept. 4 p22. 475w. 3

258 DRUID. Fluid. EMI 3128 (E)
        CAC Aug. p177. 250w. $3\frac{1}{2}$

259 DUDES. We're No Angels. Columbia PC 33577
        CRE April p12, 72. 50w. 4
        HF Feb. p123. 100w. 3
        RS Jan. 15 p56. 300w. 3

260 DUKE and the Drivers. Cruisin'. ABC ABCD 911. Cass.
     5022-911H
        CRA Jan. p76. 125w. $3\frac{1}{2}$
        LP March p7. 100w. 3

261 DUNCAN, Lesley. Moonbathing. MCA 2207
        CRA Oct. p80-1. 150w. $3\frac{1}{2}$

262 DYLAN, Bob and The Band. The Basement Tapes. Columbia
     C2-32682 (2 discs)
        AU Jan. p65-6 350w. 4

263 DYLAN, Bob. Blonde on Blonde. Columbia C2S 841 (2 discs)
        CRA March p78. 450w. 5

264 DYLAN, Bob. Desire. Columbia PC-33893. Cass. PCT-
     33893
        AU April p76-7. 700w. $3\frac{1}{2}$
        CAC March p487. 350w. 4
        CIR March 23 p12-3. 900w. $4\frac{1}{2}$
        LP March p7. 450w. 3
        MG March p42. 300w. 2
        RR March p72. 225w. $4\frac{1}{2}$
        RS March 11 p55. 1750w. 4
        SOU March p41-2. 800w. 4
        SR April p88-9 850w. $2\frac{1}{2}$

265 DYLAN, Bob. Hard Rain. Columbia PC-34349. Cart. PCA-
     34349. Cass. PCT-34349
        AU Dec. p81. 150w. 1
        CAC Nov. p295. 200w. $4\frac{1}{2}$
        CIR Nov. 25 p13, 15. 1225w. $2\frac{1}{2}$
        CRA Dec. p82. 500w. $3\frac{1}{2}$
        CRE Dec. p59. 425w. 2
        MG Nov. p55. 600w. 4
        RM Nov. p30. 125w. 1
        RR Dec. p100. 125w. $1\frac{1}{2}$
        RS Dec. 2 p91. 1000w. 2

         SR   Dec.   p52.   650w.   4
         SR   Dec.   p108-9.   1200w.   4

266   EAGLES.   Hotel California.   Asylum 7E-1084
         MM   Dec. 11   p21.   850w.   2

266a   EAGLES.   One of Those Nights.   Asylum 7E-1039
         CS   June   p38.   225w.   4

267   THE EAGLES.   Their Greatest Hits, 1971-1975.   Asylum
         7E-1052 (Reissue).   Cart. TP-1052.   Cass. CS-1052
         MM   March 20   p22.   50w.   4
         SR   Aug.   p74.   200w.   4

268   EARTHQUAKE.   8.5.   Beserkeley 0047
         RS   Sept. 9   p59.   175w.   3

269   EARTHQUAKE.   Rocking the World.   Beserkeley 0045
         CRA   Feb.   p77.   125w. $4\frac{1}{2}$

270   EASY Street.   Capricorn 0174
         MM   Nov. 20   p29.   50w. $3\frac{1}{2}$

271   ECLIPSE.   CBS FS 4596
         CRA   Dec.   p72-3.   300w. $2\frac{1}{2}$

272   EDDIE and the Hot Rods.   Teenage Depression.   Island ILPS
         9457 (E)
         MM   Nov. 27   p27.   800w.   4

273   EDDIE Boy Band.   MCA 2153
         MM   Feb. 28   p25.   250w. $3\frac{1}{2}$

274   EDELMAN, Randy.   Farewell Fairbanks.   20th Century
         T494
         CAC   July   p140.   200w. $3\frac{1}{2}$
         MG   May   p46.   50w. $3\frac{1}{2}$
         MM   May 15   p26.   325w. $1\frac{1}{2}$
         MHF   May V6/#2   p61.   150w. $2\frac{1}{2}$

275   EDGE, Graeme and Adrian Gurvitz.   Kick Off Your Muddy
         Boots.   Threshold THS-15
         CAC   March   p487.   250w. $2\frac{1}{2}$
         CRA   Jan.   p75-6.   225w.   2
         LP   Jan.   p8.   225w.   2
         SR   Feb.   p80.   75w.   2

276   EDMUNDS, Dave.   Get It.   Swan Song
         WHO   Winter   p42.   150w.   4

277   EDMUNDS, Dave.   Subtle as a Flying Mallet.   RCA LPL-1-
         5003

CRE   Feb.   p63.   25w.   3
LP   March   p7.   100w.   3
MG   Feb.   p38.   50w. $4\frac{1}{2}$
PMS   V4/#3   p192.   25w.   3
RS   Feb. 26   p78-9.   400w. $2\frac{1}{2}$

278   EDWARDS, Jonathan.   Rockin' Chair.   Reprise MS 2238
AU   June   p84.   100w.   1
GM   June   p44.   50w. $1\frac{1}{2}$
SR   July   p88.   75w.   4
MHF   June/July   p69.   175w. $3\frac{1}{2}$

279   ELECTRIC Light Orchestra.   Face the Music.   United Artists
UA-LA546-G
CAC   Feb.   p443.   150w.   2
CIR   March 23   p14.   475w.   4
CRA   Feb.   p75-6.   225w. $2\frac{1}{2}$
GR   March   p1518.   50w.   3
LP   June   p8.   200w. $2\frac{1}{2}$
MG   Jan.   p33.   50w.   5
RS   Jan. 1   p55.   175w.   3
SOU   Feb.   p45.   350w. $2\frac{1}{2}$
SR   Feb.   p80.   100w.   2

280   ELECTRIC Light Orchestra.   A New World Record.   United
Artists LA-679-G
MM   Nov. 20   p28.   450w. $3\frac{1}{2}$
PRM   Nov.   p22.   50w.   3
PRM   Nov.   p33.   800w. $3\frac{1}{2}$
RS   Dec. 16   p82, 85.   150w.   3

281   ELECTRIC Light Orchestra.   Olé ELO.   United Artists LA
630-G
CIR   Sept. 28   p14.   225w. $1\frac{1}{2}$

282   ELEVENTH HOUR.   Aspects.   Arista AL 4077
SR   Nov.   p121.   50w.   1

283   ELVITA.   MCA MCX-503 (E)
MM   Nov. 20   p26.   100w.   0

284   EMERALD City.   Waiting for the Dawn.   Hippopotamus HLP
97202 (Canada)
CC   Sept.   p31.   50w.   3

285   ENGLAND Dan and John Ford Coley.   Nights Are Forever.
Warner Bros. K50297 (E)
RS   Sept. 23   p120.   100w. $2\frac{1}{2}$
SR   Dec.   p104.   74w.   3

286   ENO, Brian.   Another Green World.   Island ILPS-9351.   Cart.
481-9351

CAC   Feb.   p443.   175w. $3\frac{1}{2}$
CIR   April 8   p16.   325w.   4
CRE   July   p12.   25w. $4\frac{1}{2}$
DB   Oct. 21   p24, 26.   175w.   4
HF   June   p101.   100w.   2
HF   June   p99.   150w.   3
MG   June   p44.   50w.   3
RR   Feb.   p67.   50w. $4\frac{1}{2}$
RS   May 6   p67, 69   500w.   4
SR   Sept.   p92.   175w.   0

287   ENO, Brian.   Discreet Music.   Obscure 3 (E)
DB   Oct. 21   p24, 26   175w.   4
MM   Feb. 21   p28.   250w.   3

288   ENO, Brian.   Taking Tiger Mountain (by Strategy).   Island ILPS 4309
CRE   Nov.   p63.   100w.   4

289   ENO.   Evening Star.   Antilles 7018
DB   Oct. 21   p24, 26.   175w.   3

290   ESSEX, David.   All the Fun of the Fair.   Columbia PC-33813. Cass. PCT-33813
GR   Jan.   p1258.   25w. $2\frac{1}{2}$
HF   Feb.   p124.   150w. $\frac{1}{2}$
LP   March   p7.   100w.   2

291   ESSEX, David.   On Tour.   CBS 95000 (2 discs) (E)
MM   May 29   p29.   350w. $1\frac{1}{2}$

292   ESSEX, David.   Out on the Street.   Epic (E)
CAC   Dec.   p338.   275w.   3
MM   Oct. 23   p24.   375w. $2\frac{1}{2}$

293   ETHOS, Ardour.   Ethos.   Capitol ST 11498
CK   Aug.   p44-5.   250w.   4

294   EVERLY, Phil.   Mystic Line.   Pye 12121
CAC   Feb.   p447.   175w. $1\frac{1}{2}$
SR   March   p83.   200w.   3

295   EVERLY Brothers.   Songs Our Daddy Taught Us.   Philips International 6467 500 (E)
CMP   March   p20.   350w.   4
MM   Jan. 31   p23.   50w.   2

296   EVERLY Brothers.   Walk Right Back.   Warner K56168 (E) (Reissue)
GR   Jan.   p1258.   75w.   3

297   FACES.   Originals.   Warner (E) (Reissue)

MM Jan. 24 p26. 100w. 3

298 FAIRWEATHER-LOW, Andy. La Booga Rooga. A&M SP-4542
     CRA Jan. p79. 225w. 2
     CRE Jan. p12. 50w. 4
     LP Jan. p10. 150w. 3

299 FALCONER, Roderick. New Nation. United Artists LA
     651-G
     CRA Nov. p75. 125w. 3
     MM Nov. 20 p29. 100w. 2
     RM Dec. p34. 125w. 3½
     RS Nov. 18 p72. 125w. 2

300 FARLOW, Chris. Live. Polydor 2460259 (E)
     CAC March p487-8. 175w. 3
     RR Jan. p62. 25w. 1

301 FARLOW, Chris. Out of Time/Best of. Immediate IML-1002
     (E) (Reissue)
     RR March p73. 50w. 3

302 FARO, Rachael. II. RCA APL1-1105. Cass. APK1-1105
     LP Jan. p19. 150w. 3

303 FATBACK Band. Night Fever. Spring 6711
     CRE Nov. p63. 50w. 3
     MM Sept. 4 p22. 425w. 2

304 FATBACK Band. Raising Hell. Event 6905
     CAC April p16. 150w. 3
     MM Feb. 7 p23. 350w. 3

305 FENNELLY, Michael. Stranger's Bed. Mercury SRM1-
     1041
     RS Jan. 15 p53-4. 100w. 3

306 FERGUSON, Jay. All Alone in the End Zone. Asylum 7E
     1063
     AU Nov. p96-7. 300w. 2
     MM Aug. 7 p18. 200w. 4
     RM Dec. p31. 100w. 3
     RS Aug. 12 p71. 200w. 2

306a FERRIER, Al and His Boppin Billies. The Birth of Rockabilly.
      Goldband LP 7769
      CM Aug. p52. 375w. 4

307 FERRY, Bryan. Let's Stick Together. Atlantic SD 18187
     AU Dec. p81. 400w. 3½
     CIR Dec. 14 p12. 625w. 3
     CRA Dec. p68. 275w. 3½
     RS Nov. 18 p72. 250w. 3

Rock   59

308   FINNIGAN, Mike.   Warner Bros.   BS 2944
         RS Oct. 7 p84. 175w. 3

309   FIREFALL. Atlantic SD 18174. Cart. TP-18174. Cass.
      CS-18174
         CRA July p76, 78 250w. 2
         GP   Aug. p80. 75w. 2½
         MHF June-July p70. 300w. 3
         MM   July 10 p22. 125w. 3
         PRM May p31. 50w. 1
         RS   July 1 p73. 300w. 2½
         SR   Sept. p92. 200w. 3

310   FISHMAN, Paul. In Search of Ancient Gods. Warner
      (E)
         MM May 1 p30. 175w. 2½

311   FLAMIN' GROOVIES. Shake Some Action. Sire SASD-
      7521
         AU   Nov. p95. 300w. 3
         CRA Oct. p79. 175w. 3
         CIR Aug. 24 p15. 250w. 3
         CRE Sept. p62. 400w. 4
         MM   June 26 p22. 50w. 2
         PRM Sept. p35-6. 600w. 4
         SR   Nov. p98. 175w. 5

312   FLASH Cadillac. Songs of the Beaches. Private Stock
      2003
         CRE Jan. p70. 300w. 4

313   FLEETWOOD Mac. Reprise M5-2225
         AU   Feb. p85-6. 400w. 2
         CRE Feb. p12. 50w. 4½
         PMS V4/#4 p256. 250w. 4½

314   FLEETWOOD Mac. In Chicago. Sire SASH 3715/2 (2
      discs)
         LP   April p7. 275w. 3
         MG   March p43. 50w. 4

315   FLO and Eddie. Illegal, Immoral and Fattening. Columbia PC-
      33554
         CRE Jan. p12. 25w. 2
         SR   Jan. p80. 200w. 2

316   FLO and Eddie. Moving Targets. Columbia PC-34262. Cart.
      PCA-34262
         CRA Nov. p77. 225w. 2
         CRE Nov. p60-1. 350w. 3
         MG   Dec. p63. 50w. 3

        RS   Nov. 4 p75-6.   150w.   3
        SR   Dec.   p106.   150w.   2½

317 FLYING Burrito Brothers.   Airborne.   Columbia PC-34222.
     Cart. PCA-34222.   Cass. PCT-34222
        CMP Nov. p40-1.   150w.   3
        GP   Sept. p87.   25w.   3
        MM   Aug. 21 p18.   375w.   3
        RS   Aug. 26 p65.   150w.   2½
        SR   Nov. p98.   175w.   2

318 FLYING Burrito Brothers.   Flying Again.   Columbia PC-
     33817.   Cart. PCA 33817
        AU   April p87.   200w.   2
        CAC Feb. p443.   150w.   2½
        CIR Jan. 20 p20.   50w.   1½
        CM   March p57-8.   775w.   2
        CMP March p19.   200w.   2
        CMR April p40.   200w.   2½
        CRE Jan. p71.   50w.   1½
        GP   May p81.   25w.   3½
        LP   March p7.   150w.   3
        MG   Jan. p34.   50w.   2
        RR   Feb. p66.   50w.   3
        SR   Feb. p80.   275w.   4

319 FLYING Burrito Brothers.   Live in Amsterdam.   Ariola
     86439 XCT (Holland)
        AU   April p87.   200w.   1

320 FOCUS.   Mother Focus.   ATCO SD36-117.   Cart. TP36-117.
     Cass. 36-117
        LP   March p7.   100w.   2½
        SR   Jan. p80.   175w.   2

321 FOGELBERG, Dan.   Captured Angel.   Full Moon PE33499.
     Cart. PEA33499.   Cass. PET33499
        AU   Feb. p86.   100w.   0
        CIR Jan. 20 p20.   225w.   3
        LP   Jan. p8-9.   225w.   4½
        SR   Jan. p80, 82.   150w.   0

322 FOGERTY, John.   Fantasy FT526 (E)
        CRE Jan. p12.   25w.   3½
        GR   Jan. p1258.   25w.   3
        PMS V4/#3 p189.   50w.   2

323 FOGHAT.   Fool for the City.   Bearsville BR-6959.   Cass.
     M5-6959
        AU   April p86-7.   200w.   2½
        LP   Jan. p9.   100w.   3½
        MM   March 6 p27.   275w.   3

RR   March   p73.   25w.   3

324-5 FOOL'S Gold.   Morning Sky 5500
         CMR Oct.   p32.   200w.   4
         MH   Oct./Nov.   p68-9.   100w.   3
         MM   July 24   p25.   25w. $2\frac{1}{2}$
         PRM Sept.   p36.   475w.   3
         RS   June 3   p75, 77.   250w. $2\frac{1}{2}$

326   FORMAN, David.   Arista AL 4084
         CIR Nov. 25   p12-3.   1000w. $4\frac{1}{2}$
         CRA Nov.   p82.   250w. $3\frac{1}{2}$
         RS   Oct. 7   p69.   750w. $3\frac{1}{2}$

327   FRAMPTON, Peter.   Frampton Comes Alive.   A&M SP-3703.
         Cart. 3703
         AU   June   p81-2.   600w. $2\frac{1}{2}$
         AU   June   p82.   200w. $3\frac{1}{2}$
         CAC May   p56-7.   225w.   4
         CIR April 27   p12, 13.   200w.   4
         HF   April   p135.   150w. $3\frac{1}{2}$
         MG   March   p42.   300w. $3\frac{1}{2}$
         MM   March 13   p23.   550w.   4
         RO   June   p87.   350w. $4\frac{1}{2}$
         RR   April   p77-8.   150w. $3\frac{1}{2}$
         RS   March 11   p60.   250w. $3\frac{1}{2}$
         SR   June   p82.   150w.   4

328   FREE Beer.   Southwind SWS 6042
         LP   Jan.   p9.   200w.   3

329   FRIPP and Eno.   No Pussyfooting.   Antilles AN-7001
         DB   April 8   p30-2.   75w.   2
         LP   April   p7.   125w. $1\frac{1}{2}$
         MM   Feb. 21   p28.   250w.   3

330   FRITH, Fred.   Guitar Solos.   Caroline C1508
         CRA Jan.   p77.   150w. $2\frac{1}{2}$

331   FROESE, Edgar.   Epsilon in Malaysian Pale.   Virgin (E)
         CRE June   p58-9.   125w. $2\frac{1}{2}$

332   FROGMORTON.   At Last.   Philips 6308 261 (E)
         CAC Aug.   p181.   225w. $2\frac{1}{2}$

333   FUNKY Kings.   Arista AL 4078
         RS   Oct. 7   p73.   250w.   4

334   FURAY, Richie.   I've Got a Reason.   Asylum 7E-1067.   Cart.
         ET8-1067.   Cass. TC5-1067
         CAC Oct.   p252.   100w. $1\frac{1}{2}$
         CIR Dec. 14   p17.   225w.   2
         CRA Oct.   p77.   275w.   3

GR   Oct.   p669.   100w.   2
MM   Sept. 11   p28.   225w.   2
RS   Sept. 23   p115, 117.   275w. $2\frac{1}{2}$
SR   Nov.   p98, 100.   150w.   2

335   FUREY, Lewis.   A&M SP 4522
      CRE   Jan.   p71.   50w.   1

336   FUREY, Lewis.   The Humours of.   A&M SP 4594
      CRE   Nov.   p63.   25w.   2
      CRE   Nov.   p63.   75w.   2
      RM   Nov.   p31.   125w. $2\frac{1}{2}$
      RS   Sept. 23   p119.   300w. $2\frac{1}{2}$

337   GALLAGHER, Rory.   Against the Grain.   Chrysalis Records,
      CHR-1098.   Cart.   M81098
      GP   Feb.   p70.   200w. $3\frac{1}{2}$
      GR   Jan.   p1258.   25w.   3
      LP   March   p8.   125w. $4\frac{1}{2}$
      MG   May   p46.   50w. $2\frac{1}{2}$
      RS   Jan. 15.   p54.   325w. $3\frac{1}{2}$
      SR   April   p84.   100w.   3

338   GALLAGHER, Rory.   The Best Years.   Polydor 2383414 (E)
      (Reissue)
      RR   Dec.   p99.   25w. $2\frac{1}{2}$

339   GALLAGHER, Rory.   Calling Card.   Chrysalis CHR 1124
      GRA   Dec.   p1079.   75w.   4
      MM   Oct. 2   p29.   550w.   4
      RR   Dec.   p99.   50w.   3
      RS   Dec. 2   p107.   250w. $3\frac{1}{2}$

340   GALLAGHER, Rory.   The Story So Far.   Polydor PD 6519
      (Reissue)
      MM   May 8   p25.   150w.   3

341   GALLAGHER and Lyle.   Breakaway.   A&M SP-4566
      CAC   June   p97.   125w. $3\frac{1}{2}$
      MHF   June-July   p66.   325w.   3
      MM   May 15   p26.   275w.   4
      PRE   April   p24.   50w. $2\frac{1}{2}$
      PRM   April   p39.   450w.   3
      SOU   April   p46.   250w. $2\frac{1}{2}$
      SR   July   p88-9.   150w.   4

342   GARCIA, Jerry.   Reflections.   Rourd RX-LA565-G
      MM   April 17   p21.   300w. $2\frac{1}{2}$
      RR   June   p82.   25w.   2
      RS   June 3   p77.   150w.   2
      SR   July   p89.   125w.   2

343   GARFIELD.   Strange Streets.   Mercury SRM 1-1082

   CC June p30. 50w. 3

344 GARFUNKEL, Art. Breakaway. Columbia PC-33700
   CIR Jan. 20 p21. 125w. $1\frac{1}{2}$
   CRE Feb. p63. 50w. 2
   GR Jan. p1258. 200w. $3\frac{1}{2}$
   HF Feb. p123. 125w. 1
   LP June p9. 350w. $3\frac{1}{2}$
   SR Feb. p88. 250w. 1

345 GARRETT, Lee. Heat for the Feets. Chrysalis 1109
   MM July 10 p22. 125w. $3\frac{1}{2}$

346 GARTHWAITE, Terry. Arista AL-4055
   CRE Feb. p12. 75w. 4
   CRE Feb. p62. 300w. $3\frac{1}{2}$
   LP April p7-8. 50w. 2
   MG Jan. p34. 50w. 3
   MM Aug. 14 p25. 300w. $3\frac{1}{2}$
   RR Sept. p88. 125w. $3\frac{1}{2}$
   RS Jan. 15 p54-5. 150w. 3
   SR March p83. 225w. 2

347 GASOLIN'. Epic PE-34149
   CIR Dec. 14 p16. 325w. $3\frac{1}{2}$
   CRE Dec. p14. 150w. $4\frac{1}{2}$
   MG Dec. p63. 25w. $3\frac{1}{2}$
   MM Oct. 9 p30. 250w. $3\frac{1}{2}$
   RS Dec. 2 p104. 225w. 3

348 GAYDEN, Mac. Skyboat. ABC ABCD-927
   GP May p81. 100w. $4\frac{1}{2}$
   MM July 10 p21. 100w. $2\frac{1}{2}$

349 GEESUN, Ron. Patruns. Ron (E)
   MM May 8 p25. 75w. 2

350 GENESIS. Rock Roots. Decca Roots 1 (Reissue) (E)
   CAC July p143. 125w. 3

351 GENESIS. A Trick of the Tail. Atco SD 36-129. Cart. TP
  36-129. Cass. CS 36-129
   CAC April p14. 200w. 4
   CIR Aug. 10 p12. 425w. 3
   GR April p1670. 75w. 3
   HF July p105. 150w. 2
   MM Feb. 7 p23. 550w. $3\frac{1}{2}$
   RR April p77. 225w. 4
   RS May 20 p72. 200w. 3
   SR Aug. p74. 250w. 3

352 GENESIS. Wind and Wuthering. Atco SD 36-114
   MM Dec. 18 p18. 900w. 4

353   GENTLE Giant. The First Five Years. Vertigo 6641334 (2
      discs) (E) (Reissue)
          RR Feb. p66. 25w. 3

354   GENTLE Giant. Interview. Capitol ST 11532
          CK Aug. p46. 125w. 3
          RS July 29 p52. 150w. $2\frac{1}{2}$

355   GEORDIE. Save the World. EMI EMC 3134 (E)
          MM Sept. 18 p21. 225w. 1

356   GIBBONS, Steve. Any Road Up. MCA MCA-2187. Cart.
      MCAR-2187
          CAC July p96. 150w. 3
          CAC June p96. 150w. 3
          CRA July p78. 300w. $2\frac{1}{2}$
          CRE June p57. 300w. $2\frac{1}{2}$
          MG   June p44. 50w. $2\frac{1}{2}$
          MM   Aug. 14 p28. 350w. $3\frac{1}{2}$
          SR   Aug. p74. 200w. 3

357   GILLIAN, Ian. Child in Time. Oyster 1602
          CAC Oct. p252, 254. 225w. $2\frac{1}{2}$
          MM   July 31 p21. 150w. $2\frac{1}{2}$
          RR   Sept. p88. 25w. $2\frac{1}{2}$

358   GILTRAP, Gordon. Visionary. Electric Record Co. TRIX2
      (E)
          CAC Dec. p336. 175w. 2
          GRA Dec. p1076, 1079. 100w. 4
          MM   Nov. 13 p25. 300w. 3

359   GLASGOW, Alex. Now and Then. MWM 1011 (E)
          MM Aug. 7 p19. 75w. 2

360   GLASS, Philip. Music in Twelve Parts, parts 1 and 2.
      Caroline CA 2010 (E)
          MM Oct. 30. p24. 275w. $3\frac{1}{2}$

361   GLITTER Band. Listen to the Band. Bells BELLS 259 (E)
          RR Feb. p67. 25w. $4\frac{1}{2}$

362   GLOBAL Village Trucking Co. Caroline C 1516 (E)
          MM April 17 p23. 375w. 3

363   GLOVER, Roger. The Butterfly Ball and the Grasshopper's
      Feast. UK UKL56000
          MG   March p43. 50w. 3
          SOU March p42-3. 475w. 3

364   GOLD, Andrew. Asylum 7E-1047
          CRE Feb. p61. 375w. $2\frac{1}{2}$
          GP   May p81. 25w. $3\frac{1}{2}$

MG   Jan.   p34.   50w.   3
MM   Feb. 28 p24.   225w. $4\frac{1}{2}$
SR   March p83-4.   175w.   2

365   GOLDEN Earring.   To the Hilt.   MCA-2183.   Cart. MCAT-
      2183.   Cass. MCAC-2183
      CAC   May   p57.   125w. $4\frac{1}{2}$
      RS   April 8   p77.   200w. $2\frac{1}{2}$
      SR   Aug.   p74, 76.   175w.   0

366   GONG.   Shamal.   Virgin PZ-34156 (E)
      CAC   April p14.   200w. $4\frac{1}{2}$
      MM   Feb. 28 p24.   475w.   3

367   GONZALEZ.   Our Only Weapon Is Our Music.   EMI (E)
      MM   Sept. 11 p26.   75w.   4

368   GOOD Old Boys.   Pistol Packin' Mama.   Round RX LA 597 G
      AU   July p68.   150w.   5
      MM   July 24 p25.   25w. $2\frac{1}{2}$

369   GOOD Rats.   Ratcity in Blue.   Ratcity RCR-8001.   Cart. 8331-
      8001-H
      HF   June   p101.   200w. $3\frac{1}{2}$
      SR   Oct.   p94.   325w.   3

370   GOODHAND-TAIT, Philip.   Oceans Away.   Chrysalis 1113
      MM   Nov. 13 p25.   300w.   3
      RS   Nov. 18 p78.   150w. $2\frac{1}{2}$

371   GOODMAN, Steve.   Jessie's Jig and Other Favorites.   Asylum
      7E-1037
      CMP   Nov.   p40.   450w.   4
      MM   Jan. 17 p32.   350w. $4\frac{1}{2}$
      RR   Feb.   p66.   50w.   3

372   GOODMAN, Steve.   Words We Can Dance To.   Asylum 7E-1061.
      Cart. ET801061.   Cass. TC5-1061
      AU   Sept.   p81.   300w.   4
      CRA   July p78-9.   250w.   3
      MHF   June-July p68.   250w. $3\frac{1}{2}$
      MM   Jan. 12 p21.   100w. $4\frac{1}{2}$
      RS   June 3 p80.   150w.   3
      SR   Aug.   p68.   375w.   5

373   GRAHAM, Ralph.   Wisdom.   RCA APL1-1918
      CRA   Dec.   p79.   200w.   3

374   GRAHAM Central Station.   Mirror.   Warner Brothers BS 2937
      RR   Nov.   p106.   50w. $2\frac{1}{2}$

375   GRAND Funk Railroad.   Born to Die.   Capitol ST-11482.   Cart.
      8XT-11482

CRA   April p72.   550w.   1
CRE   June p56-7.   300w. $2\frac{1}{2}$
MM   April 24 p23.   275w.   3
SR   June p82.   175w.   0

376 GRAND Funk Railroad. Caught in the Act.   Grand Funk SABB
11445 (2 discs). Cass. 4XZT 11445
LP   March p8.   150w. $1\frac{1}{2}$
MM   Jan. 3 p24.   275w.   1

377 GRAND Funk Railroad. Good Singin', Good Playin'.   MCA
MCA-2216. Cart. MCAT-2216. Cass. MCAC-2216
CIR   Oct. 26 p10.   325w. $2\frac{1}{2}$
CRA   Nov. p81.   150w.   2
CRE   Nov. p59 375w.   3
MG   Nov. p56.   150w. $3\frac{1}{2}$
MM   Sept. 11 p29.   675w.   3
RS   Oct. 7 p79.   200w. $2\frac{1}{2}$
SR   Dec. p107.   200w.   3

378 GRATEFUL Dead. Blues for Allah.   Grateful Dead GD-LA494
CRE   Feb. p12.   25w.   2
GR   Jan. p1258.   50w. $2\frac{1}{2}$
LP   Jan. p7.   3500w. $3\frac{1}{2}$
RR   Jan. p62.   200w. $4\frac{1}{2}$

379 GRATEFUL Dead. Steal Your Face.   Grateful Dead GD-LA
620-J (2 discs). Cart. EA 620-J. Cass. CA 620-J
AU   Sept. p80.   250w.   1
CAC   Oct. p254.   250w. $3\frac{1}{2}$
CIR   Oct. 12 p16.   200w.   3
CR   Nov. p100.   200w.   3
MM   July 17 p25.   650w.   2
RR   Oct. p101.   275w.   1
RS   Aug. 26 p60.   275w. $2\frac{1}{2}$

380 GREYHOUND. Mango Rock.   Transatlantic (E)
MM   March 13 p23.   225w.   3
MM   May 8 p25.   75w. $2\frac{1}{2}$

381 GRIMES, Carol.   Decca SKL-R5258 (E)
CAC   Dec. p336.   125w.   3
GRA   Dec. p1079.   50w. $3\frac{1}{2}$

382 GRIMMS. Sleepers.   DJM 20470 (E)
CAC   Oct. p259.   125w. $2\frac{1}{2}$
MM   May 29 p26.   400w. $3\frac{1}{2}$

383 GROCE, Larry. Junkfood Junkie.   Warner BS-2933.   Cart.
M8-2933
SR   June p82.   75w.   0

384 GROSS, Henry. Release.   Lifesong LS-6002

CRA   April   p76.   200w.   1½
HF   June   p106.   150w.   2
RS   March 25   p68.   200w.   2½
SOU   April   p43.   200w.   4½
SR   May   p83.   50w.   2½

385   GROUNDHOGS.   Black Diamond.   United Artists LA 680-G
MM   Nov. 20   p29.   75w.   2

386   GROUNDHOGS.   Crosscut Saw.   United Artists LA 603-G
MM   May 22   p25.   50w.   1

387   GROUNDHOGS.   Thank Christ for the Bomb.   Sunset SLS-50376
(E) (Reissue)
CAC   Feb.   p443.   100w.   3
RR   Feb.   p66.   25w.   2½

388   THE GUESS Who.   The Way They Were.   RCA APL1-1778.
Cart. APS1-1778.   Cass. APK1-1778
SR   Oct.   p94-5.   225w.   2

389   GUTHRIE, Arlo.   Amigo.   Reprise MS 2239
CIR   Dec. 14   p16.   250w.   4½
CRA   Nov.   p80.   150w.   4
MG   Dec.   p63.   50w.   4

390   HACKETT, Steve.   Voyage of the Acolyte.   Charisma 1112
CAC   Jan.   p402.   75w.   3½
HF   July   p105.   75w.   2½
RS   May 20   p72.   150w.   2½

391   HAGAR, Sammy.   Nine on a Ten Scale.   Capitol ST 11489
MM   Oct. 23   p27.   100w.   2

392   HALL and Oates.   RCA APL1-1144
CAC   April   p14.   150w.   3
CRE   June   p69.   175w.   3

393   HALL and Oates.   Bigger than Both of Us.   RCA APL1-1467
CAC   Nov.   p295.   150w.   3
CIR   Nov. 25   p15, 17.   325w.   2
CRA   Nov.   p67-8.   1500w.   5
CRE   Dec.   p59-60.   375w.   2½
MG   Nov.   p56.   50w.   2½
MM   Sept. 11   p26.   700w.   4½
PRM   Nov.   p22.   75w.   3
RR   Nov.   p105-6.   150w.   4
RS   Oct. 21   p103, 105.   1500w.   4

394   HALL and Oates.   Whole Oates.   Atlantic
MM   Oct. 16   p22.   50w.   3
RR   Nov.   p106.   75w.   3

68   Record Reviews, 1976

395 HAMILTON, Dick. You Can Sing on the Left Or Bark on the
     Right. ABC 920
          CRE Sept. p14.   125w. $3\frac{1}{2}$

396 HANSSON, Bo. Attic Thoughts. Charisma CAS-1113
          GR March p1518.   75w. $2\frac{1}{2}$

397 HARDIN, Tim. Nine. Antilles AN-7023
          SR Nov. p100.   200w.   3

398 HARDIN and Russell. Ring of Bone. Demo H&R 512
          RS Aug. 26 p68.   200w.   4

399 HARLEY, Steve and Cockney Rebel. A Closer Look. Capitol
     ST-11456 (Reissue)
          MG Jan. p33.   50w. $2\frac{1}{2}$

400 HARLEY, Steve and Cockney Rebel. Love's a Prima Donna.
     EMI EMC-3156 (E)
          MM Nov. 13 p22.   450w.   3

401 HARLEY, Steve and Cockney Rebel. Timeless Flight. Capitol
     ST 11500
          MM Jan. 24 p27.   450w. $2\frac{1}{2}$

402 HARMONIUM. Si on arait besoin d'une cinquieme saison.
     Celebration CEL 1900 (Canada)
          OLR Sept. p190.   25w.   2

403 HARPER, Roy. When an Old Cricketer Leaves the Crease.
     Chrysalis CHR-1105
          MG May p46.   50w. $2\frac{1}{2}$
          SR June p74.   500w. $4\frac{1}{2}$

404 HARRISON, Don. Atlantic SD-18171. Cart. TP-18171. Cass.
     CS-18171
          CIR July 6 p14.   50w.   3
          MM July 3 p21.   200w. $2\frac{1}{2}$
          RS June 17 p5013.   350w. $3\frac{1}{2}$
          SR Sept. p92, 94.   175w.   4

405 HARRISON, George. Best of. Capitol ST 11578 (Reissue)
          MM Dec. 18 p16.   175w.   3

406 HARRISON, George. Extra Texture (Read All About It).
     Apple SW-3420. Cart. 8XW-3420
          AU Nov. p79-80.   600w.   1
          GR Jan. p1258.   50w. $2\frac{1}{2}$
          LP Jan. p9.   150w.   1
          SR Feb. p81.   250w.   4

407 HARRISON, George. 33 1/3. Dark Horse 3005
          MM Nov. 27 p23.   900w. $3\frac{1}{2}$

408   HARTMAN, Dan.   Images.   Blue Sky PZ 34322
      CRE   Dec.   p60.   325w. $2\frac{1}{2}$
      RS   Nov. 4 p76, 79.   150w.   3

409   HARVEY, Alex.   Live.   Atlantic SD-18148.   Cass. CS-18148
      AU   April   p84.   300w. $4\frac{1}{2}$
      CRA   Feb.   p73-4.   250w.   4
      CRE   Feb.   p63.   25w.   3
      LP   Jan.   p13.   150w. $1\frac{1}{2}$

410   HARVEY, Alex.   Penthouse Tapes.   Vertigo 9102-007 (E)
      CAC   May   p62.   125w.   3
      GR   June   p98.   25w.   1
      MM   March 20   p22.   550w.   4

411   HARVEY, Alex.   Sahb Stories.   Mountain TOPS112 (E)
      GR   Nov.   p899.   25w.   3
      MM   July 24   p23.   475w.   4

412   HAVENS, Richie.   Polydor 2482-273 (E) (Reissue)
      CAC   April   p14-5.   225w.   3
      MM   March 13   p23.   125w.   2

413   HAVENS, Richie.   The End of the Beginning.   A&M SP 4598
      CAC   Dec.   p340.   175w.   1
      CRA   Dec.   p79.   200w.   3
      PRM   Nov.   p22.   75w.   1

414   HAWKWIND.   Astounding Sounds, Amazing Music.   Charisma
      CDS 4004 (E)
      CAC   Nov.   p294-5.   200w. $2\frac{1}{2}$
      MM   Sept. 25   p24.   325w. $1\frac{1}{2}$

415   HAWKWIND.   Roadhawks.   United Artists UAK29919 (E) (Re-
      issue)
      CAC   July   p137.   250w. $3\frac{1}{2}$
      GR   July   p226.   100w.   2
      MM   May 22   p25.   50w. $2\frac{1}{2}$

416   HAWKWIND.   Warrior on the Edge of Time.   Atco SD 36-115
      CRE   July   p68.   25w. $2\frac{1}{2}$

417   HAZZARD, Tom and Richard Barnes.   Warner Brothers K
      56233 (E)
      MM   June 12   p21.   125w. $2\frac{1}{2}$

418   HEAD, Murray.   Say It Ain't So.   A&M 4558
      CAC   May   p57.   175w. $4\frac{1}{2}$
      CIR   June 17   p16.   375w. $4\frac{1}{2}$
      MG   April   p39.   50w. $3\frac{1}{2}$
      SOU   April   p46.   425w. $3\frac{1}{2}$

419   HEAD East.   Get Yourself Up.   A&M SP 4579

CIR   Oct. 26   p12.   100w.   3

420   HEART.   Dreamboat Annie.   Arista ARTY139 (E)
      MM   Nov. 20   p25.   300w. $3\frac{1}{2}$
      RS   Oct. 21   p109.   200w. $3\frac{1}{2}$

421   HELLO People.   Bricks.   ABS ABCD 882
      MG   Feb.   p36.   25w.   1
      RS   Feb. 12   p94-5.   250w.   3

422   HENDRIX, Jimi.   Are You Experienced?   Track 612001 (E)
      (Reissue)
      CRA   March   p77.   425w.   4

423   HENDRIX, Jimi.   Crash Landing.   Reprise MS 2204
      GR   Feb.   p1389.   25w.   3

424   HENDRIX, Jimi.   Electric Ladyland.   Reprise RS 6307
      CRA   March   p80.   250w.   4

425   HENDRIX, Jimi.   Midnight Lightning.   Reprise MS 2229.
      Cart. M8-2229.   Cass. M5-2229
      AU   April   p77, 84.   400w.   1
      CAC   Feb.   p443-4.   175w.   4
      CIR   April 8   p14.   100w.   2
      CRA   Feb.   p73.   100w. $2\frac{1}{2}$
      LP   April   p8.   125w.   2
      MG   Feb.   p38.   50w.   3
      SR   March   p84.   300w.   2

426   HENRY Cow.   Concerts.   Caroline CAD 3002 (2 discs) (E)
      MM   Sept. 11   p26.   775w.   4

427   HIATT, John.   Overcoats.   Epic
      CRE   March   p12.   50w. $3\frac{1}{2}$

428   HIDDEN Strength.   United Artists LA 555G
      CRE   Dec.   p14.   75w. $2\frac{1}{2}$

428a HILL, Dan.   Hold On.   GRT 9230-1065 (Canada)
      CC   Dec.   p30.   100w. $3\frac{1}{2}$
      RM   Nov.   p33.   200w. $3\frac{1}{2}$

429   HILLAGE, Steve.   L.   Virgin V2066 (E)
      CAC   Dec.   p336-7.   250w.   4
      GRA   Dec.   p1079.   100w.   4
      MM   Sept. 18   p22.   800w. $4\frac{1}{2}$

430   HILLMAN, Chris.   Slippin Away.   Asylum 7E-1062
      MG   Sept.   p58.   50w.   3
      RS   July 15   p68.   225w. $3\frac{1}{2}$
      SR   Oct.   p95, 98.   300w.   3

431 HOBBS, Christopher, John Adams and Gavin Bryars. Ensemble Pieces. Obscure (E)
     MM Feb. 21 p28. 250w. 3

432 HOLLIES. Out on the Road. Hansa 87119 (E)
     SR May p90-1. 350w. 5

433 HOLLIES. Write On. Polydor 2442-141 (E)
     CAC March p492. 200w. 3
     MM Feb. 14 p29. 350w. 3
     GR April p1670. 75w. 2½
     SR May p90-1. 350w. 4

434 HOPKINS, Nicky. No More Changes. Mercury SRM-1-1028
     LP Jan. p9-10. 200w. 2

435 HOSFORD, Larry. Shelter SRL 52003
     CRA Dec. p81. 175w. 2½

436 HOT Tuna. Hoppkorv. Grunt BFL1-1920
     MM Nov. 20 p29. 275w. 4½

437 HOT Tuna. Yellow Fever. Grunt BFL1-1238. Cart. BFS1-1238. Cass. BFK1-1238
     CIR March 2 p14. 50w. 2½
     CRA Feb. p77. 300w. 3½
     CRE April p72. 50w. 3
     HF Feb. p120. 150w. 2½
     LP March p8. 125w. 4
     MG Jan. p33. 50w. 3
     RS Jan. 1 p55. 275w. 3
     SR March p84. 225w. 2

438 HOWE, Steve. Beginnings. Atlantic SD-18154. Cart. TP 18154
     CRA Feb. p74-5. 200w. 3
     CRE Nov. p61. 100w. 2
     GP March p73. 175w. 4
     LP April p8. 175w. 3½
     RR March p73. 50w. 3
     RS March 11 p64. 175w. 2½
     SR April p84. 150w. 3

439 HOWELL, Eddie. Gramophone Record. Warner Brothers K56154 (E)
     MM April 24 p23. 150w. 3½

439a HUD, Lorence. A&M SP9004 (Canada)
      OLR June p107. 25w. 2

440 HUDSON Brothers. Ba-Fa. Rocket PIG-2169. Cass. PIGC-2169
     AU Aug. p68-9. 200w. 1

HF   Feb.   p123.   100w.   0
LP   April   p8.   75w.   2

441   HUMMINGBIRD.   We Can't Go on Meeting Like This.   A&M
      SP-4595
          CK   Dec.   p49.   25w. $2\frac{1}{2}$
          CRA   Dec.   p74.   225w. $2\frac{1}{2}$
          MM   Sept. 11   p26.   575w.   3
          RS   Oct. 21   p109.   175w.   4

442   HUNT, Tommy.   A Sign of the Times.   Spark (E)
          MM   Nov. 13   p28.   75w.   1

443   HUNTER, Ian.   All-American Alien Boy.   Columbia PC-34142.
      Cart. PCA-34142.   Cass. PCT 34142
          CAC   July   p137.   250w.   4
          CIR   June 17   p13.   675w. $4\frac{1}{2}$
          CRA   Aug.   p77.   175w. $2\frac{1}{2}$
          CRE   July   p66.   325w.   3
          CRE   Aug.   p14.   50w.   3
          GR   Aug.   p351.   100w. $4\frac{1}{2}$
          MH   Oct./Nov.   p68.   150w.   4
          MM   May 15   p25.   925w.   4
          RS   July 15   p57.   400w.   4
          SR   Oct.   p98.   225w.   4

444   HUSTLER.   Play Loud.   A&M SP4556
          CRA   April   p76.   25w. $1\frac{1}{2}$
          CRE   July   p68.   25w.   3

445   HYDRA.   Land of Money.   Capricorn CP 0157
          MM   Jan. 3   p23.   250w.   1

446   IAN, Janis.   Aftertones.   Columbia PC-33919.   Cart. PCA-
      33919.   Cass. PCT-33919
          AU   June   p82-3.   250w.   4
          CAC   May   p57.   175w. $2\frac{1}{2}$
          CIR   April 8   p14.   325w.   2
          MG   April   p39.   50w.   4
          RR   May   p74.   75w.   4
          RS   April 8   p66, 68.   150w. $1\frac{1}{2}$
          SR   May   p84.   100w.   4

447   IAN, Janis.   Between the Lines.   Blue Sky PC 33394
          AU   June   p82-3.   250w.   4
          GR   Aug.   p351.   75w. $4\frac{1}{2}$

448   IRON Butterfly.   Sun and Steel.   MCA 2164.   Cass. MCAC-
      2164
          GR   April   p1670.   50w.   3
          LP   March   p8.   100w. $4\frac{1}{2}$
          MM   Feb. 28   p25.   200w. $1\frac{1}{2}$

449 ISOTOPE. Deep End. Decca Gull 1017 (E)
         CAC Oct. p254. 25w. $1\frac{1}{2}$

450 IVERS, Peter. Warner Brothers BS2930
         CRA Nov. p75. 150w. 3
         CRE Dec. p63. 75w. 1
         RS Oct. 7 p70, 73. 275w. 3

451 J. GEILS BAND. Blow Your Face Out. Atlantic SD2-507 (2
     discs). Cart. TP2-507. Cass. CS2-507
         CIR Sept. 13 p16. 225w. 3
         CRE Sept. p65. 100w. 3
         MM July 17 p25. 175w. 3
         RR Sept. p89. 100w. $3\frac{1}{2}$
         SR Aug. p74. 150w. 2

452 J. GEILS BAND. Hotline. Atlantic SD18147. Tape TP18147.
     Cass. CS18147
         LP Jan. p10. 150w. $3\frac{1}{2}$
         SR Jan. p82. 100w. 0

453 JAMES, Tommy. In Touch. Fantasy 9509
         WHO Winter p43. 300w. $4\frac{1}{2}$

454 JAMES Gang. Rides Again. ABC S-711
         CRA March p81. 175w. $3\frac{1}{2}$

455 JAN and Dean. Ride the Wild Surf. United Artists UAS
     29987 (E) (Reissue)
         MM Sept. 18 p21. 25w. 3

456 JAN and Dean. Old Wax and New Waves. Wizards 348
         WHO Winter p43-4. 175w. $3\frac{1}{2}$

457 JANS, Tom. Dark Blonde. Columbia PC 34292
         RS Nov. 18 p75. 225w. 3

458 JANS, Tom. The Eyes of an Only Child. Columbia PC 33699
         MG Dec. p63. 75w. 4

459 JEFFERSON Starship. Red Octopus. Grunt BFL1-0999
         CRE Jan. p12. 50w. 3

460 JEFFERSON Starship. Spitfire. Grunt BFL-1-1557. Cart.
     BFS1-1557. Cass. BFK1-1557
         AU Oct. p137-8. 500w. 3
         CAC Sept. p214. 200w. $3\frac{1}{2}$
         CIR Oct. 12 p14-5. 475w. 2
         CRA Sept. p81. 250w. $2\frac{1}{2}$
         CRE Sept. p64. 250w. 4
         GR Sept. p493. 50w. 3
         MM July 3 p23. 425w. 3
         RS Aug. 26 p57-8. 1000w. 5

SR   Oct.   p98.   200w.   2

461   JEFFERSON Starship.   Yellow Fever.   Grunt BFL1-1238
      GR   March   p1517.   150w. $2\frac{1}{2}$

462   JET.   CBS (E)
      CRE   Jan.   P71.   50w.   4

463   JETHRO Tull.   Chrysalis CHR-1078 (E) (Reissue)
      GR   March   p1518.   50w.   3

464   JETHRO Tull.   Best of.   Chrysalis CHR-1075 (Reissue)
      HF   April   p130.   150w. $1\frac{1}{2}$
      RR   March   p73.   50w. $2\frac{1}{2}$

465   JETHRO Tull.   Minstrel in the Gallery.   Chrysalis CHR-1082.
      Cart. M8C-1082.   Cass. M5C-1082
      AU   April   p84-5.   350w.   2
      LP   Jan.   p10.   200w.   3
      SR   Jan.   p82.   175w.   2

466   JETHRO Tull.   Too Old to Rock 'n' Roll, Too Young to Die.
      Chrysalis CHR-1111.   Cart. M8C-1111.   Cass. M5C-1111
      CIR   Sept. 13   p12-3.   450w.   2
      CRA   Aug.   p76-7.   150w.   3
      CRE   Aug.   p65.   150w.   2
      HF   Sept.   p110.   250w.   1
      MG   Sept.   p58.   50w. $1\frac{1}{2}$
      MM   May 1   p29.   550w.   2
      RS   Aug. 26   p60.   250w. $2\frac{1}{2}$
      SR   Oct.   p98, 100.   250w.   4

467   JIGSAW.   Sky High.   Chelsea CHS-509
      CAC   March   p492.   50w.   2
      LP   April   p8.   75w.   1

468   JIVA.   Dark Horse 22003
      RS   Feb. 12   p92.   175w. $2\frac{1}{2}$

469   JOHN, Elton.   Blue Moves.   MCA Rocket 2-1004 (2 discs)
      CAC   Dec.   p340-1.   700w. $4\frac{1}{2}$
      MG   Dec.   p62.   325w. $1\frac{1}{2}$
      MM   Oct. 23   p24.   625w.   4
      PRM   Nov.   p22.   50w.   1
      PRM   Nov.   p35.   650w. $3\frac{1}{2}$
      RM   Dec.   p31.   100w.   3
      RS   Dec. 30   p65.   1500w.   1

470   JOHN, Elton.   Captain Fantastic and the Brown Dirt Cowboy.
      MCA 2124
      AU   Feb.   p93.   250w.   4

471   JOHN, Elton.   Here & There.   MCA 2197.   Cart. T-2197.

Cass. C-2197
CIR   Aug. 24 p13. 200w. 2
CRE   Aug.   p65. 175w. 1
MG   Sept. p58. 50w. 3
MM   May 15 p26. 425w. 3
SR   Oct. p100. 400w. 5

472   JOHN, Elton. Rock of the Westies.   MCA MCA-2163.   Cart.
MCAT-2163
AU   July p69. 250w. $3\frac{1}{2}$
CAC   Jan. p402-3. 150w. 3
CIR   Feb. 10 p10, 12. 500w. $3\frac{1}{2}$
CRA   Jan. p76. 75w. $1\frac{1}{2}$
HF   Feb. p118. 150w. 3
LP   Jan. p10. 225w. $2\frac{1}{2}$
MG   Jan. p34. 100w. $4\frac{1}{2}$
SR   Feb. p81-2. 225w. 2

473   JOURNEY. Look into the Future.   Columbia KC-33904
MM   Feb. 28 p24. 300w. $4\frac{1}{2}$
SOU   May p38, 40. 300w. 2

474   JUDAS Priest. Sad Wings of Destiny.   Janus 7019
CAC   June p96. 200w. 3
RS   Sept. 23 p120. 125w. 3

474a   KGB.   MCA-2166.   Cart. MCAT-2166
CRA   April p69-70. 550w. $1\frac{1}{2}$
CRE   June p72. 50w. $1\frac{1}{2}$
HF   May p102. 150w. 2
MM   April 3 p29. 325w. 3
PRM   Nov. p22. 125w. 3
RS   April 8 p71, 73. 300w. 2
SR   June p83. 50w. 2

474b   KGB. Motion.   MCA 2221
MM   Nov. 27 p28. 75w. $1\frac{1}{2}$
RS   Nov. 18 p76. 250w. $2\frac{1}{2}$

475   KANE, Ray. Tradewind TS 1130
GP   Dec. p104. 100w. 3

476   KANSAS. Masque. Kirshner PZ-33806.   Cart. PZA-33806
LP   April p8-9. 150w. 3
SR   June p83. 50w. 0
MG   Feb. p36. 50w. $1\frac{1}{2}$
MG   April p39. 50w. $3\frac{1}{2}$

477   KAYAK. Royal Red Bouncer.   Janus JXS-7023
AU   April p86. 200w. 2
LP   April p7. 175w. $2\frac{1}{2}$
PRM   Jan. p30. 125w. 4

478 KEARNEY, Chris. Sweet Water.   Capitol ST 6424 (Canada)
        OLR   March p40.   25w. $3\frac{1}{2}$

479 KENNEDY, Clive.   Polydor UK-1023 (E)
        CAC   Dec.   p337.   225w.   2

480 KEY, Scott.   The Forest and the Sea.   Blivet
        GP   Dec.   p105.   25w. $2\frac{1}{2}$

481 KIHN, Greg.   Berserkley BZ 0046
        AU   June   p83.   200w. $2\frac{1}{2}$

482 KING, Carole.   Thoroughbred.   Ode SP77034.   Cass. CS77034
        CAC   May p60.   125w. $2\frac{1}{2}$
        CIR   May 13 p16, 18.   225w. $3\frac{1}{2}$
        GR   May p1812.   50w.   3
        HF   May p104.   100w. $2\frac{1}{2}$
        LP   April p9.   225w. $3\frac{1}{2}$
        MM   Feb. 7 p25.   450w.   3
        PRM   Jan. p22.   850w.   4
        RS   March 25 p58.   600w.   4
        SR   May p86.   150w. $3\frac{1}{2}$

483 KING, Floyd.   Well Done.   Chimneyville
        CRE   Feb. p12.   50w.   3

484 KING, Jonathan.   All the Way.   Polydor UKAL 1024 (E)
        CAC   Oct. p260.   50w. $1\frac{1}{2}$

485 KING, Jonathan.   Greatest Hits--Past, Present, Future.   Poly-
     dor UKAL 1017 (E) (Reissue)
        CAC   March p493.   100w. $2\frac{1}{2}$

486 KING Crimson.   The Young Person's Guide.   Island (E) (Re-
     issue)
        MM   May 6 p27.   650w. $2\frac{1}{2}$

487 KINGFISH.   United Artists/Round RX-LA564-G.   Cart. RX-
     EA564-H
        AU   June p86.   250w. $3\frac{1}{2}$
        MHF   May p61.   150w.   3
        MM   April 17 p22.   200w. $3\frac{1}{2}$
        RR   June p82.   25w. $3\frac{1}{2}$
        SR   Aug. p76, 78.   175w.   0

488 KINKS.   Vol. 2.   Pye 509 (Reissue)
        MG   June p44.   50w. $3\frac{1}{2}$

489 KINKS.   Greatest Celluloid Heroes.   RCA APL1-1743.   Cart.
     APS1-1743.   Cass. APK7-1743 (Reissue)
        SR   Nov. p100, 104.   75w.   2

490 THE KINKS.   Schoolboys in Disgrace.   RCA LPL1-5102.   Cart.

LPS1-5102.   Cass. LPK1-5102
    CAC   April   p16.   175w. $3\frac{1}{2}$
    CIR   March 2   p14.   600w.   4
    CRA   Feb.   p67.   1200w. $4\frac{1}{2}$
    CRE   Feb.   p59-60.   450w. $2\frac{1}{2}$
    GR   May   p1812.   25w. $1\frac{1}{2}$
    MG   Jan.   p33.   50w.   4
    MM   Jan. 3   p23.   425w. $3\frac{1}{2}$
    RS   March 11   p62.   400w.   3
    SR   March   p88.   750w.   2

491   KIRWAN, Danny.   Midnight in San Juan.   DJM DJF 20481 (E)
    CAC   Nov.   p296.   125w. $3\frac{1}{2}$
    MM   Dec. 11   p22.   75w. $\frac{1}{2}$

492   KIRWAN, Danny.   Second Chapter.   DJM 1
    CAC   Oct.   p259.   50w.   3

493   KISS.   Alive.   Casablanca NBLP-7020
    CAC   Aug.   p177.   150w. $2\frac{1}{2}$
    CRE   Feb.   p63.   100w.   4
    MG   Feb.   p36.   50w.   4
    RS   Jan. 1   p62.   150w.   0

494   KISS.   Destroyer.   Casablanca NBLP-7025.   Cart. 7025.
Cass. 7025
    CAC   Aug.   p177.   150w. $3\frac{1}{2}$
    CIR   Aug. 24   p10, 12.   500w. $1\frac{1}{2}$
    CRE   June   p60.   50w. $2\frac{1}{2}$
    CRE   July   p66.   225w.   2
    CRE   Aug.   p14.   25w.   3
    MM   April 17   p23.   400w. $2\frac{1}{2}$
    PRM   April   p40.   550w.   3
    RS   June 3   p70.   200w. $2\frac{1}{2}$
    SR   Aug.   p78.   175w.   0

495   KLAATU.   Capitol ST 11542
    CC   Nov.   p35.   75w. $3\frac{1}{2}$
    RM   Nov.   p32.   475w.   3

496   KOKOMO.   Rise and Shine.   Columbia PC 34031 (E)
    CAC   March   p488.   200w. $3\frac{1}{2}$
    MM   Feb. 14   p28.   375w. $1\frac{1}{2}$
    RR   April   p77.   175w.   3
    RS   June 17   p60.   150w. $2\frac{1}{2}$

497   KOOPER, Al.   Act Like Nothing's Wrong.   United Artists
UA-LA702-G
    PRM   Nov.   p34.   550w.   3

497a   KOTTKE, Leo.   Chewing Pine.   Capitol Records, ST-11446
    CMR   Feb.   p29.   150w. $2\frac{1}{2}$
    GP   Jan.   p70.   175w. $4\frac{1}{2}$

SOU   March   p44.   250w. $2\frac{1}{2}$
SR   Feb.   p83.   200w.   3

498   KRAAN.   Let It Go.   Passport/PPSD-98075
GP   Dec.   p104.   125w. $3\frac{1}{2}$
RS   Dec. 26   p86.   175w.   3

499   KRAAN.   Live.   Gull GUD 2001/2   (2 discs) (E)
CAC   Sept.   p214, 216.   350w. $3\frac{1}{2}$
MM   July 17   p22.   250w.   3

500   KRAFTWERK.   Radio-activity.   Capitol ST-11457.   Cart. 8XT-
11457
CAC   March   p488.   125w. $2\frac{1}{2}$
CK   March   p47.   150w.   3
CRA   May   p78.   50w. $3\frac{1}{2}$
CRE   Feb.   p60-1.   325w. $3\frac{1}{2}$
DB   June 3   p26-7.   350w.   3
GR   March   p1518.   50w. $2\frac{1}{2}$
LP   April   p9.   100w.   3
MG   Feb.   p38.   50w. $4\frac{1}{2}$
RS   Feb. 12   p92.   150w.   2
SOU   Jan.   p36.   250w.   4
SR   May   p86.   100w.   0

501   KRISTOFFERSON, Kris.   Surreal Thing.   Monument PZ-34254.
Cart. PZA-34254.   Cass. PZT-34254
CAC   Oct.   p260.   150w. $1\frac{1}{2}$
CIR   Nov. 25   p19.   200w.   2
CM   Oct.   p56.   100w.   4
CRA   Oct.   p80.   175w.   2
GR   Oct.   p669.   50w.   2
RS   Sept. 9   p60-1.   150w. $1\frac{1}{2}$
SR   Dec.   p110.   200w. $2\frac{1}{2}$

502   KRISTOFFERSON, Kris.   Who's to Bless ... and Who's to
Blame.   Monument PZ-33379.   Cart. PZA-33379.   Cass. PZT-
33379
CIR   March 2   p14.   75w. $1\frac{1}{2}$
CM   May   p49.   400w.   1
CMP   March   p20.   300w.   3
CMR   Sept.   p34.   275w.   1
CRE   March   p62.   125w. $2\frac{1}{2}$
MM   Jan. 31   p23.   100w.   1
SR   March   p84, 86.   175w.   2

503   KURSAAL Flyers.   Great Artiste.   UK UKAL-1018 (E)
CAC   Jan.   p97-8.   225w.   2
GR   May   p1812.   50w.   3

504   KURSAAL Flyers.   Golden Mile.   CBS (E)
MM   Nov. 6   p27.   800w. $3\frac{1}{2}$

Rock   79

505 L. A. Express. Caribou P2 33940
     MHF May p60-1. 175w. $2\frac{1}{2}$
     MM Sept. 4 p18. 300w. $4\frac{1}{2}$

506 L. A. Jets. RCA APL1-1547
     CRA Aug. p76. 150w. $2\frac{1}{2}$
     RS July 1 p73. 175w. $2\frac{1}{2}$

507 LA Dusseldorf. Decca (E)
     CAC Oct. p252. 100w. 1

508 LANE'S Slim Chance, Ronnie. One for the Road. Island 9366
     CRA July p80-1. 200w. $2\frac{1}{2}$

508a LAWRENCE, Claire. Leaving You Free. Haida HL 5103
     (Canada)
     OLR June p107. 25w. 4

509 LED Zeppelin. Atlantic SD 8216
     CRA March p76. 475w. $2\frac{1}{2}$

510 LED Zeppelin. Presence. Swan Song SS 8416
     CIR July 22 p13-4. 625w. $4\frac{1}{2}$
     CRA July p70. 1000w. 3
     CRE July p65. 350w. $3\frac{1}{2}$
     CRE Sept. p14. 50w. $3\frac{1}{2}$
     GR June p98. 100w. 3
     MHF June-July p66. 350w. $3\frac{1}{2}$
     RR June p82. 125w. 3
     RS May 20 p64. 350w. 3
     SR July p89-90. 175w. 3

511 LED Zeppelin The Song Remains the Same. Swan Song SSZ-
     201 (2 discs)
     MG Dec. p62. 275w. 3
     RM Dec. p33. 100w. 4
     RR Dec. p99. 150w. 2

512 LENNON, John. Shaved Fish. Capitol SW-3421. Cart. 8xW-
     3421. Cass. 4x-3421
     CRA March p82. 125w. $4\frac{1}{2}$
     CRE March p60. 400w. $3\frac{1}{2}$
     GR Jan. p1258. 100w. $2\frac{1}{2}$
     LP March p9. 150w. 2
     MG Jan. p33. 75w. $2\frac{1}{2}$
     SR Jan. p83. 300w. 4

513 LEWIS, Jerry Lee. Golden Hits. Philips 6336 245 (E) (Re-
     issue)
     CAC July p140, 143. 375w. 2
     MM June 26 p22. 50w. 3

514 LEWIS, Jerry Lee. I'm a Rocker. Mercury 6338-602 (E)

(Reissue)
>CMR   April   p40.   125w.   1
>MM   Jan. 31   p23.   50w. $3\frac{1}{2}$

514a LEWIS, Jerry Lee.   Odd Man In.   Mercury SRM 1-1064.
Cart. MC 8 1-1064
>CM   April   p47.   500w. $1\frac{1}{2}$

515 LEWIS, Jerry Lee.   The Original.   Charly (E) (Reissue)
>MM   Oct. 2   p30.   25w.   3

516 LEWIS, Jerry Lee.   Whole Lotta ... Goin' On.   Charly (E)
(Reissue)
>CAC   April   p27-8.   100w.   3

516a LIGHTFOOT, Gordon.   Gord's Gold.   Reprise 2RS-2237 (2
discs) (Reissue).   Cart. J82237.   Cass. J52237
>MM   Feb. 21   p30.   250w.   3
>RR   Feb.   p66.   25w.   3
>SR   March   p80-1.   450w.   5

516b LIGHTFOOT, Gordon.   Summertime Dream.   Reprise MS
2246.   Cart. M8 2246.   Cass. M5 2246
>CC   Sept.   p28.   50w.   4
>MM   July 31   p21.   150w. $2\frac{1}{2}$
>RS   Aug. 12   p64.   200w. $3\frac{1}{2}$
>SR   Oct.   p87.   525w.   5

517 LIMEY.   RCA SF 8463 (E)
>CAC   April   p16, 18.   175w. $2\frac{1}{2}$
>MM   March 13   p23.   100w.   2

518 LITTLE Big Band.   Canon (E)
>MM   Sept. 18   p21.   275w. $2\frac{1}{2}$

519 LITTLE Feat.   The Last Record Album.   Warner BS-2884
>CRA   Feb.   p65-6.   875w. $3\frac{1}{2}$
>CRE   Feb.   p60.   275w.   3
>LP   March   p9.   150w.   3
>MG   Jan.   p34.   50w.   3
>RS   Jan. 29   p48.   200w.   3
>SR   Feb.   p83-4.   100w.   5

520 LITTLE Feat.   Two Originals of.   Warner (2 discs) (E) (Reissue)
>MM   Jan. 31.   p23.   225w.   4

521 LITTLE River Band.   Capitol ST 11512 (E)
>CAC   Dec.   p337.   250w.   3
>MM   Nov. 6   p20.   250w.   3
>RR   Dec.   p99.   25w.   3

522 LLOYD, Ian.   Polydor   PD 6066

RS   July 1   p76.   125w. $2\frac{1}{2}$

523 LOFGREN, Nils.   Back It Up.   A&M
     CIR   April 27   p16.   50w.   4
     PRM   Jan.   p30.   200w.   4
     RS   May 20   p71.   100w.   3

524 LOFGREN, Nils.   Cry Tough.   A&M SP-4573.   Cart. 4573.
     Cass. 4573
     AU   July   p66.   350w.   4
     AU   July   p66.   450w. $4\frac{1}{2}$
     CAC   July   p137-8.   125w. $3\frac{1}{2}$
     CIR   July 6   p14.   375w.   3
     CRE   July   p64.   400w.   2
     CRE   Aug.   p14.   50w.   3
     GP   Aug.   p81.   100w.   4
     GR   June   p98.   50w.   3
     MHF   June-July   p66.   200w. $3\frac{1}{2}$
     MM   April 3   p33.   775w. $4\frac{1}{2}$
     PRM   April   p39.   600w. $4\frac{1}{2}$
     RR   June   p83.   225w.   5
     RS   May 20   p71.   100w. $2\frac{1}{2}$
     SOU   May   p40.   400w.   4
     SR   Aug.   p78.   175w.   3

525 LOFGREN, Nils.   Grin/1+1.   CBS 88204 (E) (Reissue) (2 discs)
     MM   July 24   p25.   50w. $4\frac{1}{2}$

526 LOGGINS, Dave.   Country Suite.   Epic PE-33946.   Cart.
     PEA-33946.   Cass. PET-33946
     SR   Sept.   p95.   250w.   3

527 LOGGINS and Messina.   Native Sons.   Columbia PC-33578.
     Cart. PCA-33578.   Cass. PCT-33578
     CAC   May   p60.   175w. $2\frac{1}{2}$
     CIR .April 27   p16.   225w. $1\frac{1}{2}$
     GR   May   p1812.   100w. $2\frac{1}{2}$
     MG   April   p38.   325w.   3
     MM   May 29   p29.   200w.   3
     RS   April 8   p76.   350w.   2
     SR   May   p86.   75w.   3

528 LOGGINS and Messina.   So Fine.   Columbia PC-33810.   Cart.
     PCA-33810.   Cass. PCT-33810
     CRE   Jan.   p70.   275w.   1
     GR   Feb.   p1389.   100w.   3
     SR   Jan.   p84-5.   225w.   2

529 LOKOMOTIVE Kreuzberg.   Fette Jahre.   Plane (E)
     MM   May 8   p25.   75w. $2\frac{1}{2}$

530 LOMAX, Jackie.   Lovin' for Lovin'.   Capitol ST 11558
     MM   Dec. 18   p16.   350w. $1\frac{1}{2}$

RS   Nov. 18 p78.   225w. $2\frac{1}{2}$

531   LONE Star.   Epic EPC-81545 (E)
      MM   Nov. 13 p26.   400w. $2\frac{1}{2}$
      RR   Dec.   p99.   25w. $2\frac{1}{2}$

531a LOST Gonzo Band.   MCA 487
      CMR   Feb.   p32.   125w. $2\frac{1}{2}$

532   LOST Gonzo Band.   Thrills.   MCA MCA-2232
      MG   Dec.   p63.   50w.   3

533   LUCIFER'S Friend.   Banquet.   Passport PPSD-98012
      LP   April   p9.   100w.   3

534   LYNYRD Skynyrd.   Gimme Back My Bullets.   MCA-2170.
      Tape MCAT-2170
            CRE   June   p72.   50w.   4
            GR   April   p1670.   75w.   3
            MG   May   p46.   50w.   3
            MM   Jan. 31   p23.   475w.   4
            PRM   March   p37.   400w.   2
            RS   March 25   p55.   250w.   2
            SR   June   p84.   150w.   3

535   LYNYRD Skynyrd.   One More for the Road.   MCA MCA2-6001
      (2 discs)
            CIR   Dec. 14   p13-4.   300w.   3
            CRE   Dec.   p62.   550w.   4
            MG   Dec.   p63.   50w.   3
            MM   Nov. 13   p29.   325w.   2
            RM   Dec.   p33.   100w. $2\frac{1}{2}$
            RS   Nov. 4   p68.   250w.   4

536   LYNYRD Skynyrd.   Pronounced LEH-NERD SKIN-NERD.   MCA
      CAC   Oct.   p254.   50w.   3

537   McCAFFERTY, Dan.   A&M SP4553
      CRA   Feb.   p74.   150w.   1

538   McCARTNEY, Paul.   Venus and Mars.   Capitol SMAS 11419
      AU   Feb.   p81-2.   600w.   4

539   McCLINTON, Delbert.   Genuine Cowhide.   ABC ABCD-959
      CIR   Nov. 10   p16.   450w.   3
      CM   Nov.   p60.   350w.   5
      CRA   Oct.   p78.   100w.   3
      CRE   Nov.   p62.   550w. $4\frac{1}{2}$
      CRE   Dec.   p14.   75w. $3\frac{1}{2}$
      MG   Nov.   p56.   50w.   2
      MM   Aug. 14   p28.   750w. $3\frac{1}{2}$

540   McCLINTON, Delbert.   Victim of Life's Circumstances.

ABC 907
    CM   April p50. 475w. 2
    CRE   March p12. 25w. 3

541   McCULLOUGH, Henry. Mind Your Own Business. Dark
      Horse 22005
      RS Feb. 12 p95. 200w. 3

542   McDONALD, Country Joe. Love Is a Fire. Fantasy F-9511.
      Cart. 8160-9511. Cass. 5160-9511H
      MM Nov. 20 p26. 225w. 1
      SR Dec. p112. 75w. 2

543   McDONALD, Country Joe. Paradise with an Ocean View.
      Fantasy F-9495. Cart. 8160-9495H
      LP March p9. 175w. $3\frac{1}{2}$
      MG Jan. p33. 50w. $2\frac{1}{2}$
      PMS V4/#3 p191. 50w. 4
      RS Jan. 29 p50. 275w. 1
      SR April p84. 200w. 4

544   MACDONALD, Lenny. Hard Road. Arista (E)
      MM April 17 p21. 50w. $2\frac{1}{2}$

545   McGARRIGLE, Kate and Anna McGarrigle. Warner BS-2862
      CC March p35. 50w. 4
      CIR April 27 p12. 275w. $3\frac{1}{2}$
      CM May p49. 300w. 5
      MM Feb. 7 p24. 1000w. $4\frac{1}{2}$
      MM Dec. 25 p19. 250w. $4\frac{1}{2}$
      RR May p74. 25w. 2
      RS Feb. 26 p77. 350w. 3
      SR May p78-9. 400w. 5
      SR May p78-9. 250w. 4

546   McGUINN, Roger. Columbia PC33541
      AU Feb. p81-2. 600w. 2

547   McGUINN, Roger. Cardiff Rose. Columbia PC-34154. Co-
      lumbia PC-34154. Cart. PCA-34154
      AU Sept. p72. 650w. 4
      CIR Sept. 13 p17. 300w. $4\frac{1}{2}$
      CRA Aug. p71. 275w. $3\frac{1}{2}$
      CRE Sept. p62. 375w. $3\frac{1}{2}$
      GR Aug. p351. 75w. 2
      MH Oct./Nov. p65-6. 250w. $3\frac{1}{2}$
      MM Aug. 21 p19. 375w. $2\frac{1}{2}$
      RR Sept. p88. 75w. 3
      RS July 15 p58. 600w. 4
      SR Sept. p96-7. 325w. 2

548   McKENDREE Spring. Too Young to Feel This Old. Pye 12124
      SR July p90. 125w. 3

549   McLAUCHLAN, Murray.   Boulevard.   Island ILPS 9423
      CC   Oct.   p32.   50w.   4

549a McLAUCHLAN, Murray.   Only the Silence Remains.   True
      North STN 19 (2 discs) (Canada)
      OLR   March   p40.   50w.   4

550   MACLEAN, Dan.   Solo.   United Artists LA652-H2 (2 discs)
      MM   Dec. 4   p24.   750w. $2\frac{1}{2}$

551   McLOONE, Annie.   Fast Annie.   RCA APL1-1362.   Cart.
      APK1-1362
          AU   July   p70.   50w.   0
          RS   May 20   p72.   175w. $2\frac{1}{2}$
          SR   June   p73-4.   600w.   4

552   McTELL, Ralph.   20th Century T-456
      LP   March   p9.   100w. $2\frac{1}{2}$

553   McVIE, Christine.   The Legendary.   Sire SASD 7522
          CIR   Nov. 10   p17.   350w. $2\frac{1}{2}$
          CK   Dec.   p49.   25w.   2
          CRA   Nov.   p77-8.   150w.   1
          CRE   Nov.   p60.   450w. $2\frac{1}{2}$

554   MAGMA.   Live.   Utopia CYL2-1245 (2 discs)
          CRE   Feb.   p60.   400w. $2\frac{1}{2}$
          MM   Feb. 28   p24.   550w.   4

555   MAGNA Carta.   Putting It Back Together.   Ariola 50014
      MM   Nov. 6   p22.   350w.   3

556   MAMA'S Pride.   Atco SD-36-122.   Cass. CS-35-122
          HF   Jan.   p102.   150w. $2\frac{1}{2}$
          LP   March   p9.   100w.   3
          MG   Jan.   p34.   50w.   3

557   MAMAS and Papas.   Twenty Golden Hits.   ABC (Reissue)
      MM   Sept. 18   p21.   25w.   3

558   MAN.   Maximum Darkness.   United Artists UAS 29872 (E)
      CAC   March   p488.   150w. $3\frac{1}{2}$

559   MAN.   1970.   Sunset SLS 50380 (E) (Reissue)
      MM   March 13   p23.   200w. $1\frac{1}{2}$

560   MAN.   Welsh Connection.   MCA MCA-2190
          GP   Dec.   p105.   25w.   3
          MHF   June-July   p68.   275w.   3
          RS   June 17   p58, 60.   175w.   3

561   MANCHESTER, Melissa.   Better Days & Happy Endings.
      Arista AL-4067.   Cart. 8301-4067

CIR   May 13 p14, 16.   350w.   2
CRE   June   p72.   25w.   2
MG   May   p46.   50w. $4\frac{1}{2}$
RR   May   p74.   50w. $1\frac{1}{2}$
RS   May 6   p69.   225w.   3
SR   June   p84.   125w.   4

562   MANEIGE.   Les Porches.   EMI Harvest S7-6438 (Canada)
CC   Jan.   p39.   50w. $3\frac{1}{2}$
MM   Sept. 11 p26.   25w. $3\frac{1}{2}$
OLR   Dec.   p259.   25w.   4

563   MANFRED Mann.   Mannerisms.   Phonogram SON 016 (E)
CAC   Nov.   p296.   225w. $3\frac{1}{2}$

564   MANFRED Mann's Earth Band.   Nightingales and Bombers.
Warner Brothers BS 2877
CRE   Jan.   p69.   275w.   3
CRE   Feb.   p72.   50w. $4\frac{1}{2}$

565   MANFRED Mann's Earth Band.   The Roaring Silence.   Warner
Brothers BS-2965
CK   Dec.   p48.   125w.   4
CRA   Dec.   p80.   250w.   3
GR   Nov.   p899.   50w.   3
MG   Dec.   p63.   50w.   3
MM   Oct. 2 p29.   275w. $3\frac{1}{2}$
PRM   Nov.   p22.   100w. $1\frac{1}{2}$
RS   Dec. 16 p65, 67. 600w. $2\frac{1}{2}$

566   MANSON, Charles.   Lie.   EPS
CRA   March p81.   125w. $3\frac{1}{2}$

567   MARCOVITZ, Diana.   Joie de vivre.   Kama Sutra KSBS 2614
RS   Dec. 16 p88, 90.   125w.   2

568   MARRIOTT, Steve.   Marriott.   A&M SP-4572.   Cart. 4572.
Cass. 4572
CRA   July p82.   200w.   3
MM   June 26 p22.   325w.   2
SR   Sept. p95, 96.   150w.   2

569   MARSHALL Tucker Band.   Long Hard Ride.   Capricorn CP-
0170
CMP   Dec.   p12.   200w.   3
CRE   Sept.   p59.   350w.   3
GP   Aug.   p81.   50w.   3
MG   Sept.   p58.   50w.   1
RS   Aug. 12 p62.   200w.   3

570   MARSHALL Tucker Band.   Searchin' for a Rainbow.   Capricorn
0161
CAC   Feb.   p448.   150w. $2\frac{1}{2}$

CS   Aug.   p38.   250w.   5
MM   Jan.   24 p27.   150w. $1\frac{1}{2}$

571   MASON, Barry.   The Songwriter.   Magnet MAG 5012 (E)
MM   Nov. 13 p28.   150w.   0

572   MASON, Dave.   Alone Together.   ABC
MM   Oct. 2 p30.   75w.   3

573   MASON, Dave.   Headkeeper.   ABC (2 discs) (Reissue)
MM   Sept. 18 p21.   25w.   3

574   MASON, Dave.   Split Coconut.   Columbia PC-33698
MG   Jan.   p33.   50w.   3
SR   Feb.   p84.   75w. $4\frac{1}{2}$

575   MATHEWS, Ian.   Go for Broke.   Columbia PC 34102.   Cart.
PCA 34102
MM   June 12 p25.   475w.   3
RS   July 15 p67.   150w.   3
SR   Sept.   p96.   275w.   4

576   MAYALL, John.   Polydor (E) (Reissue)
CAC   June   p76.   225w.   4

577   MAYALL, John.   Notice to Appear.   ABC 926
CRE   June   p72.   25w.   3

578   MELANIE.   Peace Will Come.   Buddah (E)
CAC   March   p492.   175w. $2\frac{1}{2}$

579   MELANIE.   Sunset and Other Beginnings.   Arista AL-3001.
Cart. 8303-3001-H
HF   March   p107.   75w. $1\frac{1}{2}$
MG   Feb.   p38.   75w.   3
SR   April   p86.   200w.   3

580   MELCHER, Terry.   Royal Flush.   RCA BEL1-0948
RS   June 17 p58.   200w.   3

581   MELTON, Barry.   The Fish.   United Artists/Rockfield UAS
29908 (E)
MM   Feb. 28 p25.   200w.   2

582   MENDELSON, Joe.   Sophisto.   Taurus TR 1004 (Canada)
OLR   June   p105.   50w. $3\frac{1}{2}$

583   MERCURY, Eric.   Mercury SRM 1-1026
AU   June   p85.   150w. $4\frac{1}{2}$

584   MERRITT, Max.   Out of the Blue.   Arista ARTY 134 (E)
GR   Nov.   p899.   50w.   3
MM   Nov. 27 p27.   325w.   3

585 MILES, John. Rebel. London PS 669
         CAC   April p18.   150w. $2\frac{1}{2}$
         CIR   July 22 p14.   75w.   2
         GR   May p1812.   25w. $2\frac{1}{2}$
         HF   Sept. p108.   200w.   2
         MG   July p46.   50w.   2
         MH   Oct./Nov.   p70.   175w. $3\frac{1}{2}$
         MM   April 3 p31.   575w.   4
         RS   July 1 p76.   250w.   3

586 MILES, John. Strangers in the City. Decca TXS118 (E)
         MM   Dec. 25 p17.   475w. $3\frac{1}{2}$

587 MILLER, Frankie. The Rock. Chrysalis CHR-1088
         AU   March p78-9.   350w.   1
         CRE   March p12.   50w. $3\frac{1}{2}$
         LP   March p9.   125w. $3\frac{1}{2}$
         SR   March p86.   225w.   0

588 MILLER, Steve. Fly Like an Eagle. Capitol ST-11497.
     Cart. 8XT-11497.   Cass. 4XT-11497
         CRA   Aug. p66.   550w.   3
         CRE   Sept. p64.   350w. $2\frac{1}{2}$
         GR   Aug. p351.   50w.   2
         HF   Sept. p109.   100w. $2\frac{1}{2}$
         MG   Sept. p58.   50w.   3
         MM   May 22 p22.   850w.   4
         RS   July 15 p65.   225w.   4
         SR   Nov. p104.   100w.   2

589 MITCHELL, Joni. Reprise RS 6293
         CRA   March p78.   75w.   4

590 MITCHELL, Joni. Hejira. Asylum 7E-1087
         MM   Nov. 27 p24.   1300w. $2\frac{1}{2}$

591 MITCHELL, Joni. The Hissing of Summer Lawns. Asylum
     7E-1051.   Cart. ET8-1051
         AU   March p75-6.   650w. $2\frac{1}{2}$
         AU   March p76.   900w.   5
         CIR   March 2 p12, 14.   775w. $3\frac{1}{2}$
         CRE   March p12-3.   200w.   3
         LP   March p10.   125w.   3
         MG   Feb. p36.   50w. $3\frac{1}{2}$
         OLR   Sept. p189.   50w. $4\frac{1}{2}$
         RS   Jan. 15 p50.   900w.   3
         SR   Feb. p75.   500w.   5

592 MODERN Lovers. Home of the Hits HH-1910A
         CIR   Aug. 24 p12-3.   375w.   3
         CIR   Oct. 26 p10-1.   625w. $2\frac{1}{2}$
         CRE   Aug. p66-7.   400w.   3
         CRE   Aug. p14.   125w. $4\frac{1}{2}$

            MG   Sept. p58. 50w. 3
            MM   July 31 p21. 550w.   4

593 MONKEES. Greatest Hits. Arista 4089. Cart. 8301-4089.
     Cass. 5301-4089 (Reissue)
            SR   Nov. p104. 125w. 1

594 MONTROSE. Jump On It. Warner Brothers BS 2963
            AU   Dec. p82. 250w. $1\frac{1}{2}$
            CRA Dec. p70. 325w. $3\frac{1}{2}$
            GP   Nov. p133. 75w. $2\frac{1}{2}$
            MM   Nov. 20 p25. 225w. $1\frac{1}{2}$
            RM   Dec. p29. 200w. $1\frac{1}{2}$
            RR   Dec. p100. 75w. 3
            RS   Dec. 16 p90. 175w. 2

595 MONTROSE. Warner Brothers Presents. Warner Brothers
     BS 2892
            CRE Jan. p68. 250w. $3\frac{1}{2}$

596 MOON. Too Close to Comfort. Epic EPC-81456 (E)
            GR   Nov. p899. 50w. 3
            MM   Nov. 27 p27. 325w. 3
            RR   Nov. p106. 75w. $2\frac{1}{2}$

597 MOONQUAKE. Starstruck. Fantasy F9486
            OLR June p106. 25w. $2\frac{1}{2}$

598 MOORE, Tim. Behind the Eyes. Asylum 7E 1042
            AU   March p78. 900w. $3\frac{1}{2}$

599 MORAZ, Patrick. "i". Atlantic SD-18175. Cart. TP-18175.
     Cass. CS 18175
            CAC May p57. 275w. 3
            CRE Nov. p61. 100w. $2\frac{1}{2}$
            GR   June p98. 75w. 3
            HF   Sept. p112. 200w. $3\frac{1}{2}$
            RS   July 15 p67-8. 100w. 3
            SR   Oct. p100. 150w. 0

599a MORNING Glory. Antilles AN 7004
            DB   April 8 p30-2. 50w. 4

600 MORRISON, Van. Two Originals of. Warner (£) (Reissue)
            MM   Jan. 24 p26. 100w. $2\frac{1}{2}$

601 MORSE Code. La marche des hommes. Capitol ST 70038
     (Canada)
            OLR Dec. p262. 25w. 2

602 MOTHER'S Finest. Epic PE 34179
            AU   Oct. p135-6. 300w. 4
            MM   Nov. 27 p28. 75w. 3

RS Nov. 4 p76. 150w. 3

603 MOTHERS of Invention. Uncle Meat. Reprise 2024
     CRA March p78. 200w. 5

604 MOTT. Drive On. Columbia PC-33705. Cart. PCA-33705.
     Cass. PCT-33705
     CIR Jan. 20 p21. 225w. 2
     CRA Jan. p77-8. 150w. 2
     CRE Jan. p66-7. 250w. $2\frac{1}{2}$
     LP Jan. p11. 150w. $2\frac{1}{2}$
     MG Jan. p33. 50w. $1\frac{1}{2}$
     SR Jan. p85. 250w. 2

605 MOTT. Shouting and Pointing. Columbia PC-34236. Cart.
     PCA-34236. Cass. PCT-34236
     AU Oct. p138-9. 500w. 1
     MM Sept. 18 p21. 225w. $2\frac{1}{2}$
     RS Sept. 9 p59-60. 175w. 2
     SR Nov. p106. 200w. 1

606 MOVIES. Arista AL-4085. Cart. 8301-4085. Cass. 5301-
     4085H
     CIR Dec. 14 p16. 125w. 2
     MM Feb. 7 p25. 275w. $1\frac{1}{2}$
     RS Aug. 26 p66. 150w. 3
     SR Nov. p104, 106. 25w. 1

607 MOXY. Mercury SRM 1-1087
     CC March p32. 50w. 3
     SOU April p42. 275w. $2\frac{1}{2}$

607a MOXY. II. Polydor 2480 372 (Canada)
      CC Dec. p32. 75w. 3

608 MUD. Use Your Imagination. Precision 1003 (E)
     CAC Feb. p448. 150w. $3\frac{1}{2}$

609 MULDAUR, Geoff. Geoff Muldaur Is Having a Wonderful Time.
     Reprise MS-2220
     CRA Nov. p78. 150w. 2
     MM Jan. 3 p23. 300w. 4
     SR Jan. p85, 88. 275w. 4

610 MULDAUR, Maria. Sweet Harmony. Reprise MS 2235. Cart.
     M82235. Cass. M52235
     AU Sept. p84. 150w. $2\frac{1}{2}$
     CAC June p98. 200w. 3
     CIR June 1 p14-5. 550w. $3\frac{1}{2}$
     CRE June p57. 200w. 2
     GR May p1812. 25w. $1\frac{1}{2}$
     HF June p101. 150w. 3
     MG May p46. 50w. 4

      MM Feb. 28 p25. 575w. 3
      RR   May p74. 25w. $1\frac{1}{2}$
      RS   April 22 p57. 725w. 4
      SR   June p80. 600w. 5

611 MUNGO Jerry. Impala Sage. Polydor 2383 364 (E)
      CAC April p19. 200w. $2\frac{1}{2}$

611a MUNGO Jerry. Pye 504 (Reissue)
      HF April p130. 50w. 0

612 MURPHEY, Michael. Swans Against the Sun. Epic PE-33851.
      Cart. PEA-33851. Cass. PET-33851
      AU   May p80-1. 350w. 4
      CMR Feb. p28. 500w. 2
      LP   March p10. 125w. 4
      MM Feb. 7 p24. 300w. 2
      RS   Jan. 29 p46. 200w. 3
      SOU Feb. p43-4. 400w. 5
      SR   March p86. 150w. 0

613 MURPHY, Elliot. Nightlights. RCA APL-1-1318
      CRE July p12, 81. 75w. 3
      MG   May p46. 50w. 3
      PRM March p36. 400w. 2
      RS   April 8 p74. 550w. $2\frac{1}{2}$
      SR   July p90. 150w. 3

613a MUSSELWHITE, Charles. Leave the Blues to Us. Capitol
      ST 11450
      CZM June p38. 200w. $2\frac{1}{2}$

614 NASTY Pop. Island (E)
      MM July 10 p21. 125w. 3

615 NATURAL Gas. Private Stock PS2011. Cart. 8300-2011H.
      Cass. 5300-2100H
      RS   Aug. 12 p68, 71. 150w. $2\frac{1}{2}$
      SR   Nov. p106. 150w. $2\frac{1}{2}$

616 NAZARETH. Close Enough for Rock and Roll. A&M SP 4562
      PRM March p32. 300w. 4
      RR   June p82. 50w. 3

617 NAZARETH. Exercises. EMI TOPS 103 (E)
      CAC Feb. p444. 75w. 3

618 NAZARETH. Greatest Hits. A&M SP 9020
      MM Jan. 3 p23. 150w. $2\frac{1}{2}$

619 NAZARETH. Hair of the Dog. EMI (E). A&M SP 4511
      CAC Feb. p444. 75w. 4

620 NAZARETH. Loud and Proud. EMI TOPS 105 (E)
     CAC Feb. p444. 75w. 3

621 NAZARETH. Rampart. EMI TOPS 106 (E)
     CAC Feb. p444. 75w. $2\frac{1}{2}$

622 NAZARETH. Razamanaz. EMI TOPS 104 (E)
     CAC Feb. p444. 75w. $3\frac{1}{2}$

623 NEKTAR. Recycled. Passport PPS-98011
     SR March p86. 225w. 2

624 NEKTAR. A Tab in the Ocean. Passport PPSD 98017
     RS Dec. 16 p100. 150w. $2\frac{1}{2}$

625 NELSON, Tracy. Time Is on My Side. MCA MCA-2203.
     Cart. MCAT-2203
     AU Sept. p81. 150w. 1
     CIR Sept. 13 p16. 200w. 1
     MM Oct. 9 p30. 200w. 2
     RS Aug. 26 p68. 225w. 3
     SR Nov. p106, 108. 125w. $2\frac{1}{2}$

626 NESMITH, Mike. Best of. RCA RS 1064 (E) (Reissue)
     MM Nov. 13 p28. 100w. 1

627 NEW Riders of the Purple Sage. MCA 2196. Cart. MCAT
     2196
     CM Nov. p61. 100w. 1
     MG Oct. p65. 50w. 3
     MM Aug. 7 p18. 200w. $2\frac{1}{2}$
     RS Aug. 26 p65. 125w. 2

628 NEW Riders of the Purple Sage. Oh, What a Mighty Time.
     Columbia PC-33688. Cass. PCT-33688
     CMP March p18. 250w. 2
     GP Jan. p71. 125w. 4
     LP March p10. 125w. 2
     MG Feb. p53. 50w. 0
     MM Jan. 10 p23. 275w. $1\frac{1}{2}$
     RR Feb. p66. 25w. $1\frac{1}{2}$

629 NEWBEATS. Bread and Butter. DJM DJM 22052 (E)
     (Reissue)
     MM Oct. 2 p30. 50w. 1

630 NICE. The Immediate Story, vol. 1. Sire SASH-3710/2 (2
     discs) (Reissue)
     LP April p10. 150w. 3
     MG March p43. 75w. 3

631 THE NIGHTHAWKS. Open All Nite. Adelphi AD4105

SR   Sept.   p97.   325w.   3

632 THE NIGHTHAWKS.   Rock 'n' Roll.   Alladin ALPS-101
     SR   March   p87.   275w.   4

633 NILSSON, Harry.   Sandman.   RCA APL1-1031.   Cart. APS1-
     1031.   Cass. APS1-1031
     CAC   April   p18.   125w.   2
     CIR   April 27   p14.   200w.   2
     HF   May   p102.   100w.   1
     MG   April   p39.   75w.   3
     RS   April 22   p61.   300w.   0
     SR   May   p86, 92.   100w.   3

634 NILSSON, Harry.   That's the Way It Is.   RCA APL1-1119.
     Cart. APS1-119.   Cass. APK1-119
     CAC   Dec.   p341.   125w.   2
     MG   Sept.   p58.   50w. $2\frac{1}{2}$
     MM   Oct. 16   p22.   100w.   0
     RS   Aug. 12   p59.   300w.   3
     SR   Sept.   p108.   900w.   2

635 The NITTY Gritty Dirt Band.   Dream.   United Artists LA469G
     CMP   March   p18.   300w.   4
     LP   Jan.   p11.   200w.   3
     PMS   V4/#3   p189-90.   50w. $3\frac{1}{2}$

636 NUCLEUS.   Alleycat.   Vertigo 6360 124 (E)
     MM   April 3   p32.   400w.   3

637 NUCLEUS.   Direct Hits.   Vertigo (E)
     MM   May 8   p22.   275w.   3

638 NUGENT, Ted.   Epic PE 33692
     MM   May 1   p30.   225w.   4

639 NUGENT, Ted.   Free for All.   Epic PE 34121
     CRA   Dec.   p80.   350w.   2
     CRE   Dec.   p58.   575w. $3\frac{1}{2}$
     MM   Oct. 16   p25.   200w. $3\frac{1}{2}$
     RS   Nov. 18   p74-5.   575w.   4

640 NYRO, Laura.   Smile.   Columbia PC-33912 PCT-33912
     AU   June   p81.   350w.   4
     CIR   June 17   p16.   200w.   4
     CRA   May   p69-70.   1300w.   4
     CRE   July   p66.   200w. $2\frac{1}{2}$
     HF   June   p102.   150w. $1\frac{1}{2}$
     MHF   May V6/#2   p59.   400w.   2
     MM   Feb. 14   p29.   425w.   4
     RR   May   p74.   75w.   3
     RS   May 6   p62.   325w.   2
     SOU   May   p38.   300w.   2

SR   June   p84.   150w.   3

641   O.   Within Reach.   United Artists UAG-29942 (E)
      CAC   Sept.   p216.   250w.   3
      GR   Oct.   p669.   50w.   1

642   OCTOBRE.   London PGP 13001 (Canada)
      OLR   March   p42.   25w.   1

643   O'KEEFE, Danny.   So Long Harry Truman.   Atlantic SD
      18125.   Cass.   CS 18125
      LP   Jan.   p11.   75w. $3\frac{1}{2}$

644   OLDFIELD, Mike.   Boxed.   Virgin VBOX1 (4 discs) (E) (Re-
      issue)
      MM   Oct. 30   p25.   975w.   4

645   OLDFIELD, Mike.   Ommadawn.   Virgin PZ-33913.   Cart.
      PZA-33913
      AU   March   p76-7.   500w.   3
      CRA   April   p76.   250w.   4
      GP   Feb.   p71.   100w.   4
      GR   Jan.   p1258.   100w.   3
      LP   March   p10.   100w. $3\frac{1}{2}$
      MG   April   p39.   50w.   3
      MM   Feb. 21   p30.   825w. $4\frac{1}{2}$
      SOU   Feb.   p46.   400w. $3\frac{1}{2}$
      SR   April   p86.   225w.   3

646   OLSSON, Nigel.   Rocket PIG-2158.   Cass. PIGC-2158
      CAC   June   p98.   125w. $2\frac{1}{2}$
      LP   Jan.   p11.   150w.   2

647   OMEGA.   Hall of Floaters in the Sky.   Decca SKLR 5219 (E)
      MM   March 6   p27.   50w.   0

648   OMEGA.   I Don't Know Your Name.   Pepita SLPX-17483 (Hun-
      gary)
      SR   May   p92.   125w.   4

649   ORLEANS.   Waking And.   Asylum 7E-1070
      RS   Oct. 21   p107.   250w.   3

650   OUTLAWS.   Arista AL 4042
      CMP   Jan.   p26.   150w.   3
      CRE   Jan.   p12.   50w.   2
      CRE   June   p72.   25w.   4

651   OUTLAWS.   Lady in Waiting.   Arista AL 4070
      CIR   July 6   p14.   100w.   2
      GR   July   p226.   50w. $1\frac{1}{2}$
      HF   July   p106.   150w. $3\frac{1}{2}$

                    MM   May 22   p23.   200w. $2\frac{1}{2}$
                    RR   June   p82.   25w.   0
                    SR   July   p90.   50w.   3

652 OVERSTREET, Tommy.   Turn Onto.   Dot 2056
                    MM   Nov. 27   p28.   125w.   3

653 OZARK Mountain Daredevils.   The Car Over the Lake Album.
     A&M SP-4549.   Cass. 4549
                    CAC   March   p488, 492.   225w. $3\frac{1}{2}$
                    CMP   April   p20.   700w.   3
                    GR   Feb.   p1389.   25w. $2\frac{1}{2}$
                    LP   March   p10.   125w.   2
                    MG   Jan.   p33.   50w. $2\frac{1}{2}$
                    SR   March   p90.   200w.   5

654 OZARK Mountain Daredevils.   Men from Earth.   A&M SP 4601
                    CAC   Dec.   p358.   150w.   3
                    MM   Nov. 20   p26.   200w.   3

654a P. F. M.   Chocolate Kings.   Asylum 7E-1071
                    CK   Oct.   p47.   150w.   3
                    MM   May 1   p30.   400w. $2\frac{1}{2}$
                    RS   Oct. 7   p87.   125w.   3

655 PABLO Cruise.   Lifeline.   A&M SP 4575
                    MM   April 17   p22.   200w. $3\frac{1}{2}$
                    SOU   May   p40-1.   250w. $1\frac{1}{2}$

656 PACHECO, Tom.   Swallowed Up in the Great American Heart-
     land.   RCA APL1-1254
                    CIR   June 17   p16.   300w. $4\frac{1}{2}$
                    CRE   July   p81.   25w. $2\frac{1}{2}$
                    RS   April 22   p61.   350w. $3\frac{1}{2}$

657 PAGE, Larry.   Rampage.   Penny Farthing (E)
                    MM   Dec. 25   p17.   50w.   1

658 PAGLIARO, Michel.   I.   Columbia KC-33901
                    OLR   June   p106.   50w.   4
                    SOU   April   p43.   350w. $2\frac{1}{2}$

659 PAGLIARO, Michel.   Pag.   RCA PCS 4019 (Canada)
                    OLR   March   p42.   25w.   3

660 PALMER, Robert.   Pressure Drop.   Island ILPS-9372
                    CRA   Feb.   p65-6.   875w. $3\frac{1}{2}$
                    LP   April   p10.   200w. $3\frac{1}{2}$
                    MG   Feb.   p36.   50w. $4\frac{1}{2}$
                    MM   Jan. 10   p23.   425w.   4
                    RS   Feb. 12   p88.   300w.   3

661 PALMER, Robert.   Some People Can Do What They Want.

Island ILPS-9420
 MG Dec. p63. 50w. 3
 MM Dec. 11 p22. 550w. 3
 RM Dec. p33. 125w. 3
 RS Dec. 2 p99-100. 275w. 3

662 PAPPALARDI, Felix. Creation. A&M SP4586
 CIR Oct. 26 p12. 100w. $1\frac{1}{2}$

663 PARIS. Capitol ST-11464
 CRA April p76. 50w. $1\frac{1}{2}$
 CRE June p57-8. 100w. $2\frac{1}{2}$
 GP April p79. 125w. 4
 PRM Jan. p30. 150w. 4
 RS March 25 p66. 175w. 2

664 PARIS. Big Towne, 2061. Capitol ST 11560
 CRA Dec. p78-9. 200w. 1
 MG Nov. p56. 50w. 2
 RS Dec. 16 p98. 100w. $2\frac{1}{2}$

665 PARKER, Graham. Howling Wind. Mercury SRM1-1095
 CAC July p138. 200w. 4
 CIR Oct. 26 p11-2. 450w. 4
 CRA Sept. p82. 425w. $2\frac{1}{2}$
 GR June p98. 50w. $3\frac{1}{2}$
 MM May 15 p25. 375w. 3
 RS July 29 p50. 225w. $3\frac{1}{2}$
 SR Nov. p108. 75w. $2\frac{1}{2}$

666 PARKER, Graham and the Rumour. Heat Treatment. Mercury SRM 1-1117
 RS Dec. 30 p67-8. 225w. 4

667 PARKS, Van Dyke. Clang of the Yankee Reaper. Warner Bros. BS2878. Cart. M82878. Cass. M52878
 CIR Feb. 10 p12. 200w. 2
 LP Jan. p12. 200w. 2
 MM Jan. 3 p23. 275w. 3
 RS Jan. 29 p48, 50. 325w. 3
 SR March p81. 550w. 5

668 PARSONS, Alan. Tales of Mystery and Imagination. 20th Century T-508. Cart. 8-508
 MG July p47. 325w. 3
 MM July 24 p23. 225w. 4
 RS Sept. 23 p118. 175w. $2\frac{1}{2}$
 SR Sept. p97, 98. 200w. 2

669 PARSONS, Gram and the Flying Burrito Brothers. Sleepless Nights. A&M SP4578
 CAC Aug. p183. 275w. 3
 CIR July 22 p16. 300w. 3
 CM Aug. p55-6. 525w. 4

CMR   Sept.   p32.   125w.   1
CRA   July   p74, 76.   1200w.   3
CRE   Aug.   p67.   200w.   1
CMP   Aug.   p30.   400w.   5
GP   Sept.   p87.   25w. $2\frac{1}{2}$
RS   June 17   p53, 55.   300w.   3
SR   Sept.   p98.   300w.   3

670   PASSPORT.   Infinity Machine.   Acto SD 36-132
DB   Nov. 18   p28.   200w. $1\frac{1}{2}$
MM   July 17   p22.   275w.   4

671   PAVLOV'S Dog.   At the Sound of the Bell.   Columbia PC 33
964
CRE   June   p58.   200w.   2
CRE   June   p60.   25w. $4\frac{1}{2}$
MM   July 24   p24.   150w.   2

672   PAYNE, Freda.   Out of Payne Comes Love.   ABC ABCD 901.
Cass. H8022-901
HF   Feb.   p121.   200w.   4

673   PENSE, Lydia and Cold Blood.   Cold Blood.   ABC ABCD-917
CRA   May   p78.   100w.   3
MM   June 26   p22.   50w.   2

674   PERRY, John G.   Sunset Wading.   Decca SKL 5233 (E)
JJ   Sept.   p41.   75w.   2

675   PETERIK, Jim.   Don't Fight the Feeling.   Epic PE 34196
RS   Nov. 4   p82.   225w.   3

676   PHILLIPS, Glenn.   Lostat Sea.   Snow Star (E)
MM   July 3   p23.   200w.   3

677   PILOT.   January.   Capitol ST 11488
SR   July   p90, 93.   100w.   3

678   PILOT.   Morin Heights.   EMI EMA779 (E)
CAC   Nov.   p296.   225w. $2\frac{1}{2}$
GR   Oct.   p669.   75w.   1
MM   Sept. 18   p21.   425w.   5

679   PINDER, Michael.   The Promise.   Threshold THS 18.   Cart.
THS8-18.   Cass. THS5-15
CAC   June   p96.   200w.   2
GR   July   p226.   25w.   3
SR   Sept.   p101.   175w.   2

680   PINK Floyd.   Wish You Were Here.   Columbia PC-33453.
Cart. PCA-33453.   Cass. PCT-33453
CRE   Feb.   p72, 74.   50w. $4\frac{1}{2}$
GP   Jan.   p71.   175w.   4

LP   Jan.   p12.   325w. $2\frac{1}{2}$
SR   Jan.   p88-9.   325w.   4

681   POCO.   Live.   Epic PE 33336
GR   May   p1812.   50w.   3
MM   April 3   p29.   300w.   3
SR   July   p93.   75w. $3\frac{1}{2}$

682   POCO.   Rose of Cimarron.   ABC ABCD-946
CMP   July   p29.   375w.   3
CMR   Sept.   p30.   125w.   2
CRA   Aug.   p74-5.   150w.   3
GP   Aug.   p81.   25w. $3\frac{1}{2}$
GR   Aug.   p351.   75w. $3\frac{1}{2}$
MG   Sept.   p58.   25w.   3
MM   July 10   p22.   125w.   3
RS   July 15   p65.   150w.   3

683   POINAREFF, Michel.   Atlantic SD 18153
RS   Feb. 26   p79.   250w.   1

684   POINT Blank.   Arista AL 4087
MM   Sept. 11   p26.   25w. $3\frac{1}{2}$
RM   Nov.   p32.   50w.   2
RS   Sept. 23   p117.   175w.   3

685   POLECAT.   Money Talkin'.   DJM DJF 20475 (E)
CAC   Oct.   p260.   50w.   3

686   POMERANZ, David.   It's in Every One of Us.   Arista AL-4054
MG   April   p39.   50w.   3
MM   May 29   p26.   75w.   2
SR   May   p92.   100w.   4

687   POST, Mike.   Fused.   Warner K56163 (E)
MM   March 6   p27.   125w.   3

688   POST, Mike.   Railhead Overture.   MGM M36-5005, M8H 5005
HF   Jan.   p104.   100w.   3

689   POUSETTE-DART Band.   Capitol ST 11507
MM   Oct. 16   p22.   75w.   1
RS   May 6   p73.   150w. $2\frac{1}{2}$

690   POZO Seco Singers.   The Best Of.   Emerald Gem GES 1143
(E) (Reissue)
CMP   Aug.   p29.   300w.   1

691   PRATT, Andy.   Resolution.   Nemperor NE-438.   Cart. TP-
438.   Cass. CS-438
AU   Sept.   p72-3.   550w.   4
CIR   Sept. 13   p14, 16.   250w. $2\frac{1}{2}$
CRA   Aug.   p64-5.   400w. $4\frac{1}{2}$

98 Record Reviews, 1976

MG   Sept.   p58.   50w. $2\frac{1}{2}$
MM   July 3 p22.   450w. $3\frac{1}{2}$
RR   Sept.   p88.   175w. $3\frac{1}{2}$
RS   July 1 p61.   1750w. 5
SR   Nov.   p108. 125w. $1\frac{1}{2}$

691a   PRELUDE. Back in the Light. Pye NSPL 18498 (E)
      MM   Dec. 25 p17.   75w. $1\frac{1}{2}$

692   PRELUDE. Owlcreek Incident.   Pye 12120
      CAC   March p492-3. 200w. $3\frac{1}{2}$
      LP   April p10.   175w. $2\frac{1}{2}$

693   PRESLEY, Elvis. A Legendary Performer, vol. 2.   RCA
      CPL1-1349 (E) (Reissue)
      CAC   April p19.   275w. $2\frac{1}{2}$

694   PRESLEY, Elvis. Live from Elvis Presley Boulevard, Mem-
      phis.   RCA APL1-1506
      GR   Aug.   p351.   100w.   3

695   PRESLEY, Elvis. The Sun Sessions.   RCA APM1-1675 (Re-
      issue)
      AU   July   p68.   250w.   4
      CM   Aug.   p53.   450w.   4
      CRE   Sept. p61-2. 350w.   3
      MG   June   p44.   25w. $3\frac{1}{2}$
      SR   July   p93-4. 175w.   4

696   PRETTY Things. SF Sorrow/Parachute.   Harvest Heritage
      SHDW-406 (E) (Reissue)
      GR   Feb.   p1389.   25w. $2\frac{1}{2}$

697   PRETTY Things. Savage Eye.   Swan Song SS8414
      CIR   June 17 p14.   325w. $2\frac{1}{2}$
      MM   March 27 p29.   350w.   2
      PRM   March   p37.   350w.   4
      SR   July   p94.   50w.   1

698   PREVIN, Dory. We're Children of Coincidence and Harpo
      Marx.   Warner BS-2908
      CR   Sept. p539.   225w.   5
      CRE   June   p58.   125w. $2\frac{1}{2}$

699   PRICE, Alan. Performing.   Polydor 2683-062 (E)
      GR   April p1670.   75w.   4

700   PRICE, Alan. Shouts Across the Street.   Polydor (E)
      CAC   Dec.   p341.   300w. $3\frac{1}{2}$

701   PROCUL Harum. Rock Roots.   Decca Roots 4 (E) (Reissue)
      CAC   July   p143.   125w.   3

702 PROCUL Harum. Procul's Ninth. Chrysalis CHR-1080
     LP Jan. p12. 225w. $2\frac{1}{2}$

703 PROTHEROE, Brian. Pick-Up. Chrysalis CHR-1090
     CK August p46. 50w. $2\frac{1}{2}$

704 PULSAR. Pollen. Decca SKLR 5228 (E)
     CAC Aug. p177. 250w. $3\frac{1}{2}$
     MM Nov. 13 p28. 100w. $2\frac{1}{2}$

705 PURE Prairie League. If the Shoe Fits. RCA APL1-1247.
     Cart. APS1-R1247. Cass. APK1-1247
     CRA May p78. 100w. 3
     HF May p102. 100w. $2\frac{1}{2}$
     MM April 17 p23. 100w. $3\frac{1}{2}$
     SR May p93. 150w. 3

705a PURE Prairie League. Two Lane Highway. RCA APL1-
      0933
      CMR March p29. 225w. 4

706 QUANTUM Jumps. Electric TRIX 1 (E)
     MM Nov. 27 p28. 125w. 1

707 QUATRO, Michael. Dancers, Romancers, Dreamers and
     Schemers. Prodigal 6-10010
     MM Nov. 27 p26. 350w. $2\frac{1}{2}$

708 QUEEN. A Day at the Races. Elektra 7ES-1091
     MM Dec. 4 p24. 1659w. $4\frac{1}{2}$

709 QUEEN. A Night at the Opera. Elektra 7E-1053. Cart.
     ET8-1053
     CIR May 13 p14. 300w. 3
     CRA April p77-8. 200w. $1\frac{1}{2}$
     CRE March p62. 400w. 2
     GP Feb. p70. 300w. $3\frac{1}{2}$
     GR March p1518. 50w. $3\frac{1}{2}$
     HF April p129. 150w. $3\frac{1}{2}$
     MG March p42. 300w. 3
     RS April 8 p76-7. 200w. $3\frac{1}{2}$
     SR April p86. 100w. 2

710 THE QUICK. Mondo Deco. Mercury SRM1-1114
     MM Nov. 13 p28. 100w. 1
     PRM Nov. p22. 100w. $2\frac{1}{2}$
     WHO Winter p42-3. 150w. 2

711 QUICKSILVER Messenger Service. Solid Silver. Capitol
     ST-11462. Cart. 8xT-11462. Cass. 4xT-11462
     GR April p1670. 50w. 3
     LP March p10. 250w. 3
     MG Jan. p33. 75w. 3

SR   March   p91.   550w.   3
RS   Jan. 15   p56.   150w.   3

712   QUIET Sun.   Mainstream.   Antilles AN 7008
CRE   April   p62.   25w.   3
DB   April 8   p30-2.   75w. $3\frac{1}{2}$

713   QUIRE.   RCA BGL1-1700
SR   Nov.   p123.   75w.   3

714   RABBIT.   Boys Will Be Boys.   Capricorn 0175
MM   Aug. 14   p29.   50w.   3
LP   April   p11.   125w.   2

714a   RACING Cars.   Downtown Tonight.   Chrysalis (E)
MM   Oct. 16   p22.   550w.   4

715   RADICE, Mark.   Ain't Nothin' But a Party.   United Artists
LA 629K
CAC   Sept.   p218.   125w.   2

716   RAITT, Bonnie.   Home Plate.   Warner Bros. BS 2864.   Cart.
M8 2864.   Cass. M5 2864
CIR   March 2   p20.   225w. $2\frac{1}{2}$
CRA   Jan.   p72.   250w. $3\frac{1}{2}$
RM   Nov.   p30.   400w. $2\frac{1}{2}$
CRE   Jan.   p12.   50w.   5
GR   April   p1670.   75w.   3
LP   March   p10-1.   100w.   3
MM   Jan. 10   p23.   375w. $4\frac{1}{2}$
SR   Jan.   p89.   150w.   3

717   RAMONES.   Sire SASD 7520.   Cart. 8147-7520-H
CIR   Aug. 10   p11.   350w.   4
CRA   Aug.   p74.   150w.   3
CRA   Aug.   p64.   375w.   2
CRE   Aug.   p14, 77.   150w.   5
CRE   Aug.   p66.   375w.   4
CRE   Dec.   p63.   175w. $2\frac{1}{2}$
MG   July   p46.   50w.   5
RR   Nov.   p106.   50w. $2\frac{1}{2}$
RS   July 29   p46-7.   325w.   3
SR   Oct.   p102.   150w.   0

718   RANDY Pie.   Polydor PD-6515
LP   April   p11.   100w.   3

719   RANKIN, Kenny.   Inside.   Little David LD-1009.   Cart. TP-
1009
SR   April   p86, 90.   100w.   3

720   RARE Bird.   Sympathy.   Charisma (E)
MM   Aug. 14   p27.   300w.   3

721 RASPBERRIES. Best of. Capitol ST 11524
       AU Nov. p95. 300w. 4
       CIR Oct. 12 p14. 500w. $4\frac{1}{2}$

722 READ, John Dawson. Read On. Chrysalis CHR 1102
       MM Sept. 25 p24. 25w. 1

723 REAL Thing. United Artists LA 676G
       MM Nov. 27 p26. 250w. 2

724 REDBONE, Leon. On the Track. Warner Bros. BS 2888
       CIR Feb. 10 p20-1. 650w. $4\frac{1}{2}$
       CRE Feb. p60. 300w. 3
       LP March p11. 150w. 4
       MM Jan. 3 p23. 300w. $3\frac{1}{2}$
       SR Jan. p89-90. 275w. $2\frac{1}{2}$

725 REDDING, Noel. Blowin'. RCA APL1-1863
       MM Nov. 27 p23. 375w. $2\frac{1}{2}$

726 REDDING, Noel. Clonakilty Cowboys. RCA APL1-1237.
       Cass. APK-1-1237
       GP Jan. p71. 225w. 4
       LP April p11. 200w. 3
       MM May 1 p31. 275w. 3
       RS Jan. 29 p50-1. 100w. 2

727 REED, Lou. Coney Island Baby. RCA APL1-0915. Cart.
       APS1-0915
       AU Dec. p84-5. 400w. 0
       CAC April p15. 175w. $2\frac{1}{2}$
       CIR April 8 p12. 500w. 3
       CIR May p1812. 25w. $2\frac{1}{2}$
       CRA May p71. 400w. 3
       CRE March p63. 900w. 1
       HF July p111. 50w. $3\frac{1}{2}$
       MG April p38. 100w. 3
       MM Jan. 17 p32. 750w. $4\frac{1}{2}$
       PRM March p38. 250w. $3\frac{1}{2}$
       RO June p86. 325w. 3
       RR May p74. 50w. 1
       RS March 25 p52. 950w. 5
       SR April p90. 350w. $4\frac{1}{2}$

728 REED, Lou. Rock and Roll Heart. Arista AL 4100
       CIR Dec. p15-6. 650w. $1\frac{1}{2}$
       MM Nov. 6 p20. 850w. 3
       RS Dec. 2 p94. 1250w. 3

729 REID, Terry. Seed of Memory. ABC 935
       MM Sept. 11 p26. 400w. $3\frac{1}{2}$
       RS July 29 p51. 125w. 2

730 RENAISSANCE. Live at Carnegie Hall. Sire 3902 (2 discs)
       MM Dec. 4 p21. 400w. 1

731 RENAISSANCE. Scheherazade and Other Stories. Sire SASD-
       7510. Cart. 8147-7510H
       GR Feb. p1389. 125w. $2\frac{1}{2}$
       SR Jan. p90, 93. 200w. 2

731a RENTON, John. Half in, Half out. Reprise MS 2222
       OLR June p107. 25w. 3

732 RICHARD, Cliff. I'm Nearly Famous. Rocket 2210
       GR Aug. p351. 75w. $3\frac{1}{2}$
       MH Oct./Nov. p66. 200w. 3
       MM May 8 p22. 875w. 3
       RS Aug. 26 p68. 150w. $2\frac{1}{2}$

733 RICHARD, Cliff. 31st of February. Capitol (Reissue)
       RM Dec. p30. 100w. $2\frac{1}{2}$

734 RICHMAN, Jonathan and the Modern Lovers. Berserkeley B2
       0048
       CRA Oct. p77. 500w. 4

735 RITCHIE Family. Brazil. Polydor 2383-358 (E)
       CAC March p493. 25w. $2\frac{1}{2}$

736 RIVERS, Johnny. Wild Night. United Artists UA-LA486-G.
       Cart. UA-EA486-H. Cass. UA-CA486-H
       SR Sept. p101-2. 200w. 5

737 ROBERTS, Larada. Pye 12126
       SR July p94. 100w. 3

738 RODEN, Jess. Keep Your Hat On. Island ILPS-9349
       AU Nov. p96. 200w. $3\frac{1}{2}$
       CAC May p57. 175w. 3
       GR June p98. 25w. $3\frac{1}{2}$
       MM March 13 p25. 525w. $3\frac{1}{2}$
       RM Nov. p30. 175w. 4
       RS Oct. 7 p82, 84. 175w. 3

739 RODEN, Jess. Play It Dirty, Play It Class. Island ILPS
       9442
       MM Dec. 18 p18. 425w. 2

740 ROGERS, D. J. It's Good to Be Alive. RCA APL1-1099
       HF May p103. 350w. 2

741 ROGUE. Fallen Angels. Epic EPC 69235 (E)
       MM April 17 p21. 50w. $2\frac{1}{2}$

742 ROLLING Stones. Aftermath. London PS 471

CRA   March p72.   550w.   3

743   ROLLING Stones.   Black and Blue.   Rolling Stones COC59106
       AU   Aug.   p65.   550w.   2
       CIR   July 22 p12-3.   825w.   4
       CRE   July   p62.   750w.   3
       CRE   Aug.   p78.   50w. $4\frac{1}{2}$
       GR   June   p98.   100w.   3
       MG   July   p47.   300w. $3\frac{1}{2}$
       MHF   June-July   p65.   400w. $4\frac{1}{2}$
       MM   April 24   p23.   1100w. $4\frac{1}{2}$
       PRM   May   p31.   50w. $2\frac{1}{2}$
       PRM   May   p48.   400w. $3\frac{1}{2}$
       RR   June   p82.   200w. $1\frac{1}{2}$
       RS   May 20   p63-4.   1150w.   3
       SR   July   p92.   950w. $4\frac{1}{2}$

744   ROLLING Stones.   Made in the Shade.   Rolling Stones
       COC59104 (Reissue)
       AU   Aug.   p65-7.   1000w.   2
       RR   Jan.   p62.   25w.   2

745   ROLLING Stones.   Metamorphosis.   Abkco/London ANA 1
       AU   Aug.   p65-7.   1000w.   4

746   ROLLING Stones.   12 x 5.   London LL 3402
       CRA   May   p76.   175w. $3\frac{1}{2}$

747   RONETTES.   Phil Spector's Wall of Sound, vol. 1.   Polydor (E)
       CAC   March   p493.   75w.   3

748   RONSTADT, Linda.   Different Drum.   Capitol Vine VMP 1010
       (E) (Reissue)
       CMP   Feb.   p19.   75w.   3

749   RONSTADT, Linda.   Hasten Down the Wind.   Asylum 7E-1072.
       Cart. ET-1072.   Cass. TC-1072
       AU   Nov.   p94.   250w. $3\frac{1}{2}$
       CIR   Nov.   10   p12.   475w.   2
       CM   Nov.   p63-4.   200w.   2
       CRA   Oct.   p67.   400w.   3
       CRE   Nov.   p58.   850w. $2\frac{1}{2}$
       GR   Oct.   p669.   75w.   3
       MG   Nov.   p56.   50w.   2
       MM   Sept. 25   p25.   300w.   3
       RS   Sept. 23   p111.   950w. $3\frac{1}{2}$
       SR   Nov.   p81.   75w. $4\frac{1}{2}$

750   RONSTADT, Linda.   Prisoner in Disguise.   Asylum 7E-1045.
       Cass. TC-51045
       AU   March   p75-6.   650w.   1
       CMP   Feb.   p19.   350w.   4
       CRE   Jan.   p12, 80.   125w. $3\frac{1}{2}$

CRE Jan. p65. 400w. $2\frac{1}{2}$
LP Jan. p12. 200w. 4
PMS V4/#3 p189. 50w. 3

751 ROWANS. Asylum 7E-1038
CMR April p41. 75w. 2
PMS V4/#4 p255-6. 300w. 4

752 ROWANS. Sibling Rivalry. Asylum 7E-1073
AU Dec. p80. 450w. 3
RS Nov. 4 p72. 275w. 2

753 ROXY Music. Siren. ATCO SD 36-127. Cart. TP 36-127.
Cass. CS 36-127
CIR April 8 p16. 450w. 4
CRA Feb. p75. 325w. 4
CRE March p13. 100w. $4\frac{1}{2}$
CRE June p60. 25w. $1\frac{1}{2}$
LP March p11. 125w. $3\frac{1}{2}$
MG Feb. p36. 25w. 4
RR Jan. p62. 25w. 2
RS Jan. 1 p52. 975w. 3
SR March p92. 125w. 0

754 ROXY Music. Viva! ATCO SD 36-139. Cart. TP 36-139.
Cass. CS 36-139
AU Dec. p81. 400w. $1\frac{1}{2}$
CIR Nov. 10 p17. 300w. 3
CRA Oct. p80. 150w. $2\frac{1}{2}$
GR Oct. p669. 50w. 1
MG Nov. p56. 75w. $2\frac{1}{2}$
RR Oct. p101-2. 175w. $4\frac{1}{2}$
RS Sept. 9 p58. 275w. $3\frac{1}{2}$
SR Nov. p108, 110. 100w. 3

754a ROY, U. Dread in a Babylon. Virgin V2048 (E)
MM April 3 p33. 300w. 2

755 THE RUNAWAYS. Mercury SRM-1-1090 Cart. MC8-1-1090.
Cass. MCR-1-1090.
CIR Sept. 13 p14. 375w. 3
CRA Aug. p76. 150w. $2\frac{1}{2}$
CRE Aug. p66. 450w. 2
CRE Sept. p14. 50w. $2\frac{1}{2}$
GR Sept. p493. 50w. 0
MM Sept. 25 p25. 500w. $1\frac{1}{2}$
PRM May p47. 550w. 3
RS July 29 p47. 125w. $2\frac{1}{2}$
SR Sept. p91. 475w. 2

756 RUNDGREN, Todd. Another Live. Bearsville BR-6961
CAC May p57-8. 200w. $3\frac{1}{2}$
CK Jan. p47. 200w. 3

CRE   Feb.   p61.   200w.   2
GR   July   p226.   25w.   3
LP   March   p11.   150w. $2\frac{1}{2}$
MG   Jan.   p35.   50w. $3\frac{1}{2}$
RS   Jan. 15   p50, 52.   250w.   3
SR   March   p92.   250w.   0

757   RUNDGREN, Todd.   Faithful.   Bearsville BR-6963.   Cart.
      M8-6963.   Cass. M5-6963
      AU   June   p84-5.   600w.   5
      CIR   Aug. 24   p12-3.   350w.   3
      CRA   Aug.   p63-4.   450w. $3\frac{1}{2}$
      CRE   Aug.   p67.   425w. $2\frac{1}{2}$
      CRE   Sept.   p69.   125w. $3\frac{1}{2}$
      GR   July   p226.   100w. $1\frac{1}{2}$
      MM   May 15   p26.   550w.   3
      PRM   April   p42.   600w. $3\frac{1}{2}$
      RS   July 1   p68.   375w.   3
      SR   Oct.   p102.   225w.   3

758   RUNDGREN, Todd.   Initiation.   Bearsville BR 6957
      AU   March   p78.   900w. $3\frac{1}{2}$

759   RUSH, Tom.   Best of.   Columbia PC 33907 (Reissue)
      MG   April   p39.   50w.   4

760   RUSH.   All the World's a Stage.   Mercury SRM 2-7508 (2
      discs)
      CC   Dec.   p32.   75w.   3
      MM   Dec. 11   p22.   50w. $2\frac{1}{2}$
      RM   Nov.   p33.   175w.   3

761   RUSH.   Caress of Steel.   Mercury SRM-1-1046.   Cass. MCR4-
      1-1046
      CC   Jan.   p39.   50w.   3
      LP   Jan.   p13.   125w. $2\frac{1}{2}$

762   RUSH.   2112.   Mercury SRM-1-1079
      CC   June   p30.   50w.   3
      CIR   June 1   p16.   125w. $1\frac{1}{2}$
      CRA   Dec.   p72-3.   300w.   1
      PRM   May   p31.   50w.   1

763   RUSSELL, Brian and Branda.   World Called Love.   Rocket
      2181
      RR   Dec.   p100.   100w.   4

764   RUSSELL, Leon and Mary Russell.   Wedding Album.   Paradise
      PA-2943.   Cart. M8-2943.   Cass. M5-2943
      CIR   July 6   p14.   150w.   3
      MM   May 29   p26.   225w. $2\frac{1}{2}$
      SR   Aug.   p81.   175w.   0

765   RUTLEDGE, James.   Hooray for Good Times.   Capitol ST-

11487
    MG   May p46.   75w. $2\frac{1}{2}$

766   RYAN, Paul.   Scorpio Rising.   Charisma (E)
      MM   Nov. 13 p28.   100w.   1

767   SADISTA Sisters.   Transatlantic TRA-313 (E)
      CAC   Dec. p337.   200w.   4

768   SADISTIC Mika Band.   Hot Menu.   Harvest SHSP4049 (E)
      GR   Feb. p1389.   25w.   3

769   SAILOR.   The Third Step.   Epic EPC 69192 (E)
      MM   Oct. 30 p24.   325w.   2

770   SAILOR.   Trouble.   Epic PE 34039
      CRA   July p81.   125w. $2\frac{1}{2}$
      MG   July p46.   50w.   3
      RS   May 6 p73.   250w. $2\frac{1}{2}$

771   SAINTE-MARIE, Buffy.   Sweet America.   ABC 929
      CMP   May p19.   200w.   2

771a ST. JOHN, Roy.   Immigration Declaration.   Caroline CA
      2008 (E)
      MM   May 29   p29.   400w. $4\frac{1}{2}$

772   SANBORN, David.   Warner (E)
      MM   Nov. 13 p26.   325w.   3

773   SANCIOUS, David and Tone.   Transformation (The Speed of
      Love).   Epic KE-3393
      SOU   May p44.   175w.   1

774   SANFORD-TOWNSEND Band.   Warner BS 2966
      CK   Dec. p49.   50w. $2\frac{1}{2}$

775   SANTANA.   Amigos.   Columbia PC-33576.   Cart. PCA-33576.
      Cass. PCT-33576
      CAC   May p58.   175w. $1\frac{1}{2}$
      DB   Oct. 7 p22, 24.   400w.   4
      MHF   June-July p68.   175w.   4
      MM   March 20 p22.   350w. $1\frac{1}{2}$
      RR   June p82.   100w. $2\frac{1}{2}$
      RS   June 17 p57-8.   250w.   3
      SOU   May p41.   300w. $2\frac{1}{2}$
      SR   Sept. p102.   150w.   2

776   SANTANA.   Festival.   Columbia PC 34423
      MM   Dec. 4 p22.   650w.   1

777   SANTANA.   Lotus.   CBS (E)
      MM   Jan. 3 p23.   50w. $4\frac{1}{2}$

778 SASSAFRAS. Riding High. Chrysalis CHR-1100 (E)
    RR Sept. p88-9. 75w. 3

779 SAVOY Brown. Wire Fire. London PS-659
    MG Jan. p34. 50w. 3
    RS Feb. 12 p93. 200w. $2\frac{1}{2}$

780 SAYER, Leo. Another Year. Warner Bros. BS-2885. Cart.
    M8-2885
    CRA Jan. p76. 175w. 2
    CRE Jan. p80. 50w. 3
    LP Jan. p13. 150w. 3
    MG Jan. p33. 50w. 3
    SR Feb. p85-6. 200w. 5

781 SAYER, Leo. Endless Flight. Warner Brothers BS 2962
    MM Nov. 13 p26. 450w. 2

782 SCAGGS, Boz. Silk Degrees. Columbia PC-33920
    CRE Sept. p69. 50w. 4
    MG July p46. 50w. $2\frac{1}{2}$
    MM May 29 p26. 300w. $3\frac{1}{2}$
    PRM April p39. 325w. $3\frac{1}{2}$
    RS April 22 p67. 275w. 3
    SR July p94. 125w. 2

783 SCOTT, Tom. New York Connection. Ode 77033
    CAC May p58. 125w. $2\frac{1}{2}$
    DB May 6 p23-4. 375w. $2\frac{1}{2}$
    HF March p104. 250w. $3\frac{1}{2}$
    MHF May p60-1. 175w. $2\frac{1}{2}$
    MM April 3 p32. 300w. 3

784 SEALS and Crofts. Get Closer. Warner Bros. BS-2907.
    Cart. M8-2907. Cass. M5-2907
    SR Aug. p81. 275w. 3

785 SEALS and Crofts. Greatest Hits. Warner BS-2886 (Reissue)
    MG Jan. p33. 50w. 3

786 SEARCHERS. Pye 501 (Reissue)
    LP March p11. 150w. $4\frac{1}{2}$

787 SEBASTIAN, John. Welcome Back. Reprise MS-2249. Cart.
    M8-2249. Cass. M5-2249
    CRE Sept. p62, 64. 350w. 3
    MM June 26 p22. 325w. $2\frac{1}{2}$
    SR Sept. p102. 175w. 3

788 SECRET Oyster. Seu Son Peters 9009
    MM Jan. 3 p24. 375w. $2\frac{1}{2}$

789 SEDAKA, Neil. The Hungry Years. Rocket PIG-2157. Cart.

PGAT-2157
    CRE Feb. p74.   50w.   3
    HF   Jan. p103. 200w. $3\frac{1}{2}$
    MG   Jan. p34.   100w.   3
    SR   Feb. p86.   300w. $4\frac{1}{2}$

790 SEDAKA, Neil. Steppin' Out. Rocket PIG-2195. Cart. PIGT-
     2195. Cass. PIGC-2195
    MG   July p46.   50w. $2\frac{1}{2}$
    RS   July 1 p73, 75. 150w. 2
    SR   Aig. p73.   350w.   4

791 SEGER, Bob, & the Silver Bullet Band. Live Bullet. Capitol
     SKBB-11523 (2 discs). Cart. 8XVV-11523. Cass. 4XVV-11523
    CRA July p82.   200w. $3\frac{1}{2}$
    CRE July p67.   600w.   3
    MM   Sept. 11 p26.   525w.   3
    RS   June 17 p55.   600w. $3\frac{1}{2}$
    SR   Oct. p102. 225w.   2

792 SEGUIN, Richard and Marie and Claire. En Attendant. WEA
     WSC 9013 (Canada)
    OLR March p42.   25w.   3

793 LA SEINE. Ariola ST 50008
    MM   Nov. 27 p28.   150w. $\frac{1}{2}$

794 SHA Na Na. Now. Kama Sutra KSBS-2605
    LP   Jan. p13.   150w.   3

795 SHADOWFAX. Watercourse Way. Passport PPSD-98013
    CK   Oct. p47.   50w.   3

796 SHADOWS. Live at the Paris Olympia. EMI (E)
    RM   Dec. p30.   100w. $1\frac{1}{2}$

797 SHANGHAI. Fallen Heroes. Thunderbird (E)
    MM   April 3 p31.   275w.   2

798 SHAZAM. The Move. A&M SP 4259
    CRA March p81.   300w.   4

799 SHOOTER. GRT 9230-1059 (Canada)
    OLR June p106.   25w. $3\frac{1}{2}$

800 SHOWADDYWADDY. Trocadero. Bell (E)
    MM   Aug. 7 p18.   175w.   2

801 SILVER. Arista AL 4076
    RS   Dec. 16 p90, 93. 150w. $2\frac{1}{2}$

802 SILVER Convention. Midland International BKL1-1369
    SR   July p94.   25w. $2\frac{1}{2}$

803 SIMON, Carly. Another Passenger. Elektra 7E-1064. Cart.
     ET8-1064. Cass. TC5-1064
          CAC Sept. p218. 200w. $2\frac{1}{2}$
          CIR Nov. 10 p17-8. 125w. 3
          GR   Aug. p351. 25w. 3
          MG   Sept. p58. 50w. $3\frac{1}{2}$
          MM   Aug. 7 p18. 300w. 2
          RS   Aug. 12 p60, 62. 450w. 4
          SR   Nov. p88-9. 425w. 5

804 SIMON, Carly. Best of. Elektra 7ES-1048 (Reissue)
          MG   Feb. p38. 25w. $3\frac{1}{2}$
          RR   Feb. p66. 25w. 3

805 SIMON, Lucy. RCA APL1-1074. Cart. APS1-1074. Cass.
     APK1-1074
          HF   Jan. p104. 100w. $3\frac{1}{2}$
          SR   Jan. p93. 225w. 3

806 SIMON, Paul. Still Crazy After All These Years. Columbia
     PC-33540. Cart. PCA-33540. Cass. PCT-33540
          CAC June p98. 325w. 4
          CIR April 8 p16. 200w. $1\frac{1}{2}$
          CRE Feb. p62. 800w. 3
          HF   Feb. p118. 150w. $3\frac{1}{2}$
          LP   Jan. p13. 300w. 4
          RR   March p72. 100w. 4
          SR   Feb. p88. 250w. $3\frac{1}{2}$

807 SINCLAIR, Stephen. Sad and Lonely Saturday Night. MCA
     2171
          MG   April p39. 25w. 3

808 LES SINNERS. Celebration CEL 1905 (Canada)
          OLR June p106. 25w. $3\frac{1}{2}$

809 SIR Doug and the Texas Tornadoes. Texas Rock for Country
     Rollers. ABC DOSD 2057   Cart. DOSD-8-2057
          CIR Sept. 28 p13-4. 600w. $4\frac{1}{2}$
          CM   Nov. p60-1. 350w. 2
          CMP Nov. p40. 275w. 3
          CMR Nov. p32. 100w. $2\frac{1}{2}$
          CRA Oct. p78. 200w. 3
          CRE Dec. p70. 125w. 4
          MM   Nov. 6 p22. 275w. 1
          RS   Aug. 26 p62, 65. 200w. $2\frac{1}{2}$

810 SKELLERN, Peter. Hard Times. Island ILPS9352 (E)
          GR   Jan. p1258. 75w. $2\frac{1}{2}$

811 SKYHOOK. Ego Is Not a Dirty Word. Mercury SRM1-1066
          CIR May 13 p18. 150w. $2\frac{1}{2}$
          MG   March p43. 50w. 1

812   SLADE, Dave Green.   Cactus Choir.   Warner (E)
      MM   Dec. 4 p22.   800w.   3

813   SLADE.   In Flame.   Warner Bros.   BS 2865
      AU   Feb.   p84-5.   400w.   3

814   SLADE.   Nobody's Fools.   Warner Brothers BS 2936
      CAC   May p62.   175w. $3\frac{1}{2}$
      CIR   June 17 p14.   200w.   2
      CRE   July p64.   375w. $1\frac{1}{2}$
      RR   May p74.   50w.   3
      RS   May 6 p65.   150w.   0

815   SLATER, Nelson.   Wild Angel.   RCA APL1-1306
      CRE   Sept.   p62.   575w.   2
      RS   Sept. 23 p118-9.   275w.   3

816   SLICK, Earl.   Capitol ST-11493
      CRA   July p82.   200w.   1
      MM   July 24 p25.   50w.   2
      PRM   April p41.   300w. $2\frac{1}{2}$

817   SLICK, Earl.   Razor Sharp.   Capitol ST 11570
      CRA   Dec.   p70.   325w. $3\frac{1}{2}$
      PRM   Sept.   p36.   500w.   2
      RS   Nov. 18 p80.   225w.   3

818   SLIK.   Arista AL 4115
      MM   May 22 p23.   400w. $2\frac{1}{2}$

819   SLIM Chance.   One for the Road.   Island ILPS-9366
      RR   April p78.   100w.   3

820-1   SLOCKE.   J'un Oeil.   RCA KPL 1-0126 (Canada)
      CC   April p35.   50w.   3

822   SMALL Faces.   The Immediate Story.   Sire SASH-3709-2 (2
      discs) (Reissue)
      MG   March p43.   75w.   3

823   SMALL Faces.   Ogden's Nut Gone Flake.   Immediate IML-1001
      (E) (Reissue)
      MM   Jan. 31 p23.   100w. $3\frac{1}{2}$
      RR   Feb.   p72.   100w. $3\frac{1}{2}$

824   SMALL Wonder.   Columbia PC 34100
      MM   Aug. 14 p27.   300w. $3\frac{1}{2}$

825   SMITH, Mike and Mike D'Abo.   CBS (E)
      CAC   Dec.   p341-2.   225w.   3
      MM   Dec. 4 p24.   100w.   2

826   SMITH, Patti.   Horses.   Arista AL-4066

CRA   Jan.   p72.   450w. $4\frac{1}{2}$
CRA   March   p82.   300w.   5
CRE   Feb.   p58-9. 900w. $4\frac{1}{2}$
CRE   Feb.   p74.   100w. $4\frac{1}{2}$
LP   April   p11.   100w.   4
RR   March   p72.   150w. $4\frac{1}{2}$
RS   Feb. 12 p85.   2000w. $4\frac{1}{2}$
SR   April   p96.   600w.   4

827 SMITH, Patti.   Radio Ethiopia.   Arista AL 4097
     CIR   Dec. 30 p12-4.   1000w. $1\frac{1}{2}$
     CRA   Dec.   p67.   750w.   2
     MM   Oct. 23 p24.   250w.   1

828 THE SMOKE.   My Friend Jack.   Gull 25-224-OB (West Germany)
     WHO   Winter   p44.   175w. $4\frac{1}{2}$

829 SMOKIE.   Midnight Cafe.   MCA 2152
     MM   June 12   p25.   175w. $2\frac{1}{2}$

830 SNELL, Adrian.   Fire Flake.   Dove (E)
     MM   Feb. 7   p24.   50w.   2

831 SNOW, Phoebe.   Second Childhood.   Columbia PC 33952.
Cart. PCA-33952.   Cass. PCT-33952
     CIR   April 27. p14.   275w. $2\frac{1}{2}$
     CRA   April   p78.   275w.   2
     CRE   June   p58.   125w.   2
     DB   May 20   p27.   300w.   4
     HF   May   p102.   200w.   4
     MG   April   p38.   350w. $4\frac{1}{2}$
     MM   Feb. 14   p28.   500w.   4
     RS   April 8   p69.   2500w. 4
     SOU   April   p45.   350w.   4
     SR   May   p83.   450w.   3

832 SNOW, Tom.   Capitol ST-11545
     CK   Dec.   p49.   25w.   3
     CRA   Oct.   p79.   175w.   3

833 SNOW, Tom.   Taking It All in Stride.   Capitol ST 11398
     MG   April   p39.   50w. $2\frac{1}{2}$

834 SOFT Machine.   Softs.   Harvest SHSP 4056 (E)
     MM   June 26   p19.   200w. $3\frac{1}{2}$
     RR   Sept.   p90.   50w.   3

835 SOLUTION.   Cordon Bleu.   Rocket 2189
     RM   Nov.   p32-3.   250w. $2\frac{1}{2}$

836 SONS of Champlin.   Ariola American ST-500002
     LP   Jan.   p13.   150w.   3
     MM   May 29   p29.   150w.   2

837 SONS of Champlin. Circle Filled With Love. Ariola Ameri-
     can ST 50007
          CRA Aug. p75. 200w. $3\frac{1}{2}$

838 SOUTH, Joe. Midnight Rainbows. Island ILPS-9328
          CRA Jan. p75. 275w. 3
          SR March p92. 450w. 2

839 SOUTHER, John David. Black Rose. Asylum 7E-1059. Cart.
     ETA-1059. Cass. TC5-1059
          CIR July 6 p14. 100w. $2\frac{1}{2}$
          RS June 3 p82. 275w. $2\frac{1}{2}$
          SR Sept. p102. 175w. 2

839a SOUTHER, Hillman and Furay. Trouble in Paradise. Asylum
     7E-1036
          CMR Feb. p31. 125w. 1

840 SOUTHERN Comfort. Distilled. Harvest SHSM-2009 (E)
          RR Dec. p101. 25w. $3\frac{1}{2}$

841 SOUTHSIDE Johnny & the Asbury Jukes. I Don't Want to Go
     Home. Epic PE-34180. Cart. PEA-34180
          AU Sept. p82-3. 300w. $2\frac{1}{2}$
          CIR Sept. 13 p12. 375w. 3
          CRA Sept. p82. 425w. $2\frac{1}{2}$
          CRE Sept. p59. 500w. 4
          CRE Sept. p69. 25w. $3\frac{1}{2}$
          MH Oct./Nov. p67. 250w. $3\frac{1}{2}$
          RS July 29 p48-9. 525w. 5
          SR Sept. p87-8. 400w. 4

842 SPANKY & Our Gang. Change. Epic PE-33580
          SR March p92. 200w. 2

843 SPARKS. Big Beat. Columbia PC 34359
          CRA Dec. p80-1. 250w. $2\frac{1}{2}$
          MM Oct. 30 p24. 325w. 3

844 SPARKS. Indiscreet. Island ILPS-9345
          CRE Feb. p63. 25w. $2\frac{1}{2}$
          GR Feb. p1389. 25w. 1
          LP April p11. 100w. $2\frac{1}{2}$
          RS Jan. 1 p59. 225w. $2\frac{1}{2}$
          SR April p92. 100w. 2

845 SPARKS. Originals of. Bearsville K85505 (E) (Reissue)
          MM Jan. 24 p26. 100w. $2\frac{1}{2}$

846 SPEDDING, Chris. Rak SRAK519 (E)
          GR June p98. 75w. $3\frac{1}{2}$

847 SPEEDY KEEN. Y' Know What I Mean? Island ILPS-9338

```
        HF   July   p111.   50w.   3
        MG   May    p46.    50w.   3
        RO   June   p86.    375w.  3½
        RR   April  p78.    50w.   3
        RS   April 22 p65.  275w.  3
        SR   June   p83.    50w.   4
```

848   SPIDERS from Mars.   Pye 12125
```
        CRA  May    p77.   175w.   4
        GR   May    p1812. 50w.    3
        MM   March 13 p25.  325w.   4
```

849   [No entry.]

850   SPIRIT.   Farther Along.   Mercury SRM1-1094
```
        AU   Nov.   p96-7.  300w.  0
        CRE  Nov.   p62.    375w.  2
        RS   Jan. 1  p57.    175w.  4
        RS   Sept. 9 p60.    100w.  1½
```

851   SPIRIT.   Son of Spirit.   Mercury SPM-1-1053.   Cart. MC8-
      1-1053
```
        LP   April  p11.    150w.  2½
        SR   April  p92.    125w.  2
```

852   SPLINTER.   Harder to Live.   Dark Horse SP-22006.   Cart.
      2206
```
        CRE  Feb.   p63.    25w.   2½
        LP   March  p12.    50w.   2
        MG   Feb.   p36.    50w.   4
        SR   Feb.   p86-7.  200w.  5
```

853   SPLIT Enz.   Mental Notes.   Chrysalis (E)
```
        MM   Oct. 2  p30.   425w.   3½
```

854   SPRINGSTEEN, Bruce.   Born to Run.   Columbia PC
      33795
```
        AU   Feb.   p93.    100w.  1
```

855   SQUIRE, Chris.   Fish Out of Water.   Atlantic SD-18159.
      Cart. TP-18159
```
        CRA  April  p76.    225w.  2½
        CRE  Nov.   p61.    100w.  2½
        HF   June   p105.   200w.  2½
        MG   April  p39.    50w.   1½
        RS   March 25 p66.   125w.   1½
        SR   June   p86.    175w.  3
```

856   STACKRIDGE.   Do the Stanley.   MCA MCF 2747 (E)
```
        MM   Oct. 16 p22.   50w.    3
```

857   STACKRIDGE.   Extravaganza.   Sire SASD-7509

LP   Jan.   p14.   200w. $2\frac{1}{2}$

858   STACKRIDGE.   Mr. Mick.   Rocket Roll 3 (E)
      MM   May 15   p24.   275w. $2\frac{1}{2}$

859   STAIRSTEPS.   2nd Resurrection.   Dark Horse SP22004.   Cart.
      8T22004
      HF   July   p104.   250w.   3

860   STAMPEDERS.   Hit the Road.   MWC MWCS709V (Canada)
      CC   Sept.   p28.   50w.   3

861   STANLEY, Michael.   Ladies' Choice.   Epic PE 33917
      CRA   Aug.   p75.   150w. $2\frac{1}{2}$

862   STANTON, Chris and Glen Turner.   Tundra.   Decca 5259
      (E)
      CAC   Dec.   p337.   300w. $3\frac{1}{2}$

863   STARBOARD List.   Songs of the Tall Ships.   Adelphi AD
      1025
      AU   Nov.   p97.   250w. $3\frac{1}{2}$

864   STARBUCK.   Moonlight Feels Right.   Private Stock 2013
      MM   Oct.   9   p33.   75w.   2

865   STARCASTLE.   Epic PE 33914
      PRM   May   p31.   50w.   1
      RS   May 6   p71.   125w. $3\frac{1}{2}$

866   STARLAND Vocal Band.   Windsong BHL1-1351
      HF   May   p105.   100w. $\frac{1}{2}$
      MG   June   p44.   50w.   1
      SR   May   p80.   250w.   5

867   STARR, Kenny.   The Blind Man in the Bleachers.   MCA
      2177
      CRE   April   p62.   25w.   1
      HF   April   p130.   200w. $2\frac{1}{2}$

868   STARR, Ringo.   Blast from Your Past.   Apple SW-3422.
      Cart. 8XW-3422
      CRE   March   p60.   250w. $2\frac{1}{2}$
      HF   March   p106.   100w. $2\frac{1}{2}$
      LP   April   p12.   100w.   2
      RR   Feb.   p66.   25w. $2\frac{1}{2}$
      RS   Dec. 2   p96, 99.   275w. $3\frac{1}{2}$
      SR   April   p92.   150w.   3

869   STARR, Ringo.   Rotogravure.   Atlantic SD 18193
      CAC   Nov.   p298.   200w. $2\frac{1}{2}$
      MM   Oct. 23   p27.   500w.   3
      RR   Dec.   p101.   50w. $1\frac{1}{2}$

870 STARR, Ruby. Scene Stealer. Capitol ST 11549
    MM Oct. 2 p30. 200w. $1\frac{1}{2}$
    RM Dec. p30-1. 200w.

871 STARR, Ruby and Grey Ghost. Capitol ST 11427
    CRE Jan. p70. 275w. 4

872 STARRY Eyed and Laughing. Thought Talk. Columbia PC-33837
    CIR Jan. 20 p20. 225w. 3
    CRA Jan. p76. 225w. 1
    CRE Jan. p71. 25w. 3
    GP Jan. p71. 50w. 3
    SR Feb. p87. 125w. 3

873 STARWOOD. Homebrew. Windsong BHL 1-1125
    MG June p44. 50w. 3

874 STARZ. Capitol ST-11539
    AU Oct. p138-9. 500w. 1
    CRA Oct. p79. 100w. $3\frac{1}{2}$
    RS Sept. 23 p118. 150w. $2\frac{1}{2}$

875 STATUS Quo. Capitol ST-11509. Cart. 8xT-11509. Cass. 4xT-11509
    CRA July p82. 200w. 2
    SR Sept. p102. 250w. 2

876 STATUS Quo. Blue for You. Vertigo 9102006 (E)
    CAC April p19. 200w. $2\frac{1}{2}$
    GR May p1812. 25w. $1\frac{1}{2}$
    MM March 6 p28. 375w. $3\frac{1}{2}$
    RR May p74. 25w. $2\frac{1}{2}$

877 STATUS Quo. The Rest of. Pye PKL 5546 (E) (Reissue)
    CAC Dec. p342. 300w. 1
    MM Nov. 20 p29. 75w. $2\frac{1}{2}$

878 STAYMER, Hans. RCA KPLI-0087 (Canada)
    OLR June p106. 25w. $3\frac{1}{2}$

879 STEELY Dan. The Royal Scam. ABC ABCD-931. Cart. 8022-931H. Cass. 5022-931H
    CIR Aug. 24 p12. 500w. 4
    CRA Aug. p65. 600w. 5
    CRE Aug. p64. 650w. 3
    CRE Sept. p69-70. 50w. 3
    DB Oct. 7 p29. 300w. 4
    GR Sept. p492-3. 175w. $3\frac{1}{2}$
    MG July p47. 650w. $4\frac{1}{2}$
    MM May 8 p24. 1250w. 4
    PRM May p48. 600w. 4
    RR Aug. p78. 325w. $4\frac{1}{2}$

     RS July 1 p66-7. 525w. 3½
     SR Aug. p80. 750w. 2

880 STEPPENWOLF. Hour of the Wolf. Epic PE-33583. Cass.
     PET-33583
     LP Jan. p14. 125w. 2
     OLR March p40. 25w. 3

881 STEPPENWOLF. Skullduggery. Epic PE-34120. Cart. PEA-
     34120
     GR July p226. 50w. 2½
     MM July 17 p22. 275w. 3
     SR Sept. p102, 104. 200w. 3

882 STEVENS, Cat. Numbers: A Pythagorean Theory Tale. A&M
     SP-4555. Cart. 8T-4555
     CIR March 2 p14, 20. 175w. 1½
     GR March p1518. 50w. 3
     LP March p12. 175w. 1½
     RR Jan. p62. 50w. 3
     RS Feb. 26 p78. 275w. 0
     SR April p92-3. 250w. 3

883 STEVENSON, B. W. We Be Sailin'. Warner BS2901. Cart.
     M8-2901. Cass. M5-2901
     MG May p46. 50w. 3½
     SR May p94. 75w. 1

884 STEWART, Al. Year of the Cat. Janus 7022
     RM Dec. p30. 100w. 3

885 STEWART, Gary. Steppin' Out. RCA APL1-1225
     HF June p101. 150w. 2½
     SR May p74. 200w. 3

886 STEWART, Rod. Atlantic Crossing. Warner BS-2875. Cass.
     M5-2875
     LP Jan. p14. 200w. 3

887 STEWART, Rod. Best of. Mercury 5RM2-7507 (2 discs) (Re-
     issue)
     CAC May p62. 200w. 4
     CIR Sept. 28 p12-3. 300w. 4
     CRA Sept. p72. 600w. 1
     GR May p1812. 75w. 3½
     MM March 13 p24. 425w. 2½

888 STEWART, Rod. A Night on the Town. Warner BS 2938
     CIR Sept. 28 p12-3. 300w. 4
     CRA Sept. p72. 600w. 1½
     CRE Sept. p58. 800w. 4½
     MG Sept. p55. 350w. 2½
     MG Oct. p65. 50w. 4½

MM June 12 p22. 500w. 3
RR Oct. p102. 100w. 4
RS Aug. 26 p52, 55. 1250w. $4\frac{1}{2}$

889 STILLS, Stephen. Illegal Stills. Columbia PC-34148. Cart.
PCA-34148. Cass. PCT-34148
CAC July p138. 150w. $2\frac{1}{2}$
CIR Aug. 10 p12. 200w. 1
GR July p226. 200w. $3\frac{1}{2}$
SR Sept. p104. 200w. 2

890 STILLS, Stephen. Live. Atlantic SD-18156. Cart. TP-18156
CRE April p59. 275w. 2
GP March p73. 150w. $3\frac{1}{2}$
LP April p12. 200w. $2\frac{1}{2}$
SR April p93. 125w. 3

891 STILLS-YOUNG Band. Long May You Run. Reprise MS-2253
CAC Dec. p337. 125w. 3
CRA Oct. p82. 700w. $2\frac{1}{2}$
CRE Dec. p70. 75w. $4\frac{1}{2}$
GR Nov. p899. 125w. $1\frac{1}{2}$
MG Nov. p56. 50w. 3
MM Sept. 18 p21. 1000w. 3
PRM Sept. p35. 550w. $3\frac{1}{2}$
RR Nov. p106. 25w. 2
RS Oct. 21 p107. 250w. 3
SR Nov. p110-111. 275w. $4\frac{1}{2}$

892 STRANDLUND, Robb. Polydor PD 6085
CIR Dec. 30 p18. 250w. 3

893 STRAWBS. Deep Cuts. Oyster 1603
MM Nov. 27 p26. 525w. 2
RS Nov. 18 p78, 80. 175w. 3

894 STRAWBS. Nomadness. A&M SP-4544
CAC Jan. p403. 100w. $3\frac{1}{2}$
CRA Jan. p77. 250w. $2\frac{1}{2}$
CRE Jan. p70. 50w. 3
LP Jan. p14. 175w. 3

895 STREETWALKERS. Mercury SRM 1-1060
CAC Feb. p444. 200w. 4
CRA April p78. 250w. $3\frac{1}{2}$
MG Feb. p38. 50w. 3

896 STREETWALKERS. Red Card. Mercury SRM 1-1083
CAC Aug. p177, 180. 225w. $3\frac{1}{2}$
GR Aug. p351. 125w. 3
MM July 31 p21. 250w. $2\frac{1}{2}$
RS July 1 p71. 150w. 4

897   STRETCH. Elastique. Anchor 2014
      MM   Feb. 21   p28.   325w. $2\frac{1}{2}$

898   STRING Driven Thing. Kep Yer 'an On It.   Charisma CAC1112
      GR   March   p1518.   25w.   3
      MM   April 3   p31.   300w.   2

899   STYX. Equinox. A&M SP-4559. Cass. 4559
      LP   April   p12.   175w.   2
      SOU   May   p38.   250w. $2\frac{1}{2}$

900   SUMMERFIELD, Saffron. Fancy Meeting You Here.   Mother
      Earth MUM 1202 (E)
      MM   Aug. 7   p19.   175w. $3\frac{1}{2}$

901   SUPERCHARGE. Local Lads Make Good.   Virgin PZ 34293
      MM   May 15   p24.   425w.   3

902   SUPERTRAMP. Crisis? What Crisis? A&M SP-4560
      CAC   Feb.   p444, 446.   275w.   3
      GR   March   p1518.   50w.   3
      HF   March   p105.   150w. $3\frac{1}{2}$
      MG   March   p43.   50w. $2\frac{1}{2}$
      RS   Jan. 29   p46.   150w.   1
      SR   April   p93-4.   175w.   3

903   SURFARIS. Surfers Rule. MCA MCF 2761 (E) (Reissue)
      MM   Sept. 18   p21.   25w. $3\frac{1}{2}$

904   SUTHERLAND Brothers and Quiver. Reach for the Sky.
      Columbia PC-33982.   Cart. PCT-33982
      AU   April   p84.   250w.   2
      CAC   Feb.   p446.   175w. $2\frac{1}{2}$
      CIR   June 1   p16-7.   17w. $4\frac{1}{2}$
      MM   Jan. 3   p23.   50w. $3\frac{1}{2}$
      PRM   March   p38.   350w.   4
      RS   April 22   p60-1.   350w. $3\frac{1}{2}$
      SR   June   p87.   75w.   3

905   SUTHERLAND Brothers and Quiver. Sailing.   Island ZC19358
      (E)
      CAC   Oct.   p261.   200w.   3
      MM   July 24   p25.   125w.   3

906   SUTHERLAND Brothers and Quiver. Slipstream.   Columbia
      PC 34376
      CAC   Nov.   p298.   200w. $3\frac{1}{2}$
      GR   Nov.   p899.   75w.   3
      MM   Sept. 18   p24.   1000w. $4\frac{1}{2}$
      RS   Dec. 16   p81.   425w.   4

907   SWAN, Billy. Monument PZ 34183.   Cart. PZA 34183
      CRE   Aug.   p78.   50w. $4\frac{1}{2}$

CRE   Sept.   p65.   25w. $3\frac{1}{2}$
SR   Nov.   p111.   200w.   4

908   SWAN, Billy.   Rock 'n' Roll Moon.   Monument PZ-33805
      CRE   Jan.   p69.   275w.   3
      CRE   Feb.   p74.   25w.   4
      LP   March   p13.   100w.   3

909   SWEET.   Give Us a Wink.   Capitol ST-11496.   Cart. 4XT-
      11496
      CAC   May   p62.   200w. $2\frac{1}{2}$
      CRE   June   p72.   25w.   3
      GR   May   p1812.   25w.   1
      MM   March 27 p29.   200w. $1\frac{1}{2}$
      PRM   March   p36.   450w.   4
      RR   May   p74.   50w. $2\frac{1}{2}$
      SR   June   p87.   75w.   4

910   SWEET.   Strung Up/Studio Album.   RCA SPC 0001 (E) (2
      discs) (Reissue)
      CAC   March   p493.   125w.   3

911   SWEET Blindness.   Quality SV1923 (Canada)
      CC   Sept.   p28.   50w.   3

912   SWEET Spirit.   II.   Christopher CH 1012 (Canada)
      CC   April   p34.   50w.   3

913   SYMPHONIC Slam.   A&M (Canada)
      RM   Nov.   p29.   375w.   3

914   SYNERGY.   Electronic Realization for Rock Orchestra.   Pass-
      port PP SD 98009
      MM   May 8   p25.   75w. $2\frac{1}{2}$

915   SYNERGY.   Sequencer.   Passport PP SD 98014
      AU   Oct.   p134-5.   800w.   4
      RS   July 29   p52.   125w. $2\frac{1}{2}$

916   T. REX.   Futuristic Dragon.   EMI BLN 5004 (E)
      CAC   April   p19-20.   175w.   2
      MM   Feb. 7   p24.   300w.   2

916a TALLEY, James.   Got No Bread, No Milk, No Money, But
      We Sure Got a Lot of Love.   Capitol ST 11416
      CRA   April   p75.   200w. $2\frac{1}{2}$

917   TALLEY, James.   Tryin Like the Devil.   Capitol ST 11494.
      Cart. 8ST 11494
      CM   Aug.   p55.   275w.   4
      CRE   June   p72.   25w. $4\frac{1}{2}$
      RS   April 22 p58, 60.   1000w.   4

918   TALTON, Stewart, and Sandlin. Happy to be Alive. Capricorn CP 0167
          CRA Aug. p77. 150w. 4
          MG July p46. 50w. 2½

919   TAMBLYN, Ian. Posterity (no serial no.) (Canada)
          RM Dec. p30. 200w. 3

920   TANGERINE Dream. Alpha Centauri/Atem. Virgin VD 2504
      (2 discs) (E) (Reissue)
          MM July 17 p22. 625w. 3

921   TANGERINE Dream. Richochet. Virgin V2044 (E)
          CRE June p58-9. 125w. 2½
          GR March p1518. 50w. 2½

922   TANGERINE Dream. Stratosphere. Virgin V2068 (E)
          MM Oct. 16 p25. 575w. 2

923   TANGERINE Dream. Zeit. Virgin VD 2503 (2 discs) (E) (Reissue)
          MM July 17 p22. 625w. 3½

924   TASTE. Polydor 2384076 (E)
          CAC May p58. 150w. 3

925   TATTOO. Prodigal P6-10014S1
          RS Dec. 16 p94, 97. 225w. 1

926   TAYLOR, Carmol. Song Writer. Elecktr, 7E-1069
          CMP Sept. p31. 350w. 4

927   TAYLOR, James. Gorilla. Warner Bros. BS-2866
          AU April p84. 250w. 5

928   TAYLOR, James. In the Pocket. Warner Bros. BS-2912.
      Cart. M8-2912. Cass. M5-2912
          CAC Sept. p218. 250w. 3½
          CIR Sept. 13 p16-7. 350w. 4½
          CRA Sept. p72-4. 625w. 2½
          MM Aug. 14 p20. 550w. 3
          RS Aug. 12 p62. 325w. 0
          SR Oct. p103. 225w. 4

929   TAYLOR, James. Rainy Day Man. DJM (E) (Reissue)
          CAC Oct. p261. 100w. 3

930   TAYLOR, Johnnie. Eargasm. Columbia PC 33951
          CRE July p82. 25w. 3

931   LE TEMPS. Parapluie. WEA PAP 1010 (Canada)
          OLR Dec. p260. 25w. 3

932 10 CC. How Dare You. Mercury SRM-1-1061
     CIR April 27 p12.   225w.   4
     GR   April p1670. 100w. $4\frac{1}{2}$
     HF   June p105.   150w.   3
     MM   Jan. 10 p23.   1050w. $4\frac{1}{2}$
     PRM March p37.   350w. $2\frac{1}{2}$
     RO   June p87.   400w. $4\frac{1}{2}$
     RS   March 25 p60.   225w.   2
     RR   April p77.   225w.   3
     SR   May p94, 96.   125w.   5

933 10 CC. 100cc. UK UKS 53110.   Cart. 0853110.   Cass. 0553110
     LP Jan. p14.   125w.   4
     SR Jan. p94.   200w.   4

934 THEE Image. Inside the Triangle.   Manticore MA6-506-S1
     LP April p12.   100w.   3

935 THEM. Backtrackin'.   London PS 639
     CAC July p143.   125w. $3\frac{1}{2}$

936 THIN Lizzy. Jailbreak. Mercury SRM1-1081
     AU   Sept. p83-4.   350w.   4
     CAC May p58.   225w. $3\frac{1}{2}$
     CIR Aug. 24 p14.   150w. $3\frac{1}{2}$
     CRA July p82.   200w. $3\frac{1}{2}$
     GR   June p98.   25w.   3
     MM   March 27 p29.   450w.   4
     RS   June 3 p80.   225w. $2\frac{1}{2}$

936a THIN Lizzy. Johnny the Fox.   Mercury SRM1-1119
     MM   Oct. 16 p22.   650w. $4\frac{1}{2}$

937 THIN Lizzy. Remembering, part 1.   Decca SKL 5249 (E)
     CAC Oct. p260.   150w.   4
     MM   Aug. 14 p27.   450w. $3\frac{1}{2}$

938 THOMAS, Ian. Calabash.   GRT 9230-1063 (Canada)
     CC   May p33.   75w.   4
     CRA Dec. p68.   275w.   3

939 THOMPSON, Robbin.   Nemperor NE 440
     CRA Dec. p77.   250w. $2\frac{1}{2}$

940 THREE Dog Night. American Pastime.   ABC 928
     PRM May p31.   25w.   0

941 TIGER. Warner BS2940
     MG   Oct. p65.   25w.   1

942 TIGER. Goin' Down Laughin'.   EMI EMC-3153 (E)
     GRA Dec. p1079.   50w.   2
     MM   Dec. 4 p21.   500w. $2\frac{1}{2}$

943   TIPPETS, Julie. Sunset Glow.   Utopia BUL1-1248
       CRA   April p78.   150w. $4\frac{1}{2}$

944   TOPP, David and Max Eastley.   New and Rediscovered Musical
       Instruments.   Obscure (E)
       MM   Feb. 21 p28.   250w.   3

945   TOUBABOU.   Attente.   Barclay 8022 (Canada)
       CC   March p33.   50w.   5

946   TRAPEZE.   Warner Bros. BS 2887
       AU   Dec.   p82.   250w. $1\frac{1}{2}$
       MM   Nov. 20 p29.   50w. $1\frac{1}{2}$
       RR   Dec.   p99.   25w. $2\frac{1}{2}$

947   TRAPEZOID.   Skyline DD-107
       AU   Nov.   p121.   400w.   3

948   TRAVERS, Pat.   Polydor PD 6079
       AU   Dec.   p82.   250w. $1\frac{1}{2}$
       CAC   Oct.   p254.   200w.   3
       MM   July 24 p24.   150w.   3
       RR   Sept.   p88.   50w. $2\frac{1}{2}$

949   TRENT, Buck.   Bionic Bango.   Dot 2058
       CRE   Nov.   p63.   125w.   1

950   TRIUMPH.   Attic LAT-1012 (Canada)
       CC   Nov.   p34.   75w.   3
       RM   Nov.   p30.   425w.   2

951   TRIUMVIRAT.   Old Loves Die Hard.   Capitol ST-11551
       CK   Dec.   p48.   100w. $3\frac{1}{2}$

952   THE TROGGS. The Trogg Tapes.   Private Stock PS-2008.
       Cart. 8300-2008-H.   Cass. 5300-2008-H
       CAC   Dec.   p342.   150w. $3\frac{1}{2}$
       RS   July 29 p52.   100w. $2\frac{1}{2}$
       SR   Oct.   p103, 107.   225w.   3
       WHO   Winter p44.   200w. $3\frac{1}{2}$

953   TROWER, Robin.   Live.   Chrysalis CHR-1089.   Cart. M8C-
       1089.   Cass. M5C-1089
       CIR   July 6 p14-5.   200w.   3
       CRE   July p65.   150w. $1\frac{1}{2}$
       GP   Aug.   p81.   100w.   4
       GR   May p1812.   25w. $2\frac{1}{2}$
       MM   March 6 p28.   1025w.   4
       RS   June 3 p80.   275w. $2\frac{1}{2}$
       SR   Nov.   p112.   100w. $2\frac{1}{2}$

954   TROWER, Robin.   Long Misty Days.   Chrysalis CHR-1107
       CRA   Dec.   p81.   225w.   4

       GP   Dec.   p105.   150w.   3
       MM   Oct. 9   p30.   700w.   4
       RS   Dec. 2   p100.   225w.   3

955   THE TUBES.   A&M SP 4534
       SR   Jan.   p93.   150w.   2

956   TUBES.   Young and Rich.   A&M SP4580 (E)
       CAC   Aug.   p180.   200w. $2\frac{1}{2}$
       CIR   July 6   p12.   600w.   4
       CRA   July   p78.   175w.   2
       CRE   Sept.   p59.   525w.   3
       CRE   Sept.   p70.   50w.   3
       MM   July 10   p22.   125w. $4\frac{1}{2}$
       PRM   May   p47.   575w.   2
       RS   July 1   p67.   350w.   3

957   TWILLEY, Dwight.   Sincerely.   Shelter SRL-52001.   Cart.
     8-52001.   Cass. 5-52001
       AU   Oct.   p130-2.   750w.   5
       CIR   Oct. 12   p13-4.   625w.   5
       CRA   Sept.   p80.   325w.   3
       CRE   Nov.   p61-2.   275w. $1\frac{1}{2}$
       MG   Oct.   p65.   50w.   3
       MM   Sept. 25   p25.   300w.   3
       RS   Sept. 9   p56, 58.   300w.   4
       SR   Dec.   p114, 116.   100w.   3

958   UFO.   No Heavy Petting.   Chrysalis CHR-1103
       MG   Sept.   p58.   50w.   1
       MM   June 19   p21.   200w.   3

959   UNICORN.   Too Many Crooks.   Harvest SHSP 4054 (E)
       MM   May 8   p22.   250w.   2

960   UNICORN.   2.   Capitol ST-11453
       AU   May   p81.   150w.   2
       CRA   April   p75-6.   150w. $2\frac{1}{2}$
       MG   May   p46.   50w.   1
       RS   April 8   p74.   200w.   3

961   UPP.   This Way Upp.   Epic PE 34177
       MM   July 17   p22.   225w.   3
       RR   Aug.   p78.   50w.   3

962   URIAH Heep.   Best of.   Mercury SRM1-1070 (Reissue)
       RR   Feb.   p66.   25w.   2

963   URIAH Heep.   High and Mighty.   Warner BS-2949
       CK   Oct.   p47.   50w.   3
       MM   July 31   p21.   250w.   2
       RS   Sept. 9   p63.   150w.   3

963a VALDY. Family Gathering. A&M SP 9013 (Canada)
        OLR June p108. 25w. 4

963b VALDY. Landscapes. Haida HLS104 (Canada)
        OLR June p108. 25w. 4

964 VALERY, Dana. Phantom BLP-1-1124
       LP Jan. p14. 50w. 2

965 VAN Der Graaf Generator. Godbluff. Mercury SRM1-1069
       CRE July p82. 25w. 1½

966 VAN Der Graaf Generator. Still Life. Mercury SRM1-1096
       CAC July p138. 200w. 3½

967 VANGELIS. Albedo 0.39. RCA LPL1-5136
       MM Sept. 18 p24. 450w. 2½

968 VANGELIS. Heaven and Hell. RCA LPL1-5110
       CAC Jan. p403. 125w. 2
       SR June p90. 170w. 3

969 VAN LEER, Thijs. Introspection 2. CBS (E)
       MM Feb. 7 p24. 50w. 2

970 VAN LEER, Thijs. O My Love. Philips 6303 143 (E)
       CAC July p137. 200w. 4

971 VANNELLI, Gino. The Gist of the Gemini. A&M
       SP-4596
         CK Dec. p49. 25w. 2½
         CRA Dec. p72-3. 300w. 0
         RS Nov. 4 p82. 225w. 0

972 VANNELLI, Gino. Storm at Sunup. A&M SP-4533
         MG April p39. 50w. 2½
         OLR June p107. 25w. 3

973 VELEZ, Martha. Escape from Babylon. Sire SASD
       7515
         AU June p85. 150w. 3
         CRA July p76. 150w. 3
         RR Oct. p102. 150w. 3

974 VELVET Underground. MGM 2354-033 (E) (Reissue)
         CAC April p15. 175w. 3
         CRE June p60. 25w. 2½
         MM May 29 p26. 50w. 1½

975 VENTURES. The Very Best of. Sunset SLS 50386 (E) (Re-
       issue)

MM   May 22   p25.   50w.   1
MM   May 22   p25.   50w.   1

976   VICTORIA, C. B.   Dawning Day.   James (Canada)
      RM   Dec.   p34.   125w. $4\frac{1}{2}$

977   WAINWRIGHT, Loudon, III.   T-Shirt.   Arista AL-4063.   Cart.
      8301-4063.   Cass. 5301-4063
      CIR   Aug. 10   p14.   225w.   1
      HF   Sept.   p109.   200w. $3\frac{1}{2}$
      MM   Sept. 25   p25.   600w.   4
      RS   July 1   p71, 73.   175w. $2\frac{1}{2}$
      SR   Sept.   p107, 109.   300w.   3

978   WAITS, Tom.   Nighthawks at the Diner.   Asylum 7E-2008 (2
      discs)
      CIR   June 1   p17.   75w. $2\frac{1}{2}$
      CRE   March   p62.   350w. $2\frac{1}{2}$
      CRE   March   p74.   50w.   3
      DB   Feb. 26   p21.   350w.   5
      LP   March   p19.   225w. $2\frac{1}{2}$
      SR   March   p94.   250w.   2

979   WAITS, Tom.   Small Change.   Asylum 7ES-1078
      CIR   Dec. 30.   p14-5.   300w. $1\frac{1}{2}$
      CRA   Nov.   p82.   800w. $2\frac{1}{2}$
      PRM   Oct.   p34.   1000w.   3
      RS   Dec. 30   p68.   275w.   3

980   WAKEMAN, Rick.   No Earthly Connection.   A&M SP 4583
      CAC   July   p138.   250w.   2
      CK   Aug.   p45.   175w.   2
      GR   June   p98.   75w. $3\frac{1}{2}$
      MM   April 3   p29.   650w.   3
      RS   July 29   p52.   125w.   2

981   WALDMAN, Wendy.   The Main Refrain.   Warner Bros. BS
      2974
      RS   Dec. 30   p68.   225w. $3\frac{1}{2}$

982   WALKER, David T.   On Love.   Ode SP 77035
      GP   Oct.   p97.   25w. $2\frac{1}{2}$

983   WALKER, Jerry Jeff.   It's a Good Night for Singin'.   MCA
      2202.   Cart. MCAT 2202
      CM   Nov.   p61.   175w.   3
      MG   Sept.   p58.   50w. $3\frac{1}{2}$
      RS   Sept. 9   p61.   275w.   2
      SR   Nov.   p112, 114.   225w. $3\frac{1}{2}$

984   WALKER, Jerry Jeff.   Ridin' High.   MCA MCA-2156
      CM   Feb.   p48.   525w. $3\frac{1}{2}$
      CS   Aug.   p38.   150w. $4\frac{1}{2}$

HF   Jan.   p103.   50w.   3
LP   Jan.   p21.   175w. $2\frac{1}{2}$
SR   Jan.   p77.   325w.   4

985 WALKER, Sammy.   Sammy Walker.   Warner BS 2961
     AU   Dec.   p84.   75w.   2
     CRA   Dec.   p68.   275w.   3

986 WALLACE, Vince.   Plays.   Amp 001
     SOU   April   p47.   100w.   3

987 WALLACK, June.   RCA KPL 1-0136 (Canada)
     CC   Sept.   p31.   50w. $2\frac{1}{2}$

988 WALSH, Joe.   You Can't Argue with a Sick Mind.   ABC ABCL-
     5156
     CIR   Aug. 10   p14.   150w.   3
     CRE   July   p65.   150w. $3\frac{1}{2}$
     GR   July   p226.   75w.   2
     MG   July   p46.   50w. $3\frac{1}{2}$
     MHF   June-July   p68.   125w.   3

989 WAMMACK, Travis.   Not for Sale.   Capricorn CP-0162
     AU   Feb.   p93.   200w.   4

990 WARD, Clifford T.   No More Rock 'n' Roll.   Philips 9109-
     560
     GR   March   p1518.   75w. $3\frac{1}{2}$
     MM   Jan. 31   p23.   225w.   4

991 WASHINGTON, Geno.   Geno Live.   DJM DJH 44313 (E)
     MM   Dec. 4   p24.   100w.   2

992 WEBSTER, Max.   Taurus TR101 (Canada)
     CC   June   p31.   50w.   3

992a WEDNESDAY.   Loving You Baby.   Skyline SKY 10160 (Canada)
     CC   Dec.   p32.   75w.   3

993 WENDLING, Michael.   There's Something About the Arco
     Desert.   Sheepeater SR000-2
     GP   Dec.   p105.   25w. $2\frac{1}{2}$

994 WERNER, David.   Imagination Quota.   RCA APL1-0922
     MG   Feb.   p38.   50w.   0
     RS   Jan. 15   p53-4.   200w.   3

995 WERTH, Howard and the Moonbeams.   King Brilliant.   Rocket
     P1G-2180
     CRA   May   p77-8.   350w.   4

996 WEST, Leslie.   RCA/Phantom BPL-1-1258.   Cass. BPK-1-
     1258

         CRA   Feb.   p77.   300w.   3
         HF   Feb.   p121. 50w. $3\frac{1}{2}$
         LP   April p12-3. 200w.   2
         MG   Jan.   p33.   50w. $2\frac{1}{2}$

997   WET Willie.   The Wetter the Better.   Capricorn 0166
         CRE   July   p66.   175w. $1\frac{1}{2}$
         MG   June   p44.   50w. $1\frac{1}{2}$
         MM   July 17 p22.   300w.   3

998   WHITE, Alan.   Ramshackled.   Atlantic SD 18167
         CRE   Nov.   p61.   100w.   2
         MM   March 20 p23.   475w.   4
         RS   July 15 p67-8.   100w.   2

999   WHITLOCK, Bobby.   One of a Kind.   Capricorn CP.0160.
      Cass. M5-0160
         LP   Jan.   p15.   25w. $1\frac{1}{2}$

1000 WHITLOCK, Bobby.   Rock Your Sox Off.   Capricorn 0168
         MM   Sept. 25 p24.   75w.   2

1001 WHO.   By Numbers.   MCA MCA-2161.   Cart. MCAT-2161.
      Cass. MCAC-2161
         AU   March p79-80.   600w.   0
         CIR   Jan. 20 p20.   575w.   3
         CRA   Jan.   p65.   2250w.   4
         CRE   Feb.   p74.   25w.   4
         GR   Feb.   p1389.   50w.   3
         HF   Feb.   p124.   50w.   1
         LP   March p12.   200w.   5
         MG   Jan.   p33.   75w. $3\frac{1}{2}$
         RR   Jan.   p62.   75w. $3\frac{1}{2}$
         SR   Jan.   p86.   750w.   5

1002 WHO.   Live at Leeds.   Decca DL 79175
         CRA   March p79-80.   125w. $4\frac{1}{2}$

1003 WHO.   My Generation.   Decca DL 74664
         CRA   March p76.   175w. $3\frac{1}{2}$

1004 WHO.   The Story of.   Polydor 2683069 (2 discs) (E) (Re-
      issue)
         MM   Oct. 2 p30.   550w. $3\frac{1}{2}$
         RR   Dec.   p101.   100w. $2\frac{1}{2}$

1005 WIDOWMAKER.   United Artists LA 642G
         CAC   May   p60.   50w. $3\frac{1}{2}$
         CRA   Nov.   p78.   175w. $2\frac{1}{2}$
         CRE   Nov.   p63.   25w.   1
         RS   Sept. 9 p63.   175w.   3

1006 WIGWAM.   The Lucky Stripes and Starpose.   Virgin V2051 (E)

MM   June 19   p20.   450w.   4

1007   WILD Angels.   Let's Get Back to Rock 'n' Roll.   Precision
(E)
CAC   July p146, 148.   325w.   2

1008   WILD Cherry.   Epic PE 34195
CRE   Dec.   p71.   75w. $2\frac{1}{2}$
MM   Oct. 16   p25.   175w.   0
RS   Sept. 9   p55-6.   175w.   1

1009   WILHELM, Mike.   Zigzag/United Artists ZZ1 (E)
MM   July 31   p21.   200w.   3

1010   WINCHESTER, Jesse.   Learn to Love It.   Bearsville BR
MM   March 13   p24.   600w.   4

1011   WINCHESTER, Jesse.   Let the Rough Side Drag.   Bears-
ville BR-6964
CIR   Dec. 14   p12-3.   350w.   4
CRA   Dec.   p68.   275w. $3\frac{1}{2}$
CRE   Dec.   p60.   300w.   3
MG   Dec.   p63.   50w.   2

1012   WING and a Prayer.   Babyface.   Wing and a Prayer HS-3025.
Cart. TP-3025.   Cass. CS-3025
SR   Aug.   p82.   150w.   0

1013   WINGFIELD, Pete.   Breakfast Special.   Island ILPS 9333
LP   April p13.   175w.   3
MG   Feb.   p36.   50w. $3\frac{1}{2}$
PMS   V4/#3   p192.   25w.   2
SR   Aug.   p94.   125w.   2

1014   WINGS.   At the Speed of Sound.   Capitol SW 11525
AU   July p67.   400w.   4
CIR   July 6   p12.   400w. $4\frac{1}{2}$
CRE   Aug.   p78, 80.   75w.   3
CRE   June p56.   350w.   2
GR   July p226.   50w.   3
MM   March 27   p28.   900w. $3\frac{1}{2}$
RR   June p82-3.   75w.   1
RS   May 20   p67.   650w.   3
SR   July p95-6.   200w. $3\frac{1}{2}$

1015   WINGS.   Over America.   EMI PCSP 720C (E) (3 discs) (Reissue)
MM   Dec. 18   p16.   1200w.   3

1016   WINTER, Edgar.   Entrance/White Trash.   Epic BG 33770
(2 discs) (Reissue)
MM   May 22   p25.   75w.   3

1017   WINTER, Edgar and Rick Derringer.   Blue Sky PZ-33798.
       Cart. PZT-33798
          CRA   Jan.   p78.   25w. $1\frac{1}{2}$
          LP   Jan.   p15.   100w. $2\frac{1}{2}$

1018   WINTER, Johnny.   Captured Live!   Columbia/Blue Sky PZ
       33944
          AU   June   p81-2.   600w. $2\frac{1}{2}$
          CIR   June 1   p16.   200w.   4
          CRE   June   p59.   200w. $4\frac{1}{2}$
          HF   May   p103.   100w. $2\frac{1}{2}$
          MM   May 22   p25.   75w.   3
          PRM   April   p24.   50w.   1
          SR   July   p96.   75w.   4

1019   WINTER, Johnny and Edgar Winter.   Together.   Blue Sky
       PZ-34033.   Cart. PZA-34033.   Cass. PZT-34033
          AU   Sept.   p84.   150w.   2
          CIR   Oct. 26   p14.   175w.   2
          GP   Aug.   p81.   50w. $2\frac{1}{2}$
          MM   July 3   p22.   225w. $2\frac{1}{2}$
          RS   July 29   p50.   175w. $3\frac{1}{2}$
          SR   Nov.   p114.   75w.   3

1020   WIRELESS.   WEA (Canada)
          RM   Nov.   p29.   475w.   3

1021   WISHBONE Ash.   Locked In.   Atlantic SD18164
          PRM   April   p24.   25w.   1
          RR   June   p82.   25w. $2\frac{1}{2}$

1022   WISHBONE Ash.   New England.   Atlantic SD 18200
          MM   Nov. 13   p29.   550w.   3

1023   WOLF, Kate and the Wildwood Flowers.   Back Roads.   Pwl
       L-001
          AU   June   p83.   200w.   3

1024   WOOD, Ron and Ronnie Lane.   Mahoney's Last Stand.   WEA
       K50308 (E)
          RM   Nov.   p29-30.   300w. $3\frac{1}{2}$
          RS   Nov. 4   p68, 70.   175w.   3

1025   WOOD, Roy.   Mustard.   United Artists UALA-575-G.   Cart.
       EA-575-H
          CAC   March   p492.   175w.   2
          CRA   May   p77.   325w.   2
          CRE   June   p60.   50w.   2
          GR   March   p1518.   50w. $3\frac{1}{2}$
          RO   June   p86.   350w.   1
          RR   March   p73.   50w.   2
          RS   March 25   p62.   325w.   2

SR   April   p80.   350w.   5

1026 WOOD, Roy. The Roy Wood Story. Harvest SHDW 408 (E)
      (Reissue) (2 discs)
          MM   May 1   p30.   300w. $4\frac{1}{2}$

1027 WOODS, Gay and Terry. The Time Is Right. Polydor
      2383-375 (E)
          CAC   April   p15.   250w. $3\frac{1}{2}$

1028 WRAY, Bill. Legend/MCA-2188. Cart. T-2188
          MG   July   p46.   25w. $2\frac{1}{2}$
          SR   Sept.   p109.   100w.   0

1029 WRAY, Link. Stuck in Gear. Virgin (E)
          MM   June 5   p20.   250w. $1\frac{1}{2}$

1030 WRIGHT, Gary. The Dream Weaver. Warner BS-2868.
      Cart. M8-2868.   Cass. M5-2868
          SR   June   p88.   600w.   4

1031 WRIGHT, Gary. That Was Only Yesterday. A&M SP-3584
      (2 discs) (Reissue)
          CRA   July   p82.   200w. $2\frac{1}{2}$

1032 WYMAN, Bill. Stone Alone. Rolling Stone COC 79103
          CRE   June   p59.   225w.   1
          HF   June   p101.   50w. $1\frac{1}{2}$
          MG   June   p44.   75w.   1
          MHF   June-July   p67-8.   200w.   3
          PRM   April   p24.   50w.   1
          RS   April 22   p63, 65.   650w.   4
          SR   July   p86.   600w.   5

1033 YAMASHTA, Winwood and Shrieve. Go. Island LPS 9387
          CRA   Sept.   p81.   100w. $2\frac{1}{2}$
          MM   July 24   p23.   275w.   3
          RS   Sept. 23   p117.   300w.   3
          SR   Dec.   p116.   250w. $2\frac{1}{2}$

1034 YARDBIRDS. Featuring Eric Clapton. Charly (E) (Reissue)
          MM   Jan. 3   p23.   25w.   4

1035 YARDBIRDS. Featuring Jeff Beck. Charly (E) (Reissue)
          MM   Jan. 3   p23.   25w.   4

1036 YARDBIRDS. Supergroup of the 60s. Charly (E) (Reissue)
          CAC   July   p148.   200w. $3\frac{1}{2}$

1037 YOUNG, Jesse Colin. On the Road. Warner BS-2913
          AU   June   p84.   150w.   3
          MG   July   p46.   25w. $1\frac{1}{2}$
          MM   June 26   p22.   300w. $2\frac{1}{2}$

RS   June 3 p82. 200w. 3
SR   Aug. p82. 275w. 2

1038   YOUNG, Larry. Spaceball. Arista AL 4027
       CRA   Sept. p78. 450w. 3

1039   YOUNG, Neil. Tonight's the Night.   Reprise MS 2221
       OLR   March p40-1. 50w. $2\frac{1}{2}$

1040   YOUNG, Neil. Zuma. Reprise MS-2242.   Cart. M8-2242.
       Cass. M5-2242
       AU   May p80. 200w. $2\frac{1}{2}$
       CIR   Feb. 10 p10. 525w. $4\frac{1}{2}$
       CRA   April p76. 300w. 3
       CRE   March p61. 525w. 1
       CRE   March p74. 50w. $4\frac{1}{2}$
       GR   March p1518. 75w. $3\frac{1}{2}$
       LP   March p13. 200w. 3
       MG   Feb. p38. 100w. 3
       PMS   V4/#4 p191. 25w. 3
       RR   Jan. p62. 50w. $1\frac{1}{2}$
       RS   Jan. 15 p49. 750w. 4
       SR   March p95, 98. 300w. 3

1041   YOUNG, Steve. Renegade Picker. RCA APL 1-1759
       CIR   Oct. 12 p16. 150w. 3

1042   ZAP-Pow. Now. Vulcan VULP 004 (E)
       MM   Sept. 25 p24. 325w. 2

1043   ZAPPA, Frank. Zoot Allures. Warner Bros. BS 2970
       RS   Dec. 30 p70. 275w. $2\frac{1}{2}$

1044   ZAPPA, Frank. Captain Beefheart and the Mothers of Inven-
       tion. Bongo Fury. Discreet DS-2234
       CRE   Jan. p65-6. 200w. $2\frac{1}{2}$
       DB   Feb. 26 p27-8. 225w.   4
       LP   March p13. 125w. 5
       RS   Jan. 1 p56. 150w. 0
       SR   March p98-9. 325w. 4

1044a ZAPPA, Frank and the Mothers of Invention.   One Size Fits
       All. DiscReet DS 2216
       DB   Feb. 26 p27-8. 225w. 3

1045   ZEVON, Warren. Asylum 7E-1060
       CRE   Sept. p70. 50w. 4
       MM   July 24 p25. 50w. 2
       RS   July p63. 650w. 4
       SR   Aug. p69-70. 425w. 5

1046   ZOMBIES. Rock Roots. Decca Roots 2 (E)
       CAC   July p143. 125w. $2\frac{1}{2}$

1047 ZOSS, Joel. Arista 4056
          CRA   April   p76.   200w. $2\frac{1}{2}$
          CRE   April   p74.   25w.   3
          RS   March 11   p64.   125w. $2\frac{1}{2}$

MOOD--POP

This section comprises what can largely be called derivative music. For mood, most of it is reinterpretive, second-generation sounds taken from the worlds of the other categories. The nasal twang of country has been dropped, the solo acoustic instrument of folk has been augmented by strings, the beat of rhythm & blues has been modified, the noise and distortion of rock has been softened, the swing of jazz is missing, and the harshness of the blues has been smoothed. All of this music has been given a characteristic full, lush sound, suitable for home stereo consoles or middle-of-the-road (M.O.R.) programming. Included here is dance music, lyrical music, plus other variants that do not jar the nerves, and is suitable for background music just one cut above the level of Muzak. Often this music has been called the Music of Middle America, or of the silent majority. It sells exceptionally well, notably through rackers and jobbers. Standards and ballads are its main repertoire, with borrowings from other fields (especially from the musical stage) for crooners and chanteuses. Usually the format is to create a specific sound for a specific entertainer (for example, Frank Sinatra, Tom Jones, Patti Page) and "bend" the selections chosen to that sound. Under this method, it is possible for each performer to record an album a month, relying on the set arrangements of the studio orchestra. Fortunately, this does not happen because the economics of the market will not sustain the glut. Still, it is not unheard of for an artist to release four or five records a year. The results in mood music is a mixed bag of Latin themes, light cocktail jazz, soft rock, and soft country and western.

This section also includes pop music that has been character-ized as "bubble gum" or pre-teen variety that appeals mainly to the very young. Such music is based on derivative rock, and is charac-terized by Top 40 tunes, usually written by someone who is not the singer or performer. These lightweight selections bear common characteristics: they are short; they have sparse instrumentation; they have trite, redundant lyrics; and they leave no lasting impres-sion. This is a singles market for 45 rpm releases, and conse-quently most albums have one or possibly two hits, followed by nine or so selections to pad the album.

Both mood and pop share several things in common. They both tend to be regarded as background music and not taken seriously; they are listened to with regularity by the automobile driver and his captive passengers; they are listened to by the lonely housewife;

they can be soothing and incredibly beautiful if the melody and the arrangements are considered equally in a lush sort of way; and they are the bread-and-butter releases of the major record companies, for these discs make money. Included here are a small minority of BAND recordings: marching bands, military bands, pipers, school bands, etc.

The reviewing media do not take this music seriously; they have little to say about the music except disparaging comments. The only magazines that give regular coverage are Audio and the two British publications Gramophone and Hi-Fi News and Record Review. The English market, judging from the number of releases, appears to be larger than that in North America, and draws on British, American and Continental sources. Their reissues are more carefully planned, with the original monophonic sound maintained, good liner notes, and packaging design.

According to the reviews in 1976, the following appear to be the best records;

ASTAIRE, Fred. Attitude Dancing. UALA 580G
AZNAVOUR, Charles. I Sing for You. RCA APL1-5115
BENNETT, Tony. Sings 10 Rodgers and Hart Songs. Improv 7113
CROSBY, Bing. At My Time of Life. United Artists UAS 29956 (E)
CROSBY, Bing and Fred Astaire. A Couple of Song and Dance Men. United Artists UALA 588G
FITZGERALD, Ella and Joe Pass. Again. Pablo 2310-772
HARVEY, Jane. Fats Waller Revisited. Classic Jazz CJ15
LAINE, Cleo. Born on a Friday. RCA LPL1-5113

1048 AINSWORTH, Alyn. The Entertainer. Pye PKLX5538 (E)
        GR Oct. p66, 669. 50w. 3

1049 ALBERTO y Lost Paranoias. Transatlantic TRA 316 (E)
        MM May 15 p24. 425w. 3

1050 ALFORD. Colonel Bogey on Parade, vol. 2. Polydor (E)
        CAC Feb. p458. 325w. 4

1051 ALGUERO, Augusto. Great Orchestras of the World. Polydor 3192-340 Cass. only (E) (Reissue)
        CAC Dec. p342. 50w. $2\frac{1}{2}$

1052 ALLEN, Peter. Taught by Experts. A&M SP 4584
        RS July 29 p50-1. 250w. 3

1053 ALMOND, Mark. To the Heart. ABC (E)
        MM Oct. 9 p33. 75w. 3

1054 ALPERT, Herb. Coney Island. A&M SP-4521
        SR July 7 p72. 275w. 4

1055 ALPERT, Herb. Just You and Me. A&M SP-4591. Cart.
8T 4591. Cass. CS 4591
    CAC Oct. p256. 150w. $1\frac{1}{2}$
    SR Nov. p94. 125w. 2

1056 ALSTON, Shirley. With a Little Help from My Friends.
London SHA 8491 (E)
    BM June p36. 125w. 3

1057 ANDREWS, Harvey. Someday. Transatlantic (E)
    MM Dec. p22. 550w. 2

1058 ANKA, Paul. Anka. United Artists UA-LA314-G. Cart.
EA314-G
    SR Feb. p86. 150w. $2\frac{1}{2}$

1059 ANKA, Paul. Feelings. United Artists UA LA367G. Cart.
EA367H. Cass. CA367H
    LP Aug. p14. 125w. 4
    MM Feb. 14 p28. 50w. $1\frac{1}{2}$
    SR Sept. p88. 150w. 4

1060 ARLEN, Harold. Harold Arlen Sings. Mark 56 Records 683
(2 discs)
    SR July p72. 300w. 3

1061 ARNOLD, Eddy. I Wish That I Had Loved You Better. MGM
2110 315 (E)
    CMP March p23. 250w. 2

1062 ASKEY, Arthur. Before Your Very Eyes. Argo ZDA 173
(E) (Reissue)
    GRA Dec. p1074. 100w. $2\frac{1}{2}$

1063 ASTAIRE, Fred. Attitude Dancing. United Artists UA
LA580G. Cart. EA 580H
    CAC Feb. p446. 200w. 3
    SR Oct. p96. 250w. 5

1064 ASTAIRE, Fred. They Can't Take These Away from Me.
United Artists UAS 29941 (E)
    CAC Aug. p181. 175w. $3\frac{1}{2}$
    SR Oct. p96. 250w. 5

1065 AUT'CHOSE. Une nuit comme une autre. Columbia FS
90309 (Canada)
    OLR Sept. p189. 25w. 3

1066 AZNAVOUR, Charles. I Sing for You. RCA APL1 5115.
Cass. LPK1-5115
    SOU Jan. p36. 225w. 5
    SR Nov. p94-5. 125w. 3

1067   AZNAVOUR, Charles. A Tapestry of Dreams. RCA CPL1-
       0170. Cart. CPS1-0710. Cass. CPK1-0710
          SR Feb. p86. 125w. 5

1068   BAKER, George. Paloma Blanca. Warner BS 2905
          MM Feb. 14 p28. 50w. 2

1069   BAKER, George. River Song. Warner K56282 (E)
          GR Dec. p1076. 25w. 4

1070   BARNET, Charlie. Aircheck 3
          JA Fall p56. 50w. 4

1071   BARRETO, Ray. Fania XSLP 00486
          CRA April p77. 250w. 2½

1072   BASILE, Jo. Paris Accordion. Pye Golden Hour GH 850 (E)
          GR Dec. p1070. 25w. 2½

1073   BASSEY, Shirley. At the Pigalle. EMI OU 2133 (E) (Re-
       issue)
          CAC Oct. p256. 100w. 4

1074   BASSEY, Shirley. Good, Bad But Beautiful. United Artists
       UA LA 542G. Cass. CA 542H
          LP March p23. 50w. 4½

1075   BASSEY, Shirley. Love, Life and Feelings. United Artists
       UAS 29944 (E)
          CAC July p140. 200w. 4

1076   BASSEY, Shirley. Nobody Does It Like Me. United Artists
       UA-LA214-G. Cass. EA214-G
          SR Feb. p86-7. 225w. 4

1077   BELAFONTE, Harry. At Carnegie Hall. RCA DHY 0003 (E)
       (Reissue)
          GR Oct. p666. 200w. 4½

1078   BELLAMY BROTHERS. Warner Bros. BS 2941. Cart. M8-
       2941. Cass. M5 2941
          SR Oct. p91. 200w. 2

1079   BENNETT, Tony. At Long Last Love. Philips SONO 14 (E)
          CAC Oct. p256. 100w. 4
          GR Oct. p666. 75w. 4

1080   BENNETT, Tony. Life Is Beautiful. Improv. 7112
          CAD Jan. p31. 250w. 2½
          LP April p20. 150w. 2½
          MM Sept. 11 p26. 350w. 2½

1081   BENNETT, Tony. Sings 10 Rogers and Hart Songs. Improv

    7113
        RFJ Dec. p13. 425w. 4
        SR   Nov. p95. 125w. 5

1082 BENNETT, Tony and Bill Evans.   Fantasy F 9489.   Cart.
      8160-9489H
        AU   Feb.   p98-9.   500w. 5
        CRE Jan.   p68.   150w. 2½
        DB   March 11 p22.   30w.   5
        JJ   April p28.   225w. 4½
        LP   March p14.   125w. 4½
        MJ   April p29.   50w. 3
        MM   May 1 p30.   225w. 1½
        SOU Feb.   p50.   100w. 4
        SR   Feb.   p78.   150w. 2

1083 BERNIE, Ben. His Hotel Roosevelt Orchestra 1924-1930.
      Sunbeam MFC 11 and HB 310 (2 discs)
        JJ   May p26.   275w. 5
        ST   June-July p198.   275w. 2

1084 BIGGS, E. Power. Stars and Stripes Forever.   Columbia
        MM   Sept. 24 p25.   25w. 2½

1085 BLACK, Cilla. It Makes Me Feel Good.   EMI EMC 3108
      (E)
        MM   May 15 p26.   50w. 2½

1086 BLACK, Stanley. Black Magic.   Decca PFS 4374 (E)
        GR   Dec. p1076.   150w. 3½

1087 BLACK Dyke Mills Band. Brass Band Works.   Decca
      SB324 (E)
        GR   Oct.   p662.   300w. 3½

1088 BLAKE, Eubie. Eubie Blake Song Hits, with Eubie and His
      Girls, Emma Kemp, Mary Louise, Mable Lees. Eubie
      Blake Music EBM 9
        CAD Aug.   p23, 24.   150w. 4

1089 BOONE, Pat. Originals. ABC 301 (E) (Reissue) (2 discs)
        MM   May 22 p25.   50w. 2

1090 BOSTON Pops. For the Road. Polydor (E)
        CAC Aug.   p182.   50w. 3

1091 BOSTON Pops. Plays the Carpenters Songbook.   Polydor
      2482-281
        CAC Oct. p260.   25w. 3½

1092 BOSTON Pops. Plays the Neil Diamond Songbook.   Polydor
      PD6053
        LP   March p23.   100w. 1½

138

1093 BOSWELL, Connee. Sand in My Shoes. MCA MCFM 2739
(E) (Reissue)
ST Aug.-Sept. p232-233. 375w. 4½

1094 BOSWELL Sisters. Jazum 43 44 (2 discs) (Reissue)

1095 BOSWELL Sisters. Sweet Harmony--Hot Rhythm. Vocalion
VLP5 (E) (Reissue)
CAC May p74. 125w. 3½
JJ March p26, 27 375w. 4
ST June-July p199. 125w. 4

1096 BREWER, Teresa. Unliberated Woman. Signature BSL1-
0935
SR Sept. p89. 200w. 4

1097 BROTHERHOOD of Man. Save Your Kisses for Me. Pye
NSPL 12134
CAC July p140. 100w. 1½

1098 BROWNE, Brian. Morning, Noon and Night-time Too.
Capitol SM6431 (Canada)
OLR June p106. 25w. 4

1099 BUTLER, Edith. Avant d'être Dépaysée. Columbia FS
90156 (Canada)
OLR March p41. 25w. 3

1100 BUTLER, Jerry. Make It Easy on Yourself. DJM (E) (Reissue)
MM Nov. 13 p29. 100w. 3½

1101 CAHN, Sammy. Words and Music. RCA LRL1-5079
SR July p88. 350w. 4

1102 The CAPTAIN & Tennille. Love Will Keep Us Together.
A&M SP-3405
SR Oct. p76, 77. 150w. 4

1103 CAPTAIN and Tennille. Song of Joy. A&M SP-4570
CAC July p143. 200w. 3
HF June p106. 175w. 3½
MM May 29 p29. 300w. 1½
SR Aug. p72. 175w. 4

1104 CARLOS, Walter. By Request. Columbia M32088. Cass.
MT 32088
LP March p29. 125w. 4½

1105 CARNES, Kim. A&M SP4548. Cart. 8T4548. Cass.
CS4548
HF March p107. 200w. 3

LP   March   p6.   25w. $2\frac{1}{2}$
RS   Jan. 1   p62.   175w.   3

1106   CARPENTERS.   Collection.   A&M (E) (Reissue)
       MM   April 3   p31.   125w. $2\frac{1}{2}$

1107   CARPENTERS.   A Kind of Hush.   A&M SP 4581
       MM   June 26   p21.   300w.   2
       SR   Oct.   p91.   150w.   2

1108   CARPENTERS.   Live at the Palladium.   A&M (E)
       MM   Dec. 25   p17.   325w.   2

1109   CARRADINE, David.   Grasshopper.   Jet 10 (E)
       MM   May 8   p25.   75w. $1\frac{1}{2}$

1110   CARRADINE, Keith.   I'm Easy.   Asylum 7E-1066
       CIR   Sept. 13   p17.   150w. $1\frac{1}{2}$
       RS   Aug. 12   p64, 67.   225w.   1
       SR   Sept.   p91.   175w.   2

1111   CASSIDY, David.   Home Is Where the Heart Is.   RCA APL1-
       1309.   Cart. APS1-1309.   Cass. APK1-1309
       CAC   June   p98.   75w.   3
       SR   Aug.   p73.   200w.   3

1112   CAVALIERE, Felix.   Destiny.   Bearsville BR 6958.   8: M8
       6958.   C: MS 6958
       SR   Nov.   p92.   100w.   2

1113   CHACKSFIELD, Frank.   Plays Irving Berlin.   London SPC
       44254
       CAC   Dec.   p340.   50w.   4
       GRA   Dec.   p1076.   50w. $3\frac{1}{2}$

1114   CHALMER, Peter.   From There to Just About Here.   Old
       Road PC375 (Canada)
       CC   March   p32.   50w.   3

1115   CHARLEBOIS, Jeanne and Jean Carignan.   Hommage à Madame
       Bolduc.   Philo F12014
       CC   June   p32.   50w.   3

1116   CHER.   Golden Hits.   Sunset SLS 50378 (E) (Reissue)
       CAC   April   p17.   75w.   3

1117   CHER.   I'd Rather Believe in You.   Warner Brothers BS
       2898
       MM   Nov. 20   p28.   200w. $1\frac{1}{2}$
       PRM   Nov.   p22.   75w. $1\frac{1}{2}$
       RR   Dec.   p100.   75w.   2
       RS   Nov. 18   p82.   225w.   1

1118   CHRISTIE, Tony. Best of. MCA MCF2769 (E) (Reissue)
         GR Dec. p1076. 25w. 3
         MM Nov. 27 p28. 125w. $2\frac{1}{2}$

1119   CLARKE, Allan. I've Got Time. Asylum 7E-1056
         RR Sept. p89. 25w. 2

1120   CLINTON, Larry. Sunbeam SB 208
         JJ Jan. p40. 50w. $3\frac{1}{2}$

1121   CLOONEY, Rosemary. Look My Way. United Artists UAS
       29918 (E) (Reissue)
         CMP Sept. p21. 250w. 2
         MM July 10 p22. 25w. 2

1122   COATES, Odia. United Artists UA-LA228-G
         SR Nov. p92. 200w. $4\frac{1}{2}$

1123   COCHRAN, Eddie. The Many Sides of Eddie Cochran. Rock
       Star JGR 1001 (E)
         CMP April p18. 200w. 3

1124   COLEMAN, Cy. The Party's On Me. RCA APL1-1252.
       Cart. APS1-1252
         SR June p77. 125w. 3

1125   COMO, Perry. Swings. RCA HY1035 (E) (Reissue)
         GR Oct. p666. 100w. 4

1126   CONNIFF, Ray. I Write the Songs. Columbia KC 34040
         CAC June p98. 25w. 3
         MM April 3 p31. 50w. 2

1127   CONNIFF, Ray. Send in the Clowns. Columbia KC 34170
         MM July 3 p21. 25w. 2

1128   CONNOR, Chris. The Finest of Chris Connor. Bethlehem
       2BP-1001 (2 discs) (Reissue)
         SR April p100. 175w. $2\frac{1}{2}$

1129   CONRAD, Joey. Salutes the Bean-Marks. Quality SV1912
       (Canada)
         OLR June p106. 25w. 3

1130   COOK, Barbara. Barbara Cook at Carnegie Hall. Columbia
       M-33438. Cart. MA-33438
         LP July p21. 150w. 4
         SR June p78. 1,000w. 4

1131   COUSINEAU, Luc. Airedale LUL500 (Canada)
         CC Sept. p29. 50w. 3

1132   CROSBY, Bing. Jazum 39/40 (Reissue) (2 discs)

JJ   July   p40.   100w. $3\frac{1}{2}$

1133   CROSBY, Bing.   At My Time of Life.   United Artists UAS
       29956 (E)
           SR   Oct.   p96.   250w.   5

1134   CROSBY, Bing.   The Great Country Hits.   Capitol Vine VMP
       1004 (E) (Reissue)
           CMP   Feb.   p19.   150w.   2

1135   CROSBY, Bing.   Many Happy Returns.   Vocalion VLP1 (E)
       (Reissue)
           CAC   May   p74.   125w. $3\frac{1}{2}$
           MM   Feb. 14   p30.   300w.   3

1136   CROSBY, Bing.   A Southern Memoir.   Decca SHU 8489 (E)
           CAC   March   p492.   50w.   3

1137   CROSBY, Bing.   That's What Life's All About.   United
       Artists UA LA 554G.   Cart. Ea 554H
           SOU   Jan.   p11.   75w. $3\frac{1}{2}$
           SR   Oct.   p96.   250w.   5

1138   CROSBY, Bing and Fred Astaire.   A Couple of Song and
       Dance Men.   United Artists UA LA 588G.   Cart. Ea 588H
           CAC   March   p492.   175w.   3
           SR   Oct.   p96.   250w.   5

1138a CRUMB, R.   Blue Goose 2014
           OTM   Summer   p28-9.   25w. $2\frac{1}{2}$

1139   CRUMB, R. and His Cheap Suit Serenaders.   No. 2.   Blue
       Goose 2019
           CRA   July   p79.   100w. $2\frac{1}{2}$
           JJ   July   p40.   50w.   1
           OTM   Summer   p29.   25w. $2\frac{1}{2}$

1140   DALSETH, Laila.   Just Friends.   EMI EO 6238217 (Norway)
           JJ   May   p40.   200w. $4\frac{1}{2}$

1141   DANA.   Love Songs and Fairy Tales.   GTO (E)
           MM   Nov. 27   p28.   100w.   0

1142   DAVIS, Sammy, Jr.   That's Entertainment.   MGM M3G 4965
           SR   March   p74.   175w.   4

1143   DEARIE, Blossom.   1975.   Daffodil BMD102
           CRE   June   p58.   125w. $1\frac{1}{2}$
           HF   Jan.   p103.   150w.   3
           SR   Jan.   p79-80.   200w.   5

1144   DEARIE, Blossum.   Special Magic of.   Verve 2317-107 (E)
           CAC   Feb.   p448.   150w. $3\frac{1}{2}$

1145 DEE, Lenny. I'll Play for You. MCA-2162
          CK March p48. 50w. 4

1146 DELAGAYEL, George. Speak Softly Love. Polydor 2482-
      287 (E)
          MM May 1 p30. 50w. 1½

1147 DELGADO, Roberto. Great Orchestras of the World. Poly-
      dor 3146-045 (Tape only) (E) (Reissue)
          CAC Dec. p342. 50w. 2½

1148 DELICATO, Paul. Ice Cream Sodas and Lollipops. Artists
      of America AOA5001
          LP April p21. 150w. 2

1149 DEODATO. Prelude. CTI 6021
          CAC May p56. 225w. 3

1150 DEODATO. 2. CTI 6029
          CAC April p18. 150w. 3½
          MM April 24 p22. 150w. 3

1151 DE PAUL, Lynsey. Love Bomb. Mercury SRM 1-1055
          MG March p43. 50w. 2½
          MM Jan. 31 p23. 225w. 3½

1152 DESHANNON, Jackie. New Arrangement. Columbia PC33500
          CRE March p12. 50w. 3
          SR Jan. p80. 200w. 3

1153 DESIGN. By Design. EMI EMC 3113 (E)
          MM May 29 p26. 50w. 3

1154 DIAMOND, Neil. Beautiful Noise. Columbia PC 33965.
      Cart. PCA 33965. Cass. PCT 33965
          CIR Oct. 26 p12. 350w. 2
          MG Oct. p65. 50w. 1½
          MM July 31 p21. 250w. 2½
          RR Sept. p88. 50w. 3
          RS Aug. p64. 250w. 3
          SR Oct. p92, 94. 350w. 3

1155 DIAMOND, Neil. Serenade. Columbia PC 32919. Cart.
      PCA 32919. Cass. PCT 32919
          SR Feb. p89. 125w. 4

1156 DONALDSON, Eric. Keep On Riding. Dynamic 3003 (E)
          BM Aug. p46. 125w. 3

1157 DORSEY, Tommy. Golden Era 15020
          JJ Feb. p27, 28. 225w. 4

1158 DORSEY, Tommy. Joyce 1022

JJ   Jan.   p40.   75w. $2\frac{1}{2}$

1159   DORSEY, Tommy.   Complete, vol. 1:1935.   RCA AXM2-5521
(2 discs) (Reissue)
AU   Nov.   p114-5.   300w.   2

1160   DOUGLAS, Mike.   Sings It All.   Atlantic SD 18168
SR   Aug.   p73-4.   225w.   3

1161   DUBOIS, Claude.   Le monde de.... Columbia GFS 90225
(2 discs) (Canada)
OLR   March   p41.   25w.   3

1162   DUBOIS, Claude.   La tout en moi.   CBS FS 751 (Canada)
OLR   Dec.   p259.   25w.   3

1163   DUFRESNE, Diane.   Mon Premier Show.   J'arrive J909-910
(2 discs) (Canada)
CC   Sept.   p29, 31.   25w.   3

1164   DUFRESNE, Diane.   Sur la même longeur d'ondes.   Kebec-
disc KD 703 (Canada)
CC   April   p34.   50w.   3

1164a   ECKSTINE, Billy and Quincy Jones.   At Basin Street East.
Philips SON 028 BS (2 discs) (E) (Reissue)
MM   Sept. 11   p25.   300w.   3

1164b   ECKSTINE, Billy.   The Special Magic of.... Polydor MGM
(E)
CAC   June   p98.   100w.   3

1165   EDDY, Nelson.   The Artistry of Nelson Eddy.   Everest 3392
(Reissue)
SR   Sept.   p92.   200w.   0

1166   EDWARDS, Cliff.   Shakin' the Blues Away.   Totem 1005
(Canada)
CAD   Sept.   p25.   100w.   3

1167   EDWARDS, Cliff.   Ukelele Ike.   Yazoo L1047 (Reissue)
JJ   June   p41.   100w.   4

1168   EDWARDS, Jackie.   Do You Believe in Love.   KLIK 9009 (E)
BM   June   p34.   200w.   3

1169   EIKHARD, Shirley.   Child of the Present.   Attic LAT-1007
(Canada)
CC   Jan.   p38.   50w.   3

1170   ELAINE.   La vraie Elaine.   London SOS 5140 (Canada)
OLR   March   p41.   25w.   2

1171   FAIREY Band. Concert Entertainment. Decca SB 323 (E)
         GR   Dec.   p1075.   125w.   4

1172   FAITH, Percy. Summer Place '76. Columbia KC 33915
         MM   Feb. 7   p24.   25w.   3

1173   FAYE, Francis. Bad, Bad Francis Faye. Bethlehem BCP
         6006
         CAD   April   p37.   75w. $3\frac{1}{2}$
         HF   May   p113.   125w. $2\frac{1}{2}$
         SR   June   p92.   600w.   4

1174   FELICIANO, Jose. And the Feeling's Good. RCA CPL1-
         0407. Cart. CPS1-0407. Cass. CPK1-0407
         SR   April   p75-6.   175w.   5

1175   FELICIANO, Jose. Angela. Private Stock 2010
         CAC   Dec.   p338.   125w.   3

1176   FELTS, Narvel. Greatest Hits, vol. 1. Dot 2036
         MM   May 8   p25.   50w.   4

1177   FERLAND, Jean-Pierre. Quand on aime on a toujours 20
         ans. Barclay 80228 (Canada)
         CC   Oct.   p33.   50w.   3

1178   FERRANTE & Teicher. Piano Portraits. United Artists UA-
         LA 585 G
         CK   Aug.   p46.   50w.   4

         FIEDLER, Arthur and the Boston Pops see Boston Pops

1179   FIFTH Dimension. Earthbound. ABC ABCD 897
         AU   Feb.   p87.   50w.   0

1180   FITZGERALD, Ella. At the Montreux Jazz Festival. Pablo
         2310-751
         CAC   Jan.   p412, 414.   100w.   2
         DB   April 8   p23-4.   100w. $3\frac{1}{2}$
         LP   March   p15.   75w.   5

1181   FITZGERALD, Ella. Ella in London. Pablo 2310 711
         JJ   Feb.   p36, 37.   350w.   4

1182   FITZGERALD, Ella. Sings the Harold Arlen Songbooks, vol.
         1&2. Verve (2 discs) (E) (Reissue)
         CAC   April   p30.   50w. $3\frac{1}{2}$

1183   FITZGERALD, Ella. Swings Lightly. Verve 2352 146 (E)
         (Reissue)
         CAC   Aug.   p195.   400w.   4
         JJ   June   p31.   325w.   5

1184 FITZGERALD, Ella and Louis Armstrong.   Special Magic of
      Verve 2317 085 (E) (Reissue)
          JJ   June   p41.   100w. $3\frac{1}{2}$

1185 FITZGERALD, Ella and Louis Armstrong.   Special Magic,
      vol. 2.   Polydor 2317-114 (E) (Reissue)
          CAC   Dec.   p354-5.   250w.   3

1186 FITZGERALD, Ella and Joe Pass.   Again.   Pablo 2310-772
          CAD   Sept.   p6.   50w.   4
          GP   Oct.   p97.   100w.   5
          JJ   Nov.   p26-7.   350w. $3\frac{1}{2}$
          SR   Dec.   p124.   125w. $4\frac{1}{2}$

1187 FITZGERALD, Ella and Oscar Peterson.   Pablo 2310 759
          CAC   Sept.   p226, 228.   350w.   3
          CR   Oct.   p584.   175w.   5
          GRA   Dec.   p1076.   75w.   4
          MM   Aug. 7   p20.   225w.   3

1188 FITZGERALD, Ella and Chuck Webb.   Ella Sings, Chuck
      Swings.   Olympic 7119 (Reissue)
          AU   March   p84.   300w.   4

1189 FIVEPENNY Piece.   King Cotton.   EMI 3129 (E)
          CAC   Oct.   p260.   75w.   3

1190 FORCIER, Denis.   Depuis longtemps.   London PGP 13002
      (Canada)
          OLR   March   p41.   25w.   2

1191 FORESTIER, Louise.   Gamma GS 167 (Canada)
          OLR   March   p41.   25w.   2

1192 FORESTIER, Louise.   Au Théâtre Outremont.   Gamma GS
      302 (Canada)
          CC   June   p31.   50w.   3

1193 FORTUNES.   Remembering.   Decca REM 2 (E) (Reissue)
          CAC   Dec.   p338.   200w. $3\frac{1}{2}$

1194 FOUR Seasons.   Story of Private Stock PS 7000.   Cass. 5300
      7000N
          CAC   April   p16.   250w.   3
          LP   April   p7.   100w.   4
          MM   Feb. 21   p30.   125w. $2\frac{1}{2}$

1195 FOUR Seasons.   Who Loves You.   Warner BS 2900.   Cass.
      M5 2900
          CAC   May   p60.   225w.   4
          LP   March   p8.   100w. $3\frac{1}{2}$
          MG   Feb.   p38.   50w.   4
          SR   March   p83.   200w.   2

1196 GAGNON, Andre. Neiges. London Phase 4 SP44252 (Canada)
       CC March p34. 75w. 4

1197 GARLAND, Judy. Concert Trophy TR 7-2145 (2 discs)
       SR Oct. p90, 91. 1800w. 4

1198 GARLAND, Judy. More Than a Memory. Stanyan 10095
       SR Jan. p82, 86. 250w. 4

1199 GARRETT, Kelly. Kelly. RCA APL1-1424. Cart. APS1-1424
       SR Sept. p100. 700w. 5

1200 GARRETT, Tommy. Takes You to Hawaii. Sunset SLS 50388
       (E) (Reissue)
       CAC Oct. p258-9. 50w. 3

1201 GARRETT, Tommy. Takes You to Italy. Sunset SLS 50390
       (E) (Reissue)
       CAC Oct. p258. 50w. 3

1202 GARRETT, Tommy. Takes You to Mexico. Sunset SLS
       50387 (E) (Reissue)
       CAC Oct. p258-9. 50w. 3

1203 GARRETT, Tommy. Takes You to Spain. Sunset SLS 50389
       (E) (Reissue)
       CAC Oct. p258-9. 50w. 3

1204 GAUTHIER, Claude. Les beaux instants. Presqu'île PE
       7500 (Canada)
       CC March p33. 50w. 3

1205 GERSHWIN, George. From Tin Pan Alley to Broadway.
       Mark 56 Records 680 (2 discs)
       SR Aug. p77. 300w. 4

1206 GERSHWIN, George. Plays Gershwin. RCA AVM1-1740
       CK Dec. p49. 50w. 3

1207 GETZ, Stan. Getz au Go Go. Verve 2352 095 (E) (Reissue)
       JJ June p31, 32. 250w. $4\frac{1}{2}$

1208 GILLIES, Stuart. Missing That Girl. EMI EMC 3143 (E)
       GR Dec. p1076. 25w. 3

1209 GLOVER, Sue. Solo. DJM 469 (E)
       CAC Oct. p260. 50w. 3

1210 GOLDSBORO, Bobby. A Butterfly for Bucky. United Artists
       LA639G
       CAC Dec. p338. 225w. 3

1211 GORE, Lesley. Love Me by Name. A&M SP4564. Cart.
      8T4564. Cass. CS4564
          HF Sept. p108. 300w. 1½

1212 GREGG Smith Singers. America Sings: The Great Sentimen-
      tal Age--Stephen Foster to Charles Ives. Vox SVBX 5304
      (3 discs)
          SR March p86. 600w. 4

1213 GRIMETHORPE Colliery Band. Decca SB325 (E)
          GR Dec. p1075. 125w. 2

1214 GUYS 'n' Dolls. The Good Times. Margret MAG 5005 (E)
          MM Nov. 27 p28. 50w. 0

1215 HAGAW, Asocjacja and Andrzei Rosiewicz. Muza SXL 1244
      (Poland)
          JF no. 41 p27-8. 50w. 3½

1216 HALL, Adelaide. Hall of Ellington. Columbia SCX 6586 (E)
          JJ April p32. 425w. 4½

1217 HAMILTON, Joe. Fallin' in Love. Playboy 407
          MM Feb. 21 p30. 150w. 1½

1218 HAMLISCH, Marvin. The Entertainer. MCA MCA-2115.
      Cart. MCAT-2115. Cass. MCAC-2115
          SR Jan. p86. 400w. 4

1219 HAMMONDS Sauce Works Band. Hootenanny. EMI One Up
      OU 2146 (E)
          GR Dec. p1075. 75w. 4

1220 HARPO. Movie Star. DJM 20478 (E)
          MM Sept. 25 p24. 50w. 3

1221 HARRIS, Jet and Tony Meehan. Remembering. Decca REM
      1 (E) (Reissue)
          CAC Dec. p340. 300w. 3

1222 HARRIS, Richard. Macarthur Park. Music for Pleasure
      MFP 50251 (E) (Reissue)
          RR March p72-3. 150w. 2½

1223 HARTMAN, Dan. Images. Blue Sky PZ 34322
          PRM Nov. p22. 75w. 1½

1224 HARVEY, Jane. Fats Waller Revisited. Classic Jazz CJ15
          JJ Aug. p35. 475w. 5
          SOU Feb. p50. 100w. 3½

1225 HAUSE, Alfred. Hi-Fi Stereo in Concert. Polydor 2482-290 (E)
          CAC July p146. 25w. 2½

1226   HAYMES, Dick.   Best of.   MCA MCFM 2720 (E) (Reissue)
       MM April 3 p31.   400w.   4

1227   HAYMES, Dick.   Moondreams.   Capitol Vine (E) (Reissue)
       MM Sept. 4 p18.   750w.   5

1228   HEATH, Ted.   Big Band Themes.   Decca PPS 4304 (E)
       JJ June p41.   100w.   3½

1229   HEATH, Ted.   89th Palladium Sunday Concert.   Decca
       Eclipse ECS 2164 (E) (Reissue)
       JJ July p31.   250w.   5

1229a HEATH, Ted.   Salutes Benny Goodman.   Decca PFS4357 (E)
       GR Oct. p666.   25w.   3

1230   HEATH, Ted.   Salutes Tommy Dorsey.   London SPC 44228
       JJ June p32.   250w.   5

1231   HEATH, Ted.   Salutes Banny Goodman.   Decca Phase Four
       PF 4357 (E)
          CAC Dec. p340.   225w.   4½

1232   HENDRICKS, Jon.   Tell Me the Truth.   Arista AL4043
       CO July p12.   350w.   3
       DB March 11 p26.   350w.   4
       MM Nov. 27. p23.   425w.   2

1233   HILDEGARDE.   I'm in the Mood for Love.   Stanyan SR 10056
       (Reissue)
          SR Feb. p96.   600w.   3

1234   HILL, Vince.   Collection.   EMI One Up OU2143 (E) (Reissue)
          CAC Nov. p295.   100w.   4
          GRA Dec. p1076.   25w.   4

1235   HILL, Vince.   Wish You Were Here.   CBS 81023 (E)
       MM Feb. 14 p28.   75w.   2

1236   HOLDRIDGE, Lee.   Conducts the Music of John Denver.
       Windsong BHL1-1366
          MM May 1 p30.   75w.   2½

1237   HOLMAN, Libby.   Something to Remember Her By.   Mon-
       mouth Evergreen MES-7067
          LP Aug. p15.   100w.   3½
          SR Feb. p89, 92.   425w.   4

1238   HOLMES, Leroy.   Themes of the Great Big Bands.   MGM
       (E)
          MM Sept. 11 p26.   50w.   3½

1239   HOLMES, Nick.   Soulful Crooner.   Just Sunshine JSS3

HF   June   p105.   275w. $2\frac{1}{2}$

1240   HOLMES, Rupert.   Epic KE 33443
       SR   Oct.   p78.   100w.   1

1241   HOLMES, Rupert.   Widescreen.   EPIC KE 32864
       SR   March   p75-6.   125w. $4\frac{1}{2}$

1242   HOPKINS, Linda.   Me and Bessie.   Columbia PC 34032
       BS   June   p36.   200w.   4

1243   HORNE, Lena.   Stormy Weather/Lena's Greatest Hits.
       Stanyan SR-10126 (Reissue)
       LP   March   p24.   125w. $3\frac{1}{2}$
       SR   Feb.   p81.   150w.   5

1244   HORNE, Lena and Legrand, Michel.   Lena & Michel.   RCA
       BGL1-1026.   Cart. BGS1-1026.   Cass. BGK1-1026
       SR   Oct.   p73-4.   425w.   4

1245   HUMES, Helen.   1947.   Trip TLP 5579
       JA   Fall   p56.   50w. $3\frac{1}{2}$

1246   HUMES, Helen.   The Incomparable Helen Humes.   Jazzology
       J-55
       SR   Aug.   p89.   200w.   4

1247   HUMES, Helen.   It's All Over Town.   Columbia PC33488
       SR   July   p76.   1000w. $4\frac{1}{2}$

1248   HUMES, Helen.   On the Sunny Side of the Street.   Black
       Lion BLP 30167 (E)
       JA   Summer   p35.   300w.   4

1249   HUMPERDINCK, Engelbert.   World of.   Decca SPA 455 (E)
       (Reissue)
       MM   Feb.   7   p24.   25w.   3

1250   JACKS, Susan.   Casino CA 1005 (Canada)
       OLR   June   p107.   50w.   4

1251   JAMES, Harry.   Vol. 2.   Joyce LP 1024
       JJ   May   p40.   100w. $2\frac{1}{2}$

1252   JOHNSON, Syl.   Total Explosion.   HI SH2 32096
       BM   June   p35.   125w.   2

1253   JOLSON, Al.   I Feel a Song Coming On.   DJM 22040 (E)
       MM   Dec.   18   p16.   350w. $2\frac{1}{2}$

1254   JOLSON, Al.   Sitting on Top of the World.   Vocalion VLP3
       (E)
       CAC   May   p74.   125w.   3

1255 JONES, Isham. Sunbeam HB 306
      JJ January p40. 50w. $3\frac{1}{2}$

1256 JONES, Jack. What I Did for Love. RCA APL1-1111.
      Cart. APS1-1111. Cass. APK1-1111
      LP March p24. 50w. $3\frac{1}{2}$
      SR Jan. p82. 200w. 0

1257 JONES, Salena. Where the Peaceful Rivers Flow. DJM
      20460 (E)
      MM March 6 p27. 75w. $2\frac{1}{2}$

1258 JONES, Tom. Memories Don't Leave Like People Do. Par-
      rot PAS 71068. Cart. 0-871068. Cass. 0-571068
      LP March p24. 100w. 2
      SR May p86. 125w. 3

1259 JONES, Tom. Somethin' 'Bout You Baby I Like. Parrot
      PAS 71066. Cart. 0871066. Cass. 0571066
      SR May p82. 50w. 5

1260 JONES, Tom. The World of. Decca SPA 454 (E) (Reissue)
      CAC March p492. 50w. 3
      MM Feb. 7 p24. 25w. 3

1261 JONIC, Bettina. The Bitter Mirror--Songs by Dylan and
      Brecht. Xtra 1157 (E) (2 discs)
      SR Aug. p76. 250w. 2

1262 JULIEN, Pauline. En scène. Deram XDEF 124 (Canada)
      CC May p33. 25w. $2\frac{1}{2}$

1263 KAEMPFERT, Bert. Contemporary. Polydor 2310-456 (E)
      CAC Oct. p260. 50w. $2\frac{1}{2}$

1264 KAEMPFERT, Bert. Everybody Loves Somebody. Polydor
      2482-288 (E)
      MM April 24 p23. 50w. 2

1265 KAEMPFERT, Bert. Great Orchestras of the World. Poly-
      dor 3146-069 (Tape only) (E) (Reissue)
      CAC Dec. p342. 50w. $2\frac{1}{2}$

1266 KAEMPFERT, Bert. Love Walked In. Polydor 2310-430 (E)
      MM Feb. 7 p24. 25w. 3

1267 KAMAHL. I Think of You. Philips 6357-014
      MM Nov. 13 p29. 125w. 1

1268 KARMEN, Steve. I Never Had the Time. Audio fidelity
      AFSD 6272
      LP March p24. 100w. 2

1269 KELLER, Greta. In Concert. Stanyan 1004
          HF   April   p135.   50w.   2
          SR   March   p100.   325w.   5

1270 KERR, Richard. Somewhere in the Night.   Epic PE 33850
          MM   March 27   p28.   50w.   1

1271 KING, Wayne. Introducing.   EMI One Up OU 2145 (E)
          GR   Dec.   p1076.   25w. $2\frac{1}{2}$

1272 KISSOON, Mac and Katie Kissoon.   The Two of Us.   State
      2192
          CAC   Dec.   p341.   100w.   1

1273 KITT, Eartha. Bad But Beautiful.   Polydor 2354-037
          CAC   Oct.   p259.   100w.   4

1274 KRAL, Irene. Where Is Love.   Choice CRS 1012
          DB   May 6   p33.   100w.   4
          SR   Oct.   p100.   175w.   0

1275 LADYFLASH. Beauties in the Night.   RSO RS1-3002.   Cart.
      8T1-3002.   Cass. Ct1-3002
          SR   Dec.   p112.   125w.   3

1275a LAINE, Cleo. At the Wavendon Festival.   Black Lion BLP
       12150 (E)
          JJ   Nov.   p32.   425w. $4\frac{1}{2}$

1276 LAINE, Cleo. A Beautiful Thing.   RCA CPL1-5059.   Cart.
      CPS1-5059.   Cass. CPK1-5059
          SR   Jan.   p88.   250w.   5

1277 LAINE, Cleo. Born on a Friday.   RCA LPL1-5113.   Cart.
      LPS1-5113.   Cass. LPK1-5113
          CAC   July   p152.   225w. $4\frac{1}{2}$
          JJ   June   p35.   500w.   4
          SR   May   p86.   100w.   2

1278 LAINE, Cleo. Easy Livin'.   Stanyon Records 10122
          SR   Jan.   p83.   200w.   3

1279 LANGFORD, Georges. Acadiana.   Gamma GS-216 (Canada)
          CC   April   p35.   50w.   3

1280 LAPIERRE, Yves. Evidence.   Celebration CEL 1898 (Canada)
          OLR   March   p41.   25w.   3

1281 LAPOINTE, Jean. Démaquillé.   Kebec-disc KD 907 (Canada)
          CC   June   p33.   50w.   3

1282 LARA, Catherine. Nil.   Columbia FS 90304 (Canada)
          OLR   Sept.   p190.   25w.   4

1283 LAST, James. Classics Up to Date, vol. 3. Polydor 2371-
       538 (E)
            CAC   May p60. 125w. $2\frac{1}{2}$
            MM   April 3 p31. 25w. 2

1284 LAST, James. In the Mood for Trumpets. Polydor 2371-548
       (E)
            CAC   May p60. 125w. $3\frac{1}{2}$
            MM   April 3 p31. 25w. 2

1285 LAST, James. Last for the Road. Polydor 3150-624 (Tape
       only) (E)
            CAC   Aug. p182. 50w. $3\frac{1}{2}$

1286 LAST, James. Make the Party Last. Polydor 2371-612 (E)
            CAC   June p98. 50w. 3

1287 LAST, James. Non-Stop Dancing 17. Polydor 2371-626 (E)
            CAC   May p60. 125w. 3
            MM   April 3 p31. 25w. 2

1288 LAST, James. Rock Me Gently. Polydor 2371-584 (E)
            MM   Oct. 23 p27. 100w. 3

1289 LEANDROS, Vicky. Across the Water. Avco AV 11024
            LP   April p9. 75w. $2\frac{1}{2}$

1290 LECLERC, Felix. Le tour de l'île. Philips 6325242 (Cana-
       da)
            CC   Oct. p32. 50w. 3

1291 LEE, Brenda. Little Miss Dynamite. MCA MCF 2729 (E)
       (Reissue)
            MM   March 20 p22. 50w. 4

1292 LEE, Dickey. Angels, Roses and Rain. RCA APL1-1725.
       Cart. APS1-1725. Cass. APK1-1725
            SR   Nov. p104. 100w. 1

1293 LEE, Peggy. Let's Love. Atlantic SD 18108. Cart. TP
       18108. Cass. CS 18108
            SR   Feb. p94. 200w. 5

1294 LEE, Peggy. Mirrors. A&M SP. 4547. Cart. 4547. Cass.
       4547
            CRA   April p74. 250w. $1\frac{1}{2}$
            DB   April 8 p29. 275w. $1\frac{1}{2}$
            SR   March p96. 600w. 4

1295 LEGRAND, Michel. And Friends. RCA BGL1-1392
            DB   Oct. 21 p23-4. 375w. 2
            MM   Sept. 25 p24. 75w. $3\frac{1}{2}$

1296 LEGRAND, Michel. The Concert Legrand. Gryphon BGL
     1-1028. Cass. BGK 1 1028
          DB Jan. 15 p23. 200w. $2\frac{1}{2}$
          LP March p24. 100w. 3

1297 LEGRAND, Michel. Paris Was Made for Lovers. Inter-
     national Artists (E) (Reissue)
          CAC Dec. p340. 25w. $2\frac{1}{2}$

1298 LEMAY, Jaqueline. La moitré du monde est une femme.
     SPPS SP 19902 (Canada)
          CC June p33. 50w. 3

1299 LENO, Sam. Ordinary Man. Anchor ANCL-2002. 8: 8308-
     2002H
          SR July p81. 150w. 3

1300 LENORMAN, Gerard. Columbia FS 90303 (Canada)
          OLR Sept. p190. 25w. 3

1301 LETTERMEN. The Time Is Right. Capitol SW 11470
          LP April p21. 200w. $2\frac{1}{2}$

1302 LEVEILLEE, Claude. Ce matin un homme. Manoir M 911
     912 (Canada)
          CC Sept. p29, 31. 50w. 3

1303 LEVEILLEE, Claude. Frédéric. CBS FS748 (Canada)
          OLR Dec. p259. 25w. 4

1304 LEVEILLEE, Claude. On remonte en amour. Barclay
     80216 (Canada)
          CC March p33. 50w. 3

1305 LEYLAND Motors Band. Decca SB326 (E)
          GR Oct. p665. 175w. 3

1306 LEYRAC, Monique. L'hiver. CBS FS741 (Canada)
          OLR Dec. p259. 25w. 5

1307 LEYRAC, Monique. Mes premiers chansons. Harmonie KHF
     90239 (Canada)
          OLR March p41-2. 25w. 4

1307a LIFE Guards Band. Soldiers of the Queen. DJM 2030 (E)
          MM July 24 p25. 50w. $3\frac{1}{2}$

1308 LIST, Liesbeth. Solitude's My Home. Stanyan 10078
          SR Feb. p94. 125w. 4

1309 LOCKYER, Malcolm. Dreamy Piano. Polydor (E)
          MM Dec. 25 p17. 100w. 1

1310   LOS Indios Tabajaras. Secret Love All-Time Favorites.
       RCA, APL 1-1033
            GP May p81. 100w. $3\frac{1}{2}$
            MM Aug. 14 p29. 25w. 3

1311   McGEE, Francine. Un quebecoise errante. Gamma GS219
       (Canada)
            CC June p31. 50w. 3

1312   McINTYRE, Hal. Joyce LP 1006
            JJ June p40. 100w. 4

1312a McKUEN, Rod. McKuen Country. EMI EMC 3136 (E)
            CMR Oct. p32. 125w. 1

1313   MACLAINE, Shirley. Live at the Palace. Columbia PC
       34223. Cart. PCA 34223. Cass. PCT 34223
            MM Sept. 11 p26. 50w. 1
            SR Oct. p111. 250w. 3

1314   MACLEOD, Robert. Between the Poppy and the Snow.
       Charisma CAS 1114 (E)
            CAC June p98. 75w. 2

1315   McPEEK, Ben. Thinking of You. Attic LAT 1008 (Canada)
            CC May p32. 50w. 3

1316   McRAE, Carmen. As Time Goes By. Catalyst CAT-7904
            CAD Aug. p17, 18. 75w. 5
            JA Fall p53. 150w. 3
            SR Dec. p128. 125w. 4

1317   McRAE, Carmen. Can't Hide Love. Blue Note LA635-G.
       Cart. EA635H
            CAD Sept. p6. 25w. 4
            SR Dec. p98-9. 450w. 4

1318   McRAE, Carmen. I Am Music. Blue Note BN LA462-G
            DB Feb. 12 p28. 300w. 2

1319   McRAE, Carmen. Velvet Soul. Groove Merchant GM 4401
       (2 discs)
            LP March p17. 125w. 4

1320   McRAE, Carmen. It Takes a Whole Lot of Human Feeling.
       Groove Merchant GM-522
            LP July p13. 150w. 4

1321   McRAE, Carmen. November Girl. Black Lion BLP 30172
       (E)
            JJ April p34. 225w. 4

1322   McCRAE, Carmen. You'd Be So Easy to Love. Bethlehem

    BCP 6004 (Reissue)
       ARG   Nov.   p57.   200w.   3
       CAD   Aug.   p26.   75w.   4
       MJ   Dec.   p26.   50w.   2

1323 MAJOR Lance. Best of. Epic EPC 81519 (E) (Reissue)
       MM   Dec. 4 p22.   175w.   4

1324 MANHATTAN Transfer. Manhattan Transfer.   Atlantic SD
      18133. Cart. TP 18133. Cass. CS 18133
       SR   Aug.   p78.   200w.   4

1325 MANHATTAN Transfer. Coming Out. Atlantic SD 18183
       MM   Nov. 27 p26.   400w.   2
       RS   Oct. 21 p105, 107. 275w. $3\frac{1}{2}$

1326 MANILOW, Barry. This One's for You. Arista AL-4090.
      Cart. 8301-4090H. Cass. 5301-4090H
       MM   Dec. 4 p24.   100w. $2\frac{1}{2}$
       RS   Sept. 23 p117.   150w.   2
       SR   Dec.   p99-100.   400w.   4

1327 MANILOW, Barry. Tryin' to Get the Feeling. Arista AL-
      4060. Cass. 5301-4060H
       GR   May   p1812.   50w.   3
       HF   Feb.   p120.   150w. $3\frac{1}{2}$
       LP   March p7.   50w. $3\frac{1}{2}$
       MG   Jan.   p34.   50w.   3
       MM   May 15 p24.   50w.   2
       RS   Jan. 1 p56.   250w. $2\frac{1}{2}$

1328 MANTOVANI. American Encores. London PS 915.
       CAC   Dec.   p431.   125w. $3\frac{1}{2}$

1329 MARKIDE, Andreas and His Bouzoukis. Midnight in Athens.
      Polydor 2343-084 (E)
       MM   May 1 p30.   100w.   2

1330 MARMALADE. World of. Decca SPA 470 (E) (Reissue)
       CAC   Oct.   p256.   25w. $2\frac{1}{2}$

1331 MARTIN, Dean. 20 Original Hits. Reprise (E) (Reissue)
       MM   Nov. 20 p29.   50w. $1\frac{1}{2}$

1332 MARTYN-Ford Orchestra. Smoovin'. Mountain (E)
       MM   May 22 p25.   125w.   2

1333 MATHIS, Johnny. Feelings. Columbia PC 33887
       CAC   April p18.   75w.   3

1334 MATHIS, Johnny. I Only Have Eyes for You. Columbia PC
      34117
       MM   July 10 p22.   25w.   2

1335 MELLY, George. Is At It Again.   Reprise (E)
      MM Nov. 20 p25. 450w. 3

1336 MENDES, Sergio.   Elektra 7E-1027
      SR May p83. 75w. 0

1337 MENDES, Sergio and Brazil '77. Home Cooking. Elektra
      7E-1055. Cart. ET-81055
      MM May 8 p25. 50w. 2
      SR June p84. 50w. 2

1338 MERCER, Mabel. Mabel for Always. Stanyan SR 10108
      (Reissue)
      SR Dec. p90-1. 200w. 4

1339 MERCER, Mabel. A Tribute to Mabel Mercer on the Oc-
      casion of Her 75th Birthday. Atlantic MM4-100 (4 discs)
      (Reissue)
      SR Dec. p90-1. 1800w. 4

1340 MERRILL, Helen. Helen Merrill. Trip TLP-5526
      SR Jan. p99. 300w. 4

1341 MERRILL, Helen and Teddy Wilson. Helen Sings, Teddy
      Swings. Catalyst CAT-7903
      CAD Aug. p17, 18. 200w. 4
      SR Dec. p128-9. 150w. 4

1342 MICHEL, Jaques. Migration. Trans World T1-6026 (Canada)
      CC May p33. 50w. 3

1343 MIDLER, Bette. Songs for a New Depression. Atlantic SD
      18155. Cart. TP18155. Cass. CS 18155
      CIR May 13 p18. 100w. $1\frac{1}{2}$
      CRA April p71. 100w. $2\frac{1}{2}$
      CRE April p59, 61. 675w. $2\frac{1}{2}$
      HF May p104. 300w. 2
      RR March p73. 50w. $2\frac{1}{2}$
      RS March 11 p59. 425w. $2\frac{1}{2}$
      SR May p79-80. 400w. 4

1344 MILLER, Glenn. The Army-Air Force Band. RCA DHY0004
      (E)
      GR Oct. p666. 75w. 3

1344a MILLER, Glenn. Best of, vol. 1/2. CBS 22023 (E) (Re-
      issue)
      RR June p83. 50w. $2\frac{1}{2}$

1345 MILLER, Glenn. The Complete vol. 1 (1938-39). RCA Blue-
      bird AxM2-5512 (2 discs) (Reissue)
      SR March p99-100. 450w. 3

1346   MILLER, Glenn. The Legendary, vol. 10.   RCA LSA 3237
(E) (Reissue)
CAC April p18.   75w.   3
JJ June p39, 40.   75w.   4

1347   MILLER, Glenn. The Legendary, vol. 11.   RCA LSA 3238
(E) (Reissue)
CAC April p18.   75w.   3

1348   MILLER, Glenn. The Legendary, vol. 12.   RCA LSA 3239
(E) (Reissue)
CAC April p18.   75w. $2\frac{1}{2}$

1349   MILLER, Glenn. The Legendary, vol. 13.   RCA LSA 3240
(E)
CAC April p18.   75w.   3

1349a MILLER, Glenn. Legendary, vol. 10, 11, 12, 13.   RCA
LSA 3237/40 (E) (4 discs) (Reissue)
RR June p83.   25w. $2\frac{1}{2}$

1350   MILLER, Glenn. A Legendary Performer and His Orchestra.
RCA CPM2-0693 (2 discs) (Reissue)
CAC June p112.   175w.   3
RR June p83.   50w.   3
SR May p90-1.   300w. $4\frac{1}{2}$

1351   MILLER, Glenn. The Original Reunion.   Pye PKL5543 (E)
GR Oct. p666.   75w.   3

1352   MILLER, Glenn. Story.   RCA LSA 3274 (E) (Reissue)
JJ July p40.   75w.   5

1352a MILLER, Glenn and the Flying Airforce Band.   RCA DHY
004 (2 discs) (E) (Reissue)
MM Nov. 27 p32.   600w. $3\frac{1}{2}$
RR Oct. p102.   75w.   4

1353   MILLER, Ray. "The Sunny Meadows Radio Show, " 1929.
Sunbeam MFC 14
ST Aug.-Sept. p238-9.   300w.   5

1354   MOFFETT, Charles. Volume 1.   Charles Moffett Recordings
LRSR 6142
CAD Jan. p14, 16.   250w.   3

1355   MONTENEGRO, Hugo. Rocket Man--A Tribute to Elton John.
RCA APL1-1024
MM May 1 p30.   75w. $2\frac{1}{2}$

1356   MONTGOMERY, Melba. The Greatest Gift of All.   Elektra
CM-6
LP March p21.   100w. $3\frac{1}{2}$

1357 MORATH, Max. Jonah Man. Vanguard VSD 79378
          CK Dec.   p49.   25w.   3
          MJ Dec.   p26.   50w.   4
          SR Nov.   p104.   100w. $3\frac{1}{2}$

1358 MORATH, Max. Irving Berlin/The Ragtime Years. Vanguard
      VSD 79346; VSQ 40042
          LP Aug.   p14.   100w. 5
          SR March   p90.   650w. 4

1359 MORRIS, Joan and William Bolcon. After the Ball: a
      Treasury of Turn of the Century Popular Songs. Nonesuch
      H 71304
          SR Feb.   p56-7. 1200w. $4\frac{1}{2}$

1360-1 MOSS, Danny and Eddie Thompson. Misty and Moody. One-
      up OU 2116 (E)
          MM Aug. 28 p22.   200w. 3

1362 MOUSKOURI, Nana. Passport. Philips 9101-061 (E)
          CAC Oct.   p258.   50w. $3\frac{1}{2}$

1363 MOUSTAKI, Georges. Polydor 2489-091 (E)
          CAC April p18.   50w.   3

1364 MUD. Use Your Imagination. Private Stock
          MM Feb. 14 p28.   50w.   1

1365 MURPHY, Mark. Muse 5078
          DB Aug. 12 p69.   200w. 4
          JJ June   p35, 36. 350w. 4
          SOU Feb.   p50.   100w. $3\frac{1}{2}$

1366 MURRAY, Anne. Highly Prized Possession. Capitol 1-ST
      11354. Cart. 8XT-11354. Cass. 4XT-11354
          CMP May   p16.   129w. 2
          SR May   p83.   125w. 4

1367 MURRAY, Anne. Together. Capitol ST 11433. Cart. 8XT
      11433. Cass. 4XT 11433
          CMP Sept. p23.   225w. 3
          MM April 3 p33.   300w. 2
          OLR June   p107.   50w.   3
          SOU Jan.   p34-5. 450w. $3\frac{1}{2}$
          SR Feb.   p82.   700w. 4

1368 The NEW Paul Whiteman Orchestra. Monmouth-Evergreen
      7074 (Reissue)
          HF March   p113.   175w. 2
          JJ April   p38, 39. 450w. $3\frac{1}{2}$
          MJ March   p23.   100w. 3
          SR April   p103.   125w. 2

1369 NEW Paul Whiteman Orchestra. Music of the Roaring Twen-
      ties. Wave LP 27
          ST   April-May p154.   350w.   5

1370 NEWBEATS. Bread and Butter--20 Tasty Slices. DJM 22052
      (E)
          CAC Dec.   p338.   50w.   4

1371 NIGHTINGALE, Maxine. Right Back Where We Started From.
      United Artists UA-LA 626-G.   Cart. UA-EA 626-H.   Cass.
      UA-CA 626-H
          SR   Oct.   p100.   175w.   3

1372 NOBLE, Ray. World Records SH198 (E) (Reissue)
          GR   Oct.   p669.   150w. $3\frac{1}{2}$

1373 NOBLE, Ray. The Radio Years, 1935-36.   London HMG
      5019 (E) (Reissue)
          GR   June p101.   150w.   3
          JJ   July p36.   475w.   4
          MM   June 19 p22.   275w. $3\frac{1}{2}$

1373a NORMAND, Emile. CBS Radio Canada 306 (Canada)
          OLR Dec.   p258.   50w. $3\frac{1}{2}$

1374 O'CONNOR, Carroll. For Old P. F. A. R. T. S. Audio Fidelity
      AFSD 6276
          SR   Aug.   p79.   275w.   0

1375 OHTA, Herb. Feelings. A&M SP 4541
          AU   Feb.   p87.   100w.   3

1376 OLIVOR, Jane. First Night. Columbia PC 34274
          CIR Nov. 25 p18.   125w. $2\frac{1}{2}$
          CRE Dec.   p14, 70.   125w.   2
          RS   Oct. 7 p87.   150w. $2\frac{1}{2}$

1377 O'NEAL Twins. Silver Anniversary Concert. Creed 3065
          AU   Nov.   p122.   300w.   4

1378 ORIGINAL Piano Trio. Nostalgia. Klavier KS-128
          SR   Oct.   p84.   275w.   3

1379 ORLANDO, Tony. Before Dawn. Epic BG 33785 (2 discs)
      (Reissue)
          MM   May 22 p25.   75w.   3

1380 ORLANDO, Tony. He Don't Love You. Elektra 7E-1034.
      Cart. ET8-1034. Cass. TC5-1034
          SR   Sept.   p97.   100w.   3

1381 ORLANDO, Tony. Prime Time. Bell 1317. Cart. 8301-

1317H.   Cass. 5301-1317H
     SR   May p83, 85.   150w.   5

1382 ORLANDO, Tony and Dawn.   Greatest Hits.   Arista AL 4045
      (Reissue)
          MM   May 22 p25.   100w. $2\frac{1}{2}$

1383 ORLANDO, Tony and Dawn.   Skybird.   Arista AL 4059.   Cart.
      8301-4059.   Cass. 5301-4059
          MG   Jan. p34.   50w.   3
          SR   March p87, 90.   500w.   5

1384 ORLANDO, Tony and Dawn.   To Be with You.   Elektra 7E-
      1049
          HF   July p104.   250w. $3\frac{1}{2}$
          MM   June 12 p22.   375w. $2\frac{1}{2}$
          SR   June p86.   100w.   2

1385 OSMOND, Donny.   Disco Train.   Polydor PD 6067
          MM   Oct. 23 p34.   125w. $2\frac{1}{2}$

1386 OSMOND, Donny.   I'm Leaving It All Up to You.   MGM M3G
      4968.   Cart. M8H 4968.   Cass. M5H 4968
          SR   March p79.   75w.   4

1387 OSMOND, Donny and Marie Osmond.   Deep Purple.   Polydor
      2391-220 (E)
          CAC   July p143.   100w. $2\frac{1}{2}$

1388 O'SULLIVAN, Gilbert.   Greatest Hits.   MAM (E) (Reissue)
          MM   Dec. 18 p16.   175w. $1\frac{1}{2}$

1389 O'SULLIVAN, Gilbert.   A Stranger in My Own Backyard.
      MAM MAM-10
          SR   May p85.   125w.   5

1390 PAHNUI, Gabby.   The Gabby Pahnui Hawaiian Band.   Panini
      Records PS-1007
          GP   April p79.   100w. $3\frac{1}{2}$

1391 PARIS, Jackie and Ann Marie Moss.   Paris and Moss Live at
      the Maisonnette.   Different Drummer DD 1004
          SR   Jan. p98.   150w. $3\frac{1}{2}$

1392 PARKER, Jim.   Little Big Band.   Canon CNN 5966 (E)
          GR   Dec. p1076.   25w. $2\frac{1}{2}$

1393 PASADENA Roof Orchestra.   Island ILPS-9324.
      Cart. Y81-9324
          JJ   July p37.   375w. $4\frac{1}{2}$
          SR   Aug. p79, 80.   200w.   3

1394 PASADENA Roof Orchestra.   Good News.   Transatlantic (E)

CAC   May   p74.   150w.   4

1395   PASADENA Roof Orchestra.   Live.   Transatlantic (E)
MM   March 20   p22.   550w. $4\frac{1}{2}$

1396   PAUL, Les and Mary Ford.   The World Is Still Waiting for
the Sunrise.   Capitol ST-11308.   (Reissue)   Cart. 8XT-11308
SR   Feb.   p95.   325w. $4\frac{1}{2}$

1397   PETERS and Lee.   Serenade.   Philips 9709 210 (E)
CAC   July   p143.   150w. $3\frac{1}{2}$

1397a   PHILLIPS, Sid.   Hors d'oeuvres.   Golden Hour GH 622 (E)
(Reissue)
JJ   Dec.   p39-40.   200w.   3
RR   Dec.   p102.   25w.   3

1398   PLATTERS.   16 Original Hits.   Philips SON 002 (E)
MM   July 24   p25.   25w. $2\frac{1}{2}$

1399   PLUME.   Plume Poudrigue.   Deram XDEF 101 (Canada)
CC   April   p35.   50w.   3

1400   The POINTER Sisters.   Live at the Opera House.   Blue
Thumb BTS 8002.   Cart. J 88002.   Cass. J 58002
SR   Jan.   p90, 91.   300w.   4

1401   The POINTER Sisters.   Steppin'.   Blue Thumb BTSD-6201.
Cart. 8307-6021H.   Cass. 5307-6201H
SR   Nov.   p100, 102.   200w.   4

1402   POURCEL, Frank.   Very Best.   EMI Studio 2 TWOX1054 (E)
(Reissue)
GR   Dec.   p1076.   50w. $3\frac{1}{2}$

1403   PRESLEY, Elvis.   From Elvis Presley Boulevard, Memphis.
RCA APL1-1506.   Cart. APS1 1506
CM   Sept.   p57-8.   300w.   3
CMP   Dec.   p12.   150w.   1

1404   PRESLEY, Elvis.   Having Fun with Elvis on Stage.   RCA
CPM1-0818.   Cart. CPS1-0818.   Cass. CPK1-0818
SR   Feb.   p95, 97.   137w. $4\frac{1}{2}$

1405   PRESLEY, Elvis.   A Legendary Performer, vol. 2.   RCA
CPL1-1349.   Cart. CPS 1 1349
CM   June   p48.   400w. $4\frac{1}{2}$
SR   May   p92-3.   200w. $2\frac{1}{2}$

1406   PRESLEY, Elvis.   Live on Stage in Memphis.   RCA CPL1-
0606.   Cart. CPS1-0606.   Cass. CPK1-0606
SR   Feb.   p95, 97.   137w. $4\frac{1}{2}$

1407   PRESLEY, Elvis. Pictures of. RCA HY 1023 (E) (Reissue)
       CAC Feb. p448. 175w. 2

1408   PRESLEY, Elvis. Promised Land. RCA APL1-0873. Cart.
       APS1-0873. Cass. APK1-0873
           CMP April p18. 150w. 2
           SR June p83. 275w. $3\frac{1}{2}$

1409   PRESLEY, Elvis. Today. RCA APL1-1039. Cart. APS1-
       1039. Cass. APK1-1039
           SR Oct. p84. 175w. $4\frac{1}{2}$

1410   PREVIN, Dory. Warner Bros. BS 2811
           SR March p82. 175w. 4

1411   PREVIN, Dory. On My Way to Where. Sunset SLS 50385
       (E)
           MM July 3 p21. 25w. 3

1412   PREVIN, Dory. We're Children of Coincidence and Harpo
       Marx. Warner BS 2908
           HF June p104. 175w. 4
           RR May p73. 50w. $2\frac{1}{2}$
           SR June p86. 150w. 2

1413   PRICE, Leontyne and Andre Previn. RCA ARL1 1029
           LP Jan. p26. 100w. $2\frac{1}{2}$

1414   PURIM, Flora. Open Your Eyes You Can Fly. Milestone
       9056
           DB June 3 p20. 325w. 4

1415   RAEBURN, Boyd. First Heard 8.
           JJ April p34, 36. 425w. $2\frac{1}{2}$

1416   RALSTON, Bob. Feelings. Ranwood R8158
           CK Dec. p49. 75w. 3

1417   RAY, Ricardo and Bobby Cruz. 1975. Vaya XVS-33
           SR June p83. 150w. $4\frac{1}{2}$

1418   READING, Wilma. Pye (E)
           MM Nov. 27 p28. 75w. 1

1418a REBROFF, Ivan. At Carnegie Hall. Columbia M 33364
           LP April p26-7. 200w. $3\frac{1}{2}$

1419   REDBONE, Leon. On the Track. Warner BS 2888
           DB April 8 p24, 25. 375w. 4

1420   REDDY, Helen. Best of. Capitol ST 11467 (Reissue)
           GR March p1518. 75w. $3\frac{1}{2}$
           MM Feb. 7 p24. 50w. 3

1421 REDDY, Helen. Free and Easy. Capitol ST-11348. Cart.
8XT-11348. Cass. 4XT-11348
SR May p85. 150w. $4\frac{1}{2}$

1422 REDDY, Helen. Music, Music. Capitol ST 11547. Cart.
8XT 11547. Cass. 4XT 11547
SR Dec. p103. 275w. $1\frac{1}{2}$

1423 REED, Les. The International Pop Proms. Granada (E)
MM May 8 p25. 100w. 1

1424 RESER, Harry. Banjo Crackerjax. Yazoo L 1048 (Reissue)
JJ June p41. 50w. 3
RT May/June p6-7. 100w. $2\frac{1}{2}$

1425 RICH, Freddie. Friendly Five Footnotes on the Air: Vol. 1
&2. Aircheck #12/13 (2 discs) (Canada)
CAD Sept. p25. 275w. 5
JJ May p34. 250w. 4

1426 RICHARD, Cliff. I'm Nearly Famous. Rocket PIG 2210.
Cart. PIGT 2210
SR Nov. p108. 125w. 3

1427 RICHMOND, Robin. The Hollywood Years. DJM (E)
MM Dec. 18 p16. 575w. $2\frac{1}{2}$

1428 RIVERS, Johnny. New Lovers and Old Friends. Epic PE
33681
CRA Jan. p79. 125w. 0

1429 ROBINSON, Vicki Sue. RCA APL 1-1829
RS Dec. 16 p88. 150w. 3

1430 ROBINSON, Vicki Sue. Never Gonna Let You Know. RCA
APL1-1256
BM Sept. p48. 200w. 2
CRE Aug. p77-8. 25w. $3\frac{1}{2}$
HF June p108. 150w. 3

1431 ROGERS, Billie. Joyce 1018
JJ Jan. p40. 50w. 3

1432 ROGERS, Eric. The Spirit of Vaudeville. Decca PFS 4371
(E)
GR Dec. p1076. 50w. 3

1433 ROUSSOS, Dennis. Happy to Be. Philips 9101 027 (E)
MM July 10 p22. 50w. $2\frac{1}{2}$

1434 ROYAL Engineers Military Band and Orchestra. Concert
Parade. Pye TBX 3010 (E)
GR Oct. p662, 665. 175w. $2\frac{1}{2}$

1435 ROYAL Engineers Band/Coldstream Guards Band.   Precision
      Pye (E)
            CAC   Feb. p458.   75w.   3

1436 ROYAL Scots Dragoon Guard.   Amazing.   Pye 5531 (E)
            CAC   Feb.   p458.   75w.   3

1437 RUBETTES.   MCA State MCA-2193.   Cart. MCAT 2193
            CAC   March p453.   50w.   4
            JR   Sept.   p102.   100w.   2

1438 RUBETTES.   Best of.   State (E) (Reissue)
            MM   Dec. 11 p21.   275w.   3

1439 SAMMES, Mike.   Songs.   EMI One Up OU 2142 (E)
            GR   Dec.   p1076.   225w. $4\frac{1}{2}$

1440 SANDPIPERS.   Greatest Hits.   A&M (E) (Reissue)
            MM   Aug. 14 p29.   25w.   0

1441 SANDS, Evie.   Estate of Mind.   Haven ST-9202.   Cart. 8XT-
      9202
            SR   June p86.   200w. $2\frac{1}{2}$

1442 SANTAMARIA, Mongo.   Afro-India.   Vaya KVS 38
            CRA   Jan.   p78.   175w.   4
            DB   April 22   p24.   300w.   4

1443 SANTAMARIA, Mongo.   Live at Yankee Stadium.   Vaya KVS-
      26
            SR   March p83.   125w. $2\frac{1}{2}$

1444 SANTOS, Larry.   You Are Everything I Need.   Casablanca
      7030
            MM   Dec. 4 p24.   75w.   2

1445 SAVALAS, Telly.   Audio Fidelity AFSD 6271
            HF   June p106, 108.   150w. $2\frac{1}{2}$
            LP   Aug.   p15.   75w.   0
            SR   Aug.   p83.   200w.   3

1446 SECOMBE, Harry.   A Man and His Dreams.   Philips SONO17
      (E)
            GR   Oct.   p666.   50w. $2\frac{1}{2}$

1447 SEGAL, George.   A Touch of Ragtime.   Signature BSLI-0654
            SR   Jan.   p91.   300w.   4

1448 SHEARING, George.   Continental Experience.   MPS BAP 5081
      (E)
            JJ   July p38.   150w.   0

1449 SHEARING, George.   My Ship.   MPS G 22369

MJ   Dec.   p44.   25w. $2\frac{1}{2}$

1450   SHERBET.   Howzat.   MCA 2226
       MM   Oct. 23   p27.   325w.   3

1451   SHERWOOD, Bobby.   Golden Era   15018
       JJ   Jan.   p40.   50w.   3

1452   SHORT, Bobby.   Celebrates Rodgers and Hart.   Atlantic SD
       2-610.   (2 discs).   Cart.   TP2-610
       SR   April   p90, 92.   300w.   4

1453   SHORT, Bobby.   My Personal Property.   Atlantic SD 1689.
       Cart.   TP 1689.   Cass.   CS 1689
       SR   Nov.   p110.   125w.   4

1454   SIMMONS, Elaine.   The Singer of the Song.   Polydor 2383-
       402 (E)
       CAC   Dec.   p342.   50w.   1

1455   SIMON, Lucy.   RCA APL1-1074.   Cass.   APK 1-1074
       LP   March   p12.   150w. $4\frac{1}{2}$

1456   SINATRA, Frank.   The Main Event Live.   Reprise FS 2207.
       Cart.   L8F 2207.   Cass.   L5F 2207
       SR   March   p84.   125w.   2

1457   SINATRA, Frank.   The Paramount Years.   Chairman 6011
       JA   Fall   p56.   25w.   3

1458   SINATRA, Frank.   To Be Perfectly Frank.   Chairman 6010
       JA   Fall   p56.   25w.   3

1459   SINGERS Unlimited.   Feeling Free.   MPS/BASF BAP 50776
       (E)
       JJ   May   p40.   100w.   3

1460   SINGERS Unlimited.   Four of Us.   MPS BAP 5067 (E)
       JJ   Jan.   p40.   100w. $2\frac{1}{2}$

1461   SLICKERS.   Many Rivers to Cross.   KLIK 9010 (E)
       BM   July   p52.   150w.   2

1462   SMECK, Roy.   Yazoo 1052 (Reissue)
       CRA   July   p79-80.   200w. $2\frac{1}{2}$
       GP   Aug.   p80.   100w. $4\frac{1}{2}$
       JJ   July   p41.   75w. $4\frac{1}{2}$

1463   SONNY and Cher.   The Beat Goes On.   Atco 11000
       CIR   May 13   p18.   75w.   4

1464   SOPHY.   Sentimentos (Feelings).   Velvet LPV-1494
       SR   April   p92.   175w.   3

1465 SOUTHERN, Jeri. You Better Go Now. Stanyan SR 10106
      (Reissue)
         SR July p82. 225w. 4

1466 STAPLES, Mavis. Only for the Lonely. Stax STX-1053
      (Reissue)
         BM Aug. p46. 75w. 3

1467 STARR, Kay. Back to the Roots. GNP Crescendo GNPS-
      2090 (Reissue)
         LP Aug. p15. 100w. 4

1468 STATON, Dakota. Ms. Soul. Groove Merchant GM-532.
      Cass. F-5532
         LP Aug. p15. 125w. 3

1469 STEVENS, Ray. Just for the Record. Warner Bros. BS
      2914. Cart. M8 2914. Cass. M5 2914
         CMP Aug. p32. 200w. 2
         MM July 24 p25. 25w. $2\frac{1}{2}$
         SR Oct. p102-3. 150w. 4

1470 STEVENS, Ray. Misty. Barnaby BR 6012. Cart. 8190-
      6012 H. Cass. 5190-6012 H
         SR Nov. p104. 100w. $3\frac{1}{2}$

1471 STEVENS, Suzanne. En Route. Capitol ST 70-032 (Canada)
         OLR Sept. p190. 25w. 4

1472 STEWART, Al. Al Stewart's Museum of Modern Brass 2.
      RCA APL1-0951
         LP July p9. 175w. 3

1473 STONE, Elly. The New Legend of the Ancient Mariner.
      Eebee Records 001
         SR Oct. p103. 275w. 0

1474 STREISAND, Barbra. Butterfly. Columbia PC 33005. Cart.
      PCA 33005. Cass. PCT 33005
         SR April p86. 700w. 3

1475 STREISAND, Barbra. Lazy Afternoon. Columbia PC 33815.
      Cart. PCA 33815
         AU July p69. 350w. 4
         LP March p25. 250w. $2\frac{1}{2}$
         MM Jan. 24 p26. 250w. 3
         RS Jan. 15 p52-3. 275w. 3
         SR Feb. p89. 200w. 3

1476 STRERATH, Walter. Fly to Brazil. Fly 0751 (E)
         JJ June p41. 100w. 3

1477 SUN. Live On. Dream On. Capitol ST 11461

MM   June 26   p22.   50w.   3

1478   SURPRISE Sisters.   RCA APL 1-1404
       GR   July   p226.   50w.   3
       MM   April 3   p29.   400w. $3\frac{1}{2}$

1479   SWINGLE II.   Rags and All That Jazz.   Columbia PC 34194
       DB   Nov. 18   p18, 20-1.   250w.   3
       SR   Nov.   p130.   175w. $1\frac{1}{2}$

1480   SYLVERS.   Showcase.   Capitol ST 11465
       BM   May   p36.   150w.   3

1481   SYLVESTER, Terry.   I Believe.   Polydor 2383394 (E)
       MM   July 24   p25.   50w.   1
       RR   Sept.   p89.   50w.   2

1482   SYMS, Sylvia.   Sylvia Syms Lovingly.   Atlantic SD 18177.
       Cart. TP 18177.   Cass. CS 18177
       SR   Aug.   p70.   600w.   5

1483   TAYLOR, Geoff.   Songsmith.   Pye (E)
       MM   Dec. 25   p17.   125w. $1\frac{1}{2}$

1484   THOMAS, B. J.   From Texas to Tennessee.   DJM 26079 (E)
       MM   Dec. 4   p24.   50w.   2

1485   THOMAS, B. J.   Reunion.   ABC 858
       CMP   Sept.   p27.   162w.   3

1486   THOMAS, Ray.   Hopes, Dreams and Wishes.   Threshold THS
       17
       CAC   Sept.   p216.   200w.   2
       GR   Aug.   p351.   50w.   2
       MM   July 31   p21.   150w. $2\frac{1}{2}$
       SR   Dec.   p114.   225w.   1

1487   THOMPSON, Sue.   The Story of.   DJM 28024 (2 discs) (E)
       (Reissue)
       MM   Oct. 16   p25.   50w. $2\frac{1}{2}$

1488   TODD, Dick.   Blue Orchids.   RCA AXM2-5509 (2 discs) (Re-
       issue)
       OLR   June   p107.   75w.   4

1489   TOLKIEN, J. R. R.   Poems and Songs of Middle Earth.
       Caedmon TC 1231.   Cass. CDL 51231
       SR   July   p88.   1100w.   4

1490   TORME, Mel.   Live at the Maisonette.   Atlantic SD 18129.
       Cart. TP 18129.   Cass. CS 18129
       LP   Aug.   p15-6.   50w.   0
       SR   Aug.   p82.   750w.   5

1491 TREPANIER, Guy.   Pour un gars heureux.   WEA WSC 9016
      (Canada)
          OLR   March p42.   25w.   5

1492 TUCKER, Sophie.   World Records SH234 (E) (Reissue)
          GR   Oct.   p669.   175w. $4\frac{1}{2}$

1493 TWIGGY.   Mercury SRM 1-1093.   Cart. MC8 1-1093.   Cass.
      MCR4 1-1093
          CAC   Sept.   p218.   200w.   3
          CRE   Dec.   p61-2.   500w.   0
          MM   Sept. 11 p28.   325w.   3
          RS   Nov. 4 p79-80.   175w. $3\frac{1}{2}$
          SR   Dec.   p114.   150w.   1

1494 TYPICALLY Tropical.   Barbados Sky.   Gull Gulp 1014 (E)
          MM   Feb. 21 p30.   50w.   2

1494a TYSON, Sylvia.   Woman's World.   Capitol ST 11434
          CMR   March p29.   125w.   2
          LP   Jan.   p14.   200w. $3\frac{1}{2}$
          OLR   March p40.   50w. $3\frac{1}{2}$

1495 VALLI, Frankie.   Close Up.   Private Stock PS 2000.   Cart.
      8300-2000.   Cass. 5300-2000(H)
          LP   July p17.   125w.   4
          SR   Aug.   p84.   150w.   2

1496 VALLI, Frankie.   Inside You.   Mowest 852
          MM   May 15 p26.   50w.   1

1497 VALLI, Frankie.   Our Day Will Come.   Private Stock PS
      2006.   Cass. 5300 2006H
          LP   April p12.   150w. $2\frac{1}{2}$

1498 VALOIS, Daniel and Alain Jodoin.   La vielle école.   CBS FS
      90323 (Canada)
          CC   Oct.   p33.   50w.   3

1499 VAUGHAN, Frankie.   Someone Who Cares.   Pye NSPL 18497
      (E)
          CAC   Dec.   p342.   50w.   3

1500 VAUGHAN, Sarah.   More, from Japan Live.   Mainstream
      MRL 419
          DB   March 25 p33.   250w.   4
          LP   April p17.   175w.   3

1501 VAUGHAN, Sarah.   Send in the Clowns.   Mainstream MRL
      412
          SR   July p87.   150w. $4\frac{1}{2}$

1502 VAUGHAN, Sarah.   Tenderly.   Bulldog BDL1-1009

JJ Sept. p40. 400w. $4\frac{1}{2}$

1503 VIGNEAULT, Gilles. En direct. CBS FS 749 (Canada)
OLR Dec. p260. 25w. 4

1504 VINTON, Bobby. Melodies of Love. ABC ABCD-851. Cart.
8022-851H. Cass. 5022-851H
SR April p88. 175w. $4\frac{1}{2}$

1505 VIRTUOSI Brass Band of Great Britain. Philips SON 025 (E)
GR Dec. p1075. 100w. $3\frac{1}{2}$

1506 WALKER Brothers. No Regrets. GTO (E)
MM Feb. 14 p30. 400w. 3

1507 WARNER, Kai. Hits All the Way. Polydor (E)
MM Nov. 20 p26. 75w. 1

1508 WARNER, Kai. For the Road. Polydor (E) (Tape only)
CAC Aug. p182. 50w. $2\frac{1}{2}$

1509 WARNER, Kai. Great Orchestras of the World. Polydor
3146-044 (Tape only) (E) (Reissue)
CAC Dec. p342. 50w. $2\frac{1}{2}$

1510 WARNER, Kai. Romantic Songs. Polydor 2482-284 (E)
MM April 24 p23. 50w. $1\frac{1}{2}$

1511 WARNER, Kai. Summer Dancing. Polydor 2371-420 (E)
CAC Oct. p261. 50w. $1\frac{1}{2}$

1512 WARWICK, Dionne. Warner Bros. BS 2893. Cart. M8 2893.
Cass. M5 2893
SR March p94. 175w. 2

1513 WARWICK, Dionne. Then Came You. Warner Brothers BS
2846. Cart. M8 2846. Cass. M5 2846
SR June p87. 150w. 3

1514 WARWICK, Dionne. Track of the Cat. Warner BS 2893.
Cart. M5P 2893. Cass. M8P 2893
BM April p32. 225w. 4
BS April p67. 150w. 4
HF March p105. 250w. $2\frac{1}{2}$
RR Feb. p66. 50w. $3\frac{1}{2}$

1515 WATERMAN, Dennis. Down Wind of Angels. DJM 20483 (E)
CAC Dec. p342. 250w. 2
MM Nov. 20 p29. 100w. 3

1516 WELSH Guards Band. Guardsmen. Decca DAF223 (E)
GR Oct. p665. 50w. 3

1517 WHITTAKER, Roger. A Special Kind of Man. RCA LSP-
      4505
            LP Aug. p9. 75w. 0

1518 WILLIAMS, Andy. You Lay So Easy On My Mind. CBS
      80490 (E)
            CMP April p10. 200w. 3

1519 WILLIAMS, Don. Harmony. Dot 2049
            MM July 3 p22. 200w. $3\frac{1}{2}$

1520 WILLIAMS, Fess. Hot Town. IAJRC 16
            JJ Feb. p43-4. 350w. 3

1521 WILLIAMS, Paul. Best of. A&M SP4543 (E) (Reissue)
            CAC Feb. p448. 175w. 3

1522 WILLIAMS, Paul. A Little Bit of Love. A&M SP-3655
            SR March p85. 175w. 5

1523 WILLIAMS, Paul. Ordinary Fool. A&M SP 4550. Cart.
      8T 4550
            CAC April p20. 150w. 3
            GR May p1812. 50w. $2\frac{1}{2}$
            HF March p105. 125w. $2\frac{1}{2}$
            LP April p13. 125w. $3\frac{1}{2}$
            MG March p43. 50w. 3
            RS Feb. 12 p93. 100w. 1
            SR April p94. 150w. 4

1524 WILLIAMS, Roger. Best of. MCA MCA2-4106 (2 discs)
      (Reissue)
            CK Dec. p49. 25w. $2\frac{1}{2}$

1525 WILLIAMS, Roger. Virtuoso. MCA 2175
            MM May 1 p30. 75w. $1\frac{1}{2}$

1526 WILSON, Nancy. Come Get To This. Capitol ST 11386
            BM Jan. p25. 350w. 2

1527 WING and a Prayer Fife and Drum Corps. Babyface. Wing
      3025
            BM April p51. 75w. 2
            MM March 27 p28. 50w. 0

1528 WOLFF, Henry and Nancy Hennings. Tibetan Bells. Antilles
      AN 7006
            DB April 8 p30-2. 50w. $2\frac{1}{2}$

1529 WOODWARD, Edward. Precision DJM 22054 (E)
            CAC Feb. p447. 50w. $3\frac{1}{2}$

1530 WORK, Henry Clay. Who Shall Rule This American Nation.

SR Jan. p79. 375w. 3

1531 WURZELS. Adge Culter and the Wurzels. Columbia SCX
      6126 (E) (Reissue)
          GR Dec. p1076. 50w. 4

1532 WURZELS. Adge Cutler's Family Album. Columbia SCX
      6135 (E) (Reissue)
          GR Dec. p1076. 50w. $3\frac{1}{2}$

1533 WYNSOR, Lance. I'll Be Around. Decca SUL 5244 (E)
          GR Dec. p1076. 50w. 4

1534 YARROW, Peter. Love Songs. Warner BS-2891
          LP March p13. 75w. $2\frac{1}{2}$
          RS Feb. 12 p95. 200w. $2\frac{1}{2}$
          SR March p95. 200w. 3

1535 ZENTNER, Si. Big Band Hits. Sunset SLS 50361 (E) (Re-
      issue)
          JJ May p40. 100w. $3\frac{1}{2}$

COUNTRY

This section comprises material known to listeners and collectors variously as "C & W," the "Nashville Sound," or hillbilly music. The tie that binds this diverse field together and distinguishes it from "folk" is that it is commercial music played for a paying audience and recorded for the industry.

Bill Malone in his excellent study, Country Music, U. S. A. [Austin: University of Texas, 1968], offers the uninitiated a handy way to categorize this genre.

Before the 1920's: The Southern rural culture, existing outside of the mainstream of American life, had its own music, expressive of the culture and isolation. We put these into FOLK.

The 1920's: The emergence of individual country performers relying upon traditional music are recorded for the growing numbers owning "Victrolas" in rural America. Jimmy Rodgers and the Carter Family begin the "country music industry." We put these under OLD TIME MUSIC.

The 1930's: The emergence of individual stars, singing cowboys, advanced recording techniques, and the radio bring change but the songs still reflect the performer's origins.

The 1940's: World War II and the move to defense jobs and Southern military camps helps make country music nationally popular. This is the boom period of the industry.

The 1950's: Country music enters the urban market and loses many of its distinctive traits. Hank Williams spans the gulf between country and popular music but country-pop and the Nashville sound are replacing tradition.

The 1960's (and into the mid-1970's): Country-pop is counterbalanced by the urban folk revival and a renewed interest in traditional country music.

Country has immense popularity in the United States. This music, which is often accused of having no "class," is the daily sound heard by many million Americans. Hundreds of AM radio stations feature it and millions of albums are sold annually. It is the working man's music and the very lyrics tell us much about his concerns: patriotism, automation, unemployment, too rapid social change, unfaithful wives and husbands, alcohol, and the dreariness of the factory and trucking. It is important music for the popular record collection in a library since it has a direct appeal to that segment of the population that traditionally does not use the library much. According to the reviews, the following appear to be the best discs in 1976:

ANDERSON, Lynn. I've Never Loved Anyone More. Columbia KC 33691
ATKINS, Chet and Les Paul. Chester and Lester. RCA APL1-1167
BARE, Bobby. The Winner and Other Losers. RCA APL1-1786
CASH, Johnny. One Piece at a Time. Columbia KC 34193
EDWARDS, Stoney. Blackbird. Capitol ST 11499
HAGGARD, Merle. My Love Affair with Trains. Capitol ST 11544
HALL, Tom T. Faster Horses. Mercury SRM1-1076
JENNINGS, Waylon. Are You Ready for the Country. RCA APL1-1816
MILSAP, Ronnie. Night Things. RCA APL1-1223
SHEPARD, Jean. Mercy, Ain't Love Good. United Artists LA 609G
STUCKEY, Nat. Independence. MCA 2184

1536 ACUFF, Roy. Smoky Mountain Memories. Hickory H3G 4517
    CMP Feb. p32-3. 275w. 4

1537 ACUFF, Roy. That's Country. Hickory H3G 4521. Cart. H88 4521
    CM Jan. p56-7. 525w. 2½
    CMR May p31. 225w. 4

1538 AMAZING Rhythm Aces. Stacked Deck. ABC 913. Cart. ABCD-8-913
    CM Jan. p57-8. 500w. 3
    CMP Feb. p21. 250w. 3
    MG Jan. p40. 75w. 3
    MG Feb. p53. 75w. 3

1539 AMAZING Rhythm Aces. Too Stuffed to Jump. ABC ABCD 940
    CMR Sept. p31. 300w. 2½
    CS Oct. p45. 475w. 3½

1540 ANDERSON, Bill. Live from London. MCA MCF 2722 (E)
    CMP Feb. p20. 275w. 5

1541 ANDERSON, Bill. Peanuts and Diamonds. MCA 2222
    CS Dec. p43. 200w. 3

1542 ANDERSON, Bill. Sometimes. MCA 2182
    MG May p56. 50w. 3

1543 ANDERSON, Lynn. I've Never Loved Anyone More. Colum-
      bia KC 33691
            CMP   Jan.   p27.   200w.   3
            CMR   April p41.   125w.   3
            PMS   V4/#3 p190. 50w.   4½

1544 ASLEEP at the Wheel. Texas Gold. Capitol ST 11441
            CMP   May   p17.   400w.   3
            CMR   Feb. p32.   150w.   3
            CRE   Feb. p12.   50w.   4
            LP   Jan. p19.   100w.   4
            MM   July 3 p21.   300w.   3½

1545 ASLEEP at the Wheel. Wheelin and Dealin'. Capitol ST
      11546. Cart. 8ST 11546
            CM   Oct.   p58.   125w.   4
            DB   Nov. 4 p24.   225w.   3½
            RS   Oct. 7 p79.   200w.   2½

1546 ATKINS, Chet. Famous Country Music Makers. RCA DPS
      2063 (E) (2 discs) (Reissue)
            CMP   July p28.   325w.   3
            CMR   Sept. p33.   125w.   3

1547 ATKINS, Chet. The Night Atlanta Burned. RCA APL 1-1233
            CM   Feb. p46.   600w.   3
            GP   Jan. p70.   75w.   4

1548 ATKINS, Chet and Merle Travis. Atkins/Travis Travelling
      Show. RCA
            MHF   May   p61.   250w.   4

1549 ATKINS, Chet and Les Paul. Chester and Lester. RCA
      APL1-1167. Cart. APS1-1167
            AU   June p86.   200w.   3½
            CM   Aug. p54.   275w.   4
            CR   Sept. p539. 175w.   4
            DB   Oct. 7 p30-1. 350w.   5
            GP   May   p81.   300w.   4½
            HF   June p108.   225w.   3½
            MG   June p55.   25w.   3
            MHF   May   p61.   250w.   4
            RS   May 6 p71, 73.   300w.   4
            SR   June p73.   300w.   4½

1550 AUTRY, Gene. Cowboy Hall of Fame. Republic IRDA-R-
      6012 (Reissue)
            CRA   Nov.   p74.   50w.   3

1551 AUTRY, Gene. Favorites. Republic IRDA R 6013 (Reissue)
            CMR   June p30.   350w.   2½
            CRA   Nov. p74.   50w.   3
            MM   April 17 p21.   50w.   2½

1552 AUTRY, Gene. Live from Madison Square Garden. Republic
      IRDA-R-6014 (Reissue)
            CRA   Nov.   p74.   50w.   0

1553 AUTRY, Gene. South of the Border/All American Cowboy.
      Republic IRDA-R-6011 (2 discs) (Reissue)
            CRA   Nov.   p74.   50w. $2\frac{1}{2}$

1554 BALLARD, Larry. Young Blood and Sweet Country Music.
      Elektra 7E-1024
            CMR   Jan.   p33.   450w.   3

1555 BANDY, Moe. Hank Williams, You Wrote My Life. Colum-
      bia KC 34091. Cass. CA 34091
            CM   Aug.   p53-4.   375w.   3
            CMR   June   p33.   150w. $2\frac{1}{2}$
            MG   June   p55.   25w. $2\frac{1}{2}$
            RS   June 3 p69.   150w. $2\frac{1}{2}$

1556 BANDY, Moe. Here I Am Drunk Again. Columbia KC 34285.
      Cass. CA 34285
            CM   Dec.   p65.   400w.   4
            CMR   Dec.   p26.   125w.   3

1557 BARE, Bobby. Cowboys and Daddys. RCA APL1-1222.
      Cart. APS1 1222
            CM   March p59.   575w. $3\frac{1}{2}$
            CMR   May   p29-30. 250w.   4
            RS   Feb. 26 p76-7. 200w.   3

1558 BARE, Bobby. Hard Time Hungrys. RCA APL1-0906
            CMR   Feb.   p32.   250w. $2\frac{1}{2}$

1559 BARE, Bobby. The Winner and Other Losers. RCA APL1
      1786
            CS   Oct.   p45.   650w.   5
            MG   Sept. p63.   50w.   3
            RS   Nov. 4 p70.   225w.   4

1560 BAREFOOT, Jerry. Keys to the Country. Monument P2
      34252
            CMP   Oct.   p30.   250w.   4

1561 BARKLIE, Pattie. Flowers and Burgundy Wine. Pye PKL
      5526 (E)
            CMR   March p33.   100w. $\frac{1}{2}$

1562 BARNETT, Don and the Nu Jays. Just Another Good Time.
      Medallion 275 218
            CS   Oct.   p44.   100w.   3

1563 BARRETT, Al. Open Country. Sweet Folk and Country SFA
      026 (E)

CMP   Feb.   p30.   50w.   2

1564   BARRETT, Al.   Open Country, v.2.   Sweet Folk and Country
SFA 045 (E)
CMR   Aug.   p28.   75w.   2

1565   BEGLEY, Philomena.   Introduces Her Ramblin' Man.   Top
Spin TSLP 76 (E)
CMR   Feb.   p30.   125w.   1

1566   BENTON, Barbi.   Something New.   Playboy 411
RS   Nov. 4   p80.   175w.   0

1567   BLAKELEY, Ronee.   Welcome.   Warner Bros. BS2890.
Cart. B8-2890
CM   Feb.   p51.   650w.   1
CMP   April   p21.   350w.   3
MM   Jan. 3   p24.   325w. $4\frac{1}{2}$
RR   Feb.   p66.   50w. $2\frac{1}{2}$
RS   Jan. 1   p56.   200w. $2\frac{1}{2}$

1568   BOOTS Randolph.   Cool Boots.   Monument KZ 33803
MG   April   p54.   50w.   3

1568a   BOYD, Bill.   RCA AXM2-5503 (2 discs) (Reissue)
CMP   Feb.   p33.   550w.   5

1569   BRETT, Ann and Roy Brett.   At Last.   Beck PT 19 (E)
CMP   May   p28.   75w.   2

1570   BRUCE, Ed.   United Artists UA LA 613G
CS   Oct.   p44.   75w. $2\frac{1}{2}$

1571   BRUMLEY, Tom.   Tom Cattin'.   Steel Guitar Record Club 2
(E)
CMR   April   p36.   150w.   3

1572   BRYCE, Sherry.   This Song's for You.   MGM M3G 5000
MG   Jan.   p40.   50w. $2\frac{1}{2}$

1573   BURKE, Fiddlin' Frenchie.   Twentieth Century T-479
CM   Feb.   p48.   400w. $3\frac{1}{2}$
MG   Jan.   p40.   50w.   3
PMS   V4/#3   p191.   25w. $3\frac{1}{2}$

1574   BURNETTE, Sonny, Hal Rugg and Weldon Myrick.   Steel
Guitars of the Grand Ole Opry.   Mega MLPS 610
CS   Nov.   p40.   100w. $1\frac{1}{2}$

1575   BUTLER, Joan Carol.   Capitol ST-11476
CRA   April   p75.   75w. $2\frac{1}{2}$

1576   CAFFREY Family.   Country Thought.   Century Productions

LP 33004
   BGU   May   p35.   100w. $1\frac{1}{2}$
   PIC   Aug. 9 p82.   175w.   2

1577   CAJUN Moon.   Chrysalis CHR 1116
   CMP   July   p29.   375w.   4

1578   CALLERY, Bill.   Columbia KC 34113
   CMR   Sept.   p32.   250w.   3

1579   CAMERON Clan.   Lightning Express.   Outlet STOL 114 (E)
   CMR   March   p33.   100w.   1

1580   CAMPBELL, Glen.   Arkansas.   Capitol Vine VMP 1001 (E)
  (Reissue)
   CAC   Jan.   p415.   150w. $3\frac{1}{2}$
   CMP   April   p19.   200w.   3
   CMR   Sept.   p33.   75w. $2\frac{1}{2}$

1581   CAMPBELL, Glen.   Bloodline.   Capitol SW 11516.   Cart.
  8XW-11516.   Cass. 4XW 11516
   CMP   Aug.   p29.   300w.   4
   CMR   June   p29.   250w.   3
   MG   July   p58.   100w.   0
   SR   Sept.   p91.   175w.   2

1582   CANTERBURY Country Orchestra.   Mistwold.   F&W F74FW5
   CM   Jan.   p60.   500w.   3
   PIC   April   p66-7.   175w.   3

1583   CARROLL, Milton.   Blue Skies.   Columbia KC 34114
   CS   Dec.   p43.   100w. $2\frac{1}{2}$

1584   CARTER, Wilf.   Have a Nice Day.   RCA KXL1-1057 (Canada)
   CC   Nov.   p34.   50w.   3

1585   CARTER, Wilf.   How My Yodelling Days Began.   RCA Camden CAS 2222 (Reissue)
   CMR   Oct.   p31.   250w.   4

1586   CARTER, Wilf.   There Goes My Everything.   RCA KXL 1-0119 (Canada)
   CMP   Feb.   p32.   400w.   4

1587   CARVER, Johnny.   Strings.   ABC Dot ABCD 864
   CMR   Feb.   p31.   75w.   1

1588   CASH, Johnny.   Collection.   Pickwick PDA 005 (E) (Reissue)
   CMP   Oct.   p21.   75w.   3

1589   CASH, Johnny.   Hello, I'm Old Golden Throat.   Charly (E)
   CAC   Nov.   p310.   150w. $3\frac{1}{2}$

1590 CASH, Johnny. I Forgot to Remember to Forget. Hallmark
      SHM 884 (E) (Reissue)
          CMP April p19. 100w. 3

1591 CASH, Johnny. Look at Them Beans. Columbia KC 33814
          CAC Jan. p415. 200w. 3
          CM   Feb. p45-6. 600w. $2\frac{1}{2}$
          CMP Jan. p26-7. 200w. 4
          PMS V4/#3 p189. 50w. 4

1592 CASH, Johnny. The Making of a Legend. Charly (E) (Re-
      issue)
          CAC April p27. 200w. 3

1593 CASH, Johnny. One Piece at a Time. Columbia KC 34193.
      Cart. CA-34193. Cass. CT 34193
          CM   Sept. p56. 100w. 4
          CMP Sept. p21. 300w. 5
          CMR Aug. p26-7. 1175w. 4
          SR   Oct. p91-2. 250w. 5

1594 CASH, Johnny. The Original. Charly (E) (Reissue)
          MM   Nov. 27 p24. 175w. $2\frac{1}{2}$

1595 CASH, Johnny. Strawberry Cake. Columbia KC 34088.
      Cart. CA-34088. Cass. CT-34088
          CM   July p55, 58. 500w. 3
          CMP May p18. 350w. 5
          CMR Aug. p30. 300w. 4
          SR   Aug. p72-3. 225w. 4

1596 CASH Singers, Johnny. A Tie That Binds. Mark Town TO
      14176 (Netherlands)
          CMR Oct. p33. 150w. 0

1597 CATO, Connie. Good-Hearted Woman. Capitol ST 11387
          CMR March p31. 325w. $2\frac{1}{2}$

1598 CHALKER, Curly. Nashville Sundown. Sonet SNTF 694 (E)
          CMR Aug. p34. 150w. 3

1599 CHARLEY Boy. Introducing. Release BRL 4076 (E)
          CMP Oct. p29. 100w. 3
          CMR Aug. p28. 150w. $2\frac{1}{2}$

1600 CHAVIN, Chinga. Country Porn. Country Porn CP 666
          CM   Dec. p65. 250w. 1
          RS   Oct. 21 p109. 225w. 0

1601 CHRISTENSON, Terry. First Visit. Corner Store C1001
      (Canada)
          CC   April p34. 50w. 3

1602 CHRISTENSON, Terry. The Ghosts of 40 Thieves. Corner
      Store C1002 (Canada)
         CC Sept. p30. 50w. 3

1603 CLARK, Guy. Old no. 1. RCA APL1-1303
         CIR April 8 p14. 175w. 4
         CMP July p29. 400w. 5
         CMR June p29-30. 225w. $2\frac{1}{2}$
         CRA April p75. 200w. $2\frac{1}{2}$
         CRE April p12. 25w. 4
         MM June 5 p19. 750w. $4\frac{1}{2}$
         PMS V4/#4 p192. 50w. 4
         RS Feb. 26 p76-7. 150w. 3

1604 CLARK, Guy. Texas Cookin'. RCA APL1 1944. Cass.
      APS1 1944
         CIR Dec. 30 p17-8. 625w. 4
         CM Dec. p63. 350w. 4
         MG Oct. p70. 150w. 3
         MG Dec. p63. 50w. 2
         MM Nov. 6 p27. 750w. $4\frac{1}{2}$

1605 CLARK, Roy. In Concert. ABC Dot DOSD 2054. Cart.
      DOSD-2054M
         CM Nov. p63. 275w. 4
         CMP Sept. p31. 325w. 2
         GP Oct. p97. 50w. $4\frac{1}{2}$
         MG Oct. p70. 50w. 1

1606 CLARK, Roy. Heart to Heart. ABC DOSD 2041
         MG Jan. p40. 50w. $3\frac{1}{2}$
         MG Feb. p54. 50w. $1\frac{1}{2}$

1607 CLINE, Patsy. Have You Ever Been Lonely. MCA MCF
      2725 (E) (Reissue)
         CMP Feb. p19. 200w. 3
         CMR Feb. p28. 125w. 3

1608 COATES, Ann. That Star Belongs to Me. Westwood WRS
      081 (E)
         CMP March p27. 50w. 3
         CMR March p32. 75w. $1\frac{1}{2}$

1609 COE, David Allen. Longhaired Redneck. Columbia KC
      33916. Cass. CA 33916
         CM Aug. p54-5. 250w. 3

1610 COLTER, Jessi. Jessi. Capitol ST-11477. Cart. 8XT-11477
         CMP July p27. 350w. 3
         CMR June p30. 125w. $2\frac{1}{2}$
         MG April p54. 50w. 3
         MM April 17 p21. 450w. 3
         RS April 8 p77. 150w. $3\frac{1}{2}$

SR   June   p78.   175w.   4

1611   COLTER, Jessi.   Diamond in the Rough.   Capitol ST-11543.
       Cart. 8XT-11543.   Cass. 4XT-11543
           CRA   Oct.   p78-9.   175w. $1\frac{1}{2}$
           CS   Dec.   p43.   250w. $1\frac{1}{2}$
           RS   Oct. 7   p82.   175w.   3
           SR   Dec.   p104.   150w.   3

1612   CONNOR, Randy.   My First Album.   ABC DOSD 4028
           CMP   Nov.   p41.   100w.   2
           CS   Nov.   p41.   100w.   2

1613   CONNORS, Stompin' Tom.   The North Atlantic Squadron.
       Boot BOS 7153 (Canada)
           CC   March   p38.   50w.   3

1614   CONNORS, Stompin' Tom.   The Unpopular.   Boot BOS 7171
       (Canada)
           CC   Nov.   p32.   50w.   3

1615   COOLEY, Spade.   Club of Spade 00102/3 (2 discs)
           JEMF   Winter '74   p211.   100w.   3

1616-7   COUNTRY Confusion.   Country Side of Home.   Westwood
         WRS 088 (E)
           CMP   Oct.   p29.   50w.   2

1618   COUNTRY Life.   Sing Me a Country Song.   Westwood WRS
       083 (E)
           CMP   March   p27.   100w.   3
           CMR   Aug.   p28.   50w. $1\frac{1}{2}$

1619   COUNTRY Revue.   Westwood WRS 087 (E)
           CMP   Oct.   p29.   75w.   3

1620   COUNTRY Road.   Our Home Country.   Tank BSS 110 (E)
           CMR   Feb.   p31-2.   150w. $2\frac{1}{2}$

1621   CRAMER, Floyd.   Class of '74 and '75.   RCA APL1 1191
           MG   Jan.   p40.   50w.   3

1622   CRAMER, Floyd.   Floyd Cramer Country.   RCA APL1 1541
           CK   Aug.   p45.   200w. $4\frac{1}{2}$
           MG   June   p55.   175w.   4

1622a   CROW, Alvin and the Pleasant Valley Boys.   Long Neck LP
        001.   Cart. 8T 001
           CM   May   p50-1, 54.   375w.   4

1623   CULPEPPER Country.   Your Request, Our Pleasure.   Pixie
       PIX 0004 (E)
           CMR   May   p29.   250w.   1

1624 CURLESS, Dick. End of the Road. Hilltop JS 6147 (Reissue)
      CMR Jan. p31. 125w. 1

1625 DANIELS, Charlie. Nightride. Kama Sutra KSLP 7009 (E)
      CMR April p41. 75w. $2\frac{1}{2}$

1626 DANIELS, Charlie. Saddletramp. Epic PE 34150. Cart. EA
      34150
      CM Sept. p57. 100w. 3

1627 DAVE and Sugar. RCA APL1 1818
      CYR Nov. 4 p36. 200w. $2\frac{1}{2}$

1628 DAVIS, Skeeter. The Versatile Skeeter Davis. RCA LSA
      3269 (E) (Reissue)
      CMP Aug. p32. 350w. 5
      CMR Aug. p30. 100w. $2\frac{1}{2}$

1629 DAVIS, Skeeter and Bobby Bare. Tunes for Two. RCA LSA
      3252 (E) (Reissue)
      CMP April p20. 350w. 5
      CMR Aug. p32. 100w. $3\frac{1}{2}$
      MM April 17 p21. 50w. 3

1630 DAVIS, Mac. Forever Lovers. Columbia PC 34105
      MM June 26 p22. 50w. $1\frac{1}{2}$

1631 DAY, Jimmy. All Those Years. Midland MD JD 10010
      CMP Oct. p32. 300w. 5

1632 DEAN, Jimmy. I.O.U. Casino GRT 8014
      CMP Sept. p29. 450w. 2

1633 DENVER, Jeannie. Queen of the Silver Dollar. Westwood
      WRS 094 (E)
      CMP March p27. 200w. 4
      CMR Feb. p27. 775w. $3\frac{1}{2}$

1634 DEREK, John. Songs I Have Written ... With a Little Help
      From My Friends. Westwood WRS 098 (E)
      CMP Oct. p29. 150w. 4
      CMR Nov. p29. 225w. 1

1635 DEREK, John and Country Fever. The Country Trail. Mas-
      kerade FWS 3881 (E)
      CMR Dec. p26-7. 550w. 5
      MM Dec. 11 p22. 75w. 3

1636 DEVINE, Sydney. Doubly Devine. Philips 6625 019 (E)
      CMP July p28. 375w. 4

1637 DEVINE, Sydney. The Very Best of. Emerald Gem GES
      1142 (E) (Reissue)

CMP   July   p28.   100w.   3
CMR   June   p31.   75w. $1\frac{1}{2}$

1638   DEXTER, Ray.   Sound Show, Act I.   Sweet Folk and Country
SFA 142 (E)
CMR   May   p32-3.   300w. $3\frac{1}{2}$

1639   DIAMOND Accordion Band.   25 Great Country Hits.   Emerald
Gem GES 1145 (E) (Reissue)
CMR   June   p33.   25w.   0

1640   DOTTSY.   The Sweetest Thing.   RCA APL1-1358
CMP   Sept.   p23.   400w.   5
CMR   Aug.   p32.   200w.   3
CS   Aug.   p38.   150w.   2
MG   May   p56.   50w. $2\frac{1}{2}$

1641   DRUSKY, Roy.   Country Classics.   Philips International 6336
261 (E) (Reissue)
CMP   Jan.   p25.   50w.   4

1642   DUDLEY, Dave.   1776.   United Artists UALA 625 G
CMP   Dec.   p30.   200w.   5
CS   Oct.   p45.   75w. $2\frac{1}{2}$

1643   DUDLEY, Dave.   Uncommonly Good Country.   United Artists
UALA 512 H
CM   June   p47.   400w.   2

1644   DUFFY Brothers.   Wild Over Us.   Country Music Records
CFHR 074 (E)
CMP   Feb.   p30.   75w.   3

1645   DUNCAN, Johnny.   The Best of Johnny Duncan.   Columbia
KC 34243 (Reissue)
CMP   Sept.   p30-1.   200w.   3
CMR   Sept.   p32.   125w.   1

1646   EDWARDS, Stoney.   Blackbird.   Capitol ST 11499
CRE   Sept.   p14.   75w.   4
CYR   Nov. 4   p36.   200w.   5

1647   EDWARDS, Stoney.   Mississippi You're On My Mind.   Capitol
ST 11401
CMR   April   p41.   150w.   3

1648   EMMONS, Buddy.   Sing Bob Wills.   Flying Fish 017
CMP   Sept.   p20.   375w.   5
CS   Nov.   p40.   100w. $2\frac{1}{2}$
GP   Aug.   p81.   25w.   3

1649   EMMONS, Buddy.   Steel Guitar.   Flying Fish 007
OTM   Spring   p61.   50w.   1

1650 EVERLY, Phil. Mystic Line. Pye 12121
      MG May p56. 25w. 3

1651 EVERLY Brothers. Songs Our Daddy Taught Us. Philips
      6467500 (E)
      CMR March p29. 125w. 3

1652 FAIRCHILD, Barbara. Columbia KC 33974
      PMS V4/#3 p189. 25w. 4

1653 FAMILY Brown. I Am the Words, You Are the Music. RCA
      KVL 1-0167 (Canada)
      CC Dec. p30. 100w. 3

1654 FARGO, Donna. On the Move. Warner Bros. BS 2926.
      Cart. M8-2926. Cass. M5-2926
      CMR Aug. p30. 150w. $2\frac{1}{2}$
      SR Aug. p74. 250w. 3

1655 FARGO, Donna. Whatever I Say Means I Love You. ABC/
      Dot DOSD-2029. Cart. 8310-2029H
      SR April p83. 150w. 3

1656 FELLER, Dick. Some Days Are Diamonds. Elektra/Asylum
      7E 1044
      MG Jan. p40. 50w. 3
      PMS V4/#3 p190. 25w. 4

1657 FELTS, Narvel. Greatest Hits, vol. 1. ABC DOSD 2036
      (Reissue)
      CMR Feb. p30. 150w. $2\frac{1}{2}$
      MG Jan. p40. 50w. 3

1658 FELTS, Narvel. Narvel the Marvel. ABC DOSD 2033
      CMR Oct. p32-3. 75w. 2
      MG June p55. 50w. 1

1659 FENDER, Freddy. Are You Ready for Freddy. ABC DOSD
      2044
      CM Feb. p45. 550w. 3
      CMP March p19. 250w. 2
      CMR April p39. 200w. 2
      PMS V4/#4 p192. 25w. $2\frac{1}{2}$
      RS Jan. 1 p57, 59. 250w. $2\frac{1}{2}$

1660 FENDER, Freddy. If You're Ever in Texas. ABC Dot 2061
      MG Dec. p67. 125w. 3

1661 FENDER, Freddy. Rock 'n' Country. ABC/Dot 2050
      CM June p47. 400w. $3\frac{1}{2}$
      CMR May p30. 175w. $2\frac{1}{2}$
      CRE July p12. 75w. 4
      MG May p56. 125w. $3\frac{1}{2}$

MM   June 26   p21.   125w. $2\frac{1}{2}$

1662   FENDER, Freddy.   Since I Met You Baby.   GRT 8005 (Re-issue)
      MG   Jan.   p40.   75w.   3

1663   FORD, Tennessee Ernie.   For the 83rd Time.   Capitol ST 11561
      MG   Dec.   p67.   250w. $1\frac{1}{2}$

1664   FOSTER, Jodie.   Good Morning Country Rain.   Westwood WRS 073 (E)
      CMR   Jan.   p31.   300w. $2\frac{1}{2}$

1665   FRANCIS, Connie & Hank Williams Jr.   Great Country Favourites.   MGM Special 3140 115 (E) (Reissue)
      CAC   Dec.   p355.   75w.   3
      CMP   Sept.   p22.   250w.   2
      MM   Aug. 21   p18.   25w. $2\frac{1}{2}$

1666   FRICKER, Thom.   Summer of Roses.   Sweet Folk and Country SFA 041 (E)
      CMR   May   p33.   250w. $2\frac{1}{2}$

1667   FRIZZELL, Lefty.   Remembering the Greatest Hits of.   Columbia KC 33882 (Reissue)
      CM   March   p59.   375w. $2\frac{1}{2}$
      CMP   Feb.   p34.   375w.   3
      PMS   V4/#3   p190.   25w.   3

1668   GALBRAITH, Bob.   Throw Me a Bone.   RCA APL1-1747
      MG   Oct.   p70.   100w. $3\frac{1}{2}$

1669   GARRETT's Texas Opera Co.   Classical Country.   Ranwood R8156
      CS   Nov.   p40.   100w. $2\frac{1}{2}$

1670   GAYLE, Crystal.   United Artists UALA614G.   Cart. UAEA614H.   Cass.   UACA614H
      CAC   Oct.   p276.   175w.   3
      CMP   Nov.   p40.   250w.   4
      CMR   Jan.   p29.   850w. $4\frac{1}{2}$
      CS   Dec.   p43.   200w.   3
      MM   Sept. 18   p24.   400w. $3\frac{1}{2}$
      RS   Nov. 4   p76.   175w. $2\frac{1}{2}$
      SR   Dec.   p106-7.   150w. $4\frac{1}{2}$

1671   GAYLE, Crystal.   Somebody Loves You.   United Artists UALA543G
      CMR   April   p42.   350w. $4\frac{1}{2}$

1672   GIBSON, Don.   Don't Stop Loving Me.   DJM20477 (E)
      CAC   Oct.   p276.   50w.   3

     CMP   Oct.   p23.   275w.   3
     CMR   Nov.   p32-3. 100w.   1
     MM   Aug. 21 p18.   25w. $3\frac{1}{2}$

1673 GIBSON, Don. Four Sides of. DJM (2 discs) (E)
     MM   Nov. 27 p28.   50w.   3

1674 GIBSON, Don. The Very Best of Don Gibson. London SHE
     8487 (E) (Reissue)
     CMP   Feb.   p14.   450w.   4
     CMR   Jan.   p31.   125w.   3

1675 GILLEY, Mickey. Crazy Cajun CCLP1006 (Reissue)
     CM   Feb.   p46.   550w. $2\frac{1}{2}$

1676 GILLEY, Mickey. Smokin'. Playboy 415
     MG   Dec.   p67.   100w.   3

1677 GIMBLE, Johnny. Texas Dance Party. Columbia KC 34284
     RS   Dec. 16 p93-4.   150w.   5

1678 GLASER, Tompall. The Great Tompall & His Outlaw Band.
     Polydor 2315 364 (E)
     CAC   Oct.   p276.   200w.   2
     CM   May   p55-6.   425w.   4
     CMP   Aug.   p32.   500w.   3
     CMR   Nov.   p29.   575w.   4
     CRE   July p12.   25w.   3
     MG   May   p56.   50w.   3
     RS   April 22 p65, 67.   325w.   4

1679 The GOOD Old Boys. Pistol Pickin Mama. Round Records
     LA 597G
     CMP   Sept.   p21.   300w.   3
     CMR   Sept.   p31-2.   200w. $3\frac{1}{2}$

1680 GOODACRE, Tony. Grandma's Feather Bed. Outlet SBOL
     4021 (Northern Ireland)
     CMP   Feb.   p30.   150w.   5

1681 GOODFOOT. Get on the Goodfoot. Real RR 2009 (E)
     CMP   Oct.   p29.   75w.   3

1682 GRAND, Johnny. Country Contrast. Lismore LILP 5034 (E)
     CMR   March p32.   75w. $2\frac{1}{2}$

1683 GREEN, Lloyd. Steel Rides. Monument K2 33368
     CMP   May   p19.   350w.   5
     CMR   Aug.   p29.   150w. $3\frac{1}{2}$
     MM   May 15 p24.   50w.   4

1684 GREEN, Lloyd. Ten Shades of Green. Midland MDLG 10009
     (E)

CMP   Oct.   p32.   300w.   5

1685   GREENE, Jack.   The Best of Jack Greene.   MCA MCF 2748
       (E) (Reissue)
            CMP   Aug.   p29.   400w.   5
            CMR   June   p31.   100w.   3
            MM   May 15   p26.   50w. $2\frac{1}{2}$

1686   GREER, John and Ann Coates.   Two Loves.   Homespun HRL
       109 (E)
            CMP   March   p27.   50w.   2
            CMR   Feb.   p28.   50w.   0

1687   GRIFF, Ray.   Capitol ST 11486
            CMR   Sept.   p33.   150w.   3

1688   GRINDERSWITCH.   Pullin Together.   Capricorn 0173
            CS   Nov.   p40.   100w. $2\frac{1}{2}$

1689   GUEST, Billy.   A Tribute to Don Messer.   Audat 477-4011
       (Canada)
            CMR   Nov.   p31.   450w. $3\frac{1}{2}$

1690   HAGGARD, Merle.   It's All in the Movies.   Capitol ST 11483.
       Cart. 8ST 11483
            CM   July   p58.   350w.   2
            CMR   May   p29.   225w. $2\frac{1}{2}$
            MG   May   p56.   50w.   3

1691   HAGGARD, Merle.   My Love Affair with Trains.   Capitol ST
       11544.   Cart. 8XT-11544.   Cass. 4XT-11544
            CM   Oct.   p56.   150w.   4
            CMP   Sept.   p29.   325w.   5
            CMR   Oct.   p28.   650w. $4\frac{1}{2}$
            CS   Oct.   p44.   325w. $3\frac{1}{2}$
            SR   Dec.   p107, 110.   225w.   3

1692   HAGGARD, Merle.   A Tribute to the Best Damn Fiddle Player
       in the World.   Capitol ST 638
            CMR   Feb.   p32.   125w. $2\frac{1}{2}$

1693   HAGUE, Mel and the New Westerners.   Look LK/LP 6023 (E)
            CMP   Oct.   p29.   150w.   2
            CMR   June   p31.   200w.   3

1694   HALL, Tom T.   Country Classics.   Philips International
       6336 262 (E) (Reissue)
            CMP   Jan.   p25.   75w.   5

1695   HALL, Tom T.   Faster Horses.   Mercury SRM 1-1076
            CM   Oct.   p57.   250w.   4
            CRE   July   p12.   50w.   4
            MG   June   p55.   175w.   4

1696 HALL, Tom T. Greatest Hits, vol. 2. Mercury SRM 1-1044
(Reissue)
      MG Jan. p40. 50w. 3
      MG Feb. p53. 50w. 3

1697 HAMILTON, George IV. 16 Great Performances. ABC ABCL
5178 (E) (Reissue)
      CMR Sept. p30. 250w. 2
      MM May 22 p25. 75w. 2

1698 HAMILTON, George IV. This Is. RCA DHYK0008 (2 tapes
only) (E) (Reissue)
      CAC Dec. p355. 150w. $4\frac{1}{2}$

1699 HAMILTON, George IV. Trendsetter. RCA LSA 3229 (E)
      CAC Jan. p415. 100w. 3
      CMR March p32. 225w. $2\frac{1}{2}$

1700 HARGROVE, Linda. Love, You're the Teacher. Capitol ST-
11463
      CMR June p30. 125w. 2
      MG Jan. p40. 125w. $3\frac{1}{2}$

1701 HARRIS, Emmylou. Elite Hotel. Reprise MS2236. Cart.
M8-223. Cass. M5-223
      AU May p79-80. 300w. 4
      CAC May p72. 125w. 3
      CIR May 13 p16. 275w. $2\frac{1}{2}$
      CMP April p19. 450w. 4
      CMR May p29. 300w. 4
      CRA April p75. 150w. 3
      CRE April p62. 200w. 3
      CRE April p72. 50w. 3
      GR April p1670. 100w. $4\frac{1}{2}$
      LP April p19. 200w. $3\frac{1}{2}$
      MG April p54. 50w. 3
      MM Jan. 17 p34. 625w. 5
      PRM Jan. p29. 400w. 3
      RR March p73. 50w. $2\frac{1}{2}$
      RS Feb. 26 p79. 350w. $3\frac{1}{2}$
      SR May p83-4. 200w. 4

1702 HARRIS, Emmylou. Pieces of the Sky. Reprise MS 2213
      CAC May p72. 125w. 3

1703 HART, Freddie. The First Time. Capitol ST-11449
      MG Jan. p40. 50w. 3

1704 HART, Freddie. Presents the Heartbeats. Capitol ST 11431
      CMR Feb. p30. 75w. 0

1705 HAWAIIAN Meets Country. Westwood WRS 075 (E)
      CMR March p32. 100w. $1\frac{1}{2}$

1706 HAYNES, Reg and the Outfit. Phoney World. DTS 009 (E)
        CMP Oct. p29. 200w. 5

1707 HAZELWOOD, Lee. These Boots Are Made for Walkin'.
        MGM 2354036 (E) (Reissue)
        CMP Nov. p41. 150w. 1

1708 HEAD, Roy. Head First. ABC Dot 2051
        MG July p58. 125w. 3

1709 HENDERSON, Kelvin. Slow Moving Outlaw. Windmill WMO
        250 (E)
        CMP Feb. p30. 100w. 4

1710 HILLSIDERS. To Please You. Precision Stile (E)
        CAC April p27. 200w. 3

1711 HOLLY, Buddy. Nashville Sessions. Coral CDLM 8038 (E)
        RR Feb. p67. 25w. 3

1712 HOSFORD, Larry. Crosswords. Shelter SRL 52003
        CS Nov. p30. 100w. 4
        CYR Oct. 21 p28. 150w. 4½

1713 HOUSTON, David. Greatest Hits. Epic EPC 69190 (E) (Re-
        issue)
        CMP Jan. p27. 200w. 3

1714 HOUSTON, David. What a Night. Epic KE 33948
        CMR Aug. p29. 150w. 2½

1715 HUBBARD, Ray Wylie and the Cowboy. Twinkies. Reprise
        MS2231
        CMR March p29-30. 150w. 3
        CRA April p75. 225w. 2
        RS Feb. 26 p76-7. 175w. 3

1716 HUNTER, Tommy. RCA KPL1-0088 (Canada)
        OLR June p107-8. 25w. 4

1717 INMAN, Jerry. You Betchum! Elektra 7ES-1068
        RS Nov. 18 p76-7. 250w. 4

1718 JACKSON, Wanda. I'll Still Love You. DJM (E) (Reissue)
        MM Nov. 20 p26. 50w. 2

1719 JAMES, Sonny. The Southern Gentleman. Columbia KC 33846
        MG Jan. p40. 50w. 2½

1720 JAMES, Sonny. 200 Years of Country Music. Columbia KC
        34035. Cart. CA-34035
        CM June p48, 50. 800w. 2½
        CMP Sept. p22. 350w. 5

CMR   April   p39.   300w. $3\frac{1}{2}$
CS   June   p38.   150w. $4\frac{1}{2}$
MG   April   p54.   50w. $3\frac{1}{2}$
MM   July 24   p25.   25w.   3
SR   May   p84.   225w. $2\frac{1}{2}$

1721   JENNINGS, Frank.   Heaven Is My Woman's Love.   One-Up
OU 2139 (E)
CMP   Oct.   p22.   300w.   5
CMR   Sept.   p29.   600w.   4

1722   JENNINGS, Waylon.   Are You Ready for the Country.   RCA
APL1-1816.   Cart. APS1-1816.   Cass. APK1-1816
CAC   Dec.   p355.   200w. $3\frac{1}{2}$
CIR   Sept. 28   p15.   200w.   4
CM   Oct.   p56.   200w.   4
CMP   Dec.   p13.   250w.   3
CS   Nov.   p41.   100w.   3
CYR   Nov. 4   p36.   200w.   2
RS   Sept. 23   p115.   325w.   3
SR   Oct.   p104-6.   1200w.   4

1723   JENNINGS, Waylon.   The Best of Waylon Jennings.   RCA
LSP-4341.   Cart. APS-1577.
SR   Oct.   p104-6.   200w.   4

1724   JENNINGS, Waylon.   Dreaming My Dreams.   RCA APL1-1062.
Cart. APS1-1062.   Cass. APK1-1062
CMR   Sept.   p33-4.   300w.   3
PMS   V4/#3   p189.   50w.   4
SR   Oct.   p104-6.   200w.   4

1725   JENNINGS, Waylon.   Good Hearted Woman.   RCA LSP 4647.
Cart. APS 1886.   Cass. APK 1886
SR   Oct.   p104-6.   200w.   4

1726   JENNINGS, Waylon.   Honky Tonk Heroes.   RCA APL1-0240.
Cart. APS1-0240.   Cass. APK1-0240
SR   Oct.   p104-6.   200w.   4

1727   JENNINGS, Waylon.   Ladies Love Outlaws.   RCA LSP 4751.
Cart. APS 2016.   Cass. APK 2016
SR   Oct.   p104-6.   200w.   4

1728   JENNINGS, Waylon.   Lonesome, On'ry and Mean.   RCA LSP
4854.   Cart. APS 2136.   Cass. APK 2136
SR   Oct.   p104-6.   200w.   4

1729   JENNINGS, Waylon.   Music from Mackintosh & T.J.   RCA
APL1-1520.   Cart. APS1-1520.   Cass. APK1-1520
CM   July   p52.   425w.   2
SR   Oct.   p104-6.   200w.   4

1730 JENNINGS, Waylon. The Ramblin' Man. RCA APL1-0734.
      Cart. APS1-0734. Cass. APK1-0734
          SR Oct. p104-6. 200w. 4

1731 JENNINGS, Waylon. Singer of Sad Songs. RCA LSP 4418.
      Cart. APS 1625. Cass. APK 1625
          SR Oct. p104-6. 200w. 4

1732 JENNINGS, Waylon. The Taker/Tulsa. RCA LSP 4487.
      Cart. APS 1695. Cass. APK 1695
          SR Oct. p104-6. 200w. 4

1733 JENNINGS, Waylon. This Time. RCA-APL1-0539. Cart.
      APS1-0539. Cass. APK1-9539
          SR Oct. p104-6. 200w. 4

1734 JENNINGS, Waylon, Willie Nelson and the Waylors. RCA
      APL1-1520
          CMR Oct. p29. 400w. 2

1735 JOHNSON, Kenny and Northwind. Lakeside Highway. North
      West Gramaphone NWG 76103 (E)
          CMP Oct. p29. 100w. 4
          CMR Aug. p12. 500w. 4

1736 JOHNSON, Lois. Lois Johnson. 20th Century T465
          CMP Feb. p32. 325w. 3

1737 JONES, George. Alone Again. Epic KC 34290. Cart. EA
      34150
          CM   Dec. p63. 475w. 4
          CMR Dec. p25. 600w. $4\frac{1}{2}$
          MG   Oct. p70. 100w. $2\frac{1}{2}$

1738 JONES, George. The Battle. Epic KE-34034. Cart. EA-
      34034
          CM   June p45.   350w. $2\frac{1}{2}$
          CMP   May p17.   350w. 5
          CMR   June p31-2. 150w. $2\frac{1}{2}$
          MM   May 1 p30. 50w. 3
          RS   June 3 p69. 175w. 4

1739 JONES, George. The Best of the Best. RCA LSA 3251 (E)
      (Reissue)
          CMP May p20. 350w. 3

1740 JONES, George. Memories of Us. Epic KE-33547. Cart.
      EA-33547
          CM   Feb. p45. 225w. 2
          CMP March p20. 200w. 5

1741 JONES, George and Tammy Wynette. Golden Ring. Epic
      KE34291. Cart. EA34291. Cass. ET34291

CYR   Nov. 18 p36.   150w.   1½
SR   Dec.   p110.   100w.   3

1742   JONES, George and Melba Montgomery.   We Must Have Been Out of Our Minds.   RCA LSA 3230 (E) (Reissue)
CMP   Feb.   p14.   300w.   5

1743   JONES, Grandpa.   Everybody's Grandpa.   Monument BZ 33873 (2 discs) (Reissue)
CMR   Jan.   p31.   200w.   2½

1744   JONES, Grandpa.   What's for Supper.   Monument KZ 32939
CMR   April   p36.   250w.   2½

1745   JONES, Grandpa.   Story.   CMH 9007 (2 discs).   Cart. CMH-8-9007
CM   Sept.   p57.   150w.   3
OTM   Summer   p24-5.   125w.   3½
PIC   Dec.   p50.   150w.   3½

1746   JUICE Newton and Silver Spurr.   RCA APL1 1004.   Cart. APS1 1004
CM   Aug.   p55.   275w.   3½

1747   KERSHAW, Doug.   Louisiana Man.   DJM DJB 26080 (E) (Reissue)
CMP   Dec.   p12-3.   225w.   5

1748   KERSHAW, Doug.   Ragin' Cajun.   Warner Bros. BS 2910.   Cart. B8 2910
CM   Nov.   p62-3.   150w.   3
CRE   Dec.   p14.   25w.   3½
CS   Nov.   p41.   100w.   3½

1749   KERSHAW, Rusty and Doug.   Louisiana Man.   DJM DJB 26080 (E) (Reissue)
CAC   Nov.   p310.   175w.   3½
CMR   Nov.   p30.   600w.   4½
MM   Oct. 16   p25.   125w.   4½

1750   KINDA Country.   Cartwheel.   Westwood WRS 103 (E)
CMR   Nov.   p32.   250w.   2½

1751   KING, Pete.   My Kind of Country.   Tank BSS114
CMR   Jan.   p30.   650w.   4

1752   LANG, Peter.   Lycurgus the Wolf Driver.   Flying Fish Records, FF 014
GP   Feb.   p70.   175w.   4

1753   LEE, Brenda.   LA Sessions.   MCA 2233
RS   Dec. 30   p70.   175w.   0

1754 LEE, Joni. MCA 2194
      CMP Dec. p30. 175w. 4

1755 LEE, Wilma and Stoney Cooper. Satisfied. DJM (E)
      (Reissue)
      MM Dec. 11 p22. 75w. 4

1756 LEGG, Adrian. The All Around Gigster. Guitar 104
      (E)
      CMR Oct. p30. 375w. 1½

1757 LEWIS, Jerry Lee. Boogie Woogie Country Man. Mercury
      SRM 1-1030
      CMP Feb. p32. 250w. 5

1758 LEWIS, Jerry Lee. Country Roots. Charly (E)
      CAC April p27-8. 100w. 3

1759 LEWIS, Jerry Lee. Golden Hits. Philips Int'l 6336245 (E)
      (Reissue)
      CMP Nov. p40. 100w. 3

1760 LEWIS, Jerry Lee. Odd Man In. Mercury SRM1-1064
      RS March 25 p56, 58. 200w. 1½

1761 LIMEY. RCA SF 8463 (E)
      CMP July p27. 300w. 2

1762 LOCKLIN, Hank. MGM 4986
      CMR Jan. p30-1. 150w. 3

1763 LOCKLIN, Hank. Famous Country Music Makers. RCA DPS
      2060 (E) (2 discs) (Reissue)
      CMP Feb. p19. 300w. 5
      CMR June p31. 125w. 4

1764 LYMAN, Ray and Philomena Begley. Best of. Country
      SMLP 001 (E) (Reissue)
      CMP May p28. 100w. 4
      CMR Oct. p34. 100w. 3

1765 LYNCH, Lee. Introducing. Hit HTL 5007 (E)
      CMP May p28. 75w. 3

1766 LYNN, Loretta. Country Roads. MCA Coral CDL 8045 (E)
      (Reissue)
      CMP May p18. 300w. 5
      MM March 13 p25. 50w. 2½

1767 LYNN, Loretta. When the Tingle Becomes a Chill. MCA
      2179
      CM June p45. 350w. 2

CMR April p42. 125w. $2\frac{1}{2}$
CRE June p72. 50w. 4
CS Aug. p38. 150w. $1\frac{1}{2}$
MG May p56. 50w. $3\frac{1}{2}$

1768 LYNN, Loretta & Conway Twitty. Feelin's. MCA
2143
CMP Jan. p27. 175w. 3

1769 LYNN, Loretta and Conway Twitty. United Talent. MCA
2209
CMP Dec. p13. 200w. 3
MG Sept. p63. 75w. 3
MM Oct. 16 p25. 125w. $1\frac{1}{2}$

1770 McCALL, C. W. Black Bear Road. MGM M3G-5008. Cart.
M88-5008
CM May p49-50. 300w. 1
CMP April p19. 350w. 2
CMR May p31-2. 100w. $2\frac{1}{2}$
MG Jan. p40. 50w. $3\frac{1}{2}$
MM April 3 p33. 200w. 4

1771 McCALL, C. W. Wilderness. Polydor PD-1-6069. Cart.
8T-1-6069. Cass. CT-1-6069
CAC Sept. p230. 100w. 3
CMP Aug. p31. 375w. 2
CMR Oct. p33. 150w. 0
CRE July p65. 275w. 2
MG July p58. 100w. $1\frac{1}{2}$
SR Sept. p96. 150w. 0

1772 McCALL, C. W. Wolf Creek Pass. MGM 4989
CMR May p31-2. 100w. $2\frac{1}{2}$

1773 McCLINTON, Delbert. Genuine Cowhide. ABC 959
MG Oct. p70. 200w. 5
RS Aug. 23 p117. 300w. $3\frac{1}{2}$

1774 McCORMACK, Mose. Beans and Make Believe. CMH
6205
CS Oct. p44. 75w. $2\frac{1}{2}$

1775 McCOY, Charlie. Harpin' the Blues. Monument KZ 33802.
Cart. ZA 33802
AU April p85-6. 350w. 3
CM April p48-9. 475w. 3
MG April p54. 200w. 3
PMS V4/#3 p193. 25w. 3
SR April p84. 275w. $4\frac{1}{2}$

1776 McCRIMMON, Dan. Dreams, Lies and Whispers. Biscuit

City BC 1304CF
   LP   Jan.   p20.   200w.   2

1777 McEVOY, Johnny.   Sings Hank Williams.   Hawk HALPX 130
(E)
   CMR   March   p32.   100w. $2\frac{1}{2}$

1778 McEVOY, Johnny and Gloria South.   Golden Duets.   Hawk
HALPX 140 (E)
   CMR   Feb.   p31.   50w.   2

1779 McFARLAND, Billy.   Golden Guitar.   Outlet SBOL 4012 (E)
   CMR   Aug.   p28.   50w. $1\frac{1}{2}$

1780 McGILL, Hugo and the Willhire Band.   Truckin' Country.
GW   101 (E)
   CMR   Oct.   p31.   450w.   2

1781 MAGGARD, Cledus and the Citizen's Band.   The White Knight.
Mercury SRM 1-1072
   CMR   Oct.   p33.   100w. $2\frac{1}{2}$
   MG   May   p56.   200w. $2\frac{1}{2}$

1782 MAHAN, Larry.   King of the Rodeo.   Warner BS 2529
   CS   Nov.   p41.   75w. $2\frac{1}{2}$

1783 MANDRELL, Barbara.   This Is Barbara Mandrell.   ABC
Dot 2045
   CMP   Sept.   p21.   300w.   4
   CMR   Nov.   p30.   125w.   3

1784 MANIFOLD, Keith.   Danny Boy.   Westwood WRS 096 (E)
   CMP   March   p27.   200w.   3
   CMR   March   p29.   175w. $1\frac{1}{2}$

1785 MASKELL, Rick and Pam Maskell.   Sounds of London.   Look
LK/LP 510 (E)
   CMP   March   p27.   100w.   4

1786 MAVERICKS.   Country Dream.   Westwood WRS 079 (E)
   CMP   May   p28.   75w.   3
   CMR   Aug.   p28.   50w. $2\frac{1}{2}$

1787 MEYERS, Augie and the Western Head Band.   Live at the
Longneck.   Texas Re-cord LP 1002
   CRA   April   p75.   225w.   2
   RS   Feb. 12   p94.   200w.   3

1788 MILLER Brothers.   Louisville.   Westwood WRS 977 (E)
   CMP   May   p28.   75w.   3
   CMR   March   p32-3.   100w. $2\frac{1}{2}$

1789 MILLS, Mick.   Music.   Westwood WRS 084 (E)

1790   MILSAP, Ronnie.   Warner BS 2870
            MG   Feb.   p53.   75w.   3

1791   MILSAP, Ronnie.   Mr. Mailman.   DJM DJSLM 2036 (E) (Re-
        issue)
            CAC   Oct.   p276.   150w. $3\frac{1}{2}$
            CMP   Dec.   p19-20.   175w.   1
            CMR   Sept.   p32.   250w. $2\frac{1}{2}$

1792   MILSAP, Ronnie.   Night Things.   RCA APL1-1223
            CMP   March   p25.   250w.   5
            CMR   Sept.   p31.   150w. $2\frac{1}{2}$
            MG   Jan.   p40.   100w.   4

1793   MILSAP, Ronnie.   20-20 Vision.   RCA APL1-1666
            CM   Sept.   p58.   175w.   3
            CMP   Nov.   p41.   200w.   3
            MM   Sept. 18   p21.   25w.   3

1794   MOFFATT, Katy.   Columbia KC 34172
            CMR   Sept.   p31.   125w. $3\frac{1}{2}$
            RS   Sept. 23   p119.   250w.   3

1795   MOLE City Ramblers.   Kentucky in the Morning.   Westwood
        WRS 093 (E)
            CMP   Oct.   p29.   125w.   4

1796   MONTGOMERY, Melba.   The Greatest Gift of All.   Elektra/
        Asylum CM 6
            MG   Feb.   p53.   50w.   3

1797   MOODY, George.   Country Roads.   Raven KS 1017 (E)
            CMP   Oct.   p29.   125w.   4

1798   MOONSHINE Steel.   Raw Edges.   Look LK 6033 (E)
            CMP   May   p28.   125w.   3
            CMR   Aug.   p28.   75w. $1\frac{1}{2}$

1799   MORGAN, George.   Remembering the Greatest Hits of.
        Columbia KC 33894 (Reissue)
            CMP   Feb.   p34.   50w.   3
            PMS   V4/ #3   p190.   25w.   3

1800   MOUNTAINEERS.   Sweet Country Music.   Release DRL 2006
        (E)
            CMR   Feb.   p28.   150w.   2

1801   MURPHEY, Michael.   Swans Against the Sun.   Epic PE 33851
            MG   Feb.   p53.   50w. $1\frac{1}{2}$

1802   MURRAY, Anne.   Together.   Capitol ST 11433.   Cart. 8ST 11433
            CM   April   p49-50.   350w. $1\frac{1}{2}$
            CYR   Nov. 18   p36.   150w.   3

1803 NELSON, Pete. The Road That Leads Me Home. Westwood
      WRS 090 (E)
            CMP   May p28. 75w. 2
            CMR   March p33. 75w. 1

1804 NELSON, Willie. Classic. United Artists UAS 29945 (E)
            MM June 26 p21. 125w. 2½

1805 NELSON, Willie. Country Willie. United Artists UALA
      410G. Cass. UALA410H
            CM March p58-9. 250w. 1½

1806 NELSON, Willie. Famous Country Music Makers. RCA DPS
      2062 (E) (2 discs) (Reissue)
            CMP Feb. p19. 350w. 5
            CMR Jan. p31. 350w. 3½

1807 NELSON, Willie. Live. RCA APL1-1487
            CM   Sept. p56. 100w. 4
            MG   July p58. 50w. 3
            MM   Nov. 13 p25. 100w. 2½

1808 NELSON, Willie. Red Headed Stranger. Columbia KC 33482
            CMP April p20-1. 350w. 3
            CMR April p41-2. 125w. 4
            MM   March 13 p23. 450w. 3

1809 NELSON, Willie. The Sound in Your Mind. Columbia KC
      34092. Cart. CA-34092. Cass. CT-34092
            AU   Sept. p82. 550w. 4
            CIR June 1 p17. 325w. 1½
            CM   July p51-2. 550w. 4½
            CMP Aug. p29, 30. 400w. 3
            CMR June p30. 350w. 4
            MG   June p55. 50w. 3½
            MM   June 26 p21. 125w. 2½
            RS   June 3 p73, 75. 700w. 2½
            SR   Aug. p79. 250w. 2

1810 NELSON, Willie. The Troublemaker. Columbia/Lone Star
      KC 34112. Cass. CA 34112
            CM   Dec. p62. 550w. 5
            MM   Nov. 13 p25. 100w. 2½

1811 NELSON, Willie. What Can You Do to Me Now. RCA APL1-
      1234. Cass. APS1 1234
            CM   March p58-9. 250w. 2
            CMR Feb. p30. 175w. 2
            MG   Feb. p53. 75w. 4

1812 NESMITH, Michael. Best. RCA RS 1064 (E) (Reissue)
            CMP Dec. p19. 225w. 5

1813 NEWTON-JOHN, Olivia. Clearly Love.   MCA MCA-2148.
      Cart. MCAT-2148.   Cass. MCAC-2148
          CRE   Jan.   p67.   325w.   2
          LP   Jan.   p11.   125w.   3
          MG   Jan.   p33.   50w. $2\frac{1}{2}$
          SR   March p86-7. 175w.   3

1814 NEWTON-JOHN, Olivia. Come On Over.   MCA MCA-2186.
      Cart. MCAT-2186.   Cass. MCAC-2186
          CM   July   p51.   450w.   3
          CMP   Aug.   p30.   350w.   3
          MM   May 22 p22.   200w.   1
          PRM   April p24.   25w. $1\frac{1}{2}$
          SR   Aug.   p79.   175w.   2

1814a NOLAN, Dick.   RCA KXL 1-0096 (Canada)
          OLR   June   p108.   25w. $3\frac{1}{2}$

1815 ORBISON, Roy. Focus on.... London (2 discs) (E)
          CAC   Oct.   p26.   100w. $3\frac{1}{2}$
          MM   Sept. 18 p21.   25w.   3

1816 ORBISON, Roy. I'm Still in Love with You.   Mercury
      SRM-1-1045.   Cart. MC-8-1045
          CM   Jan.   p57.   450w. $3\frac{1}{2}$
          CRE   Feb.   p61.   275w.   3
          MG   Jan.   p40.   50w.   3
          MG   Feb.   p73.   50w.   1

1817 OVERSTREET, Tommy. Greatest Hits, vol. 1.   ABC Dot
      2027 (Reissue)
          CMR   March p29.   125w. $1\frac{1}{2}$

1818 OVERSTREET, Tommy. I'm a Believer. ABC Dot 2016
          CMP   Jan.   p25.   200w.   3

1819 OVERSTREET, Tommy. Live from the Silver Slipper. Dot
      DOSD 2038.   Cart. DOSD-8-2038
          CM   April p50.   475w.   2
          CMP   Feb.   p34.   325w.   1

1820 OVERSTREET, Tommy. Turn on To. ABC DOSD 2056
          CMP   Dec.   p12.   175w.   5
          CS   Dec.   p43.   150w.   3

1821 OWENS, Buck. Best of, vol. 3.   Capitol ST 11471 (Reissue)
          CMR   June   p31.   125w.   3

1822 OWENS, Buck. Buck 'em. Warner BS 2952.   Cart. BS 2952
          CM   Oct.   p57.   100w.   3
          CMP   Dec.   p31.   225w.   5
          CMR   Oct.   p33.   150w. $3\frac{1}{2}$
          CS   Nov.   p41.   100w.   3

1823   OXFORD, Vernon. I Just Want to Be a Country Singer.   RCA
       LSA 3281 (E)
              CMR Dec.   p26.   275w.   4
              MM   Nov. 27 p28.   75w. $2\frac{1}{2}$

1824   OZARK Mountain Daredevils.   It'll Shine When It Shines.
       A&M SP 3654
              CMR Feb.   p32.   100w. $3\frac{1}{2}$

1825   NOACK, Eddie.   Look LK 6041 (E)
              CMR Dec.   p25.   150w. $1\frac{1}{2}$

1826   NUTT, Wayne.   Oil Field Man.   Epic EPC 69232
              CMP May p17.   325w.   4
              CMR April p36.   550w.   4
              MM   March 6 p27.   100w. $1\frac{1}{2}$

1827   PACHECO, Tom.   Swallowed Up in the Great American
       Heartland.   RCA APL 1 - 1254.   Cart. APS1-1254
              CM   May p54-5.   250w.   3
              CMP Sept.   p30.   450w.   3

1828   PARKER, Wayne.   Oklahoma Twilight.   Ariola America ST
       50005
              RS   May 6 p73-4.   250w.   2

1829   PARTON, Dolly.   Dolly.   RCA APL1-1221.   Cart. APS1-1221
              CM   Jan.   p56.   350w.   2
              CMP March p20.   300w.   5
              CMR June p29.   200w.   3
              CRE Feb.   p72.   50w. $2\frac{1}{2}$
              CS   June p38.   225w.   1
              MG   Feb.   p53.   50w.   3
              MM   Feb. 28 p24.   175w. $2\frac{1}{2}$

1830   PARTON, Dolly.   All I Can Do.   RCA APL1-1665
              CMP Nov.   p41.   250w.   5
              CMR Nov.   p29-30.   400w. $1\frac{1}{2}$
              CRE Dec.   p60.   350w. $2\frac{1}{2}$
              CRE Dec.   p70.   75w.   3
              CS   Dec.   p42.   300w. $4\frac{1}{2}$
              CYR Oct. 21 p28.   150w.   3
              MM   Oct. 16 p25.   125w.   3
              RS   Oct. 21 p875. $4\frac{1}{2}$

1831   PARTON, Dolly.   The Best of Dolly Parton Vol. 2.   RCA
       LSA 2222 (E) (Reissue)
              CAC Jan.   p415.   75w.   3
              CMP Feb.   p21.   200w.   5
              CMR Sept.   p34.   300w.   3
              MM   March 13 p25.   125w.   3

1832   PARTON, Dolly.   Hello, I'm Dolly/As Long As I Love.

Monument BZ33876 (2 discs) (Reissue)
CMR   Feb.   p29.   150w.   2

1833   PARTON, Dolly.   The World of Dolly Parton.   Monument
MNT 88192 (E) (Reissue)
CMP   May   p19-20.   450w.   4

1834   PARTON, Stella.   I Want to Hold You in My Dreams Tonight.
Soul, Country and Blues LPN 6006 (E)
CMR   March   p29.   350w. $3\frac{1}{2}$

1835   PAYCHECK, Johnny.   Juke Box Charlie.   Emerald Gem GES
1144 (E) (Reissue)
CMP   Sept.   p21.   400w.   4
CMR   Aug.   p29.   250w. $1\frac{1}{2}$

1836   PAYCHECK, Johnny.   Eleven Months and 29 Days.   Epic
KC 33943.   Cart.   EA 33943
CM   Dec.   p65.   400w.   4
MG   Oct.   p70.   225w.   4

1837   PAYNE, Jimmy and Friends.   Live at Broadmoor Hospital.
Ocean OCL 3001 (E)
CMP   March   p18.   200w.   4

1838   PAYNE, Roy.   Outlaw Heroes.   RCA KXL1-0163 (Canada)
CC   Dec.   p32.   75w. $2\frac{1}{2}$

1839   PAYNE, Wayne.   Willie's Yellow Pickup Truck.   RCA KXL1-
0098 (Canada)
OLR   June   p108.   25w. $4\frac{1}{2}$

1840   PEDERSEN, Herb.   Southwest.   Epic PE 34225
CS   Dec.   p43.   200w.   3

1841   PEDERSON, Louis III.   Rodeo No. 1 Sport.   Broadland BR
1916 (Canada)
OLR   Dec.   p256.   25w.   4

1842   PERKINS, Carl.   Greatest Hits.   Embassy EMB 31259 (E)
(Reissue)
CMP   Nov.   p40.   100w.   3

1843   PERKINS, Carl.   Guitar Pickin, Rock Singin Country Boy.
Charly (E)
CAC   April   p28.   150w.   3

1844   PERKINS, Carl.   The Original.   Charly CR 30110 (E) (Reissue)
MM   Nov. 27   p24.   175w. $2\frac{1}{2}$

1845   PERKINS, Carl.   Rocking Guitarman.   Charly (E)
CMR   May   p33.   100w. $2\frac{1}{2}$

1846 PLACE, Mary Kay. Tonite at the Capri Lounge. Columbia
      PC 34353
           CRA Dec. p76. 475w. $2\frac{1}{2}$
           RS Dec. 16 p85. 225w. 3

1847 PLANE, Dave. One Tree Hill. Westwood WRS 076 (E)
           CMP Jan. p27. 250w. 5

1848 PLAYBOYS. Made in the Country. Tank BSS 118 (E)
           CMR May p30-1. 250w. $3\frac{1}{2}$

1849 POWELL, Patsy. Thank You for Loving Me. Country Music
      Folk Heritage CFHR 073 (E)
           CMR Aug. p27, 29. 550w. 4

1850 PRICE, Ray. Best of. Columbia KC 34160 (Reissue)
           MG Sept. p63. 50w. $2\frac{1}{2}$

1851 PRICE, Ray. For the Good Times/I Won't Mention It Again.
      Columbia CG 33633 (2 discs) (Reissue)
           CMR April p40. 125w. 2

1852 PRICE, Ray. Rainbows and Tears. ABC 2053. Cart. DOSD
      2053M
           CM Oct. p58. 150w. 3
           CM Nov. p61-2. 250w. 1
           CMP Oct. p30. 200w. 3

1853 PRICE, Ray. Say I Do. ABC DOSD 2037. Cart. DOSD-8-
      2037
           CM April p47-8. 700w. 0

1854 PRIDE, Charley. RCA DHYK0002 (E) (2 Tapes only) (Reissue)
           CAC Dec. p355. 125w. 4

1855 PRIDE, Charley. Best of, vol. 3. RCA APL 1-2023 (Re-
      issue)
           CMR Dec. p26. 150w. 3
           MM Nov. 20 p29. 75w. $3\frac{1}{2}$

1856 PRIDE, Charley. Charley. RCA APL1-1038
           CAC Jan. p415. 25w. $2\frac{1}{2}$
           CMR Jan. p30-1. 175w. 1

1857 PRIDE, Charley. The Happiness of Having You. RCA APL1-
      1241
           CMR May p32. 100w. $2\frac{1}{2}$
           MM March 20 p22. 50w. 2

1858 PRIDE, Charley. Sample. RCA (E) (Reissue)
           CAC Jan. p415. 75w. $3\frac{1}{2}$

1859 PROPHET, Ronnie. RCA KPL1-0164 (Canada)

CYR Nov. 18 p36. 150w. $1\frac{1}{2}$

1860 PRUETT, Jeanne. Honey on His Hands. MCA 479
CMR Aug. p31. 150w. 2

1861 PRUETT, Jeanne. Welcome to the Sunshine. MCA MCF
2768 (E)
CMP Dec. p12. 200w. 5
MM Oct. 2 p30. 50w. 3

1862 RABBITT, Eddie. Rocky Mountain Music. Elektra 7E-1065.
Cart. ET 81065
CM Aug. p53. 200w. $2\frac{1}{2}$
CMR Oct. p28-9. 225w. $1\frac{1}{2}$
CS Oct. p44. 500w. $4\frac{1}{2}$
MG Sept. p63. 50w. 3

1863 RAINWATER, Marvin. Especially for You. Westwood WRS
101 (E)
CMR Nov. p30. 300w. $2\frac{1}{2}$

1864 RAYE, Susan. Honey, Toast and Sunshine. Capitol ST 11472
CMR Sept. p33. 125w. $1\frac{1}{2}$

1865 REED, Jerry. Red Hot Picker. RCA APL 1-1226
GP May p81. 50w. $3\frac{1}{2}$
MG Jan. p40. 50w. 3

1866 REED, Jerry. Both Barrels. RCA APL1-1861. Cart. APS1
1861
CM Dec. p67. 200w. 4
CYR Oct. 21 p28. 150w. $1\frac{1}{2}$
GP Dec. p104. 125w. $2\frac{1}{2}$
GP Dec. p104. 50w. 3

1867 REEVES, Jim. I Love You Because. RCA APL1-1224 (Reissue)
MG April p54. 50w. 3

1868 RICH, Charlie. Favourites. RCA Starcall HYK1024 (E) (Re-
issue)
CAC July p153. 175w. $3\frac{1}{2}$
CMP July p27. 75w. 2
MM April 3 p29. 50w. $2\frac{1}{2}$

1869 RICH, Charlie. Greatest Hits. Epic PE-34240. Cart. PA-
3240 (Reissue)
CAC Sept. p230. 250w. $3\frac{1}{2}$
CM Oct. p57. 75w. 4
CMP Sept. p23. 300w. 4
CMR Oct. p31. 125w. $3\frac{1}{2}$
MG Sept. p63. 25w. 3

1870 RICH, Charlie. I Do My Swingin at Home. Embassy EMB
      31212 (E) (Reissue)
            CMP April p21. 350w. 5

1871 RICH, Charlie. Lonely Weekends. Charly CR 300004 (E)
      (Reissue)
            CMR May p33. 100w. 2½

1872 RICH, Charlie. Silver Linings. Epic KE-33545. Cart.
      EA-33545
            CM July p52. 300w. 1½
            CMP July p27. 400w. 3

1873 RITTER, Tex. An American Legend. Capitol SKC 11241
      (3 discs) (Reissue)
            CRA Nov. p74. 100w. 3

1874 RITTER, Tex. Deck of Cards. Music for Pleasure
      MFP50237 (E) (Reissue)
            CMR Feb. p30. 200w. ½

1875 RITTER, Tex. Everyday in the Saddle. Ember CW 146
      (E) (Reissue)
            CMP Aug. p30. 350w. 4
            CMR Aug. p34. 400w. 2½

1876 RITTER, Tex. The Singing Cowboy. MCA Coral 6283341
      (2 discs) (W. Germany) (Reissue)
            CMR Oct. p29-30. 600w. 4½
            JEMF Spring p50-1. 200w. 3

1877 ROBBINS, Marty. Collection. Hallmark PDA 018 (E) (Re-
      issue)
            CMP Oct. p21. 75w. 3

1878 ROBBINS, Marty. El Paso City. Columbia KC 34303
            CMP Oct. p30-1. 250w. 3
            CS Dec. p43. 300w. 2
            MM Oct. 16 p25. 75w. 2½

1879 ROBBINS, Marty. The Fastest Gun Around. Hallmark SHM
      878 (E) (Reissue)
            CMP April p21. 300w. 3
            CMR Feb. p31. 100w. 1½

1880 ROBBINS, Marty. No Sign of Loneliness Here. Columbia
      C33476
            CMR May p30. 125w. 2½

1881 ROBBINS, Marty. Two Gun Daddy. MCA 342
            CAC Sept. p230. 200w. 3
            CMP Oct. p22. 300w. 5

1882 ROBERTS, Billy. Thoughts of California. Tulip Records,
      TLP-2001
          GP Jan. p71. 25w. 3

1883 RODRIGUEZ, Johnny. Country Classics. Philips International
      6336 259 (E) (Reissue)
          CMP Jan. p25. 75w. 4

1884 RODRIGUEZ, Johnny. Greatest Hits. Mercury SRM1-1078
      (Reissue)
          MG June p55. 25w. $2\frac{1}{2}$

1885 RODRIGUEZ, Johnny. Love Put a Song in My Heart. Mer-
      cury SRM-1-1057. Cart. Mc-8-1057
          CM May p55. 250w. $1\frac{1}{2}$

1886 ROE, Tommy. Energy. Monument PZ 34182
          CM Sept. p58. 150w. 3

1887 ROGERS, Kenny. Love Lifted Me. United Artists UALA607G
          CS Oct. p45. 350w. 2

1888 ROGERS, Roy. Happy Trails to You. Twentieth Century
      T467 (Reissue)
          CRA Nov. p74. 50w. 3

1889 ROMAINE, Anne. Gettin' on Country. Rounder 3009
          CS Nov. p40. 75w. $2\frac{1}{2}$

1890 RONSTADT, Linda. Different Drummer. Capitol VMP 1010
      (E) (Reissue)
          CMR Feb. p30. 75w. 2

1891 RONSTADT, Linda. Hasten Down the Wind. Asylum 7E-1072.
      Cart. ET 8 1072
          CM Nov. p63-4. 500w. 2
          CS Dec. p43. 200w. $4\frac{1}{2}$

1892 RONSTADT, Linda. Prisoner in Disguise. Asylum 7E-1045.
      Cart. ET8 1045   Cass. TC5 1045
          CM March p57-8. 750w. $3\frac{1}{2}$
          CS June p38. 200w. 2
          HF Jan. p104. 200w. 3

1893 ROSS, Danny. Flat Top Pickin. Stoneway STY 107
          CMR Oct. p30. 50w. $\frac{1}{2}$

1894 ROSS, Jeris. ABC DOSD 2046
          PMS V4/#3 p190. 50w. 4

1895 RYE Whiskey Band. I Dreamed of Highways. Country Music
      CFHRO 72 (E)
          CMP May p28. 75w. 4

CMR Feb. p32.   350w. $2\frac{1}{2}$

1896 SADDLETRAMPS.   Westwood WRS 069 (E)
        CMP   Feb.   p30.   75w.   2
        CMP   May   p28.   75w.   3

1897 SANDERS, Harlan.   Off and Running.   Epic KE 34305
        CMR   Dec.   p26.   125w. $3\frac{1}{2}$

1898 SAYER, Pete.   And His Grand Ole Opry Road Show.   Trans-
        atlantic Xtra 1156 (E)
        CMP   Jan.   p29-30.   105w.   4

1899 SCHULLER, Gunther.   Country Fiddle Band.   Columbia M
        33981.   Cart. MA 33981
        BGU   Dec.   p29.   200w. $1\frac{1}{2}$
        CM   Nov.   p62.   200w.   3
        CRE   Dec.   p70.   125w.   4
        SR   Nov.   p114.   175w. $3\frac{1}{2}$

1900 SHEPARD, Jean.   I'm a Believer.   United Artists UA-
        LA525G.   Cart. UA-EA525H
        CM   March   p60.   350w.   3
        CMP   July   p27.   300w.   5
        MM   May 15   p26.   50w. $2\frac{1}{2}$

1901 SHEPARD, Jean.   Mercy, Ain't Love Good.   United Artists
        UALA 609G
        CAC   Sept.   p230.   275w.   3
        CMP   Oct.   p22.   350w.   5
        CMR   Oct.   p30.   125w.   3
        CS   Oct.   p44.   25w. $2\frac{1}{2}$
        MM   Aug. 21   p18.   25w.   3

1902 SHEPPARD, T. G.   Melodyland ME 40151 (E)
        CMR   Feb.   p33.   300w.   2

1903 SHILOH Country.   First Acre.   Westwood WRS 085 (E)
        CMP   Oct.   p29.   75w.   2
        CMR   March   p32.   100w.   2

1904 SHUCKS.   Two Days, Two Tracks.   Sweet Folk and Country
        SFA 052 (E)
        CMR   Aug.   p28.   125w. $2\frac{1}{2}$

1905 SIOUX, Tammi.   Act Naturally.   Sweet Folk and Country SFA
        037 (E)
        CMR   Aug.   p28.   250w.   1

1906 SLIM Pickins.   The Fiddlin Fool.   Westwood WRS 086 (E)
        CMP   May   p28.   125w.   4
        CMR   Aug.   p29.   350w.   4

1907   SMITH, Cal.   Cal's Country.   MCA 485
      CMP   May   p18.   375w.   5

1908   SMITH, Cal.   Jason's Farm.   MCA 2172
      CMR   April   p37.   250w.   3

1909   SMITH, Connie.   The Song We Fell in Love To.   Columbia
      KC 33918
      CMP   May   p19.   350w.   5
      MM   May 15   p24.   50w. $2\frac{1}{2}$

1910   SMITH, Margo.   Twentieth Century T490
      MG   Feb.   p53.   50w.   3

1911   SMITH, Sammi.   As Long as There's a Sunday.   Elektra
      7E-1058
      CMP   Oct.   p31.   500w.   5

1912   SMITH, Sammi.   Sunshine.   Mega MLPS 611.   Cart.   ML8
      611
      CM   Jan.   p59-60.   700w.   2

1913   SMITH and Son.   Battling Banjos/Guitars Galore.   Monument
      BZ33861 (2 discs) (Reissue)
      CMR   Feb.   p29.   250w. $3\frac{1}{2}$

1914   SNOW, Hank.   You're Easy to Love.   RCA APL1-0908
      CAC   Jan.   p415.   50w. $4\frac{1}{2}$

1915   SOUTHERN Eagle String Band.   Hee Haw Hallelujah.   String
      901 (E)
      CMP   Feb.   p30.   75w.   5

1916   SOVINE, Red.   Little Rosa.   Hit HITL 5008 (E) (Reissue)
      CMP   May   p17-8.   225w.   4

1917   SOVINE, Red.   Teddy Bear.   Starday SD 968X.   Cart.   SD 8
      968X
      CM   Nov.   p61.   100w.   0
      MG   Oct.   p70.   100w. $1\frac{1}{2}$
      MM   Dec. 11   p22.   75w. $2\frac{1}{2}$

1918   SPEARS, Billie Jo.   United Artists UALA508
      CMR   Feb.   p33.   200w.   1
      MG   Feb.   p53.   75w.   3

1919   SPEARS, Billie Jo.   The Best of Billie Jo Spears.   Capitol
      Vine VMP 1012 (E) (Reissue)
      CMP   May   p17.   300w.   5
      CMR   Sept.   p33.   125w.   3

1920   SPEARS, Billy Jo.   Blanket on the Ground.   United Artists
      UALA 390G

CAC   Feb.   p446.   175w.   3

1921   SPEARS, Billie Jo.   What I've Got in Mind.   United Artists
       UALA 608G
              CMP Oct.   p22.   225w.   4
              CMR Oct.   p31.   200w. $2\frac{1}{2}$
              CS Oct.   p44.   350w.   3

1922   SPENCER, Johnny.   Country Gamble.   Sweet Folk and Country
       SFA 035 (E)
              CMP   March p27.   50w.   2

1923   STAMPLEY, Joe.   All These Things.   ABC DOSD 2059.
       Cart. DOSD 2059M
              CM Oct.   p58.   150w.   3

1924   STAMPLEY, Joe.   Billy Get Me a Woman.   Epic KE 33546
              MG Feb.   p53.   50w. $2\frac{1}{2}$

1925   STANLEY, Pete and Roger Knowles.   Picking & Singing.
       Transatlantic XTRA 1146 (E)
              CMP Jan.   p25.   225w.   5
              OTM Spring p60-1.   375w.   4

1926   STARR, Kenny.   Man in the Bleachers.   MCA 2177
              MG April p54.   50w. $2\frac{1}{2}$

1927   STATLER Brothers.   The Best of the Statler Brothers.   Mer-
       cury SRM1-1037 (Reissue)
              CMP Feb.   p20.   175w.   5
              CMR April p40.   125w.   3
              MM Jan. 31 p23.   50w.   4

1928   STATLER Brothers.   Country Classics.   Philips International
       6336 263 (E) (Reissue)
              CMP Jan.   p25.   850w.   5

1929   STATLER Brothers.   Harold, Lew, Phil and Don.   Mercury
       SRM 1-1077
              MG Jan.   p55.   25w. $2\frac{1}{2}$

1930   STEAGALL, Red.   Lone Star Beer and Bob Wills Music.
       ABC DOSD 2055.   Cart. DOSD 8 2055
              CM Oct.   p57-8.   100w.   3

1931   STEAL 'n' Corn.   Westwood WRS 078 (E)
              CMP May p28.   75w.   2
              CMR Aug.   p28.   50w. $2\frac{1}{2}$

1932   STEVENSON, B. W.   We Be Sailin'.   Warner BS 2901.   Cart.
       B8 2901
              CM Aug.   p55.   250w.   2

1933 STEWART, Gary. Steppin Out. RCA APL1-1225
      CIR April 27 p14. 225w. $2\frac{1}{2}$
      CMP April p21. 300w. 4
      CRM Dec. p26. 75w. $2\frac{1}{2}$
      HF June p99. 225w. 3
      MG April p54. 50w. 3
      RS March 25 p56. 600w. $3\frac{1}{2}$

1934 STONE Mountain Boys. Songs of the Pioneers. Old Home-
      stead OHRC 90032
      OTM Autumn p26. 125w. 3

1935 STUCKEY, Nat. Independence. MCA 2184
      CMP Sept. p22. 350w. 5
      CMR Nov. p31. 250w. $3\frac{1}{2}$
      CS Aug. p38. 150w. 3
      MG June p55. 25w. $3\frac{1}{2}$

1936 SWAN, Billy. Monument PZ 34183. Cart. PZA 34183
      CM Sept. p57. 300w. 5
      RS June 17 p57. 350w. 3

1937 SWAN, Billy. Rock 'n' Roll Moon. Monument PZ 33805.
      Cart. PZA-33805
      CM Jan. p56. 450w. $3\frac{1}{2}$
      CMP Jan. p25-6. 200w. 2

1938 TAYLOR, Carmol. Song Writer. Elektra 7E-1069. Cart.
      7E 8 1069
      CM Nov. p61. 125w. 3

1939 TAYLOR, Chip. This Side of the Big River. Warner Bros.
      BS 2882
      CMP Feb. p20. 150w. 4
      CMR March p31. 275w. 3

1940 TENNESSEE Singers. Country Comfort. DJM DJSL 067 (E)
      (Reissue)
      CMP Feb. p20. 175w. 1

1941 TENNESSEE Stud. Free Country. Westwood WRS 062 (E)
      CMP March p27. 100w. 3
      CMR March p32. 75w. $1\frac{1}{2}$

1942 THEORET, Sandy. Sing Me a Love Song. Boot BOS 7164
      (Canada)
      CMR Oct. p33. 200w. $1\frac{1}{2}$

1943 THOMPSON, Hank. Back in the Swing of Things. ABC Dot
      2060
      CMP Dec. p13. 200w. 5
      CMR Dec. p25-6. 250w. 4
      CS Dec. p42. 100w. $2\frac{1}{2}$

      MG   Dec.   p67.   175w.   3
      MM   Dec. 4 p21.   475w. $4\frac{1}{2}$
      MM   Dec. 25 p19.   300w. $4\frac{1}{2}$

1944   THOMPSON, Hank.   Sings the Hits of Nat King Cole.   ABC
      DOSD 2032
          CM   March p59-60.   525w.   3
          CMR   Feb.   p31.   75w.   0

1945   THOMPSON, Sue.   Story.   DJM DJD 28024 (2 discs) (E) (Re-
      issue)
          CMP   Dec.   p19.   250w.   2

1946   THREEWHEEL.   Westwood WRS 068 (E)
          CMP   March p27.   75w.   2
          CMR   Jan. p32-3.   125w.   3

1947   TILLIS, Mel & Statesiders.   M-M-Mel.   MGM G 5002
          CMP   Jan.   p26.   250w.   5
          CMR   March p30.   150w. $2\frac{1}{2}$

1948   TILLIS, Mel.   Best of.   MGM G 5021.   Cart. 8T 1 5021
      (Reissue)
          CM   Nov.   p62.   150w.   3

1949   TILLIS, Mel.   Love Revival.   MCA 2204
          CMP   Oct.   p21.   250w.   3
          MG   Sept.   p63.   50w. $3\frac{1}{2}$

1950   TRAVERS, Dave.   Long Black Veil.   Spark ZCS 81062 (E)
          CMP   Dec.   p19.   250w.   5

1951   TRAVIS, Merle.   The Merle Travis Guitar.   Capitol SM 650
      (Reissue)
          CM   Feb.   p52.   500w.   3

1952   TRENT, Buck.   Bionic Banjo.   ABC Dot DOSD 2058
          CMP   Sept.   p29-30.   450w.   2
          CS   Nov.   p40.   100w. $3\frac{1}{2}$

1953   TUBB, Ernest.   MCA 496
          CMR   April   p36.   225w.   3

1954   TUCKER, Tanya.   Here's Some Love.   MCA 2213
          CS   Dec.   p43.   100w.   3
          MG   Dec.   p67.   50w. $2\frac{1}{2}$
          MM   Nov. 20 p28.   200w. $4\frac{1}{2}$

1955   TUCKER, Tanya.   Lovin' and Learnin'.   MCA 2167.   Cart.
      MCAT 2167.   Cass. MCAC 2167
          CM   April   p52.   250w.   4
          CMP   Dec.   p12.   275w.   4
          HF   May   p105.   200w. $2\frac{1}{2}$

MG April p54. 50w. 3
MM April 3 p32. 325w. 3
RS April 11 p62-3. 325w. $3\frac{1}{2}$
SR May p96. 200w. $1\frac{1}{2}$

1956 TWITTY, Conway. The Best of Conway Twitty. MCA MCF
2737 (E) (Reissue)
CMP Aug. p29. 300w. 5

1957 TWITTY, Conway. Now and Then. MCA MCA 2206. Cart.
MCAT 2206
CM Sept. p56. 100w. 4
CMP Oct. p21. 250w. 5

1958 TWITTY, Conway. This Time I've Hurt Her More Than She
Loves Me. MCA 2176. Cart. MCA 8 2176
CM June p47-8. 400w. $3\frac{1}{2}$
CS June p38. 150w. 3

1959 TYSON, Ian. Ol 'Eon. A&M SP 9017 (Canada)
OLR June p108. 25w. $4\frac{1}{2}$

1960 VINCENT, Gene. A Tribute to My Best Friend. Capitol 2C
06681618 (France) (Reissue)
CMR March p30. 125w. $2\frac{1}{2}$

1961 WAGONER, Porter. Sing Some Love Songs. RCA APL1-1056
CMP Jan. p26. 175w. 2
CMR Sept. p34. 150w. 0

1962 WAGONER, Porter and Dolly Parton. Say Forever You'll Be
Mine. APL1-1116
CMP Feb. p20. 250w. 3
CMR April p40. 125w. 3
MM Jan. 31 p23. 50w. $1\frac{1}{2}$

1963 WALKER, Billy. Portrait of/Darling Days. Monument BZ
33858 (2 discs) (Reissue)
CMR Feb. p29. 150w. $2\frac{1}{2}$

1964 WALLACE, Jerry. MGM M3G 5007
MG Jan. p40. 50w. 3

1965 WARHURST, Ray and Dick Damron. Northwest Rebellion.
Westwood WRS 102 (E)
CMP April p19. 300w. 4
CMR Oct. p32. 150w. $1\frac{1}{2}$

1966 WATSON, Gene. Love in the Hot Afternoon. Capitol ST-
11443. Cart. 8xT-11443
CMR Feb. p32. 125w. $2\frac{1}{2}$
MG Jan. p40. 50w. $3\frac{1}{2}$
SR Jan. p94. 300w. 3

210   Record Reviews, 1976

1967 WEAVER, Dennis. McCloud Country. DJM DJ4 20479 (E)
          CAC Nov. p310. 75w. $2\frac{1}{2}$
          CMR Nov. p30. 100w. $1\frac{1}{2}$

1968 WELLER, Freddy. ABC Dot DOSD 2026
          CMR Aug. p29. 100w. $2\frac{1}{2}$

1969 WELLER, Freddy. Greatest Hits. Columbia KC 33883
          CMR April p39. 100w. $2\frac{1}{2}$

1970 WELLER, Freddy. Liquor, Love and Life. Columbia KC
      34244. Cart. CA 34244
          CM   Oct. p56. 150w. $3\frac{1}{2}$
          CMP Dec. p30. 225w. 5

1971 WELLS, Kitty. The Kitty Wells Story. MCA MCF 2743 (E)
      (Reissue)
          CMP Aug. p29. 300w. 5
          CMR Nov. p31. 100w. $4\frac{1}{2}$

1972 WELLS, Tracy. Give Daddy Back to Me. Homespun HRL
      108 (Northern Ireland)
          CMP Feb. p30. 50w. 2
          CMR March p30. 75w. 3

1973 WEST, Dodie. Walk Through the World. Decca SKL 5232
          CMP Aug. p31. 300w. 4
          CMR Aug. p31. 150w. 3

1974 WEST, Dottie. Carolina Cousins. RCA APL1-1041
          CMP Jan. p27. 225w. 3

1975 WEST, Hedy. Love, Hell and Biscuits. Bear Family BF
      15003 (West Germany)
          CMR Nov. p29. 400w. 4
          OTM Summer p23. 350w. 5

1976 WHITE, Tony Joe. Best of. Warner (E) (Reissue)
          MM   March 13 p25. 75w. 3

1977 WHITMAN, Slim. Everything Leads Back to You. United
      Artists UALA513G. Cart. UALA513H
          CM   April p52. 625w. 4

1978 WHITMAN, Slim. The Very Best of Slim Whitman. United
      Artists UAS 29898 (E) (Reissue)
          CMP March p18. 275w. 5

1979 WIER, Rusty. Twentieth Century T 495. Cart. T8 495
          CM   April p50, 52. 400w. 2

1980 WILDWOOD. Easy Come, Easy Go. Westwood WRS 095 (E)
          CMP Oct. p29. 75w. 2

CS Dec. p42. 200w. $2\frac{1}{2}$

1981 WILLIAMS, Don. Harmony. ABC Dot 2049
MG July p58. 150w. 4

1982 WILLIAMS, Don. V. 1/2. ABC ABCL 5153/4 (E) (2 discs)
(Reissue)
CMR Feb. p28. 100w. 4
MM Jan. 31 p23. 100w. $1\frac{1}{2}$

1983 WILLIAMS, Don. Greatest Hits. ABC DOSD 2035 (Reissue)
MG Jan. p40. 50w. 4

1984 WILLIAMS, Hank. The Collector's Hank Williams, Vol. 1.
MGM 2353 118 (E) (Reissue)
CMP Feb. p14. 500w. 5
CAC Jan. p415. 150w. $3\frac{1}{2}$
CMR Feb. p29-30. 300w. 4

1985 WILLIAMS, Hank. Live at the Grand Ole Opry. MGM 2353
128 (E) (Reissue)
CRA Nov. p77. 150w. 4

1986 WILLIAMS, Hank, Jr. MGM M3G 5009. Cart. M8H5009
CAC Sept. p230. 100w. 3
CM May p54. 425w. 4
CMR Oct. p33. 275w. 3
CRE Aug. p78. 50w. $4\frac{1}{2}$
RS April 8 p64, 66. 1500w. 4
SR June p90. 125w. 4

1987 WILLIAMS, Hank, Jr. 14 Greatest Hits. MGM MG 1 5020.
Cart. 8T 1 5020 (Reissue)
CM Nov. p60. 150w. 4
CMP Oct. p32. 300w. 5

1988 WILLIAMS, Leona. San Quentin's First Lady. MCA MCA-
2212. Cart. MCAT 2212
CM Dec. p65. 300w. 3
CMR Oct. p33. 50w. 0

1989 WILLS, Bob. In Concert. Capitol SKBB 11550. Cart. 8XVV
11550 (2 discs) (Reissue)
CM Dec. p62-3. 550w. 4
CS Dec. p43. 100w. 3
MG Dec. p67. 250w. 3
RS Oct. 7 p87. 250w. 3

1990 WILLS, Bob. The Legendary. Columbia P 212922. Cart.
P8 212922 (Reissue)
CM March p60. 475w. $2\frac{1}{2}$

1991 WILLS, Bob. Remembering the Greatest Hits of. CBS (Re-

issue) (E)
    CMP Oct. p30. 250w. 1

1992 WILLS, Bob/Asleep at the Wheel.   Fathers and Sons.   Epic
    BG 33782 (2 discs)
    CMR Feb. p33. 150w. $3\frac{1}{2}$

1993 WILLS, Dave. Everybody's Country. Epic KE 33548. Cart.
    EA 33548
    CM   Feb. p48. 450w. $1\frac{1}{2}$
    MG   Feb. p53. 75w. $3\frac{1}{2}$

1994 WITHERS, Tex. Tex Withers. RCA LSA 3265 (E) (Reissue)
    CMP July p27. 250w. 2
    MM   April 3 p29. 50w. 2

1995 WYLDE, Stacy. Heaven from Now On. Look LK 6025 (E)
    CMR Aug. p30-1. 450w. 3

1996 WYNETTE, Tammy. I Still Believe in Fairy Tales. Epic
    KE-33582. Cart. EA-33582
    CM   Feb. p45. 225w. $3\frac{1}{2}$
    CMP Feb. p13. 300w. 4

1997 WYNETTE, Tammy. Stand by Your Man/Bedtime Story.
    Epic BG 33773 (2 discs) (Reissue)
    CMR April p41. 150w. $3\frac{1}{2}$

1998 WYNETTE, Tammy. 'Til I Can Make It on My Own.   Epic
    KE34075.   Cart. EA34075
    CM   July p58. 275w. 3
    CMP May p19. 300w. 3
    CMR June p29. 200w. $2\frac{1}{2}$

1999 WYNETTE, Tammy. You and Me.   Epic KE 34289
    MG   Dec. p67. 250w. $3\frac{1}{2}$
    MM   Nov. 20 p28. 200w. 2

2000 YOUNG, Faron. I'd Just be Fool Enough.   Mercury SRM 1-
    1075
    MG   July p58. 50w. $2\frac{1}{2}$

2001 YOUNG, Jessi Colin. The Soul of a City Boy.   Capitol VMP
    1007 (E) (Reissue)
    CMR Feb. p28. 125w. $2\frac{1}{2}$

2002 YOUNG, Steve. Renegade Picker. RCA APL1-1759. Cart.
    APS1 1759
    CM   Nov. p60. 150w. 4
    RS   Aug. 26 p66. 175w. 3

2003 YOUNG, Steve. Honky-Tonk Man. Mountain Railroad LP 1
    CM   Sept. p56-7. 175w. 3
    CYR Nov. 18 p36. 150w. 4

OLD TIME MUSIC and BLUEGRASS

The significant movement in this field is not the decay of the Nashville Sound, but the re-emergence of older styles that are rapidly capturing a new audience. These older styles center upon "bluegrass" and the old time Southern string band.

Old time music is pre-bluegrass, commercial folk music and comes from the Southern mountains. It usually features fiddles, banjos and guitars. The term "bluegrass" does not refer to a geographic area but comes from the name of Bill Monroe's string band, the Blue Grass Boys. Bluegrass music is recognizable and distinctive; it features a high-pitched, strident style of two- three- or four-part harmony and five instruments--fiddle, guitar, mandolin, string bass, and five-string banjo. Bluegrass has been around for three decades but has never been an overwhelming commercial success.

Today the primitive, non-commercial sound of bluegrass music is stirring up a revival of interest in the more traditional roots of country music. There is something about this hard-driving sound that has captured the imagination not only of rural people but urban youngsters. The growth of summer-time bluegrass festivals has been phenomenal and to attend one is to have an almost déjà vu feeling of Woodstock. Even more significant is the growth of record companies recording and releasing this style of music.

According to the reviews, the best of 1976 were:

BAILEY Brothers. Take Me Back to Happy Valley. Rounder 0030
CLIFTON, Bill. Going Back to Dixie. Bear Family BF 15000-2
    (2 discs) (W. Germany)
FLATT, Lester. Flying Fish FF 015
HIGHWOOD String Band. Dance All Night. Rounder 0045
KEITH, Bill. Something Auld, Something Newgrass, Something Borrowed, Something Bluegrass. Rounder RB1
MONROE, Bill. The Weary Traveler. MCA 2173
MUNDE, Alan. Banjo Sandwich. Ridge Runner 0001
RECTOR, Red and Bill Clifton. Another Happy Day. Breakdown
    001 (E)
STONE Mountain Boys. Briar Records BT 7204
THOMAS, Buddy. Kitty Puss: Old Time Fiddle Music from Kentucky. Rounder 0032
WISEMAN, Mac. Stony. CMH 9001 (2 discs)

2004 ADKINS, Ernest. Blueridge Fiddler. Major MRLP2164
      BGU Oct. p23. 150w. $2\frac{1}{2}$

2005 ALLEN, Red and Frank Wakefield. Red Clay 104 (Japan)
      BGU Sept. p27. 300w. $2\frac{1}{2}$

2006 AMAZING Grass. Live from the Deadwood. Wrinkel RSS
      2026
      BGU March p21. 250w. 3
      DIC July p59. 125w. 3

2007 AMERICAN Bluegrass Express. Eagle ABE 109
      BGU Jan. p21. 125w. $2\frac{1}{2}$

2008 ATKINS, Bobby. Back Home in Gold Hill. Heritage 601
      MN V7/#4 p17-8. 150w. $2\frac{1}{2}$
      OTM Summer p27-8. 75w. 3

2009 AULDRIDGE, Mike. Dobro. Takoma/Devi D 1033
      CS Dec. p42. 150w. $3\frac{1}{2}$

2010 BAILEY Brothers. Old Homestead CS 103
      OTM Autumn p22. 100w. $3\frac{1}{2}$

2011 BAILEY Brothers. Have You Forgotten: Early Days of Blue-
      grass, vol. 6. Rounder 1018 (Reissue)
      BGU June p45-6. 300w. $3\frac{1}{2}$
      MN V7/ #4 p18. 350w. 3
      OTM Spring p51. 250w. $3\frac{1}{2}$
      PIC Aug. -Sept. p72-3. 200w. $3\frac{1}{2}$

2012 BAILEY Brothers. Take Me Back to Happy Valley. Rounder
      0030
      MN V7/#4 p18. 350w. 3
      OTM Spring p51. 425w. $4\frac{1}{2}$

2013 BANJO Dan and the Mid-nite Plowboys. Snowfall. Fretless
      109
      BGU Feb. p22. 200w. 3
      OTM Spring p57. 50w. $2\frac{1}{2}$

2014 BARBOUR, Burke and Troy Brammer. Bluegrass, Western
      Swing Style. Dominion
      BGU Feb. p24. 50w. 2

2015 BERLINE, Byron and Sundance. MCA MCA-2217. Cart.
      MCAT-2217
      RS Oct. 7 p76. 150w. 3
      SR Dec. p102-3. 100w. $2\frac{1}{2}$

2016 BEVERLY, Charlie. Miner's Dobro. Starr 1066
      BGU July p32. 200w. 1
      PIC Aug. -Sept. p87. 75w. $3\frac{1}{2}$

2017 BLACK Mountain Bluegrass Boys.   Talk of the Country.
      Lark 2141
          OTM Winter p27. 550w. 4
          PIC Jan. p48. 375w. 3

2018 BLAKE, Norman. Old and New.   Flying Fish Records, 010
          BGU Sept. p26. 75w. $2\frac{1}{2}$
          CMP Dec. p31. 125w. 5
          GP May p81. 125w. $4\frac{1}{2}$
          MN V7/#6 p16. 300w. 3
          OTM Spring p59. 150w. 2
          PIC Aug.-Sept. p72. 100w. 3

2019 BLAKE, Norman. Whisky Before Breakfast.   Rounder 0063
          BGU Sept. p26. 75w. $2\frac{1}{2}$
          MN V7/#6 p16. 225w. 4
          OTM Spring p59. 150w. $2\frac{1}{2}$
          PIC July p61. 125w. 4

2020 BLAKE, Norman and Red Rector.   County 755
          MN V7/#6 p16. 350w. $3\frac{1}{2}$
          OTM Autumn p27. 500w. $3\frac{1}{2}$

2021 BLAKE, Norman, Tut Taylor, Sam Bush, Butch Robins, Vas-
      sar Clements, David Holland, Jethro Burns.   Flying Fish
      HDS 701
          BGU Feb. p23. 125w. 3
          CRA Feb. p74. 150w. 4
          PIC Aug.-Sept. p86. 50w. 4

2022 BLUE Denim. Old Homestead OHS 90055
          MN V7/#1 p21-2. 275w. $2\frac{1}{2}$
          PIC June p72. 175w. 2

2023 BLUE Ridge Gentleman. Solid as a Rock.   Atteiram 1517
          BGU Jan. p18. 250w. $2\frac{1}{2}$

2024 BLUE Ridge Highballer. County 407 (Reissue)
          JEMF Winter '75 p210. 100w. 3

2025 BLUE Sky Boys. County 752
          OTM Autumn p25. 250w. 5

2026 BLUE Sky Boys. RCA AXM2-5525 (2 discs) (Reissue)
          AU Nov. p118-9. 600w. $2\frac{1}{2}$

2027 BLUE Sky Boys. Rounder 0052
          OTM Autumn p25. 250w. 5

2028 BLUEGRASS Cardinals. Briar BR 4205
          BGU May p32. 500w. $4\frac{1}{2}$

2029 BLUEGRASS Drifters. Bluegrass Covered with Snow.   Jewel

524
    BGU   Jan.   p17.   225w. $2\frac{1}{2}$

2030   BLUEGRASS Express.   WAM 15-545 (West Germany)
    BGU   Nov.   p36-7.   150w. $1\frac{1}{2}$

2031   BLUEGRASS Generation.   Atteiram API L-1521
    PIC   March   p54.   100w.   3

2032   BLUEGRASS Incorporated.   Back Home in Georgia.   Atteiram
API L 1530
    BGU   Oct.   p26.   50w. $2\frac{1}{2}$

2033   BLUEGRASS Special.   Mountains, Mines and Memories.   King
Bluegrass KB 554
    BGU   Dec.   p31.   100w.   1

2034   BLUEGRASS Swedes.   GM GLP 755 (Sweden)
    BGU   April   p28.   175w. $3\frac{1}{2}$

2035   BOYS from Indiana, with Paul Mullins and Noah Crase.   Atlanta Is Burning.   King Bluegrass KB530
    OTM   Spring   p54-5.   150w.   3

2036   BOYS from Indiana, with Paul Mullins and Noah Crase.
Bluegrass Music Is Out of Sight.   King Bluegrass KB 539
    BGU   Feb.   p20.   250w. $3\frac{1}{2}$
    OTM   Spring   p54-5.   150w. $2\frac{1}{2}$

2037   BOYS from Indiana with Paul Mullins and Noah Crase.   One
More Bluegrass Show.   King Bluegrass KB 545
    PIC   Aug./Sept.   p73-4.   300w.   5

2038   BRAKEMEN.   Play Bluegrass Favorites.   Atteiram 1522 A
    BGU   Jan.   p20.   175w.   2

2039   BRAY Brothers.   Prairie Bluegrass.   Rounder 0053
    OTM   Spring   p52.   200w.   3
    PIC   Oct.   p56.   150w.   5

2040   BROTHER Oswald and Charlie Collins.   Oz and Charlie.
Rounder 0060
    OTM   Autumn   p25.   75w. $3\frac{1}{2}$

2041   BROTHER Oswald and Charlie Collins.   That's Country.
Rounder 0041
    PIC   Feb.   p56-7.   375w.   4

2042   BROWN, Abe and Friends.   Banjo Revolution.   Base CEA 1001
    BGU   June   p42.   150w. $2\frac{1}{2}$

2043   BROWN, Hylo and the Timberliners.   Original Radio Recordings.   Grassound 103

MN V7/#7 p16. 400w. 3

2044 BRYSON, Wally and the Blaylock Brothers. Just Jammin'.
Davis Unlimited DU 33026
BGU Dec. p31. 50w. 2

2045 BUFFALO Gals. First Born. Revonah RS 913
BGU Jan. p21. 75w. 2
OTM Spring p57-8. 700w. $2\frac{1}{2}$

2046 BUMGARDNER, Cathy Ann and the Sounds of the South. Al-
bum of Memories. Old Homestead OHS 90048
BGU March p21. 75w. 2
OTM Spring p54. 200w. 0
PIC June p73. 100w. $3\frac{1}{2}$

2047 BURNETT, Richard and Leonard Rutherford. A Ramblin
Reckless Hobo. Rounder 1004 (Reissue)
BGU Jan. p15. 300w. $2\frac{1}{2}$
JEMF Summer p107. 50w. 3
OTM Winter p26-7. 600w. 3

2048 BUSBY, Buzz and Leon Morris. Honky-Tonk Bluegrass.
Rounder 0081 (E)
CMR June p32. 325w. 4

2049 BUSKIRK, Paul. Good Dobro Pickin. Stoneway 158
PIC Dec. p52. 200w. 3

2050 BUTLER Brothers. Sounds of Bluegrass. Carpenter 200012
BGU Jan. p22. 100w. $1\frac{1}{2}$

2051 CALLAHAN Brothers. Old Homestead OHS 90031 (Reissue)
PIC Oct. p55. 175w. $3\frac{1}{2}$

2052 CAROLINA Tar Heels. Can't You Remember. Bear Family
15505 (West Germany) (Reissue)
BGU April p30. 75w. $1\frac{1}{2}$
OTM Summer p19. 250w. 5

2053 CARPENTER, French and Jenes Cottrell. Elzic's Farewell.
Kanawha 301
BGU Aug. p36. 200w. $2\frac{1}{2}$
OTM Spring p48-9. 350w. $3\frac{1}{2}$
PIC Dec. p53. 75w. $3\frac{1}{2}$

2054 CARSON, Fiddlin Joe. The Old Hen Cackled and the Rooster's
Going to Crow. Rounder 1003 (Reissue)
BGU July p31. 300w. 4
CMR May p29. 175w. $2\frac{1}{2}$

2055 CARTER Family. 1936 Radio Transcriptions. Old Homestead
OHS 90045

BGU   March   p16.   125w.   1
OTM   Winter   p26.   325w. $4\frac{1}{2}$
PIC   July   p56.   150w. $3\frac{1}{2}$

2056   CHANDLER, Dillard.   The End of an Old Song.   Folkways
       FA 2418
       BGU   March   p18.   250w. $2\frac{1}{2}$
       SO   V25/#1   p69.   75w.   3

2057   CITY Limits Bluegrass Band.   Hello.   Biscuit City BC1305CF
       BGU   March   p21.   100w.   3

2058   CLEMENTS, Vassar.   Hillbilly Jazz.   Flying Fish 101
       RS   Feb. 12   p93.   300w.   4

2059   CLEMENTS, Vassar.   Superbow.   Mercury SRM 1-1058.
       Cart. MC8-1-1058
       CMP   Feb.   p34.   375w.   3
       PIC   Oct.   p52.   200w.   3
       SR   March   p82.   175w.   2

2060   CLIFTON, Bill.   Come by the Hills.   County 751
       OTM   Winter   p28.   450w. $2\frac{1}{2}$
       PIC   Feb.   p54.   450w. $4\frac{1}{2}$

2061   CLIFTON, Bill.   Going Back to Dixie.   Bear Family BF
       15000-2 (2 discs) (West Germany)
       BGU   April   p30.   250w.   3
       CMP   July   p29.   400w.   5
       CMR   Feb.   p27.   450w.   4
       OTM   Spring   p56.   275w.   3

2062   CLIFTON, Bill and Paul Clayton.   Bluegrass Session: 1952.
       Bear Family 15001 (West Germany)
       BGU   June   p42, 44.   40w. $3\frac{1}{2}$
       CMP   May   p20.   325w.   4
       CMR   March   p31.   225w. $3\frac{1}{2}$
       JEMF   Spring   p52.   100w.   3
       OTM   Spring   p56.   200w. $3\frac{1}{2}$

2063   CLINE, Curly Ray.   Why Me Ralph.   Rebel 1545
       BGU   May   p34.   150w.   3
       MN   V7/#4   p17.   125w. $2\frac{1}{2}$

2064   COBB, Ray and Ray McGinnis.   Traditional Sounds of Blue-
       grass.   Old Homestead OHS 90057
       BGU   Dec.   p32.   200w. $1\frac{1}{2}$
       PIC   Oct.   p55.   75w. $2\frac{1}{2}$

2065   COLLINS, G. F. and the Blue Ridge Entertainers.   Bluegrass
       Pickin.   Heritage VII
       BGU   Dec.   p26.   150w. $3\frac{1}{2}$
       OTM   Summer   p27.   75w. $2\frac{1}{2}$

2066 COLLINS, Randall. Georgia Fiddler.   Atteiram 1536
         BGU   Sept.   p27.   150w. $2\frac{1}{2}$
         MN   V7/#6   p16.   325w.   4

2067 CONNIE and Babe. Backwoods Bluegrass.   Rounder 0043
         OTM   Summer   p25.   150w.   4
         SO   V25/#1   p68.   50w. $3\frac{1}{2}$

2068 CONNOR Brothers. Bluegrass.   Copper Hill 0027
         BGU   Nov.   p28.   225w.   3

2069 COUNTRY Cooking.   Rounder 0006
         CMR   Oct.   p32.   200w. $2\frac{1}{2}$

2070 COUNTRY Cooking. With the Fiction Brothers.   Flying Fish
      019
         BGU   Nov.   p32.   375w.   4
         OTM   Summer   p28.   150w. $2\frac{1}{2}$
         SO   Sept./Oct.   p51.   150w.   4

2071 COUNTRY Gazette. Live. Antilles AN 7014.   Cart. AN8-
      7014
         CM   Nov.   p61.   275w.   3
         OTM   Spring   p55.   50w.   2
         SR   Nov.   p96.   125w.   5

2072 COUNTRY, Gazette. The Sunny Side of the Mountain.   Trans-
      atlantic TRA 318 (E)
         CMP   Sept.   p23.   375w.   5
         OTM   Spring   p55.   50w. $1\frac{1}{2}$

2073 CREED, Kyle. Virginia Reel. Leader LED 2053
         ETH   Sept.   p623-5.   500w.   4

2074 CRISP, Rufus. Folkways FA 2342
         ETH   Sept.   p620-2.   500w.   4

2075 CROUCH, Dub and Norman Ford.   Footprints in the Snow.
      King Bluegrass 548
         PIC   Nov.   p58.   50w. $2\frac{1}{2}$

2076 CROUCH, Dub and Norman Ford.   Traditional Bluegrass.
      King Bluegrass KB 537
         PIC   Feb.   p57.   125w.   3

2077 CROWE, J. D. and the Kentucky Mountain Boys.   Bluegrass
      Holiday.   King Bluegrass KB 524
         LP   April   p18.   125w.   3

2078 CROWE, J. D. and the New South. Holiday in Japan.   Towa
      1065
         PIC   Aug./Sept.   p80.   175w. $4\frac{1}{2}$
         BGU   Oct.   p24.   350w.   1

2079 CRYSTAL Creek. Rock, Salt and Nails. Crystal Creek
      BGU Feb. p24. 75w. 2½

2080 CURLY Dan, Wilma Ann and the Danville Mountain Boys.
      New Bluegrass Songs. Old Homestead OHS 90053
      BGU Nov. p29. 225w. 3

2081 DACUS, Johnny. John's Mule. Old Homstead OHS 90042
      BGU March p19. 300w. 3½
      MN V7/#2 p17. 150w. 2½
      OTM Spring p51-2. 175w. 1½
      PIC Oct. p54. 175w. 3½

2082 DADI, Marcel. Dadi's Folks. Guitar World 2
      PIC Aug.-Sept. p76-7. 225w. 4

2083 DARBY, Tom and Jimmy Tarlton. New Birmingham Jail.
      Folk Variety FV 12504 (West Germany)
      CMR May p32. 300w. 3

2084 DAVIS, Eldon. Changing Habits. Breeze (no serial number)
      PIC Aug.-Sept. p80-1. 50w. 2

2085 DERRICK, Vernon. Grass Country. Renovah 906
      PIC April p66. 150w. 4

2086 DICKENS, Hazel and Alice Foster. Won't You Come and Sing
      For Me. Folkways FTS 31034
      PMS V4/#3 p191. 25w. 4

2087 DILLARDS. Country Tracks/The Best of the Dillards. Elek-
      tra K52035 (E) (Reissue)
      CMP July p27-8. 425w. 5
      CMR Dec. p25. 150w. 3½
      MM June 12 p24. 325w. 3½

2088 DIXIE Bluegrass Boys. Bluegrass Festival. KIM PAT KLP
      7452
      BGU Feb. p24. 50w. 2
      PIC April p69. 75w. 2½

2089 DIXIE Bluegrass Boys. Going Up. KLP 7339
      PIC June p68-9. 125w. 2½

2090 DIXIE Bluegrass Boys. Grass Along the River. Lucy Opry
      76-01
      BGU Sept. p30. 75w. 2½

2091 DIXIE Travellers. Free Wheeling. Renovah R-914
      OTM Spring p53. 300w. 2½

2092 DOUGLAS, Wilson. The Right Hand Fork of Rush's Creek.
      Rounder 0047

BGU Dec. p29. 175w. $2\frac{1}{2}$
JEMF Summer p106. 250w. 3
OTM Spring p48-9. 125w. 2

2093 DUSTY Chaps. Honky Tonk Music. Bandoleer 1021
RS Feb. 12 p94. 200w. $3\frac{1}{2}$

2094 ECHO Mountain Band'. Westwood WRS 071
BGU Sept. p26-7. 325w. $2\frac{1}{2}$
CMP March p27. 100w. 5
CMR Feb. p33. 350w. $3\frac{1}{2}$

2095 EDMONDS, Norman. Train on the Island. Davis Unlimited
33002
BGU Nov. p36. 125w. $2\frac{1}{2}$

2096 EVANS, Virg. The Flying Fiddler. American Heritage Music
AH10-34S
PIC Jan. p47. 400w. 4

2097 FAIRCHILD, Raymond. Rural Rhythm 260/61/62/63 (4 discs)
BGU Nov. p33. 300w. $2\frac{1}{2}$
CM Oct. p58. 125w. 4

2098 FELDMAN, Peter. How to Play Country Fiddle, vol. 2.
Sonyafone 102
BGU March p21. 100w. $2\frac{1}{2}$

2099 FERGUSON, Dave. Somewhere Over the Rainbow and Other
Fiddle Tunes. Ridge Runner RR0003
BGU Oct. p23. 200w. 3
OTM Spring p55. 50w. $2\frac{1}{2}$

2100 FISHER, Betty and Dixie Bluegrass Band. Carolina Mountain
Home. Atteiram API L 1512
BGU Jan. p21. 150w. $2\frac{1}{2}$

2101 FLATT, Lester. Flying Fish FF 015
CMR Oct. p29. 425w. $4\frac{1}{2}$
OTM Summer p26. 125w. 3

2102 FLATT, Lester. A Living Legend. CMH 9002 (2 discs)
BGU Sept. p29. 225w. $2\frac{1}{2}$
OTM Summer p24-5. 125w. 3
PIC Nov. p51-2. 100w. $4\frac{1}{2}$

2103 FRALEY, J. P. and Annadeene Fraley. Wild Rose of the
Mountain. Rounder 0037
JEMF Summer p106. 250w. 3

2104 FROG and the Greenhorns. My Tennessee Gals. Starr 1080
BGU July p34. 150w. 2

2105 GARDNER, Glen and Francis. Heritage 602
        OTM Summer p27-8. 75w. 1

2106 GOINS Brothers. Rebel SLP 1543
        BGU Aug. p33. 200w. 3
        MN V7/#4 p17. 325w. 4

2107 GOOD Brothers. RCA KPL1-0168 (Canada)
        CC Sept. p30. 50w. 3

2108 GORDONS. Southern Illinois Bluegrass. Crusade 798
        BGU Dec. p31. 75w. $1\frac{1}{2}$

2109 GRAND Poo-bah Beaner Band. It Must Be a Breakdown.
      Rising Star 3301
        PIC Nov. p52. 75w. $2\frac{1}{2}$

2110 GRANT, Bill, Delia Bell. There Is a Fountain. Kiamichi
      KMB 103
        BGU Nov. p26. 275w. 3
        PIC Aug.-Sept. p86. 175w. 3

2111 GRASS Reflection. Zap 110
        BGU Aug. p36-7. 100w. $2\frac{1}{2}$

2112 GRAVES, Josh. Vetco LP 3025
        BGU Sept. p30. 150w. 2
        MN V7/#6 p17. 400w. 2

2113 GREATER Chicago Bluegrass Band. Fargo 975
        BGU March p21. 75w. $1\frac{1}{2}$
        PIC July p57. 100w. 3

2114 GREEN Side Up. How Does Bluegrass Grow. Redcrest DPX
      600
        BGU May p32. 150w. $2\frac{1}{2}$

2115 GROCE, Larry and the Currence Brothers. Peacable (no
      serial no.)
        PIC March p56-7. 250w. 3

2116 HAGAN Brothers. Kanawha 321
        OTM Spring p53. 100w. $2\frac{1}{2}$

2117 HALE, J. C. and the Blue Fescue. Down to Grass Tacks.
      Major MRLP 2207
        BGU Aug. p36. 75w. $1\frac{1}{2}$
        PIC Nov. p50-1. 75w. $3\frac{1}{2}$

2118 HALEY, Ed. Parkerburg Landing. Rounder 1010
        BGU Aug. p35. 200w. 3
        JEMF Summer p105. 250w. $3\frac{1}{2}$
        OTM Spring p48. 400w. 3

2119   HALL, Tom T.   Magnificent Music Machine.   Mercury SRM-
       1-111
           MN   V7/7   p16.   750w.   3

2120   HARRELL, Kelly.   The Complete.   Bear Family 12508/09/10
       (West Germany) (3 discs) (Reissue)
           BGU   June   p45.   225w. $2\frac{1}{2}$
           JEMF   Summer   p106-7.   150w.   3
           OTM   Winter   p25.   1200w. $3\frac{1}{2}$

2121   HARRELL, Kelly and the Virginia String Band.   County 408
       (Reissue)
           JEMF   Summer   p106-7.   150w.   3
           OTM   Spring   p46.   275w.   3

2122   HARTFORD, John.   Mark Twang.   Flying Fish 020
           CRE   Dec.   p14.   50w. $3\frac{1}{2}$
           CS   Nov.   p40.   100w.   3
           MN   V7/#2   p18.   200w. $2\frac{1}{2}$
           PIC   Nov.   p52.   200w. $2\frac{1}{2}$
           SR   Oct.   p95.   175w.   3

2123   HARVEST.   Breaking Ground.   Major MRLP 2217
           BGU   Nov.   p36.   50w.   2

2124   HENLEY, Jim.   One for the Record.   TIG 7612
           BGU   Dec.   p31.   100w.   2

2125   HICKORY Wind.   At the Wednesday Night Waltz.   Adelphi AD
       2002
           LP   Jan.   p20.   200w. $2\frac{1}{2}$

2126   HICKORY Wind.   Fresh Produce.   Flying Fish 018
           AU   Dec.   p103-4.   200w.   4
           BGU   Dec.   p20.   125w. $2\frac{1}{2}$
           CS   Nov.   p40.   100w.   3
           OTM   Spring   p58-9.   150w.   1
           SR   Nov.   p100.   150w. $4\frac{1}{2}$

2127   HIGHLANDERS.   Doin Things Our Way.   Heritage I
           OTM   Winter   p29.   400w. $3\frac{1}{2}$
           PIC   Aug.-Sept.   p75-6.   125w.   3

2128   HIGHWOOD String Band.   Dance All Night.   Rounder 0045
           BGU   June   p44-5.   100w.   3
           OTM   Spring   p58.   425w.   3
           PIC   March   p54-5.   250w. $4\frac{1}{2}$

2129   HIGHWOODS String Band.   Fire on the Mountain.   Rounder
       0023
           BGU   June   p44-5.   100w.   3

2130   HILL, Dudley.   From a Northern Family.   Voyager 3175

        BGU   Nov. p34. 125w.   3
        OTM   Summer p22. 75w.   3

2131 HOLCOMB, Roscoe. Close to Home. Folkways FA 2374
        BGU   Jan. p17. 200w.   2
        ETH   Sept. p620-1. 500w.   4
        OTM   Autumn p22. 300w.   3

2132 HOLLOW Poplar. The Second Battle Ground Fiddlers Gather-
      ing, 1974. Log Cabin 8003
        BGU   Feb. p25. 100w.   3

2133 HOTMUD Family. Buckeyes in the Briar Patch. Vetco
      507
        BGU   Aug. p35. 200w.   2
        PIC   Aug.-Sept. p78. 125w. $3\frac{1}{2}$

2134 HOWARD, Clint and Fred Price. The Ballad of Finley Pres-
      ton. Rounder 0009
        CMR   Feb. p31. 350w. $3\frac{1}{2}$

2135 HOWARD, John and the Bluegrass Express. Hills of the Old
      Home. Lemco 051
        PIC   Aug./Sept. p86. 100w.   2

2136 HUCKABEE, Dan. Why Is This Man Smiling. Ridge Runner
      RR0004
        OTM   Summer p28. 100w.   3

2136a HUNTER, Thomas Hall. Deep in Tradition. June Appal 007
        OTM   Autumn p24. 250w.   3

2136b HUTCHINSON Brothers. Vetco 505
        PIC   Aug./Sept. p83. 125w.   4

2136c IRON Mountain String Band. Walkin in the Parlour. Folk-
      ways FA 2477
        BGU   April p27. 200w. $3\frac{1}{2}$
        ETH   Sept. p623-5. 500w.   0
        OTM   Summer p29. 50w.   3

2136d JACKSON, Roma. The Old Home Town. Heritage 603
        OTM   Summer p27-8. 75w.   3

2136e JARRELL, Benny. Lady of the Lake. Heritage VIII
        BGU   Dec. p28. 175w.   4
        OTM   Summer p22. 125w.   3

2136f JARRELL, Tommy. Come and Go with Me. County 748
        AU   Nov. p117. 400w.   4

2136g JARRELL, Tommy. Sail Away Ladies. County 756
        OTM   Autumn p24. 350w. $3\frac{1}{2}$

2136h JENKINS, Snuffy and Pappy Sherrill.   Crazy.   Rounder 0059
       OTM   Autumn   p23.   175w.   4

2137 JENKINS, Cockerham and Jarrell.   Stay All Night and Don't
      Go Home.   County 741
         AU   Nov.   p117.   400w.   4

2138 JOHNSON, Earl and His Clodhoppers.   Red Hot Breakdown.
      County 543 (Reissue)
         OTM   Autumn   p21.   300w.   3

2139 JOHNSON, Mike and Sounds of Bluegrass.   Envy 81175
         PIC   Nov.   p54.   75w.   2

2140 JONES, Al and Frank Necessary.   Rounder 0050
         BGU   Aug.   p32.   175w.   3
         CMR   Nov.   p31.   350w.   4
         ETM   Summer   p26   200w. $3\frac{1}{2}$

2141 JONES, Bill and the Bluegrass Travellers.   Get in Line
      Brothers.   SPBGMA 7600
         BGU   Nov.   p34.   200w. $2\frac{1}{2}$

2142 JONES Brothers and the Log Cabin Boys.   In Concert.   Paly-
      house LP 257
         BGU   Nov.   p36.   25w.   1

2143 KEITH, Bill.   Something Auld, Something Newgrass, Some-
      thing Borrowed, Something Bluegrass.   Rounder RB 1
         BGU   Nov.   p27.   300w.   4
         OTM   Summer   p27.   550w.   3

2144 KENTUCKY Colonels.   1965-66, Featuring Roland and Clarence
      White.   Rounder 0070
         BGU   Nov.   p26.   250w.   4

2145 KENTUCKY Colonels.   Livin in the Past.   Takoma Briar BT
      7202
         BGU   Nov.   p26.   250w.   4

2146 KENTUCKY Gentlemen.   A Day in October.   King Bluegrass.
      KB 544
         BGU   Nov.   p27.   200w. $2\frac{1}{2}$
         PIG   June   p72-3.   250w.   4

2147 KENTUCKY Gentlemen.   True Bluegrass.   King Bluegrass
      KB534
         BGU   March   p13.   300w. $4\frac{1}{2}$
         MN   V6/#11   p29.   150w.   3

2148 KESSINGER, Clark.   Live at Union Grove.   Folkways FA 2337
         BGU   Dec.   p28.   225w. $2\frac{1}{2}$
         OTM   Autumn   p24.   100w.   3

                     PIC   Nov.   p51.   125w.   4½

2149   KESSINGER, Clark.   Memorial Album.   Kanawha 327 (Re-
       issue)
                     BGU   Aug.   p36.   200w.   2½
                     OTM   Spring p49.   100w.   1
                     PIC   Dec.   p51.   125w.   4½
                     SO   Sept./Oct.   p51.   100w.   2½

2150   KESSINGER, Clark.   Old Time Music with Fiddle and Guitar.
       Rounder 0004
                     CMR   March   p30.   350w.   2½

2151   KESSINGER, Clark.   Sweet Bunch of Daisies.   County 747
       (Reissue)
                     OTM   Spring p49.   100w.   1½

2152   KING, Clinton and the Virginia Mountaineers.   Renovah 905
                     PIC   June   p68.   125w.   2½

2153   LAMB, Grant.   Tunes from Home.   Voyager VRLP 3125
                     OTM   Summer   p22.   75w.   4

2154   LAMBETH, Dave and the Lonesome Ramblers.   Blue Ridge
       Mountain Music.   King Bluegrass 556
                     BGU   Nov.   p36.   50w.   1½
                     MN   V7/#7   p17.   350w.   2

2155   LAMBETH, Dave and the High Lonesome Ramblers.   Standing
       in the Shadows.   King Bluegrass 541
                     PIC   Aug.-Sept.   p82-3.   75w.   2½

2156   LAMBETH, Dave and the High Lonesome Ramblers.   A Trib-
       ute to the Stanley Brothers.   King Bluegrass 535
                     MN   V6/#11   p28-9.   250w.   3½

2157   LANDRY, Henri.   Philo 2002
                     OTM   Spring   p50.   300w.   3½

2158   LANE, Lawrence and Kentucky Grass.   1776-1976.   Rome
       RLP 4134
                     BGU   Dec.   p28.   150w.   2½
                     PIC   Aug.-Sept.   p79.   125w.   4

2159   LANE, Lawrence and Kentucky Grass.   Washington's Files.
       Rome RSP 1124
                     PIC   Feb.   p54.   250w.   4

2160   LAST Mile Ramblers.   While They Last.   Blue Canyon BCS-
       406
                     OTM   Summer   p30.   50w.   3

2161   LAUR, Katie.   Good Time Girl.   Vetco 3023

BGU   Oct. p23.   125w.   3
PIC   Aug.-Sept.   p74-5.   100w. $3\frac{1}{2}$

2162   LAUREL Mountain Boys.   Sometime, Somewhere.   Lemco
055
BGU   Nov.   p34.   225w. $2\frac{1}{2}$

2163   LIVIN' Grass.   Appalachian Swing.   Stoof MU 7418
BGU   Dec.   p28-9.   200w. $2\frac{1}{2}$

2164   LOST and Found.   The Second Time Around.   Outlet STLP
1006
BGU   Nov.   p32-3.   250w.   4
MN   V7/#7   p17.   350w.   3

2165   LUNDY, Ted.   The Old Swinging Bridge.   Rounder 0020
CMR   Aug.   p33.   150w. $1\frac{1}{2}$

2166   LUNDY, Ted and Bob Paisley.   Slipping Away.   Rounder 0055
BGU   May   p33.   225w.   3
MN   V7/#6   p18.   400w.   3
OTM   Summer   p25.   150w.   4

2167   McCOURY, Del and the Dixie Pals.   Renovah 916
BGU   Feb.   p21.   150w. $3\frac{1}{2}$
MN   V7/#2   p18.   250w.   4
OTM   Spring   p52.   225w.   2
PIC   April   p66.   125w.   4
SO   V25/#1   p68.   25w. $3\frac{1}{2}$

2168   McGEE, Sam and Kirk McGee.   From Sunny Tennessee.
Bear Family 15517 (West Germany) (Reissue)
BGU   April   p30.   75w. $1\frac{1}{2}$
OTM   Winter   p25-6.   450w.   3

2169   McKELLAR, Mike and His Bluegrass Dedications.   Silver
Moon.   Mila 1
BGU   Nov.   p36.   100w. $1\frac{1}{2}$

2170   McLAIN Family.   Country Life.   Country Life CRL4
PIC   May   p64.   100w.   4

2171   McLAIN Family.   On the Road.   Country Life CLR6
CS   Nov.   p40.   100w.   3

2172   MACON, Dave.   At Home.   Davis Unlimited DUTFS 101
BGU   Feb.   p21.   150w. $3\frac{1}{2}$
OTM   Summer   p19-20.   250w.   4
PIC   May   p62.   200w. $3\frac{1}{2}$

2173   MACON, Dave.   First Row, Second Left.   Bear Family
15518 (West Germany) (Reissue)
BGU   June   p47.   75w.   3

OTM Spring p47. 250w. 3

2174 MACON, Dave. Fun in Life. Bear Family 15519 (West
      Germany) (Reissue)
          BGU June p47. 75w. 3
          OTM Spring p47. 350w. 3

2175 McPEAK Brothers. Bluegrass at Its Peak. RCA APL1 0587
          PIC Oct. p50. 200w. $3\frac{1}{2}$

2176 MacREYNOLDS, Jim and Jesse MacReynolds. Bluegrass
      Specials/Bluegrass Classics. Columbia BN 26031/047 (2
      discs) (Reissue)
          BGU Jan. p15. 175w. 4

2177 MacREYNOLDS, Jim and Jesse MacReynolds. Jim and Jesse
      Show. Old Dominion OD 49804
          CMR Nov. p32. 300w. 3

2178 MacREYNOLDS, Jim and Jesse MacReynolds. Live in Japan.
      Old Dominion OD 49807
          BGU April p31. 200w. 3

2179 MacREYNOLDS, Jim and Jesse MacReynolds. Songs About
      Our Country. Old Dominion OD 49808
          CS Nov. p40. 100w. 3

2180 MARTIN, Asa and the Cumberland Rangers. Dr. Ginger Blue.
      Rounder 0034
          JEMF Winter '75 p210-11. 100w. 3

2181 MARTIN, Benny. Fiddle Collection. CMH 7006 (2 discs)
          BGU Nov. p33. 125w. 3
          MN V7/#6 p18. 375w. $2\frac{1}{2}$
          OTM Summer p24-5. 125w. $2\frac{1}{2}$

2182 MARTIN, Benny, John Hartford and Lester Flatt. Tennessee
      Jubilee. Flying Fish 012
          BGU March p16. 225w. $3\frac{1}{2}$
          MG June p55. 50w. $4\frac{1}{2}$
          MN V7/#1 p22, 24. 650w. 3
          OTM Spring p53. 150w. 2
          PIC Aug.-Sept. p79-80. 200w. $3\frac{1}{2}$

2183 MESING, Ron. Saturday Night, Sunday Morning. Country
      Bay CB201
          BGU Jan. p22. 100w. 3

2184 MILLER, John. Let's Go Riding. Rounder 3002
          PIC Aug./Sept. p84. 150w. 3

2185 MILLER, Wendy and Mike Lilly. Country Grass. Old Home-
      stead OHS 90049

BGU Nov. p35. 350w. 4
OTM Autumn p26. 100w. 1
PIC Dec. p52. 50w. $3\frac{1}{2}$

2186-7 [No entries.]

2188 MISTY Mountain. Through the Bottom of a Glass. Westwood
WRS 082 (E)
CMR April p42. 225w. $2\frac{1}{2}$

2189 MONROE, Bill. Bluegrass Special BS3 (partial Reissue)
OTM Summer p23. 200w. $2\frac{1}{2}$

2190 MONROE, Bill. All Time Bluegrass Favorites. MCA MZPS
7920 (E) (Reissue)
CMR June p32-3. 125w. 2

2191 MONROE, Bill. The Weary Traveler. MCA 2173
BGU April p27. 125w. $4\frac{1}{2}$
CM June p45, 47. 550w. 2
MN V6/#11 p28. 475w. $2\frac{1}{2}$
PIC July p59. 200w. $4\frac{1}{2}$

2192 MONROE, Brother Birch. Plays Old Time Fiddle Favorites.
Atteiram APIL 1516
BGU Jan. p18. 200w. 3

2193 MONROE, James. Midnight Blues. Atteiram APIL 1524A
BGU Feb. p23. 200w. 3

2194 MONROE, James. Sings Songs of Memory Lane. Atteiram
APIL 1532
MN V7/#2 p18. 200w. $2\frac{1}{2}$

2195 MONROE Brothers. Feast Here Tonight. RCA AXM2-5510
(2 discs) (Reissue)
CMP Feb. p33. 150w. 5

2196 MONROE Doctrine. Falls River FR 00201
PIC Feb. p56. 175w. $2\frac{1}{2}$

2197 MOORE, Charlie. Original Rebel Soldier. Wango 114
BGU Sept. p29. 150w. $2\frac{1}{2}$

2198 MOORE, Charlie and the Dixie Partners. The Fiddler. Old
Homestead 90052
BGU March p17. 150w. 3
MN V7/#3 p17. 425w. $3\frac{1}{2}$
OTM Spring p52-3. 175w. $3\frac{1}{2}$
SO V25/#1 p68. 50w. $3\frac{1}{2}$

2199 MOORE, Charlie and the Dixie Partners. Traditional Sound

of. Old Homestead OHS 90046
BGU   Nov.   p35.   300w. $3\frac{1}{2}$

2200 MORRIS Brothers and Homer Sherril.   Wiley, Zeke and
Homer.   Rounder 0022
CMR   Sept.   p29.   600w. $4\frac{1}{2}$

2201 MOSS, Frazier.   All Fiddler.   Davis Unlimited DU 33023
BGU   Oct.   p26.   75w.   3

2202 MOUNTAIN Musicians' Cooperative.   Brown Lung Cotton Mill
Blues.   June APPAL 006
BGU   Sept.   p26.   200w. $1\frac{1}{2}$

2203 MUNDE, Alan.   Banjo Sandwich.   Ridge Runner 0001
BGU   May   p32.   250w.   4
BGU   May   p32.   250w.   4
MN   V7/#2   p17.   275w.   3
OTM   Spring   p55.   50w. $2\frac{1}{2}$
PIC   June   p66.   200w. $4\frac{1}{2}$

2204 NATURAL Grass.   It's Only Natural.   SF 1796
BGU   June   p47.   150w.   2
PIC   Aug.-Sept.   p74.   175w.   4

2205 NEW Grass Revival.   Fly Through the Country.   Flying
Fish 016
BGU   Dec.   p31.   50w. $1\frac{1}{2}$
OTM   Spring   p58.   150w. $2\frac{1}{2}$
PIC   Aug.-Sept.   p81-2.   200w.   3

2206 NEW Lost City Ramblers.   On the Great Divide.   Folkways
FTS 31041
OTM   Winter   p27.   500w. $3\frac{1}{2}$

2207 NEW North Carolina Ramblers.   North Carolina Boys.   Leader LED 4040 (E)
ETH   Sept.   p623-5.   500w.   4

2208 NEW River Boys.   Aunt Dinah's Quilting Party.   June APPAL
005
BGU   Feb.   p25.   50w. $1\frac{1}{2}$
PIC   Oct.   p52.   400w.   2

2209 NEW River Ramblers.   Old Time Hodown Instrumentals.
Heritage IV
OTM   Winter   p30.   300w.   2

2210 NEW River Train.   One Sunday in May.   Zebra Breath
ZB001
BGU   July   p32.   200w. $1\frac{1}{2}$
PIC   Oct.   p54.   175w.   3

2211 NEW South. Rounder 0044
      OTM   Spring p55-6. 175w. $2\frac{1}{2}$

2212 NEW Strangers. Come Closer.   EMI 501
      BGU Dec. p31. 75w. $2\frac{1}{2}$
      PIC Dec. p51. 50w.   4

2213 NITTY Gritty Dirt Band. Dream. United Artists UA-LA496G.
      Cart. UA-EA-469G. Cass. UA-CA496H
      CAC April p19. 225w. 3
      LP Jan. p11. 200w. 3
      MM Jan. 10 p23. 225w.   1
      SR Jan. p88. 175w. 3

2214 NOBLEY, Robert and Claudine Nobley. Lamp Lighting Time:
      Old Time Songs. Davis Unlimited 33020
      BGU Jan. p22. 50w. $2\frac{1}{2}$
      OTM Winter p28. 250w.   2
      PIC Jan. p46. 275w. $2\frac{1}{2}$

2215 O'CONNOR, Mark. Rounder 0046
      MN   V7/#4 p17. 125w. $2\frac{1}{2}$

2216 O'CONNOR, Mark. Pickin in the Wind.   Rounder 0068
      BGU Sept. p28. 150w. $3\frac{1}{2}$
      PIC Nov. p56. 75w. $3\frac{1}{2}$

2217 OLD Kentucky String Band. Twilight Is Stealing. Old Home-
      stead OHS 80008
      OTM   Autumn p25. 125w. $3\frac{1}{2}$

2217a The ORIGINAL Missouri Corn Dodgers. Old Time String
      Band Music. Davis Unlimited 33018
      BGU April p27. 200w. $3\frac{1}{2}$
      PIC Jan. p46. 450w.   4

2218 OSBORNE, Sonny. Early Recordings of, 1952-53, vol. 1/3.
      Gateway (Reissue) (3 discs)
      BGU April p29. 275w.   4

2219 PACK Duet. When I've Climbed the Last Hill. Vetco 3022
      PIC Aug.-Sept. p73. 175w. 3

2220 PANCERZEWSKI, Joe. The Fiddlin Engineer. Voyager
      VRLP3155
      BGU March p18. 200w. $1\frac{1}{2}$

2221 PARISH, Peter. Clawhammer Banjo--Wade Ward's Way.
      Tennvale TV003
      OTM Spring p59-60. 375w. 3

2222 PERRY, Bill. Bluegrass Jam. King Bluegrass 551
      PIC Dec. p53-4. 125w. $4\frac{1}{2}$

2223 PERRY County Music Makers. Going Back to Tennessee.
      Davis Unlimited DU 33024
            BGU   Aug.   p33.   250w. $2\frac{1}{2}$
            PIC   Aug.-Sept.   p84.   125w.   3

2224 PHILLIPS, Stacy. All Old Friends. Renovah RS 930
            BGU   Oct.   p26.   100w.   2
            OTM   Spring p61.   225w.   3

2225 PIKE, Fred, Sam Tidwell and the Kennebec Valley Boys.
      The Last Log Drive. Renovah RS 922
            BGU   Nov.   p36.   50w. $1\frac{1}{2}$

2226 PINE Hill Ramblers. Red and Rusty; a Bluegrass Saga.
      Renovah 911
            BGU   March   p15.   250w. $3\frac{1}{2}$
            PIC   March   p54.   150w.   4
            MN   V6/#11   p29.   375w. $2\frac{1}{2}$

2227 PINE Island. No Curb Service Anymore. Green Mountain
      1052
            PIC   Dec.   p54-5.   275w. $3\frac{1}{2}$

2228 PINE River Boys, With Maybelle Outback. Heritage III
            OTM   Winter   p29.   125w.   2

2229 PINE River Valley Boys. Bluegrass from the North. Old
      Homestead OHS 90054
            OTM   Summer   p27.   50w.   1
            PIC   Aug.-Sept.   p87.   75w.   3

2230 PINNACLE Boys. Atteiram APIL 1525
            BGU   Aug.   p34.   200w.   3
            MN   V7/#2   p18.   250w.   3

2231 PINNACLE Boys. Rounder 0049
            BGU   March   p15.   250w.   3
            OTM   Spring   p53-4.   200w. $1\frac{1}{2}$
            PIC   July   p58-9.   200w.   4

2232 PIPER Road Spring Band. Fiend's Club Productions
            BGU   Sept.   p30.   100w.   2
            CS   Oct.   p45.   100w.   2
            PIC   Nov.   p56.   75w. $4\frac{1}{2}$

2233 POOLE, Charlie and the North Carolina Ramblers. Vol. 4.
      County 540 (Reissue)
            JEMF   Autumn   p172.   300w.   4

2234 POOR Richard's Almanac. Ridge Runner 002 (Reissue)
            BGU   Nov.   p32.   250w. $4\frac{1}{2}$

2234a PRICE, Larry. Mr. Poverty. King Bluegrass KB 543

BGU   April   p31.   250w.   3

2235 PRICE, Malcolm.   And Then We Got Up and Slowly Walked
      Away.   Sweet Folk and Country SFA 017 (E)
            OTM   Spring   p61.   200w. $2\frac{1}{2}$

2236 RECTOR, Red.   Appaloosa.   Old Homestead 90044
            BGU   Jan.   p18.   250w.   3
            MN   V7/#4 p17.   100w.   3
            OTM   Spring   p57.   150w.   2
            PIC   Oct.   p50.   200w. $4\frac{1}{2}$

2237 RECTOR, Red & Bill Clifton.   Another Happy Day.   Break-
      down 001 (E)
            CMP   Aug.   p32.   350w.   5
            CMR   June   p29.   400w. $4\frac{1}{2}$
            OTM   Spring   p56-7.   150w. $2\frac{1}{2}$

2238 RED Clay Ramblers.   Stolen Love.   Flying Fish 009
            BGU   Oct.   p26.   125w.   3
            CM   Aug.   p56.   350w.   3
            CRE   July   p81-2.   50w.   3
            OTM   Summer   p29.   100w. $3\frac{1}{2}$
            PIC   Aug.-Sept.   p83.   225w.   4

2239 RED, White and Blue Grass Band.   1976.   Playhouse LP
      258
            BGU   Oct.   p26.   75w. $2\frac{1}{2}$

2240 RENO, Don.   Profile.   Wango 113
            BGU   Aug.   p32.   275w.   4
            MN   V7/#6 p16-7.   500w. $3\frac{1}{2}$

2241 RENO, Don and Bill Harrell.   Don Reno Story.   CMH 9003
            BGU   Oct.   p25.   200w. $2\frac{1}{2}$
            MN   V7/#2 p18.   150w. $3\frac{1}{2}$
            OTM   Summer   p24-5.   125w.   5

2242 RENO, Don and Bill Harrell.   Spice of Life.   King Bluegrass
      KB 540
            BGU   Jan.   p16.   100w.   3
            MN   V7/#1 p21.   250w.   3
            PIC   Aug.-Sept.   p78.   125w.   3

2243-4 RICE, Tony.   California Autumn.   Rebel SLP 1549
            BGU   Dec.   p26.   200w. $2\frac{1}{2}$

2245 RILEY, Bartow.   Panhandle Texas Fiddling.   Kanawha 315
            BGU   Aug.   p36.   200w. $2\frac{1}{2}$
            PIC   Nov.   p51.   175w.   3

2246 ROBERTS, Doc.   Classic Fiddle Tunes Recorded During the
      Golden Age.   Davis Unlimited DU 33015 (Reissue)

JEMF   Winter   '75   p210.   100w.   3

2247   ROONEY, Jim.   One Day at a Time.   Rounder 3008
       OTM   Summer   p30.   25w.   3

2248   ROSENBAUM, Art.   Art of the Mountain Banjo.   Kicking
       Mule   SNKF 113
       MM   Feb. 21   p29.   150w.   3

2249   RUTLAND, Georgia Slim.   Rare Fiddle.   Kanawha 325
       BGU   Aug.   p36.   200w. $2\frac{1}{2}$
       OTM   Spring   p49.   200w.   2
       PIC   Dec.   p55.   150w.   4
       SO   Sept./Oct.   p51.   100w.   4

2250   ST. PIERRE, Simon.   The Joys of Quebec.   Renovah 915
       BGU   Jan.   p16.   200w.   3
       MN   V7/#3   p17.   275w. $3\frac{1}{2}$
       PIC   March   p55-6.   200w.   3

2251   ST. PIERRE, Simon.   The Woods of Maine.   Renovah 920
       BGU   Nov.   p28.   150w.   3

2252   SCHWARZ, Tracy.   Look Out Here It Comes.   Folkways FA
       2419
       BGU   Feb.   p21.   150w. $3\frac{1}{2}$
       LP   April   p17-20.   175w. $3\frac{1}{2}$
       MN   V7/#2   p17.   300w. $4\frac{1}{2}$
       OTM   Summer   p29.   100w. $3\frac{1}{2}$

2253   SCOTT, Carl and Ronnie Massey.   Mountain Guitars.   Outlet
       STLP1004
       BGU   Nov.   p36.   50w. $3\frac{1}{2}$

2254   II GENERATION.   We Call It Grass.   Rebel SLP 1546
       MN   V7/#1   p22.   500w.   3
       PIC   June   p66, 68.   200w. $2\frac{1}{2}$

2255   SELDOM Scene.   Live at the Cellar Door.   Rebel SLP
       1547/48 (2 discs)
       BGU   Feb.   p20.   450w. $3\frac{1}{2}$
       MG   May   p56.   75w. $2\frac{1}{2}$
       MN   V6/#11   p27.   1200w.   3

2256   SHADY Grove Ramblers.   Ramblers' Special.   Grove 7617
       BGU   Sept.   p27.   150w.   3

2257   SHENANDOAH Cut-Ups.   Bluegrass Autumn.   Renovah 904
       PIC   May   p64.   175w.   4

2258   SHENANDOAH Cut-Ups.   Bluegrass Spring.   Renovah 921
       PIC   Dec.   p50.   150w. $4\frac{1}{2}$

2259 SHUPING, Garland and Wild Country. Old Homestead OHRC
      90069
            CS Nov. p41. 100w. $2\frac{1}{2}$

2260 SILER, L. B. and the Round Mountain Boys.   The Good
      Sounds of Bluegrass. Jalyn JLP 156
            PIC April p68. 75w. 1

2261 SLONE Family. Ramblin Around With.   King Bluegrass KB
      538
            BGU Jan. p22. 100w. 1
            PIC March p56. 175w. $2\frac{1}{2}$

2262 SMELSER, Ken. Traditional Dance Music.   Davis Unlimited
      DU33022
            BGU Feb. p22. 125w. 2
            PIC July p58. 125w. 3

2263 SMITH, Glen. Kanawha 322
            OTM Spring p49-50. 100w. $2\frac{1}{2}$

2264 SMITH, Walter. Carolina Buddies and Others, vol. 1.   Bear
      Family 15521 (West Germany) (Reissue)
            BGU April p30. 75w. $1\frac{1}{2}$
            JEMF Spring p50. 150w. 3
            OTM Spring p46. 275w. 3

2265 SMITH Brothers Bluegrass Orchestra. Oldgrass, Newgrass,
      Bluegrass. CMH 6203
            BGU Nov. p36. 150w. $1\frac{1}{2}$
            CM Nov. p64. 525w. 2

2266 SOUTHERN Express, With Peter Lissman. North and South.
      Mountain 307
            BGU July p34. 200w. 3
            PIC June p69-70. 175w. 4

2267 SOUTHERN Express. A Tribute to Bluegrass. Alpine RSR
      343
            BGU Dec. p32. 100w. $1\frac{1}{2}$

2268 SOUTHERN Show Boys. On the Road with Bluegrass. Old
      Homestead OHS 90050
            BGU March p19. 75w. 2
            OTM Summer p25. 50w. 1
            PIC Feb. p54-5. 100w. 3

2269 SPARKS, Larry and the Lonesome Ramblers. Pickin and
      Singin. Pine Tree PTSLP 519
            MN V7/#2 p17. 350w. $2\frac{1}{2}$

2270 SPARKS, Larry. Sparklin Bluegrass. King Bluegrass KB
      531

SO V25/#1 p68. 50w. $3\frac{1}{2}$

2271 SPARKS, Larry. You Could Have Called. King Bluegrass
      KB 550
          CS Nov. p40. 100w. 3
          PIC Nov. p56-7. 200w. $4\frac{1}{2}$

2272 SPENCER, Tom. The Old Professor and His West Virginia
      (by Way of Indiana) Guitar. Davis Unlimited DU 33025
          BGU Dec. p32. 50w. 2

2273 STANLEY, Ralph and the Clinch Mountain Boys. Live at
      McClure Virginia. Rebel 1554/55 (2 discs)
          BGU Sept. p28-9. 200w. 3

2274 STANLEY Brothers. On the Air. Wango 115
          BGU Sept. p29-30. 225w. 3
          MN V7/#7 p16. 175w. 3

2275 STEPHENSON, Larry and New Grass. Best of Bluegrass.
      Major MRLP 2198
          BGU Aug. p37. 50w. 2

2276 STONE Mountain Boys. Briar Records, BT 7204
          BGU March p19. 250w. 3
          GP March p73. 50w. 3
          MN V7/#4 p18. 200w. 4
          PIC Nov. p50. 175w. 4

2277 STONEMAN, Ernest and the Blue Ridge. Corn Shuckers.
      Rounder 1008 (Reissue)
          BGU Oct. p24-5. 350w. 3
          OTM Spring p45. 650w. 5
          PIC July p59-60. 125w. 4

2278 STOVER, Don and the White Oak Mountain Boys. Rounder
      0039
          BGU Feb. p20. 175w. $2\frac{1}{2}$

2279 STOVER, Everett Alan. Down Home Guitar. Towa 105S
          PIC May p62. 125w. 3

2280 STUART, Joe. Sittin on Top of the World. Atteiram APL
      1514
          BGU Jan. p19. 225w. $2\frac{1}{2}$
          CS Dec. p42. 150w. $2\frac{1}{2}$
          MN V7/#3 p17. 400w. 4
          PIC March p56. 225w. $3\frac{1}{2}$

2281 SUNDOWN Valley Boys. Smokin' Bluegrass. Pine Tree
      PTSLP 535
          BGU Dec. p31. 50w. 2

2282 SULLIVAN Family. The Prettiest Flowers Will Be Blooming.
      Atteiram APIL 1518
            BGU Jan. p22.   500w.   1½

2283 SWEET, Gene and the Blue Grass Unlimited. Out on the
      Ocean. Jewel 548
            BGU Oct. p26.   250w.   2½
            PIC Dec. p55.   200w.   4

2284 TANNER, Gid and the Skillet Lickers. Vetco 107 (Reissue)
            OTM Spring p45-6.   300w.   2½

2285 TAYLOR, Tut. Dobrolic Plectral Society. Takoma, D-1050
            BGU Dec. p29.   150w.   3
            GP Aug. p81.   25w.   2½

2286 TAYLOR, Tut. The Old Post Office. Flying Fish 008
            CM Jan. p60.   425w.   2½
            CMP Dec. p31.   125w.   5
            MN V6/#11 p29.   300w.   2½
            OTM Spring p59.   175w.   2½

2287 THOMAS, Buddy. Kitty Puss: Old Time Fiddle Music from
      Kentucky. Rounder 0032
            BGU Dec. p31.   200w.   3½
            OTM Summer p22.   200w.   4
            PIC Nov. p57-8.   125w.   4½

2288 THOMASON, Ron. The Mandolin and Other Stuff. Kanawha
      324
            BGU March p20.   225w.   1½
            OTM Summer p26.   300w.   3
            PIC July p56-7.   275w.   2½

2289 TIPTON, Carl. Sunday Singing. Skylite Country SC7304
            PIC May p63-4.   75w.   3

2290 TOTTLE, Jack. Back Road Mandolin. Rounder 0067
            OTM Autumn p27.   425w.   3

2291 TRISCHKA, Tony. Heartlands. Rounder 0062
            BGU June p47.   200w.   2
            OTM Summer p28.   150w.   1

2292 TUCKER, George. Rounder 0064
            OTM Autumn p22-3.   225w.   3½

2293 UNCLE Leroy and the Pike County Partners. Star Spangled
      Bluegrass. Major MRLP 2195 (Reissue)
            BGU Sept. p27.   150w.   2½

2294 VAL, Joe and New England Bluegrass Boys. Rounder 0025
            BGU April p28.   200w.   3½

SO   V25/#1   p68.   50w.   3

2295 VIRGINIA Drifters.   A Delmore Brothers Tribute.   Old
      Homestead OHS 80007
            BGU Dec. p30.   225w. $3\frac{1}{2}$
            OTM Autumn p26.   200w.   3
            PIC Oct. p54.   125w. $2\frac{1}{2}$

2296 WAKEFIELD, Frank, With Country Cooking.   Rounder 0007
            CMR Sept. p32.   200w. $3\frac{1}{2}$

2297 WARREN County String Ticklers.   Now Entering Warren
      County.   Warren County 101
            PIC Aug.-Sept. p77.   150w.   1

2298 WATSON, Doc. Doc and the Boys.   United Artists UALA
      601G
            MG Sept. p63.   50w.   3
            SR Nov. p90.   250w.   5

2299 WHEAT Straw. It Ain't Hay.   Old Homestead OHS 90051
            BGU Feb. p25.   75w.   1
            PIC Aug.-Sept. p75.   125w.   2

2300 WILD Turkey String Band.   Kanawha 323
            BGU Jan. p21.   75w.   2
            OTM Summer p30.   75w.   2
            PIC Jan. p47-8.   350w. $2\frac{1}{2}$

2301 WILLIAMS, Vivian and Barbara Lamb.   Twin Sisters.
      Voyager 316S
            BGU Feb. p21.   100w. $2\frac{1}{2}$
            OTM Summer p22.   75w. $3\frac{1}{2}$
            PIC June p73.   150w.   4

2302 WILLIAMSON, George and Mary Williamson.   Appalachian
      Echoes.   Old Homestead OHS 80006
            OTM Autumn p25.   25w. $2\frac{1}{2}$

2303 WISE, Chubby. Grassy Fiddle.   Stoneway STY 157
            BGU July p34.   150w.   1

2304 WISE, Joe and the Country Boys.   Old Time Music.   CB
      1001
            BGU April p32.   50w. $2\frac{1}{2}$

2305 WISEMAN, Mac and the Shenandoah Cut-Ups.   New Traditions,
      vol. 1.   Vetco 508
            BGU Nov. p28.   175w.   3
            PIC Nov. p58.   75w.   4

2306 WISEMAN, Mac. Sixteen Great Performances.   Dot ABDP
      4009 (E) (Reissue)

CMP   Feb.   p33.   300w.   4

2307   WISEMAN, Mac.   Story.   CMH 9001 (2 discs).   Cart.   CMH
       8-9001
              BGU   Nov.   p28.   175w. $2\frac{1}{2}$
              CM   Oct.   p56.   200w.   3
              CMP   Oct.   p31.   250w.   4
              MN   V7/#4   p17.   375w.   3
              OTM   Summer   p24-5.   125w.   4
              PIC   Dec.   p53.   175w. $3\frac{1}{2}$

2308   WOOTEN, Fiddlin Art.   A Living Legend.   Old Homestead
       104
              OTM   Summer   p22.   125w.   2

2309   YARBROUGH, Rual and the Dixiemen.   The Old Oak Tree.
       Old Homestead OHS 90043
              BGU   March   p20.   250w.   3
              OTM   Spring   p54.   125w.   3

FOLK and ETHNIC

It is difficult to arrive at a definition satisfactory to performers, reviewers, and listeners that explicitly defines the broad spectrum of recordings indexed under FOLK. Even the experts find themselves in basic disagreement. For example, Grove's Dictionary of Music and Musicians [vol. 3, New York: St. Martin's, 1954; p182] describes this genre as "any music which has entered into the heritage of the people, but can be assigned to no composer, school, or as a rule, even period. In general, it may be defined as a type of music which has been submitted for many generations to the process of oral transmission."

In contrast to Grove's learned point of view, Pete Seeger, dean of American folksingers, points out [in The Incompleat Folksinger, New York: Simon & Schuster, 1972; p5] that "folk music" was a term invented by 19th-century scholars and today covers such a multitude of kinds of music as to be almost meaningless. For Seeger, it is homemade music played mainly by ear and arising out of older traditions, but with a meaning for today. In fact, he even rejects the term "folksinger," preferring the more awkward appellation "professional singer of amateur music."

The final word on the subject may come from the great Big Bill Broonzy who is credited with the statement, "Folk music just got to be sung by peoples; ain't never heard no horse singing."

Attempting to categorize the records reviewed in 1976 and indexed in this volume has caused some difficulty. The user of this index will find, along with the many familiar names with long connections in performing traditional music, many other names unfamiliar to folk followers. Possibly one reason for the confusion that seems to have hold of what was once a well-defined musical genre may be the transitional nature of the current folk scene. Popular acceptance of folk music is at a near record low. The world of popular music, caught up in the rock explosion that began with Elvis Presley and the Beatles, has passed folk music by. The folk revival of the early 1960's is now a part of the historical parade of popular musical tastes and the genre has been relegated to the few still surviving "coffee houses," the scattered folk festivals, and to re-releases of singers and instrumentalists who once commanded a much broader audience.

At least two major trends seem to offer a ray of light for

240

followers of the folk field. The first is the emergence of the modern-day singer-songwriter who writes his/her own material. Often the singer-songwriter makes an attempt to find a base in the folk tradition. The sound of the acoustic guitar, though usually accompanied by electrical instruments, is once again being heard. However, because of the tenuous relationship many of these artists have to traditional music, they have been placed in the section of the book reserved for ROCK.

Among the performers in this growing troubadour genre are such as John Prine, Kris Kristofferson, Carole King, Joni Mitchell, Randy Newman, Carly Simon, Murray McLauchlin, and Bruce Cockburn. Listening to their often poetic and always intriguing music reveals that their roots are not "arising from older traditions" but are deep, in the popular concerns of the counter-culture.

A second trend may be more significant for the immediate presence of folk music. There was a period in the development of modern popular music when every pop vocalist who carried an acoustic guitar was referred to as a "folksinger." Today, when very little real folk music is currently reaching a mass audience, these artists have been absorbed in the pop culture. In England, however, the situation is somewhat different. There are emerging several notable groups and individuals who have won both respect and an audience for their highly personal arrangements of traditional material. They are deeply rooted in traditional music and draw upon the past as well as on popular song styles to arrive at a medium that is both ancient and modern at the same time. As well, non-English roots in America (specifically Cajun and Chicano music) promotes its brand of folk music, and it can be found here.

Finally, the distance between folk music and country (or country and western) continues to grow. As country and western falls even further under the influence of rock the audience for an older "Grand Old Opry" style becomes smaller. At the same time country-based music has begun to invade the rock and folk fields. Listening habits, attendance at folk festivals, and new recordings may indicate an awakening interest in a more rural and traditionally based music.

According to the reviews, the best folk albums of 1976 are:

BAKER, Duck. There's Something for Everyone in America.
    Kicking Mule 124
BOYS of the Lough. Lochaber No More. Philo 1031
KIRKPATRICK, John and Ashley Hutchings. The Compleat Dancing
    Master. Antilles AN 7003
MacDONALD, John. The Singing Mule Catcher of Morayshire.
    Topic 12TS 263 (E)
PHILLIPS, Utah. El Capitan. Philo 1016
PRIOR, Maddy and June Tabor. Silly Sisters. Chrysalis CHR 1101
    (E)

THOMPSON, Richard and Linda Thompson. Pour Down Like Silver.
    Island ILPS 9348
TRAUM, Happy. Relax Your Mind. Kicking Mule 110

2310 ABSHIRE, Nathan. Pine Grove Blues. Swallow LP 6014
        CRA April p70. 425w. 3

2310a ARDOIN, Alphonse Boisec. La Musique Creole. Arkoolie
     1070
        CO June p13. 175w. 3

2311 ASHLEY, Steve. Speedy Return. Gull 6-406
        MM April 3 p33. 375w. 3

2312 ASPEY, Gary and Vera Aspley. From the North. Topic
     12TS255 (E)
        EDS Winter/Spring p34. 100w. 4

2313 BAKER, Duck. There's Something for Everyone in America.
     Kicking Mule 124
        CAD Sept. p28, 29. 175w. 5
        GP Nov. p104. 25w. 3
        MM Feb. 21 p29. 150w. $3\frac{1}{2}$
        SR Dec. p102. 200w. 4

2314 BALDWIN, Stephen. English Village Fiddler. Leader
     LED2068 (E)
        OTM Summer p30. 150w. 4
        TM #4 p12, 13. 275w. 4

2315 BALFA Brothers. J'ai vu le loup, le renard et le belette.
     Cezame CEZ1008 (France)
        OTM Spring p50. 250w. 3

2316 BALFA Brothers. More Traditional Cajun Music. Swallow
     LP 6019
        CRA April p70. 425w. 3

2317 BELLAMY, Peter. Green Linnet STF 1001
        AU Nov. p120-1. 550w. 3
        SO V25/#1 p67. 150w. 3

2318 BELLAMY, Pete. Tell It Like It Was. Trailer LER 1089
     (E)
        SO V25/#1 p67. 150w. 3

2319 BURPPS Barn Dance Band. Enjoy Yourself Friendly Style.
     GUS JDC 0079 (E)
        EDS Winter p112. 75w. $3\frac{1}{2}$

2320 BURPPS Barn Dance Band. Two Change Partner Square Dan-
     ces and Two That Aren't. GUS JDC 0080 (E)

EDS   Winter   p112.   75w. $3\frac{1}{2}$

2321   BERUBÉ, Jocelyn.   Nil en Ville.   SOLO SO 25502 (Canada)
CC   Dec.   p31.   50w.   3

2322   BLONDAHL, Omar.   16 Songs of Newfoundland.   Banff RBS
1231 (Canada)
SO   Sept./Oct.   p51.   75w.   2

2323   BOISEC.   La musique creole.   Arhoolie 1070
OLR   Sept.   p189.   25w.   4

2324   BOTHY Band.   Polydor 2383379 (E)
MM   March 27   p27.   400w.   4

2325   BOTHY Band.   Old Hag You Have Killed Me.   Polydor
2383417 (E)
MM   Oct. 16   p29.   300w.   3

2326   BOYS of the Lough.   Lochaber No More.   Philo 1031
AU   Nov.   p117.   300w.   4
MM   Feb. 28   p23.   400w.   4

2327   BRIGHTWELL, Jumbo.   Songs from Eel's Foot.   Topic
12TS261 (E)
EDS   Summer   p76.   300w.   4

2328   BRISSON, Gaston.   Corridor.   Capitol EMI ST 70040 (Canada)
CC   March   p35.   50w.   4

2329   BROWNSVILLE Banned.   In Any Case.   Sweet Folk and
Country SFA 049 (E)
MM   Feb. 28   p23.   125w. $3\frac{1}{2}$

2330   BRUNEAU, Philippe.   Danses pour veilles Canadiennes.
Philo 2006
OTM   Spring   p50.   225w. $1\frac{1}{2}$

2331   BYRD, Joseph.   Yankee Transcendoodle.   Takoma C 1051
CK   Dec.   p49.   25w.   2

2332   BYRNE, Packie Manus.   Songs of a Donegal Man.   Topic
12TS257 (E)
TM   no. 4   p24.   675w.   5

2333   CAMERON, John Allan.   Weddings, Wakes and Other Things.
Columbia GES 90343 (2 discs) (Canada)
OLR   Dec.   p256.   50w. $4\frac{1}{2}$

2334   CAMPBELL, Lorna.   Adam's Rib.   Cottage COT 701 (E)
MM   Nov. 13   p30.   400w.   3

2335   CANN, Bob.   West Country Moledeon.   Topic 12TS275 (E)

EDS Summer p74. 100w. 3
TM no. 4 p28, 29. 900w. 4

2336 CHERNY, Al. Golden Ukrainian Memories. Tee Vee Ta
1017 (Canada)
OLR Sept. p188. 25w. 3

2337 CHIEFTAINS. Island (E)
CAC July p152. 125w. 4

2338 CHIEFTAINS. 2. Island (E)
CAC July p152. 125w. 4

2339 CHIEFTAINS. 3. Island (E)
CAC July p152. 125w. 4

2340 CHIEFTAINS. 4. Island (E)
CAC July p152. 125w. 4

2341 The CHIEFTAINS. 5. Island 1LPS9334
CRA April p76. 200w. 3
HF March p106. 175w. $2\frac{1}{2}$
RS Feb. 12 p88. 300w. 4
SR March p100. 150w. 3

2342 CLAYRE, Alasdair. Adam and the Beasts. Acorn (no serial
no.) (E)
EDS Winter p112. 150w. $3\frac{1}{2}$

2343 COLTMAN, Bob. Before They Close the Minstrel Show.
Minstrel JD 202
OTM Summer p29. 150w. 4

2344 COLLINS, Shirley. Amaranth. Harvest Heritage SHSM 2008
(E) (partial Reissue)
MM Aug. 28 p21. 425w. 3

2345 COLLINS, Shirley. Favourite Garland. Deram SML 1117 (E)
EDS Winter/Spring p33. 150w. 3

2346 The COPPERS. Bob and Ron Copper. EFDSS LP 1002
TM no. 3 p39, 40. 75w. 4

2347 The COPPERS. A Song for Every Season. Leader LEAB 404
(4 discs) (E)
TM no. 3 p39, 41. 725w. 4

2348 The COPPERS. Twankydillo. Folktracks FSA082 (E)
TM no. 3 p39, 41. 250w. 5

2349 The COPPERS. The Two Brethren. Folktracks FSA081 (E)
TM no. 3 p39, 40. 75w. 4

2350 CROWIN, Paddy. The Rakish Paddy. Fiddler FRLP 002
      (E)
          OTM Summer p30. 100w. 4

2351 DE DANAAN. Polydor 2904005 (E)
          EDS Summer p76. 50w. $4\frac{1}{2}$

2352 DIGNANCE, Richard. In Concert. Transatlantic (2 discs)
      (E)
          MM May 8 p24. 300w. 3

2353 DIGNANCE, Richard. Treading the Boards. Transatlantic
      (E)
          CAC April p19. 50w. $2\frac{1}{2}$

2354 DOBSON, Bonnie. Morning Dew. Polydor (E)
          MM Nov. 20 p29. 75w. 1

2355 DOLAN, Brian. Red Roses and Green Fields. Setanta SET
      1AB (E)
          CMR Aug. p28. 25w. $2\frac{1}{2}$

2356 DOUCET, Tom. The Down East Star. Fiddler FRLP 001
      (Canada)
          OTM Autumn p24. 200w. $3\frac{1}{2}$

2357 DRAKE, Nick. Five Leaves Left. Antilles AN 7010
          SR Nov. p98. 75w. 2

2358 DRONEY, Chris. The Flowing Tide: Irish Traditional Con-
      certina Music. Topic/Free Reed 12TFRS503 (E)
          EDS Summer p73. 50w. 3

2359 DUBLINERS. Now. Polydor (E)
          CAC June p152. 100w. 3

2360 DUBLINERS. Parcel of Rogues. Polydor 2383 387 (E)
          CAC July p152. 100w. $2\frac{1}{2}$
          MM May 15 p27. 225w. $2\frac{1}{2}$

2361 DUNN, George. Leader 4042 (E)
          EDS Winter/Spring p33. 50w. 5

2361a ELLIOTT, Jack. The Essential. Vanguard VDS 89/90 (2
      discs) (Reissue)
          SR Nov. p114-5. 200w. $4\frac{1}{2}$

2362 ENGELHARDT, Toulouse. Toullusions. Briar Records, BR
      4203
          GP Aug. p80. 125w. $4\frac{1}{2}$

2363 ENNIS, Seamus. The Wandering Minstrel. Topic 12TS250
      (E)

EDS   Winter/Spring p34.   75w.   4

2364 ESSIG, David. Stewart Crossing. Woodshed WS 006 (Cana-
      da)
          CC Dec. p32. 75w. 3

2365 FAHEY, John. Christmas, vol. 2.   Takoma C 1045
          RS Dec. 30 p64. 100w. $3\frac{1}{2}$

2366 FAHEY, John. The New Possibility. Takoma C 1020
          RS Dec. 30 p64. 100w. 4

2367 FAIRPORT Convention. Chronicles. A&M SP 3530 (2 discs)
      (Reissue)
          CIR Oct. 26 p12, 14. 300w. $3\frac{1}{2}$

2368 FAIRPORT Convention. Gottle o' Geer   Island ILPS 9389
          CAC Sept. p214. 275w. 3
          MM June 26 p22. 400w. 3
          SR Dec. p104, 106. 200w. $2\frac{1}{2}$

2369 FINGER, Peter. Bottleneck Guitar Solos. Kicking Mule 116
          PIC Aug./Sept. p77. 25w. 3

2370 FIVE-HAND Reel. Rubber RUBO19
          MM Aug. 7 p19. 375w. $3\frac{1}{2}$
          MM Dec. 25 p19. 275w. $4\frac{1}{2}$

2371 FUREY, Finbar and Eddie Furey. Hornpipes, Airs and Reels.
      Nonesuch HF2059
          ETH June p153-5. 750w. 4

2372-3 GILFELLAN, Tom. In the Middle of the Tune. Topic
      12TS282 (E)
          MM May 15 p27. 300w. 4

2374 GRAINGER, Percy. Unto Brigg Fair. Leader LEA 4050 (E)
          ETH Jan. p155-60. 300w. 4

2375 GROSSMAN, Steve. Some Shapes to Come. pm PMR 002
      (Canada)
          SOU Feb. p48. 25w. 2

2376 HANDLE, Johnny. The Collier Laddie. Topic 12TS270 (E)
          EDS Summer p75. 50w. 2

2377 HARDIN & Russell. Ring of Bone. Demo H&R512 (Canada)
          CC Oct. p32. 50w. 3

2378 HARDING, Mike. One Man Show. Philips 6625 022 (E) (2
      discs)
          CAC Sept. p218. 175w. 4

2379 HARRIS, Roy. Folksong Symphony 1940. Vanguard SRV
      347SD
          CS Oct. p45. 250w. $3\frac{1}{2}$

2380 HARRIS, Woody. American Guitar Solos. Arhoolie, 4008
          GP Aug. p81. 50w. $3\frac{1}{2}$
          JJ Aug. p34-5. 350w. 5

2381 HARTE, Frank. And Listen to My Song. Ram RMLP 1013
      (E)
          EDS Summer p76. 50w. $3\frac{1}{2}$

2382 HASLAM, Cliff and John Millar. Colonial and Revolutionary
      War Sea Songs and Chanteys. [no label cited]
          SO Sept./Oct. p51. 75w. 4

2383 HEANEY, Joe. Philo 2004 (E)
          SO V25/#1 p67. 75w. 3

2384 HIGH Level Ranters. The Bonny Pit Laddie. Topic
      212TS271/2 (2 discs) (E)
          EDS Winter p111-2. 150w. $3\frac{1}{2}$

2385 HINE, Graham. Bowery Fantasy. Blue Goose Records 2021
          GP Sept. p86. 125w. $2\frac{1}{2}$

2386 HOLLAND, Bill. If It Ain't One Thing.... Adelphi 4104
          CAD Oct. p42, 43. 200w. 2

2387 HOLY Modal Rounders. Alleged in Their Own Time. Round-
      er 3004
          OTM Summer p30. 50w. 4

2388 HUMAN Condition. Working People Gonna Rise. [no label
      cited]
          SO V24/#6 p46-7. 200w. $2\frac{1}{2}$

2389 JACK the Lad. Rough Diamonds. Charisma (E)
          CAC Jan. p402. 100w. $3\frac{1}{2}$

2390 JAMES, John. Head in the Clouds. Transatlantic TRA 305
      (E)
          MM June 24 p30. 225w. $3\frac{1}{2}$

2391 JANSCH, Bert. Santa Barbara Honeymoon. Charisma CAS
      1107 (E)
          CAC Jan. p402. 200w. 3

2392 JOHNSON, Vera. Bald Eagle. Boot BOS 7151 (Canada)
          CC May p33. 75w. $2\frac{1}{2}$

2393 JONES, David. Easy and Slow. Minstrel JD 201
          SO V24/#6 p46. 200w. 3

2394   JOY, Mabel.   Real RR 2004
             CMR Oct.   p34.   125w.   2

2395   KELLY, John.   Fiddle and Concertina Player.   Topic
       12TFRS504 (E)
             EDS Summer p73.   50w.   4

2396   KIRKPATRICK, John.   Plain Capers.   Free Reed FRR 010
       (E)
             MM Nov. 13 p30.   350w.   3

2397   KIRKPATRICK, John and Ashley Hutchings.   The Compleat
       Dancing Master.   Antilles AN 7003
             AU Dec.   p103.   500w. $3\frac{1}{2}$
             DB April 8 p30-2.   50w. $3\frac{1}{2}$
             SR Sept.   p109.   200w.   3

2398   KOUDELKA, Glenn.   Painted Lives.   CB 101 (Canada)
             CC Oct.   p32.   50w.   3

2399   KURAPEL, Alberta.   Chili.   Apir KAU4444 (Canada)
             CC Nov.   p35.   50w.   3

2400   LIMITED Edition.   Presents.   Limited Edition AR2350
             BGU May p34.   125w.   1
             PIC July p60-1.   175w. $\frac{1}{2}$

2401   LINDISFARNE.   Finest Hour.   Charisma CAS 1108 (E)
             CAC Jan. p403.   125w.   2

2402   MACARTHUR, Margaret.   The Old Songs.   Philo 1001
             OTM Summer p30.   50w.   3

2403   McCASLIN, Mary.   Prairie in the Sky.   Philo 1024
             ARG Dec. p45.   175w. $3\frac{1}{2}$
             OTM Summer p30.   50w.   3

2404   McCLINTOCK, Harry K.   Haywire Mac.   Folkways FD5272
             ETH Sept. p620-22.   500w.   4

2405   McCONNELL, Cathal and Robin Morton.   An Irish Jubilee.
       Topic 12T290 (E) (Reissue)
             MM Sept. 4 p22.   250w.   3

2406   McDONALD, Country Joe.   The Essential.   Vanguard VSD
       85/86 (2 discs) (Reissue)
             CMR Sept. p30.   100w.   2

2407   MacDONALD, John.   The Singing Molecatcher of Morayshire.
       Topic 12TS263 (E)
             EDS Summer p75.   175w. $3\frac{1}{2}$
             TM no. 3 p11, 12.   1275w.   4

2407a McGREEVY, John and Seamus Cooley.   Philo 2005
      OTM Summer p30. 50w. 3

2408 McKENNA, Mae. Everything That Touches Me. Pye 12117
      CMP Sept. p22. 300w. 3
      LP April p10. 125w. 2
      MM Aug. 31 p21. 225w. $2\frac{1}{2}$

2409 MALKA and Joso. Jewish Songs.   Capitol SM 6432 (Canada)
      OLR Sept. p188. 25w. $4\frac{1}{2}$

2410 MANITAS de Plata. Flamenco. Columbia KGS 90269 (2
discs) (Canada)
      OLR Sept. p189. 25w. 4

2411 MANITAS de Plata. Gypsy Blues. Columbia ES 90177 (Canada)
      OLR Sept. p189. 50w. 5

2412 MAYNARD, George. Ye subjects of England. Topic 12T286
(E)
      EDS Winter p112. 125w. $3\frac{1}{2}$

2413 MURPHY Clan. Disques Pleiade 2424127 (Canada)
      CC Dec. p31. 100w. 3

2413a NATCHEZ Trace. Best of. Sweet Folk and Country SFA
048 (E)
      CMR April p36-7. 150w. 3
      MM May 15 p27. 225w. $1\frac{1}{2}$

2413b OLDHAM Tinkers. For Old Time's Sake. Topic 12TS276 (E)
      EDS Winter p111. 175w. 3

2414 ORANGE and Blue. The English Dancing Master. EFDSS
PLA 1 (E)
      EDS Summer p74. 550w. $3\frac{1}{2}$

2415 OSBORNE, Brian. Ae Fond Kiss. Tradition TSRO24 (E)
      EDS Winter p111. 200w. 3

2416 PARDON, Walter. A Proper Sort. Leader LED 2063
      TM no. 3 p18-20. 1575w. 5

2417 PERTH County Conspiracy. Break Out to Berlin. Rumour
(Canada)
      CC March p34. 50w. $2\frac{1}{2}$

2418 PETERS, Brock and Odetta. Ballad for Americans. United
Artists UALA604G
      CRA Aug. p70. 300w. 5

2419 PHILLIPS, Utah. El Capitan. Philo 1016

BGU Feb. p26. 75w. 2½
CM Jan. p58-9. 500w. 3
OTM Summer p30. 50w. 4

2420 PHILLIPS, Utah. Good Though. Philo 1004
          SR Sept. p99, 101. 275w. 3

2421 PIGG, Billy. The Border Minstrel. Leader LEA 4006 (E)
          ETH Jan. p153-5. 250w. 4

2422 PLANXTY. Collection. Polydor 2383 397 (E) (Reissue)
          MM Sept. 25 p25. 275w. 4½

2423 POACHER, Cyril. The Broomfield Wager. Topic 12TS252
      (E)
          EDS Winter/Spring p33. 225w. 3

2424 POZO Seco Singers. Best of. Emerald Gem GES1143 (E)
      (Reissue)
          CMR Aug. p30. 350w. 2

2425 PRESS Gang. Hawk HALP 135 (E)
          EDS Summer p76. 50w. 3½

2426 PRIOR, Maddy and June Tabor. Silly Sisters. Chrysalis
      CHR1101 (E)
          GR June p98. 25w. 3
          MM March 27 p27. 625w. 3
          SO Sept./Oct. p51-2. 200w. 5

2427-8 RAVEN, Jon. Ballad of the Black Country. Broadside
          BRO 116 (E)
          EDS Summer p75. 125w. 4½

2429 RAWSOME, Leo. Classics of Irish Piping, vol. 1. Topic
      12T259 (E)
          EDS Winter p112. 125w. 4½

2430 RED Star Singers. The Fare of Life. Paredon P 1023
          SO V24/#6 p46. 200w. 3

2431 RINGER, Jim. Any Old Wind That Blows. Philo 1021
          OTM Winter p27. 350w. 3

2432 ROBERTS, John and Tony Barrand. Mellow with Ale from
      the Horn. Front Hall FHR 04
          AU Nov. p117-18. 500w. 2½

2433 ROTH, Kevin. Sings and Plays Dulcimer. Folkways FA
      2367
          BGU July p34. 225w. 2½

2434 ROY, Raoul. Folklore, vol. 5. Select S-398235 (Canada)

CC   Nov.   p33.   50w. $2\frac{1}{2}$

2435   RUSKIN, Rick.   Microphone Fever.   Takoma Records, C-1044
       GP   Jan.   p70.   250w.   4

2436   The RUSSELL Family.   The Russell Family of Doolin, Co.
       Clare.   Topic 12TS251 (E)
       EDS   Winter/Spring   p34.   250w.   3
       TM   no. 4   p23, 24.   800w.   4

2437   ST. MARIE, Buffy.   A Golden Hour of the Best of.   Golden
       Hour GH 852 (E) (Reissue)
       MM   Nov. 20   p29.   125w. $3\frac{1}{2}$

2438   SANDBURG, Carl.   Carl Sandburg Sings Americana.   Everest
       FS 309 (Reissue)
       SR   Jan.   p93.   175w.   5

2439   SCAFELL Pike.   Four's a Crowd.   Mercury 6363008 (E)
       MM   Oct. 16   p29.   250w.   0

2440   SCHUSTIK, Bill.   Stormalong.   American Muse (no serial no.)
       SO   Sept./Oct.   p51.   100w.   4

2441   SCOTT, Peter.   Jimmy the Moonlight.   Rubber RUBO20 (E)
       MM   Nov. 13   p30.   125w. $2\frac{1}{2}$

2441a SCOTTISH National Chorus and Orchestra.   Great Scottish
       Songs.   Polydor 2383 396 (E)
       GR   Oct.   p663.   175w. $3\frac{1}{2}$

2442   SEARCHERS.   Pye 501 (E) (Reissue)
       HF   Feb.   p119.   100w.   2

2443   SEEGER, Pete.   Live in Concert.   Embassy EMB 3115 (E)
       CMR   June   p30.   25w. $1\frac{1}{2}$

2444   SHEARSTON, Gary.   The Greatest Stone on Earth and Other
       Two-Hob Wonders
       Charisma CAS 1106 (E)
       GR   Feb.   p1389.   25w.   3

2445   SILVER Birch.   Brayford BR/02 (E)
       EDS   Summer   p75.   150w.   2

2446   SKINNER, Scott and Bill Hardie.   The Music of.   Topic 12
       TS268 (E) (Reissue)
       MM   Jan. 24   p30.   250w. $2\frac{1}{2}$

2447   SMITH, Ralph Lee, with Mary Louise Hollowell.   Dulcimer
       Old Time and Traditional Music.   Skyline DD 102
       BGU   Jan.   p22.   100w. $3\frac{1}{2}$

2448 SORRELS, Rosalie. Always a Lady. Philo 1029
      ARG Dec. p45.   250w. $3\frac{1}{2}$
      CRA Oct. p81.   175w. $3\frac{1}{2}$

2449 STEELEYE Span. All Around My Hat. Chrysalis CHR1091.
      Cart. CYS M8C 1091. Cass. CYS M5C 1091
      RR Jan. p62.   100w. 1
      SR April p79.   275w. 5

2450 STEELEYE Span. Commoners Crown. Chrysalis CHR 1071
      EDS Winter/Spring p33.   125w. $3\frac{1}{2}$

2451 STEELEYE Span. Rocket Cottage. Chrysalis CHR1123.
      Cart. 8C1123. Cass. M5C1123
      GR Dec. p1074.   100w. 4
      MM Oct. 16 p22.   550w. $3\frac{1}{2}$
      RM Dec. p30.   100w. $3\frac{1}{2}$
      RR Dec. p100.   75w. 3
      SR Dec. p118.   475w. $4\frac{1}{2}$

2452 TANSEY, Seamus. Leader LEA2005 (E)
      TM no. 3 p12.   125w. 4

2453 TANSEY, Seamus. Outlet OLP1007 (E)
      TM no. 3 p12.   125w. 4

2454 TANSEY, Seamus. Traditional Music from Sligo. Outlet
      SOLP1022 (E)
      TM no. 3 p12, 13.   475w. 4

2455 THIBEAULT, Fabienne. Lamothe (no serial no.) (Canada)
      CC June p33.   50w. 3

2456 THOMPSON, Richard. Island ICD8 (2 discs)
      CAC p254.   200w. $3\frac{1}{2}$
      MM July 3 p22.   475w. 4
      SR Dec. p114.   200w. $2\frac{1}{2}$

2457 THOMPSON, Richard and Linda Thompson. Pour Down Like
      Silver. Island ILPS-9348
      CAC Jan. p403.   150w. $3\frac{1}{2}$
      CIR June 1 p16.   100w. $4\frac{1}{2}$
      CRA Aug. p75.   200w. 4
      CRE July p82.   25w. 4
      GR March p1518.   25w. 3
      MM Jan. 3 p23.   50w. 4
      RS June 3 p70.   300w. 5
      SR Aug. p81-2.   250w. 3

2458 TIMPANY, John and Audrey Smith. The Turtle Dove. Real
      RR2005 (E)
      EDS Summer p75.   75w. $3\frac{1}{2}$

2459 TRAUM, Happy. Relax Your Mind. Kicking Mule 110
      CAD Sept. p28, 29. 150w. 5
      GP Nov. p104. 50w. $2\frac{1}{2}$
      MM Feb. 28 p29. 150w. 3
      PIC Dec. p50-1. 100w. $4\frac{1}{2}$

2460 TRAUM, Happy and Artie Traum. Hard Times in the Country.
Rounder 3007
      CRE March p72. 50w. 3
      GP Jan. p71. 75w. $3\frac{1}{2}$
      OTM Spring p59. 250w. 4

2461 UNGAR, Jay and Lyn Hardy. Ballads and Fiddle Tunes.
Philo 1023
      BGU Jan. p22. 50w. $1\frac{1}{2}$
      OTM Summer p30. 50w. $3\frac{1}{2}$

2462 VANAVER, Bill and Livia Drapkin. Lardfull II. Philo 1031
      OTM Summer p30. 50w. 3

2463 WAGNER, Bodie. Hobo. Philo 1015
      ARG Dec. p45-6. 150w. $3\frac{1}{2}$
      OTM Summer p30. 50w. 3

2464 WALKER, Sammy. Song for Patty. Folkways BR5310
      LP March p32. 100w. 0
      PMS V4/#3 p192. 50w. $3\frac{1}{2}$
      SR May p96. 225w. 1

2465 WATERSONS. For Pence and Spicy Ale. Topic 12 TS265
(E)
      SO V25/#1 p67. 150w. 3

2466 WAY, Brian. Where Do You Go. Quality SV 1927 (Canada)
      CC June p32. 50w. 3

2467 WILKIE, Colin and Shirley Hart. Outside the City. Plane
S15F500 (E)
      EDS Winter/Spring p34. 125w. 4

2468 WILLS, Charlie. Leader LEA 4041 (E)
      ETH June p155-60. 300w. 4

2469 WOODS, Gay and Terry Woods. The Time Is Right. Polydor 2383375 (E)
      MM May 15 p23. 400w. $4\frac{1}{2}$

2470 YETTIES. The Village Band. Decca 5253 (E)
      CAC Dec. p338. 50w. $3\frac{1}{2}$

2471 YETTIES. The World of.... Argo SPA 436 (E) (Reissue)
      EDS Summer p75. 50w. 3

2472   YETTIES.   Of Yetminster.   Zrgo ZDA 168 (E)
          EDS   Winter/Spring   p33.   50w. $2\frac{1}{2}$

2473   ZENTZ, Bob.   Mirrors and Changes.   Folk Legacy 51
          PIC   Nov.   p53.   175w.   3

JAZZ

   This section contains material from diverse origins:
Dixieland, ragtime, instrumental blues, swing, avant-garde, and so
forth.   Music of a light "cocktail jazz" texture usually performed
by non-jazz musicians will be found in MOOD--POP.   Similarly, the
employment of jazz in ROCK will be found in the ROCK category.
BLUES has its own section, although the 12-bar construction and the
"blue" notes are employed extensively in jazz.

   Of all the popular music fields, jazz is the best docu-
mented.   There are sufficient discographies, journals, exchange
markets, record stores and mail-order outlets to meet the demand,
but work continues into the esoteric reaches of descriptive writings
and performances.   Unfortunately, measured against "classical music" standards, jazz is far behind in critical and scholarly writing
ventures.   Articles and books thus far have been of the survey
type, employing biographies and personal experiences, histories of
ventures, discographic information, and photography, but while
there have been lots of words about the subject of jazz, there has
been little written about the actual jazz music.   Many writers and
critics do not play any instrument, and some cannot even read or
write music.   This is completely opposite from the situation with
writers in folk and blues music.

   Jazz is an aural music; its written score represents a
skeleton of what actually takes place during a performance.   Thus,
there appears to be no need for the "classical music" approach.
Yet it cannot be denied that written transcriptions are valuable for
instructional purposes and for structural analysis.   Such data are
usually not available in published form, and the demand for it at the
present time is slight.   Educational use is limited to original transcriptions, often not yet published.   Often, too, critics and reviewers
will argue against systematic analysis of jazz, for then the music
will not be enjoyable anymore.   This visceral reaction, also common
to rock music writers, is negated by the continual enjoyment people
derive from classical music.   What is really meant is that the
writers would not be able to understand the musicological terms for
they cannot play jazz.   Reaction of this kind is missing in folk and
blues, for the use of the solo instrument enables detailed study by
the listener in order to emulate his favorite performers.   One
reason advanced for musicological discussions within jazz is that
such writings will enhance the level of jazz criticism and make it
more acceptable for classical music writers.   Yet the other side

of the coin is that the performers themselves cannot usually read
or write music, playing only by ear and by a feel for it. Both ar-
guments are specious.

For the moment, then, jazz critics and reviewers are in-
tensely interested in discovering and disseminating all facts they can
locate about the performers and the performances of the music per
se. The British publication Jazz Journal often contains discographical information consuming more lineage than the review itself, and
even within the review there are plenty of informative bits of data
that appear to have no relevance to the music at hand. Virtually
every jazz record released gets reviewed somewhere and there is
also a proliferation of reissues, and new releases of recently discovered unreleased material never before commercially available.
"Bootleggers" have emerged to sell the previously unreleased material, most of it very old and rare. It is not our intention to probe
this matter of ethical issues, for that battle is being waged in the
media. But "unauthorized" versions--usually selling 500 or fewer
copies--serve the purpose of meeting the demand for keeping in
print virtually every worthwhile (and some not-so-worthwhile) jazz
recording, and this matter of availability is constantly being referred to in the media. 1976 has also seen a proliferation of original
issues based on taped transcriptions from the 1940's, 1950's and
1960's.

America is thought of as the home of jazz, yet the leading magazines and scholars are European. Europe is now the scene
of exciting new jazz and many reissues of earlier material. England
and France have the key reissues, all nicely packaged and often re-
taining the original monophonic sound. Sweden is close behind, and
so is Japan. The International Jazz Federation is well organized
and is certain to expand. In the lists of "best" records below the
reader should note that the bulk of the reissues come from England
and France and that much post-Parker material comes initially from
Europe. That jazz is neglected at home is evidenced by both the
lack of issued product and by the lack of review media devoted to
jazz. Down Beat concentrates on American modern jazz labels,
while Jazz Report, a mimeographed alternative, concentrates on
traditional material. General review publications, such as Stereo
Review or Audio have jazz sections, while Rolling Stone will review
the occasional jazz record. Canada, on the other hand, has probably
the best jazz magazine in the world in Coda, put out by two immi-
grants from Britain. And Britain itself has the prestigious Jazz
Journal plus excellent sections in Gramophone, Records and Recording, and Storyville. 1976, though, saw the birth of an important
periodical in jazz--Cadence--which should rectify the reviewing situation in America.

We have noted a tendency for non-jazz magazine reviews
to go overboard on "black jazz" (e.g., Rolling Stone) with the re-
sulting swings of 0 to 5 on the rating scales when compared with
the jazz magazines. This is easily proved with regularity as the
jazz review magazines give a wide range of rankings to individual

records (from low to high), while the non-jazz publications give a consistently high rating that smacks of appeasement.

The greatest single influence on jazz has been Charlie Parker and his early followers. By changing chord progressions, Parker's innovative style had set jazz free from the printed score and the arranged notes. Some may argue that other musicians were influential at other times, but such influences only took the shape of imitation plus modest refinement. Parker influenced whole schools of jazz, and brought on bop, cool, time changes, and free jazz. To many fans, there was no jazz before Parker. Thus, we have divided the "best" items in the jazz category (based on the reviews themselves) into "Pre-Parker" and "Post-Parker" (including Parker himself). According to the 1976 reviews, the following appear to be the best discs:

PRE-PARKER:

> BASIE, Count. Jam Session at Montreux, 1975. Pablo 2310 750
> BASIE, Count, and Zoot Sims. Basie and Zoot. Pablo 2310 745
> ELDRIDGE, Roy. What's It All About? Pablo 2310 766
> ELLINGTON, Duke, and Ray Brown. This One's for Blanton. Pablo 2310 721
> NEW York Jazz Repertory Company. Satchmo Remembered. Atlantic SD 1671
> NIMMONS, Phil. The Atlantic Suite. Sackville 2008 (Canada)
> PETERSON, Oscar, and Dizzy Gillespie. Pablo 2310 740
> SIMS, Zoot. Soprano Sax. Pablo 2310 770
> TERRY, Clark, and His Jolly Giants. Vanguard VSD 79365

POST-PARKER:

> ABRAMS, Muhal Richard. Sight Song. Black Saint BSR 0003 (Italy)
> BLEY, Paul. Alone Again. Improvising Artists 373840
> BRAXTON, Anthony. Creative Orchestra Music, 1976. Arista AL 4080
> BRUBECK, Dave, and Paul Desmond. The Duets: 1975. Horizon SP 703
> BURTON, Gary. Dreams So Real. ECM 1072
> EVANS, Bill. Intuition. Fantasy F 9475
> FORTUNE, Sonny. Awakening. Horizon SP 704
> JARRETT, Keith. Arbour Zena. ECM 1070
> JONES, Elvin. On the Mountain. PM PMR 005
> OPEN Sky. In Concert. Vanguard VSD 79358
> Les OUBLIES de Jazz Ensemble. That Nigger Music. Touche 101 (France)
> SHEPP, Archie. A Sea of Faces. Black Saint BSR 0002 (Italy)
> TYNER, McCoy. Trident. Milestone M 9063
> WHEELER, Kenny. Gnu High. ECM 1069

2474 ABERCROMBIE, John.   Gateway.   ECM 1061
          DB   May 6 p23-4.   5
          MF   April p61-2.   600w. $2\frac{1}{2}$
          MM   Jan. 17 p42.   400w. $3\frac{1}{2}$
          SOU   March p47.   50w. $2\frac{1}{2}$

2475 ABERCROMBIE, John and Ralph Towner.   Sargasso Sea.
      ECM 1080 (E)
          MM   Oct. 23 p28.   425w. $3\frac{1}{2}$

2476 ABERCROMBIE, John.   Timeless.   ECM 1047
          SOU   May p46.   25w. $2\frac{1}{2}$

2477 ABRAMS, Muhal Richard.   Sightsong.   Black Saint BSR 0003
      (Italy)
          CAD   Aug.   p34.   400w.   5
          CAD   Sept. p33.   250w.   5
          JJ   March p26.   350w. $4\frac{1}{2}$

2478 ABRAMS, Muhal Richard.   Things to Come from Those Now
      Gone.   Delmark DS 430
          CAD   Feb.   p25-6.   300w. $2\frac{1}{2}$
          CRA   Feb.   p76.   225w.   3

2479 ABSOLUTE Elsewhere.   In Search of Ancient Gods.   Warner
      K 56192 (E)
          RR   May p75.   175w. $2\frac{1}{2}$

2480 ADAMS, Pepper.   Ephemera.   Zim 2000
          CAD   April p36-7.   150w. $3\frac{1}{2}$

2481 ADAMS, Pepper.   Julian.   Enja 2060 (Austria)
          JF   May p41.   550w. $2\frac{1}{2}$
          JJ   March p26.   175w. $4\frac{1}{2}$

2482 ADDERLEY, Cannonball.   Capitol Vine VMP 1023 (E) (Re-
      issue)
          CAC   Nov. p311.   125w.   2
          GR   Nov. p900.   150w. $2\frac{1}{2}$
          JJ   Aug. p39.   600w.   1
          MM   July 10 p24.   175w. $3\frac{1}{2}$

2483 ADDERLEY, Cannonball.   Big Man.   Fantasy F 79006 (2
      discs)
          CRE   Jan. p70.   400w. $2\frac{1}{2}$
          DB   Jan. 15 p20.   225w.   4
          HF   July p106-7.   375w.   3
          LP   March p13.   125w.   2
          SOU   Feb. p50.   125w. $2\frac{1}{2}$

2484 ADDERLEY, Cannonball.   In Memoriam.   Mercury 6336 375
      (Netherlands) (Reissue)
          SOU   March p48.   50w.   3

2485 ADDERLEY, Cannonball. The Japanese Concerts. Milestone
      M 47029 (2 discs) (Reissue)
          JJ Feb. p26. 375w. $4\frac{1}{2}$
          SOU March p48. 75w. 4

2486 ADDERLEY, Cannonball. Lovers. Fantasy F-9505
          CAD Aug. p39, 40. 275w. 0

2487 ADDERLEY, Cannonball. Music, You All. Capitol ST 11484
          BS June p36. 225w. $3\frac{1}{2}$
          CAD April p30-1. 150w. $2\frac{1}{2}$
          DB Sept. 9 p32. 375w. 5

2488 ADDERLEY, Cannonball. Phenix. Fantasy F 79004
          AU June p88. 600w. 4
          DB Jan. 15 p20. 225w. 4

2489 ADDERLEY, Cannonball. Spontaneous Combustion. Savoy
      SJ 2206 (2 discs) (Reissue)
          JA Summer p41-2. 100w. 3
          PRM May p63. 75w. 3
          SR Nov. p133. 25w. 3

2490 ADDERLEY, Cannonball and John Coltrane. Cannonball and
      Coltrane. Mercury 6336.319 (Holland) (Reissue)
          CO Feb. p18. 150w. 5

2491 AHVENLAHTI, Olli. Bandstand. Love LRLP 126 (Finland)
          JF no. 41 p28. 50w. 3
          JJ May p40. 75w. $2\frac{1}{2}$

2492 AIRTO. Identity. Arista AL 4063. Cart. 8301-4063H
          AU Dec. p97-8. 750w. $3\frac{1}{2}$
          DB April 8 p20-1. 475w. $3\frac{1}{2}$
          SOU Jan. p39. 25w. 2
          SR April p99. 225w. 3

2493 AKIYOSHI, Toshiko and Lew Tabackin. Kogun. RCA 6246
          DB April 22 p24-5. 500w. 4

2494 AKIYOSHI, Toshiko and Lew Tabackin. Long Yellow Road.
      RCA JPL1-1350
          AU June p88-9. 550w. 4
          CAD April p34. 150w. 3
          HF July p108. 125w. $3\frac{1}{2}$
          JA Summer p40. 275w. $4\frac{1}{2}$
          MJ Oct. p22. 25w. $2\frac{1}{2}$
          SR Aug. p83. 300w. 5

2495 AKIYOSHI-Tabackin Big Band. Tales of Courtesan. RCA
      JPL1-0723 (Japan)
          CAD Sept. p6. 50w. 5
          MJ Oct. p22. 25w. $2\frac{1}{2}$

        SR   Dec.   p124.   75w. $4\frac{1}{2}$

2496   ALCORN, Alvin. Alvin Alcorn and His New Orleans Jazz
       Band.   New Orleans NOR 7205
           JJ   Jan.   p28.   225w.   5

2497   ALCORN, Alvin. Now He Is King.   Rarities 20
           JJ   Aug.   p30.   150w.   4

2498   ALDRED, Bill and Al Winters. Jazz Trombones. Jim Taylor
       Presents JTP 101
           JJ   Feb.   p26.   225w. $3\frac{1}{2}$

2499   ALEXANDER, Monty. Love and Sunshine.   MPS BAP 5078 (E)
           CAD   Dec.   p26.   100w. $2\frac{1}{2}$
           GR   Aug.   p352.   200w.   4
           JJ   May p26.   225w. $4\frac{1}{2}$
           MJ   Dec.   p44.   75w.   3
           MM   June 5 p22.   325w. $3\frac{1}{2}$

2500   ALLEN, Henry Red. Vol. 4.   RCA FXM-17285 (France)
           JJ   Nov.   p24.   325w. $2\frac{1}{2}$
           RR   Dec.   p101-2.   50w. $3\frac{1}{2}$

2501   ALLISON, Mose. Atlantic ATL 50 249 (E) (Reissue)
           MM   Sept. 4 p21.   500w.   3

2502   ALLISON, Mose. Creek Bank.   Prestige 24055 (2 discs)
       (Reissue)
           DB   Feb.   p31-2.   500w.   4
           LP   March p14.   150w.   3

2503   ALLISON, Mose. Your Mind Is on Vacation.   Atlantic SD
       1691
           CRA   Dec.   p66.   375w. $3\frac{1}{2}$
           RS   Nov. 18 p82.   150w. $3\frac{1}{2}$

2504   ALLRED, Bill. Reedy Creek Romp! Reedy Creek RCR-101
           CO   Feb.   p20.   300w.   2

2505   ALMEIDA, Laurindo. Latin Guitar.   Dobre 1000
           CAD   Nov.   p20-1.   50w.   3

2506   ALTSCHUL, Barry, Paul Bley and Gary Peacock. Virtuosi.
       Improvising Artists IAI 373844
           CAD   Dec.   p26-7.   150w.   2

2507   AMALGAM. A Records A 002 (E)
           JF   May   p43.   475w.   4
           JJ   Feb.   p34.   400w.   3

2508   AMALGAM. Innovation.   Tangent TGS 121 (E)
           JJ   March p26.   325w. $3\frac{1}{2}$

RR   May   p75.   400w. $3\frac{1}{2}$

2508a   AMMONS, Albert.   Boogie Woogie Piano Stylings.   Mercury
         6336 326 (Holland) (Reissue)
             BM   April   p35.   350w.   3

2509   AMMONS, Albert.   King of Blues and Boogie Woogie, 1907-
       1949.   Oldie Blues OL2807 (Holland) (Reissue)
             BU   Jan.-Feb.   p25-6.   700w.   4
             JJ   Jan.   p28.   275w. $3\frac{1}{2}$
             MM   Aug. 7   p19.   350w.   4

2510   AMMONS, Gene.   Story: the 78 Era.   Prestige PR 24058 (2
       discs) (Reissue)
             DB   Oct. 21   p33-4.   175w.   4

2511   AMMONS, Gene.   Swinging the Jugg.   Roots 1002
             CAD   Sept.   p29.   225w.   4

2512   ANDERSON, Cat.   Cat on a Hot Tin Horn.   Trip TLP 5586
             JA   Fall   p56.   50w. $3\frac{1}{2}$

2513   ARDLEY, Neil.   Kaleidoscope of Rainbows.   Gull GULP 1018
       (E)
             JJ   Sept.   p28.   375w.   5

2514   ARK and the Ologists.   Oceanic 500
             CAD   Feb.   p24.   150w. $1\frac{1}{2}$

2515   ARKIN, Bob.   The Resurrection of Cyronocchio.   Oceanic C
       500
             CAD   Jan.   p16.   200w. $2\frac{1}{2}$

2516   ARMSTRONG, Louis.   All Stars in Concert, 1956.   Jazz Ar-
       chives 100 (Reissue)
             SOU   March   p48.   50w.   3

2517   ARMSTRONG, Louis.   The All-Stars in Philadelphia 1948-9.
       Jazz Archives JA-20
             CO   Feb.   p20, 21.   450w.   4

2518   ARMSTRONG, Louis.   And Friends.   Philips SON 010 (E)
             GR   Oct.   p666.   75w.   2
             RR   Dec.   p102.   75w. $2\frac{1}{2}$

2519   ARMSTRONG, Louis.   At the Friedrichstadt--Palast in East
       Berlin.   Black Jack LP 3007 (Italy)
             ST   April-May   p158.   350w.   2

2520   ARMSTRONG, Louis.   Best.   Pye Golden Hour GH 648 (E)
       (Reissue)
             CAC   Dec.   p354.   100w.   2

2521   ARMSTRONG, Louis.   The Essential.   Vanguard VSD 91/92
        (2 discs) (Reissue)
                AU   Dec.   p99.   250w. $1\frac{1}{2}$
                CAD   Sept.   p21.   125w.   4
                MJ   Dec.   p26.   50w.   3

2522   ARMSTRONG, Louis.   On the Road.   Fairmont (2 discs) FA-
        1005/6
                DB   Nov. 4   p29.   75w.   2
                LP   July   p10-1. 125w.   2

2523   ARMSTRONG, Louis.   Satchmo's Greatest, Vol. 6.   RCA
        FXM 1-7142 (France) (Reissue)
                FT   April/May   p20.   350w. $3\frac{1}{2}$
                JJ   Feb.   p26.   250w. $4\frac{1}{2}$

2524   ARMSTRONG, Louis.   Town Hall Concert; the Unissued Part.
        RCA FXMI 7142 (France) (Reissue)
                DB   Nov. 4   p29.   75w.   5

2525   ARMSTRONG, Louis.   V.S.O.P., Vol. 1/8.   CBS 88001/2/3/4
        (8 discs) (France) (Reissue)
                JJ   Aug.   p32.   625w.   5

2525a   ARMSTRONG, Louis and Earl Hines, 1928.   Smithsonian Col-
        lection R 002 (Reissue)
                CAD   March   p29.   200w. $3\frac{1}{2}$
                DB   May 20   p30-1.   275w.   5
                HF   April   p140.   550w. $3\frac{1}{2}$
                MJ   April   p28.   125w. $2\frac{1}{2}$
                SR   Aug.   p88.   650w.   5

2526   ARMSTRONG, Louis.   Weather Bird.   Columbia
                RFJ   June/Oct.   p8.   50w.   5

2527   ARMSTRONG, Louis and King Oliver.   Milestone M47017 (2
        discs) (Reissue)
                CO   March   p27.   325w. $2\frac{1}{2}$
                SR   July   p90, 91.   275w.   4

2528   ARMSTRONG, Louis/Lu Watters.   Louie and Lu.   Fairmont
        108
                LP   Aug.   p9-10.   150w.   4

2529   ARPIN, John.   Eubie Blake Music EBM-10
                CAD   Aug.   p24.   125w.   5

2530   ART Ensemble of Chicago.   Certain Blacks.   Inner City IC
        1004 (Reissue)
                DB   Nov. 18   p26-7.   175w. $1\frac{1}{2}$
                JJ   Sept.   p28.   300w. $4\frac{1}{2}$
                MJ   Dec.   p44.   75w.   1

2531 ART Ensemble of Chicago. Live at Mandel Hall. Trio PA 6022-3 (Japan (2 discs)
     CAD   Aug.   p16.   50w.   4

2532 ART Ensemble of Chicago. The Paris Session. Arista Freedom 1903
     DB   Feb. 12   p24-5.   450w. $3\frac{1}{2}$

2533 ATTITUDES. Dark Horse SP22008
     CRA   May   p79.   125w. $3\frac{1}{2}$

2534 AUSTRALIAN Jazz Quartet. Bethlehem BCP 6002 (Reissue)
     CAD   April   p42.   100w. $2\frac{1}{2}$

2535 AUSTIN, Charles and Joe Gallivan. At Last. Man Made Records [no serial no.]
     CAD   Jan.   p14.   75w.   3
     DB   March 25   p34-5.   2
     JJ   Feb.   p38.   150w. $3\frac{1}{2}$

2536 AUSTIN, Claire. Goin Crazy with the Blues. Jazzology 52
     CAD   Nov.   p15-6.   125w. $3\frac{1}{2}$

2537 AWAY. Innovation. Tangent TGS 121 (E)
     MM   March 20   p24.   100w.   3

2538 AWAY. Somewhere in Between. Vertigo 6360 135 BD (E)
     JJ   Dec.   p26.   325w.   3
     MM   Oct. 16   p30.   600w. $3\frac{1}{2}$

2539 AYERS, Roy. Everybody Loves Sunshine. Polydor PD 6070
     CRE   Dec.   p63.   150w.   2

2540 AYERS, Roy. Mystic Voyage. Polydor PD-6057
     BD   June 3   p25-6.   325w. $1\frac{1}{2}$
     SR   June   p76.   100w. $4\frac{1}{2}$

2541 AYLER, Albert. New Grass. Impulse AS 9175
     RR   Sept.   p90.   125w.   3

2542 AYLER, Albert. Prophecy. ESP 3030
     CAD   March   p24.   125w. $2\frac{1}{2}$

2543 AYLER, Albert. Vibrations. Arista AL1000 (Reissue)
     CO   Feb.   p19.   275w.   4
     SR   Aug.   p40-1.   150w.   4

2544 AYLER, Albert. Witches and Devils. Arista 1018 (Reissue)
     DB   March 11   p29.   250w.   4

2545 BACKHAND. Impulse ASH 9305
     CRA   April   p73-4.   475w. $2\frac{1}{2}$

2546 BAILEY, Buster. All About Memphis. Master Jazz Record-
      ings MJR 8125 (Reissue)
            CO   Feb.   p21.   225w.   2
            SR   April p89.   275w.   4

2547 BAILEY, Derek. Improvisation. Cramps CRSLP 6202 (Italy)
            JJ   June   p40.   125w.   5
            RR   Sept. p70.   25w.   3

2548 BAILEY, Derek and Evan Parker. The London Concert. In-
      cus 16 (E)
            JJ   Sept. p28.   300w.   5

2549 BAKER, Chet. In Paris (1955-56). Blue Star 80.704/705
      (2 discs) (France) (Reissue)
            CAD Aug.   p43.   200w.   5

2550 BAKER, Chet. She Was Too Good to Me. CTI CTI 6050.
      Cart. CT8 6050. Cass. CTC 6050
            SR   May   p88.   225w.   5

2551 BAKER, Kenny. Baker's Jam. 77 Records 77 S 56 (E)
            GR   April p1673. 275w.   3
            JJ   Feb.   p26, 27. 350w. 5
            ST   Feb.-March p113. 200w. 5

2552 BARBER, Chris. One-Up OU 2093 (E) (Reissue)
            ST   Dec. 1975-Jan. 1976 p74. 350w.   4

2553 BARBER, Chris. In Berlin. Black Lion BLP 12110/1 (2
      discs) (E) (Reissue)
            JJ   July   p28.   250w. $3\frac{1}{2}$
            RR   Aug.   p80.   25w. $2\frac{1}{2}$

2554 BARBER, Chris. Jubilee Tour Album. Black Lion 12132/3
      (2 discs) (E)
            JA   Fall   p47.   225w.   4
            JJ   Jan.   p28.   150w.   4
            MM   April 17 p24. 550w. $3\frac{1}{2}$
            RR   June   p83.   100w.   3

2555 BARBIERI, Gato. Caliente. A&M SP4597
            CAD Oct.   p17.   125w.   4
            MM   Dec. 4 p28.   150w.   0
            RS   Dec. 2 p104.   175w.   3

2556 BARBIERI, Gato. Chapter Four: Alive in New York. ABC
      Impulse ASD 9303
            DB   Jan. 15 p24-5. 475w. $4\frac{1}{2}$

2557 BARBIERI, Gato. El Gato. Flying Dutchman BDL1-1147
            DB   April 8 p22.   450w.   4
            JJ   May   p26.   200w.   1

2558 BARBIERI, Gato and Dollar Brand.   Confluence.   Arista AL
      1003 (Reissue)
          CO   Feb.   p19, 20.   275w.   5
          SR   Aug.   p90-1.   150w.   4

2559 BARLEY, Brian.   CBC Radio Canada 309 (Canada)
          OLR Dec.   p256-7.   75w.   5

2560 BARNES, George.   Swing Guitars.   Famous Door HL-100
          CO   April p24.   200w.   4

2561 BARNET, Charlie.   Aircheck 5 (Canada)
          CAD Dec.   p32.   125w. $2\frac{1}{2}$
          JJ   Sept. p28.   350w.   5

2562 BARNET, Charlie.   DJM DJML-061 (E) (Reissue)
          JJ   March p26.   375w.   3

2563 BARNET, Charlie/Woody Herman.   One Night Stand Battle of
      the Bands.   Joyce LP 1012 (Reissue)
          DB   June 3   p30-1.   100w. $2\frac{1}{2}$

2564 BARRON, Kenny.   Lucifer.   Muse MR 5070
          MG   June   p50.   75w.   2

2565 BARRON, Kenny.   Peruvian Blue.   MUSE 5044
          SR   April p89.   125w. $4\frac{1}{2}$

2566 BARTOW, Jim.   An American Poet's Song Book.   Blue Blood
      132
          CAD Aug.   p23.   175w.   5

2567 BARTZ, Gary.   The Shadow Do.   Prestige P-10092
          AU   Jan.   p68.   300w.   2
          CRE Jan.   p71.   50w.   3
          DB   Jan. 15   p26.   225w.   1
          SR   Feb.   p92.   100w.   3

2568 BASIE, Count.   Queen-disc 015 (Reissue)
          JJ   Jan.   p28.   275w.   5

2569 BASIE, Count.   The Atomic Mister Basie/Chairman of the
      Board.   Vogue VJD 517 (2 discs) (France) (Reissue)
          JJ   June   p30.   275w.   5
          MM   May 8   p28.   375w.   3

2570 BASIE, Count.   Basie Beat.   Verve 2352 098 (E) (Reissue)
          RR   Feb.   p68.   50w. $2\frac{1}{2}$

2571 BASIE, Count.   Basie Big Band.   Pablo 2310 756
          CAC Oct.   p274.   100w.   3
          CAD Jan.   p18.   150w. $3\frac{1}{2}$
          DB   March 25   p32-3.   225w. $2\frac{1}{2}$

HF   March   p110.   325w.   4
JJ   April   p28.   175w.   5
MJ   July   p52.   50w.   2
MM   May 8   p28.   375w. $3\frac{1}{2}$

2572   BASIE, Count.   Basie Jam.   Pablo 2310 718
       AU   April   p92.   200w.   5

2573   BASIE, Count.   Blues by Basie.   Tax m-8025 (Denmark)
       JJ   Sept.   p28.   425w. $4\frac{1}{2}$
       MM   Dec. 18   p20.   475w. $3\frac{1}{2}$

2574   BASIE, Count.   The Count at the Chatterbox.   Jazz Archives
       JA 16
       CO   Feb.   p21.   300w.   5

2574a BASIE, Count.   Featuring Lester Young.   Swing Treasury
       101
       JJ   Jan.   p28, 29.   175w.   4

2575   BASIE, Count.   For the First Time.   Pablo 2310 712
       DB   April 10   p19.   225w. $4\frac{1}{2}$

2576   BASIE, Count.   Jam Session at Montreux 1975.   Pablo 2310
       750
       AU   April   p92-3.   200w.   3
       CAC   Jan.   p412, 414.   100w. $3\frac{1}{2}$
       CAD   Jan.   p19.   250w.   4
       DB   April 8   p22-4.   100w.   4
       MM   Jan. 3   p26.   550w.   4
       RR   Feb.   p68.   50w. $4\frac{1}{2}$

2577   BASIE, Count.   V-Discs, Volume 2.   Jazz Society AA-506
       (Denmark)
       JJ   May   p26.   625w.   4
       ST   Oct./Nov.   p38.   50w. $3\frac{1}{2}$
       ST   Dec. 1975-Jan. 1976   p78.   175w.   4

2578   BASIE, Count and Oscar Peterson.   Encounter.   Pablo 2310
       722
       AU   April   p93.   200w.   4

2579   BASIE, Count and Zoot Sims.   Basie & Zoot.   Pablo 2310
       745.   Cart. S10-745
       CAC   Sept.   p226.   275w. $4\frac{1}{2}$
       CAD   April   p28.   175w. $4\frac{1}{2}$
       DB   Oct. 21   p32-3.   200w.   5
       CR   Oct.   p58.   100w.   5
       HF   June   p109.   150w.   5
       JJ   July   p28.   475w.   5
       MJ   July   p52.   50w.   3
       MM   Aug. 28   p22.   650w.   4
       RR   Aug.   p80.   50w.   3
       SR   Aug.   p83-4.   100w.   4

2580 BASIE, Count and Joe Williams. Swingin with the Count.
      Verve 3113187 (E) (Reissue)
            CAC Oct. p272. 300w. 3
            GR   Nov. p900. 75w. $3\frac{1}{2}$
            MM   July 24 p26. 400w. 4

2581 BASIE, Count/Cab Calloway. Jazzum (Reissue)
            JA   Fall p56. 100w. $2\frac{1}{2}$

2582 BECHET, Sidney. RCA FXM 3-7054 (France) (3 discs) (Re-
      issue)
            SOU March p48. 50w. 3

2583 BECHET, Sidney. Bechet and Blues. DJM DJMLO63 (E)
            GR   March p1521. 200w. $2\frac{1}{2}$
            RR   Feb. p68. 50w. 3

2584 BECHET, Sidney. Master Musician. RCA Blackbird AXM2-
      5516 (2 discs) (Reissue)
            MJ   March p22. 200w. 4

2585 BECHET, Sidney and Mezz Mezzrow. Classic Jazz CJ 28
      (2 discs) (Reissue)
            CAD Dec. p32. 75w. $2\frac{1}{2}$
            MJ   Dec. p26, 44. 200w. $4\frac{1}{2}$

2586 BECK, Joe. Kudu 21
            BM   Dec. p28. 200w. 3
            DB   Jan. 15 p21. 150w. 2

2587 BECKETT, Harry. Memories of Bacares. Ogun OG 800 (E)
            JJ   Oct. p30. 250w. $4\frac{1}{2}$
            MM   Nov. 6 p25. 450w. 2

2588 BEIDERBECKE, Bix, and the Chicago Cornets. Milestone
      M47019 (2 discs) (Reissue)
            CO   March p28. 325w. $2\frac{1}{2}$
            SR   July p90, 91. 275w. 4

2589 BEIRACH, Richard. Eon. ECM 1054ST
            DB   Sept. 6 p26. 300w. 5

2590 BELLSON, Louis. The Louis Bellson Explosion. Pablo 2310
      755
            CAC Oct. p272. 75w. 4
            CAD Jan. p17. 175w. $3\frac{1}{2}$
            DB   March 11 p23. 250w. 3
            JJ   April p28. 175w. 4
            MJ   July p52. 50w. $3\frac{1}{2}$

2591 BEN, Jorge. Samba Nova. Island ILPS 9361
            RS   Dec. 16 p98. 100w. $2\frac{1}{2}$

2592 BENEKE, Tex. With No Strings. Hep 8 (E) (Reissue)

      JJ Dec. p39. 100w. $1\frac{1}{2}$

2593 BENSON, George. Bad Benson. CTI DTI-6045 S1. Cart.
      CT8-6045. Cass. CTC-6045
          SR March p88. 125w. 5

2594 BENSON, George. Breezin'. Warner Brothers BS 2919
          BM Oct. p41. 225w. 4
          CRE Aug. p14. 50w. $2\frac{1}{2}$
          CIR Nov. 10 p18. 300w. 3
          JH Summer p33. 250w. $3\frac{1}{2}$
          MHF June-July p66-7. 275w. 4
          MJ July p54. 75w. $2\frac{1}{2}$
          MJ Oct. p22. 25w. $2\frac{1}{2}$
          MM July 3 p21. 25w. 2
          MM Aug. 21 p20. 150w. 3
          RR Nov. p105. 150w. $3\frac{1}{2}$
          RS Nov. 4 p75. 200w. 3
          SR Nov. p118. 200w. 3

2595 BENSON, George. Good King Bad. CTI 6062
          BM Aug. p44. 150w. 3
          CAD Oct. p48. 75w. 4
          MJ Oct. p22. 25w. $2\frac{1}{2}$

2596 BENSON, George. Willow Weep for Me. CBS 63533 (E)
          SR Jan. p97. 300w. $4\frac{1}{2}$

2596a BERGMAN, Borah. Discovery. Chiaroscuro CR 125
          LP March p14. 100w. 3
          SR Jan. p96. 175w. 4

2597 BERIGAN, Bunny. Almanac QSR 2714
          JJ Feb. p27. 275w. 4

2598 BERIGAN, Bunny. Volume 1 (1934-38). RCA FXM 1-7172
      (France) (Reissue)
          JJ April p28, 29. 275w. 5

2599 BERIGAN, Bunny. Airchecks. Shoestring SS100/101 (2
      discs)
          CAD Sept. p22. 325w. 5

2600 BERIGAN, Bunny. Leader & Sideman. Jazz Archives JA-19
          CO Feb. p21. 425w. 0

2601 BERIGAN, Bunny. Nostalgia, 1934-38. RCA FXMI 7172
      (Reissue) (France)
          RR June p83. 50w. 3

2602-3 BERIGAN, Bunny. Shanghai Shuffle. DJM DJB 26078 (E)
      (Reissue)
          RR Dec. p102. 50w. 3

2604 BERMAN, Sonny. Beautiful Jewish Music. Onyx 211 (Re-
      issue)
         CO   Feb.   p21, 22.   375w. $2\frac{1}{2}$

2605 BERNHARDT, Clyde. Barrow YLP 401
         JJ   April   p29.   400w. $3\frac{1}{2}$

2606 BERNHARDT, Clyde.   More Blues and Jazz from Harlem.
      400 W 150 NLP 400
         LB   Nov./Dec.   p38.   75w. $3\frac{1}{2}$

2607 BERNHARDT, Clyde. Sittin' on Top of the World.   Barron
      VLP 401
         LB   Nov./Dec.   p38.   75w. $3\frac{1}{2}$
         ST   June-July   p191.   450w. $4\frac{1}{2}$

2608 BERRY, Bill.   Beez Records 23033
         JJ   April   p29.   275w.   3
         MJ   Jan.   p21.   125w.   4

2609 BERRY, Bill.   Hot and Happy.   Beez 1
         CAD   Jan.   p13.   250w.   3
         DB   Feb. 26   p28.   200w.   5
         RFJ   July   p14.   450w. $3\frac{1}{2}$

2610 BERRY, Leon 'Chu'.   With Wingy Manone and His Orchestra
      RCA FPM 1-7026 (France) (Reissue)
         JJ   Feb.   p34, 35.   500w.   5

2611 BIGARD, Barney.   Clarinet Gumbo.   RCA APL1-1744
         CAD   Aug.   p37.   175w.   5
         MJ   Oct.   p22.   25w.   3

2612 BIRTHRIGHT.   Breath of Life.   Freelance Records FLS-2
         CAD   Oct.   p36.   125w.   3
         JJ   Nov.   p24.   150w.   3

2613 BIRTHRIGHT.   Free Spirits.   Freelance FS1
         JJ   Nov.   p24.   150w. $3\frac{1}{2}$

2614 BLACK Artists Group.   In Paris 1973.   Bag 324 000
         JJ   Feb.   p46.   300w.   5

2615 BLACKBYRDS.   City Life.   Fantasy F 9490
         CAD   Feb.   p28-9.   200w. $3\frac{1}{2}$

2616 BLAKE, Eubie.   Live Concert.   Eubie Blake Music EBM 5
         OB   April 10   p20.   200w.   3

2617 BLAKE, Eubie.   Sissle and Blake: Early Rare Recordings,
      Vol. 2.   Eubie Blake Music EBM-7 (Reissue)
         CAD   Aug.   p23.   125w.   4

2618   BLAKE, Eubie. Eubie Blake and His Proteges.   Eubie
       Blake Music EBM 8
          CAD Aug. p24. 175w. 5

2619   BLAKE, Eubie/Jim Hession.   Eubie Blake Music EBM 6
          DB April 10 p20. 200w. 3

2620   BLAKEY, Art.   Art Blakey and the Jazz Messengers '70.
       Catalyst CAT-7902
          CAD Aug. p17, 18. 170w. 5

2620a BLAKEY, Art and the Jazz Messengers. Live.   DJM
       DJSLM 2018 (E)
          RR Feb. p68. 50w. 3

2621   BLAKEY, Art and Max Roach.   Percussion Discussion.
       Chess Jazz Masters 2ACMJ-406 (2 discs) (Reissue)
          CAD Oct. p21. 250w. 4

2622   BLANKE, Toto. Electric Circus.   Vertigo 6360 634 (West
       Germany)
          MM Dec. 25 p18. 125w. $2\frac{1}{2}$

2623   BLEY, Paul. Alone Again. Improvising Artists 373840
          JA Summer p33-4. 300w. 4
          JF no. 44 p31. 75w. 4
          JJ May p27. 550w. 5
          MM May 22 p26. 300w. 3
          SR June p93. 100w. $4\frac{1}{2}$

2624   BLEY, Paul. Copenhagen and Haarlem.   Arista 1901 (Re-
       issue)
          CD May p22. 725w. 4
          CO May p22-3. 700w. 3
          LP March p14. 150w. 4

2625   BLEY, Paul. Live at the Hillcrest Club 1958.   Inner City
       IC 1007 (Reissue)
          CAD Oct. p35, 36. 175w. 4
          JJ Nov. p24. 225w. $3\frac{1}{2}$
          RFJ Dec. p13. 450w. 3

2626   BLEY, Paul. Open, to Love. ECM 1023 ST
          DB March 27 p17-8. 200w. 5
          SR June p88. 100w. $4\frac{1}{2}$

2627   BLEY, Paul. Quiet Song. Improvising Artists 373839
          JA Summer p33-4. 300w. 3
          JJ May p27. 550w. $3\frac{1}{2}$
          MM May 22 p26. 300w. 4
          SR Aug. p84. 150w. 4

2628   BLEY, Paul. Turning Point. Improvising Artists 373841

JA Summer p33-4. 300w. $3\frac{1}{2}$
JJ May p27. 550w. $4\frac{1}{2}$
MM May 22 p26. 300w. $3\frac{1}{2}$

2629 BLYTHE, Jimmy. Stomp Your Stuff. Swaggie S1324 (Australia) (Reissue)
CO Feb. p22. 400w. 5

2629a BOGER, Rickie. Slow Down Baby. Muse MR 5084
CAD Sept. p21. 150w. 2

2630 BOLAND, Francy. Papillon noir. Freedom FLP 40176 (E)
RR Nov. p107. 125w. $2\frac{1}{2}$

2631 BOLAND, Francy and Kenny Clarke. Open Door. Muse MR 5056
MJ Jan. p21. 125w. $3\frac{1}{2}$

2632 BOLLING, Claude. Original Ragtime. Columbia PC 3327
CK Oct. p46. 150w. 4

2633 BONNER, Joe. Angel Eyes. Muse MR 5114
CAD Nov. p23-4. 100w. $2\frac{1}{2}$

2634 BOOTSY's Rubber Band. Stretchin' Out. Warner K56200 (E)
MM May 22 p30. 150w. 3

2635 BOTHWELL, Johnny. Whatever Happened to Johnny Bothwell?
Bob Thiele Music BBM1-0741 (Reissue)
AU Aug. p79-80. 300w. 4

2636 BOWIE, Lester. Fast Last! Muse MR5055
CO May p24. 550w. 5
SR June p88. 300w. 1

2637 BOWIE, Lester. Rope-a-Dope. Muse MR 5081
CAD Sept. p20. 100w. 3

2638 BRACKEEN, Charles. Rhythm X. Strata-East SES 19736
CO June p13. 200w. $2\frac{1}{2}$

2639 BRACKEEN, Joanne. Snooze. Choice CRS 1009
CAD March p26, 28. 100w. $3\frac{1}{2}$
CK Aug. p45. 150w. 5
DB Oct. 7 p30. 300w. 5

2640 BRADLEY, Will. Aircheck 15 (Canada)
DB June 3 p30. 50w. $3\frac{1}{2}$
ST June-July p191-2. 125w. 2

2641 BRAFF, Ruby. Sonet SNTF 713 (E)
MM Dec. 25 p18. 450w. 3

272   Record Reviews, 1976

2642 BRAFF, Ruby and George Barnes. The Best I've Heard.
      Vogue--VJD 519 (France) (2 discs) (Reissue)
            JJ July p28. 475w. 5
            RR Dec. p102. 50w. 4½
            RR June p84. 100w. 4

2643 BRAFF, Ruby & George Barnes. Live at the New School.
      Chiaroscuro CR 126
            CO Feb. p22, 23. 99w. 4

2644 BRAFF, Ruby & George Barnes. Plays Gershwin. Concord
      5
            CO Feb. p22, 23. 99w. 4
            JJ June p41. 75w. 4½

2645 BRAFF, Ruby & George Barnes. Quartet. Chiaroscuro CR
      121
            CO Feb. p22. 99w. 2

2646 BRAFF, Ruby & George Barnes. Salutes Rogers and Hart.
      Concord 7
            CO Feb. p22, 23. 99w. 4
            MJ March p30. 50w. 3

2647 BRAFF, Ruby & George Barnes. To Fred Astaire with Love.
      RCA APL 1-1008
            CO Feb. p22, 23. 99w. 4

2648 BRAND, Dollar. African Portraits. Sackville 3009 (Canada)
            CAD Oct. p42. 200w. 3
            JJ Nov. p24. 200w. 3
            MM Dec. 4 p28. 75w. 3

2649 BRAND, Dollar. Ancient Africa. Japo 60005
            CO Feb. p23. 300w. 4

2650 BRAND, Dollar. The Children of Africa. Enja 2070 (Austria)
            JJ Sept. p29. 375w. 5
            MM Dec. 4 p28. 75w. 3½

2651 BRAND, Dollar. Good News from Africa. Enja 2048 (Aus-
      tria)
            CO May p23, 24. 250w. 5

2652 BRAND, Dollar. Mannenberg-'It's Where It's Happening'.
      as-shams SRK 786134 (South Africa)
            CO May p23. 200w. 5

2653 BRAND, Dollar. Sangoma. Sackville 3006 (Canada)
            CAD Aug. p26, 45. 200w. 5
            DB Jan. 15 p28. 200w. 4

2654 BRAND, Dollar. Underground in Africa. Mandla KRS 114

(South Africa)
    CO May p23. 200w. 4

2655 BRAND X. Unorthodox Behaviour.   Passport PPSD 98019
      RS Dec. 2 p107. 175w. 3

2656 BRASIL, Vera. Revelation 24
      DB May 6 p27. 450w. 5

2657 BRASS Construction. United Artists UALA545G
      DB April 22 p25. 175w. 1

2658 BRASS Fever. Impulse ASD-9308
      DB March 11 p23-4. 250w. 2
      ST April p107. 75w. 3

2659 BRAXTON, Anthony. Creative Orchestra Music 1976. Arista
    AL 4080
      DB Oct. 7 p20. 375w. 5
      RFJ July p11. 925w. $4\frac{1}{2}$
      RS Aug. 12 p59. 275w. $3\frac{1}{2}$
      SR Nov. p118. 225w. 5

2660 BRAXTON, Anthony. Five Pieces 1975. Arista AL 4084
      CRA April p73-4. 475w. 4
      CRE Feb. p63. 75w. $2\frac{1}{2}$
      DB Jan. 15 p20-1. 275w. 5
      LP March p14. 150w. 3
      MM May 29 p31. 675w. $3\frac{1}{2}$
      SR Feb. p76. 450w. 5
      RFJ Jan. p11-2. 700w. 3
      SOU March p47. 200w. 4

2661 BRAXTON, Anthony. In the Tradition--Volume 2. Steeple-
    chase SCS 1045 (Denmark)
      DB Oct. 7 p20. 375w. $2\frac{1}{2}$
      JJ June p30, 31. 325w. 3

2662 BRAXTON, Anthony. New York, Fall 1974. Arista AL 4032
      SR Aug. p90-1. 150w. 5

2663 BRAXTON, Anthony. Saxophone Improvisations Series F.
    Inner City 1008
      CAD Sept. p10. 75w. 3
      CAD Nov. p28. 100w. $2\frac{1}{2}$
      SR Dec. p124. 125w. $2\frac{1}{2}$
      JJ Nov. p24-5. 300w. $3\frac{1}{2}$

2664 BRAXTON, Anthony. Trio and Duet. Sackville 3007 (Cana-
    da)
      CAD Aug. p46. 275w. 5
      OLR Dec. p257. 75w. $4\frac{1}{2}$

2665 BRAXTON, Anthony. Town Hall 1972. Trio PA 3008-9
      (Japan) (2 discs)
          CAD Aug. p16. 50w. 4

2666 BRAXTON, Anthony & Derek Bailey. Duo v. 1, 2. Emanem
      3313/3314
          CAD Jan. p27-8. 175w. 3½
          CO   Feb. p23. 925w. 2½
          JF   no. 44 p30. 75w. 4
          JJ   Feb. p35. 500w. 5

2667 BRAXTON, Anthony and Chick Corea. Gathering. CBS/Sony
      20-XJ (Japan)
          CAD Aug. p17. 50w. 4

2668 BRAXTON, Anthony and Chick Corea. Live in German Con-
      cert. CBS/Sony SOPL 19-XJ (Japan)
          CAB Aug. p17. 50w. 3

2669 BRECKER Brothers. Back to Back. Arista AL 4061. Cart.
      8301-4061. Cass. 5301-4601
          SR May p100. 125w. 2½

2670 BRIGGS, Arthur. In Berlin: 14 Rare Recordings from 1927.
      Black Jack LP 3006 (Italy) (Reissue)
          ST April-May p156. 425w. 4½

2671 BRITT, Pat. Jazzman. Vee-Jay 3070
          CAD June p26, 28. 200w. 3½

2672 BRONSTEIN, Stan and Elephant's Memory Band. Our Own
      Music. Muse MR 5072
          CAD Nov. p28. 125w. 2

2673 BROOKS, Roy. The Free Slave. Muse 5003
          CO June p12. 300w. 4

2674 BROWN, Brian. Carton Streets. Forty Four 6357 700 (E)
          JJ June p40. 75w. 3

2675 BROWN, Clifford. Trip TLP-5550 (Reissue)
          CO May p24. 350w. 3

2676 BROWN, Clifford. Brownie Eyes. Blue Note BN-LA267-G
          SR Jan. p98. 250w. 4

2677 BROWN, Clifford. The Complete Paris Collection. Vogue
      VJT-3001 (3 discs) (France) (Reissue)
          JJ July p28-9. 950w. 4½
          RR June p84. 100w. 3½

2678 BROWN, Clifford. With Strings. Trip TLP-5502 (Reissue)
          SR Jan. p98. 250w. 4

2679 BROWN, Clifford and Max Roach.   Brown & Roach Inc.
Trip TLP-5520 (Reissue)
     SR Jan. p98. 250w. 4

2680 BROWN, Clifford and Max Roach.   Jordu.   Trip Jazz TLP-
5540 (Reissue)
     CO June p13, 14. 400w. 4

2681 BROWN, Clifford and Max Roach.   Study in Brown.   Trip
TLP-5530 (Reissue)
     CO May p19, 20, 21. 575w. 4

2682 BROWN, Marion.   Duets.   Arista Freedom 1904
     DB Sept. 9 p26, 30. 350w. 5

2683 BROWN, Marion.   Gesprachsfetzen.   Calig CAL 10601 (West
Germany)
     CAD Sept. p10. 50w. 4

2684 BROWN, Marion.   In Sommerhausen.   Calig CAL 10605
     CAD Sept. p10. 75w. 4

2685 BROWN, Marion.   Porto Novo.   Arista AL1001 (Reissue)
     CO Feb. p19. 275w. 4
     SR Aug. p90-1. 150w. 4

2686 BROWN, Marion.   Vista.   Impulse ASD 9304
     DB Feb. 26 p30. 350w. 3

2687 BROWN, Ray.   Brown's Bag.   Concord CJ-19
     CAD Oct. p48. 120w. 2

2688 BROWN, Sandy.   Clarinet Opening.   CSA CLPS 1009 (Denmark)
     JJ March p27. 425w. 4

2689 BROWN, Sandy.   McJazz Lives On! A Tribute to Sandy
Brown.   One Up OU 2092 (E) (Reissue)
     GR April p1673. 250w. 3
     ST Feb.-March p199. 425w. 4

2690 BRUBECK, Dave.   All the Things We Are.   Atlantic SD-1684
     CAD Aug. p43. 175w. 4
     CK Oct. p47. 100w. 5
     JA Fall p47. 300w. $3\frac{1}{2}$

2691 BRUBECK, Dave.   Time Out/Time Further Out.   CBS 22013
(2 discs) (E) (Reissue)
     CAC Aug. p195. 475w. $3\frac{1}{2}$
     MM April 24 p24. 650w. 4

2692 BRUBECK, Dave and Paul Desmond.   The Duets: 1975.
Horizon SP-703

CAD   Feb.   p18.   75w.   3
CK   March   p46.   400w.   4
CRE   March   p62.   300w.   4
CRE   April   p12.   25w. $2\frac{1}{2}$
DB   Feb. 26   p20.   325w.   4
HF   April   p142.   275w.   3
MJ   Sept.   p75.   100w.   3
MM   Feb. 21   p31.   550w.   4
RFJ   Feb.   p11.   350w.   4
RR   March   p74.   100w.   4
SOU   April   p48.   75w.   3
SR   April   p99.   100w. $4\frac{1}{2}$

2693 BRUBECK, Dave and Jimmy Rushing.   Columbia CS 8353
      RFJ   June   p9.   150w.   4

2694 BRYANT, Ray.   Here's Ray Bryant.   Pablo 2310 746
      GR   Nov.   p900.   125w.   3
      JJ   Oct.   p30.   600w.   5
      MJ   July   p52.   50w.   3
      MM   July 24   p26.   225w. $3\frac{1}{2}$
      SOU   July   p40.   325w. $3\frac{1}{2}$

2695 BRYANT, Willie and Jimmie Lunceford.   RCA Bluebird AXM2-
      5502 (2 discs) (Reissue)
      DB   March 11   p28-9.   850w.   5

2696 BRYDEN, Beryl.   Down Yonder in New Orleans.   Elite SOLP
      514 (E)
      JF   no. 41.   p25.   100w.   3

2697 BUCKNER, Milt & Jo Jones.   Blues for Diane.   Jazz Odyssey
      011 (France)
      CO   Feb.   p24.   200w.   3
      GR   Oct.   p670.   250w. $3\frac{1}{2}$
      JJ   June   p29.   100w. $3\frac{1}{2}$

2698 BUCKNER, Teddy.   On the Air, v. 1.   Aircheck #10 (Canada)
      CAD   Sept.   p25.   175w.   4
      JJ   April   p29.   300w.   3

2699 BUNCH, John.   John's Bunch.   Famous Door HL 107
      CAD   Aug.   p40.   125w.   4
      JJ   Oct.   p30.   500w.   5

2700 BUNCH, John.   Plays Kurt Weil.   Chiarscuro CR 144
      JA   Fall   p47.   150w.   4
      SR   Nov.   p118.   100w.   2

2701 BURBANK, Albert.   Living New Orleans Jazz 1969.   Smoky
      Mary SM 1969 (E)
      FT   April/May   p18-9.   450w.   2

2702 BURGEVIN, Mike. Finger Poppin'. Jezebel 101
CAD Oct. p30. 425w. 3

2703 BURRELL, Dave. After Love. America 30 AM 6115 (France)
CAD Sept. p10. 105w. 4

2704 BURRELL, Dave. High Won--High Two. Arista AL 1906
(partial reissue)
CRA Nov. p72. 50w. 3
RFJ Dec. p13. 400w. 4

2705 BURRELL, Kenny. Ellington Is Forever. Fantasy Records,
F-79005
CAD Feb. p22. 150w. 3
DB April 22 p24. 275w. 4
GP March p73. 275w. $3\frac{1}{2}$
MJ March p23. 150w. 3

2706 BURRELL, Kenny. Sky Street. Fantasy F-9514
CAD Oct. p37. 150w. 2

2707 BURRELL, Kenny and John Coltrane. Prestige, P-24059 (2
discs) (Reissue)
CAD Nov. p27. 125w. 2
DB Oct. 21 p34. 150w. 5
GP Aug. p81. 25w. $2\frac{1}{2}$
RFJ Oct. p9. 550w. 3

2708 BURROW, Don. At the Sydney Opera House. Mainstream
416
DB March 25 p34-5. 25w. $1\frac{1}{2}$
SR Sept. p86. 375w. 3

2709 BURTON, Gary. Dreams So Real. ECM-1-1072
CAD Oct. p31. 100w. 5
DB Nov. 18 p18. 300w. 4
JA Fall p47-8. 250w. 5
MM July 31 p22. 150w. $2\frac{1}{2}$

2710 BURTON, Gary. 7 Songs for Quartet and Chamber Orchestra.
ECM 1040
CO Feb. p24. 375w. 2
SR Feb. p98. 175w. 5

2711 BURTON, Gary. Tennessee Firebird. RCA
RFJ June p7. 100w. 4

2712 BURTON, Gary and Steve Swallow. Hotel Hello. ECM 1055
SR Jan. p96-7. 75w. 5

2713 BURTON, Gary and Eberhard Weber. Ring. ECM 1051
JJ Feb. p35. 250w. 5

2714 BUTLER, Billy and Al Casey. Guitar Odyssey. Jazz Odyssey 012 (France)
      JJ Jan. p29. 325w. $3\frac{1}{2}$
      RR Feb. p68. 50w. $2\frac{1}{2}$

2715 BUTTERFIELD, Billy and Dick Wellstood. Rapport. 77 Records 54 (E)
      GR March p1521. 300w. $3\frac{1}{2}$
      ST Dec. 1975-Jan. 1976. p76-7. 225w. 5

2716 BYRD, Charlie. Top Hat. Fantasy Records, F-9496
      GP Feb. p70. 225w. 4
      HF March p112. 200w. $1\frac{1}{2}$
      SOU March p46. 50w. $2\frac{1}{2}$

2717 BYRD, Donald. Black Byrd. Blue Note BN-LA 047
      JJ Jan. p29. 250w. 1

2718 BYRD, Donald. House of Byrd. Prestige P-24066 (2 discs)
      CAD Oct. p25. 250w. 4

2719 BYRD, Donald. Long Green. SJL 1101. Savoy (Reissue)
      CAD Sept. p25, 26. 50w. 4
      DB Dec. 2 p25-6. 200w. $4\frac{1}{2}$

2720 BYRD, Donald. Places and Spaces. Blue Note BN LA546-G
      BM March p19. 325w. 4
      DB Feb. 12 p26-7. 175w. 3
      GR Sept. p493. 225w. 3
      JJ April p29. 100w. 1

2721 CALIFORNIA State University Northridge Jazz Ensemble. Dizzyland. CFS 3581
      JF April p64-5. 1250w. 3

2722 CALIMAN, Hadley. Projecting. Catalyst 7604
      CAD Aug. p37, 38. 150w. 4
      MJ July p55. 75w. 3
      SR Nov. p118, 120. 75w. $3\frac{1}{2}$

2723 CALLENDER, Red. Basin Street Brass. Legend LGS-1003
      CO Feb. p24, 25. 225w. 2

2724 CALLOWAY, Cab. Golden Era LP 15013 (E)
      JJ March p27. 275w. 4

2725 CALLOWAY, Cab/Count Basie. Jazum 45 (Reissue)
      JJ Oct. p30-1. 375w. $3\frac{1}{2}$

2726 CANADIAN Brass. Rag-ma-tazz. Boot BMC 3004 (Canada)
      RT Jan./Feb. p7. 100w. $3\frac{1}{2}$

2727 CANDOLI, Conte and Frank Rosolino. Conversation. RCA APL1-1509

CAD   Sept.   p6.   50w.   5
SR   Nov.   p120.   100w.   3

2728   CARR, Peter.   Not a Word on It.   Big Tree 89518
GP   Dec.   p104.   125w. $3\frac{1}{2}$

2729   CARROLL, Barbara.   Barbara Carroll.   Blue Note LA645-G
CAD   Sept.   p6.   50w.   4
CK   Dec.   p48.   100w. $3\frac{1}{2}$
MJ   Oct.   p23.   50w.   3

2730   CARTER, Benny.   Big Band Bounce.   Capitol M-11057 (Re-issue)
JJ   May   p40.   150w. $4\frac{1}{2}$

2731   CARTER, Benny.   The King.   Pablo 2310-768
CAC   Dec.   p354.   275w.   5
CAD   Sept.   p6.   25w.   3
DB   Dec. 2   p19-20.   350w.   3
JA   Fall   p48.   750w.   5
JJ   Nov.   p25.   275w. $3\frac{1}{2}$
MJ   Oct.   p22.   25w.   3
MM   Oct. 9   p34.   425w. $2\frac{1}{2}$

2732   CARTER, Betty.   Bet-Car MK 1002
CAD   May   p28-9.   250w. $4\frac{1}{2}$

2733   CARTER, Betty.   Finally.   Roulette Birdland SR 5000
CAD   April   p32-3.   100w.   4
JA   Summer   p34-5.   200w. $3\frac{1}{2}$

2734   CARTER, Betty.   Round Midnight.   Roulette Birdland SR 5001
CAD   April   p32.   100w.   4
JA   Summer   p34-5.   200w.   4

2735   CARTER, Betty.   What a Little Moonlight Can Do.   ABC Impulse 9321 (Reissue)
CAD   Nov.   p19.   200w.   3

2736   CARTER, Ron.   Anything Goes.   Kudu KU-25S1.   Cart. KU8-25.   Cass. KUC-25
BM   July   p50.   200w.   2
CAC   May   p62.   75w.   3
DB   April 22   p29-30.   350w.   1
MJ   Jan.   p20.   75w.   3
SR   March   p82.   250w.   4

2737   CARTER, Ron.   Spanish Blue.   CT1 6051 S1
CO   June   p14.   125w.   2
SR   Oct.   p92.   100w.   4

2738   CARVIN, Michael.   The Camel.   Steeplechase SCS 1038 (Denmark)

DB May 6 p31-2. 100w. 4
JJ March p27, 28. 525w. $4\frac{1}{2}$

2739 CASE, John and Jerry Case. Birderic. Priority PRS 405
      CAD Sept. p11. 100w. 4

2740 CATHERINE, Philip. Nairam. Warner Brothers BS 2950
      (Reissue)
      CAD Aug. p25. 105w. 4
      DB Nov. 18 p28-9. 275w. 3
      GP Sept. p86. 175w. 4
      JA Fall p48. 200w. 2

2741 CHADBOURNE, Eugene. Solo Acoustic Guitar: Vol 1. Para-
      chute Records P0001
      CAD Oct. p12. 25w. 3
      GP Sept. p86. 300w. 4
      JJ Aug. p38. 150w. 5

2742 CHAMBERPOT. Bead BEAD 2 (E)
      MM Nov. 13 p30. 600w. 3

2743 CHAMBERS, Paul and John Coltrane. High Step. Blue Note
      BNLA 451 H2 (2 discs)
      LP March p15. 200w. 3

2744 CHARTERS, Ann. Genius of Scott Joplin. GNP Crescendo
      GNPS 9032
      RT May/June p5. 150w. $1\frac{1}{2}$

2745 CHAVERS, Charlie. The Most Intimate. Bethlehem BCP
      6005 (Reissue)
      MJ Dec. p26. 75w. 4

2746 CHEATHAM, Adolph. Jezebel 102 ST
      CAD Nov. p21-2. 200w. 3

2747 CHERRY, Don. Eternal Now. Sonet SNTF 653 (E)
      CAD Sept. p10. 75w. 3

2748 CHERRY, Don. Organic Music Society. Caprice RIKS DLP 1
      (2 discs) (Sweden)
      CAD Sept. p10. 100w. 4
      SR May p100. 250w. 2

2749 CHERRY, Don. The Third World--Underground. Trio PAP
      9018 (Japan)
      CAD Aug. p16. 105w. 4

2750 CHERRY, Don. Togetherness. Durium CICALA BL 7068 J
      (Sweden)
      CAD Sept. p10. 75w. 5

2751 CHRISTIAN, Charlie. With Benny Goodman and the Sextet.
      Jazz Archives JA 23
            DB June 3 p30. 75w. 5
            JJ Feb. p27. 575w. 5

2752 CHRISTIAN, Charlie and Lester Young.   Together 1940.
      Jazz Archives JA-6 (Reissue)
            SR June p90. 1150w. $4\frac{1}{2}$

2753 CIRILLO, Wally and Joe Dioro.   Rapport.   Spitball SB-1
            CAD July p16. 100w. $2\frac{1}{2}$
            CO Feb. p26, 27. 425w. 5

2754 CLARK, Sonny. Memorial Album.   Xanadu 121
            RFJ Dec. p13, 16. 450w. $3\frac{1}{2}$
            JA Fall p48. 300w. $2\frac{1}{2}$

2755 CLARKE, Stanley. Atlantic NE 431
            DB March 27 p17. 350w. 5
            JJ Feb. p46. 300w. 1

2756 CLARKE, Stanley. Journey to Love.   Nemperor NE 433
            BM Jan. p26. 75w. 3
            CRA Feb. p74. 150w. $3\frac{1}{2}$
            GP Jan. p71. 650w. $4\frac{1}{2}$
            MG Jan. p34. 50w. $3\frac{1}{2}$
            MJ Jan. p20. 75w. 3
            RS Jan. 15 p52. 225w. $2\frac{1}{2}$
            SOU Jan. p39. 25w. $1\frac{1}{2}$
            SR March p101. 200w. 2

2757 CLARKE, Stanley. School Days.   Nemperor NE 439
            BM Dec. p55. 250w. 4
            CRA Dec. p78. 400w. 3
            CRE Dec. p58-9. 350w. 4
            GP Dec. p104. 125w. 3
            GP Dec. p104. 75w. $3\frac{1}{2}$
            GRA Dec. p1079. 75w. 4
            JJ Nov. p25. 300w. 2
            RS Nov. 18 p80-1. 175w. $3\frac{1}{2}$

2758 CLAYTON, Buck. The Golden Days of Jazz.   CBS 88031 (2
      discs) (Netherlands) (Reissue)
            RR June p84. 125w. $4\frac{1}{2}$
            RR Dec. p102. 50w. 3

2759 CLAYTON, Buck. Jam Sessions.   Chiaroscuro CR132 and
      143 (2 discs)
            DB June 3 p29. 300w. 4
            JJ July p29. 575w. 5
            MM Aug. 14 p30. 550w. 3
            RR June p84. 100w. $3\frac{1}{2}$

2760   CLEVELAND, Jimmy. 1956. Trip TLP 5575 (Reissue)
       JA   Fall p56.   50w.   3½

2761   CLIMAX Jazz Band. I Can't Escape from You.   Tormax
       33005 (Canada)
       SOU   July p41.   150w.   3

2762   COATES, John Jr.   The Jazz Piano of John Coates Jr.   Om-
       nisound N 1004
       CAD   Jan.   p14.   75w.   3
       CK   March   p48.   175w.   4

2763   COBHAM, Billy.   A Funky Thide of Sings.   Atlantic SD 18149.
       Cart. TP 18149.   Cass. CS 18149
       DB   Feb. 26 p20.   400w.   3
       LP   April p14.   100w.   2
       SR   March p101.   150w.   2

2764   COBHAM, Billy.   Life & Times.   Atlantic SD 18166
       DB   Aug. 12 p26.   350w.   3
       GP   Aug.   p81.   25w.   2½

2765   COBHAM, Billy.   Shabazz.   Atlantic SD 18139.   Cart. TP
       18139.   Cass. CS 18139
       SR   Nov.   p112.   175w.   4½

2766   COBHAM, Billy.   Total Eclipse.   Atlantic SD 18121
       DB   March 27 p17.   425w.   4

2767   COBHAM, Billy and George Duke.   Live on Tour in Europe.
       Atlantic SD 18194
       PRM   Nov.   p45.   475w.   1
       RS   Dec. 16 p98.   200w.   2½

2768   COHEN, Alan.   Black, Brown and Beige.   Monmouth Ever-
       green MES 7077 (Reissue)
       DB   Nov. 4 p29.   125w.   3½
       SR   Nov.   p121-2.   125w.   3½

2769   COHN, Al.   Beautiful.   Xanadu 115
       SOU   May p46.   25w.   3½

2770   COHN, Al.   Play It Now.   Xanadu 110
       CAD   April p42-3.   75w.   2
       JA   Fall p48.   250w.   3½
       SOU   May p46.   25w.   3½

2771   COHN, Al and Zoot Sims.   Motoring Along.   Sonet SNTF 684
       (E)
       JJ   March p28.   225w.   5

2772   COLE, Cozy and Red Norvo.   Jazz Giants, Volume 3.   Trip
       TLP-5538

CO   April   p20, 21.   525w.   3

2773 COLE, Nat "King." Anatomy of a Jam Session.   Black Lion
BLP 30104 (E) (Reissue)
MM   Sept. 4 p21.   225w.   5

2774 COLE, Nat "King." Crazy bout Rhythm.   DJM 22029 (E) (Re-
issue)
CAC   Dec.   p354.   200w. $3\frac{1}{2}$
JJ   March   p28.   275w. $3\frac{1}{2}$
MM   Jan. 31   p22.   600w.   4
RR   June   p84.   25w.   3

2775 COLE, Nat "King." Unfamiliar.   Capitol EST 23480 (E) (Reissue)
JJ   June   p41.   150w.   4

2776 COLEMAN, Bill.   Mainstream at Montreux.   Black Lion BL-
212.   Cart. 8T-212
SR   April   p89, 92.   150w.   4

2777 COLEMAN, Ornette.   Chappaqua Suite.   CBS 62896/97 (2
discs) (France)
CAD   Sept.   p9, 10.   100w.   4

2778 COLEMAN, Ornette.   Crisis.   Impulse IMPL 8002 (E)
GR   Feb.   p1390.   250w. $3\frac{1}{2}$

2779 COLEMAN, Ornette.   Free Jazz.   Atlantic SD 1364
MM   Aug. 7   p20.   200w. $3\frac{1}{2}$
RFJ   June   p8.   200w. $4\frac{1}{2}$

2780 COLLETTE, Buddy.   Now and Then.   Legend LGS-1004
CO   Feb.   p27.   125w.   3

2781 COLLIE, Max.   Battle of Trafalgar.   Reality R 106 (2 discs)
(E)
CO   June   p14.   50w. $2\frac{1}{2}$
JJ   Feb.   p35.   100w.   0

2782 COLLIE, Max.   On Tour in the U.S.A.   GHB-63
CO   June   p14.   525w.   3
JJ   Feb.   p35.   100w.   0

2783 COLLIE, Max.   World Champions of Jazz.   Black Lion BLPX
12137/8 (2 discs) (E)
JJ   Sept.   p30.   525w. $3\frac{1}{2}$
MM   July 17   p26.   550w. $3\frac{1}{2}$
RR   Oct.   p102.   50w.   3
ST   Aug.-Sept.   p238.   300w.   5

2784 COLLIER, Graham.   Midnight Blue.   Mosaic GCM 751 (E)
JJ   Jan.   p29.   200w.   4

2785 COLTRANE, Alice. Eternity. Warner Bros. BS 2916
          CK   Aug.   p46.   50w.   2
          DB   Nov. 4 p25-6.   325w.   3
          MG   June p50.   75w.   3
          MHF June-July p68.   275w. $4\frac{1}{2}$
          MJ   July p54.   50w.   0
          MM   May 8 p28.   675w. $4\frac{1}{2}$
          RS   June 17 p55.   100w.   3

2786 COLTRANE, Alice and Santana. Illuminations. Columbia PC
      32900.   Cart. PCA 32900.   Cass. PCT 32900
          SR   April p92.   200w.   5

2787 COLTRANE, John. The Gentle Side of J.C. Impulse ASH
      9306-2 (2 discs)
          JJ   March p28.   350w. $4\frac{1}{2}$
          LP   March p15.   200w.   4

2788 COLTRANE, John. Giant Steps. Atlantic SD 1311
          MM   Aug. 21 p20.   400w.   5

2789 COLTRANE, John. In Europe Vol. 3. Beppo 507 (E)
          JJ   Oct.   p31.   300w. $4\frac{1}{2}$

2790 COLTRANE, John. BYG YX 4001-2 (Japan)
          CAD Aug.   p16.   100w.   4

2791 COLTRANE, John. A Love Supreme. Impulse AS 77
          CRA March p76-7.   150w. $4\frac{1}{2}$
          RFJ June p9.   75w.   4

2792 COLTRANE, John. Turning Point. Bethlehem BCP 6024
      (Reissue)
          ARG March p56.   100w. $3\frac{1}{2}$
          CAD Oct.   p39.   175w.   5
          MJ   Dec.   p26.   50w. $3\frac{1}{2}$
          PRM Oct.   p46.   300w.   3

2793 COLTRANE, John and Paul Chambers. High Step. Blue
      Note BN-LA 451-H2 (2 discs) (Reissue)
          CO   Feb.   p25, 26.   1025w.   4

2794 COLTRANE, John and Wilbur Harden. Countdown. Savoy
      SJL 2203 (2 discs) (Reissue)
          CAD Aug.   p42.   300w.   5
          JA   Summer p41-2.   100w.   4
          JJ   Dec.   p26.   525w. $3\frac{1}{2}$
          PRM May p63.   50w.   3
          RFJ Oct.   p9.   550w. $3\frac{1}{2}$
          SR   Nov.   p133.   25w.   3

2795 COMPOSERS' Collective. Poum. Composers' Collective 721
          AU   March p85.   250w.   0

2796   CONDON, Eddie. All Star Session. DJM DJM965 (E) (Reissue)
       GR March p1521. 250w. 3
       RR Feb. p68. 125w. 3

2797   CONFREY, Zez. Novelty Piano Solos.   Genesis GS 1051
       SR June p73. 275w. 2

2798   CONFREY, Zez. You Tell 'em Ivories!   Golden Crest CRS-
       31040
       SR June p73. 275w. 2

2799   CONNOR, Chris. Finest of.   Bethlehem 2BP1001 (2 discs)
       (Reissue)
       CAD Feb. p22. 150w. 3
       MJ Feb. p47. 50w. 3
       RS July 15 p68. 200w. 3

2800   CONNORS, Bill. Theme to the Guardian.   ECM 1057
       DB May 6 p23-4. 225w. 3

2801   CONNORS, Norman. Saturday Night Special.   Buddah BDS
       5643
       DB Feb. 12 p24-5. 300w. $2\frac{1}{2}$

2802   CONNORS, Norman. Slew Foot.   Buddah BDS 5611
       BD April 10 p20. 250w. 3

2803   CONNORS, Norman. You Are My Starship.   Buddah BDS
       5655
       DB Nov. 4 p20. 300w. 2

2804   CONTRACTION. La bourse ou la vie.   Deram DEF-106
       (Canada)
       CO April p19. 300w. 5

2805   COREA, Chick. Circling in.   Blue Note LA 472 (2 discs)
       BD Aug. p36. 125w. $3\frac{1}{2}$
       MG June p50. 100w. $2\frac{1}{2}$
       MM Dec. 18 p20. 1050w. 3
       PRM Jan. p37. 50w. 3

2806   COREA, Chick. The Leprechaun.   Polydor PD 6062
       CAC June p94, 96. 350w. 3
       DB June 3 p21. 375w. 5
       RS July 1 p67-8. 150w. 3
       SOU May p46. 50w. $2\frac{1}{2}$
       SR June p93. 100w. 4

2807   COREA, Chick. No Mystery.   Polydor PD-6512.   Cass.
       CF-6512
       LP Aug. p10. 125w. 3

2808   COREA, Chick. Return to Forever.   ECM 1022

CRE   June   p60.   75w.   4
LP   March   p15.   175w. $3\frac{1}{2}$
SR   April   p100-1.   250w.   3

2809   COREA, Chick.   Sundance.   Groove Merchant GM-530
LP   July   p12.   200w.   4

2810   CORYELL, Larry.   Aspects.   Arista AL 4077
DB   Dec. 2   p17-18.   275w.   2
GP   Oct.   p97.   100w.   4
MM   Aug. 14   p28.   400w.   3
RR   Sept.   p90.   50w. $1\frac{1}{2}$

2811   CORYELL, Larry.   The Essential.   Vanguard VSD 75/76 (2 discs) (Reissue)
LP   Jan.   p15-6.   150w.   3

2812   CORYELL, Larry.   Fairyland.   Mega 607
CAD   May   p25.   125w.   1

2813   CORYELL, Larry.   Level One.   Arista AL 4052
RR   May   p75.   150w.   4

2814   CORYELL, Larry.   Planet End.   Vanguard 79367
CAD   April   p35.   75w. $3\frac{1}{2}$
DB   Aug. 12   p30-1.   350w.   4
MM   July 3   p21.   25w.   3

2815   CORYELL, Larry.   Spaces.   Vanguard VSD 79345
SR   Feb.   p98.   275w.   5

2816   COUNT Ossie and the Mystic Revelation of Rastafari.   Grounation.   B&C Records NTI VULX 301 (3 discs) (E)
SO   May/June   p42-3.   175w. $4\frac{1}{2}$

2817   COWELL, Stanley.   Brilliant Circles.   Arista Freedom 1009 (Reissue)
CO   June   p15, 16.   375w. $2\frac{1}{2}$
LP   March   p15.   125w.   3

2818   COXHILL, Lol.   Fleas in the Custard.   Caroline (E)
MM   May 8   p25.   75w.   1

2818a   CRAWFORD, Hank.   I Hear a Symphony.   Kudu KU 26
BM   Aug.   p45.   75w.   2
MM   May 8   p25.   75w.   1

2819   CREATIVE Construction Co.   CCC.   Muse MR 5071
AU   Feb.   p99-100.   1000w. $4\frac{1}{2}$
DB   May 20   p29.   250w.   5

2820   CRISS, Sonny.   Crisscraft.   Muse 5068
CO   June   p12.   250w.   5

MJ   March   p23.   75w. $4\frac{1}{2}$

2821   CRISS, Sonny.   Out of Nowhere.   Muse MR 5089
       CAD   Nov.   p26.   50w. $3\frac{1}{2}$

2822   CRISS, Sonny.   Saturday Morning.   Xanadu 105
       CO   June   p12.   250w.   5

2823   CROSBY, Bob.   Jazum 48/49 (Reissue)
       JA   Fall   p56.   75w.   3
       JJ   Aug.   p33.   525w. $4\frac{1}{2}$

2824   CROSBY, Bob.   Aircheck 17 (Reissue) (Canada)
       CAD   Nov.   p24.   75w. $2\frac{1}{2}$
       JJ   Nov.   p25.   150w.   3

2825   CROSBY, Bob.   1936.   London HMG 5021 (E)
       GR   June   p101.   150w.   4
       JJ   April   p29, 30.   150w. $2\frac{1}{2}$
       MM   March 20   p24.   375w.   3
       RR   June   p83.   50w.   3

2826   CROSBY, Bob.   Silver Star Swing.   Coral PCO 7995 (West
       Germany) (Reissue)
       RR   June   p83.   50w. $3\frac{1}{2}$

2827   CULLUM, Jim.   Happy Landing!   Audiophile AP121
       CO   Feb.   p26.   250w.   3

2828   CURSON, Ted.   Tears for Dolphy.   Arista/Freedom AL 1021
       AU   Sept.   p86-7.   650w.   4
       CRA   July   p81.   200w. $2\frac{1}{2}$
       CRE   July   p12.   50w.   4
       DB   May 20   p22.   275w.   5
       SR   Aug.   p84, 87.   325w.   4

2829   CYRILLE, Andrew.   Celebration.   Institute of Percussion
       Studies IPS 002
       JF   no. 44.   p77.   300w.   4
       SOU   Jan.   p39.   50w.   2

2830   CYRILLE, Andrew and Milford Graves.   Dialogue of Drums.
       Institute of Percussion Studies IPS 001
       CAD   Jan.   p17.   200w. $4\frac{1}{2}$
       DB   Oct.   p20, 22.   300w.   4
       JF   April   p64.   675w. $3\frac{1}{2}$
       JF   no. 44   p77.   300w.   4

2831   CZAR.   From Russia with Jazz.   Different Drummer Records
       DD 1002
       CK   Jan.   p47.   200w.   4
       DB   March 25   p29-30.   150w.   3
       MJ   Feb.   p30.   75w.   2

2832 DADI, Marcel. Country Show. Guitar World GW 4
        GP   Sept. p87.   200w. $4\frac{1}{2}$

2833 DAMERON, Tadd and Bill Evans. The Arrangers' Touch.
        Prestige P-24049 (2 discs) (Reissue)
        CO   March p18.   700w.   5

2834 DANDRIDGE, Putney. Volume 1/2. Rarities no. 26/7 (E)
        (2 discs)
        JJ   May p27.   725w.   5

2835 DANIELS, Eddie. A Flower for All Seasons. Choice CRS
        1002
        CO   June p16.   375w.   4

2836 DANSERS Inferno. Creative One. Thimble (no serial no.)
        DB   March 25 p34-5.   25w.   1

2837 DAPOGNY, James. Piano Music of Ferdinand "Jelly Roll"
        Morton. Smithsonian Coll. 003
        CAD Aug. p42.   105w.   5
        JA   Fall p48, 50.   400w.   4
        JJ   Sept. p30.   425w.   5
        SR   Nov. p120-1.   325w.   5

2838 DAVIS, Eddy. Plays Ragtime. Pa Da P7402
        CO   June p16.   250w.   2

2839 DAVIS, Eddy. Plays and Sings Just for Fun. Pa Da P7402
        CO   June p16.   250w.   4

2840 DAVIS, Rev. Gary. Ragtime Guitar. Kicking Mule 106
        LB   May-June p40.   175w. $4\frac{1}{2}$

2841 DAVIS, Miles. Vol. 3. Archives of Jazz AJ 503 (Reissue)
        DB   Feb. 12 p29-31.   200w.   5

2842 DAVIS, Miles. Agharta. Columbia PG 33967 (2 discs).
        Cart. PGT 33967
        CRA April p77.   200w. $2\frac{1}{2}$
        DB   May 6 p23.   450w.   4
        JF   no. 41 p24.   75w.   4
        JF   no. 44 p74.   550w.   0
        RR   July p80.   50w. $3\frac{1}{2}$
        SR   June p94.   100w.   3

2843 DAVIS, Miles. At Birdland 1951. Beppo 501 (E)
        JJ   Sept. p29.   525w. $4\frac{1}{2}$

2844 DAVIS, Miles. Dig. Prestige P 24054 (2 discs) (Reissue)
        LP   April p14.   100w. $2\frac{1}{2}$

2845 DAVIS, Miles. Get Up with It. Columbia KG33236

CO   Feb.   p27.   250w.   0

2846   DAVIS, Miles.   Green Haze.   Prestige P-24064 (2 discs)
       (Reissue)
       CAD   Oct.   p25.   250w.   5

2847   DAVIS, Miles.   Kind of Blue.   Columbia PC8163
       RFJ   June   p8.   100w.   4

2848   DAVIS, Miles.   Lady Bird.   Jazz Showcase 5004
       JJ   Jan.   p29, 30.   450w. $4\frac{1}{2}$

2849   DAVIS, Miles.   Miles in Tokyo.   CBS/Sony SOPL 162 (Japan)
       CAD   Aug.   p17.   150w.   4

2850   DAVIS, Miles.   Pangarea.   CBS/Sony SOPZ 96-97 (Japan)
       (2 discs)
       CAD   Aug.   p16.   105w.   4

2851   DAVISON, Wild Bill.   Birthday.   Hore Kiks HK LP 5 (Den-
       mark)
       CO   June   p17.   300w.   3
       JJ   Jan.   p40.   100w. $3\frac{1}{2}$

2852   DAVISON, Wild Bill.   Live at the Rainbow Room.   Chiaro-
       scuro CR-124
       CO   June   p16, 17.   275w.   3

2853   DEAN, Roger.   Lysis Live.   Mosaic GCM 762 (E)
       JJ   Dec.   p26.   350w.   3

2854   DeFRANCO, Buddy.   Free Sail.   Choice CRS 1008
       SR   July   p86.   275w.   4

2855   DEGEN, Bob.   Sequoia Song.   Enja 2072 (Austria)
       JJ   Sept.   p30-1.   325w.   5

2856   DE JOHNETTE, Jack.   ECM 1074
       CAD   Nov.   p15.   75w.   2
       DB   Dec. 2   p16.   300w.   5
       GP   Dec.   p105.   25w.   3
       MM   Oct. 9   p3-4.   500w. $1\frac{1}{2}$
       PRM   Oct.   p46.   525w.   3
       RS   Nov. 18   p81.   300w. $3\frac{1}{2}$

2857   DEODATO.   Very Together.   MCA 2219
       MM   Dec. 11   p22.   250w.   3

2858   DE PARIS, Wilbur.   At Symphony Hall.   Atlantic ATL 50
       237 (E) (Reissue)
       MM   Aug. 14   p30.   225w.   3

2859   DESEO, Csaba.   Four String Tschaba.   Four String Tschaba.

MPS 20 223663 (West Germany)
    JF   April   p63.   300w.   3

2860 DESMOND, Paul.   Live.   Horizon SP 850
    DB   Oct. 7 p22.   225w.   4
    GP   Oct.   p97.   75w.   3
    JJ   Oct.   p31-2.   400w.   5
    MJ   Sept.   p35.   50w.   3
    RR   Nov.   p107.   100w. $3\frac{1}{2}$

2861 DE SOUZA, Raul.   Colors.   Milestone M-9061
    SR   Oct.   p96.   175w.   1

2862 DICKERSON, Walt.   Peace.   Steeplechase SCS 1042 (Denmark)
    DB   May 6 p32.   175w.   5
    JJ   May   p27.   175w.   1

2863 DIGGS, David.   Out on a Limb.   PBR International PBR 9
    CAD   Nov.   p23.   150w. $1\frac{1}{2}$

2864 DIGGS, David.   Supercook.   Instant Joy Records S-1002
    CAD   Sept.   p8.   100w.   4

2865 DIKKER, Loek.   Tan Tango.   WM 001 (E)
    MM   Dec. 25 p18.   125w. $2\frac{1}{2}$

2866 DI MARCO, Marco.   At the Living Room.   Modern Jazz
Record MJC-0098 (France)
    CO   June p17.   175w.   3

2867 DIMEOLA, Al.   Land of the Midnight Sun.   Columbia PC
34074
    RS   July 1   p67-8.   150w.   3

2868 DIORIO, Joe.   Solo Guitar.   Spitball SB 2
    CAD   Jan.   p16.   100w. $2\frac{1}{2}$
    DB   Feb. 26 p28.   200w. $3\frac{1}{2}$
    JJ   Jan.   p40.   100w. $4\frac{1}{2}$
    MM   Dec. 4 p28.   50w. $2\frac{1}{2}$

2869 DIORIO, Joe.   Straight Ahead to the Light.   Spitball Records
SB5
    CAD   Aug.   p24.   250w.   5
    GP   Oct.   p97.   125w.   3
    JJ   Oct.   p39.   100w.   4
    MM   Dec. 4 p28.   50w. $2\frac{1}{2}$

2870 DIORIO, Joe and Wally Cirillo.   Soloduo.   Spitball Records,
SB-3
    GP   Aug.   p80.   100w.   4
    MM   Dec. 4 p28.   50w. $2\frac{1}{2}$

2871 DOBBINS, Bill.   Textures.   Advent 5003

        CAD Oct. p17. 200w. 5
        CO June p17, 18. 300w. 4

2872 DOLPHY, Eric. Jitterbug Waltz. Douglas ADLP 6002 (Re-
     issue)
        CAD Oct. p37. 375w. 5

2873 DOLPHY, Eric and Ron Carter. Magic. Prestige P24053
     (2 discs) (Reissue)
        CRE Jan. p71. 25w. 4
        DB April 22 p33-4. 375w. 5

2874 DORHAM, Kenny. Afro Cuban. Blue Note 1535 (Reissue)
        MM Sept. 25 p26. 275w. $4\frac{1}{2}$

2875 DORHAM, Kenny. But Beautiful. Milestone 47036 (2 discs)
     (Reissue)
        CAD Oct. p25. 250w. 5
        JJ Nov. p25-6. 500w. $2\frac{1}{2}$
        RR Dec. p103. 150w. $3\frac{1}{2}$

2876 DORHAM, Kenny. Ease It! Muse 5053 (Reissue)
        CO Feb. p27, 28. 250w. $2\frac{1}{2}$

2877 DORHAM, Kenny. Memorial Album. Xanadu 125
        CAD April p41-2. 175w. $1\frac{1}{2}$

2878 DOROUGH, Bob. Yardbird Suite. Bethlehem BCP 6023 (Re-
     issue)
        CAD Oct. p38. 150w. 5
        PRM Oct. p46. 300w. $3\frac{1}{2}$

2879 DORSEY, Jimmy. 1935. London HMG 5022 (E)
        GR June p101. 150w. 3
        JJ June p39. 75w. 3

2880 DORSEY, Tommy. Best of, Vol 6. RCA FXM 1-7283
     (France) (Reissue)
        JJ Dec. p26-7. 400w. $4\frac{1}{2}$
        RR Dec. p102. 50w. $2\frac{1}{2}$

2881 DORSEY, Tommy. The Complete Tommy Dorsey (Vol. 1--
     1935). RCA Bluebird AXM2-5521 (2 discs) (Reissue)
        CAD Aug. p36. 175w. 3

2882 DORSEY, Tommy. 1942-1946. First Heard 1974-73 (E)
        JJ Feb. p35-6. 250w. 5

2883 DREW, Kenny. If You Could See Me Now. Steeplechase
     SCS 1034 (Denmark)
        JJ April p30. 325w. 4
        MM Dec. 4 p30. 250w. $3\frac{1}{2}$

2884 DREW, Kenny. Morning. Steeplechase SCS 1048 (Denmark)
      JJ   Sept. p31. 250w. 4

2885 DREW, Kenny and Niels-Henning Orsted Pedersen. Duo Live
      in Concert. Steeplechase SCS 1031 (Denmark)
      JJ   March p28. 150w. 2½

2886 DUDZIAK, Urszula. Urszula. Arista AL 4065. Cart. 8301-
      4065
          CIR   Feb. 10 p48. 225w.   4
          DB   Jan. 29 p20. 300w.   2½
          JF   April p60. 450w.   4
          JF   no. 41 p24-5. 100w.   4
          RFJ   Jan. p11. 400w.   4½
          SOU   Jan. p39. 25w.   2
          SR   March p101-2. 100w.   0

2887 DUKE, George. The Aura Will Prevail. MPS BASF MC25613
          DB   April 8 p29-30. 200w.   3½
          JF   May p40. 350w.   3

2888 DUKE, George. Faces in Reflection. BASF 22018
          DB   April 10 p18. 275w.   3½

2889 DUKE, George. Feel. BASF 25355
          DB   April 10 p18. 275w.   3½

2890 DUKE, George. I Love the Blues, She Heard My Cry.
      MPS/BASF MC-25671
          CK   March p48. 165w.   4½
          DB   April 8 p29-30. 200w.   3
          SR   April p101. 75w.   4

2891 DUTCH Swing College Band. 1965-70. DSC PA 2018
      (Netherlands)
          RR   June p83. 50w. 2

2892 DYKSTRA, Brian. Something Like a Rag. Advent 5021
          CAD   Oct. p17. 200w. 5

2893 EAST New York Ensemble de Music. At the Helm. Folk-
      ways FTS 33867
          CAD   Oct. p42. 300w. 4

2894 EATON, John. Solo Piano. Chiarscuro 137
          CAD   Feb. p20-1. 50w. 1½

2895 EDELHAGEN, Kurt. Golden Era 2702 (2 discs) (West Ger-
      many)
          JJ   Jan. p30. 100w. 4½

2896 EDISON, Harry, Hot Lips Page, and Roy Eldridge. Lips
      and Lots of Jazz. Xanadu 123

CAD Dec. p28, 30. 125w. 4

2897 EDWARDS, Eddie. London 5014 (E) (Reissue)
JJ Oct. p31. 100w. 3

2898 EDWARDS, Teddy. Feelin's. Muse 5045
SR Sept. p102. 150w. 4

2899 ELDRIDGE, Roy. Pablo 2310 746
JJ April p30. 275w. 4

2900 ELDRIDGE, Roy. Tax m-8020 (Sweden)
JJ April p30. 275w. 4

2901 ELDRIDGE, Roy. Happy Time. Pablo 2310 746
CAC Oct. p275. 100w. 2
DB April 22 p32-3. 175w. 3
GR Sept. p493. 200w. 4

2902 ELDRIDGE, Roy. Live at the Three Deuces. Jazz Archives JA 24 (Reissue)
DB June 3 p31. 75w. 4

2903 ELDRIDGE, Roy. What's It All About. Pablo 2310-766
CAC Nov. p310-11. 300w. $3\frac{1}{2}$
CAD Sept. p6. 50w. 4
GRA Dec. p1080. 150w. 4
JJ Nov. p26. 500w. $3\frac{1}{2}$
MJ Oct. p22. 50w. $2\frac{1}{2}$
MM Dec. 11 p29. 375w. 3

2904 ELLINGTON, Duke. Black Jack 3004 (Italy) (Reissue)
DB Jan. 29 p26. 50w. 1

2905 ELLINGTON, Duke. Jazz Society AA 520/1 (Denmark) (Reissue)
JJ March p28, 30. 375w. 5

2906 ELLINGTON, Duke. Rarities 29 (E)
JJ May p28. 275w. $4\frac{1}{2}$

2907 ELLINGTON, Duke. Volume 1. Stardust 201 (Reissue)
DB Jan. 29 p27. 50w. $3\frac{1}{2}$

2908 ELLINGTON, Duke. Volume 2. Swing Treasury 105 (Reissue)
DB Jan. 29 p26. 25w. 4
JJ Jan. p30. 50w. $4\frac{1}{2}$

2909 ELLINGTON, Duke. Volume 3. Swing Treasury 104
DB Jan. 29 p26. 25w. 4
JJ Jan. p30. 50w. $4\frac{1}{2}$

2910   ELLINGTON, Duke. vol. 1.   RCA 731-043 (France) (Reissue)
          MM July 3 p23.   575w. $3\frac{1}{2}$

2911   ELLINGTON, Duke. V. 14/15.   RCA FXM 1-7134/5
          (France) (2 discs) (Reissue)
             JJ Feb. p28. 300w. $4\frac{1}{2}$

2912   ELLINGTON, Duke. Volume 16.   RCA FXM 1-7201 (France)
          (Reissue)
             JJ May p27-8. 425w. 5
             RR June p83. 50w. 4

2913   ELLINGTON, Duke. The Afro Eurasian Eclipse.   Fantasy
          F 9498
             CAD May p24-5. 125w. 3
             DB Aug. 12 p2678. 150w. $3\frac{1}{2}$
             SOU July p40. 150w. 3

2914   ELLINGTON, Duke. All That Jazz.   DJM DJL M08020 (2
          discs) (E)
             GR Dec. p1080. 200w. 4
             JJ June p31. 500w. 4
             MM June 5 p22. 625w. 4
             RR June p83. 75w. 4

2915   ELLINGTON, Duke. At Carnegie Hall (1946).   Queen-disc Q
          018 (Italy) (Reissue)
             JJ May p28. 500w. 4
             MM July 24 p26. 350w. 3

2916-7 ELLINGTON, Duke. The Bethlehem Years: Vol. 1.   Bethle-
          hem BCP 6013 (Reissue)
             ARG March p56. 150w. 3
             CAD Aug. p26. 100w. 4
             DB Aug. 12 p28. 75w. 4
             MJ Dec. p26. 100w. 4

2918   ELLINGTON, Duke. Blue Skies.   Swing Treasury 110 (Re-
          issue)
             DB Jan. 29 p26. 25w. 4
             JJ Jan. p30. 100w. $4\frac{1}{2}$

2919   ELLINGTON, Duke. The Complete.   CBS 67264, 68275,
          88000, 88035, 88082, 88137, 88140 (14 discs) (France) (Re-
          issue)
             JJ Aug. p30-1, 40. 3100w. 4

2920   ELLINGTON, Duke. Cotton Club, 1938: "If Dreams Came
          True," v. 1.   Jazz Archives JA-12
             COD March p16. 175w. 4

2921   ELLINGTON, Duke. Cotton Club, 1938: "Three Blind Mice"
          Volume 2. Jazz Archives JA-13

COD   March   p16.   175w.   4

2922 ELLINGTON, Duke.   A Date With, vol. 1-6.   Fairmont FA
      1001/02/03/04/07/08 (6 discs)
            DB   Jan. 29 p26-7.   100w. $4\frac{1}{2}$
            LP   March p15.   100w. $2\frac{1}{2}$

2923 ELLINGTON, Duke.   Duke's Big 4.   Pablo 2310 703
            COD   June p19.   200w.   3
            DB   Jan. 29 p25.   50w.   4

2924 ELLINGTON, Duke.   Eastborne Performance.   RCA APL1-
      1023
            AU   July p73-4.   550w.   4
            DB   Jan. 29 p24.   50w.   3
            GR   April p1673.   350w.   3
            MM   Feb. 7 p26.   450w. $3\frac{1}{2}$

2925 ELLINGTON, Duke.   Ellington for Always.   STANYAN 10105
      (Reissue)
            SR   Feb. p98-9.   237w.   4

2926 ELLINGTON, Duke.   The Ellington Suites.   Pablo 2335 743
            CAC   Nov. p311.   250w.   3
            GRA   Dec. p1080.   150w.   3
            JJ   Aug. p33.   750w.   1
            DB   Aug. 12 p28.   75w.   3
            MJ   July p52.   50w.   4
            MM   Sept. 18 p25.   550w. $3\frac{1}{2}$
            RR   Oct. p102.   100w. $2\frac{1}{2}$
            SOU   July p40.   150w.   3

2927 ELLINGTON, Duke.   In Hollywood.   Max MLP 1001 (Reissue)
            DB   Jan. 29 p27.   50w.   4

2928 ELLINGTON, Duke.   Homage to.   Golden Crest CRS 31041
            DB   Jan. 29 p25.   50w.   2

2929 ELLINGTON, Duke.   Jazz Violin Sessions.   Atlantic SD 1688
            CAD   Oct. p36.   225w.   4

2930 ELLINGTON, Duke.   The Johnny Blanton Years.   Queen Disc
      007 (Italy) (Reissue)
            DB   Jan. 29 p26.   50w.   5

2931 ELLINGTON, Duke.   Live from the Crystal Ballroom.   Jazz
      Society AA 520/21 (Sweden) (Reissue) (2 discs)
            RR   Dec. p102.   75w.   4

2932 ELLINGTON, Duke.   Love You Madly.   V J International VJS
      3061 (Reissue)
            DB   Jan. 29 p25.   50w. $3\frac{1}{2}$

2933 ELLINGTON, Duke. October 20, 1945. Queen Disc 006
      (Italy) (Reissue)
            DB Jan. 29 p27.   25w.   3½

2934 ELLINGTON, Duke. On the Air 1938/39. Max 1002 (Reissue)
            DB Jan. 29 p27.   25w.   3½

2935 ELLINGTON, Duke. On the Air, 1940. Max 1003 (Reissue)
            DB June 29 p27.   25w.   4½

2936 ELLINGTON, Duke. On the Air--From the Blue Note. Air-
      check 4 (Canada)
            CO June p19.   350w.   4
            DB Jan. 29 p25.   50w.   4
            MM Sept. 18 p25.   550w.   3½

2937 ELLINGTON, Duke. One Night Stand With. Joyce 1023 (Re-
      issue)
            DB Jan. 29 p27.   50w.   2½
            JJ Feb. p28.   225w.   2½

2938 ELLINGTON, Duke. Recollections of the Big Band Era. At-
      lantic SC 1665 (Reissue)
            DB Jan. 29 p25.   50w.   3½

2939 ELLINGTON, Duke. Souvenirs. Warner Bros. K64021 (E)
      (5 discs)
            GRA Dec. p1080.   200w.   2½
            JJ July p29-30.   600w.   3½

2940 ELLINGTON, Duke. Suddenly It Jumped. Big Band Archives
      LP-1217
            CO March p16.   175w.   4
            DB Jan. 29 p26.   25w.   4
            JJ Feb. p36.   250w.   4

2941 ELLINGTON, Duke. Toodle-oo. Vocalion VLP 4 (E) (Re-
      issue)
            CAC July p152.   225w.   4
            JJ March p30.   450w.   5
            RR June p83.   75w.   3½
            ST June-July p199.   125w.   4

2942 ELLINGTON, Duke. The Unusual Ellington. Jazz Guild 1004
            JJ Aug. p33-4.   350w.   4

2943 ELLINGTON, Duke. The Washington D.C. Armory Concert;
      April 30, 1955. Jazz Guild 1002
            CAD Aug. p33, 34.   475w.   4
            JJ Aug. p34.   350w.   4

2944 ELLINGTON, Duke. Will the Big Bands Ever Come Back?
      Reprise K54064 (E) (Reissue)

MM   Aug. 28 p22.   200w. $2\frac{1}{2}$

2945   ELLINGTON, Duke.   The World of Duke Ellington, Volume 2.
       Columbia KG 33341 (2 discs) (Reissue)
              AU   Dec. p95-6.   600w.   4
              CAC April p28.   150w. $2\frac{1}{2}$
              CO   March p16, 17. 475w.   3

2946   ELLINGTON, Duke and Ray Brown.   This One's for Blanton.
       Pablo 2310 721
              CAC April p28.   225w. $3\frac{1}{2}$
              CAD Jan. p17-8.   150w.   4
              CRE April p72.   50w. $4\frac{1}{2}$
              DB   Jan. 29 p25.   50w.   5
              GR   March p1521.   225w.   3
              RFJ Feb. p12.   350w. $4\frac{1}{2}$

2947   ELLINGTON, Duke, and Django Reinhardt.   Chicago Opera
       House.   Prima DC 01/02 (2 discs) (Reissue)
              DB   Jan. 29 p25-6.   50w. $3\frac{1}{2}$

2948   ELLINGTON, Mercer.   Continuum.   Fantasy F9481
              AU   Aug. p83.   350w. $2\frac{1}{2}$
              GR   April p1673.   350w.   3
              JJ   Jan. p30.   250w.   5
              MM   Feb. 7 p26.   450w.   3
              RR   Feb. p68.   50w.   3
              ST   April-May p157-58.   400w.   5

2949   ELLIOT, Mike.   Atrio.   Celebration CB 5003
              DB   March 27 p20.   100w.   4

2950   ELLIOTT, Don.   Rejuvenation.   Columbia PC33799
              DB   March 11 p24, 26.   350w.   3

2951   ELLIS, Herb and Ray Brown.   Hot Tracks.   Concord CJ 12
              JJ   Dec. p27.   250w. $3\frac{1}{2}$

2952   ELLIS, Herb and Freddie Green.   Rhythm Willie.   Concord
       CJ 10
              CAD Jan. p16-7.   250w.   4
              CAD Feb. p24.   75w. $3\frac{1}{2}$

2953   ELLIS, Herb and Jake Hanna.   After You've Gone.   Concord
       CJ 6
              MJ   Feb. p30.   50w.   3

2954   ELLIS, Herb and Joe Pass.   Seven Come Eleven.   Concord
       Jazz CJ-2
              CO   March p15, 16.   250w.   0

2955   ELLIS, Herb and Ross Tompkins.   A Pair to Draw To.   Con-
       cord Jazz 17

CAD   Sept.   p19.   300w.   3
GP   Oct.   p97.   100w.   3
JJ   Oct.   p32.   250w.   4

2956   ELLIS, Serger.   Almanac OSR 2408
JJ   Feb.   p28.   200w.   3

2957   ELSDON, Alan.   Alan Elsdon.   Rediffusion 'Gold Star' 15-12
JJ   Feb.   p36.   300w.   3

2958   ELY, Chet and Mike Walbridge.   Til Times Get Better.   GHB-67
CO   June   p19, 20.   350w.   5

2959   ERNRYD, Bengt.   1964-5.   Dragon LP 1 (Sweden)
CAD   June   p29.   75w. $1\frac{1}{2}$
JJ   Oct.   p40.   100w.   2
MM   Dec. 25   p18.   100w. $2\frac{1}{2}$

2960   ERVIN, Booker.   Lament for Booker Ervin.   Enja 2054
AU   July   p74-5.   350w.   4
JJ   Feb.   p28.   150w.   3

2961   ERVIN, Booker.   The Song Book.   Prestige PR 7318
JJ   June   p31.   275w.   5
RR   Aug.   p80.   75w.   3

2962   ESCOVEDO, Coke.   Mercury SRM 1-1041
DB   May 20   p28.   300w.   2

2963   ETCETERA String Band.   The Harvest Hop.   Moon MLP 200
RT   Sept./Oct.   p7-8.   100w. $4\frac{1}{2}$

2964   EVANS, Bill.   Intuition.   Fantasy F-9475
AU   Feb.   p98-9.   500w.   5
CO   June   p20.   500w.   4
SR   Aug.   p88.   200w.   4

2965   EVANS, Bill.   Montreux III.   Fantasy F 9510
CRA   Dec.   p66.   375w. $3\frac{1}{2}$

2966   EVANS, Bill.   Peace Peace and Other Pieces.   Milestone
M47024 (Reissue)
DB   March 11   p27-8.   400w. $4\frac{1}{2}$

2967   EVANS, Bill.   Since We Met.   Fantasy F 9501
AU   Sept.   p86.   600w.   3
CAD   Dec.   p23.   75w. $3\frac{1}{2}$
CRE   Sept.   p65.   25w. $3\frac{1}{2}$
DB   Aug. 12   p29-30.   375w. $4\frac{1}{2}$
SOU   July   p40.   150w. $3\frac{1}{2}$

2968   EVANS, Bill.   Spring Leaves.   Milestone M47034 (2 discs)
(Reissue)

CAD   Oct.   p26.   150w.   3
CK   Dec.   p49.   25w. $3\frac{1}{2}$
JJ   Dec.   p27.   500w.   4
RR   Dec.   p103.   50w. $3\frac{1}{2}$

2969   EVANS, Bill.   Trio/Duo.   Verve VE 2-2509 (2 discs) (Re-issue)
CAD   Sept.   p27.   150w.   5
DB   Nov. 18   p31-2.   350w.   3

2969a   EVANS, Bill/Tadd Dameron.   The Arrangers' Touch.   Prestige PR 24049 (2 discs) (E) (Reissue)
MM   Jan. 10   p32.   750w.   3

2970   EVANS, Frank.   Noctuary.   Blue Bag BB 101 (E)
JJ   Dec.   p27.   425w.   4

2971   EVANS, Gil.   The Gil Evans Orchestra Plays the Music of Jimi Hendrix.   RCA CPL 1-0667
CO   March   p17, 18.   700w. $2\frac{1}{2}$
SR   March   p88-9.   125w.   0

2972   EVANS, Gil.   There Comes a Time.   RCA APL1-1057.   Cass. APK1-1057
CRE   July   p67.   425w.   4
DB   May 6   p22.   350w. $3\frac{1}{2}$
SR   Aug.   p87.   375w.   4

2973   EWELL, Don.   Don Ewell.   Chiaroscuro CR 130
SR   Jan.   p97.   250w. $4\frac{1}{2}$

2974   EWELL, Don and Willie "the Lion" Smith.   Duets.   Sackville 2004 (Canada) (Reissue)
CAD   Aug.   p26.   150w.   4

2975   FADDIS, Jon.   Youngblood.   Pablo 2310 765
DB   Dec. 2   p22.   325w.   4
JA   Fall   p50.   325w.   4
JJ   Aug.   p34.   425w.   5
MM   July 31   p22.   300w.   2

2976   FARLOW, Tal.   Fuerst Set.   Xanadu 109
CAD   Jan.   p28.   250w. $4\frac{1}{2}$
GP   Jan.   p70.   300w.   4

2977   FARRELL, Joe.   Canned Funk.   CTI CTI-6053 S1.   Cart. CT8-6053.   Cass. CTC-6053
SR   July   p86.   150w.   1

2978   FAST, Larry.   Sequencer.   Passport PPSD 98014
CK   Oct.   p46.   350w.   4

2979   FELIX, Lennie.   The Many Strides of Lennie Felix.   88 Up

Right 88UR 003 (E)
ST Aug.-Sept. p228-29. 300w. 4½

2980 FERGUSON, Maynard. Primal Scream. Columbia PC 33953
MG Jan. p52. 25w. 3
MM July 3 p24. 75w. 2

2981 FILMER, Vic. Saga of. Jazzology SCE 58
RT Sept./Oct. p6. 125w. 2

2982 FISCHER, Clare, and the Yamaha Quartet. Revelation 23
DB Nov. 4 p26. 200w. 4
HF April p146. 250w. 2

2983 FITE, Buddy. Plays for Satin Dolls. Different Drummer
1001
CAD April p16. 150w. 2½
DB Jan. 15 p29. 200w. 2
MJ March p47. 50w. 3

2984 FLANAGAN, Tommy. Tokyo Recital. Pablo 2310 724
AU Aug. p82-3. 500w. 4
GR Jan. p1263. 250w. 3
HF May p108-9. 250w. 4

2985 FLORES, Chuck. Flores Azules. Dobres DR 1001
CAD Nov. p19-20. 50w. 3
RFJ Dec. p17. 225w. 4

2986 FLYING Island. Vanguard VSD 79359
SR Jan. p97. 100w. 3

2987 FORTUNE, Sonny. Awakening. A&M Horizon SP 704
AU June p89, 95. 750w. 4
CRE April p72. 50w. 4½
DB April 8 p24. 250w. 5
MJ Sept. p35. 25w. 2½
MM April 3 p34. 225w. 2½
RFJ Feb. p11. 250w. 4
SOU Feb. p50. 150w. 3½
SR May p100. 75w. 3

2988 FORTUNE, Sonny. Waves of Dreams. Horizon SP 711
CAD Dec. p27. 125w. 2½

2989 FOSTER, Ronnie. Cheshire Cat. Blue Note BN 1A 425-G
JJ Jan. p30. 75w. 0

2990 FREE Kata. Spontaneous Improvisations. Philips 6357 021
(E)
JJ June p40. 75w. 5

2991 FREE Music Communion. Communion Structures. Fremuco

1001 (West Germany)
    JJ June p40. 100w. 5

2992 FREEMAN, Bud. Bud Freeman. Tax m-8019 (Reissue)
    JJ Feb. p37. 300w. 4

2993 FREEMAN, Bud. Chicagoans in New York. Dawn Club
12009 (Reissue)
    OLR Dec. p257. 50w. 4

2994 FREEMAN, Bud. Midnight at Eddie Condon's. Mercury
6336-327 (Holland) (Reissue)
    CO June p20. 400w. 4

2995 FREEMAN, Bud. Song of the Tenor. Philips 6308 254
    GR Dec. p1080. 200w. 4
    JJ May p28. 375w. 4
    MM April 17 p24. 425w. $3\frac{1}{2}$

2996 FREEMAN, Bud. Superbud. 77 Records 77S 55 (E)
    GR April p1673. 100w. $1\frac{1}{2}$
    JJ Feb. p28. 225w. $2\frac{1}{2}$
    MM Feb. 21 p31. 325w. $2\frac{1}{2}$
    ST Feb.-March p116-7. 325w. 5

2997 FREEMAN, Van. Have No Fear. Nessa 6
    DB March 25 p34-5. 25w. 4

2998 FRIEDMAN, David. Futures Passed. Enja 2068
    JJ Sept. p31. 225w. 3

2999 The FUNKY New Orleans Jazz Band. Make Me a Pallet on
the Floor. (Herwin 301)
    SO May/June p42. 175w. $4\frac{1}{2}$

3000 GAILLARD, Slim, Bam Brown and Leo Watson. McVonty.
Hep 6 (E)
    MM May 1 p32. 575w. 2

3001 GALAPAGOS DUCK. St. James. Forty Four 6357 704 (E)
    JJ June p40. 75w. 4

3002 GALLOWAY, Jim and Dick Wellstood. Three Is Company.
Sackville 2007 (Canada)
    JJ Sept. p31-2. 375w. 5
    OLR Dec. p257. 75w. 4
    SOU April p47. 550w. 3

3003 GARBAREK, Jan. Esoteric Circle. Arista LAL 1031 (Reissue)
    CAD Aug. p37. 100w. 4

3004 GARBAREK, Jan. Witchi-Tai-To. ECM 1041 ST

SR   March   p89.   125w.   5

3005   GARBAREK, Jan and Keith Jarrett.   Belonging.   ECM 1050
       JF   no. 41   p60.   250w.   4

3006   GARBAREK, Jan and Bobo Stenson.   Dansere.   ECM 1075
       DB   Dec. 2   p16.   450w. $3\frac{1}{2}$
       MM   July 31   p22.   125w.   3
       SR   Dec.   p124.   175w.   5

3007   GARNER, Erroll.   The Elf.   Savoy SJL 2207 (2 discs) (Re-
       issue)
       JA   Summer   p41-2.   100w.   3
       SR   Nov.   p133.   50w.   3

3008   GARNER, Erroll.   Feeling Is Believing.   Pye 28214 (E)
       RR   April   p78.   100w.   3

3009   GARNER, Erroll.   The Greatest.   Atlantic ATL 50 243 (West
       Germany) (Reissue)
       MM   Aug. 21   p20.   350w. $3\frac{1}{2}$

3010   GARNER, Erroll.   Play It Again.   Columbia PG 33424 (2
       discs) (Reissue)
       MJ   Jan.   p20.   75w. $3\frac{1}{2}$

3011   GARNETT, Carlos.   Journey to Enlightenment.   Muse MR5057
       CO   March   p18, 19.   400w. $2\frac{1}{2}$
       CO   June   p20, 21.   125w.   2

3012   GARNETT, Carlos.   Let the Melody Ring On.   Muse MR 5079
       DB   June 3   p22, 24.   225w. $4\frac{1}{2}$

3013   GASCA, Luis.   Collage.   Fantasy F-9504
       CAD   Aug.   p30.   150w.   0

3014   GELLER, Herb.   Condoli/Vines.   Trip TLP-5539 (Reissue)
       CO   May   p19, 20, 21.   525w.   4

3015   GELLER, Herb.   Rhyme and Reason.   Atlantic SD 1681
       CAD   Jan.   p23.   200w. $3\frac{1}{2}$

3016   GETZ, Stan.   Au Go Go.   Verve V6-8600
       CAC   April   p30.   100w. $2\frac{1}{2}$
       GR   Aug.   p352.   125w. $3\frac{1}{2}$

3017   GETZ, Stan.   The Best of Two Worlds.   Columbia PC 33703
       DB   Oct. 21   p20.   375w.   3
       SR   Dec.   p124, 126.   200w. $4\frac{1}{2}$

3018   GETZ, Stan.   Captain Marvel.   Columbia KC 32706
       CAC   July   p152.   250w.   4
       CO   June   p21.   300w.   3

JJ   May   p38, 40.   1275w.   5
SR   June   p88.   200w. $4\frac{1}{2}$

3019   GETZ, Stan.   Sweet Rain.   Verve 2317 115 (E) (Reissue)
MM   Nov. 20   p30.   400w. $4\frac{1}{2}$

3020   GETZ, Stan.   West Coast Jazz.   Verve
RFJ   June   p8.   100w.   4

3021   GETZ, Stan.   The Chick Corea/Bill Evans Sessions.   Verve
VE-2-2510 (2 discs) (Reissue)
CAD   Sept.   p27.   125w.   4
DB   Nov. 18   p32.   275w.   5

3022   GETZ, Stan and J. J. Johnson.   Verve (E)
CAC   Sept.   p228.   250w. $4\frac{1}{2}$

3023   GIBBS, Mike.   The Only Chrome Waterfall Orchestra.
Bronze ILPS 9353 (E)
DB   March 11   p20.   300w.   5

3024   GIBBS, Terry.   Big Band Sound.   Verve 2317 112 (E) (Re-
issue)
GR   Nov.   p899-900.   125w.   4
JJ   Nov.   p28.   325w. $2\frac{1}{2}$
MM   Nov. 13   p31.   350w.   3

3025   GIBBS, Terry.   Launching a New Band.   Trip Jazz TLP-5545
(Reissue)
CO   Sept.   p12.   150w.   3

3026   GILLESPIE, Dizzy.   At the Montreux Jazz Festival 1975.
Pablo 2310 749
CAC   Jan.   p412, 414.   100w. $3\frac{1}{2}$
CAD   Jan.   p19.   150w. $3\frac{1}{2}$
DB   April 8   p22-4.   100w. $4\frac{1}{2}$
MM   Jan. 31   p22.   475w.   4
RR   Feb.   p68.   50w. $2\frac{1}{2}$

3027   GILLESPIE, Dizzy.   Bahiana.   Pablo 2625 708 (2 discs)
CAC   Dec.   p355.   150w.   4
DB   June 3   p20-2.   250w.   3
JJ   July   p30.   475w.   5
MM   Aug. 7   p20.   350w. $3\frac{1}{2}$

3028   GILLESPIE, Dizzy.   Big 4.   Pablo 2310 719
CO   Sept.   p12.   325w.   4
SR   Sept.   p102.   225w.   5

3029   GILLESPIE, Dizzy.   Dee Gee Days.   Savoy SJL 2209
(2 discs) (Reissue)
CAD   Sept.   p26.   150w.   4
DB   Dec. 2   p25.   200w.   4

JA   Fall   p50-1.   450w. $2\frac{1}{2}$

3030   GILLESPIE, Dizzy.   Dizzy Goes to College, Vol. 1 & 2.
Jazz Showcase 5000/5002 (2 discs)
JJ   Jan.   p30, 31.   450w.   4

3031   GILLESPIE, Dizzy.   The Giant.   Prestige P-24047 (2 discs)
(Reissue)
CO   June   p21.   550w.   5

3032   GILLESPIE, Dizzy.   The Gillespie Jam Sessions.   Verve
2610 023 (E) (2 discs) (Reissue)
JJ   Oct.   p32.   425w.   5
MM   Dec. 4   p30.   325w.   2

3033   GILLESPIE, Dizzy.   Live at the Spotlite.   Hi-Fly H-01 (E)
JJ   May   p28, 30.   450w.   5

3034   GILLESPIE, Dizzy.   Something Old, Something New.   Mercury 6336 304 (Holland) (Reissue)
CO   Sept.   p12.   150w.   4

3035   GILLESPIE, Dizzy.   The Sonny Rollins/Sonny Stitt Session.
Verve VE 2 2505 (2 discs) (Reissue)
DB   Oct. 7   p33.   175w.   4
JA   Summer   p401.   175w.   5
MJ   Oct.   p52.   25w. $2\frac{1}{2}$

3036   GILLESPIE, Dizzy and Sonny Stitt.   The Bop Session.   Sonet
SNTF 692 (E)
MM   April 3   p34.   500w.   3

3037   GIRARD, Willy.   Jazz Violin.   CBC Radio Canada 371 (Canada)
OLR   Dec.   p257.   50w.   5

3038   GIUFFRE, Jimmy.   River Chant.   Choice CRS 1011
DB   May 6   p33.   75w.   1
HF   May   p109.   275w.   4
SR   May   p100, 104.   125w. $4\frac{1}{2}$

3039   GLADKOWSKI, Czeslaw, and Krzysztof Zgraja.   Alter Ego.
Muza SX 1190 (Poland)
JF   No. 44   p33.   125w.   4

3040   GLASS, Philip.   Music in Twelve Parts, Parts 1 & 2.   Caroline CA 2010 (E)
RR   Sept.   p90.   125w.   3

3041   GLOBE Unity.   Evidence, vol. 1.   FMP 0020 (E)
MM   Dec. 4   p28.   375w. $3\frac{1}{2}$

3042   GOLDEN Age Jazz Band.   Arhoolie 4007

AU   Feb.   p100-1.   400w.   3

3043 GONDA, Janos.   Shaman Song.   Pepita SLPX 17484 (Hungary)
      JF   No. 44   p34.   100w.   4

3044 GOODMAN, Benny.   Jazum 41/42 (2 discs) (Reissue)
      JA   Fall   p56.   100w.   4
      JJ   July   p30.   425w.   4

3045 GOODMAN, Benny.   Jazz Society AA-508 (Denmark)
      DB   June 3   p30.   25w. $2\frac{1}{2}$
      JJ   May   p30.   625w. $4\frac{1}{2}$

3046 GOODMAN, Benny.   Rarities No. 30 (E)
      JJ   July   p30-1.   525w. $3\frac{1}{2}$

3047 GOODMAN, Benny.   vol. 12.   RCA FXM1-7283 (France) (Re-
      issue)
      JJ   Nov.   p28, 30.   300w.   3
      RR   Dec.   p102.   50w.   3

3048 GOODMAN, Benny.   1946-1949.   First Heard 1974-1
      JJ   Feb.   p37-8.   400w.   5

3049 GOODMAN, Benny.   The Best.   RCA HY 1020 (E) (Reissue)
      CAC   Feb.   p448, 50.   475w.   3
      JJ   Jan.   p40.   75w.   4
      RR   Feb.   p68.   50w. $2\frac{1}{2}$

3050 GOODMAN, Benny.   The Complete Benny Goodman, Volume
      1 - 1935.   RCA AXM2-5505 (2 discs) (Reissue)
      DB   Nov. 4   p28.   50w. $3\frac{1}{2}$
      SR   Oct.   p94.   300w. $3\frac{1}{2}$

3051 GOODMAN, Benny.   The Complete, vol. 2.   RCA AXM2 5515
      (2 discs) (Reissue)
      AU   Dec.   p94-5.   425w.   5
      DB   Nov. 4   p28.   75w. $4\frac{1}{2}$

3052 GOODMAN, Benny.   The Complete, vol. 3.   RCA AXM2 5532
      (2 discs) (Reissue)
      AU   Dec.   p94-5.   425w.   5
      DB   Nov. 4   p28.   75w.   4

3053 GOODMAN, Benny.   The Early B.G.   Vocalion VLP 2 (E)
      (Reissue)
      CAC   May   p74.   125w. $3\frac{1}{2}$
      GRA   May   p1815.   300w.   4
      JJ   March   p30.   375w.   4
      MM   Feb. 14   p31.   750w. $4\frac{1}{2}$
      RR   June   p83.   100w.   3
      ST   June-July   p199.   225w. $4\frac{1}{2}$

3054 GOODMAN, Benny. Early Years. Capitol VMPM 1002 (E)
      (Reissue)
          CAC Feb. p450. 400w. 3
          JJ Jan. p31. 100w. $\frac{1}{2}$
          MM March 13 p26. 650w. $2\frac{1}{2}$

3055 GOODMAN, Benny. The Forgotten Years--1943. Swing
      Treasury 103
          JJ Jan. p31. 100w. $1\frac{1}{2}$

3056 GOODMAN, Benny. In Hollywood. Swing Treasury 100
          DB June 3 p30. 25w. $1\frac{1}{2}$
          JJ Jan. p31. 100w. 1

3057 GOODMAN, Benny. A Jam Session, 1935-37. Sunbeam SB
      149 (Reissue)
          DB June 3 p30. 75w. 4

3058 GOODMAN, Benny. The 'Let's Dance' Broadcasts, 1934-1935,
      v. 3. Sunbeam SB 150
          JJ May p30. 500w. $4\frac{1}{2}$

3059 GOODMAN, Benny. London Date. Polydor SON 011 (Reissue)
          GRA Nov. p900. 125w. $2\frac{1}{2}$
          MM Sept. 11 p30. 375w. 3
          RR Dec. p102. 50w. 3

3060 GOODMAN, Benny. On the Air. Aircheck 16 (Canada)
          CAD Nov. p14. 100w. $2\frac{1}{2}$
          JJ Nov. p28. 200w. $1\frac{1}{2}$

3061 GOODMAN, Benny. Presents Arrangements by Fletcher Hen-
      derson. Columbia JCL 524 (Reissue)
          CO March p19. 325w. $2\frac{1}{2}$
          MJ Jan. p20. 75w. 3

3062 GOODMAN, Benny. Solid Gold Instrumental Hits. Columbia
      PG 33405 (2 discs) (Reissue)
          CO March p19. 300w. $2\frac{1}{2}$
          MJ Jan. p20. 50w. $2\frac{1}{2}$

3063 GOODMAN, Benny. The War Years. Jazz Society AA 510
      (Denmark)
          JJ Sept. p32. 625w. $4\frac{1}{2}$

3064 GORDON, Dexter. All Souls'. Dexterity ST-1-001 (Holland)
          CO March p19. 225w. 3

3065 GORDON, Dexter. Blues Walk. Black Lion BL 309
          JA Summer p35. 400w. $3\frac{1}{2}$

3066 GORDON, Dexter. The Bethlehem Years. Bethlehem BCP
      6008 (Reissue)

CAD   Oct.   p38.   125w.   4
MJ   Dec.   p26.   75w.   4
PRM   Oct.   p46.   300w. $4\frac{1}{2}$

3067   GORDON, Dexter.   Dial Masters.   Spotlite SPJ 130 (E) (Reissue)
JJ   Nov.   p30-1.   500w.   3

3068   GORDON, Dexter.   Long Tall Dexter.   Savoy SJL 2211 (2
discs) (Reissue)
CAD   Sept.   p25, 26.   175w.   3
DB   Dec. 2   p25.   175w. $4\frac{1}{2}$

3069   GORDON, Dexter.   More Than You Know.   Steeple Chase
SCS 1030 (Denmark)
JJ   Feb.   p30.   425w.   4
MM   Dec. 18   p20.   325w. $3\frac{1}{2}$
SOU   April   p47.   200w.   4

3070   GORDON, Dexter.   Stable Mable.   Steeplechase SCS 1040
(Denmark)
DB   May 6   p32.   75w. $4\frac{1}{2}$
JJ   April   p32.   250w.   5
MM   Dec. 25   p18.   150w.   3

3071   GORDON, Dexter.   Swiss Nights, Volume One.   Steeplechase
SCS 1050 (Denmark)
JJ   Sept.   p32.   250w.   5

3072   GORDON, Dexter.   Tangerine.   Prestige P-10091
CO   Sept.   p12.   225w.   2
DB   April 8   p27-8.   275w.   4

3073   GORDON, Joe.   Introducing.   Trip TLP-5535 (Reissue)
CO   May   p19, 20, 21.   525w.   3

3074   GORDON, John.   Step by Step.   Strata-East 19760
JJ   July   p31.   525w. $4\frac{1}{2}$

3075   GOTHIC Jazz Band.   Carrot 7 (E)
JJ   Dec.   p28.   250w. $3\frac{1}{2}$

3076   GRAPPELLI, Stephane.   Pye 12115
HF   Jan.   p106.   300w. $3\frac{1}{2}$
SR   May   p102.   150w.   2

3077   GRAPPELLI, Stephane.   I Got Rhythm.   Black Lion BL 047
MJ   March   p23.   25w. $3\frac{1}{2}$

3078   GRAPPELLI, Stephane.   Meets the Rhythm Section.   Black
Lion BLP 30183 (E)
JJ   March   p30.   225w. $3\frac{1}{2}$

3079 GRAPPELLI, Stephane. Satin Doll. Vanguard VSD 81/2 (2 discs)
        MJ Dec. p26. 50w. 4

3080 GRAPPELLI, Stephane. The Talk of the Town. Black Lion 313
        CAO Jan. p30. 75w. $2\frac{1}{2}$
        SR May p102. 150w. $1\frac{1}{2}$

3081 GRAPPELLI, Stephane. Violinspiration. BASF MC22545
        AU Aug. p79. 250w. 4
        GR May p1815. 175w. 4
        MJ March p23. 25w. $3\frac{1}{2}$
        SR May p102. 150w. 3

3082 GRAPPELLI, Stephane and Yehudi Menuhin. Fascinatin' Rhythm. Angel S37156
        CAC Feb. p447. 200w. $3\frac{1}{2}$
        SR May p102. 150w. $2\frac{1}{2}$
        ST April-May p158-9. 300w. 4

3083 GRAY, Wardell. Central Avenue. Prestige P 24062 (2 discs) (Reissue)
        DB Oct. 21 p34. 150w. 4

3084 GRAY, Wardell and Stan Hasselgard. Spotlite SPJ 134 (E) (Reissue)
        JJ Nov. p31. 550w. $4\frac{1}{2}$

3085 GRAYE, Tony. Oh Gee. ZIM 2001
        CAD Aug. p38. 105w. 0

3086 GREEN, Grant. The Main Attraction. Kudu KU29
        BM Nov. p45. 100w. 2
        CAD Oct. p18. 125w. 2

3087 GREEN, Lloyd. Ten Shades of Green. Mid-Land Records MD-LG-10009
        GP Sept. p86. 225w. $4\frac{1}{2}$

3088 GREENWICH, Sonny. Sun Song. Radio Canada International 399 (Canada)
        CAD Feb. p28. 75w. 4
        CO March p19, 22. 675w. $2\frac{1}{2}$

3089 GRIFFIN, Johnny and Eddie "Lockjaw" Davis. The Toughest Tenors. Milestone 47035 (2 discs) (Reissue)
        CAD Oct. p24. 175w. 5
        JJ Dec. p28. 300w. 4
        RR Dec. p102. 50w. 3

3090 GRIFFIN, Johnny and John Coltrane. Blowin' Sessions. Blue
      Note BNLA 521-H2 (2 discs) (Reissue)
          DB Aug. 12 p37. 225w. 4
          LP April p14-5. 175w. 4

3091 GROSSMAN, Stefan. Yazoo Basin Boogie. Kicking Mule 102
          LP July p12. 125w. 3

3092 GROSSMAN, Steve. Horo HLL 101-23 (Italy)
          CAD Sept. p9. 50w. 4

3093 GROSSMAN, Steve. Memphis Jelly Roll. Kicking Mile 118
          CAD May p25. 75w. $1\frac{1}{2}$

3094 GROSSMAN, Steve. Some Shapes to Come. P.M. Records
      PMR-002
          CO Sept. p12, 13. 500w. 3

3095 GRUBBS, Earl and Carl Grubbs. Motherland. Muse MR
      5094
          CAD April p36. 150w. $3\frac{1}{2}$

3096 GRUBBS, Earl & Carl Grubbs. Rebirth. Muse MR5047
          CO March p22. 275w. 3

3097 GRUNTZ, George. 2000 Keyes. Atlantic SO 04J (West Ger-
      many)
          JF No. 41 p62. 600w. 4

3098 GUARNIERI, Johnny. Johnny Guarnieri Plays Harry Warren.
      Jim Taylor Presents JTP 102
          SR Jan. p97, 98. 250w. 4

3099 GULLIN, Lars. 1959-1960. Artist ALP 30-114 (Reissue)
          JJ Feb. p46, 48. 200w. 2

3100 GUY, Joe and "Hot Lips" Page. Trumpet Battle at Minton's.
      Xanadu 107 (Reissue)
          DB June 3 p31-2. 100w. $4\frac{1}{2}$

3101-2 GYLLANDER, Dick. Nobody Knows. Dragon LP8 (Sweden)
          JJ Oct. p40. 75w. 4

3103 HACKETT, Bobby. Masters of Dixieland, Volume 1. EMI
      Electrola C 054-81 844 (E) (Reissue)
          JJ May p30, 32. 475w. $4\frac{1}{2}$

3104 HACKETT, Bobby. Strike Up the Band. Flying Dutchman
      BDL1-0829
          AU Feb. p102. 500w. 5
          SR June p88. 125w. $3\frac{1}{2}$

3105 HADEN, Charlie. Closeness. Horizon SP 710
        MM   Nov. 20 p30. 875w. 3
        MM   Dec. 25 p19. 250w. $4\frac{1}{2}$
        PRM Nov. p45. 400w. 3

3106 HAGAW. Do You Love Hagaw? Muza XLO388 (Poland)
        CO   March p15. 350w. 4

3107 HAIG, Al. Piano Interpretations. See Breeze 1001
        CAD Nov. p18. 25w. 1

3108 HAIG, Al. Trio and Quintet. Prestige PR 7841
        GR   May p1815. 200w. 3

3109 HAIG; Al and Jim Raney. Strings Attached. Choice 1010
        CAD March p24. 175w. $4\frac{1}{2}$
        DB   May 6 p32-3. 200w. 3

3110 HAKIM, Sadik. London Suite. CBC Radio Canada 378 (Canada)
        OLR Dec. p257. 50w. 3

3111 HAKIM, Sadik. Plays Duke Ellington. Radio Canada RCI
      379
        CAD May p23-4. 75w. 4

3112 HALL, Adelaide. Hall of Ellington. Columbia SCX 6586 (E)
      (Reissue)
        GR   July p229. 275w. 3
        MM   June 12 p26. 300w. 3
        RR   April p78. 100w. 2

3113 HALL, Herb. Old Tyme Modern. Sackville 3003 (Canada)
        CAD Aug. p21. 150w. 5

3114 HALL, Jim. Commitment. Horizon SP 715
        PRM Sept. p46. 700w. $3\frac{1}{2}$

3115 HALL, Jim. Concierto. CTI 6060
        JJ   Feb. p30. 350w. $4\frac{1}{2}$
        LP   Jan. p16. 175w. $4\frac{1}{2}$
        SR   Jan. p97. 150w. 5

3116 HALL, Jim. Jim Hall Live. Horizon, SP-705
        CAD Feb. p18. 75w. 4
        DB   April 22 p30. 275w. 5
        GP   Feb. p71. 600w. $4\frac{1}{2}$
        RFJ March p10. 200w. $4\frac{1}{2}$
        RR   March p74. 100w. 3
        SOU Jan. p36, 38. 250w. 3

3117 HAMILTON, Chico. Chico Hamilton and the Players. Blue
      Note BN-LA 622G

CAD   Aug.   p44.   250w.   0
HF   Sept.   p114.   250w.   4

3118   HAMILTON, Chico.   Peregrinations.   Blue Note BN-LA520-G.
Cart. BN-EA520-H
DB   March 25   p28, 29.   300w.   2
SR   Feb.   p92.   100w.   4

3119   HAMMER, Jan.   The First Seven Days.   Nemperor Records
NE 432
CK   Jan.   p46.   425w. $4\frac{1}{2}$
DB   March 25   p22.   600w.   4

3120   HAMMER, Jan.   Make Love.   MPS MC 20688
CAD   Aug.   p40.   150w.   3
DB   Oct. 21   p22.   450w. $2\frac{1}{2}$

3121   HAMMER, Jan.   "Oh Yeah?"   Nemperor NE 437
CK   Oct.   p46.   125w. $4\frac{1}{2}$
CRAW   Oct.   p69.   100w. $2\frac{1}{2}$
DB   Oct. 21   p22.   450w.   4
RR   Sept.   p90.   25w.   3
RS   Sept. 9   p64.   200w. $3\frac{1}{2}$

3122   HAMPTON, Lionel.   Jazz Ambassadors, vol. 2.   Verve 2610
022 (2 discs) (E) (Reissue)
JJ   Nov.   p31.   350w. $3\frac{1}{2}$
MM   Dec. 11   p29.   800w. $4\frac{1}{2}$

3123   HAMPTON, Slide and Joe Haider.   Give Me a Double.   MPS
29 223116
JF   April   p63.   300w.   3

3124   HANCOCK, Herbie.   Dedication.   CBS/Sony SOPM 165 (Japan)
CAD   Aug.   p17.   105w.   3

3125   HANCOCK, Herbie.   Flood.   CBS/Sony SOPZ 98-99 (Japan)
(2 discs)
CAD   Aug.   p17.   50w.   5

3126   HANCOCK, Herbie.   Man-Child.   Columbia PC 33812.   Cart.
PCA 33812
CRA   Jan.   p77.   25w.   1
DB   Jan. 15   p21.   300w.   3
RS   Jan. 15   p53.   250w.   3
SOU   Jan.   p39.   25w. $1\frac{1}{2}$
SR   April   p101.   25w.   3

3127   HANCOCK, Herbie.   Secrets.   Columbia PC 34280.   Cart.
PCA 34280.   Cass. PCT 34280
CK   Dec.   p49.   25w. $2\frac{1}{2}$
CRA   Nov.   p70.   175w.   3
DB   Nov. 18   p18.   375w.   2

                    RS Dec. 16 p98.   300w. 3
                    SR Dec. p126. 100w. 4

3128 HANCOCK, Herbie. Thrust. Columbia PC 32965
                    DB April 10 p18-9. 300w. 4

3129 HANCOCK, Herbie and Freddie Hubbard. In Concert, V. 2.
        CTI 6049
                    CO March p22, 23. 200w. 3
                    DB April 10 p18-9. 300w. $2\frac{1}{2}$

3130 HANDY, John. Hard Work. ABC Impulse ASD-9314
                    DB Sept. 9 p22. 350w. 3
                    GP Aug. p81. 50w. 3
                    MM Oct. 9 p34. 400w. $3\frac{1}{2}$

3131-2 HANNA, Jake. Kansas City Express. Concord CJ 22
                    CAD Nov. p20. 100w. $3\frac{1}{2}$
                    JJ Dec. p28. 375w. 3
                    MJ Feb. p30. 50w. 3

3133 HANNA, Roland. Child of Gemini. MPS 21 20875-3 (West
        Germany)
                    CO Sept. p13. 275w. 4

3134 HANNA, Roland. Perugia. Arista - Freedom AL 1010
                    CO Sept. p13, 14. 800w. 4
                    GR Aug. p352. 200w. $4\frac{1}{2}$
                    JA Summer p34. 150w. $3\frac{1}{2}$

3135 HARPER, Billy. Black Saint BSR 0001 (Italy)
                    CAD Oct. p33. 175w. 5
                    CO Sept. p14. 325w. 4
                    DB March 25 p34-5. 25w. 3
                    JJ Feb. p30. 250w. 5
                    RFJ June p11. 750w. 4

3136 HARRIS, Barry. Plays Tadd Dameron. Xanadu 113
                    CAD Jan. p28. 200w. $3\frac{1}{2}$
                    HF Jan. p106-7. 325w. 3

3137 HARRIS, Beaver. The 360 Degree Music Experience. 360
        LP 2001
                    CRA Nov. p72. 100w. 4
                    DB Dec. 2 p21. 450w. 4
                    SR Sept. p110, 112. 425w. 3

3138 HARRIS, Bill and Charlie Ventura. Live at the Three Deuces.
        Phoenix Jazz LP 11
                    JJ Feb. p30. 475w. 4
                    MM May 29 p30. 675w. 4

3139 HARRIS, Bill and Charlie Ventura. Aces at the Deuces.

Phoenix LP 14
>JJ   Sept.   p32.   350w.   5

3140   HARRIS, Bill.   A Knight in the Village.   Jazz Showcase 5001
(Reissue)
>CAD   Feb.   p29.   175w.   4
>JJ   Jan.   p31.   275w.   4

3141   HARRIS, Eddie.   Bad Luck Is All I Have.   Atlantic SD 1675.
Cart. TP-1675.   Cass. CS-1675
>BM   Dec.   p28.   225w.   4
>DB   March 25   p33-4.   275w.   2
>LP   March   p27.   50w. $3\frac{1}{2}$
>SR   March   p84.   125w.   0

3142   HARRIS, Eddie.   I Need Some Money.   Atlantic SD 1669.
Cart. TP 1669.   Cass. CS1669
>SR   Sept.   p102.   225w.   4

3143   HARRIS, Eddie.   That Is Why You're Overweight.   Atlantic
SD 1683
>BM   July   p51.   150w.   3
>BS   Aug.   p61.   100w. $2\frac{1}{2}$
>MM   May 8   p25.   75w.   2

3144   HARRIS, Gene.   In a Special Way.   Blue Note LA634-G
>CAD   Sept.   p6.   25w.   0
>CK   Dec.   p49.   25w. $2\frac{1}{2}$

3145   HARRISON, Wendell.   An Evening with the Devil.   Tribe
PRSD-2212
>CO   May   p18, 19.   225w. $2\frac{1}{2}$

3146   HARVEY, Jane.   Friends of Fats.   Classic Jazz 15 (Reissue)
>CAD   Nov.   p18.   125w. $3\frac{1}{2}$
>HF   July   p109-10.   200w. $1\frac{1}{2}$

3147   HAWES, Hampton.   Anglo American Jazz Phase One.   Music
De Wolfe DW/LP 3214 (E)
>JJ   Feb.   p30, 32.   250w.   4

3148   HAWES, Hampton.   The Challenge.   RCA JPL1-1508 (Japan)
>CAD   Sept.   p6.   25w.   4
>JA   Fall   p51.   300w.   4

3149   HAWES, Hampton.   Live at the Montmartre.   Arista/Freedom
AL 1020
>DB   June 3   p27, 29.   300w. $4\frac{1}{2}$
>SR   Aug.   p87, 88.   150w.   2

3150   HAWES, Hampton.   Northern Windows.   PRESTIGE P-10088.
Cart. 8162-10088
>SR   May   p88.   75w. $4\frac{1}{2}$

3151 HAWKINS, Coleman. Centerpiece. Phoenix LP 13
       JJ Sept. p32. 500w. 5
       RR Oct. p102. 100w. 4
       RR Dec. p102. 50w. $4\frac{1}{2}$

3152 HAWKINS, Coleman. Crazy Rhythm. Prestige (Reissue)
       RFJ June p7. 100w. 4

3153 HAWKINS, Coleman. The Hawk Flies. Milestone M-47015
       (2 discs) (Reissue)
       CO March p23. 375w. 4 ˙

3153a HAWKINS, Coleman. In Concert w. Roy Eldridge & Billy
       Holiday. Phoenix LP8
       CO July p11. 525w. 4

3154 HAWKINS, Coleman. Masters of Jazz, no. 4. Electrola
       CO54 82000 (West Germany) (Reissue)
       RR June p83. 50w. 3

3155 HAWKINS, Coleman. Sirius. Pablo 2310.707
       CO July p11, 12. 600w. 4

3156 HAWKINS, Coleman and Pee Wee Russell. Jam Session in
       Swingville. Prestige P-24051 (2 discs) (Reissue)
       CO March p23, 24. 400w. 3

3157 HAYES, Louis. Breath of Life. Muse 5052
       CO March p23. 200w. 3

3158 HAZELL, Eddie. Take Your Shoes Off, Baby. Monmouth
       Evergreen 7975
       HF July p108. 325w. $3\frac{1}{2}$

3159 HEAD. Red Dwarf. Canon CNN 5970 (E)
       JJ June p40. 125w. $3\frac{1}{2}$
       MM March 6 p29. 200w. 2

3160 HEATH, Jimmy. Picture of Heath. Xanadu 118
       AU July p74. 350w. 4
       CAD April p38. 125w. $3\frac{1}{2}$
       SOU May p46. 25w. $3\frac{1}{2}$

3161 HEATH BROTHERS. Marchin' On. Starta East SES 19766
       CAD Aug. p29. 100w. 5

3162 HEMPHILL, Julius. 'Coon Bid'ness. Arista AL 1012
       CRE April p62. 25w. $3\frac{1}{2}$
       DB May 20 p27-8. 375w. 4

3163 HENDERSON, Bobby. Last Recordings. Chiaroscuro CR-122
       CO July p12. 250w. 3

3164 HENDERSON, Eddie. Heritage. Blue Note LA636-G
     CAD Sept. p6. 25w. 0
     MJ Oct. p23, 52. 25w. $2\frac{1}{2}$
     RS Oct. 7 p84. 150w. $3\frac{1}{2}$

3165 HENDERSON, Eddie. Sunburst. Blue Note BN LA464-G
     DB June 29 p24. 325w. 4

3166 HENDERSON, Fletcher. 1923-1925. Fountain FJ 112 (E)
     (Reissue)
     JJ March p30, 32. 350w. 2
     MM Jan. 17 p42. 575w. $1\frac{1}{2}$
     RR April p78. 125w. 2
     ST Feb.-March p115. 400w. $2\frac{1}{2}$

3167 HENDERSON, Fletcher. The Complete Fletcher Henderson
     (1927-1936). RCA Bluebird AXM2-5507 (2 discs) (Reissue)
     AU Dec. p98-9. 550w. 4
     CAD Aug. p35. 200w. 4
     DB Nov. 4 p28. 225w. 4

3168 HENDERSON, Fletcher/CALLOWAY, Cab. Great Moments in
     Jazz, Vol. 1. Swing Treasury 107
     JJ Jan. p31, 32. 300w. $3\frac{1}{2}$

3169 HENDERSON, Joe. Black Miracle. Milestone M 9066
     CAD May p29. 75w. 3
     MG June p50. 50w. $1\frac{1}{2}$

3170 HERMAN, Woody. 1963. Trip Jazz TLP-5547 (Reissue)
     CO July p12, 13. 475w. 3

3171 HERMAN, Woody. Bijou. Columbia
     RFJ Jan. p8. 100w. $4\frac{1}{2}$

3172 HERMAN, Woody. Boiled in Earl (The Second Herd, 1948).
     Swing Treasury 108
     JJ Jan. p32. 225w. $4\frac{1}{2}$

3173 HERMAN, Woody. Double Exposure. Chess Jazz Masters
     Series 2ACMJ-402 (2 discs) (Reissue)
     CAD Oct. p22. 200w. 2

3174 HERMAN, Woody. The Great Herd, 1946. Swing Treasury
     102 (Reissue)
     JJ Jan. p32. 225w. 4

3175 HERMAN, Woody. Hollywood Palladium 1948. Hep 7 (Re-
     issue)
     JJ July p31. 500w. 5

3176 HERMAN, Woody. King Cobra. Fantasy F-9499
     AU June p87. 300w. $4\frac{1}{2}$

SR   Aug.   p89.   150w.   3

3177 HERMAN, Woody.   Live at Basin Street West, Hollywood.
Philips SONO18BS (E) (Reissue)
      GR   Nov.   p899.   350w.   4
      MM   Oct. 30   p26.   375w.   2½
      RR   Dec.   p102.   25w.   3

3178 HERMAN, Woody.   25th Anniversary.   Polydor 6336 369 (Reissue)
      SOU   May   p45.   125w.   4

3179 HERMAN, Woody.   Wood-Choppers, Volume 2.   First Heard
Records 10 (E)
      JJ   June   p32.   275w.   4½

3180 HERSH, Paul and David Montgomery.   Salon Classics for
Piano Duo.   Orion Master ORS 76247
      CK   Dec.   p49.   25w.   2½

3181 HESS, Mark.   Jazz: Blues and Stomp.   American Jazz JA 123
      CAD   April   p35.   125w.   3½
      RT   Sept./Oct.   p7.   100w.   2½

3182 HEST, Jeff.   Tip of the Iceberg.   Project 3 PR-5091SD
      SR   Feb.   p92.   100w.   2

3183 HILL, Andrew.   Divine Revelation.   Steeplechase SCS 1044
(Denmark)
      DB   Dec. 2   p20.   450w.   4
      JJ   June   p32, 34.   375w.   3½

3184 HILL, Andrew.   Live at Montreux Jazz Festival, 1975.
Arista Freedom AL 1023
      DB   Nov. 4   p24-5.   250w.   3½
      JA   Summer   p34.   150w.   2½

3185 HILL, Andrew.   Spiral.   Arista-Freedom AL1007
      CO   July   p13.   550w.   4
      CO   July   p13.   300w.   3
      LP   April   p15.   150w.   4

3186 HINES, Earl.   Jazum 47 (Reissue)
      JJ   July   p31.   275w.   4

3187 HINES, Earl.   All-Star Session.   DJM DJMLO66 (E) (Reissue)
      GR   March   p1521.   175w.   3½
      RR   Feb.   p67-8.   75w.   3

3188 HINES, Earl.   Live at Buffalo.   Improv 7114.   Cart. 8337-
7114H.   Cass. 5337 7114H
      CAD   Aug.   p37.   150w.   4
      SR   Nov.   p122.   250w.   5

3189 HINES, Earl. 1929 Recordings. RCA FPM 1-7023 (France)
      (Reissue)
          JJ   Feb.   p38.   250w.   4

3190 HINES, Earl. Once Upon a Time. Impulse IMPL 8011 (E)
      (Reissue)
          JJ   Jan.   p32, 33.   450w.   3½
          RR   Jan.   p63.   150w.   3

3191 HINES, Earl. Quintessential, 1974. Chiaroscuro 131
          HF   June   p110.   250w.   4
          SR   May   p104.   100w.   5

3192 HINES, Earl. Tea for Two. Black Lion BL-112. Cart.
      8T-112
          SR   June   p88, 89.   375w.   4

3193 HINES, Earl. West Side Story. Black Lion BLP 30170 (E)
          MM   Jan. 3   p26.   350w.   3½

3194 HINES, Earl and Jaki Byard. Duet. MPS 20 22022 2 (West
      Germany)
          JF   No. 41   p62-3.   375w.   5

3195 HINES, Earl and Roy Eldridge. At the Village Vanguard.
      Xanadu 106
          AU   April   p96.   500w.   4½

3196 HINO, Terumasa. Fuji. Catalyst CAT-7901 (Japan)
          CAD   Aug.   p17, 18.   200w.   4
          RFJ   Oct.   p8.   275w.   2
          SR   Dec.   p126.   150w.   4½

3197 HINTON, Milt. Here Swings the Judge. Famous Door HL-104
          SR   April   p101.   225w.   4½

3198 HIRT, Al and Peter Fountain. Super Jazz 1. Monument
      PZG 33485 (2 discs)
          SOU   Feb.   p50.   100w.   1

3199 HITCH, Curtis/Hoagy Carmichael. Fountain FJ 109 (E) (Re-
      issue)
          ST   Dec. 1975-Jan. 1976   p75.   550w.   3

3200 HODES, Art. Hodes's Art. Delmark DS-213
          CAD   May   p27-8.   175w.   3
          CK   March   p48.   50w.   3

3201 HODGES, Johnny. Ellingtonia. Onyx 216
          SR   Jan.   p98.   325w.   4

3202 HODGES, Johnny. Everybody Knows. Impulse 561
          MM   April 3   p34.   450w.   3

3203 HODGES, Johnny. Love in Swingtime. Tax MM 8022 (Denmark)
    ST Dec. 1975-Jan. 1976 p79. 350w. 3

3204 HOLIDAY, Billie. Vol. 2, 1953-56. ESP 3003
    MM Nov. 13 p31. 375w. 3

3205 HOLIDAY, Billie. "All of Me", Volume 3. Saga 6930 (E) (Reissue)
    ST April-May p155. 450w. 5

3206 HOLIDAY, Billie. Billie's Blues. Bulldog BDL 1077 (Reissue)
    JJ Aug. p35. 500w. $4\frac{1}{2}$
    MM Sept. 25 p26. 475w. 3

3207 HOLIDAY, Billie. A Day in the Life of. Different Drummer 1003 (Reissue)
    CAD Jan. p30. 375w. $2\frac{1}{2}$

3208 HOLIDAY, Billie. The First Verve Sessions. Verve VE2-2503 (2 discs) (Reissue)
    CRE Sept. p61. 350w. 4
    DB Oct. 7 p33. 150w. 5
    JA Summer p40-1. 175w. 5
    MJ Oct. p52. 50w. $2\frac{1}{2}$

3209 HOLIDAY, Billie. "Lady Day Blues". AJ Records AJ 504
    DB Feb. 12 p29-31. 200w. $3\frac{1}{2}$
    ST Feb.-March p118-9. 500w. 0

3210 HOLIDAY, Billie. The Lady Day Story. DJM 22047 (E) (Reissue)
    MM Nov. 13 p31. 375w. 3

3211 HOLIDAY, Billie. The Voice of Jazz, Volume Ten. Verve 2304 120 (E) (Reissue)
    JJ Feb. p38. 300w. $4\frac{1}{2}$

3212 HOLLAND, Dave and Sam Rivers. Improvising Artists 373843
    CAD Aug. p35. 150w. 5

3213 HOLMES, Richard "Groove". Six Million Dollar Man. Flying Dutchman BDL1-1146
    SR Jan. p82. 175w. 2

3214 HOOPER, Lou. Piano. Radio Canada International 380 (Canada)
    CAD Feb. p28. 125w. 3
    CO March p24. 275w. 4

3215 HOPE, Elmo. The All-Star Sessions. Milestone M-47037

(2 discs) (Reissue)
    CAD Oct. p29. 400w. 5
    CK Dec. p49. 25w. $3\frac{1}{2}$
    RR Dec. p103. 150w. 3

3216 HOPKINS, Claude. Singin' in the Rain. Jazz Archives JA
27 (Reissue)
    DB June 3 p31. 75w. 2
    JJ March p32. 200w. $3\frac{1}{2}$
    MJ Jan. p21. 125w. $3\frac{1}{2}$

3217 HOPKINS, Claude. Soliloquy. Sackville 3004 (Canada)
    CAD Aug. p45. 175w. 3

3218 HORN, Paul. In India. Blue Note BNLA 529-H2 (2 discs)
(Reissue)
    DB Aug. 12 p35. 25w. 2
    JJ June p34. 650w. $3\frac{1}{2}$
    MG June p50. 50w. 3
    PRM Jan. p37. 50w. 2
    SR June p94. 125w. $3\frac{1}{2}$

3219 HORN, Paul. Nexus. Epic KE 33561. Cart. EA 33561
    LP March p16. 200w. $2\frac{1}{2}$
    RR May p75. 350w. $4\frac{1}{2}$
    SR March p102. 200w. 4

3220 HORN, Paul. Special Edition. Island ISLD6 (2 discs). Cart.
Y81D 106
    JJ Feb. p48. 150w. 3
    SR May p76. 350w. 5

3221 HOWARD, Kid. At Zion Hill Church. Dan VC 7005 (E)
    FT June/July p16-7. 500w. $4\frac{1}{2}$

3222-3 HOWELL, Michael. In the Silence. Milestone M-9054
    SR March p89. 125w. $4\frac{1}{2}$

3224 HUBBARD, Freddie. The Badder Hubbard. CTI 6047 (Reissue)
    DB April 10 p24-5. 150w. $3\frac{1}{2}$

3225 HUBBARD, Freddie. Echoes of Blues. Atlantic SD-1687
    CAD Sept. p6. 50w. 4

3226 HUBBARD, Freddie. High Energy. Columbia KC 33048
    CO July p15. 350w. 0

3227 HUBBARD, Freddie. Liquid Love. Columbia PC 33556
    CO July p15. 300w. 3

3228 HUBBARD, Freddie. Polar AC. CTI 6056
    CO July p15. 175w. 2

JJ Feb. p32. 250w. 2½

3229 HUBBARD, Freddie. Red Clay. CTI 6001
       CAC April p28. 75w. 2½
       RR July p80. 50w. 2½

3230 HUBBARD, Freddie. Windjammer. Columbia PC 34166.
       Cart. PC434166. Cass. PCT 34166
       DB Nov. 18 p22. 175w. 1
       PRM Sept. p46. 525w. 3½
       RS Nov. 4 p79. 225w. 3
       SR Dec. p126. 50w. 2

3231 HUG, Armand. An Autobiography in Jazz. Land o' Jazz LOJ
       3475
       ST Oct./Nov. p35-6. 50w. 1½

3232 HUMAN Arts Ensemble. Concere Nitasiah. Universal Justice
       UJ 101
       JJ Nov. p31. 325w. 2

3233 HUMAN Arts Ensemble. Under the Sun. Arista AL 1022
       CAD April p43. 175w. 2
       JA Summer p36. 400w. 5
       RR Nov. p107. 150w. 2½
       SR June p94. 125w. 4½

3234 HUMPHREY, Bobbi. Fancy Dancer. Blue Note BN LA 550G.
       Cass. BNCA 550H
       LP March p16. 50w. 4

3235 HUMPHREY, Bobbi. Satin Doll. Blue Note BN LA 344G
       DB March 27 p19. 150w. 3½

3236 HUMPHREY, Percy. CSA CLPS 1016 (E) (Reissue)
       FT June/July p18. 275w. 2½

3237 HUTCHERSON, Bobby. Montara. Blue Note BN LA 551G
       DB May 6 p26. 200w. 3

3238 HUTCHERSON, Bobby. Waiting. Blue Note LA615-G
       CAD Sept. p6. 25w. 0
       JA Fall p51-2. 425w. 3½

3239 HYMAN, Dick. Charleston--The Song That Made the 'Twenties
       Roar and Other Delectations. Columbia M 33706
       DB Feb. 26 p22. 300w. 3½
       HF April p138, 42. 350w. 3
       RT Sept./Oct. p6-7. 150w. 3
       SOU April p9. 75w. 3
       SR Feb. p93. 150w. 5

3240 HYMAN, Dick. Ragtime, Stomps and Stride. Project 3PR

5080
    RT   May/June   p7-8.   75w.   4

3241   HYMAN, Dick.   Scott Joplin: Complete Works for Piano.
    RCA CRL5-1106 (5 discs)
    RT   July/Aug.   p15-6.   325w.   4

3242   IDRIS, Muhammed.   House of the Rising Sun.   Kudu 27
    RFJ   March   p11.   200w. $3\frac{1}{2}$

3243   INGHAM, Keith.   Music of Richard Rogers.   World Records
    SH 236 (E)
    JJ   Dec.   p28-9.   575w.   3
    MM   Dec. 11   p29.   425w. $3\frac{1}{2}$

3244   IRVINE, Weldon.   Sinbad.   RCA APL1-1363
    CAD   April   p41.   125w.   2

3245   JABULA.   Thunder into Our Hearts.   Virgin CA 2009
    JF   No. 44   p33-4.   100w.   4

3246   JACKSON, Milt.   The Big 3.   Pablo 2310 757
    CAC   Oct.   p272.   275w. $4\frac{1}{2}$
    CAD   May   p28.   100w.   3
    MM   Aug. 21   p20.   75w. $4\frac{1}{2}$

3247   JACKSON, Milt.   At Montreux Jazz Festival, 1975.   Pablo
    2310 753
    CAC   Jan.   p412, 414.   100w.   5
    DB   April 8   p22-4.   100w.   4
    MM   April 17   p24.   325w.   3
    SR   May   p104.   75w. $3\frac{1}{2}$
    RFJ   Oct.   p14.   600w. $3\frac{1}{2}$

3248   JACKSON, Milt.   Feelings.   Pablo 2310-774
    CAC   Nov.   p311.   125w.   3
    CAD   Sept.   p6.   50w.   4
    GRA   Dec.   p1080.   100w.   4
    JJ   Nov.   p31-2.   300w.   2
    MJ   Oct.   p22.   25w.   3
    MM   Dec. 18   p20.   275w. $3\frac{1}{2}$

3249   JACKSON, Milt.   Live at the Museum of Modern Art 1965.
    Trip TLP-5553 (Reissue)
    CO   July   p15, 16.   300w.   3

3250   JACKSON, Milt.   Olinga.   CTI CTI 6046.   Cart. CT8-6046.
    Cass. CTC-6046
    SR   March   p91.   225w.   5

3251   JACKSON, Milt.   Opus de Funk.   Prestige P-24048 (2 discs)
    (Reissue)
    CO   July   p15.   175w.   2

MM April 24 p24. 600w. $3\frac{1}{2}$
RR Jan. p63. 50w. $2\frac{1}{2}$

3252 JACKSON, Milt. Second Nature. Savoy SJL 2204 (2 discs)
(Reissue). Cart. SJ8 2204
JA Summer p41-2. 100w. 3
JJ Dec. p29. 550w. 3
PRM May p63. 50w. 3
SR Nov. p133. 25w. 3

3253 JACKSON, Milt. Sunflower. CTI 6024
RR July p80. 25w. $2\frac{1}{2}$

3254 JACKSON, Willis. Headed and Gutted. Muse 5048
CAD April p37. 100w. $1\frac{1}{2}$

3255 JACKSON, Willis. Plays with Feeling. Cotillion SD
9908
CAD Oct. p18. 75w. 2

3256 JACQUET, Illinois. Birthday Party. JRC 11434
HF July p111. 200w. $2\frac{1}{2}$

3257 JACQUET, Illinois. Genius at Work. Black Lion BL-146
CO March p24. 175w. 4

3258 JACQUET, Illinois. How High the Moon. Prestige P24057
(2 discs) (Reissue)
AU April p94. 250w. 4
CRE Feb. p59. 350w. 4

3259 JAMAL, Ahmad. Live at Oil Can Harry's. Catalyst CAT
7606 (Japan)
CAD June p23. 50w. 3
MJ July p55. 125w. $3\frac{1}{2}$
SR Nov. p122. 75w. $3\frac{1}{2}$

3260 JAMAL, Ahmad. Plays Jamal. 20th Century T-459. Cart.
8459. Cass. C459
SR May p89. 100w. $4\frac{1}{2}$

3261 JAMAL, Ahmad. Steppin' Out with a Dream. 20th Century
T515
CAD Sept. p8. 100w. 4

3262 JAMES, Bob. Three. CTI 6063
BM Nov. p47. 200w. 2
CAD Oct. p18. 75w. 3
DB Oct. 21 p24. 200w. 2

3263 JAMES, Harry. The Best of the Big Bands. Embassy EMB
31048 (E) (Reissue)
MM Aug. 28 p22. 200w. 3

3264 JAMES, Harry. The Second Big Band Sound. Verve 2317
      083 (E) (Reissue)
          GRA Nov. p900. 100w. 3
          MM Jan. 10 p32. 400w. 3

3265 JAMES, Harry. Texas Chatter. Tax m-8015 (Sweden)
          JJ April p32. 100w. 4

3266 JAMES, Harry. The Third Big Band Sound. Verve 2317 110
      (E) (Reissue)
          CAC Oct. p257. 150w. 3
          GRA Nov. p900. 100w. 3
          JJ July p31-2. 675w. 5
          MM July 17 p26. 425w. 3

3267 JAMES, Harry/Woody Herman. Batch of Jazz. Tulip TLP 107
          AU June p87-8. 200w. 2

3268 JARREAU, Al. Glow. Reprise MS 2248
          CAD Aug. p25. 75w. 5
          DB Nov. 4 p25. 200w. 3
          RS Oct. 7 p81. 200w. 3

3269 JARRETT, Keith. Arbour Zena. ECM 1070
          CAD Aug. p41. 350w. 5
          DB Oct. 21 p20, 22. 350w. 3

3270 JARRETT, Keith. Back Hand. ABC Impulse ASH-9305.
      Cart. 8027-9305 H
          DB May 6 p24, 26. 325w. $4\frac{1}{2}$
          HF March p110, 112. 425w. $4\frac{1}{2}$
          JJ Jan. p33. 200w. 5
          LP March p16. 150w. $4\frac{1}{2}$
          SR March p102. 275w. 5

3271 JARRETT, Keith. Death and the Flower. Impulse ASD-9301
          CO July p16. 275w. 3

3272 JARRETT, Keith. El Juicio. Atlantic SD 1673
          DB Jan. 15 p23-4. 425w. 3

3273 JARRETT, Keith. Facing You. ECM 1017 ST
          DB March 27 p17. 200w. 5
          SR May p89. 100w. 5

3274 JARRETT, Keith. In the Light. ECM 103/04 (2 discs)
          SOU May p45. 150w. $2\frac{1}{2}$

3275 JARRETT, Keith. The Köln Concert. ECM 1064/65 (2 discs)
          CRA April p73-4. 475w. 4
          DB Feb. 12 p22. 325w. 5
          HF March p110, 112. 425w. 4
          LP March p16. 150w. 4

SOU   Jan.   p39.   150w.   4
SR   March   p102.   275w.   5

3276   JARRETT, Keith.   Mysteries.   Impulse ASD-9315
CK   Oct.   p46.   125w.   5
DB   Sept. 9   p25-6.   500w. $3\frac{1}{2}$
JJ   Aug.   p35-6.   275w. $4\frac{1}{2}$

3277   JARRETT, Keith and Jan Garbarek.   Luminescence.   ECM
1049
DB   Jan. 29   p22.   250w.   5

3278   JASEN, Dave.   Rompin' Stompin' Ragtime.   Blue Goose 3002
SR   Jan.   p87, 88.   300w.   3

3279   JAZZ Carriers.   Carry On!   Muza SXL0962 (Poland)
CO   March   p15.   350w.   0

3280   JAZZ Crusaders.   The Young Rabbits.   Blue Note BN-LA
530-H2 (2 discs) (Reissue)
DB   Aug. 12   p35.   75w. $1\frac{1}{2}$
JJ   June   p34.   275w. $2\frac{1}{2}$
PRM   Jan.   p37.   50w. $2\frac{1}{2}$

3281   JAZZ Messengers.   1970.   Catalyst CAT 7902 (Japan)
RFJ   Oct.   p8.   275w. $2\frac{1}{2}$

3282   JEFFERSON, Eddie.   Things Are Getting Better.   Muse MR
5043
CO   March   p26, 27.   325w.   3
DB   March 27   p18.   200w.   4

3283   JEFFERSON, Eddie.   Still on the Planet.   Muse MR 5063
CAD   Nov.   p14.   125w. $3\frac{1}{2}$

3284   JEFFERSON, Ron.   Vous etes swing.   Catalyst CAT 7601
(Japan)
CAD   Dec.   p24.   150w.   2

3285   JENKINS, LeRoy.   For Players Only.   JCOA LP1010
DB   Sept. 9   p31.   400w.   4
HF   May   p109, 112.   275w. $3\frac{1}{2}$
JJ   July   p34.   400w.   5
MG   June   p50.   75w. $3\frac{1}{2}$
MM   Sept. 17   p24.   750w. $3\frac{1}{2}$
SR   Sept.   p112.   325w.   2

3286   JENSEN, John.   Zez Confrey Novelty Piano Solos.   Genesis
GS 1061
CO   March   p25.   300w.   5

3287   JOBIM, Antonio Carlos.   Urubu.   Warner BS 2928
DB   Nov. 4   p26-7.   200w.   3

MJ   July   p54.   50w.   1
MM   Aug.   21   p20.   75w.   3

3288 JOHNSON, Alphonso.   Moonshadows.   Epic PE 34118
      CRA   July   p72-3.   100w.   3
      DB   Sept. 9   p30.   300w. $3\frac{1}{2}$

3289 JOHNSON, Buddy.   At the Savoy Ballroom 1945-46.   Jazz
      Archives JA 25 (Reissue)
      JJ   March   p32.   350w. $3\frac{1}{2}$
      MJ   Jan.   p21.   125w.   3

3290 JOHNSON, Bunk.   The Last Testament of a Great New Orleans
      Jazzman.   Columbia JCL 829 (Reissue)
      MJ   Jan.   p20.   100w. $2\frac{1}{2}$
      SR   Oct.   p94.   400w.   4

3291 JOHNSON, James P.   1921-1926.   Ember CJS 853 (E) (Re-
      issue)
      RR   April   p78.   125w.   3

3292 JOHNSON, James P.   The Original.   Folkways FJ 2850 (Re-
      issue)
      CO   March   p26.   325w.   3
      CO   July   p16, 17.   600w.   5

3293 JOHNSON, Pete.   Master of Blues and Boogie Woogie, Vol. 2.
      Oldie Blues OL 2806 (Holland) (Reissue)
      BU   Jan.-Feb.   p26.   475w. $4\frac{1}{2}$
      JJ   Feb.   p32.   200w. $3\frac{1}{2}$

3294 JONES, Elvin.   Live.   PM PMR 004
      CAD   Jan.   p13.   200w. $4\frac{1}{2}$
      CRA   Feb.   p73.   375w.   3
      DB   May 20   p26-7.   200w. $3\frac{1}{2}$
      JF   No. 44   p30.   75w.   4
      RFJ   Feb.   p12.   400w.   4
      SOU   Feb.   p48.   25w. $2\frac{1}{2}$

3295 JONES, Elvin.   The Main Force.   Vanguard VSD 79372
      MJ   Dec.   p26.   50w.   3
      RR   Dec.   p102.   75w.   3
      SR   Oct.   p108.   200w.   3

3296 JONES, Elvin.   New Agenda.   Vanguard VSD 79362
      AU   March   p83-4.   700w. $3\frac{1}{2}$
      CO   July   p17.   800w.   3

3297 JONES, Elvin.   On the Mountain.   PM PMR 005
      CAD   Jan.   p13.   75w. $4\frac{1}{2}$
      CRA   Feb.   p73.   375w. $4\frac{1}{2}$
      DB   May 20   p26.   200w.   4
      JF   No. 44   p75-6.   600w. $4\frac{1}{2}$

SOU   Feb.   p48.   150w.   3

3298   JONES, Elvin.   Prime Element.   Blue Note LA 506
       CAD   Nov.   p15.   125w.   3

3299   JONES, Jo.   The Drums.   CRD Jazz Odyssey 008 (2 discs)
       (E) (Reissue)
       GR   Oct.   p670.   325w.   3

3300   JONES, Jonah/Brown, Pete.   Low Down Blues.   Jazz Show-
       case 5006
       JJ   Jan.   p33.   200w.   4$\frac{1}{2}$

3301   JONES, Philly Joe.   Trailways Express.   Black Lion BL-142
       CO   July   p17.   300w.   3

3301a JONES, Quincy.   I Heard That.   A&M SP3705
       BM   Dec.   p51, 53.   200w.   4

3301b JONES, Quincy.   Mellow Madness.   A&M SP4526
       BM   Nov.   p30.   125w.   5

3302   JONES, Thad and Mel Lewis.   Pausa PR-7012
       CAD   Oct.   p44.   300w.   4

3303   JONES, Thad and Mel Lewis.   Fingers.   Blue Note BNLA
       392-H (2 discs) (Reissue)
       RFJ   June   p8.   125w.   4$\frac{1}{2}$

3304   JONES, Thad and Mel Lewis.   New Life.   Horizon AMLJ
       707.   Cart. 8T707.   Cass. CS707
       HF   Sept.   p113.   350w.   4
       JA   Fall   p52-3.   500w.   3$\frac{1}{2}$
       JF   No. 44   p30.   100w.   4
       JJ   Sept.   p33.   800w.   5
       MJ   Sept.   p34-5.   125w.   3$\frac{1}{2}$
       RR   Dec.   p107.   50w.   3$\frac{1}{2}$
       SR   Oct.   p108.   150w.   4

3305   JONES, Thad and Mel Lewis.   Potpourri.   Philadelphia In-
       tional KZ33152.   Cart. ZA 33152
       SR   March   p72.   400w.   4

3306   JONES, Thad and Mel Lewis.   Suite for Pops.   Horizon
       SP-701
       CAD   Jan.   p24, 26.   125w.   5
       DB   April 8   p20.   425w.   4$\frac{1}{2}$
       HF   March   p112-3.   325w.   4
       MJ   Sept.   p35.   100w.   3$\frac{1}{2}$
       RFJ   March   p10.   550w.   4
       SOU   Feb.   p48, 50.   300w.   4
       SR   April   p102.   225w.   4

3307 JONES, Thad, and the Swedish Radio Jazz Group. Greetings and Salutations. Four Leaf Clover FLC 5001 (Sweden)
JF May p40-1. 625w. 4

3308 JOPLIN, Scott. Elite Syncopations. Biograph 10140
CO July p17, 18. 200w. 4

3309 JOPLIN, Scott. The Entertainer. Biograph 10130
CO July p17, 18. 200w. 4

3310 JORDAN, Clifford. The Highest Mountain. Steeplechase SCS 1047 (Denmark)
JJ Sept. p33. 200w. 4

3311 JORDAN, Clifford. And the Magic Triangle. Steeplechase SCS 1033 (Denmark)
JJ May p32. 325w. 5

3312 JORDAN, Clifford. Night of the Mark VII. Muse 5076
DB Oct. 21 p28, 31. 300w. $3\frac{1}{2}$
MG June p50. 50w. $2\frac{1}{2}$

3313 JORDAN, Duke. Archives of Jazz, vol. 5. Archives of Jazz AJ 506 (Reissue)
DB Feb. 12 p29-31. 200w. 3

3314 JORDAN, Duke. Duke's Delight. Steeplechase SCS 1046 (Denmark)
JJ June p34, 35. 350w. 4

3315 JORDAN, Duke. The Murray Hill Caper. Spotlite DJ 5
CO July p18, 19. 625w. 0

3316 JORDAN, Louis. Star Performance SP 3001 (Switzerland)
ST Feb.-March p117-8. 220w. 4

3317 JORDAN, Louis. With the Chris Barber Band. Black Lion BLP 30175 (E) (Reissue)
JJ July p34-5. 475w. $3\frac{1}{2}$

3318 JORDAN, Sheila. Confirmation. East Wind 8024
CAD Aug. p42. 200w. 4

3319 JUJU. Chapter Two: Nia. Strata-East SES 7420
CO July p19. 425w. 3

3320 KAMUCA, Richard. Quartet 1976. JAZZZ 104
CAD Aug. p41. 150w. 5

3321 KANE, Raymond. Tradewind TS 1130
GP Dec. p104. 125w. $2\frac{1}{2}$

3322 KAROLAK, Wojciech. Easy. Muza SXL 1069 (Poland)

JF   May   p42.   575w.   3

3323   KASAI, Kimiko and Mal Waldron.   One for Lady.   Catalyst
       CAT-7900 (Japan)
              CAD   Aug.   p17.   150w.   4
              SR   Dec.   p126.   150w.   2

3324   KAYE, Milton.   Classic Rags of Joe Lamb, vol. 2.   Golden
       Crest CRS 31035
              RT   Jan./Feb.   p7-8.   100w.   1

3325   KAYE, Milton.   You Tell Em Ivories.   Golden Crest CRS
       31040
              RT   Jan.   p7-8.   100w.   3

3326   KENTON, Stan.   Artistry in Rhythm, 1944-45.   Sunbeam
       SB213 (Reissue)
              DB   June 3   p29-30.   75w.   3

3327   KENTON, Stan.   Balboa/Summer 1941.   Mark IV 581 (Re-
       issue)
              AU   April   p93.   500w.   4

3328   KENTON, Stan.   By Request, vol. 6.   Creative World ST
       1069 (Reissue)
              AU   April   p93-4.   500w.   2

3329   KENTON, Stan.   Fire, Fury and Fun.   Creative World ST
       1073
              AU   April   p93.   500w.   4½

3330   KENTON, Stan.   Hits in Concert.   Creative World ST 1074
              AU   April   p93-4.   500w.   4½
              CAD   May   p29.   125w.   2½
              MJ   Jan.   p21.   25w.   3

3331   KENTON, Stan.   Kenton '76.   Creative World ST1076
              CAD   April   p34.   150w.   3½
              JJ   Dec.   p32.   450w.   2
              SOU   July   p41.   125w.   1

3332   KENTON, Stan.   National Anthems of the World.   Creative
       World ST 1060 (2 discs)
              LP   Jan.   p17.   150w.   4½

3333   KENTON, Stan.   The Romantic Approach.   Creative World
       ST1017
              DB   June 3   p29.   75w.   2½

3334   KENTON, Stan.   Solo.   Creative World ST1071
              MJ   Jan.   p21.   50w.   3½

3335   KENTON, Stan.   Road Show, vol. 1/2.   Creative World

ST1019/20 (Reissue) (2 discs)
    DB June 3 p29. 100w. 3

3336 KENYATTA, Robin. Nomusa. Muse 5062
      DB April 8 p28. 300w. 4

3337 KERR, Brooks. Soda Fountain Rag. Chiarascuro 2001
      CAD March p28. 125w. 3
      HF July p111. 300w. 3

3338 KERR, Brooks and Paul Qunichette. Prevue. Famous Door
    HL 106
      CAD May p24. 150w. 3
      DB Nov. 4 p30. 75w. $4\frac{1}{2}$
      HF July p111. 100w. $2\frac{1}{2}$
      JF No. 44 p32. 100w. 4

3339 KESSEL, Barney. Blue Soul. Black Lion BL 310
      CAD Jan. p30. 75w. 1
      SR April p102. 100w. 2

3340 KESSEL, Barney. Just Friends. Sonet SNTF 685 (E)
      JJ March p32. 250w. 4

3341 KESSEL, Barney. Plays Kessel. Concord CJ9
      DB March 25 p34-5. 25w. 3
      HF Jan. p107. 375w. $3\frac{1}{2}$
      RFJ July p9. 525w. 4

3342 KESSEL, Barney. Swinging Easy. Black Lion BL-130
      CO March p26. 100w. 3

3343 KINCH, Don and the Conductors Ragtime Band. Rexius RL
    5123
      ST Oct./Nov. p34. 175w. $3\frac{1}{2}$

3344 KIRBY, John. Biggest Little Band in the Land. Classic
    Jazz CJ 22 (2 discs) (Reissue)
      JJ Aug. p36. 425w. 4
      MJ Dec. p44. 75w. 3
      SR Oct. p108. 300w. 3

3345 KIRBY, John. Flow Gently Sweet Rhythm. TAX m-8016
    (Sweden)
      CO July p19. 350w. 4
      JJ April p33. 275w. $4\frac{1}{2}$

3346 KIRK, Rahsaan Roland. Other Folks' Music. Atlantic SD-
    1686
      CAD Sept. p6. 25w. 0
      DB Nov. 4 p20. 350w. 5

3347 KIRK, Rahsaan Roland. The Return of the 5,000 lb. Man.

Warner BS 2918
    DB   June 3 p20. 500w. $2\frac{1}{2}$
    JA   Summer p36-7. 400w.   3
    JJ   July p35. 300w. $3\frac{1}{2}$
    MJ   July p54. 125w. $2\frac{1}{2}$
    RS   June 17 p55. 150w. $3\frac{1}{2}$

3348 KIRK, [Rahsaan] Roland. We Free Kings. Trip Jazz TLP-
5541 (Reissue)
        CO   July p19, 20. 550w.   4

3349 KLEMMER, John. Barefoot Ballet. ABCD 950
        CAD   Oct. p17. 150w.   5

3350 KLEMMER, John. Intensity. Impulse AS-9224
        CO   July p20. 350w.   3

3351 KLEMMER, John. Magic Moments. Chess Jazz Masters
Series 2 ACMJ-401 (2 discs) (Reissue)
        CAD   Oct. p22. 200w.   4

3352 KLEMMER, John. Touch. ABC Impulse 922
        DB   Feb. 28 p21-2. 325w.   2
        LP   April p15. 125w. $2\frac{1}{2}$

3353 KLOSS, Eric. One, Two, Free. Muse MR 5019
        CO   Sept. p15. 175w.   3

3354 KLOSS, Eric. Warm Bodies. Muse 5077
        CAD   Feb. p23. 150w. $3\frac{1}{2}$

3355 KLUGH, Earl. Blue Note BN-LA 596-G
        DB   Nov. 18 p22. 325w. $3\frac{1}{2}$
        GP   Sept. p86. 150w. $4\frac{1}{2}$

3356 KLUGH, Earl. Living Inside Your Love. Blue Note BNLA
667G
        PRM   Nov. p45. 625w.   1

3357 KOFFMAN, Moe. Live at George's. GRT 9230 1055 (2
discs) (Canada)
        OLR   Dec. p258. 50w.   4
        SOU   June p36. 250w.   4

3358 KOLLEKTIEF, William Brueker. Live in Berlin. BVHAAST
008 SAJB (Netherlands)
        MM   Dec. 4 p28. 100w.   4

3359 KOMEDA, Krzystof. Astigmatic. Muza SXL0298 (Poland)
        CO   March p13. 350w.   4

3360 KONITZ, Lee and Red Mitchell. I Concentrate on You.
Steeplechase SCS 1018 (Denmark)

JJ   Jan.   p33.   400w.   4

3361 KONITZ, Lee.   Lone-Lee.   Steeplechase SCS 1035 (Denmark)
      JA   Summer   p37.   200w. $4\frac{1}{2}$
      JA   March   p33.   150w.   2

3362 KONITZ, Lee.   Motion.   Polydor 2317 106 (E)
      GRA   Jan.   p1263.   225w. $3\frac{1}{2}$

3363 KONITZ, Lee.   Oleo.   Sonet SNTF 690 (E)
      JJ   March   p33.   150w.   4
      MM   March 20   p24.   225w. $2\frac{1}{2}$

3364 KONITZ, Lee.   Revelations.   Blue Note BN LA 532H2 (2
      discs) (Reissue)
      PRM   Jan.   p37.   50w. $3\frac{1}{2}$

3365 KONITZ, Lee.   Satori.   Milestone M-9060
      CO   Sept.   p15, 16.   575w.   2
      SR   July   p86.   175w. $4\frac{1}{2}$

3366 KONITZ, Lee and Attila Zoller.   Zo-Ko-Ma.   MPS BAP 5072
      (E)
      JJ   March   p32, 33.   250w.   4
      MM   March 20   p24.   225w. $2\frac{1}{2}$

3367 KOSZ, Mieczyslaw   Reminiscence.   Muza SXLO744 (Poland)
      CO   March   p15.   350w.   2

3368 KRAL, Irene.   Where Is Love.   Choice 1012
      CAD   March   p26, 28.   75w.   2

3369 KRIEGEL, Volker.   Topical Harvest.   MPS BASF 20228274
      J F   No. 44   p33.   100w.   4

3370 KRUPA, Gene.   Big Band Sound.   Verve 2317 113 (E) (Re-
      issue)
      JJ   Oct.   p32.   550w.   4

3371 KRUPA, Gene.   King Krupa 1945.   Swing Treasury 106
      JJ   Jan.   p33, 34.   300w. $4\frac{1}{2}$

3372 KRUPA, Gene.   One Night Stand.   Joyce 1029 (Reissue)
      DB   Nov. 4   p28-9.   75w.   2

3373 KRUPA, Gene.   Second Big Band Sound of.   Verve 2317 113
      (E) (Reissue)
      GRA   Nov.   p900.   100w. $2\frac{1}{2}$
      MM   Nov. 13   p31.   400w. $3\frac{1}{2}$

3374 KRUPA, Gene and Buddy Rich.   Drum Battle.   Verve 2317
      116 (E) (Reissue)

JJ Dec. p32. 225w. 3

3375 KRUPA, Gene/Ziggy Elman. Monmouth Evergreen MES 7072
      (Reissue)
            CAD March p30. 75w. $3\frac{1}{2}$
            SR May p104. 200w. 4

3376 KUHN, Joachim. Joachim Kuhn. MPS 2111330-7 (West Ger-
      many)
            CO Sept. p16, 17. 225w. 4

3377 KUHN, Joachim. Association P.C. MPS 2121763-9 (West
      Germany)
            CO Sept. p16, 17. 225w. 4

3378 KUHN, Steve. Ecstasy. ECM 1058
            CAD Nov. p20. 50w. 3

3379 KUHN, Steve. Raindrops (Live in New York). Muse MR
      5106 (Reissue)
            CAD Sept. p22. 125w. 2

3380 KUHN, Steve. Trance. ECM 1052
            CK March p48. 50w. 3
            CO March p26. 150w. 2
            HF Feb. p124, 127. 250w. 3
            JF No. 41 p61. 350w. 4
            SOU March p47. 50w. 4

3381 KURYLEWICZ, Andrej. Ten + Eight. Muza XLO439 (Poland)
            CO March p14, 15. 350w. 2

3382 KUSTBANDET. Kenneth KS 2037 (Sweden)
            CO Sept. p17. 250w. 4

3383 KVARTETT, Bjorn Alkes. Caprice RIKS LP 72 (Sweden)
            JJ July p40. 75w. 4

3384 The L.A. Four. Concord Jazz CJ-18
            CAD Aug. p36. 175w. 2
            GP Aug. p81. 25w. 3
            JA Fall p53. 400w. 1
            JJ Oct. p32, 34. 475w. 5
            RFJ Dec. p16-7. 600w. 4
            SR Sept. p88. 350w. 4

3385 LACY, Steve. The Crust. Emanem 304
            CAD Feb. p25. 100w. 2
            CO Sept. p17. 275w. 2

3386 LACY, Steve. Estilhacos--Live in Lisbon. Sassetti Guilda
      da Musica 11403001 (Portugal)
            CAD April p31. 150w. 4

3387 LACY, Steve. Lapis. Editions Saravah SH10031 (France)
      CO   March   p26, 27.   425w.   2

3388 LACY, Steve. Saxophone Special.   Emanen 3310
      CAD   Oct.   p39.   175w. $2\frac{1}{2}$

3389 LACY, Steve. School Days.   Emanen 3316
      CAD   Feb.   p27.   100w. $3\frac{1}{2}$
      DB   March 25 p34-5.   25w. $3\frac{1}{2}$
      JF   No. 44 p30-1.   75w.   4
      JJ   Jan. p34.   275w. $4\frac{1}{2}$

3390 LACY, Steve. Solo. Emanen 301
      CAD   Jan.   p23-4.   275w.   3
      CO   Sept.   p17.   400w.   4

3391 LADD'S Black Aces. Volume 3: 1923-1924.   Fountain FJ 111
      (E) (Reissue)
      ST   Feb.-March p113.   375w.   3

3392 LAKE, Oliver. Heavy Spirits. Arista 1008
      CO   July   p20.   675w.   5
      DB   April 22 p25, 28.   400w.   4

3393 LAKE, Oliver. NTU: The Point From Which Freedom Begins.
      Arista Freedom AL 1024
      DB   Nov. 18 p18.   300w. $3\frac{1}{2}$

3394 LAKE, Oliver. Passing Thru: Oliver Lake.   Passin' Thru
      Records 4237
      CAD   Aug.   p23.   150w.   4
      CAD   Sept.   p10.   50w.   3

3395 LAMBERT, Donald. Meet the Lamb. IAJRC 23 (Reissue)
      CAD   Nov.   p22.   75w. $3\frac{1}{2}$
      JJ   Dec. p33.   275w. $4\frac{1}{2}$

3396 LANDE, Art and Jan Garbarek.   Red Lanta.   ECM 1038
      DB   Jan. 15 p21-2.   250w.   5
      LP   Jan.   p17.   225w. $3\frac{1}{2}$
      SR   May   p104.   150w. $4\frac{1}{2}$

3397 LANE, Steve. Jubilee Album.   JM SLC 26 (E)
      JJ   April   p33.   250w.   4
      ST   April-May p159.   600w. $4\frac{1}{2}$

3398 LATEEF, Yusef. Vol. 2. Archives of Jazz 502 (Reissue)
      DB   Feb. 12 p29-31.   200w.   3

3399 LATEEF, Yusef. Club Date. Impulse AS 9310
      MM   Aug. 28 p22.   200w. $2\frac{1}{2}$

3400 LATEEF, Yusef. The Doctor Is In ... And Out.   Atlantic

SD-1685
    CAD Sept. p6. 25w. 0

3401 LATEEF, Yusef. Morning: The Savoy Sessions. Savoy SJL
      2205 (2 discs) (Reissue). Cart. SJ8 2205
          CAD Nov. p28-9. 175w. $2\frac{1}{2}$
          JA Summer p41-2. 100w. 3
          JJ Dec. p32-3. 375w. $3\frac{1}{2}$
          PRM May p63. 100w. 3
          SR Nov. p133. 25w. 3

3402 LAWRENCE, Azar. Bridge Into the New Age. Prestige
      P-10086
          CO March p22. 275w. 2
          SR April p102. 175w. 2

3403 LAWRENCE, Azar. People Moving. Prestige P-10099
          CAD Oct. p39. 175w. 0

3404 LAWRENCE, Azar. Summer Solstice. Prestige P 10097
          AU Aug. p80-2. 700w. 4
          DB March 25 p24, 26. 300w. 4

3405 LAWS, Hubert. The Chicago Theme. CTI CTI-6058 S1.
      Cart. CT8-6058. Cass. CTC-6058
          SR Oct. p95. 200w. 4

3406 LAWS, Ronnie. Fever. Blue Note BN LA 624G. Cart. EA
      628H. Cass. CA628H
          MM July 24 p25. 225w. $2\frac{1}{2}$
          SR Dec. p126, 128. 50w. 2

3407 LAWS, Ronnie. Pressure Sensitive. Blue Note LA 452G
          BM April p31. 300w. 5
          CRA May p79. 125w. 4
          DB Feb. 12 p22-3. 200w. 3

3408 LEDUC, Pierre. CBC Radio Canada 267 (Canada)
          OLR Dec. p258. 50w. 4

3409 LEE, John and Gerry Brown. Mango Sunrise. Blue Note
      BN-LA541-G
          BM Aug. p42. 75w. 2
          DB May 6 p29. 200w. 2
          GP Aug. p80. 250w. 4
          MM May 22 p26. 50w. 1

3410 LEE, Tony. British Jazz Artists, vol. 1. Lee Lambert
      Lyn 3416 (E)
          MM Sept. 11 p30. 600w. 4

3411 LeGRAND, Michel. And His Friends. RCA RS1061 (E)
          JJ Oct. p34. 400w. $4\frac{1}{2}$

3412 LeGRAND, Michel. Recorded Live at Jimmy's. RCA BGL-
      0850. Cart. BGS1-0850. Cass. BGK1-0850
         SR July p78. 225w. 4

3413 LEIGH, Carol. Wild Women Don't Have the Blues. Jazzology
      GHB 88
         CAD May p15-6. 125w. $3\frac{1}{2}$

3414 LEIGHTON, Bernie. Plays Duke Ellington at Jimmy Weston's.
      Monmouth Evergreen MES 7068
         SR May p89-90. 150w. $4\frac{1}{2}$

3415 LEIMGRUBER, Urs. Kirikuki. Japo 60012ST
         JJ June p35. 125w. 0

3416 LENZ, Klaus. Big Band 1974. Amiga (East Germany)
         JF No. 41 p28-9. 100w. 3

3417 LEVIN, Marc. Social Sketches. Enja 2058
         CAD Dec. p23. 175w. 3
         JJ May p32. 350w. $4\frac{1}{2}$

3418 LEWIS, George. "Live at the Hangover Club". Dawn Club
      12008
         JJ March p33. 175w. $2\frac{1}{2}$
         ST Aug.-Sept. p232. 350w. 4

3419 LEWIS, James Mingo. Flight Never Ending. Columbia PC
      34260
         RS Dec. 14 p72. 50w. $2\frac{1}{2}$

3420 LEWIS, John. European Windows. RCA APM1-1069
         SR Feb. p93. 100w. 4

3421 LEWIS, John. P.O.V. Columbia PC 33534
         BD March 11 p20. 350w. 5
         LP Jan. p17. 175w. $2\frac{1}{2}$

3422 LEWIS, Ramsey. Don't It Feel Good. Columbia PC 33800
         DB Jan. 29 p23-4. 200w. 2
         RR July p80. 25w. $1\frac{1}{2}$

3423 LEWIS, Ramsey. Salongo. Columbia PC 34173
         DB Oct. 7 p29. 275w. $3\frac{1}{2}$
         RR Nov. p105. 50w. 3

3424 LIEBMAN, Dave. Drum Ode. ECM 1046
         CO April p14. 175w. 2

3425 LIEBMAN, David. First Visit. Philips RJ 5101 (Japan)
         CAD Aug. p16. 75w. 5
         CO Sept. p18. 600w. 4

3426 LIEBMAN, David and Richard Beirach. Forgotten Fantasies.
      Horizon SP-709
            CAD Aug. p38. 150w. 5
            JJ   Sept. p34. 300w. $4\frac{1}{2}$
            MJ   Sept. p35. 250w. 3
            RR   Nov. p106-7. 200w. 4

3427 LIEBMAN, Dave and Lookout Farm. Sweet Hands. Horizon
      SP 702
            DB   March 25 p22. 300w. 3
            MJ   Sept. p35. 25w. 3
            MM   April 3 p34. 575w. 3
            RFJ March p10-1. 200w. 4
            RR   March p73-4. 450w. $3\frac{1}{2}$
            SOU Feb. p50. 150w. 2

3428 LOCKRAN, Gerry. Rags to Glad Rags. Decca (E)
            MM   Nov. 13 p28. 125w. 2

3429 LOLAX, Paul. Ragtime Guitar. Titanic, TI-13
            AU   Dec. p104. 200w. 4
            GP   Aug. p81. 25w. 3

3430 LONDON Festival Ballet Orchestra. Scott Joplin: The Enter-
      tainer Ballet. Columbia M 33185
            RT   Jan./Feb. p6. 150w. $1\frac{1}{2}$

3431 LOWE, Frank. The Flam. Black Saint BSR 0005 (Italy)
            CAD Oct. p33, 34. 225w. 4
            JJ   April p34. 350w. 5

3432 LOWE, Frank. Fresh. Arista/AL 1015
            CAD Feb. p24. 50w. $1\frac{1}{2}$
            CRE April p62. 50w. 4
            DB   April 8 p26. 300w. $4\frac{1}{2}$
            SR   April p102. 150w. 2

3433 LUCAS, Doug. Niara. Shady Brook 33-004
            CAD Sept. p8. 150w. 4

3434 LUCIE, Lawrence. Cool and Warm Guitar. Toy T 1001
            MJ   March p47. 75w. 3

3435 LUNCEFORD, Jimmie/Louis Prima. Victory Parade. Air-
      check 8 (Canada)
            CAD Sept. p23-4. 200w. 3
            JJ   May p40. 100w. 3
            ST   June-July p191-2. 150w. 0

3436 LYTTLETON, Humphrey. Take It From the Top. Black
      Lion BLP 12134 (E)
            JJ   March p33, 34. 500w. $4\frac{1}{2}$

3437   McBEE, Cecil. Mutima. Strata-East SE7417
       CO Sept. p19. 350w. 3

3438   McCANN, Les. Mustle to Survive. Atlantic SD 1679
       CK Jan. p47-8. 200w. 3

3439   McCANN, Les. River High, River Low. Atlantic SD 1679
       CAD Oct. p18. 100w. 4
       DB Aug. 12 p31, 34. 325w. 5
       LP March p16-7. 100w. $4\frac{1}{2}$

3440   McCONNELL, Rob and the Boss Brass. Attic LAT 1015
       (Canada)
       CC Nov. p32. 50w. 3

3441   MacDONALD, Ralph. Sound of the Drum. Marlin
       RM Dec. p31. 100w. 3

3441a McGHEE, Howard. Shades of Blue. Black Lion 305
       CAD Jan. p31. 125w. 3
       MJ April p29. 50w. 3

3442   McINTYRE, Ken. Home. Steeplechase SCS 1039 (Denmark)
       DB May 6 p32. 175w. $3\frac{1}{2}$
       JJ May p32-3. 275w. 4

3443   McINTYRE, Ken. Open Horizon. Steeplechase SCS 1049
       (Denmark)
       JJ Sept. p34. 475w. $4\frac{1}{2}$

3444   McKENNA, Dave. By Myself. Shiah MK1
       CAD Oct. p38. 150w. 5
       RFJ Oct. p9. 625w. 4

3445   McKENNA, Dave and Zoot Sims. Chiaroscuro CR 136
       DB Jan. 29 p23-3. 200w. 2

3446   McKINLEY, Ray. Class of '49. Hep 4 (Reissue)
       DB June 3 p30. 75w. 3

3447   McLAUGHLIN, John. Shakti. Columbia PC 34162
       CRE Sept. p65. 50w. $3\frac{1}{2}$
       DB Sept. 9 p22. 375w. $3\frac{1}{2}$
       MM May 29 p29. 550w. 3
       RR Sept. p90. 50w. $3\frac{1}{2}$

3448   McLEAN, Jackie. Two Sides of J. M. Trip TLX-5027 (Re-
       issue)
       CO Sept. p20. 300w. 3

3449   McLEAN, Rene. Watch Out. Steeplechase SCS 1037 (Den-
       mark)
       DB May 6 p31. 100w. $3\frac{1}{2}$

      JJ   March p34.   350w. $3\frac{1}{2}$
      MM   March 13 p26.   275w. $3\frac{1}{2}$

3450 McPARTLAND, Marian. Solo Concert at Haverford. Halcyon 111
      DB Jan. 29 p22-3. 200w. 5
      MM June 5 p22. 225w. 3
      SR Sept. p102. 275w. 4

3451 McPHEE, Joe. Trinity. CJR CJR 3
      CAD April p35. 125w. 2

3452 McPHEE, Joe. The Willisau Concert. Hat-B (Switzerland)
      CAD Sept. p12. 305w. 5

3453 McPHERSON, Charles. Beautiful. Xanadu 115
      CAD April p33. 75w. $3\frac{1}{2}$

3454 MacPHERSON, Fraser. Live at the Planetarium. West End 101 (Canada)
      CAD Oct. p10. 425w. 5
      JJ Dec. p33. 325w. 4

3455 McRAE, Carmen. Alone Live at the Dug. Catalyst CAT 7904 (Japan)
      RFJ Oct. p8. 275w. 3

3456 McSHANN, Jay. Jay McShann. Sackville 3005 (Canada)
      CAD Aug. p21. 275w. 5

3457 MAGADINI, Peter. Polyrhythm. Briko BR 1000
      BD March 25 p34-5. 25w. 3
      SR Sept. p112. 175w. 2

3458 MAGGIE'S Blue Five. Funny Feathers. Kenneth KS 2038 (Sweden)
      ST June-July p198-9. 225w. $4\frac{1}{2}$

3459 The MAGNETS. Electromagnets. EGM Records, SD 1001
      GP March p73. 25w. 3

3460 MAGOG. Japo 60011 (West Germany)
      JF No. 41 p27. 75w. $3\frac{1}{2}$
      MM May 1 p32. 200w. 3

3461 MAHAVISHNU Orchestra and John McLaughlin. Inner Worlds. Columbia PC 33908. Cart. PCA 33908. Cass. PCT 33908
      DB May 20 p22, 26. 325w. 1
      GRA May p1812. 150w. 3
      HF June p102. 175w. $3\frac{1}{2}$
      JA Summer p37. 250w. $\frac{1}{2}$
      MM Feb. 21 p30. 675w. 4
      RR May p75. 150w. $3\frac{1}{2}$

SR   Sept.   p112.   125w.   2

3462   MAHAVISHNU Orchestra.   Visions of the Emerald Beyond.
Columbia PC-33411.   Cass.   PCT-33411
    LP   Aug.   p6.   175w.   5
    SR   July   p98.   200w.   5

3463   MAISTER, Art.   Piano Styles.   Radio Canada RC1 398
    CAD   Feb.   p28.   50w. $2\frac{1}{2}$

3464   MANGELSDORFF, Albert.   Spontaneous.   Enja 2064
    JJ   Sept.   p34.   350w. $4\frac{1}{2}$
    MM   Dec. 4   p28.   375w. $3\frac{1}{2}$

3465   MANGELSDORFF, Albert.   The Wide Point.   MPS 20 225690
    MF   April   p62-3.   750w. $4\frac{1}{2}$

3466   MANGIONE, Chuck.   Bellavia.   A&M SP-4557.   Cart. 4557.
Cass. 4557
    DB   Feb. 26   p20.   300w.   3
    LP   April   p16.   100w.   3
    MH   Oct./Nov.   p70.   150w. $3\frac{1}{2}$
    SOU   Jan.   p38.   200w. $3\frac{1}{2}$
    SR   March   p102.   100w.   2

3467   MANGIONE, Chuck.   Chase the Clouds Away.   A&M SP-4518
    SR   Aug.   p88.   200w.   4

3468   MANGIONE, Chuck.   Encore.   Mercury SRM 1-1050
    SOU   March   p43-4.   400w.   3
    SOU   April   p48.   50w.   3

3469   MANGIONE, Gap.   She and I.   A&M SP 3407
    LP   Jan.   p17.   175w. $3\frac{1}{2}$

3470   MANN, Herbie.   Be Bop Synthesis.   Savoy SJL 1102 (Reissue)
    CAD   Sept.   p25, 26.   75w.   4
    DB   Dec. 2   p26.   200w. $3\frac{1}{2}$

3471   MANN, Herbie.   Discotheque.   Atlantic SD 1670.   Cart. TP
1670.   Cass. CS 1670
    SR   Oct.   p78, 80.   150w.   1

3472   MANNE, Shelly.   Hot Coles.   Flying Dutchman BDL1-1145
    DB   Jan. 29   p21-2.   300w.   4
    GR   Aug.   p352.   275w.   4
    JJ   May   p32.   350w. $4\frac{1}{2}$
    MM   April 24   p24.   325w.   2

3473   MANONE, Wingy and Sidney Bechet.   Together.   Jazz Archives 29
    HF   April   p142.   225w. $2\frac{1}{2}$

3474   MANTLER, Michael and Carla Bley. 13 for Piano & Two
       Orchestras & 3/4 for Piano & Orchestra. Watt Records 3
              CAD Sept. p27, 28. 425w. 5
              JF No. 41 p634. 400w. 4
              MM Jan. 17 p30. 450w. 3

3475   MANTLER, Michael and Edward Grovey. The Hapless Child.
       Watt 4
              DB Nov. 18 p28-9. 350w. 2
              MM April 17 p22. 550w. 4
              RS Nov. 4 p80. 150w. $2\frac{1}{2}$
              SR Oct. p108. 125w. 2

3476   MANUSARDI, Guido. Romanian Impressions. Amigo
       AMLP814
              CO Sept. p19. 300w. 2

3477   MARCUS, Steve. Sometime Other Than Now. Flying Dutch-
       man BDL1-1461
              DB Nov. 18 p27. 325w. 3
              GP Oct. p97. 50w. 3
              RS Dec. 2 p92. 125w. 3

3478   MARCUS, Wade. Metamorphosis. Impulse ASD 9318
              CAD Oct. p17. 125w. 4

3479   MARIANO, Charlie. Helen Twelve Trees. MPS BASF DC
       229416
              MM Dec. 4 p28. 100w. $2\frac{1}{2}$

3480   MARMAROSA, Dodo. Spotlite Records, 108
              CK March p47. 175w. $4\frac{1}{2}$

3481   MARMAROSA, Dodo. California Boppin'. Jazz Showcase
       5005
              JJ Jan. p34. 150w. 4

3482   MARMAROSA, Dodo. The Dial Masters. Spotlite 128 (E)
       (Reissue)
              JJ Jan. p34. 150w. 4

3483   MARSALA, Joe. Aircheck 14 (Canada)
              JA Fall p56. 75w. $2\frac{1}{2}$
              JJ Sept. p41. 75w. 3

3484   MARSHALL, Owen. Naked Truth. Aditi AD 2001
              JJ Feb. p38. 175w. $3\frac{1}{2}$

3485   MARTIN, Stu and John Surman. Live at Woodstock Town
       Hall. Pye 12114
              DB Feb. 12 p27-8. 450w. 4
              MM Feb. 14 p31. 550w. 2

3486   MARTINO, Pat.   Consciousness.   Muse 5039
       CO   Sept.   p19, 20.   325w.   4

3487   MARTINO, Pat.   Footprints.   Muse 5096 (Reissue)
       CAD   March   p28-9.   125w. $3\frac{1}{2}$

3488   MARTINO, Pat.   Live!   Muse MR 5026
       CO   Sept.   p14.   175w.   2

3489   MARTINO, Pat.   Starbright.   Warner BS 2921
       MG   June   p50.   50w.   3
       MM   Sept.   25   p26.   275w. $3\frac{1}{2}$
       RS   June 17   p55.   100w.   3

3490   MARTINO, Pat.   We'll Be Together Again.   Muse MR 5090
       CAD   Nov.   p18.   125w. $\frac{1}{2}$

3491   MAS, Jean Pierre and Cesarius Alvin.   Rue de Lourmel.
       Owl 03 (France)
       JF   No. 44.   p34.   100w.   4

3492   MASON, Harvey.   Marching in the Street.   Arista 4054
       CAD   Feb.   p21.   50w.   3
       DB   Feb. 26   p21.   250w. $3\frac{1}{2}$

3493   MATTHEWS, David.   Big Band Recorded Live at the Five
       Spot.   Muse MR 5073
       HF   Jan.   p107, 109.   350w. $2\frac{1}{2}$
       MJ   Jan.   p21-1.   100w. $3\frac{1}{2}$
       SR   March   p102.   175w.   4

3494   MAUPIN, Bennie.   The Jewel in the Lotus.   ECM 1043 ST
       SR   Feb. 2   p99-100.   325w.   5

3495   MAYCOCK, George.   Ring 01008 (West Germany)
       JF   No. 41   p26-7.   50w.   3

3496   MAYL, Gene.   Country Goes Dixie.   Red Onion 2
       JJ   Jan.   p34.   125w. $\frac{1}{2}$

3497   MENDELSON, Stan.   Storyville Piano.   Land O' Jazz LOJ
       2674
       ST   Oct./Nov.   p36.   50w. $3\frac{1}{2}$

3498   MERIWETHER, Roy.   Live.   Stinger LP 1001
       JJ   May   p40.   75w. $3\frac{1}{2}$

3499   MERIWETHER, Roy.   Nublian Lady.   Stinger LP 1000
       JJ   May   p40.   75w. $3\frac{1}{2}$

3500   MERRILL, Helen and Teddy Wilson.   Helen Sings, Teddy
       Swings.   Catalyst CAT 7903 (Japan)
       RFJ   Oct.   p8.   275w. $3\frac{1}{2}$

3501 METHENY, Pat. Bright Size Life. ECM 1073
        CAD Oct. p31. 150w. 5
        DB Dec. 2 p22, 24. 350w. 3
        GP Aug. p80. 25w. 4
        MM July 31 p22. 75w. 2½

3502 MICHALEK, Al. Voices. RCI 420
        CAD May p22-3. 75w. 2

3503 MIGLIORI, Jay. Count the Nights and Times. PBR International PBR-5
        JJ April p34. 375w. 5
        RFJ July p9, 14. 500w. 3½

3504 MILLER, Punch. Jazz Rarities 1929-1930. Herwin 108 (Reissue)
        FT June/July p18-9. 550w. 3½
        JJ Sept. p34 & 36. 875w. 4½

3505 MINASI, Dom. When Joanna Loved Me. Blue Note BNLA 2580
        DB March 27 p20, 22. 250w. 2

3506 MINGUS, Charles. At Carnegie Hall. Atlantic SD1667
        CO Sept. p20, 21. 375w. 4
        JF No. 44 p75. 100w. 4

3507 MINGUS, Charles. Blues and Roots. Atlantic ATL 50 232
        MM Aug. 7 p20. 200w. 3½

3508 MINGUS, Charles. Changes One/Two. Atlantic SD 1677/8 (2 discs)
        DB March 25 p22, 24. 425w. 3½
        JF No. 44 p75. 200w. 4
        MJ Jan. p20. 75w. 3
        RFJ Feb. p12. 450w. 4
        SOU July p102. 100w. 3½

3509 MITCHELL, Blue. Stratosonic Nuances. RCA APL1-1109
        DB April 22 p28-9. 225w. 2½

3510 MITCHELL, Roscoe. Sackville 2009 (Canada)
        CAD Oct. p40. 250w. 4
        JJ Dec. p33-4. 475w. 3½

3511 MITCHELL, Roscoe. Solo Saxophone Concerts. Sackville 2006 (Canada)
        CAD Aug. p46. 75w. 4

3512 MOBLEY, Hank. Messages. Prestige 24063 (2 discs) (Reissue)
        CAD Oct. p24. 75w. 5

3513 MODERN Jazz Quartet. Sait on Jamais. Atlantic ATL 50 231 (West Germany) (Reissue)
       MM Sept. 11 p30. 275w. 4

3514 MOLE, Miff. The Early Years. Jazz Studies JS-2 (Canada) (Reissue)
       CO April p14, 15. 375w. 3

3515 MONCOR, Grachan III. Echoes of a Prayer. JCOA 1009
       CRE Jan. p67. 475w. 3

3516 MONK, Thelonious. Milestone M47022 (2 discs) (Reissue)
       JJ Nov. p34. 575w. 4

3517 MONK, Thelonious. Complete Genius. Blue Note BN LA 579H2 (2 discs) (Reissue)
       CAD Nov. p22-3. 200w. 4
       CRA Nov. p72. 100w. 3
       CRE Nov. p59-60. 375w. 5

3518 MONK, Thelonious. In Person. Milestone M47033 (2 discs) (Reissue)
       CAD Oct. p26. 250w. 4
       CK Dec. p49. 25w. $3\frac{1}{2}$
       RR Dec. p103. 250w. 3

3519 MONK, Thelonious. Pure Monk. DJM DJSLM 2017 (E) (Reissue)
       GRA May p1815. 200w. $3\frac{1}{2}$
       JJ Jan. p34. 375w. 4
       RR Feb. p68. 75w. 3

3520 MONK, Thelonious. Who's Afraid of the Big Band Monk. Columbia KG 32892 (2 discs) (Reissue)
       MJ Jan. p20. 125w. 3

3521 MONTEROSE, J. R. Straight Ahead. Xanadu 126 (Reissue)
       HF Sept. p114. 350w. 4

3522 MONTGOMERY, Wes. Beginnings. Blue Note BN LA 531 (2 discs) (Reissue)
       DB Aug. 12 p35-6. 125w. 3
       PRM Jan. p37. 50w. 3

3523 MONTGOMERY, Wes. Pretty Blue. Milestone, M-47030 (2 discs) (Reissue)
       GP May p81. 50w. 4
       JJ March p34, 36. 275w. 3
       SOU March p48. 25w. 3

3524 MOODY, James. Feelin' It Together. Muse MR 5020
       CO Sept. p21. 400w. 4

3525 MOODY, James. Group Therapy. DJM DJM 22035 (E)

        JJ Oct.   p34.   250w. $3\frac{1}{2}$
        MM Dec. 25 p18.   375w.   3

3526 MOODY, James. Moody's Mood.   Chess Jazz Masters Series
       2ACMJ-403 (2 discs) (Reissue)
        CAD Oct.   p21.   400w.   3

3527 MOODY, James. Never Again! Muse MR 5001
        CO Sept.   p21.   400w.   4

3528 MOODY, James. Timeless Aura. Vanguard VSD 79366
        MJ Dec.   p26.   50w. $2\frac{1}{2}$

3529 MOORE, Oscar. vol. 8.   Archives of Jazz AJ 509 (Reissue)
        DB Feb. 12 p29-31.   200w. $3\frac{1}{2}$

3530 MORATH, Max. The World of Scott Joplin, Vol. 2.   Van-
       guard SRV-351 SD
        CK March p48.   200w.   4
        RT Sept./Oct.   p5.   150w.   2

3531 MORAZ, Patrick. Patrick Moraz. Atlantic SD 18175
        CK Aug.   p44.   325w.   5

3532 MORGAN, Lee. All That Jazz. DJM Records DJLMD 8007
       (E) (Reissue)
        JJ Jan.   p36.   225w. $2\frac{1}{2}$

3533 MORRIS, Thomas. Volume One, 1926. RCA FPM 1-7049
       (France) (Reissue)
        JJ Feb. 2 p44, 46.   400w.   4

3534 MORTON, Jelly Roll. Volume 7-1929-30. RCA 741.081
       (France) (Reissue)
        CO Sept.   p22.   375w. $2\frac{1}{2}$

3535 MORTON, Jelly Roll. 1923/24. Milestone M47018 (2 discs)
       (Reissue)
        CO March p27.   325w.   4
        SR July p90, 91.   275w.   4

3536 MOSES, Bob. Bitter Suite in the Ozone. Mozown MZ001
        MG June p50.   50w.   4

3537 MOSES, Ted. Sidereal Time. Radio Canada RCI 4000 (Cana-
       da)
        CAD Feb.   p28.   50w. $3\frac{1}{2}$

3538 MOST, Sam. Mostly Flute. Xanadu 133
        CAD Dec.   p30-1.   125w.   2

3539 MOTIAN, Paul. Tribute. ECM 1048
        SR Oct.   p95, 96.   175w.   4

3540 MOUZON, Alphonse. The Man Incognito. Blue Note UAG
      20005 (E)
           BM July p50-1. 275w. 4
           CAC Aug. p176. 25w. 3
           MM May 22 p26. 50w. 1

3541 MOUZON, Alphonse. Mind Transplant. Blue Note
      BN-LA398G
           SR Sept. p103, 104. 150w. 5

3542 MULLIGAN, Gerry. United US-7804
           JJ Feb. p38, 40. 75w. 1

3543 MULLIGAN, Gerry. Profile. Trip TLP-5531 (Reissue)
           CO May p19, 20, 21. 575w. 2

3544 MULLIGAN, Gerry and Chet Baker. Carnegie Hall Concert,
      Volume 1/2. CTI CTI-6054/5 (2 discs). Cart. CT8-6054/5.
      Cass. CTC-6054/5
           CO Sept. p22. 550w. 4
           SR Aug. p88, 89. 200w. 5

3545 MULLIGAN, Gerry and Enrico Intra. Pausa 7010
           CAD Oct. p40. 250w. 5
           DB Nov. 4 p22, 24. 450w. $3\frac{1}{2}$

3546 MULLIGAN, Gerry and Lee Konitz. Revelation. Blue Note
      LA 532 (2 discs)
           DB Aug. 12 p36. 100w. $4\frac{1}{2}$

3547 MURIBUS, George. Brazillian Tapestry. Catalyst CAT-7602
      (Japan)
           CAD June p23. 50w. $3\frac{1}{2}$
           MJ July p55. 100w. $2\frac{1}{2}$
           SR Oct. p108, 110. 150w. 2

3548 MURPHY, Malc. At the Mardi Gras. Joy 259 (E)
           CO Sept. p19. 300w. 4

3549 MURPHY, Turk. Dawn Club 12015
           JJ Jan. p40. 100w. $2\frac{1}{2}$

3550 MURPHY, Turk. Dawn Club 12018/9 (2 discs)
           JJ Feb. p40. 125w. 2

3551 NADOLSKI, Helmut. Meditation. Veriton SXV 786 (Poland)
           JF No. 41 p27. 100w. $3\frac{1}{2}$

3552 NAMYSLOWSKI, Zbigniew. Kuyaviak Goes Funky. Muza SX
      1230 (Poland)
           CAD Nov. p15-6. 150w. 3
           JJ Dec. p40. 200w. 4

3553   NAMYSLOWSKI, Zbigniew.   Winobranie.   Muza SXL0952
       (Poland)
             CO   March   p13, 14.   350w.   4

3554   NATIONAL Youth Jazz Orchestra.   Eleven Plus--Live at LWT.
       RCA SF 8464 (E)
             CAD   May   p22.   100w.   3½
             HF   July   p108.   150w.   3
             JJ   March   p34.   350w.   4

3555   NATIONAL Youth Jazz Orchestra.   Return Trip.   RCA DPS
       2072 (E) (2 discs)
             JJ   Oct.   p34-5.   700w.   4
             MM   Sept. 18   p25.   550w.   3½

3556   NATURAL Life.   Unnamed Land.   Celebration Records, CB-
       5005
             GP   Jan.   p70.   150w.   4

3557   NAVARRO, Fats.   Prime Source.   Blue Note BN LA 507-H2
       (2 discs) (Reissue)
             DB   Aug. 12   p35.   225w.   5
             HF   June   p110, 112.   175w.   3½
             JJ   July   p35-6.   925w.   5
             MM   Aug. 21   p20.   275w.   3½
             PRM   Jan.   p37.   50w.   5
             PRM   April   p55.   250w.   4
             PRM   May   p62.   800w.   3½

3558   NEGATIVE Band.   Stockhousen.   Finnador SR 9009
             DB   April 22   p32.   275w.   4

3559   NEIL, Al.   Retrospective 1965-1968.   Lodestone LP 7001
       (Canada)
             CAD   Aug.   p23.   175w.   5

3560   NELSON, Louis and Purnell, Alton.   With the Trevor Richards
       New Orleans Trio.   WAM MLP 15.513 (West Germany)
             JJ   Jan.   p36.   175w.   3½

3561   NELSON, Oliver and Lou Donaldson.   Back Talk.   Chess Jazz
       Masters Series 2ACMJ-404 (2 discs) (Reissue)
             CAD   Oct.   p21.   75w.   4

3562   NELSON, Oliver.   A Dream Deferred.   RCA CYL2-1449 (2
       discs)
             DB   Dec. 2   p18-9.   550w.   5

3563   NELSON, Oliver.   Images.   Prestige P24060 (Reissue) (2
       discs)
             CAD   Nov.   p27.   125w.   3
             DB   Oct. 21   p34.   150w.   5

3564 NEW Black Eagle Jazz Band. Black Eagle BE 1
       JJ May p46. 50w. $3\frac{1}{2}$

3565 NEW Black Eagle Band. Dirty Shame 2002
       AU Aug. p80. 250w. 3
       CO Sept. p22. 200w. 4
       JJ May p46. 50w. $3\frac{1}{2}$

3566 NEW Black Eagle Jazz Band. GHB 59
       JJ May p46. 50w. 3

3567 NEW Black Eagle Jazz Band. In Concert. Black Eagle 2
       CAD April p40. 125w. $3\frac{1}{2}$
       HF Jan. p109. 300w. $3\frac{1}{2}$

3568 NEW England Conservatory Jazz Ensemble. Happy Feet: A
       Tribute to Paul Whiteman. Golden Crest 31043
       CAD Oct. p41. 75w. 4
       SR June p94. 225w. 4

3569 NEW England Conservatory Jazz Ensemble. Homage to El-
       lington in Concert. Golden Crest 31041
       CAD Oct. p41. 150w. 4

3570 NEW England Conservatory Ragtime Ensemble. More Scott
       Joplin Rags. Golden Crest CRS 31031
       RT March/April p5-6. 50w. 3

3571 NEW England Conservatory Ragtime Ensemble. The Road
       from Rags to Jazz. Golden Crest 31042 (2 discs)
       CAD Oct. p41. 125w. 5
       RT Jan./Feb. p5. 200w. 3
       SR April p107. 325w. 3

3572 NEW Figaro. Live at Fasching, vol. 1. Dragon LP 4
       (Sweden)
       MM Dec. 25 p18. 100w. $2\frac{1}{2}$

3573 NEW Leviathan Oriental Fox-Trot Orchestra. Camel Race
       19325 (E)
       FT April/May p18. 175w. $2\frac{1}{2}$

3574 The NEW McKinney's Cotton Pickers. You're Driving Me
       Crazy. Bountiful B 38001
       JJ March p34. 300w. 2

3575 The NEW McKinney's Cotton Pickers. Rated G. Bountiful
       38003
       CAD Oct. p31, 32. 350w. 4

3576 NEW Orleans Ragtime Orchestra. Vanguard VSD 69/70 (2
       discs)
       CO Sept. p23. 425w. 4

RT   May/June   p8.   150w.   3

3577   NEW Orleans Rascals.   The World Is Waiting for the Sunrise.
RCA JRS 7265 (Japan)
ST   April-May   p152.   200w. $4\frac{1}{2}$

3578   NEW Orleans Rascals.   You Rascal You.   Philips FX 8529
(Japan)
CO   Sept.   p23.   275w.   2

3579   NEW Orleans Rhythm Kings.   Milestone M47020 (2 discs) (Re-
issue)
CO   March   p28.   375w.   4
SR   Aug. 7   p90, 91.   275w.   4

3580   The NEW Sunshine Jazz Band.   Old Rags.   Flying Dutchman
BDL 1-0549
ST   Feb.-March   p115-6.   225w.   4

3581   The NEW York Jazz Quartet.   In Concert in Japan.   Salvation
SAL 703 S1.   Cart. SA8-703
SR   Feb.   p95.   125w.   4

3582   NEW York Jazz Repertory Company.   Satchmo Remembered.
Atlantic SD 1671
CAD   Sept.   p21.   200w.   5
DB   Feb. 12   p24.   250w.   5
JJ   March   p38.   400w.   5
RR   Feb.   p67.   150w. $3\frac{1}{2}$

3583   NEW York Mary.   Arista Freedom AL 1019
CRA   May   p79.   125w.   4
DB   June 3   p22.   300w.   3

3584   NEWMAN, David.   Mr. Fathead.   Warner Bros. BS 2917
DB   Oct. 21   p31.   200w. $1\frac{1}{2}$
JJ   Aug.   p39.   75w.   0
MM   Aug. 21   p20.   100w.   3

3585   NICHOLS, Herbie.   The Third World.   Blue Note BN LA--
485--H2 (2 discs) (Reissue)
DB   Aug. 12   p35.   200w.   5
JJ   June   p36.   375w. $4\frac{1}{2}$
MJ   April   p28.   175w. $3\frac{1}{2}$
MM   Sept. 18   p25.   350w. $3\frac{1}{2}$
PRM   Jan.   p37.   50w.   5

3586   NICHOLS, Keith.   Cat at the Keyboard.   EMI One-Up OU
2085 (E)
GR   May   p1815.   225w. $2\frac{1}{2}$

3587   NICHOLS, Keith.   Ragtime Rules--OK.   One-Up OU 2135 (E)
JJ   Oct.   p35.   400w. $4\frac{1}{2}$
ST   Oct.-Nov.   p39.   200w. $3\frac{1}{2}$

3588 NICHOLS, Red. Jazz Studies JS 3 (Canada) (Reissue)
ST April-May p153-4. 550w. $4\frac{1}{2}$

3589 NICHOLS, Red. 1929-1932. LAJRC (Reissue)
JJ Oct. p35-6. 825w. $3\frac{1}{2}$
ST Oct.-Nov. p33-4. 200w. $2\frac{1}{2}$

3590 NIEWOOD, Gerry. Slow, Hot Wind. A&M SP 3409
LP March p18. 150w. 4

3591 NIMMONS, Phil. The Atlantic Suite. Sackville 2008 (Canada)
CAD Aug. p45, 46. 175w. 5
JJ Sept. p37. 325w. 5
OLR Dec. p258. 50w. 4
SOU May p44. 325w. $4\frac{1}{2}$

3592 NINESENCE. Oh, for the Edge. Ogun OG 900 (E)
JJ Dec. p34. 225w. 3
MM Oct. 16 p30. 550w. $3\frac{1}{2}$

3593 NO-GAP Generation Jazz Band. Swing Live. Dharma GFL
1084
JF No. 41 p26. 50w. 4

3594 NOONE, Jimmy. LAJRC 18 (Reissue)
CAD Nov. p25. 125w. 2

3595 NORRIS, Walter. Drifting. Enja 2044
CO Sept. p22. 125w. 3
JF No. 41 p64. 600w. 3

3596 NORTH Texas State University Lab Band. Lab '75. Lab Jazz
LJ 108
CAD Aug. p34, 35. 225w. 4
CK March p48. 50w. 4
RFJ Jan. p11. 475w. 4

3597 NORVO, Red. The Second Time Around. Famous Door HL
108
JJ Oct. p36. 450w. 5

3598 NORVO, Red. Vibes a la Red. Famous Door HL 105
DB Jan. 15 p28. 225w. 3
SR Jan. p97-8. 150w. 5

3599 NOTO, Sam. Entrance. Xanadu 103
CAD Jan. p28, 30. 200w. 4

3600 NOVI Singers. Rien Va Ne Plus. Muza SXL1009 (Poland)
CO March p15. 350w. 0

3601 NUCLEUS. Alleycat. Vertigo 6360 124 (E)
JF No. 41 p26. 50w. 4

JJ   Feb.   p34.   300w. $4\frac{1}{2}$

3602   NUCLEUS.   Direct Hits.   Vertigo 9286019 (E) (Reissue)
RR   Sept.   p90.   25w.   3

3603   NUNEZ, Flip.   My Own Time and Space.   Catalyst 7603
(Japan)
CAD   Aug.   p29.   125w.   5
MJ   July   p55.   125w.   3

3604   OLIVER, King.   Volume 1.   Classic Jazz Masters CJM 19
(Denmark) (Reissue)
JJ   Dec.   p34-5.   475w. $3\frac{1}{2}$
ST   Feb.-March   p112.   375w. $4\frac{1}{2}$

3605   OLIVER, King.   The Gennett and Paramount Recordings, 1923.
Smithsonian Collection R001 (Reissue)
CAD   March   p20.   150w. $3\frac{1}{2}$
CO   Oct.   p12.   200w. $4\frac{1}{2}$
DB   May 20   p30-1.   275w.   4
HF   April   p140.   550w. $3\frac{1}{2}$
JJ   Feb.   p34.   200w.   1
MJ   April   p28.   125w.   3

3606   OM.   Kirikuki.   Japo 60012 (West Germany)
MM   May 1   p32.   100w.   3

3607   OPEN Sky.   pm PMR-001
SOU   Feb.   p48.   25w. $2\frac{1}{2}$

3608   OPEN Sky.   Spirit in the Sky.   pm PMR-003
CO   Oct.   p12.   250w.   1
SOU   Feb.   p48.   25w. $2\frac{1}{2}$
SR   Sept.   p103.   175w. $4\frac{1}{2}$

3609   OREGON.   In Concert.   Vanguard VSD 79358
DB   Feb. 12   p22.   325w.   5
GP   Feb.   p70.   300w.   4
SR   April   p103-4.   250w.   4

3610   ORIGINAL Dixieland Jazz Band.   Revisted.   Rarities 36 (Reissue)
JJ   Dec.   p34.   200w.   3

3611   ORIGINAL Tuxedo Band.   Patch's Jazz.   Patch's Jazz 1001
CO   Oct.   p12.   325w. $1\frac{1}{2}$

3612   ORSTED-PEDERSEN, Nils Henning.   Jaywalkin'.   Steeplechase
SCS 1041 (Denmark)
DB   May 6   p32.   175w.   2
JJ   May   p33-4.   250w.   2

3613   ORY, Kid.   Folklyric 9008 (Reissue)

AU April p94-5. 500w. 4
CO Oct. p12-3. 650w. 2½
JJ Feb. p34. 275w. 3½
RR Dec. p102. 75w. 3½

3614 ORY, Kid. Live at Club Hangover, Volume 1/4. Dawn Club
DC 12013/4 (2 discs)
ST Dec. 1975-Jan. 1976 p79. 275w. 4

3615 ORY, Kid. Live at Club Hangover, Volume 2/3. Dawn Club
12016/17 (2 discs)
JJ March p36. 225w. 3½
ST Aug.-Sept. p239. 475w. 4

3616 ORY, Kid and Joe Darensbourg. New Orleans. Vogue VJD
521 (2 discs) (France) (Reissue)
FT June/July p17-8. 650w. 4
JJ July p36. 400w. 3
MM Oct. 30 p26. 425w. 2
RR June p84. 50w. 3

3617 OSBORNE, Mike. All Night Long. Ogun 700 (E)
CAD Sept. p20, 21. 300w. 5
JJ May p33. 250w. 5
MM April 24 p24. 500w. 4

3618 OSBORNE, Mike. Border Crossing. Ogun OG 300 (E)
JF No. 41 p65. 300w. 4

3619 OSBORNE, Mike and Stan Tracey. Original. Cadillac SGC
1002 (E)
CO Oct. p13. 450w. 3

3620 OSCARSSON, Ivan. Ivan the Terrible. Dragon LP 7 (E)
JJ Nov. p37. 150w. 2½

3621 OSKAR, Lee. United Artists LA 594 G
DB Sept. 9 p31. 225w. 4

3622 Les OUBLIES de Jazz Ensemble. That Nigger Music.
Touche Records 101
CAD Oct. p10, 12. 275w. 5
DB March 11 p26-7. 400w. 5
JF No. 44 p32. 50w. 4

3623 OVARY LODGE. Ogun OG 600 (E)
JJ Oct. p36. 350w. 1
MM Aug. 28 p22. 650w. 3½

3624 OXLEY, Tony. Incus 8 (E)
MM Dec. 18 p20. 300w. 4½

3625 OXLEY, Tony and Allan Davie. Duo. ADMW 005 (E)

MM Dec. 18 p20. 300w. $\frac{1}{2}$

3626 PAGE, Hot Lips. After Hours in Harlem. Onyx OR1 207
(Reissue)
      CO April p15. 250w. 5

3627 PAICH, Marty. Vol. 9. Archive of Jazz AJ 510 (Reissue)
      DB Feb. 12 p29-31. 200w. 4

3628 PALMIERI, Eddie. The Sun of Latin Music. Coco CLP
109XX. Cart. ST 1109XX. Cass. CAS1109XX
      SR May p90. 400w. 4

3629 PARADOX. Drifting Feather. Muza SXLO745 (Poland)
      CO March p15. 350w. 3

3630 PARKER, Charlie. Bird: The Savoy Recordings. Savoy SJL
2201 (2 discs). Cart. SJ8 2201 (Reissue)
      CRE Sept. p60-1. 325w. $4\frac{1}{2}$
      JA Summer p41-2. 100w. 5
      JJ Dec. p35-6. 325w. $3\frac{1}{2}$
      PRM May p63. 200w. 4
      RS Sept. 9 p51. 600w. 5
      SR Nov. p132-3. 150w. $3\frac{1}{2}$

3631 PARKER, Charlie. Bird & Miles. DJM Records DJML 062
(E) (Reissue)
      JJ Jan. p36. 275w. $3\frac{1}{2}$
      RR Feb. p68. 50w. $2\frac{1}{2}$

3632 PARKER, Charlie. Bird in Sweden. Spotlite 124/125 (E)
(2 discs) (Reissue)
      JJ May p33. 425w. 5

3633 PARKER, Charlie. Bird of Paradise, vol. 9. Saga 6928 (E)
(Reissue)
      MM Feb. 21 p31. 225w. $3\frac{1}{2}$

3634 PARKER, Charlie. Bird on 52nd St./Bird at St. Nick's.
Prestige PR 24009 (2 discs) (Reissue)
      GR Jan. p1263. 300w. 3

3635 PARKER, Charlie. Bird on the Coast. Jazz Showcase 5007
      JJ Feb. p35. 250w. 5

3636 PARKER, Charlie. Bird on the Road. Jazz Showcase 5003
      JJ Feb. p35. 250w. $4\frac{1}{2}$

3637 PARKER, Charlie. Bird's Nest. Vogue VJT 3002/1/2/3 (3
discs) (France) (Reissue)
      JJ July p36-7. 525w. 4
      MM Aug. 21 p20. 350w. $3\frac{1}{2}$
      RR Aug. p80. 100w. 3

3638 PARKER, Charlie. Just Friends. SCAM JPG 4 (E)
      JJ Feb. p35. 325w. $4\frac{1}{2}$

3639 PARKER, Charlie. The Massey Hall Concert. Saga 6906
      (E) (Reissue)
      ARG Nov. p56-7. 225w. 5

3640 PARKER, Charlie. New Bird, Vol. 2. Phoenix LP 12
      JJ Feb. p34, 35. 425w. 4

3641 PARKER, Charlie. Norman Granz Jam Session. Verve VE-
      2-2507 (2 discs) (Reissue)
      CAD Sept. p27. 200w. 3
      DB Nov. 18 p30-1. 300w. 4

3642 PARKER, Charlie. On Dial vol. 1/6. Spotlite 101/6 (E)
      (6 discs) (Reissue)
      SR Feb. p94. 375w. 5

3643 PARKER, Charlie. Out of Nowhere. Saga 6929 (E) (Reissue)
      MM Feb. 21 p31. 225w. $3\frac{1}{2}$

3644 PARKER, Charlie. The Verve Years, 1948-50. Verve VE2-
      2501 (2 discs) (Reissue)
      MJ Oct. p52. 25w. $2\frac{1}{2}$
      DB Oct. 7 p32. 150w. 5
      CRE Sept. p60-1. 325w. $3\frac{1}{2}$
      JA Summer p40-1. 175w. $3\frac{1}{2}$
      RS Sept. 9 p51-2. 600w. $3\frac{1}{2}$

3645 PARKER, Charlie and Miles Davis. Vogue VJD 529/1-2
      (France) (2 discs)
      JJ Dec. p35-6. 325w. 2

3646 PARKER, Erroll. My Own Bag. Sahara 9002
      MG June p50. 50w. $2\frac{1}{2}$

3647 PARKER, Evan. Saxophone Solos. Incus 19 (E)
      MM Oct. 23 p28. 650w. 5

3648 PARKS, Van Dyke. Clang of the Yankee Reaper. Warner
      BS 2878
      DB May 6 p28-9. 325w. 4

3649 PASS, Joe. At Montreux Jazz Festival, 1975. Pablo 2310
      752
      CAC Jan. p412, 414. 100w. $4\frac{1}{2}$
      DB April 8 p22, 24. 100w. 4
      JJ Jan. p36. 350w. 5
      MM May 22 p26. 325w. $3\frac{1}{2}$

3650 PASS, Joe. Intercontinental. MPS BAP 5053
      CO Oct. p14. 250w. 2

JJ   Feb.   p38.   400w.   5

3651   PASS, Joe.   Portraits of Duke Ellington.   Pablo 2310 716
       CO   Oct.   p14.   400w. $1\frac{1}{2}$

3652   PASS, Joe.   Happy Time.   Pablo 2310 746
       MJ   July   p52.   50w.   3

3653   PASTORIUS, Jaco.   Epic PE 33949.   Cart. PEA 33949
       CAD   Aug.   p25.   125w.   5
       CRA   July   p72-3.   275w.   3
       DB   Aug. 12   p26.   475w.   4
       MM   June 26   p21.   200w.   3
       RR   Sept.   p90.   150w.   3
       SR   Sept.   p112.   225w.   3

3654   PASTORIUS, Jaco.   Improvising Artists Inc.   IAI 373846
       CAD   Dec.   p27-8.   200w. $3\frac{1}{2}$

3655   PAYNE, Cecil.   Bird Gets the Worm.   Muse MR 5061
       CAD   Sept.   p22, 23.   275w.   3

3656   PAYNE, Cecil.   Cool Blues.   DJM DJMSLM 2032 (E) (Re-
       issue)
       JJ   July   p37.   450w. $4\frac{1}{2}$

3657   PAYNE, John.   Bedtime Stories.   Bromfield BR2
       CAD   Jan.   p13-4.   100w. $3\frac{1}{2}$
       CAD   Feb.   p26-7.   150w.   2

3658   PAZANT Brothers.   Loose and Juicy.   Vanguard VSD 79364
       DB   May 6   p30-1.   225w.   1

3659   PEPPER, Art.   Living Legend.   Contemporary S7633
       SR   Dec.   p129.   175w.   4

3660   PERIGEO.   Genealogia.   RCA TPL1-1080
       AU   Jan.   p67-8.   700w. $3\frac{1}{2}$

3661   PERLMAN, Itzhak and Andre Previn.   Easy Winners.   Angel
       S 37113
       RT   May/June   p5-6.   100w. $3\frac{1}{2}$

3662   PERSIANNY, Andre.   Jazz Piano Concert.   Concert Hall 1362
       (France)
       CO   Oct.   p14.   325w.   3

3663   PERSIANNY, Andre.   The Real Me.   Black and Blue 33 024
       (France)
       CO   Oct.   p14.   325w.   3

3664   PERSIANNY, Andre.   Requiem pour un chat.   Le Chant du
       Monde AJ 1010 (France)
       CO   Oct.   p14.   325w.   3

3665 PETERSON, Hannibal Marvin. Hannibal and the Sunrise Orchestra. MPS 2022 669 7 (West Germany)
JF No. 44 p78. 500w. 2

3666 PETERSON, Oscar. Another Day. BASF 20869
GR Jan. p1263-4. 175w. 4

3667 PETERSON, Oscar. At the Montreux Jazz Festival, 1975.
Pablo 2310 747
CAC Jan. p412, 414. 100w. 4
CAD Jan. p19. 150w. $3\frac{1}{2}$
DB April 8 p22-4. 100w. $3\frac{1}{2}$
HF Feb. p127. 375w. $3\frac{1}{2}$
JJ Feb. p35, 36. 275w. $4\frac{1}{2}$
MM Jan. 3 p26. 350w. $3\frac{1}{2}$
RR Feb. p68. 50w. $2\frac{1}{2}$

3668 PETERSON, Oscar. The History of an Artist. Pablo 2625
702 (2 discs)
DB April 10 p19-20. 225w. 4
JJ Feb. p38, 40. 450w. 5

3669 PETERSON, Oscar. In Concert. Verve 2683 963 (E) (2
discs) (Reissue)
CAC Oct. p274. 125w. 4
GR Sept. p493-4. 250w. 3
JJ March p36, 37. 350w. 4

3670 PETERSON, Oscar. In Russia. Pablo 2625 711 (2 discs)
CAC Oct. p272, 274. 250w. $4\frac{1}{2}$
DB Oct. 21 p22. 200w. 3
GR Nov. p900. 125w. 3
JJ Aug. p36. 650w. 5
MJ July p52. 50w. 3
MM Aug. 14 p30. 650w. $3\frac{1}{2}$
SO July p40. 300w. $3\frac{1}{2}$

3671 PETERSON, Oscar. Oscar's Choice. BASF 22010
CAD Dec. p26. 50w. $2\frac{1}{2}$
JJ Oct. p39. 100w. $4\frac{1}{2}$
MJ Dec. p44. 100w. 4
RR Aug. p80-1. 50w. 3

3672 PETERSON, Oscar. Walking the Line. BASF 20868
GRA May p1815-6. 125w. 3
JJ Feb. p35, 36. 275w. $4\frac{1}{2}$

3673 PETERSON, Oscar. We Get Requests. Verve V6-8606
GRA May p1815-6. 125w. 3
MM Feb. 7 p26. 400w. 4

3674 PETERSON, Oscar and Count Basie. Satch and Josh. Pablo
2310 722

GR   Jan.   p1263-4.   175w.   4

3675   PETERSON, Oscar and Harry Edison.   Pablo 2310-741.   Cart.
       S 10741
           AU   Nov.   p114.   450w. $4\frac{1}{2}$
           CAC   June   p110, 112.   150w. $3\frac{1}{2}$
           CAD   Jan.   p19, 20-1.   100w.   3
           MM   May 1   p32.   550w.   3
           SR   March   p104.   125w.   4

3676   PETERSON, Oscar and Roy Eldridge.   Pablo 2310-739.   Cart.
       S 10740
           CAC   June   p110, 112.   150w. $3\frac{1}{2}$
           CAD   Jan.   p19-20.   100w. $2\frac{1}{2}$
           GR   July   p229.   275w.   3
           LP   Jan.   p18.   200w. $3\frac{1}{2}$
           RR   June   p84.   50w. $2\frac{1}{2}$
           SR   March   p104.   125w.   4

3677   PETERSON, Oscar and Jon Faddis.   Pablo 2310-743.   Cart.
       S 10743
           CAC   June   p110, 112.   150w. $4\frac{1}{2}$
           CAD   Jan.   p20, 21.   150w.   2
           GRA   July   p229.   275w. $3\frac{1}{2}$
           MM   March 20   p24.   750w. $3\frac{1}{2}$
           SR   March   p104.   125w.   4

3678   PETERSON, Oscar and Dizzy Gillespie.   Pablo 2310-740.
       Cart.   S 10740
           AU   Nov.   p114.   450w.   5
           CAC   June   p110, 112.   150w.   4
           GR   July   p229.   275w. $3\frac{1}{2}$
           LP   March   p18.   150w. $4\frac{1}{2}$
           MM   May 8   p28.   500w. $4\frac{1}{2}$
           RR   June   p84.   50w. $2\frac{1}{2}$
           SR   March   p104.   125w.   4

3679   PETERSON, Oscar and Joe Pass.   A Salle Pleyel.   Pablo
       2657 015 (2 discs)
           GRA   Jan.   p1263-4.   175w.   4

3680   PETERSON, Oscar and Clarke Terry.   Pablo 2310-742.   Cart.
       S 10742
           CAC   June   p110, 112.   150w. $3\frac{1}{2}$
           CAD   Jan.   p20, 21.   100w. $2\frac{1}{2}$
           GRA   July   p229.   275w.   3
           SR   March   p104.   125w.   4

3681   PETTIFORD, Oscar.   The Legendary.   Black Lion BLP
       30185 (E) (Reissue)
           GRA   Dec.   p1080.   125w. $3\frac{1}{2}$
           JJ   July   p37-8.   450w.   5
           RR   July   p80.   125w.   3

3682   PHILLIPS, Barre.   For All It Is.   Japo 6003
          CO   Oct.   p14-5.   400w.   3

3683   PHILLIPS, Barre.   Mountainscapes.   ECM 1076
          JF   No. 44   p31.   100w.   4
          MM   Oct. 2   p34.   575w.   5

3684   PHILLIPS, Flip.   Verve 2317 092 (E) (Reissue)
          GR   Feb.   p1390.   275w. $3\frac{1}{2}$
          JJ   Nov.   p34.   525w.   4
          MM   March 6   p29.   400w. $4\frac{1}{2}$

3685   PIANO Conclave.   Palais Anthology.   MPS BASF 20227863
       (West Germany)
          JF   No. 44   p79-80.   600w. $3\frac{1}{2}$

3686   PIERCE, Nat.   Orchestra with Buck Clayton.   RCA FXL
       1-7230 (France) (Reissue)
          JJ   Aug.   p36.   525w.   5

3687   PINE, Jack.   Bix Beiderbecke Legend.   Jim Taylor Presents
       JTP 104
          CO   Oct.   p15.   400w.   1

3688   PIZZARELLI, Bucky and Joe Venuti.   Nightwings.   Flying
       Dutchman BDL 1-1120
          HF   Feb.   p127.   300w.   2
          SR   Jan.   p98-9.   100w.   4

3689   PIZZARELLI, Bucky and Zoot Sims.   Classic Jazz Records,
       CJ-21
          GP   Aug.   p80.   100w.   4

3690   PIZZI, Ray.   Appassionato.   P. Z. Records PZ333
          CAD   Sept.   p11.   175w.   5
          CAD   Oct.   p43, 44.   300w.   5

3691   POLLACK, Ben.   1933/34.   VJM VLP 43 (E) (Reissue)
          FT   April/May   p19-20.   275w.   3
          JJ   March   p37.   175w. $2\frac{1}{2}$
          MM   March 20   p24.   375w. $2\frac{1}{2}$
          ST   April-May   p152-3.   575w.   2

3692   PONDER, Jimmy.   Illusions.   Impulse Records ASD 9313
          GP   Sept.   p87.   100w.   4

3693   PONTY, Jean-Luc.   Aurora.   Atlantic SD 18163.   Cart. TP
       18163.   Cass. CS 18163
          HF   July   p108-9.   250w. $3\frac{1}{2}$
          JA   Summer   p37-8.   450w. $3\frac{1}{2}$
          MM   April 3   p34.   700w.   0
          RR   May   p75.   25w. $2\frac{1}{2}$

358 Record Reviews, 1976

3694 PONTY, Jean-Luc. Canteloupe Island. Blue Note BN LA
632-H2 (Reissue)
    CAD Nov. p21. 250w. 3
    MM Dec. 4 p28. 75w. $2\frac{1}{2}$

3695 PONTY, Jean-Luc. Imaginary Voyage. Atlantic SD 18195
    MM Dec. 4 p28. 75w. $2\frac{1}{2}$

3696 PONTY, Jean-Luc. Sonata Erotica. Inner City IC 1003
    CAD Sept. p19. 100w. 4
    JJ Nov. p37. 150w. 2

3697 PONTY, Jean-Luc. Sunday Walk. BASF 20645
    JJ Jan. p37. 200w. 5

3698 PONTY, Jean-Luc and Stephane Grappelli. Inner City 1005
    CAD Nov. p28. 100w. $3\frac{1}{2}$
    JJ Nov. p37. 100w. $3\frac{1}{2}$

3699 POREE, Ernest. "New Orleans Saxophone". Rampart Record
ords RS 102
    ST Feb.-March p112-3. 275w. 5

3700 PORTSMOUTH Sinfonia. Hallelujah. Antilles AN 7002
    DB April 8 p30-2. 100w. 1

3701 POWELL, Bud. The Genius of. Verve VE 2-2506 (2 discs)
(Reissue)
    DB Oct. 7 p33. 150w. 5
    JA Summer p40-1. 175w. $3\frac{1}{2}$
    MJ Oct. p52. 25w. $2\frac{1}{2}$

3702 POWELL, Bud. In Paris. Xanadu 102 (Reissue)
    LP April p16-7. 150w. 3

3703 POWELL, Bud. Strictly Powell, Vol. 1. RCA FXM 1 7193
(France) (Reissue)
    JJ March p37. 400w. $4\frac{1}{2}$

3704 POZAR, Cleve. So'o Percussion. CSP 125B
    DB March 25 p34-5. 25w. $2\frac{1}{2}$

3705 PRINCE, Roland. Color Visions. Vanguard VSD 7931
    CAD Sept. p21, 22. 150w. 3
    GP Oct. p97. 50w. $4\frac{1}{2}$

3706 PROBY, Ron. Evian. CBS Radio Canada 374 (Canada)
    OLR Dec. p258. 25w. $4\frac{1}{2}$

3707 PULLEN, Don. Horo HLL 101-21 (Italy)
    CAD Sept. p9. 75w. 4

3708 PULLEN, Don. Solo Piano Album. Sackville 3008 (Canada)

        CAD   Aug.   p45.   325w.   5
        CRA   Feb.   p76.   50w.   3
        OLR   Dec.   p258.   50w.   4
        RFJ   Jan.   p11.   475w. $3\frac{1}{2}$

3709   PULLEN, Don and Sam Rivers.   Capricorn Rising.   Black
       Saint BSR 0004 (Italy)
        CAD   Oct.   p33.   100w.   3
        JJ   Aug.   p36, 38.   375w.   5

3710   PURIM, Flora.   Stories to Tell.   Milestone M9058
        AU   April   p94.   500w. $3\frac{1}{2}$

3711   PURIM, Flora.   Open Your Eyes You Can Fly.   Milestone
       M 9065
        MF   April   p61.   525w. $3\frac{1}{2}$
        MM   May 8   p28.   150w. $\frac{1}{2}$
        RR   May   p75.   100w.   3

3712   PYRAMIDS.   Birth, Speed, Merging 1976.   Pyramid Records
       30935
        CAD   Sept.   p11, 12.   150w.   4
        JF   No. 44   p32.   50w.   4

3713   QUATUOR Du Jazz Libre du Quebec.   CBC Radio Canada 271
       (Canada)
        OLR   Dec.   p258-9.   50w. $3\frac{1}{2}$

3714   The QUEEN City Ragtime Ensemble.   Zeno Records HHZ-99
        CAD   Aug.   p24.   150w.   4

3715   QUIRE.   RCA BGL1-1700
        DB   Nov. 18   p18, 20-1.   250w.   5
        MJ   Oct.   p22.   50w.   2

3716   RADER, Don.   Now.   PBR International PBR 10
        CAD   Nov.   p25.   125w.   2

3717   RAICES.   Nemperor NE 434
        DB   June 3   p29.   250w. $3\frac{1}{2}$

3718   RAMA, Rena.   Caprice RIKS LP 49 (Sweden)
        JJ   July   p40-1.   100w.   4

3719   RAMPAL, Jean-Pierre and Claude Bolling.   Suite for Flute
       and Jazz Piano.   Columbia M 33233
        DB   March 11   p26.   300w. $3\frac{1}{2}$

3720   RANELIN, Phil.   The Time Is Now.   Tribe TRCD-4006
        CO   May   p18, 19.   225w. $2\frac{1}{2}$

3721   RANEY, Jimmy.   The Influence.   Xanadu 116
        GP   Sept.   p87.   100w.   5

3722 RANEY, Jimmy. Strings Attached. Choice Records CRS
      1010
          GP Sept. p87. 200w. 5

3723 RANIER, Tom. Ranier. Warner Brothers BS 2946
          CAD Aug. p25. 105w. 4

3724 RAVA, Enrico. The Pilgrim and the Stars. ECM 1063
          JF No. 41 p61-2. 400w. $2\frac{1}{2}$
          JJ Feb. p36. 100w. $3\frac{1}{2}$
          SOU May p45-6. 200w. $2\frac{1}{2}$

3725 RAVA, Enrico. Quotation Marks. Japo 60010
          MM July 31 p22. 150w. $2\frac{1}{2}$

3726 REID, Bob. Emergency Sound, Africa Is Calling Me. Kwela
      30K010
          CAD April p43-4. 150w. 1

3727 REID, Steve. Nova. Mustevic Records 2001
          CAD Oct. p12. 300w. 3

3728 REILLY, Jack. Blue-Sean-Green. Carousel ATM-1001
          CAD Jan. p14. 75w. 3
          CAD March p25-6. 300w. 3
          JF No. 44 p31. 50w. 4
          SR Aug. p89. 250w. 3

3729 REILLY, Jack. Tributes. Carousel Records CLP 1002
          CAD Aug. p30, 32. 900w. 3

3730 REINHARDT, Django. Vogue VJD 526 (2 discs) (E) (Reissue)
          JJ Nov. p35. 250w. $3\frac{1}{2}$
          RR Dec. p102. 25w. $3\frac{1}{2}$

3731 RENDELL, Don. Just Music. Spotlite SPJ 502 (E)
          JJ Nov. p35. 500w. 4
          MM Nov. 6 p25. 500w. $3\frac{1}{2}$

3732 RENDELL, Don. With the Joe Palin Trio. Spotlite 501 (E)
          JJ Jan. p37, 38. 325w. $4\frac{1}{2}$

3733 RETURN to Forever. No Mystery. Polydor PD 6512. Cart.
      8F-6512. Cass. CF-6512
          SR July p86, 87. 175w. 3

3734 RETURN to Forever. Romantic Warrior. Columbia PC
      34076
          CAC May p74. 250w. 3
          DB May 20 p22. 475w. $3\frac{1}{2}$
          MG June p50. 50w. 2
          RS July p67-8. 150w. 3

3735 REVOLUTIONARY Ensemble. People's Republic. A&M
Horizon SP 708
      DB Nov. 4 p20. 300w. 4
      JJ Dec. p36. 300w. 4
      MJ Sept. p35. 100w. $2\frac{1}{2}$
      MM Sept. 4 p21. 650w. 4
      RS Aug. 12 p59. 250w. $3\frac{1}{2}$

3736 RICH, Buddy. Big Band Machine. Groove Merchant GM
3307
      DB Jan. 15 p25-6. 325w. 4

3737 RICH, Buddy. Great Moments. Golden Era LP 15021 (E)
      JJ June p36, 38. 425w. 3

3738 RICH, Buddy. The Monster. Verve 2352 100 (E) (Reissue)
      CAC Jan. p414. 125w. $3\frac{1}{2}$
      MM Jan. 17 p42. 400w. $3\frac{1}{2}$

3739 RICH, Buddy. Richcraft. Trip TLP 5586 (Reissue)
      JA Fall p56. 50w. 4

3740 RICH, Buddy. Speak No Evil. RCA APL1-1503
      CAD Sept. p6. 50w. 4
      JJ Nov. p35. 200w. 1
      MJ Oct. p22. 25w. 3
      MM Dec. 25 p17. 475w. 2

3741 RICH, Freddie. "Friendly Five Footnotes on the Air" 1932.
Aircheck No. 12/13 (2 discs) (Canada)
      ST Aug.-Sept. p233. 300w. $4\frac{1}{2}$

3742 RICHARDS, Trevor. On Tour--U.S.A. Crescent CJP 4
      JJ Feb. p36. 175w. $2\frac{1}{2}$

3743 RIDLEY, Larry. Sum of the Parts. Strata-East 19759
      HF Feb. p127-8. 350w. 3
      MJ Jan. p20. 75w. $3\frac{1}{2}$

3744 RILEY, Doug. Dreams. PM 007
      CAD Nov. p24-5. 150w. $3\frac{1}{2}$

3745 RINALDO, John. Jazz Is a Four Letter Word. J&J Records
[no serial number]
      CAD Oct. p13. 225w. 3

3746 RITENOUR, Lee. First Course. Epic PE 33947
      DB Nov. 4 p27-8. 400w. 3
      GP Aug. p81. 450w. 5

3747 RIVERS, Sam. Involution. Blue Note BN-LA 453-H2 (2 discs)
(Reissue)
      CO July p13, 14, 15. 450w. $2\frac{1}{2}$

3748 RIVERS, Sam. Nuits De La Fondation Maeght. Shandar SR
      10.011, 83508, 83509 (3 discs) (France)
            CAD Sept. p10. 75w. 5

3749 RIVERS, Sam. One for One. Blue Note BN-LA 459-H2
      (2 discs) (Reissue)
            CO July p13, 14, 15. 450w. 3

3750 RIVERS, Sam. Sizzle. ABC Impulse ASD 9316
            CRA Aug. p74. 150w. 4
            DB Oct. 7 p22. 350w. 3
            JA Fall p54. 200w. 4
            MM June 12 p26. 525w. 4
            RR Sept. p90. 75w. 3

3751 RIVERS, Sam and Dave Holland. Improvising Artists IAI
      373843
            JA Fall p54. 200w. 4
            MM Aug. 14 p30. 400w. 3
            SR Nov. p123, 126. 250w. 5

3752 RIZZI, Tony. Plays Charlie Christian. Millagro MR 1000
            DB Nov. 18 p18, 20-1. 250w. 4

3753 ROACH, Max. Trip TLP 5522 (Reissue)
            CO Oct. p15-6. 475w. 3

3754 ROACH, Max. We Insist!--Freedom Now Suite. Amigo
      AMLP 810 (Sweden)
            CO April p15, 16. 1050w. 5

3755 ROBERTS, Lucky. Ragtime King. Everest FS 304M
            SR Aug. p80. 200w. 3

3756 ROBINSON, Billy. Evolution's Blend. CBC Radio Canada
      375 (Canada)
            OLR Dec. p259. 25w. 4

3757 ROBINSON, Pete. Dialogues for Piano and Reeds. Testa-
      ment Records T-4401
            CAD April p29. 325w. $1\frac{1}{2}$
            CK Jan. p47. 150w. 3

3758 RODNEY, Red. The Red Tornado. Muse MR 5088
            DB Oct. 7 p31-2. 300w. $4\frac{1}{2}$

3759 RODNEY, Red. With the Be-Bop Preservation Society.
      Spotlite SPJ LP 7 (E)
            JJ April p36. 275w. 4
            MM May 1 p32. 300w. 4

3760 RODNEY, Red. Yard's Pad. Sonet SNTF 698 (E)
            MM Sept. 11 p30. 550w. $3\frac{1}{2}$

3760a ROLLINS, Sonny. Vol. 5/6.   RCA FPL 2-7036 (France)
       (2 discs) (Reissue)
             JJ Feb. p46. 400w. 4

3761   ROLLINS, Sonny. Volume 7.   RCA FXL 1-7199 (France)
       (Reissue)
             JJ May p34. 325w. $4\frac{1}{2}$

3762   ROLLINS, Sonny. The Cutting Edge.   Milestone M-9059
             CO Oct. p16. 250w. 2
             JJ May p38, 40. 400w. 5

3763   ROLLINS, Sonny. Horn Culture.   Milestone M-9051
             JJ May p38, 40. 400w. $4\frac{1}{2}$

3764   ROLLINS, Sonny. More from the Vanguard.   Blue Note BN
       LA 475 H2 (2 discs)
             CRE June p59. 400w. 5
             DB Aug. 12 p37. 100w. 5
             JA Summer p38-40. 300w. 4
             PRM Jan. p37. 50w. 4

3765   ROLLINS, Sonny. Next Album.   Milestone M 9042
             JJ May p38, 40. 400w. $4\frac{1}{2}$

3766   ROLLINS, Sonny. Nucleus.   Milestone M 9064
             CAD Feb. p17. 100w. 1
             CRE April p74. 50w. 5
             DB April 8 p20. 475w. $3\frac{1}{2}$
             JA Summer p38-40. 300w. $2\frac{1}{2}$
             JJ March p37. 375w. $2\frac{1}{2}$
             MM Jan. 17 p42. 375w. $1\frac{1}{2}$
             RR March p74. 100w. 3
             SOU March p46-7. 200w. 2

3767   ROLLINS, Sonny. Saxophone Colossus and More.   Prestige
       24050 (2 discs) (Reissue)
             AU March p81-3. 1000w. 4
             MM March 6 p29. 750w. 4
             RR Jan. p63. 300w. 3

3768   ROSENGREN, Bernt. Notes from the Underground.   EMI
       Harvest E154 34958/9 (Sweden) (2 discs)
             JF No. 41 p25-6. 75w. 4

3769   ROSS de Luxe Syncopators. Territory Jazz, 1925-32.   RCA
       FXM1-7205 (France) (Reissue)
             GR Nov. p900. 600w. $2\frac{1}{2}$

3770   ROWLES, Jimmy. Halcyon 110
             DB Jan. 29 p22-3. 200w. 2

3771   ROWLES, Jimmy. Jazz Is a Fleeting Moment. Jazzz
       Records 103

CAD   Aug.   p40.   175w.   3

3772   RUDD, Roswell.   Flexible Flyer.   Arista AL1006
  CO   Feb.   p19.   275w.   4
  SR   Aug.   p90-1.   150w.   3

3773   RUDD, Roswell.   Numatik Swing Band.   JCOA 1007
  CO   Oct.   p16.   500w.   3

3774   RUIZ, Hilton.   Piano Man.   Steeple Chase SCS 1036 (Denmark)
  DB   May 6   p31.   50w. $2\frac{1}{2}$
  JJ   March   p37, 38.   400w.   4
  MM   March 13   p26.   275w. $3\frac{1}{2}$

3775   RUSHEN, Patrice.   Before the Dawn.   Prestige, P-10098
  CK   March   p47.   175w.   3

3776   RUSSELL, George.   Listen to the Silence.   Concept CR002
  CO   Oct.   p16-7.   400w.   2

3777   RUSSELL, George.   Outer Thoughts.   Milestone M 47027
(2 discs) (Reissue)
  CO   Oct.   p17-8.   1750w. $2\frac{1}{2}$

3778   RUSSELL, George and Don Cherry.   At Beethoven Hall.
BASF 25125 (2 discs)
  JJ   July   p38.   275w.   5

3779   RUSSELL, Luis.   And His Louisiana Swing Orchestra.
Columbia KG 32388 (2 discs) (Reissue)
  CO   April   p17.   450w.   4

3780   RUSSELL, Ron.   Jazz at the Palace.   SRT CUS 018 (E)
  JJ   March   p38.   600w.   4
  MM   March   p20, 24.   100w.   3
  ST   April-May   p155-6.   475w. $4\frac{1}{2}$

3781   RUSSO, Cope Lee.   Capra Presents.   CRS 1203
  CAD   April   p38, 40.   250w. $1\frac{1}{2}$

3782   RUTHERFORD, Paul.   The Gentle Harm of the Bourgeoisie.
Emanem 3305
  MM   Dec.   p18.   900w.   3

3783   RYPDAL, Terje.   Odyssey.   ECM 1067/8 (2 discs)
  GP   May   p81.   150w. $3\frac{1}{2}$
  JJ   Feb.   p36.   175w.   2

3784   RYPDAL, Terje.   What Comes After.   ECM 1031 ST
  CO   Oct.   p18.   475w.   3

3785   RYPDAL, Terje.   Whenever I Seem to Be Far Away.   ECM

1045 ST
JJ   Feb.   p48.   150w.   4

3786   SAMOLE, Stan.   America.   Lotus YAM 1
JJ   June   p40.   100w.   4

3787   SANTAMARIA, Mongo.   Skins.   Milestone M-47038 (2 discs)
(Reissue)
CAD   Oct.   p28.   150w.   4

3788   SANBORN, Dave.   Dave Sanborn.   Warner Bros. BS 2957
CAD   Sept.   p8.   75w.   4
RS   Sept. 23   p118.   175w.   3

3789   SANDERS, Pharoah.   Elevation.   Impulse AS 9261
CO   Oct.   p18-9.   675w.   2

3790   SANDERS, Pharoah.   Love in Us All.   Impulse ASD 9280
CO   April   p17.   275w.   3

3791   SANDERS, Pharoah.   Wisdom Through Music.   Impulse
JJ   Aug.   p38.   275w.   0

3792   SANDVIK Big Band.   Dragon 3 (Sweden)
MM   Dec. 25   p18.   100w. $2\frac{1}{2}$

3793   SANTOS, Moacir.   Carnival of the Spirits.   Blue Note BN
LA 463-G
JJ   Jan.   p30.   75w. $\frac{1}{2}$

3794   SCHIANO, Mario.   Perdas de fogu.   Vista TPL1 1082
CO   Oct.   p19-20.   400w.   4

3795   SCHIFRIN, Lalo.   Black Widow.   CTI 5000
CAD   Oct.   p18.   75w. $2\frac{1}{2}$
CAC   Nov.   p296, 298.   225w.   3
JJ   Nov.   p37.   200w.   3

3796   SCHLIPPENBACH, Alex and Sven-Ake Johansson.   Live at
the Latin Quarter.   FMP 0310 (E)
MM   Dec. 4   p28.   375w. $3\frac{1}{2}$

3797   SCOTT, James.   Vol. 1.   Biograph BLP 10160
RT   May/June   p7.   75w.   3

3798   SCOTT, Ronnie.   At Ronnie's.   RCA LPL 1 5056
CO   April   p18.   125w.   4

3799   SCOTT, Tom.   New York Connection.   Ode SP 77033
SR   May   p104, 109.   75w.   3
RFJ   July   p9.   225w. $3\frac{1}{2}$

3800   SCOTT-HERON, Gil.   The First Minute of a New Day.

Arista A 4030
SR   May   p91.   200w. $4\frac{1}{2}$

3801 SCOTT-HERON, Gil and Brian Jackson.   From South Africa
to South Carolina.   Arista AL 4044.   Cart. 8301-4044H
DB   March 11   p20-1.   500w.   3
SR   Feb.   p95.   150w.   3

3802 SEBESKY, Don.   The Rape of El Morro.   CTI CTI-6061 S1.
Cart. CTI-6061 HT
DB   Jan. 29   p20.   250w.   5
LP   March   p18.   175w.   3
SR   Feb.   p95.   200w. $4\frac{1}{2}$

3803 SELS, Jack.   The Complete, Vol. 2.   Vogel 102 AS (Belgium)
(Reissue)
JJ   Dec.   p36.   250w.   3

3804 SENENSKY, Bernie.   New Life.   PM PMR 006 (Canada)
CK   Dec.   p49.   100w. $3\frac{1}{2}$

3805 SENENSKY, Bernie.   Trio.   RCI 416 (Canada)
CAD   May   p24-5.   75w. $2\frac{1}{2}$

3806 SEVDA.   At Fregatten.   Sonet SNTF 665 (Sweden)
CAD   Sept.   p10.   100w.   4
CO   Oct.   p20.   225w.   4

3807 SHAFER, Ted and the Jelly Roll Jazz Band.   Good Old Jazz,
vol. 1.   Merry Makers MMRC 101
JF   No. 41.   p26.   50w.   3

3808 SHANK, Bud.   Sunshine Express.   Concord CJ20
CAD   Nov.   p19-20.   50w.   3
JJ   Dec.   p36.   250w. $3\frac{1}{2}$

3809 SHARKEY & Co.   Pragmaphone PRG 10 (France)
CO   Oct.   p20.   200w.   3

3810 SHARKEY & Co.   Kansas City Kitty.   Pragmaphone PRG 4
(France)
CO   Oct.   p20.   200w.   3

3811 SHAVERS, Charlie.   The Finest of....   Bethlehem BCP 6005
(Reissue)
DB   Oct. 21   p33.   175w. $1\frac{1}{2}$

3812 SHAW, Artie.   The Complete, vol. 1.   RCA AXM2-5517 (2
discs) (Reissue)
DB   Nov. 4   p28.   75w. $3\frac{1}{2}$

3813 SHAW, Artie.   Melody and Madness, v. 1/2.   Jazz Guild
1001/2 (2 discs)

        CAD Aug. p32. 175w. 5
        DB   Nov. 4 p28. 75w. $3\frac{1}{2}$
        JA   Fall p56. 75w. 4
        JJ   Sept. p37-8. 450w. 1

3814 SHAW, Artie. On the Air. Aircheck #11 (Canada)
        CAD Sept. p24. 150w. 5
        DB   June 3 p31. 75w. 4
        ST   Dec. 1975-Jan. 1976 p77-8. 50w. 4

3815 SHAW, Woody. Love Dance. Muse MR 5074
        CAD Sept. p20. 300w. 4

3816 SHAW, Woody. Moontrane. Muse MR 5058
        CO   Oct. p20. 625w. $3\frac{1}{2}$

3817 SHEARING, George. My Ship. MPS G22369
        CAD Dec. p26. 75w. $2\frac{1}{2}$

3818 SHEPHERD, Dave. Benny Goodman Classics. Black Lion
        BLP 12119 (E)
        JJ   April p36. 325w. 5

3819 SHEPP, Archie. Doodlin'. Inner City 101001
        CRA Nov. p72. 50w. 3
        DB   Nov. 18 p21-2. 350w. 3

3820 SHEPP, Archie. Kwanza. Impulse AS 9262
        CO   Oct. p21. 150w. 0

3821 SHEPP, Archie. Montreux One. Arista Freedom AL 1027
        CRA Nov. p72. 50w. 3

3822 SHEPP, Archie. A Sea of Faces. Black Saint BSR 0002
        (Italy)
        CAD Oct. p33. 175w. 5
        CO   Sept. p14. 325w. 4
        CRE Aug. p78. 50w. 4
        DB   March 25 p34-5. 25w. 4
        JJ   Feb. p36. 275w. $2\frac{1}{2}$
        MM   Jan. 17 p42. 525w. $4\frac{1}{2}$

3823 SHEPP, Archie. There's a Trumpet in My Soul. Arista
        Freedom AL 1016
        CO   March p18-9. 225w. 3

3824 SHERWOOD, Bobby. Aircheck No. 3 (Canada)
        ST   Dec. 1975-Jan. 1976 p77-8. 200w. 3

3825 SHORTER, Alan. Parabolic. Verve 2304 060 (E)
        CAD Sept. p10. 75w. 4

3826 SHORTER, Wayne. Native Dancer. Columbia PC 33418

CO   Oct.   p21.   325w.   1½

3827 SHORTER, Wayne. Second Genesis.   Vee-Jay VJS 3057
      (Reissue)
           CAD June p28.   125w.   3

3828 SILVER, Horace. Silver 'n' Brass.   Blue Note BN LA 405G
           DB Jan. 29 p22.   300w.   4

3829 SILVER, Horace. Silver 'n' Wood.   Blue Note BN-LA 851-G
           CAD May p23.   125w.   2
           DB Oct. 21 p26, 28.   425w.   3
           JA Summer p35-6.   400w.   3
           JJ Aug.   p38.   400w.   5
           MJ Oct.   p23.   50w.   3
           PRM May p62.   475w.   4

3830 SILVER, Horace. Silver's Blue.   Columbia JLA 16005 (Re-
      issue)
           CO Oct.   p21.   150w.   1½
           MJ Jan.   p20.   75w.   3

3831 SIMKINS, Benny. Linger Awhile.   Flyright LP 202 (E)
           JJ April p36.   375w.   3

3832 SIMS, Zoot. And Friend.   Classic Jazz CJ 21
           CAD June p28.   75w.   3
           JJ Aug.   p38.   350w.   5

3833 SIMS, Zoot. And the Gershwin Brothers.   Pablo 2310 744
           AU Sept.   p87-8.   300w.   4½
           CAC April p28.   125w.   3½
           CAD Jan.   p18.   150w.   3
           GRA Sept.   p494.   200w.   4½
           HF April p142.   175w.   3
           JJ April p36, 37.   350w.   5
           MJ July p52.   25w.   3
           MM June 19 p22.   475w.   5

3834 SIMS, Zoot. At Ease.   Famous Door HL 2000
           JJ Feb.   p40.   350w.   5
           SR March p92.   150w.   5

3835 SIMS, Zoot. Soprano Sax.   Pablo 2310-770
           CAD Sept.   p6.   50w.   5
           JA Fall p55.   500w.   4
           JJ Nov.   p35-6.   500w.   4½
           RFJ Oct.   p9, 14.   525w.   4½
           SR Dec.   p129.   75w.   4

3836 SIMS, Zoot. Zootcase.   Prestige P 24061 (2 discs) (Reissue)
           AU Nov.   p113-4.   300w.   3½
           CAD Nov.   p27.   125w.   2½

DB   Oct. 21 p34.   150w.   4

3837   SIMS, Zoot.   Zoot Sims' Party.   Choice CRS 1006
       SR   March p92-3.   150w. $2\frac{1}{2}$

3838   SLOANE, Carol.   Subway Tokens.   Moonbeam
       CAD   March p25.   275w.   3

3839   SMITH, Jimmy.   The Black Smith.   DJM DJLPS 451 (E)
       MM   Jan. 10 p32.   250w.   1

3840   SMITH, Leo.   New Dalta Ahkri-Reflectativity.   Kabell K-2
       CO   April p13, 14.   1175w.   4

3841   SMITH, Lonnie Liston.   Reflections of a Golden Dream.
       Flying Dutchman BDL 1-1460
       DB   Sept. 9 p24-5.   350w.   1

3842   SMITH, Lonnie Liston.   Visions of a New World.   Flying
       Dutchman BDL 1-1196
       BM   April p31-2.   200w.   4
       CRA   Jan. p77.   25w.   1
       DB   Feb. 12 p22.   325w. $1\frac{1}{2}$
       JJ   May p34.   125w.   2
       LP   March p19.   125w. $2\frac{1}{2}$

3843   SMITH, Michael.   Geomusic III PL.   Pronit ZSX 0614 (Poland)
       JF   No. 44 p33.   75w. $3\frac{1}{2}$

3844   SMITH, Michael.   Reflection on Progress.   Storyville SLP
       1006 (Denmark)
       JJ   Feb. p40.   250w.   3

3845   SMITH, Michael and Kent Carter.   La Musique Blanche.   Le
       Chant Du Monde LDX 74601 (France)
       JJ   Aug. p39.   100w. $2\frac{1}{2}$

3846   SMITH, Plato.   Dixieland Dance Date.   Land o' Jazz LOJ 1972
       ST   Oct./Nov. p35-6.   50w.   2

3847   SMITH, Willie "The Lion" and Jo Jones.   The Lion and the
       Tiger.   Jazz Odyssey 006
       GRA   Oct. p670.   200w.   3
       JJ   Jan. p38.   150w.   4

3848   SMITH, Willie "The Lion" and Jo Jones.   Le Tigre, Le Lion
       & La Madelon.   Jazz Odyssey 009
       GRA   Oct. p670.   150w. $3\frac{1}{2}$
       JJ   Jan. p38.   150w.   4
       RR   Feb. p68.   100w. $2\frac{1}{2}$

3849   SOLAL, Martial.   Nothing But Piano.   MPS BASF 2022 6808
       JF   No. 44 p32-3.   100w.   4

3850 SOUTHLAND Stingers. Scott Joplin Palm Leaf Rag. Angel·
      S 36074
          RT   March/April p5-6. 50w. $3\frac{1}{2}$

3851 SPANIER, Herbie. Forensic Perturbations. Radio Canada
      International Transcription 376 (Canada)
          CO   April p17, 18. 250w. 5
          OLR Dec. p259. 50w. $3\frac{1}{2}$

3852 SPANIER, Muggsy. A Muggsy Spanier Memorial. Saga 6917
      (E) (Reissue)
          SR   Nov. p126, 130. 400w. 3

3853 SPIVAK, Charles & Jimmy Joy. Victory Parade. Aircheck
      # 6 (Canada)
          CAD Sept. p23, 24. 200w. 3
          JJ   May p40. 50w. 3
          ST   June-July p191-2. 125w. 2

3854 SPONTANEOUS Music Ensemble. Face to Face. Emanen
      303
          CAD Feb. p20. 200w. 2

3855 STACK, Eric. Fruit from Another Garden. RCI 425
          CAD May p22-3. 75w. 2

3856 STACY, Jess. Stacy Still Swings. Chiaroscuro CR 133
          SR   Nov. p112. 200w. $4\frac{1}{2}$

3857 STADLER, Heiner. Jazz Alchemy. Labor LRS 7006
          CAD Nov. p16. 175w. 4

3858 STANKO, Tomasz. Balladyna. ECM 1071
          CAD Sept. p23. 175w. 3
          JF   No. 41 p25. 125w. 4
          JF   April p62. 525w. 3
          MM   July 31 p22. 100w. $2\frac{1}{2}$

3859 STEIN, Lou. Tribute to Tatum. Chiaroscuro CR 149
          CAD Dec. p26. 75w. $3\frac{1}{2}$

3860 STERN, Bobby. Libra. Vertigo 6360 632 (West Germany)
          MM   Dec. 25 p18. 125w. $2\frac{1}{2}$

3861 STEVENS, John. Away. Vertigo 6360 131 (E)
          JJ   Aug. p38. 350w. $3\frac{1}{2}$

3862 STILES, John. In Tandem. Famous Door HL103
          CAD May p30. 75w. $3\frac{1}{2}$

3863 STITT, Sonny. Dumpy Mama. Flying Dutchman BDL1-1197
          SOU Feb. p50. 50w. 2

3864 STITT, Sonny. Mellow. Muse MR 5067
      DB   May 6   p26-7.   200w. $2\frac{1}{2}$

3865 STITT, Sonny. Night Work.   Black Lion 307
      CAD   Jan.   p31.   25w. $1\frac{1}{2}$
      MJ   April p29.   50w. $2\frac{1}{2}$

3866 STITT, Sonny. Satan. Cadet CA 50060
      CO   April   p18.   300w.   3

3866a STITT, Sonny. Soul Girl. Panda LPS 4004
      DB   March 27   p22.   150w.   2

3867 STITT, Sonny. Stomp Off Let's Go.   Flying Dutchman
      BDL1-1538
      CAD   Sept.   p6.   50w.   4
      JA   Fall   p54-5.   450w. $1\frac{1}{2}$
      MJ   Oct.   p23.   50w.   3
      SR   Nov.   p130.   225w. $1\frac{1}{2}$

3868 STITT, Sonny and Zoot Sims. Interaction.   Chess 2ACMU
      405 (2 discs)
      CAD   Nov.   p24.   75w.   2

3869 STIVIN, Jiri and Randolph Dasek.   System Tandem.   Japo
      6008 (West Germany)
      MM   May 1   p32.   225w. $2\frac{1}{2}$

3870 STONE, Fred. CBC Radio Canada 377 (Canada)
      OLR   Dec.   p259.   75w.   4

3871 STRACHAN, Donald Alexander. Soul Translation.   Triad 001
      CAD   Aug.   p43.   175w. $2\frac{1}{2}$

3872 STRAZZERI, Frank. After the Rain.   Catalyst CAT 7607
      (Japan)
      CAD   Dec.   p304.   125w.   2

3873 STRAZZERI, Frank. Frames.   Glendale 6002
      DB   June 3   p24-5.   250w. $3\frac{1}{2}$

3874 SULIEMAN, Idrees. Now Is the Time.   Steeplechase SCS 1052
      (Denmark)
      JJ   Nov.   p36-7.   375w. $3\frac{1}{2}$

3875 SULLIVAN, Ira. Horizon SP-706
      CAD   Aug.   p39.   250w.   5
      DB   Nov. 18 p22, 26.   350w.   4
      HF   Sept.   p114.   300w.   4
      JJ   Sept.   p38.   250w. $2\frac{1}{2}$
      MJ   Sept.   p35.   75w. $2\frac{1}{2}$
      RR   Nov.   p107.   250w.   4
      SR   Oct.   p110.   175w.   3

3876   SULLIVAN, Joe.   Piano.   Folkways FA 2851 (partial reissue)
          CO   Oct.   p22.   300w. $3\frac{1}{2}$

3877   SUNSHINE, Monty.   Happy Bird 5001 (West Germany)
          RR   June   p83-4.   50w.   3

3878   SUNSHINE, Monty.   The Glory of Love.   Happy Bird 5010
       (West Germany)
          RR   June   p84.   25w.   3

3879   SUTTON, Ralph.   Changes.   77 Records S 57 (E)
          JJ   Oct.   p38.   450w.   5
          MM   Dec.   4   p30.   250w. $3\frac{1}{2}$
          RR   Dec.   p102.   25w.   3

3880   SVENSON, Lalle.   Cockroach Road.   Cockroach CLP-101
       (Sweden)
          CO   April   p18, 19.   250w.   0

3881   SWANSEN, Chris.   Album LI.   Badger 1002
          SR   Sept.   p103.   150w.   4

3882   SZABADOS, Gyorgy.   The Wedding.   Hungaraton SLPX 17475
       (Hungary)
          JF   No. 41   p28.   100w.   3

3883   SZOBEL, Herman.   Arista AL 4058
          CAD   April   p30.   150w.   1
          DB   Sept. 9   p32.   225w. $3\frac{1}{2}$

3884   TATE, Buddy.   Swinging Like Tate.   Master Jazz MJR 8127
       (Reissue)
          CAD   Jan.   p24.   75w.   4
          DB   Nov. 4   p30.   50w.   4
          SR   Nov.   p112, 114.   175w.   4

3885   TATE, Buddy.   The Texas Twister.   Master Jazz Recordings
       MJR 8218
          CAD   Jan.   p24.   75w.   4
          DB   Nov. 4   p30.   50w.   2
          JJ   March   p38, 40.   350w. $4\frac{1}{2}$

3886   TATUM, Art.   Vols. 1/2.   Vogue VJD 511/1-2 (2 discs)
       (France) (Reissue)
          GRA   Jan.   p1264.   500w. $3\frac{1}{2}$

3887   TATUM, Art.   All That Jazz, vol. 2.   DJM DJLMD 8002
       (2 discs) (E) (Reissue)
          GRA   Jan.   p1264.   500w. $3\frac{1}{2}$
          JF   No. 41   p24.   75w.   4

3888   TATUM, Art.   His Rarest Solos.   Saga 6915 (E) (Reissue)
          ARG   Nov.   p56.   125w.   4

3889 TATUM, Art. Masterpieces. MCA 2-4019 (2 discs) (Re-issue)
  CO Oct. p23. 825w. $3\frac{1}{2}$

3890 TATUM, Art. Solo. Pablo 2625703 (13 discs) (Reissue)
  DB April 10 p22-4. 950w. 4

3891 TATUM, Art. Song of the Vagabonds. Black Lion BLP 30166 (E) (Reissue)
  JJ Sept. p38. 700w. 5
  MM Dec. 11 p29. 425w. $3\frac{1}{2}$
  RR Oct. p102. 100w. 3

3892 TATUM, Art. Tatum Group Masterpieces. Pablo 2625 706 (8 discs) (Reissue)
  JJ Dec. p36-7. 625w. $4\frac{1}{2}$
  MM Nov. 27 p32. 1350w. 5
  SR Jan. p98. 300w. 5

3893 TATUM, Art. Works of Art. Jazzz Records 101
  CAD Aug. p40, 41. 250w. 5

3894 TATUM, Art and Buddy Defranco. Pablo 2310 736 (Reissue)
  CO Dec. p12-3. 600w. $3\frac{1}{2}$

3895 TATUM, Art, Lionel Hampton and Buddy Rich. The Tatum-Hampton-Rich Trio. Pablo 2310 720 (E) (Reissue)
  CAC April p28, 30. 225w. $2\frac{1}{2}$
  GR Jan. p1264. 500w. $4\frac{1}{2}$

3896 TAYLOR, Cecil. Akisakila. Trio PA 3004-5 (Japan) (2 discs)
  CAD Aug. p16. 125w. 5

3897 TAYLOR, Cecil. In Transition. Blue Note BNLA 458-H2 (Reissue)
  DB Feb. 26 p31. 400w. 5

3898 TAYLOR, Cecil. Live at Cafe Montmartre/Nefertiti. Arista Freedom AL 1905 (2 discs) (Reissue)
  DB Oct. 21 p22-3. 400w. 5
  MM Oct. 2 p34. 475w. 4
  RR Nov. p107. 125w. 3

3899 TAYLOR, Cecil. Silent Tongues. Arista AL 1005 (Reissue)
  CO Feb. p20. 275w. 5
  SR Aug. p90-1. 150w. 5

3900 TAYLOR, Cecil. Solo. Trio PA 7067 (Japan)
  CAD Aug. p16. 50w. 5

3901 TEAGARDEN, Jack. IAJRC 19 (Reissue)
  ST Dec. 1975-Jan. 1976 p74-5. 350w. 0

3902 TEAGARDEN, Jack. Big Band 1939. Tax m-8024 (Sweden)
      (Reissue)
          JJ April p37. 200w. $3\frac{1}{2}$
          ST Oct.-Nov. p31. 75w. 3

3903 TEAGARDEN, Jack. Masters of Dixieland. Capitol C 054-81
      845 (E)
          JJ April p37, 38. 300w. $4\frac{1}{2}$

3904 TEAGARDEN, Jack and Frank Trumbauer. Aircheck # 9
      (Canada)
          CAD Sept. p24. 175w. 4

3905 TERRY, Clark. And His Jolly Giants. Vanguard VSD 79365
          CAD Feb. p24. 50w. $4\frac{1}{2}$
          DB Sept. 9 p32. 200w. 2
          MJ Dec. p26. 50w. 4
          SR June p95. 50w. 5

3906 TERRY, Clark. Big Bad Band Live on 57th Street. Vanguard
      VSD 79355
          AU Dec. p96-7. 800w. $3\frac{1}{2}$
          JJ Sept. p39. 500w. 5
          MM Aug. 28 p22. 350w. $3\frac{1}{2}$
          RR Oct. p102. 75w. $2\frac{1}{2}$
          SR Aug. p73. 300w. 5

3907 TERRY, Clark. Cruising. Milestone M 47032 (2 discs) (Re-
      issue)
          JJ Feb. p36, 37. 200w. $2\frac{1}{2}$
          RR March p74. 125w. $3\frac{1}{2}$
          SOU March p48. 50w. 3

3908 TERRY, Clark and Cecil Payne. Cool Blues. DJM (E)
          MM Aug. 28 p22. 225w. $4\frac{1}{2}$

3909a THELIN, Eje. Caprice RIKS LP 91 (Sweden)
          JJ Aug. p39. 75w. $4\frac{1}{2}$

3909b THIELE, Bob. I Saw Pinetop Spit Blood. Flying Dutchman
      BDL 1-0964
          SR Jan. p99. 100w. 3

3909c THIELEMANS, Toots. Captured Alive. Choice CRS 1007
          SR Aug. p89. 250w. 4

3909d THOMAS, Joe. Masala. Groove Merchant 3310
          CAD April p38. 125w. 1

3909e THOMAS, Rene. TLP. Vogue 003-S (Belgium)
          CO Dec. p13. 300w. 2

3909f THOMPSON, Don. Country Place. PM 008 (Canada)

CAD   Nov.   p25-6.   100w.   3

3909g THOMPSON, Lucky. Dancing Sunbeam.   Impulse ASH
       9307-2 (2 discs)
       LP   March   p19.   175w.   3

3909h THOMPSON, Robbin.   Nemperor NE 440
       RS   Nov. 18   p81.   175w.   1½

3909i THORNHILL, Claude.   The Memorable.   Columbia KC 32906
       AU   Nov.   p112-3.   1000w.   4½

3909j THORNTON, Clifford.   The Gardens of Harlem.   JCOA LP
       1008
       CAD   Aug.   p38. 39.   400w.   5
       JJ   June   p38.   325w.   4½
       SR   May   p109.   300w.   4½

3910 TIMMONS, Bobby.   Moanin.   Milestone M-47031 (2 discs)
      (Reissue)
      CK   March   p47.   100w.   4
      JJ   Feb.   p37.   200w.   3
      RR   March   p74.   75w.   3½
      SOU   March   p48.   50w.   3

3911 TJADER, Cal.   Amazonas.   Fantasy 9502
      CAD   May   p24.   150w.   3½
      MG   June   p50.   50w.   3

3912 TJADER, Cal.   Last Night When We Were Young.   Fantasy
      F-9482.   Cart. 8160-9482H
      DB   May 20   p29-30.   125w.   2
      SR   Feb.   p95.   100w.   3

3913 TOLLIVER, Charles.   Live in Tokyo.   Strata-East SES-19745
      CO   April   p19.   425w.   4

3914 TOLLIVER, Charles.   Paper Man.   Arista AL1002 (Reissue)
      CO   Feb.   p19.   275w.   4
      SR   Aug.   p90-1.   150w.   3

3915 TOLLIVER, Charles.   The Ringer.   Arista/Freedom AL 1017
      CRA   Jan.   p78.   150w.   4
      DB   June 3   p26.   325w.   5

3916 TOLONEN, Jukka.   Cross Section.   Sonet SNTF 699 (Sweden)
      MM   May 8   p25.   75w.   1½

3917 TOMPKINS, Fred.   The Compositions of....   Festival 9001
      CAD   April   p45.   75w.   3½
      JF   No. 44   p78-9.   175w.   3

3918 TOMPKINS, Fred.   Somesville.   Festival 9002

CAD   April   p45.   75w. $3\frac{1}{2}$
JF   No. 44   p78-9.   175w.   3
MG   June   p50.   50w.   3

3919   TORNER, Gosta.   Boy Meets Horn.   Sonora 6394035
ST   Oct./Nov.   p39.   200w. $3\frac{1}{2}$

3920   TOUBABOU.   Le Ble et le mil.   Kot'ai KOT-3305 (Canada)
CO   April   p19.   300w. $2\frac{1}{2}$

3921   TOWNER, Ralph.   Solstice.   ECM 1060
DB   April 8   p21-2.   500w.   5
HF   July   p105.   200w. $3\frac{1}{2}$
JJ   May   p34.   525w.   5
SOU   March   p47-8.   150w.   2
SR   March   p102-3.   325w.   4

3922   TOWNER, Ralph and Gary Burton.   Matchbook ECM 1056
HF   July   p105-6.   150w. $3\frac{1}{2}$
LP   Jan.   p19.   275w.   4

3923   TRACEY, Stan.   Captain Adventure.   Steam SJ 102 (E)
CAD   Dec.   p28.   225w. $3\frac{1}{2}$
JF   No. 41   p65.   200w.   5
JJ   March   p40.   350w. $4\frac{1}{2}$

3924   TRACEY, Stan.   Jazz Suite: Under the Milkwood.   Stream
101 (E) (Reissue)
CAD   Dec.   p28.   225w. $3\frac{1}{2}$
JJ   Dec.   p38-9.   275w. $4\frac{1}{2}$
MM   Oct. 30   p27.   475w. $4\frac{1}{2}$

3925   TRISTANO, Lennie.   Atlantic ATL 50 245 (West Germany)
(Reissue)
MM   Dec.   p28.   125w.   3

3926   TROPEA, John.   Marlin 2200
DB   Aug. 12   p34.   250w.   3

3927   TRUMPET Kings.   At Montreux Jazz Festival, 1975.   Pablo
2310 754
CAC   Jan.   p412, 414.   100w. $3\frac{1}{2}$
DB   April 8   p22-4.   100w.   5
RR   Jan.   p63.   225w.   3

3928   TRYFOROUS, Bob.   Scott Joplin: Composer; Bob Tryforous,
Guitarist.   Puritan 5002
RT   March/April   p5-6.   50w.   0

3929   TURNER, Joe.   Another Epoch--Stride Piano.   Pablo 2310 763
HF   Sept.   p113-4.   300w. $2\frac{1}{2}$
JJ   Sept.   p39.   500w.   5
MJ   July   p52.   50w. $3\frac{1}{2}$
MM   July 31   p22.   225w.   3

ST   Nov.-Dec.   p38-9.   250w.   3

3930   TURNER, Joe.   King of Stride.   Chiarscuro CR 147
       CAD   Dec.   p26.   100w.   4

3931   TURRENTINE, Stanley.   Blue Note BN LA 394-H2 (2 discs)
       (Reissue)
       LP   March   p19.   200w. $3\frac{1}{2}$

3432   TURRENTINE, Stanley.   The Baddest Turrentine.   CTI 6048
       (Reissue)
       DB   April 10   p25.   150w. $3\frac{1}{2}$

3933   TURRENTINE, Stanley.   Everybody Come on Out.   Fantasy
       9508
       CAD   Aug.   p25.   75w.   5

3934   TURRENTINE, Stanley.   Have You Ever Seen the Rain.
       Fantasy F 9493
       BS   March   p64.   200w.   4
       CAD   Feb.   p30-1.   150w.   2
       DB   Feb. 12   p27.   300w.   2

3935   TUSA, Frank.   Father Time.   Enja 2056
       JJ   April   p38.   250w. $2\frac{1}{2}$

3936   TYNER, McCoy.   Atlantis.   Milestone M 55002 (2 discs)
       CO   Dec.   p12.   350w. $2\frac{1}{2}$

3937   TYNER, McCoy.   Cosmos.   Blue Note BN-LA 460-H2 (2
       discs) (Reissue)
       CAD   Oct.   p37, 38.   200w.   5

3938   TYNER, McCoy.   Fly with the Wind.   Milestone M-9067
       BM   Aug.   p42.   150w.   4
       CAD   Aug.   p36.   175w.   3
       CK   Aug.   p45.   150w. $2\frac{1}{2}$
       DB   Oct. 21   p20.   450w.   4
       JA   Fall   p53-4.   300w.   1
       JJ   July   p38.   475w. $4\frac{1}{2}$
       MM   June 5   p22.   700w.   2

3939   TYNER, McCoy.   Trident.   Milestone M 9063
       CO   Dec.   p12.   450w.   4
       CRA   May   p78-9.   200w. $4\frac{1}{2}$
       DB   March 11   p20.   400w.   5
       JJ   Feb.   p37.   350w. $4\frac{1}{2}$
       MM   Jan. 17   p42.   625w. $4\frac{1}{2}$
       RR   March   p74.   100w.   4
       SOU   March   p46.   100w.   4

3940   TYNER, McCoy.   Sama Layuca.   Milestone M-9056
       CO   April   p20.   300w.   3

3941 ULANDER, Lars-Goran. The New Figaro. Dragon LP 4
      (Sweden)
          JJ Oct. p40. 75w. $4\frac{1}{2}$

3942 ULANOV, Barry. Anthology '45-48. ZIM 1002 (Reissue)
          CAD April p43. 100w. 3

3943 UNITY. Blow Thru Your Mind. EPI-02
          CO May p18, 19. 225w. 4

3944 UNIVERSAL Folk Sounds. Eternal Now. Sonet SNTF 653
      (Sweden)
          JJ Feb. p40, 42. 225w. 4

3945 UNIVERSAL Folk Sounds. Music for Xaba. Sonet SNTF 642
      (Sweden)
          JJ Feb. p40, 41. 225w. 4

3946 URBANIAK, Michal. Body English. Arista AL 4086
          DB Dec. 2 p21-2. 300w. 3
          JF No. 44 p76-7. 700w. $4\frac{1}{2}$
          RS Aug. 12 p67-8. 200w. 3
          SR Nov. p130. 25w. $1\frac{1}{2}$

3947 URBANIAK, Michal. Constellation in Concert. Muza SXL
      1010 (Poland)
          CO March p14. 350w. 4

3948 URBANIAK, Michal. Fusion III. Columbia PC 33542
          JF No. 41 p24. 75w. 4
          MF April p60-1. 450w. 3

3949 URBANIAK, Michal. Live Recording. Muza SXL0733 (Poland)
          CO March p14. 350w. 4

3950 URBANIAK, Michal and Urszula Dudziak. A Tribute to Kome-
      da. MPS/BASF 21657
          CAD Aug. p35. 175w. 4
          SR Nov. p130. 100w. 2

3951 URBANIAK, Michal/Bernard Kafka. Funk Factory. Atco
      SD 36-116
          JF April p60. 250w. 3

3952 VAN BERGEYK, Tom. Famous Ragtime Guitar Solos. Kick-
      ing Mule KM 114
          RT Jan./Feb. p8. 100w. 2

3953 VAN DER GILD, Tom, Roger Jannotta and Larry Porter.
      Children at Play. Japo 60009 (West Germany)
          MM May 1 p32. 150w. $3\frac{1}{2}$

3954 VAN'T HOF, Jasper. The Door Is Open. MPS BSF DC 228

754 (E)
 MM Dec. 4 p28. 100w. 3

3955 VAUGHAN, Sarah. Tenderly. Bulldog BDL 1009 (E)
  MM Oct. 16 p30. 350w. 3

3956 VENTURA, Charlie. Charlie Boy. Phoenix LP 6 (Reissue)
  CAD Feb. p18, 20. 200w. 3

3957 VENTURA, Charles. Jumping with Charlie Ventura. Trip
  TLP-5536 (Reissue)
  CO April p20, 21. 525w. 4

3958 VENTURA, Charlie. Sextet in Chicago 1947. ZIM 1004
  CAD Aug. p39. 200w. 3
  JF No. 44 p31-2. 50w. 4

3959 VENUTI, Joe. Venuti Blue Four. Chiaroscuro CR 134
  CO Dec. p13. 250w. $4\frac{1}{2}$
  DB March 25 p31. 100w. 4

3960 VENUTI, Joe. The Radio Years, No. 5, 1934. London
  HMG-5023 (E) (Reissue)
  GR June p101. 225w. 4
  JJ Oct. p38. 400w. $3\frac{1}{2}$
  MM June 19 p22. 275w. 3
  RR June p83. 50w. 3

3961 VENUTI, Joe and George Barnes. Gems. Concord Jazz,
  CJ-14
  HF May p112-3. 225w. 4
  GP May p81. 125w. $4\frac{1}{2}$

3962 VENUTI, Joe and Eddie Lang. The Sounds of New York,
  vol. 2. RCA FPM 1-7106 (France) (Reissue)
  JJ Feb. p42. 450w. 5

3963 VENUTI, Joe and Marion McPartland. The Maestro and
  Friend. Halcyon HAL-112
  SR Sept. p112-3. 400w. 3

3964 VENUTI, Joe and Zoot Sims. Chiaroscuro CR 142
  CAD March p26. 75w. $3\frac{1}{2}$
  CO Dec. p13. 450w. $3\frac{1}{2}$
  HF May p112-3. 225w. $3\frac{1}{2}$
  SR Sept. p112. 400w. 3

3965 VENUTI, Joe and Zoot Sims. Joe & Zoot. Chiaroscuro CR
  128
  JJ Oct. p38-9. 550w. 5
  MM Oct. 2 p34. 575w. 4
  RR Oct. p102. 100w. $3\frac{1}{2}$
  SR March p92. 150w. 2

3966 VESALA, Edward. Nan Madol. Japo 60007 (West Germany)
          JJ Feb. p48. 150w. 3
          MM July 31 p22. 100w. 3

3967 VINNEGAR, Leroy. Glass of Water. Legend LGS-1001
          CO April p21. 250w. 3

3968 VISITORS. In My Youth. Muse MR 5024
          CO Dec. p14. 400w. $3\frac{1}{2}$

3969 VITOUS, Miroslav. Magical Shepherd. Warner Bros. BS
      2925
          CK Aug. p45. 50w. 2
          CRA July p72-3. 150w. 2
          CRA July p72-3. 275w. 2
          MJ July p54. 50w. $2\frac{1}{2}$
          MM May 22 p26. 75w. 1
          RS June 17 p55. 100w. 3

3970 VITOUS, Miroslav. Purple. CBS/Sony SOPM 157 (Japan)
          CAD Aug. p17. 105w. 3

3971 WALDO, Terry. Snookums Rag. Dirty Shame 1237
          CO April p21. 300w. 5
          JJ May p46. 50w. 4

3971a WALDRON, Mal. Horo HLL 101-19 (Italy)
          JF No. 41 p65. 175w. 4

3971b WALDRON, Mal. Blues for Lady Day. Arista AL 1013
          DB Feb. 26 p22, 26. 275w. 2
          JA Summer p34. 150w. $3\frac{1}{2}$

3971c WALDRON, Mal. One and Two. Prestige P24068 (2 discs)
      (Reissue)
          CAD Oct. p26. 150w. 3
          CK Dec. p49. 25w. $3\frac{1}{2}$

3971d WALDRON, Mal. One for Lady. Catalyst CAT 7900 (Japan)
          RFJ Oct. p8. 275w. 3

3971e WALDRON, Mal. A Touch of the Blue. Enja 2062
          JJ May p34. 200w. 5

3972 WALLACE, Vince. Plays. AMP 001
          DB April 8 p30-2. 50w. 1

3973 WALLER, Fats. Vol. 3. Biograph BLP 1015Q
          RT May/June p7. 75w. 3

3974 WALLER, Fats. Vol. 11. RCA FPM 1-7048 (France) (Re-
      issue)
          JJ Feb. p42, 43. 150w. 5

3975 WALLER, Fats. Vol. 16. RCA FXM 1-7198 (France) (Re-
      issue)
            JJ   April   p38.   275w.   3
            RR   June   p84.   50w.   3

3976 WALLER, Fats. Vol. 17. RCA FXM 1-7282 (France) (Re-
      issue)
            JJ   Sept.   p40.   475w.   5

3977 WALLER, Fats. All That Jazz. DJM DJLMD 8003 (2 discs)
      (E) (Reissue)
            GR   Aug.   p352.   250w. $1\frac{1}{2}$

3978 WALLER, Fats. The Complete Fats Waller, Vol. 1. RCA
      AXM2-5511 (2 discs) (Reissue)
            CK   March   p48.   50w.   3
            CRE   March   p61.   325w. $3\frac{1}{2}$
            HF   Feb.   p128.   225w. $3\frac{1}{2}$
            MJ   March   p22-3. 75w. $3\frac{1}{2}$

3978a WALLER, Fats. In London. World Record Club SHB 29
      (E) (2 discs) (Reissue)
            ST   June-July p196-8. 350w.   4

3979 WALTON, Cedar. Beyond Mobius. RCA APL1-1435
            AU   Sept.   p88-9. 500w.   1
            MG   June   p52.   50w.   3
            PRM   May   p62.   650w.   3

3980 WALTON, Cedar. Firm Roots. Muse MR 5059
            CAD   May   p20.   75w.   1

3981 WALTON, Cedar. Mobius. RCA APL 1-1009
            DB   March 11 p24. 350w.   2
            JJ   Feb.   p38.   100w.   0
            SOU   Feb.   p50.   25w.   2
            SR   Nov.   p114.   350w. $4\frac{1}{2}$

3982 WALTON, Cedar. A Night at Boomer's, Vol. 1. Muse 5010
            CO   April   p21.   375w.   4

3983 WARREN, Earle. The Anglo-American All Stars. RCA LFL
      1-5066 (E)
            JJ   May   p44.   600w.   5

3984 WATROUS, Bill. Bone Straight Ahead. Famous Door
      HL0101
            CO   April   p21, 22. 350w.   4

3985 WATROUS, Bill. Manhattan Wildlife Refuge. Columbia KC
      33090
            SOU   Feb.   p38-9. 225w.   3

3986 WATROUS, Bill. The Tiger of San Pedro. Columbia PC
     33701
          DB   Jan. 15 p20. 375w. $4\frac{1}{2}$
          MJ   Jan. p21. 75w. $2\frac{1}{2}$

3987 WATTERS, Lu. Dawn Club 12010/1 (2 discs)
          JJ   May p40. 75w. $3\frac{1}{2}$

3988 WEATHER Report. Black Market. Columbia PC 34099
          CAC Aug. p180. 400w. $3\frac{1}{2}$
          CRA July p72-3. 275w. $3\frac{1}{2}$
          MM   June 26 p21. 200w. 3
          RR   July p80. 50w. $2\frac{1}{2}$

3989 WEATHER Report. Live in Tokyo. CBS/Sony 12-13XR (Japan)
     (2 discs)
          CAD Aug. p16, 17. 75w. 4

3990 WEATHER Report. Tale Spinnin'. Columbia PC33417. Cart.
     PCA 33417. Cass. PCT33417
          AU   Feb. p83-4. 1250w. 5
          SR   Sept. p103. 225w. 5

3991 WEBER, Eberhard. Yellow Fields. ECM 1066
          JF   No. 41 p60-1. 250w. 3
          MM   Feb. 7 p26. 600w. $3\frac{1}{2}$
          SOU May p46. 100w. $2\frac{1}{2}$

3992 WEBSTER, Ben. Atmosphere for Lovers and Thieves. Black
     Lion BL-111
          CO   April p22, 23. 250w. 5

3993 WEBSTER, Ben. Live at the Haarlemse Jazz Club. Cat LP
     11 (Holland)
          JJ   May p34, 36. 275w. 5

3994 WEBSTER, Ben. Live at Pio's. Enja 2038
          JJ   Feb. p42. 200w. 2

3995 WEBSTER, Ben. Saturday Night at the Montmartre. Black
     Lion BLP 30155
          JJ   May p44, 45. 275w. 5
          RR   June p83. 50w. 3

3996 WEBSTER, Ben and Harry Edison. Walkin' with Sweets.
     Verve 2317-109 (E) (Reissue)
          CAC Oct. p274. 175w. 4

3997 WEISBERG, Tim. Listen to the City. A&M SP 4545
          DB   Feb. 26 p30-1. 275w. 3
          MM   Jan. 24 p27. 250w. 2

3998 WELLSTOOD, Dick. Live at the Cookery. Chiaroscuro CR

139
    CAD   Feb.   p20-1. 50w. $3\frac{1}{2}$
    JJ   April   p38. 325w. 4
    SOU   May   p44. 400w. $3\frac{1}{2}$
    SR   April   p104. 200w. 3

3999 WELLSTOOD, Dick. Three Is Company. Sackville 2007 (Canada)
    CAD   Aug.   p21. 50w. 5

4000 WELLSTOOD, Dick. Walkin' with Wellstood. 77 SEU 12/51 (E)
    CO   April   p23. 300w. 5

4001 WELLSTOOD, Dick and Kenny Davern. Chiaroscuro CR 129
    SR   Feb.   p100. 200w. 5

4002 WELSH, Alex. Showcase 1. Black Lion BLP 12120 (E)
    JJ   April   p38. 250w. 5
    RR   June   p84. 50w. $2\frac{1}{2}$

4003 WELSH, Alex. Showcase 2. Black Lion BLP 12121 (E)
    JJ   Sept.   p40. 475w. 5
    MM   Dec. 25   p18. 175w. $2\frac{1}{2}$
    RR   Oct.   p102. 50w. $3\frac{1}{2}$

4004 WERNER, Lasse and Christie Boustedt. Kroff and Sjal. Dragon LP 2 (Sweden)
    CAD   June   p29. 50w. 3
    MM   Dec. 25   p18. 100w. $2\frac{1}{2}$

4005 WESTBROOK, Mike. Love/Dream and Variations. Transatlantic TRA323 (E)
    JJ   Oct.   p39. 600w. $4\frac{1}{2}$
    MM   Sept. 25   p26. 600w. $4\frac{1}{2}$
    RR   Nov.   p107. 100w. $2\frac{1}{2}$

4006 WESTBROOK, Mike. Plays for the Record. Transatlantic TRA 312 (E)
    RR   May   p75. 150w. 3

4007 WESTON, Randy. African Nite. Inner City IC 1013
    MJ   Dec.   p44. 75w. 3
    JF   No. 41   p63. 400w. 3

4008 WESTON, Randy. Blues to Africa. Arista AL 1014
    DB   Feb. 26   p22, 26. 275w. 3
    GR   Aug.   p352. 200w. 4
    JA   Summer   p34. 150w. $3\frac{1}{2}$
    SR   March   p103. 250w. 3

4009 WESTON, Randy. Carnival--Live at Montreux, 1974. Arista Freedom 1004

       GR   Aug.   p352.   200w.   3
       JA   Summer p34.   100w.   4

4010 WESTON, Randy. Informal Solo Piano. Hi-Fly P 101 (E)
       JJ   March p40.   525w.   5
       MM   July 31 p22.   275w.   3
       SOU July p102.   75w.   3

4011 WHEELER, Kenny. Gnu High. ECM ECM-1069. Cart. 8F-
1069. Cass. CF-1069
       CAD May p31.   125w.   4
       DB   Oct. 21 p31-2.   300w.   4
       JF   No. 41 p25.   75w.   4
       MG   June p50.   50w.   2
       MM   March 13 p26.   600w.   5
       SR   Aug. p89.   250w.   4

4012 WHITE, Andrew. Collage. Andrew's Music No. 14
       CAD Jan. p16.   250w.   3
       CAD April p34-5.   125w. $1\frac{1}{2}$
       CAD Feb. p25.   225w.   3

4013 WHITE, Andrew. Live at Foolery, vol. 2. Andrew's Music 9
       CAD March p30.   200w. $2\frac{1}{2}$

4014 WHITE, Lenny. Venusian Summer. Nemperor NE 435.
Cart. TP 435
       DB   March 25 p31-2.   350w. $3\frac{1}{2}$
       SR   April p104-7.   100w.   2

4015 WHITE, Michael. Go with the Flow. Impulse ASD-9281
       DB   March 27 p20.   150w. $2\frac{1}{2}$
       LP   July p10.   200w.   4

4016 WILBER, Bob. New Clarinet in Town. Classic Jazz CJ 8
       CO   Dec. p14.   325w.   3

4017 WILBER, Bob and Kenny Davern. Chalumean Blue/Soprano
Summit. Chiaroscuro 148 (2 discs)
       CAD Nov. p23.   100w.   3

4018 WILLIAMS, Al. Sundance. Renaissance 9565
       CAD Dec. p27.   150w. $3\frac{1}{2}$

4019-20 WILLIAMS, Buster. Pinnacle. Muse MR 5080
       CAD Feb. p22-3.   100w. $1\frac{1}{2}$
       DB   Aug. 12 p30.   250w. $3\frac{1}{2}$
       JJ   Dec. p39.   100w.   3

4021 WILLIAMS, Clarence. Country Goes to Town. RCA 741-058
(France) (Reissue)
       CO   Dec. p14.   850w.   3

4022 WILLIAMS, Claude. Call for the Fiddler. Steeplechase SCS
      1051 (Denmark)
            JJ Nov. p37. 350w. $3\frac{1}{2}$
            MM Nov. 20 p30. 400w. $3\frac{1}{2}$

4023 WILLIAMS, Cootie. Cootie and the Boys from Harlem. Tax
      m-8005 (Sweden) (Reissue)
            JJ April p39. 425w. 5

4024 WILLIAMS, Mary Lou. Free Spirits. Steeplechase SCS 1043
      (Denmark)
            JJ May p36. 325w. 2

4025 WILLIAMS, Mary Lou. Live at the Cookery. Chiaroscuro
      146
            CAD June p26. 100w. $3\frac{1}{2}$

4026 WILLIAMS, Mary Lou. Zodiac Suite. Folkways 32844 (Re-
      issue)
            CAD March p29. 75w. 2

4027 WILLIAMS, Mary Lou. Zoning. Mary M 103
            SR Oct. p96, 98. 425w. 4

4028 WILLIAMS, Tony. Believe It. Columbia PC 33836
            CRE July p18. 25w. 3
            DB Jan. 29 p20-1. 325w. 3
            GP Jan. p70. 200w. $4\frac{1}{2}$
            RR May p75. 50w. $2\frac{1}{2}$
            SR April p103. 150w. 2

4029 WILLIAMS, Tony. Million Dollar Legs. Columbia PC 34263
            CRA Nov. p70. 475w. 3
            RS Nov. 4 p72. 100w. 0

4030 WILSON, Teddy. London HMG 5020 (E)
            JJ June p39. 450w. 5
            MM May 22 p26. 350w. $3\frac{1}{2}$

4031 WILSON, Teddy. Tax m-8018
            JJ Feb. p44. 200w. 3

4032 WILSON, Teddy. And His All-Star Sextet. DJM DJML 076
      (E) (Reissue)
            MM May 22 p26. 350w. $3\frac{1}{2}$

4033 WILSON, Teddy. 'B' Flat Swing. Jazz Archives JA-28
            CAC Dec. p355. 150w. 4
            DB June 3 p31. 50w. 4
            JJ May p36. 325w. 5
            SOU April p48. 125w. 3

4034 WILSON, Teddy. In Tokyo. Sackville 2005 (Canada) (Reissue)

CAD   Aug.   p45.   175w.   3

4035 WILSON, Teddy. Radio Years, 1944.   London HMG 5020 (E)
(Reissue)
      GR   June p101.   175w.   4
      RR   June p83.   50w.   4

4036 WILSON, Teddy. Striding After Fats.   Black Lion BL 308
      SR   Nov.   p130.   75w. $3\frac{1}{2}$

4037 WINDING, Kai. Danish Blue.   Glendale Records 6003
      CAD   Oct.   p36.   100w.   4
      DB   June 3 p24-5.   250w. $3\frac{1}{2}$
      JJ   Aug.   p38.   100w. $3\frac{1}{2}$

4038 WINDING, Kai and J. J. Johnson. The Finest of Kai Winding
and J. J. Johnson. Bethlehem BCP-6001 (Reissue)
      CAD   April p36.   50w. $2\frac{1}{2}$
      SR   June p95.   150w.   4

4039 WOFFORD, Mike. Scott Joplin: Interpretations '76.   Flying
Dutchman BDL1-1372
      SR   Sept.   p113.   150w.   4

4040 WOODING, Sam. Bicentennial Jazz Vistas.   Twin Sign 1000
      CAD   Oct.   p10.   225w.   3
      ST   Oct. 11 p32-3.   250w. $2\frac{1}{2}$

4041 WOODS, Phil. Altology.   Prestige PR 24065 (2 discs) (Reissue)
      CAD   Oct.   p24.   100w.   4

4042 WOODS, Phil. Images.   RCA Gryphon BGL 1-1027
      DB   Jan. 15 p23.   200w.   3
      JJ   May p36.   175w.   3

4043 WOODS, Phil. New Music.   Testament T 4402
      CAD   April p33.   125w.   3
      SR   Jan.   p99.   150w.   3

4044 WOODS, Phil. The New Phil Woods Album.   RCA BGL1-1391.
Cart. BGS1-1391
      CAD   May p23.   125w.   4
      DB   Aug. 12 p28-9.   250w.   3
      MJ   Oct.   p22.   25w.   3
      SR   Sept.   p113.   275w.   3

4045 WOODS, Phil and His European Rhythm Machine.   Inner City
IC 1002
      CAD   June p28.   50w. $1\frac{1}{2}$
      DB   Nov. 4 p22.   325w.   5

4046 WORLD'S Greatest Jazz Band. Live at Lawrenceville School.

Flying Dutchman BDL1-1371 (E)
    CAD May p27. 150w. 4
    JJ July p38, 40. 375w. 5

4047 WORLD'S Greatest Jazz Band. Plays Cole Porter. World
    Jazz WJLP S 6
      AU Feb. p19-20. 1000w. 3

4048 WORLD'S Greatest Jazz Band. Plays Rodgers and Hart.
    World Jazz 7
      HF July p110-11. 350w. 3
      JJ Nov. p37. 400w. 3

4049 WYBLE, Jimmy. Diane. Vantage LP 502
      GP Nov. p104. 100w. 3

4050 YAMASHITA Trio. Clay. Enja 2052
      CO Dec. p14-5. 650w. $2\frac{1}{2}$
      JJ Jan. p40. 275w. 4

4051 YAMASHITO, Yosuke. Charisma. MPS BASF 226786 (E)
      MM June 19 p22. 750w. $4\frac{1}{2}$

4052 YOUNG, Larry. Larry Young's Fuel. Arista AL 4051
      DB April 8 p27. 275w. 2

4053 YOUNG, Leon. Ellington for Strings. One Up OU 2094 (E)
      ST Feb.-March p114. 100w. $2\frac{1}{2}$

4054 YOUNG, Lester. DJM DJLMD 8019 (E) (Reissue)
      JJ May p36, 38. 325w. $1\frac{1}{2}$

4055 YOUNG, Lester. Vol. 1. Archives of Jazz AJ 501 (Reissue)
      DB Feb. 12 p29-31. 200w. $4\frac{1}{2}$

4056 YOUNG, Lester. Vol. 4. Archives of Jazz AJ 505
      DB Feb. 12 p29-31. 200w. $4\frac{1}{2}$

4057 YOUNG, Lester. The Aladdin Sessions. Blue Note BN-LA
    456-H2 (2 discs) (Reissue)
      CO Feb. p17. 1050w. 4
      RR June p84. 50w. 4

4058 YOUNG, Lester. The Alternative Lester. Tax m-8000
      JJ May p45, 46. 625w. 5

4059 YOUNG, Lester. The Complete Savoy Recordings. Savoy
    SJL 2202 (2 discs). Cart. SJ8 2202 (Reissue)
      CAD Nov. p26. 150w. 3
      JA Summer p41-2. 100w. 5
      JJ Dec. p39. 650w. 4
      PRM May p63. 50w. 3
      SR Nov. p132. 125w. $2\frac{1}{2}$

388   Record Reviews, 1976

4060 YOUNG, Lester. Jammin' with Lester. Jazz Archives JA-18
         SR June p90. 1150w. 4½

4061 YOUNG, Lester. Lester Swings. Verve 2783 066 (E) (2
      discs) (Reissue)
         JJ July p40. 825w. 4½
         MM July 17 p26. 875w. 3½

4062 YOUNG, Lester. Newly Discovered Performances, Volume 1.
      ESP-Disk ESP-3017
         SR June p90. 1150w. 4½

4063 YOUNG, Lester. Prez in Europe. Onyx 218
         CO April p23, 24. 450w. 4

4064 YOUNG, Lester. Prez and Teddy and Oscar. Verve VE
      2-2502 (2 discs) (Reissue)
         CAD Nov. p26. 150w. 3
         DB Oct. 7 p32-3. 150w. 4
         JA Summer p40-1. 175w. 4½
         MJ Oct. p52. 50w. 3

4065 YOUNG, Lester/Yusef Lateef. Sax Masters. Vogue VJP
      512 (2 discs) (France) (Reissue)
         MM Nov. 6 p25. 300w. 2½
         RR April p78. 150w. 2½

4066 YOUNG, Smokey/Norris Turney. The Boys from Dayton.
      Master Jazz Recordings MJR 8130
         HF June p112. 300w. 2½
         JJ April p39. 275w. 4

4067 ZADLO, Leszek. Inner Silence. PSJ Klub Plytowy Z-S-3XW-
      549 (Poland)
         CO April p24. 700w. 2

4068 ZAPATA, Emiliano. Viva. Impulse EMPL 8003 (E)
         MM March 20 p24. 75w. 0

4069 ZEITLIN, Denny. Expansion. 1750 Arch Records 1758
         CK Aug. p45. 225w. 2
         JJ Oct. p39. 350w. 4

4070 ZIMMERMAN, Richard. Scott Joplin, the Entertainer. Olym-
      pic 7116
         AU Nov. p114. 150w. 3½

4071 ZUKOFSKY, Paul. Classic Rags. Vanguard SVR 350SD
         RT Sept./Oct. p5-6. 125w. 4

BLUES

This section comprises material generally classified by collectors as pre-World War II or post-World War II vocal blues, and based on the two major discographies of Godrich and Dixon, and Leadbitter and Slavens. Blues music is often of two types--country, rural, solo, and acoustic; or electric, amplified, and urban with ensemble playing. The former has been around since before the turn of the century; however, the latter is a more recent development, often called "Chicago blues" and generally attributed to Muddy Waters but also having roots in the string bands and the Mississippi Delta. Heavy white blues bands are in the ROCK category, for they have used the technical aspects of blues as a format, not as a life style. Instrumental blues is more properly JAZZ, although the odd instrumental turns up on an album of vocals.

Scholars and collectors have tried to break blues into manageable forms with partial success. Regional styles, time periods, format of presentation, type of instrumentation, individuals--the blues get worked over as much as the grieving performer. This accounts for the vast number of anthologized offerings and the responses of the so-called "bootleggers."

Anyone can play the blues, for it is a simple technical form of music. Thus, all interest in the blues is dependent on the performer. But not everyone can feel the blues, with the message to be conveyed being essentially one of emotion. Real blues singers used the blues therapeutically to escape from their situation. They stood outside, looking in while singing about their problems. It always felt so good to a blues singer when he finished his song, for he "talked it out" as many people in therapy do. Most typical white blues singers cannot feel the blues because they have not experienced it. They see injustices and become disturbed; the typical black blues singer is the actual recipient of those injustices. He not only sees it, but also he lives it. Thus, for all purposes, the typical white singer cannot get into the blues.

Many blues records are reviewed only once or twice in a well-covered field. Besides the British publication Blues Unlimited and the American Living Blues, blues music is proportionately well off in all jazz magazines, some folk, some rock, and some general publications. Foreign language magazines exist in Japan, France, Germany, Sweden and other countries. "The blues is everywhere" is a true statement indeed. While Blues Unlimited stands out for its

389

convincing rave reviews, ephemeral publications present their fair share of glossies that only serve notice to collectors that records exist and are now on the market.   Many such publications exist for a short period of time, ceasing to exist for a multitude of reasons.

For reissued material, the reviews themselves often tend only to be notices explaining that certain records are now available for purchase; hence, on our rating scale, there is a heavy preponderance of $2\frac{1}{2}$ to $3\frac{1}{2}$ ratings.   The collector knows what he wants, and the reviews only interest him for consideration of sound quality, duplicated tracks on existing albums, and additional biographical information not easily obtained elsewhere.

New material seems to be exceedingly difficult to evaluate. Reviewers appear to be on safe ground with reissues, but uncertain with new post-war material.   The case has been made, quite successfully, that electric blues has not matured beyond its mid-50's development.   Nothing new is being played and the hordes of white imitators are prolonging the status quo.   The jazz magazines tend to be more realistic about the music; if it is good, then it is ranked as such; if it is bad, then it is shot down.   Tainted by white commercialism, certain "Chicago bluesmen" are virtually ignored or condemned by the blues press while given rave send-ups by the rock media.   Thus, these groups are regarded by both types of media as having sold out from one side to another.   All the media seems to have agreed that original electric blues have oversaturated the market.   Artists such as B. B. King, James Cotton, Buddy Guy and Junior Wells, and even Muddy Waters himself have been battered around by the critics who are still waiting for that "definitive, next album."   Yet the records sell well and this is yet another example of there being no correlation between critical acclaim and sales. And in recent years the number of new titles has declined as older bluesmen die.

According to the 1976 reviews, the following are the best discs:

CHENIER, Clifton. Boogalusa Boogie. Arhoolie 1076
HOPKINS, Lightnin'. Live at the Bird Lounge. 2 discs. Bulldog
        BDL 1010 (E)
ROBINSON, Fenton. Somebody Loan Me a Dime. Alligator 4705
TAYLOR, Hound Dog. Beware of the Dog. Alligator 4707

4072 ALEXANDER, Dave. The Dirt on the Ground. Arhoolie 1071
        CO Feb.   p18.   300w.   4
        JJ Feb.   p26.   375w.   3
        RR Feb.   p67.   50w.   3

4073 ALLISON, Luther. Luther's Blues. Gordy 967
        LB Nov.-Dec.   p33-4.   100w.   4

4074 ALLISON, Luther. Night Life. Gordy 964

LB Nov.-Dec. p33-4. 100w. 2
RS June 3 p77. 300w. $3\frac{1}{2}$

4075 ARNOLD, Billy Boy. Blow the Back Off It. Red Lightnin
RL 0012 (E) (Reissue)
BM May p37. 300w. 2

4076 ARNOLD, Billy Boy. Session. Vogue 30285 (France) (Reissue)
LB March-April p36. 300w. $2\frac{1}{2}$

4077 ARNOLD, Billy Boy. Sinner's Prayer. Red Lightnin RL
0014 (2 discs) (E) (Reissue)
MM Nov. 13 p30. 300w. 3

4078 ARNOLD, Kokomo. Bad Luck Blues, 1934-39. MCA 510
116 (France) (Reissue)
BM Oct. p44. 150w. 4

4079 ARNOLD, Kokomo/Casey Bill Weldon. Bottleneck Guitar
Trendsetters of the 1930's (Anthology). Yazoo L-1049 (Re-
issue)
CO May p17, 18. 250w. 4

4080 BAKER, McHouston. Mississippi Delta Dues. Blue Star
80605 (France) (Reissue)
CZM June p41-2. 25w. $1\frac{1}{2}$
LB July-Aug. p42-3. 275w. $2\frac{1}{2}$

4081 BASIE, Count & Joe Williams. Swingin' with the Count.
Verve 2317111 (E) (Reissue)
JJ Aug. p32. 325w. $4\frac{1}{2}$

4082 BELL, Carey. Last Night. ABC Bluesway 6079
LB May/June p50. 275w. 4

4083 BIG Maceo--Volume 1. RCA FXM 1-7204 (France) (Reissue)
BM Oct. p44. 350w. 5
JJ June p30. 200w. 3
RR June p83. 25w. $4\frac{1}{2}$

4084 BLAKE, Blind. Rope Stretchin' Blues. Biograph 12037 (Reissue)
LB May/June p48-9. 250w. 5

4085 BLAND, Bobby. Dreamer. ABC Dunhill DSX-50169
LB March-April p33-4. 200w. $4\frac{1}{2}$

4086 BLAND, Bobby. Get Down with Bobby Bland. ABC Dunhill
ABCD-895
BM Oct. 1975 p27. 200w. 3
CZM Jan. p57. 600w. 3
DB Jan. 29 p24. 200w. 2

LB   March-April p33-4.   200w.   3

4087 BLAND, Bobby. His California Album.   ABC Dunhill DSX-
      50163
          LB   March-April p33-4.   200w. $4\frac{1}{2}$

4088 BREWER, Jim. Jim Brewer.   Philo 1003
          CO   Feb. p24.   350w.   4
          LB   July-Aug. p46-7.   350w.   4

4089 BROONZY, Big Bill. All Them Blues.   DJM DJLMD 8009
      (E) (Reissue)
          BU   Jan.-Feb. p28.   500w. $2\frac{1}{2}$
          RR   Feb. p67.   50w.   3

4090 BROWN, Buster. Raise a Ruckus Tonight.   DJM 22037 (E)
      (Reissue)
          BM   Oct. p43-4.   150w.   3
          MM   Dec. 25 p17.   150w.   3

4091 BROWN, Charles. Great Rhythm and Blues Oldies Volume 2.
      Blues Spectrum 102
          CO   May p16, 17.   225w.   4

4092 BROWN, Clarence "Gatemouth".   Down South ... in the Bayou
      Country.   Barclay 90 002 (France)
          CMP   May p15.   149w.   5

4093 BROWN, Clarence "Gatemouth".   Gate's on the Heat.   Blue
      Star 80603 (France) (Reissue)
          LB   July-Aug. p43.   100w. $2\frac{1}{2}$

4094 BROWN, J. T. Rockin' with J T.   Flyright LP 4712 (E)
          BM   June p36.   225w.   5
          CZM   June p34-5.   200w.   4

4095 BROWN, Olive. And Her Blues Chasers.   Jim Taylor Pre-
      sents JTP 103
          JJ   Feb. p27.   200w. $3\frac{1}{2}$
          LB   May/June p50.   225w.   5

4096 BROWN, Olive. The New Empress of Blues.   Jazz Odyssey
      013 (E)
          RR   Feb. p67.   100w.   3

4097 BURNS, Eddie "Guitar".   Detroit Blackbottom.   Big Bear (E)
          MM   Jan. 24 p30.   350w. $2\frac{1}{2}$

4098 BURRIS, J. C. One of These Mornings.   Arhoolie 1075
          JJ   Aug. p32-3.   400w.   5

4099 BUTTERFIELD, Paul. Put It in Your Ear.   Bearsville BR
      6960.   Cart. M8 6960

CRA April p69-70. 550w. $2\frac{1}{2}$
CRE July p12. 50w. $3\frac{1}{2}$
GM May p46. 50w. 4
MM March 27 p28. 50w. $1\frac{1}{2}$
RS May 6 p74. 175w. 0
SR June p77. 175w. 2

4100 CANNON, Gus. 1927-1930 Complete. Herwin 208 (Reissue)
CO Feb. p25. 475w. 5
LB March/April p47-8. 275w. $4\frac{1}{2}$

4101 CHARITY, Pernell. The Virginian. Trix
GP Dec. p104. 125w. 3

4102 CHENIER, Clifton. Bayou Soul. Crazy Cajun 1002
LB Jan./Feb. p30. 375w. 5

4103 CHENIER, Clifton. Bogalosa Boogie. Arhoolie 1076
CK Aug. p46. 50w. 4
JJ Aug. p33. 350w. 3
SR Nov. p120. 150w. 4

4104 CHENIER, Clifton. Out West. Arhoolie 1072
LB Jan./Feb. p30. 375w. 5

4105 CLIMAX Blues Band. Gold Plated. Sire 7523
MM Nov. 13 p29. 750w. $3\frac{1}{2}$
RR Dec. p99. 175w. 4

4106 COTTON, James. High Energy. Buddah BDS 5650
CAD May p26. 100w. 2
DB May 20 p32-3. 125w. $3\frac{1}{2}$
LB March/April p34. 300w. 4
MG March p43. 50w. 4

4107 COTTON, James. Live and on the Move. Buddah 5661-2
(2 discs)
CAD Oct. p32, 33. 100w. $2\frac{1}{2}$
LB July-Aug. p38-9. 300w. $4\frac{1}{2}$

4108 COTTON, James. 100% Cotton. Buddah BDS 5620
LB March-April p34. 300w. 4

4109 COX, Ida. Volume 2--1923-24. Fountain FB 304 (E) (Re-
issue)
JJ Oct. p31. 525w. 5
MM Dec. 25 p18. 300w. $2\frac{1}{2}$
RR Dec. p101. 175w. 4

4110 CRAYTON, Pee Wee. Great Rhythm and Blues Oldies,
Volume 5. Blues Spectrum 105
CO May p16, 17. 225w. 5
LB March/April p46-7. 450w. 4

4111 CRUDUP, Arthur. That's Alright Mama. DJM DJSLM 2025
      (E) (Reissue)
            DB June p36. 200w. 4
            MM May 15 p27. 350w. $4\frac{1}{2}$

4112 DAVIS, Blind John. Alive, "Live" and Well. Chrischaa CB
      30. 3301 (West Germany)
            BU May-June p32-3. 350w. $4\frac{1}{2}$

4113 DAWKINS, Jimmy. Blisterstring. Delmark DS 641
            CAD Dec. p30. 100w. $3\frac{1}{2}$
            GP Nov. p104. 125w. $2\frac{1}{2}$

4114 DIXON, Floyd. Opportunity Blues. Route 66 KIX 1 (Sweden)
            CAD Nov. p16, 18. 125w. $4\frac{1}{2}$

4115 DIXON, Willie. Peace. Ovation
            OLR March p39-40. 25w. 3

4116 DORSEY, George Tom. Come on Mama Do That Dance.
      Yazoo L-1041 (Reissue)
            CO June p18. 300w. 4

4117 DOUGLAS, K. C. The Country Boy. Arhoolie 1073
            CO June p18. 275w. 4
            LB Sept./Oct. p39. 125w. 4

4118 EDWARDS, Charles. Good Rockin' Charles. Mr. Blues 7601
            CZM June p36-7. 275w. $3\frac{1}{2}$
            LB July-Aug. p36. 400w. $4\frac{1}{2}$

4119 ELLIS, Big Chief. Trix 3316
            LB Nov.-Dec. p37-8. 350w. 3

4120 FLOYD, Harmonica Frank. Adelphi AD 1023
            JJ Nov. p27. 375w. $2\frac{1}{2}$

4121 FLOYD, Harmonica Frank. Great Original Recordings of.
      Puritan 3003 (Reissue)
            CAD April p30. 175w. 4
            JEMF Spring p52. 250w. 3

4122 FROST, Frank. Frank Frost. Jewel LPS 5013
            CO June p20. 300w. 4

4123 FULLER, Blind Boy/ Blind Willie McTell. MCA 3523 (Japan)
      (Reissue)
            LB May-June p39. 350w. $4\frac{1}{2}$

4124 FULSON, Lowell. Chess Blues Masters Series 2 ACMB-205
      (2 discs) (Reissue)
            CAD Oct. p22, 23. 100w. 4

4125 FULSON, Lowell. The Ol' Blues Singer. Granite GS 1006
         CAD   April p31-2. 150w. $3\frac{1}{2}$
         DB   May 20 p32. 125w. $3\frac{1}{2}$
         HF   June p104. 150w. $1\frac{1}{2}$
         LB   Nov.-Dec. p38. 200w. 0
         MM   March 27 p27. 200w. $2\frac{1}{2}$

4126 GANT, Cecil. Cecil Boogie. Flyright 4714 (E) (Reissue)
         JJ   Nov. p27-8. 425w. 2

4127 GANT, Cecil. Rock Little Baby. Flyright 4710 (E) (Reissue)
         BM   Nov. p48. 300w. 3
         LB   May-June p44-5. 250w. $4\frac{1}{2}$

4128 GRIFFITH, Shirley. Mississippi Blues. Blue Goose 2011
         LB   Sept./Oct. p39. 125w. 5

4129 GUITAR Shorty. Alone on His Field. Trix 3306
         GP   April p79. 50w. 4

4130 HELFER, Edwin. Boogie Piano Chicago Style. Bear 11 (E)
         JJ   June p32. 250w. 4
         MM   Aug. 7 p19. 150w. 3

4131 HINES, Earl and Jimmy Rushing. Blues & Things. Master
      Jazz MJR 8101
         LB   May-June p38-9. 175w. $4\frac{1}{2}$

4132 HOLMES, Groove & Jimmy Witherspoon. Cry the Blues.
      Bulldog BDL 1012 (Reissue)
         JJ   Aug. p32. 200w. 2

4133 HOMESICK, James. Chicago Blues Festival, Volume 1.
      Black and Blue 33034 (France)
         CO   April p17. 200w. 2

4134 HOMESICK, James. Home Sweet Homesick James. Big
      Bear 10 (E)
         JJ   April p33. 250w. $2\frac{1}{2}$
         RR   June p83. 50w. $1\frac{1}{2}$

4135 HOOKER, Earl, Little Walter and Muddy Waters. At Pepper's
      Lounge Chicago. Rarities 25 (E)
         LB   July-Aug. p47. 425w. 0

4136 HOOKER, John Lee. Blues Before Sunrise. Bulldog BDL
      1011 (Reissue)
         BM   Nov. p48. 150w. 4
         JJ   Aug. p32. 200w. 5
         MM   Aug. 28 p21. 375w. 3

4137 HOOKER, John Lee. Born in Mississippi, Raised up in Ten-
      nessee. ABC 768

        LB   Nov.-Dec. p36. 50w. 0

4138   HOOKER, John Lee. Free Beer and Chicken. ABC ABCD-
       838
          CO   March p24. 250w. 0
          LB   Nov.-Dec. p36. 50w. 0

4139   HOOKER, John Lee. In Person. Dynasty 7301
          DB   May 20 p33. 150w. $4\frac{1}{2}$

4140   HOOKER, John Lee. Kabuki Wuki. Bluesway 6052
          LB   Nov.-Dec. p36. 50w. 0

4141   HOOKER, John Lee. Never Get Out of These Blues Alive.
       ABC 736
          LB   Nov.-Dec. p36. 50w. 0

4142   HOPKINS, Lightnin'. All Them Blues. DJM MD 8016 (E)
       (Reissue)
          BM   May p37. 225w. 3
          JJ   April p34. 275w. $4\frac{1}{2}$
          MM April 3 p54. 375w. $4\frac{1}{2}$
          RR   June p83. 50w. $3\frac{1}{2}$

4143   HOPKINS, Lightnin'. The Best of Lightnin' Hopkins. Soufflé
       SO 2013
          LB   Sept./Oct. p40. 225w. 3

4144   HOPKINS, Lightnin'. Live at the Bird Lounge. Bulldog BDL
       1010 (E) (2 discs)
          BM   Nov. p48. 200w. 4
          JJ   Aug. p32. 200w. 5
          MM Nov. 13 p30. 250w. $3\frac{1}{2}$

4145   HOPKINS, Lightnin'. Low Down Dirty Blues. Mainstream
       405 (Reissue)
          CO   March p24. 275w. 3

4146   HORTON, Walter and Carey Bell. Alligator 4702
          SO   Jan./Feb. p45, 47. 325w. $4\frac{1}{2}$

4147   HOUSE, Son. The Real Delta Blues. Blue Goose 2016
          LB   May-June p43. 225w. 4

4148   HOWLIN' Wolf. Chess Blues Masters Series 2ACMB-201 (2
       discs) (Reissue)
          CAD Oct. p22. 75w. 5

4149   HOWLIN' Wolf. The Back Door Wolf. Chess 50045
          LB   Jan.-Feb. p43. 280w. $4\frac{1}{2}$

4150   HOWLIN' Wolf. Change My Way. Chess 418 (Reissue)
          LB   Jan.-Feb. p43. 200w. $4\frac{1}{2}$

4151 HOWLIN' Wolf and Muddy Waters. London Revisited. Chess 60026
        LB Jan.-Feb. p43. 190w. 2

4152 HURT, John. Volume One of a Legacy. Legacy CLPS-1068
        CAD Sept. p32. 200w. 4
        GP April p79. 150w. $3\frac{1}{2}$
        LP Jan. p16-7. 250w. $3\frac{1}{2}$

4153 HUTTO, J. B. Slidewinder. Delmark 636
        CAD Jan. p27. 400w. 3

4154 JAMES, Elmore. All Them Blues. DJM DJLMD 8008 (E) (Reissue)
        BM April p35. 400w. 5
        JJ Feb. p32. 400w. $2\frac{1}{2}$

4155 JAMES, Elmore/Eddie Taylor. Street Talkin'. Muse 5087 (Reissue)
        CAD Nov. p29. 75w. 3

4156-7 JEFFERSON, Blind Lemon. Milestone M 47022 (2 discs) (Reissue)
        CAD April p37-8. 200w. 3
        CO March p24, 25. 375w. 4
        CO March p28. 375w. 3
        LB May-June p44. 225w. 4
        LB July-Aug. p47. 275w. $4\frac{1}{2}$
        SR July p90, 91. 275w. 4

4158 JOHNSON, Henry "Rufe". The Union County Flash. Trix 3304
        GP April p79. 25w. 4

4159 JOHNSON, Herman E. Louisiana Country Blues. Arhoolie 1060
        LB Sept./Oct. p42. 250w. 5

4160 JOHNSON, Lonnie. Mr. Johnson's Blues, 1926-32. Mamlish S 3807 (Reissue)
        JJ Nov. p32. 425w. 2
        LB Nov.-Dec. p32-3. 300w. 4

4161 JOHNSON, Luther. On the Road Again. Black and Blue 33 509 (France)
        CAD May p31. 100w. $3\frac{1}{2}$

4162 JONES, Eddie Lee. Yonder Go That Old Black Dog. Testament 2224
        CAD May p30. 100w. $3\frac{1}{2}$
        LB May/June p47. 175w. 5

4163 KATZMAN, Nick and Ruby Green. Mississippi River Bottom

Blues. Kicking Mule KM 111
    GP Nov. p104. 50w. $2\frac{1}{2}$

4164 KATZMAN, Nick and Ruby Green. Panic When the Sun Goes
Down. Kicking Mule
    MM April 3 p29. 50w. $2\frac{1}{2}$

4165 KING, Albert. Albert. Utopia 1-1731
    CAD Oct. p43. 125w. 3
    RS Dec. 16 p93. 200w. 3

4166 KING, Albert. I Wanna Get Funky. Stax 5505
    LB July-Aug. p36. 200w. 4

4167 KING, Albert. Truckload of Lovin'. Utopia BUL1-1387
    AU July p75. 100w. 1
    BM Nov. p45. 125w. 2
    DB Oct. 7 p24-5. 300w. 4
    JJ Nov. p32. 250w. 0
    LB July/Aug. p36. 200w. 4
    RR Dec. p99. 75w. $3\frac{1}{2}$
    RR Dec. p101. 25w. 2

4168 KING, B. B. Friends. ABC 825
    LB May-June p36. 150w. 0

4169 KING, B. B. Lucille Talks Back. ABC 898
    CRA April p77. 250w. 3
    DB May 20 p22. 175w. $2\frac{1}{2}$
    LB May/June p36. 150w. $2\frac{1}{2}$
    LP March p27. 50w. 3
    RS Feb. 12 p92. 175w. 0
    SR March p84. 125w. 0

4170 KING, B. B. To Know You Is to Love You. ABC 794
    LB May-June p36. 150w. 3

4171 KING, B. B. and Bobby Bland. Together Again ... Live.
Impulse ASD-9317
    CAD Oct. p41, 42. 175w. 4
    GP Sept. p87. 25w. $3\frac{1}{2}$
    LB Nov.-Dec. p34. 250w. $3\frac{1}{2}$
    RS Aug. 26 p65. 275w. $2\frac{1}{2}$

4172 KING, B. B. and Bobby Bland. Together for the First
Time ... Live. ABC Dunhill DSY-50190/2 (2 discs)
    CO March p26. 275w. 4
    LB May-June p36. 150w. 3
    SR March p76. 225w. $4\frac{1}{2}$

4173 KING, Freddie. Burglar. RSO 4803
    LB May/June p49. 375w. 0
    SR June p81. 200w. $3\frac{1}{2}$

4174 KING, Freddie. Getting Ready. Shelter 52021 (Reissue)
      CZM June p34. 175w. $2\frac{1}{2}$

4175 KING, Freddie. Larger Than Life. RSO SO 4811
      BM   April p32. 250w. 3
      CAD Feb.   p29-30. 50w. 3
      CRA Jan.   p79. 100w. 3
      CZM June p32. 150w. 3
      DB   April 8 p29-30. 300w. 4

4176 KIRKLAND, Eddie. The Devil and Other Blues Demons.
      Trix 3308
      CO   Sept. p14, 15. 325w. 3
      LB   Jan./Feb. p28-30. 400w. 3

4177 LATIMORE, Benny. Latimore. Glades 6502
      LB   Sept./Oct. p541. 225w. 0

4178 LATIMORE, Benny. Latimore III. Glades 7505
      CZM June p38. 125w. 4
      LB   Sept./Oct. p41. 225w. $3\frac{1}{2}$

4179 LATIMORE, Benny. More ... More ... More Latimore.
      Glades 6503
      LB   March/April p47. 250w. 4

4180 LEE, John. Down at the Depot. Rounder 2010
      LB   Jan.-Feb. p44. 425w. 4

4181 LEWIS, Furry. Fourth & Beale. Blue Star 80602 (France)
      (Reissue)
      CZM June p41-2. 25w. $3\frac{1}{2}$
      LB   July-Aug. p43. 125w. $4\frac{1}{2}$

4182 LEWIS, Furry. In His Prime 1927-28. Yazoo 1050 (Reissue)
      GP   Jan. p71. 25w. 3

4183 The LITTLE Hatchet Band. Live. M&M3001 (West Germany)
      LB   July-Aug. p37. 200w. 4

4184 LITTLE Milton. Chess Blues Masters Series 2 ACMB-204
      (2 discs) (Reissue)
      CAD Oct. p22, 24. 100w. 4

4185 LITTLE Milton. Friend of Mine. Glades 7508
      RS   Nov. 18 p81-2. 275w. 3

4186 LITTLE Milton. Raise a Little Sand. Red Lightin' 0011 (E)
      (Reissue)
      LB   May-June p42. 400w. $4\frac{1}{2}$

4187 LITTLE Walter. Chess Blues Masters Series 2ACMB-202
      (2 discs) (Reissue)

CAD   Oct.   p22.   150w.   5

4188   LITTLE Walter.   Confessin' the Blues.   Chess 416 (Reissue)
         CO   April p21.   250w.   4
         LB   Jan./Feb.   p28.   300w.   4

4189   LITTLEJOHN, Johnny.   Funky from Chicago.   ABC Bluesway
       6069
         LB   March/April p48.   225w.   4

4190   LOCKWOOD, Robert.   Blues Live in Japan.   Advent 2807 (Re-
       issue)
         AU   Nov.   p115-6.   450w. $3\frac{1}{2}$
         BU   May-June p30.   450w. $4\frac{1}{2}$
         DB   May 20 p31.   325w. $4\frac{1}{2}$
         LB   July-Aug.   p37.   350w.   3
         JJ   Nov.   p32.   225w. $2\frac{1}{2}$
         RS   July 1 p64.   150w.   3

4191   LOCKWOOD, Robert Jr.   Contrasts.   Trix 3307
         LB   Jan./Feb.   p28-30.   400w. $3\frac{1}{2}$
         RS   July 1 p64.   100w.   4

4192   LOCKWOOD, Robert Jr.   Steady Rollin Man.   Delmark DS
       630
         RS   July 1 p64.   100w. $2\frac{1}{2}$

4193   LOFTON, Cripple Clarence.   Euphonic Sound ESR1208
         CAD   Jan.   p26.   250w.   3

4194   LUCAS, Bill.   Lazy Bill Lucas.   Philo 1007
         CO   Sept.   p18, 19.   325w.   4
         ETH   Sept.   p617-8.   500w. $3\frac{1}{2}$
         LB   July-Aug.   p44-5.   200w. $3\frac{1}{2}$

4195   MABON, Willie.   The Comeback.   Big Bear 9 (E)
         MM   Feb. 7 p32.   75w.   4

4196   McCLENNAN, Tommy.   Travelin' Highway Man.   Flyright
       LP 112 (E) (Reissue)
         BM   May p37.   200w.   4
         JJ   Feb. p32, 34.   375w. $2\frac{1}{2}$
         MM   Dec. 25 p19.   275w. $4\frac{1}{2}$

4197   McDOWELL, Fred.   Keep Your Lamp Trimmed and Burning.
       Arhoolie 1068
         CO   Sept.   p20.   350w.   5
         LB   March/April p50, 53.   275w.   4

4198   McDOWELL, Fred.   Mississippi Fred McDowell 1904-1972.
       Just Sunshine 4
         LB   March/April p50, 53.   275w.   4

4199 McTELL, Blind Willie. Death Cell Blues. Biograph BLPC-
      14
          LB Sept./Oct. p41-2. 350w. 4

4200 McVIE, Christine. The Legendary Christine Perfect Album.
      Sire SASD 7522. Cart. 8147-7522H. Cass. 5147-7522H
          SR Dec. p112, 114. 300w. $2\frac{1}{2}$

4201 MARS, Johnny. Bear 12 (E)
          JJ June p35. 200w. $\frac{1}{2}$
          RR June p83. 50w. 3

4202-3 MARTIN, Bogan & Armstrong. Flying Fish 003
          LB Sept./Oct. p42. 300w. 5
          OTM Spring p25-6. 450w. $3\frac{1}{2}$
          SO Vol. 24 no. 6. p44. 200w. 3

4204 MEMPHIS Slim. RCA 730.581 (France) (Reissue)
          LB May-June p41. 200w. 4

4205 MEMPHIS Slim. RCA FXM 1-7215 (France) (Reissue)
          BM Aug. p43. 100w. 4
          JJ June p30. 200w. 4
          RR June p83. 25w. $4\frac{1}{2}$

4206 MEMPHIS Slim. All Them Blues. DJM DJLMD 8012 (E)
      (Reissue)
          BU Jan.-Feb. p28-9. 500w. 3
          RR Feb. p67. 25w. 2

4207 MEMPHIS Slim. The Blues Is Everywhere. GNP Crescendo
      10002 (Reissue)
          LB May-June p41-2. 200w. $4\frac{1}{2}$

4208 MEMPHIS Slim. Born with the Blues. Jewel 5004
          LB May-June p41-2. 200w. 5

4209 MEMPHIS Slim. Chicago Boogie. Black Lion BLP 30196 (E)
          BM Nov. p48. 200w. 3
          JJ Sept. p34. 275w. $2\frac{1}{2}$
          MM Oct. 16 p29. 250w. 3
          RR Oct. p102. 50w. $3\frac{1}{2}$

4210 MEMPHIS Slim. Favorite Blues Singers. Folkways 2387
          LB May-June p41. 200w. 4

4211 MEMPHIS Slim. Going Back to Tennessee. Barclay 90034
      (France)
          BM May p37. 50w. 1
          RR Feb. p67. 25w. 2

4212 MEMPHIS Slim. The Legacy of the Blues. Vol. 7. Sonet
      647 (E)

LB   May-June   p41-2.   200w. $4\frac{1}{2}$

4213   MEMPHIS Slim.   Raining the Blues.   Fantasy 24705 (2 discs)
(Reissue)
LB   May-June   p41-2.   200w. $4\frac{1}{2}$

4214   MEMPHIS Slim.   Rock Me Baby.   Black Lion 155
LB   May-June   p41-2.   200w.   4

4215   MEMPHIS Slim and Buddy Guy.   Southside Reunion.   Blue
Star 80601 (France) (Reissue)
CZM   June   p41-2.   25w.   4
LB   July-Aug.   p43.   100w. $4\frac{1}{2}$

4216   The MISSISSIPPI Sheiks.   Stop and Listen Blues.   Mamlish
S-3804 (Reissue)
BU   May-June   p30-1.   400w. $4\frac{1}{2}$
CO   Sept.   p21.   225w.   5

4217   MISSISSIPPI Sheiks/Beale Street Sheiks.   Biograph 12041 (Reissue)
LB   May/June   p52.   400w.   4

4218   MUDDY Waters.   Chess Blues Masters Series 2ACMB-203
(2 discs) (Reissue)
CAD   Oct.   p22.   75w.   4

4219   MUDDY Waters.   Can't Get No Gridin'.   Chess 50023
LB   Sept./Oct.   p38.   275w.   3

4220   MUDDY Waters.   Unk in Funk.   Chess 60031
LB   Sept./Oct.   p38.   175w.   0

4221-2   MUDDY Waters.   Woodstock Album.   Chess 60035
LB   Sept./Oct.   p38.   175w.   0

4223   MUSSELWHITE, Charlie.   Leave the Blues to Us.   Capitol
ST 11450
CRA   Jan.   p78-9.   150w. $4\frac{1}{2}$
LP   March   p17.   100w.   5

4224   MUSSELWHITE, Charlie.   Goin' Back Down South.   Arhoolie
1974
CO   Sept.   p22, 23.   275w.   0

4225   The NIGHTHAWKS.   Open All Night.   Adelphi 4105
CAD   Oct.   p44.   175w.   5

4226   PAGE, Jimmy.   Special Early Works (featuring Sonny Boy
Williamson).   Springboard 4038
LB   May-June   p38.   375w. $2\frac{1}{2}$

4227   PARKER, Junior.   You Don't Have to Be Black to Love the

Blues. Groove Merchant GM-502
LP July p13. 125w. 4

4228 PEG Leg Sam. Going Train Blues. Blue Labor BL105
CAD Oct. p40. 150w. 5

4229 PEG Leg Sam. The Last Medicine Show. Flyright 507/8
(E) (2 discs)
LB March/April p45-6. 350w. 5

4230 PIANO Red. Ain't Goin' to Be Your Low Down Dog No More.
Black Lion BL-311
BM May p37. 150w. 3
CAD June p29. 125w. 3
SR Oct. p110. 125w. 4

4231 PLEASANT, Cousin Joe. New Orleans. Bluesway 6078
CO Feb. p26. 150w. 2

4232 PROFESSOR Longhair. New Orleans Piano. Atlantic 7225
(Reissue)
CO April p14. 200w. 4

4233 PROFESSOR Longhair. Rock 'n' Roll Gumbo. Blue Star
80606 (France)
LB July-Aug. p42. 275w. 5

4234 RACHELL, Yank. Blue Goose 2010
LB March-April p35. 250w. 4

4235 RACHELL, Yank. Mandolin Blues. Delmark 606
ETH Sept. p619-20. 500w. $3\frac{1}{2}$
LB March-April p34-5. 250w. 4

4236 RAINEY, Ma. Milestone M47021 (2 discs) (Reissue)
CO March p28. 375w. $2\frac{1}{2}$
LB May-June p44. 225w. $4\frac{1}{2}$
LP Aug. p11. 175w. 5
SR July p90, 91. 275w. 4
ST June-July p196. 525w. 4

4237 REED, Jimmy. Blues Is My Business. Vee Jay 7303 (Reissue)
DB May 26 p32. 225w. $4\frac{1}{2}$

4238 REED, Jimmy. Cold Chills. Antilles AN 7007
SR May p93-4. 250w. 2

4239 REED, Jimmy. Is Back. Roots 1001
CAD Oct. p31. 200w. 3

4240 RIEDY, Bob. Just Off Halsted. Flying Fish 006
LB March/April p45. 350w. 3

4241   ROBINSON, Fenton. Somebody Loan Me a Dime. Alligator
       4705
          BM   Oct.   p44.   225w.   4
          DB   March 27   p22.   175w.   5
          LB   March/April   p45.   400w.   5
          SO   Jan./Feb.   p47.   150w.   4½

4242   RUSH, Otis. Cold Day in Hell. Delmark Records, DS-638
          CAD   April   p28.   150w.   3
          CZM   June   p35-6.   175w.   2½
          GP   March   p73.   225w.   4
          JJ   Oct.   p36, 38.   300w.   4½
          LB   March-April   p33.   775w.   4
          MM   Oct. 16   p29.   300w.   3
          RR   Dec.   p101.   50w.   3
          RS   April 8   p73, 74.   500w.   4

4243   RUSH, Otis. Live. Trio PA 3086 (Japan)
          CZM   June   p35-6.   175w.   2½

4244   RUSHING, Jimmy. Gee Baby Ain't I Good to You? Master
       Jazz MJR 8104
          LB   May-June   p38-9.   175w.   4½

4245   RUSHING, Jimmy. Who Was It Sang That Song? Master
       Jazz MJR 8120
          LB   May-June   p39.   175w.   4½

4246   SCOTT, Esther Mae. Mama Ain't Nobody's Fool. Bomp 1
          LB   June-Aug.   p46.   325w.   4

4247   SEALS, Son. Alligator 4703
          SO   Jan./Feb.   p45.   100w.   0

4248   SHINES, Johnny. Advent 2803
          CO   Oct.   p21.   650w.   3½
          LB   Jan./Feb.   p27.   100w.   5
          SR   Feb.   p85.   250w.   4

4249   SHINES, Johnny. Blue Horizon 4607 (Reissue)
          LB   Jan./Feb.   p27.   100w.   2½

4250   SHINES, Johnny. And Company. Biograph 12048
          LB   Jan./Feb.   p27.   100w.   0
          SR   Jan.   p91, 94.   250w.   4

4251   SHINES, Johnny. Chicago Blues Festival, 1972. Black &
       Blue 33-502
          LB   Jan./Feb.   p27.   100w.   5

4252   SHINES, Johnny. Masters of Modern Blues, Vol. 1. Testa-
       ment 2212
          LB   Jan./Feb.   p27.   100w.   4

4253   SHINES, Johnny.   Sitting on Top of the World.   Biograph
       12044
           LB   Jan./Feb.   p27.   100w.   5

4254   SHINES, Johnny.   Standing at the Crossroads.   Testament
       2221
           LB   Jan./Feb.   p27.   100w.   5

4255   SHINES, Johnny and Big Walter Horton.   Testament 2217
           LB   Jan./Feb.   p27.   100w. $2\frac{1}{2}$

4256   SHORT, J. D.   The Legacy of the Blues Vol. 8.   Sonet SNTF
       648 (E)
           LB   May-June   p37.   325w.   3

4257   SLIM Harpo.   Knew the Blues.   Excello 28030
           CAD   May   p30.   100w.   3

4258   SMITH, Dan.   Now Is the Time.   Biograph 12053
           CAD   Oct.   p43.   200w.   5
           JJ   Nov.   p36.   300w.   3

4259   SOUTH Memphis Jug Band.   Flyright LP 113 (E)
           BM   Oct.   p44.   225w.   4
           JJ   June   p38.   275w.   4

4260   SPANN, Otis.   Cryin' Time.   Vanguard VSD 6514
           BU   Jan.-Feb.   p28.   250w.   3

4261   The STROZIERS.   Red Light.   Mainstream 415
           LB   May-June   p37-8.   250w.   3

4262   SUMLIN, Hubert.   Kings of Chicago Blues Vol. 2.   Vogue
       30175 (France)
           LB   Jan-Feb.   p43.   250w. $2\frac{1}{2}$

4263   SUNNYLAND Slim.   The Legacy of the Blues Vol. 11.   Sonet
       SNTF 671 (E)
           LB   March-April   p35.   175w. $4\frac{1}{2}$

4264   SUNNYLAND Slim.   She Got That Jive.   Airway 3220
           LB   March-April   p35.   175w.   3

4265   SYKES, Roosevelt.   Dirty Double Mother.   Bluesway 6077
           CO   April   p17.   200w.   3

4266   SYKES, Roosevelt.   Honeydripper's Duke Mixture.   Blue Star
       80604 (France) (Reissue)
           CZM   June   p41-2.   25w.   3
           LB   July-Aug.   p43.   75w. $2\frac{1}{2}$

4267   TAJ Mahal.   Mo'Roots.   Columbia KC 33051.   Cart. CA
       33051

SR   Jan.   p92.   1050w.   5

4268 TAJ Mahal. Music Keeps Me Together. Columbia PC
      33801. Cart. PCT 33801
            BM   March p20-1. 300w.   3
            CIR Jan. 20 p22. 125w.   3
            DB   May 6 p29. 300w.   2
            LP   Jan. p24. 125w.   3½
            MM   April 17 p21. 325w.   3
            RR   Feb. p66. 25w.   2
            SR   Feb. p84. 125w.   4½

4269 TAJ Mahal. Satisfied 'n' Tickled Too. Columbia PC 34103.
      Cart. PCA-3404. Cass. PCT-34103
            AU   Dec. p104. 200w.   1
            BM   July p51. 200w.   4
            CRA July p80. 125w.   2½
            HF   Sept. p112. 200w.   2
            MM   July 3 p21. 25w.   3
            CRA July p80. 150w.   2
            RR   Aug. p78. 25w.   3
            SR   Sept. p96. 175w.   3

4270 TAMPA Red. Bottleneck Guitar, 1928-1937. Yazoo 1039
      (Reissue)
            LB   March/April p44. 400w.   4

4271 TAMPA Red. The Guitar Wizard. Blues Classics 25 (Re-
      issue)
            CO   Oct. p22-3. 350w.   3½
            LB   March/April p44. 250w.   5

4272 TAMPA Red. Guitar Wizard. RCA AM2-5501 (2 discs) (Re-
      issue)
            CO   Oct. p22-3. 350w.   3½
            LB   July-Aug. p45-6. 800w.   4½

4273 TAYLOR, Eddie. Ready for Eddie. Munich Records BM
      150.203 (E)
            CO   April p19. 225w.   4
            LB   May/June p50. 225w.   3½

4274 TAYLOR, Hound Dog. Alligator 4701
            SR   Oct. p103. 100w.   2

4275 TAYLOR, Hound Dog. Beware of the Dog! Alligator 4707
            AU   Sept. p89-90. 600w.   4
            BU   May/June p27. 300w.   4
            CAD May p26-7. 250w.   3
            CZM June p39. 225w.   4
            DB   May 20 p33. 175w.   3½
            JJ   June p38. 325w.   2½
            MM   Aug. 28 p21. 575w.   3

RS   July 15   p65, 67.   175w. $2\frac{1}{2}$

4276 TAYLOR, Hound Dog.   Natural Boogie.   Alligator 4704
      SO   Jan./Feb.   p47.   100w. $3\frac{1}{2}$

4277 TAYLOR, Koko.   I Got What It Takes.   Alligator 4706
      BM   Oct.   p44.   150w.   4
      LB   May/June   p49.   250w.   5

4278 TAYLOR, Koko.   Southside Baby.   Black & Blue 33.505
      (France)
      LB   May/June   p49.   250w.   2

4279 TERRY, Sonny and Brownie McGhee.   Going Down Slow.
      Mainstream 407 (Reissue)
      SR   May   p86.   75w. $2\frac{1}{2}$

4280 TERRY, Sonny and Brownie McGhee.   Hootin' and Hollerin'.
      Olympic 7108 (Reissue)
      LB   Sept./Oct.   p40.   225w.   4

4281 THOMAS, Henry.   Ragtime Texas.   Herwin 209 (2 discs)
      (Reissue)
      BU   Jan.-Feb.   p25.   900w.   5

4282 THORNTON, Mama.   Jail.   Vanguard VSD 79351
      SR   Nov.   p111-2.   200w. $3\frac{1}{2}$

4283 THORNTON, Big Mama.   Sassy Mama.   Vanguard VSD
      79354
      LB   Sept./Oct.   p42.   225w. $2\frac{1}{2}$
      SR   June   p87.   150w.   3

4284 TOWNSEND, Henry.   Henry T.-Musicman.   Adelphi 1016
      LB   May/June   p48.   300w.   4

4285 TRAUM, Artie and Happy Traum.   Hard Times in the Country.
      Rounder 3007
      CRA   Feb.   p77.   175w.   4

4286 TRICE, Willie.   Blue & Rag'd.   Trix 3305
      GP   April   p79.   50w.   4

4287 TURNER, Joe.   Great Rhythm and Blues Oldies Volume 4.
      Blues Spectrum 104
      CO   May   p16, 17.   225w.   4

4288 TURNER, Joe.   His Greatest Recordings.   Atlantic 40525 (E)
      (Reissue)
      BM   Aug.   p43.   75w.   4
      MM   Aug. 7   p20.   325w. $3\frac{1}{2}$

4289 TURNER, Joe.   Nobody in Mind.   Pablo 2310-760

           BM   Aug.   p43.   125w.   3
           CAC   Oct.   p274.   225w.   4
           CAD   April   p44.   125w.   3
           GR   Dec.   p1080.   100w.   0
           MM   Oct. 16 p30.   225w.   3
           SR   June   p95.   100w. $2\frac{1}{2}$

4290   TURNER, Joe.   Still Boss of the Blues.   United 7790 (Re-
       issue)
           LB   March-April   p36.   125w.   4

4291-2 TURNER, Joe.   The Trumpet Kings Meet Joe Turner.   Pablo
       2310 717
           GR   March   p1521.   225w. $2\frac{1}{2}$
           LB   March-April   p36.   125w.   3

4293   TURNER, Joe and Count Basie.   The Bosses.   Pablo 2310 709
           LB   March-April   p36.   125w.   4

4294   WALKER, Charles.   Blues from the Apple.   Oblivion OD 4
           LP   July   p14.   150w.   3

4295   WALKER, Jimmy and Erwin Helfer.   Duets and Solos.   Flying
       Fish 001
           LB   July-Aug.   p44-5.   225w. $3\frac{1}{2}$

4296   WALKER, T-Bone.   Atlantic SD 8256
           CZM   June   p33-4.   125w.   4

4297   WALKER, T-Bone.   Classics of Modern Blues.   Blue Note
       BNLA 533-H2 (2 discs) (Reissue)
           CRE   June   p58.   175w.   4
           DB   Aug. 12   p36.   125w.   4
           JJ   June   p38-9.   325w.   5
           MJ   April   p28.   150w.   3
           PRM   Jan.   p37.   50w. $4\frac{1}{2}$

4298   WALKER, T-Bone.   Flywalker Airlines.   Polydor
           OLR   March   p40.   25w.   3

4299   WALKER, T-Bone.   Well Done.   Home Cooking 103
           LB   May-June   p40.   250w.   4

4300   WARREN, Baby Boy.   Detroit Blues 1949-1954.   Kingfish 1001
           BU   Jan.-Feb.   p27.   775w.   5
           LB   July-Aug.   p37.   300w. $4\frac{1}{2}$

4301   WELLS, Junior.   On Tap.   Depmark 635
           BM   April   p35.   250w.   3
           LB   May/June   p52.   225w. $2\frac{1}{2}$

4302   WHITE, Bukka.   Big Daddy.   Biograph 12049
           LB   July-Aug.   p44.   200w. $4\frac{1}{2}$

4303 WILD Bill's Blue Washboard Boys. Baby Yum Yum. Fly-
      right 4701 (E)
          LB May-June p40. 250w. 5

4304 WILKINS, Robert. Before the Reverence (1928-1935). Mag-
      pie PY 18000 (E) (Reissue)
          JJ Sept. p41. 625w. 4½

4305 WILLIAMS, Big Joe. Blues Bash. Olympic 7115 (Reissue)
          LB Sept.-Oct. p40. 125w. 4

4306 WILLIAMS, Big Joe. Malvina My Sweet Woman. Oldie
      Blues 2804 (Holland)
          CO April p23. 350w. 4
          JJ May p45. 400w. 3

4307-8 WILLIAMS, Bill. Blues, Rags, & Ballads. Blue Goose 2013
          LB May-June p43. 225w. 4

4309 WILLIAMSON, Sonny Boy No. 2. v. 1. RCA FXM 1 7203
      (France) (Reissue)
          BM Aug. p43. 225w. 5
          JJ June p30. 200w. 5
          RR June p83. 25w. 4½

4310 WILLIAMSON, Sonny Boy No. 2. Vol. 3. Blues Classics
      24 (Reissue)
          RR Feb. p67. 75w. 3½

4311 WILLIAMSON, Sonny Boy No. 2. In Paris. GNP Crescendo
      10003 (Reissue)
          LB July-Aug. p39. 325w. 2½

4312 WILLIAMSON, Sonny Boy No. 2. King Biscuit Time. Ar-
      hoolie M 2020 (Reissue)
          SR May p87. 175w. 2

4313 WILLIAMSON, Sonny Boy No. 2. One Way Out. Chess CHV
      417 (Reissue)
          LB July-Aug. p39. 325w. 4½

4313a WILSON, Joe Lee. Livin' High Off Nickels and Dimes. Ob-
       livion 5
          CO April p23. 200w. 2½
          DB March 27 p18. 200w. 3½
          JJ Feb. p48. 100w. 4
          LP Aug. p18. 50w. 4

4314 WITHERSPOON, Jimmy. Spoonful. Blue Note LA 534-G
          CAD April p31-2. 150w. 3½
          DB April 8 p24. 350w. 3
          PRM Jan. p37. 200w. 3
          RFJ March p11. 200w. 4

410   Record Reviews, 1976

4315 WITHERSPOON, Jimmy and Jay McShann. RCA ANL1-1048e
      (Reissue)
           LB Jan.-Feb. p44-5. 175w. 4

4316 WRENCHER, Big John. Big John's Boogie. Big Bear 4 (E)
           LB Jan.-Feb. p44. 190w. 4

4317 WRENCHER, Big John. Maxwell St. Alley Blues. Barrel-
      house 02 (Reissue)
           LB Jan.-Feb. p44. 190w. 4

4318 YANCEY, Jimmy. The Immortal. Oldie Blues OL 2802
      (Holland) (Reissue)
           ST Dec. 1975-Jan. 1976 p76. 550w. 4½

4319 YOUNG, Johnny. Blue Horizon 4609 (Reissue)
           LB May/June p48. 50w. 5

4320 YOUNG, Johnny. Arhoolie 1029
           LB May/June p46. 50w. 4½

4321 YOUNG, Johnny. And His Friends. Testament T2226
           BU May-June p32. 525w. 5
           CAD May p29-30. 125w. 3½
           CZM June p32. 200w. 3½
           LB July-Aug. p38. 300w. 5

4322 YOUNG, Johnny. I Can't Keep My Foot from Jumping.
      Blues Way 6075
           LB May/June p48. 150w. 2½

4323 YOUNG, Johnny. Plays & Sings the Blues with His Gut-
      Bucket Mandolin. Blues on Blues 10005
           LB May/June p48. 50w. 2

4324 YOUNG, Johnny and Big Walter. Chicago Blues. Arhoolie
      1037
           LB May/June p48. 50w. 3½

4325 YOUNG, Mighty Joe. Chicken Heads. Ovation 1437
           LB Jan./Feb. p28-9. 150w. 4

4326 YOUNG, Mighty Joe. The Legacy of the Blues #4. Sonet
      663
           LB Jan./Feb. p28. 150w. 3½

SOUL, REGGAE, and SALSA

This section covers the basic soul market--the black and ethnic alternative to rock music. Included here are rhythm 'n' blues music, reggae, salsa and other gospel-inspired and inflected artists or records. Most of this music is vocal. Attempts have been made to pass rock and jazz records off as soul (to sell the record); those sections should be consulted for those records which usually include in their titles the words: "funky," "right on," "dues," "soul," "dig it," and other forms of jive talk. This is not to say that this music is not soul--but certainly it is not pure soul and as a hybrid it is best placed where it originated, as is much of disco music.

There are few American review media for soul. Ebony has a few watered-down reviews (mostly of the New Jazz). Blues 'n' Soul and Black Music, two British magazines, are not very critical; indeed, they present reviews that include blues material more adequately handled elsewhere. No rhythm and blues fanzines contain record reviews. Mention is often made of albums, but no serial number of title is given. What are often reviewed (as in Blues 'n' Soul, Blues Unlimited, and Living Blues) are the 45-rpm singles, and this is where the soul market lies, in the three-minute miniature. Singles are important because they all sound the same, with no extended lengths for improvisation, and the guaranteed formula seems to strike pay dirt each time. Artists rarely play around with success. Many performers go into the studio to cut singles, with few ideas or plans for albums; consequently, the music is mainly a variation on a few hit themes at the same tempo. Such speeds and other technical devices (riffing horns, for example) render a whole album monotonous if one number follows another in the same manner and mode. The best purchases in this category are the anthologies, for a selection of different stylings. All male vocalists may sound like James Brown, but they don't sound like the Temptations, Diana Ross or Aretha Franklin, or vice versa.

A blues magazine and a good rock magazine will always review a good soul disc, but the reviewer may come from a white background. Such periodicals as the British Blues Unlimited, and the American Rolling Stone, Living Blues, and Creem appear to be fair, although the records never seem to come in as raves. This is still an independent label's field, but the best of the smaller majors come from the Mowest complex, Atlantic (and Atco), Chess, Philadelphia International, and Epic.

According to the 1976 reviews, the following appear to be the best discs:

ARMATRADING, Joan. A&M SP 4588
BURNING Spear. Man in the Hills. Island ILPS 9412
DR. BUZZARD'S Original Savannah Band. RCA APL1-1504
EARTH, Wind and Fire. Spirit. Columbia PC 34241
HEPTONES. Night Food. Island ILPS 9381
JACKSON, Millie. Free and In Love. Spring 6709
JADE Warrior. Waves. Island ILPS 9318
MARLEY, Bob and the Wailers. Live. Island ILPS 9376
MAYFIELD, Curtis. Give, Get, Take and Have. Curtom 5007
OHIO Players. Honey. Mercury SRM1-1038
OSIBISA. Welcome Home. Island ILPS 9355
SPINNERS. Happiness Is Being with the Spinners. Atlantic SD
    18181
TAYLOR, Johnnie. Eargasm. Columbia PC 33951
WAILER, Bunny. Black Heart Man. Island ILPS 9415
WONDER, Stevie. Songs in the Key of Life. 2 discs. Tamla T13-
    34002

4327 ACKLIN, Barbara. A Place in the Sun. Capitol ST 11377
      BM Oct. p27. 100w. 3

4328 AGROVATORS. Dreadlocks in Jamaica. Live and Love 05
      BM Aug. p43. 125w. 4

4329 AGROVATORS. Straight to Babylon Chest. Live and Love 06
      BM Aug. p45, 46. 250w. 4

4330 AGROVATORS. Strictly Rockers in a Dread Land. Live and
      Love 07
      BM Aug. p43. 75w. 3

4331 ALLEN, Rance. Brothers. Stax STX 1034
      BM March p20. 175w. 4

4332 ALTON, Roy and the Puzzle People. Carnival in Ladbroke
      Grove. Tackle 001 (E)
      BM Sept. p46. 125w. 3

4333 ARMADA Orchestra. Disco Armada. Contempo 528 (E)
      BM April p51. 125w. 1

4334 ARMADA Orchestra. Philly Armada. Contempo 536 (E)
      BM Sept. p46. 100w. 2

4335 ARMADA Orchestra. Ultra Funk. Contempo 509 (E)
      BM April p51. 75w. 2

4336 ARMATRADING, Joan. A&M SP 4588
      AU Dec. p82. 200w. 4

         CAC Dec. p336. 200w. 4
         BM Nov. p47. 200w. 4

4337 ARMATRADING, Joan. Back to the Night. A&M SP-4525
         LP Aug. p3. 125w. 4

4338 ASHFORD and Simpson. Come As You Are. Warner Bros.
      BS-2858
         BM July p51. 150w. 4
         MG June p52. 25w. 1½
         MM April 17 p41. 325w. 3
         PRM March p47. 400w. 4

4339 ASWAD. Island ILPS 9399
         BM Oct. p45. 125w. 3
         MM Sept. 25 p24. 400w. 2½

4340 ATLANTA Disco Band. Bad Luck. Ariola AAS 1502
         BM May p39. 200w. 2

4341 BAG O Wire. Klik 9007 (E)
         BM March p21. 175w. 3

4342 BAKER, Laverne. Sings Bessie Smith. Atlantic 50241 (E)
      (Reissue)
         MM Aug. 7 p20. 325w. 3

4343 BANKS, Ron and the Dramatics. Drama V. ABC ABCD 916.
      Cart. H 8022916. Cass. H5022 916
         HF Feb. p128. 50w. 3
         LP March p26. 50w. 3
         RS Feb. 12 p95. 150w. 3

4344 BANKS, Rose. Motown M6-845
         BM Sept. p45. 150w. 3
         MM Aug. 14 p29. 325w. 4

4345 BAR-KAYS. Coldblooded. Stax STX 1033
         BM May p38. 100w. 4
         MM Feb. 7 p25. 150w. 2

4346 BARABBAS. Watch Out. Atco SO 36-136
         BM Nov. p46. 125w. 4

4347 BELL, Archie and the Drells. Dance Your Troubles Away.
      Philadelphia International PZ 34323
         BM May p34. 200w. 5
         RS Feb. 26 p73. 475w. 3½

4348 BELL, Madeline. This Is One Girl. Pye NSPL 18433 (E)
         BM May p39. 100w. 2

4349 BELL, William. Bound to Happen. Stax STX 1050

414 Record Reviews, 1976

BM   Aug.   p45.   100w.   4
MM   July 10   p22.   100w. $3\frac{1}{2}$

4350   BELL, William.   Relating.   Stax STX 1010
BM   Oct.   p42.   200w.   3
MM   July 31   p37.   50w.   3

4351   BENTON, Brook.   Hot Millions of the 50s and 60s.   Philips
6336 268 (E) (Reissue)
BM   April   p51.   75w.   3

4352   BENTON, Brook.   Lovin'.   RCA HY1029 (E) (Reissue)
BM   Aug.   p51.   75w.   1
MM   April 17   p41.   150w. $2\frac{1}{2}$

4353   BENTON, Brook.   Looking Back.   DJM 073 (E) (Reissue)
BM   Oct.   p42-3.   125w.   3
CAC   Oct.   p256.   250w. $3\frac{1}{2}$
MM   May 22   p30.   125w. $2\frac{1}{2}$

4354   BENTON, Brook.   This Is....   All Platinum 3015
BM   July   p51.   175w.   3
MM   May 22   p30.   125w.   3

4355   BERRY, Chuck.   Chess CH-60032
LP   July   p18.   100w.   4

4356   BIDDU Orchestra.   Rain Forest.   Epic PE 34230
BM   Aug.   p46.   100w.   2
CAC   June   p97.   175w.   3

4357   BIG Youth.   Dread Locks Dread.   Klik 9001 (E)
BM   Oct.   p34.   150w.   4

4358   BIG Youth.   Natty Cultural Dread.   Trojan 123 (E)
BM   March   p22.   300w. $2\frac{1}{2}$
CRA   July   p69.   225w. $2\frac{1}{2}$

4359   BLACK Blood.   Bradleys BLAKL 9001 (E)
BM   July   p52.   75w.   2

4360   BLACK, Bill.   The World's Greatest Honky-Tonk Band.
Hi/London SHL 32093.   Cart. 083293.   Cass. 0532093
HF   Jan.   p102.   100w.   3
MG   Jan.   p40.   50w.   3

4361   BLACK Satin.   Buddah BDS 5654
MG   June   p52.   25w.   0

4362   BLACKBYRDS.   City Life.   Fantasy F 9490
DB   Feb. 12   p26-7.   150w.   2
MM   Jan. 17   p39.   300w. $2\frac{1}{2}$

4363 BLACKBYRDS. Flying Start. Fantasy F 9472
AU March p84-5. 400w. $4\frac{1}{2}$
DB March 27 p19-20. 125w. 1

4364 BLUE Magic. 13 Blue Magic Lane. Atco SD 36-120
BM Jan. p24. 200w. 4

4365 BOBB B Sox and the Blue Jeans. Spector 2307 004
BM Jan. p26. 50w. 3

4366 BOHANNON, Hamilton. Dance Your Ass Off. Dakar 76919
BM Oct. p42. 150w. 3
CRE Sept. p65. 125w. $2\frac{1}{2}$

4367 BOOKER T and the MGs. Melting Pot. Stax STX 1054 (Re-
issue)
BM Aug. p45. 50w. 2
MM July 10 p22. 100w. $3\frac{1}{2}$

4368 BOOKER T and the MGs. Union Extended. Atlantic K 50283
(E)
BM Sept. p47. 125w. 3

4369 BOOTHE, Ken. Freedom Street. Trojan 120 (E)
BM Nov. p32. 175w. 3

4370 BOOTSY's Rubber Band. Stretchin' Out In. Warner Brothers
BS 2920
BM July p52. 225w. 5

4371 BOTTOM Line. Crazy Dancin'. GTO GTLP 009 (E)
BM July p53. 25w. 1

4372 BRASS Construction. United Artists UALA 545 G
BM May p35. 100w. 4
MM April 24 p35. 250w. 3

4373 BRIDGEWATER, Dee Dee. Dee Dee Bridgewater. Atlantic
SD 18188
CAD Oct. p18. 50w. 2

4374 The BROTHERS. Don't Stop Now. RCA APL 1-1187
BM Sept. p46. 50w. 1

4375 BROWN, James. Get Up Offa That Thing. Polydor PD 6071
BM Dec. p53. 150w. 4
CAC Dec. p338. 200w. 3
CRE Nov. p63. 100w. 3
MM Nov. 27 p31. 300w. 3

4376 BROWN, James. Hot. Polydor PD 6054
BM June p35. 125w. 2
CAC June p97. 200w. $3\frac{1}{2}$

4377 BROWN, James. Live at the Apollo, vol. 1.   Polydor 22482
      184 (E)
           BM   Oct.   p34.   75w.   4

4378 BROWN, James. Sex Machine Today.   Polydor PD-6042
           BM   Oct.   p34.   75w.   2
           LP   Aug.   p16.   75w.   0

4379 BROWN, Keisa. Live.   Little Star 1001
           RS   Nov. 18 p77.   275w.   4

4380 BT Express. Do It.   Pye NSLP 28207 (E)
           BM   Dec.   p19.   300w. $4\frac{1}{2}$

4381 BT Express. Energy to Burn.   Columbia PC 34178
           BM   Aug.   p46.   225w.   5

4382 BT Express. Non Stop.   EMI INA 1501 (E)
           BM   Nov.   p32.   150w.   3

4383 BURKE, Solomon. Back to My Roots.   Chess ACH 19002
           CAD   Oct.   p46.   175w.   4

4384 BURNING Spear. Garvey's Ghost.   Margo ILPS 9382
           BM   July   p52.   200w.   3
           RR   July   p80.   50w.   3

4385 BURNING Spear. Man in the Hills.   Island ILPS9412
           BM   Oct.   p45.   125w.   4
           CRA   Oct.   p72, 74.   300w.   5
           MM   Sept. 25 p24.   600w. $3\frac{1}{2}$
           RS   Sept. 23 p118.   225w.   4
           SR   Dec.   p103-4.   150w. $1\frac{1}{2}$

4386 BURNING Spear. Marcus Garvey.   Island ILPS 9377
           CRA   May   p78.   150w.   4
           MG   July   p46.   25w. $2\frac{1}{2}$
           RR   July   p80.   50w. $2\frac{1}{2}$
           RS   April 8 p76.   150w. $2\frac{1}{2}$

4387 BUTLER, Jerry. Love's on the Menu.   Motown M6-850
           BM   Oct.   p40.   250w.   5
           MM   July 24 p24.   225w.   3

4388 BUTLER, Leslie. Ja Gan.   Trojan 112 (E)
           BM   March   p22.   200w.   4

4389 CAMERON, G. C.   Motown M6-880
           MM   Oct. 2 p28.   225w.   3

4390 CAMPBELL, Cornell. Dance in a Greenwich Farm.   Grouna-
      tion 503 (E)
           BM   April   p32.   225w.   4

4391   CAPONE, Dennis. Dread Capone.   Live and Love 004 (E)
       BM   May p34. 125w.   4

4392   CARR, Linda.   Cherry Pie Guy.   Chelsea 2306 112 (E)
       BM   Aug. p42-3. 100w.   2
       CAC Oct. p256.   50w.   3

4393   CARTER, Clarence. A Heart Full of Song.   ABC 943
       RS   Sept. 9 p64. 175w.   1

4394   CASTOR Jimmy. E-Man Groovin.   Atlantic SD 18186
       BM   Nov. p46. 200w.   4
       MM   Oct. 16 p26. 325w. $2\frac{1}{2}$

4395   CASTOR, Jimmy. Supersound.   Atlantic SD 18150
       BM   Jan. p24. 200w.   4

4396   CATE Brothers. In One Eye and Out the Other.   Asylum 1080
       GRA Dec. p1074. 100w. $3\frac{1}{2}$
       RS   Dec. 16 p82. 150w.   3

4397   CHANTER Sisters. First Flight.   Polydor PD 6075
       BM   Aug. p45. 175w.   3
       CAC June p97. 225w. $3\frac{1}{2}$
       RS   Aug. 26 p48. 175w. $3\frac{1}{2}$

4398   CHARLES, Ray. Vol. 2.   London SPA U 422 (E) (Reissue)
       JJ   June p41. 100w.   4

4399   CHARLES, Ray. Focus On.   London U 1/2 (2 discs) (E)
       (Reissue)
       BM   Nov. p32. 125w.   2

4400   CHARLES, Tina. I Love to Love.   Columbia PC 34424
       MM   Dec. 25 p17. 75w.   1

4401   CHI-LITES. Half a Love. Brunswick 754204
       BM   Oct. p34. 200w.   3
       CAC Feb. p446. 75w.   4
       LP   Jan. p23. 50w. $2\frac{1}{2}$

4402   CHOSEN Few. In Miami. Trojan 131 (E)
       BM   Nov. p49. 100w.   3

4403   CIMARONS. On the Rock. Vulcan 501 (E)
       BM   Sept. p48, 53. 125w.   4

4404   CLARKE, Johnnie. Rockers Time Now. Virgin V2058 (E)
       MM   Aug. 21 p18. 500w.   3

4405   CLAYTON, Obie. DJM DJF 20458
       CAC Oct. p258. 50w. $2\frac{1}{2}$

4406 CLIFF, Jimmy. Best of. Island ICD 6 (E) (Reissue) (2
      discs)
            BM   May   p38. 125w. 4
            CRA July p69. 50w.   3
            MM   April 24 p23. 400w. 3

4407 CLIFF, Jimmy. Follow My Mind. Warner Bros. MS2218
            BM   May   p34. 150w. 3
            CRA Jan. p73. 225w. $1\frac{1}{2}$
            CRE Jan. p65. 175w. 2
            CRE Feb. p12. 25w. $2\frac{1}{2}$
            SR   Jan. p79. 100w. 2

4408 CLIFF, Jimmy. Music Maker. Reprise MS 2188. Cart.
      M8 2188. Cass. M5 2188
            SR   Feb. p88. 200w. 5

4409 CLIFF, Jimmy. Wonderful World, Beautiful People. A&M
      SP4251
            SO   May/June p43. 100w. $2\frac{1}{2}$

4410 CLIFFORD, Mataya. Star Fell from Heaven. Virgin V 2063
      (E)
            BM   Nov. p46. 125w. 3

4411 COASTERS. World Famous. DJM (E) (Reissue)
            MM   Dec. 25 p17. 150w. 4

4412 COFFEY, Dennis. Finger Lickin Good. Westbound Records,
      W-212
            GP   March p73. 150w. 3

4413 COLE, Natalie. Capitol EST-11517. Cart. 8XT-11517. Cass.
      4XT-11517
            BM   July p52. 200w. 4
            MM   June 12 p24. 450w. 2
            RS   July 15 p60. 200w. $2\frac{1}{2}$
            SR   Oct. p85-6. 450w. 3

4414 COLE, Natalie. Inseparable. Capitol ST 11929
            BM   Nov. 1975. p30. 225w. 5
            CRA Feb. p76. 150w. 2
            DB   Jan. 15 p29. 225w. 1

4415 COLLINS, Lyn. Check Me Out. People 6605
            RS   Dec. 2 p92. 275w. 2

4416 The COMMODORES. Machine Gun. Motown M6-798S1. Cart.
      7798 HT. Cass. 7798 HC
            SR   Jan. p82. 250w. 4

4417 COMMODORES. Hot on the Tracks. Motown M6-867
            BM   Oct. p40. 150w. 3

GR   Sept.   p493.   25w.   2

4418   COMMODORES.   Movin' On.   Motown M6-848
       BM   Jan.   p25.   125w.   3

4419   COOKE, Sam.   The Golden Age of....   RCA RS 1054 (E) (Re-
       issue)
       MM   Dec. 4   p22.   175w.   4

4420   COOKE, Sam.   Interprets Billie Holliday.   RCA HY 1030 (E)
       (Reissue)
       BM   July   p51.   150w.   3
       JJ   June   p40.   125w. $3\frac{1}{2}$

4421   COOKE, Sam.   Twistin the Night Away.   RCA HY 1034 (E)
       (Reissue)
       BM   Oct.   p43.   150w.   3
       CAC   Dec.   p341.   50w.   3
       MM   July 31   p37.   50w. $2\frac{1}{2}$

4422   COUNT Ozzie and the Mystic Revelation of the Rastafari.
       Grounation.   Vulcan 301 (E)
       BM   April   p51.   200w.   5

4423   COUNT Ozzie and the Mystic Revelation of the Rastafari.
       Tales of Mozambique.   Dynamic 001 (E)
       BM   Sept.   p46.   150w.   4

4424   COVAY, Don.   Travellin in Heavy Traffic.   Philadelphia In-
       ternational PZ 33958
       BM   Oct.   p40.   250w.   5
       MM   Aug. 28   p21.   350w. $3\frac{1}{2}$
       RS   Aug. 2   p68.   175w.   2

4425   CRACK the Sky.   Lifesong LS6000
       CRA   Feb.   p77.   25w.   4

4426   CREACH, Papa John.   I'm the Fiddle Man.   Buddah BD 5649
       BM   May   p36-7.   75w.   3

4427   CREATIVE Source.   Consider the Source.   Polydor PD 6065
       BM   Aug.   p46.   125w.   3

4428   CREATIVE Source.   Pass the Feelin' On.   Polydor PD 6052
       BM   March   p20.   200w.   3
       CAC   May   p60.   150w. $2\frac{1}{2}$
       MM   Jan. 24   p27.   150w.   3

4429   CROUCH, Andrae and the Disciples.   The Best of....   Light
       LSD 7034 (E)
       BM   April   p31.   250w.   3

4430   CROWN Heights Affair.   Dreaming a Dream.   De-Lite 2017

      BM   March p20. 200w. 3
      MM   Jan. 17 p39. 225w. $2\frac{1}{2}$

4431 CRUSADERS. Chain Reaction. Blue Thimb BTSD 6022
      BD Feb. 12 p22-3. 200w. 2
      LP Jan. p23. 75w. 0

4432 CRUSADERS. Those Southern Knights. ABC BTSD 6024
      DB Oct. 7 p20, 22. 375w. $3\frac{1}{2}$
      RR Dec. p105. 100w. 3

4433 CRYSTALS. Sing Their Greatest Hits. Spector 2307 006 (E)
      (Reissue)
      BM Jan. p26. 50w. 3

4434 DAVE and Sugar. RCA APL 1-1818
      MM Nov. 20 p29. 50w. 2

4435 DAVIS, Betty. Nasty Gal. Island ILPS 9329
      BM Dec. p27. 275w. 4
      CRE Jan. p67-8. 350w. 2

4436 DAVIS, Tyrone. Love and Touch. Columbia PC 34268
      PRM Oct. p45. 350w. 3

4437 DAVIS, Tyrone. Turning Point. Dakar 76918
      BM Sept. p47. 125w. 3

4438 DEKKER, Desmond. Israelites. Cactus 111 (E)
      BM Oct. p28. 150w. 3

4439 DELLS. We've Got to Get Our Thing Together. Mercury
      SRM 1-1059. Cass. MCR 4 1 1059
      LP March p26. 100w. $2\frac{1}{2}$

4440 DEZRO Orchestra. Bright Lights, Soul Nights. Route ROTL
      100 (E)
      BM Aug. p45. 25w. 1

4441 DIBANGU, Manu. Makossa Music. Creale CRLP 503 (E)
      BM Dec. p27. 175w. 4

4442 DICTATORS. Go Girl Crazy. Epic KE 33348
      CRE Feb. p63. 50w. 5

4443 DIDDLEY, Bo. The Twentieth Anniversary of Rock 'n' Roll.
      RCA APL1-1229. Cart. APS1-1229
      BM Aug. p45. 100w. 1
      SR June p79. 400w. $2\frac{1}{2}$

4444 DILLINGER. CB 200. Mango 9385
      BM Sept. p48. 200w. 3

4445   DIRTY Tricks. Night Man. Polydor PD 1-6082
       AU Dec. p82. 250w. 1½

4446   DIXON, Prince. It's a Sad Situation. Joliet 5001
       BU May-June p33. 350w. 4½

4447   DR. BUZZARD'S Original Savannah Band. RCA APL1-1504
       BM Oct. p43. 150w. 5
       MM Oct. 16 p26. 350w. 2½
       RS Sept. 23 p120. 175w. 3
       SR Nov. p124. 600w. 4½

4447a DOMINO, Fats. Live in New York. Philips 6336.275 (E)
       CAC Oct. p259. 100w. 3

4448   DORSEY, Lee. Yes We Can. Polydor 2482.280 (E)
       CAC June p97. 200w. 4½
       MM March 6 p34. 200w. 2½

4449   DOUGLAS, Carol. Midnight Love Affair. Midland Inter-
       national BKL-1798
       MM Nov. 20 p29. 75w. 3

4450   DOZIER, Lamont. Right There. Warner Brothers BS 2929
       BM Aug. p42. 150w. 4
       MM Aug. 28 p21. 350w. 3
       RS Sept. 9 p63. 175w. 2½

4451   DRAMATICS. Best of. Stax STX 1047 (Reissue)
       BM May p36. 150w. 4

4452   DRENNON, Eddie. Do the Latin Hustle. Pye NSPL 29221
       (E)
       BM June p36. 125w. 2
       MM April 24 p35. 225w. 1

4453   DRIFTERS. Every Nite's a Saturday Night. Arista 4111
       MM Dec. 4 p24. 50w. 1½

4454   DRIFTERS. Save the Last Dance for Me. Music for Pleasure
       (E) (Reissue)
       CAC Feb. p447. 150w. 2½

4455   DRIFTERS. There Goes My First Love. Bell 260 (E)
       BM April p32. 200w. 2
       MM Feb. 21 p28. 200w. 2

4456   EARTH, Wind, and Fire. Gratitude. Columbia PG 33694.
       Cart. PGA 33694
       BM March p21. 250w. 4
       DB April 22 p30, 32. 325w. 3
       SOU Feb. p46, 48. 250w. 4
       SR April p83. 150w. 2

4457 EARTH, Wind, and Fire. Spirit. Columbia PC 34241
      CRA Dec.   p78.   400w. $4\frac{1}{2}$
      DB   Dec. 2 p16-7.   250w.   5
      RM   Dec.   p30.   225w.   3
      RS   Dec. 16 p78.   225w. $2\frac{1}{2}$

4458 EARTH, Wind, and Fire. That's the Way of the World.
      Columbia PC-33280.   Cart. PCA 33280.   Cass. PCT-33280
      LP   July   p18.   125w.   3
      SR   Sept. p93.   100w.   5

4459 ECSTASY, Passion and Pain. Roulette SR 3013.   Cart.
      8045-3013 H.   Cass. 5045-3013 H
      BM   Dec.   p19.   300w. $4\frac{1}{2}$
      SR   Jan.   p82.   450w.   4

4460 EDWARDS, Rupie. Dub Basket, v. 1.   Cactus 107 (E)
      BM   Oct.   p33.   100w.   3

4461 EDWARDS, Rupie. Dub Basket, Chapter 2.   Cactus 117 (E)
      BM   Nov.   p49.   200w.   3

4462 EDWARDS, Winston. Natty Locks Dub.   Fay (E)
      MM   March 13   p25.   100w. $2\frac{1}{2}$

4463 ELBERT, Donnie. Stop in the Name of Love.   Trip 9524
      BM   Dec.   p28.   150w.   1

4464 ELLISON, Lorraine. The Best of.   Warner K56230 (E) (Re-
      issue)
      BM   Aug.   p44.   150w.   5

4465 EMOTIONS. Flowers.   Columbia PC 34163
      RS   Sept. 9   p61.   225w.   5

4466 ENGLISH, Junior. The Great.   Horse 707 (E)
      BM   May   p34.   100w.   3

4467 EQUALS. Born Ya! Mercury 9109 601 (E)
      BM   Sept.   p46.   150w.   2
      MM   Oct. 30   p24.   275w.   3

4468 ETHNIC Flight Band. Music Explosion.   Ethnic Flight 4444
      (E)
      BM   July   p51.   175w.   3

4469 ETHNIC Flight Band. Out of One Man Comes Many Dubs.
      Ethnic Flight 4416 (E)
      BM   Oct.   p33.   150w.   3

4470 EVANS, Tony. Let's Go to the Disco.   Satire SATL 4005 (E)
      MM   Nov. 13   p28.   75w.   0

4471 EVERETT, Betty. It's in His Kiss. DJM 22042 (E) (Re-
      issue)
            BM Dec. p55. 125w. 3
            MM Nov. 13 p29. 100w. 3½

4472 FABULOUS Five. My Jamaican Gift. Trojan 129 (E)
            BM Nov. p49. 75w. 3

4473 FAIR, Yvonne. The Bitch Is Black. Motown M5-832
            BM Jan. p25. 200w. 4
            MM Jan. 3 p23. 50w. 4

4474 FAITH, Hope and Charity. RCA APL1-1100
            BM Nov. p31. 150w. 5
            LP Jan. p23. 75w. 2½

4475 FAITH, Hope and Charity. Life Goes On. RCA APL 1-1827
            BM Nov. p45. 100w. 3

4476 FANIA All-Stars. Delicate and Jumpy. Columbia PC 34283.
      Cart. PCA 34283. Cass. PCT 34283
            CRE Dec. p14. 25w. 2
            SR Dec. p106. 300w. 0

4477 FANIA All-Stars. Salsa Live. Island HELP 21 A
            BM March p21. 200w. 3

4478 FARRA, Maryann and Satin Soul. Never Gonna Leave You.
      Brunswick (E)
            MM Dec. 4 p24. 50w. 2

4479 FATBACK Band. Night Fever. Spring 6711
            BM Oct. p40-1. 225w. 3
            CAC Dec. p338. 75w. 3

4480 FATBACK Band. Raising Hell. Event 6405
            BM April p31. 200w. 4

4481 FATBACK Band. Yum Yum. Event 6904
            BM Oct. p28. 100w. 3

4482 FIRST Choice. So Let Us Entertain You. Warner BS 2934
            BM Aug. p44. 125w. 2
            MG June p32. 50w. 3
            MM June 12 p22. 275w. 1

4483 FLACK, Roberta. Feel Like Makin' Love. Atlantic SD 18131.
      Cart. TP 18131. Cass. CS18131
            SR Aug. p77. 200w. 5

4484 FLIRTATIONS. Love Makes the World Go Round. RCA SF
      8448 (E)
            BM Dec. p28. 200w. 1

4485 FLOYD, King. Well Done. Chimneyville 201
       LP March p27. 75w. $3\frac{1}{2}$

4486 FORRESTER, Sharon. Vulcan 002 (E)
       BM Jan. p26. 150w. 4

4487 FOUR Tops. Catfish. ABC 468
       BM Dec. p55. 150w. 3
       MM Nov. 27 p31. 450w. $1\frac{1}{2}$

4488 FOUR Tops. Super Hits. Tamla Motown (E) (Reissue)
       MM Nov. 20 p29. 75w. $2\frac{1}{2}$

4489 FRANKLIN, Aretha. Sparkle. Atlantic SD 18176
       BM Nov. p46-7. 300w. 4
       MM Oct. 16 p26. 300w. 2
       RS Aug. 12 p56. 300w. $3\frac{1}{2}$

4490 FRANKLIN, Aretha. With Everything I Feel in Me. Atlantic
       SD 118116. Cart. TP 18116. Cass. CS 18116
       SR May p80. 150w. 5

4491 FRANKLIN, Aretha. You. Atlantic SD 18151. Cart. TP
       18151. Cass. CS 18151
       CAD March p24. 125w. 2
       CIR May 13 p18. 75w. 2
       CRE March p12. 25w. 3
       HF   Feb. p118. 150w. $1\frac{1}{2}$
       LP   March p27. 100w. 4
       MM   Jan. 17 p39. 575w. $1\frac{1}{2}$
       RS   Jan. 1 p60. 1125w. 2
       SR   March p83. 150w. 0

4492 FUNKADELIC. Let's Take It to the Stage. 20th Century/
       Westbound 215
       CRE Jan. p12. 50w. 4

4493 FUNKADELIC. Tales of Kidd Funkadelic. Westbound 227
       RS Dec. 16 p81-2. 250w. $2\frac{1}{2}$

4494 GARRETT, Lee. Heat for the Feet. Chrysalis CHR 1109
       BM June p35. 175w. 3

4495 GAYE, Marvin. The Best of. Tamla T6-348 (Reissue)
       MM Oct. 23 p27. 225w. 2

4496 GAYE, Marvin. I Want You. Tamla T6-342
       BM   June p34. 225w. 4
       CRE July p12. 50w. 3
       CIR Aug. 10 p12. 250w. 3
       MM   May 1 p29. 500w. $3\frac{1}{2}$
       RS   June 3 p69. 250w. $2\frac{1}{2}$

4497 GAYNOR, Gloria. Experience.   MGM M3G 4997
         BM Dec. p27. 250w. 3
         CAC April p19. 50w. $2\frac{1}{2}$
         CRA Feb. p73. 100w. $2\frac{1}{2}$

4498 GAYNOR, Gloria. I've Got You.   Polydor PD1-6063.   Cart.
      8T1 6063.   Cass. CT1 6063
         BM Oct. p41. 250w. 3
         CAC Oct. p259. 125w. 3
         SR Dec. p106. 125w. 3

4499 GILSTRAP, James. Love Talk.   Rox 102
         BM Sept. p48. 150w. 2

4500 GIORGI. Knights in White Satin.   Oasis 5006
         MM Nov. 20 p26. 100w. 1

4501 GLADIATORS. Trench Town Mix-Up.   Virgin V 2062 (E)
         BM Nov. p49. 150w. 5

4502 GRAHAM Central Station. Aint No 'Bout-a-Doubt-It.   Warner
      Brothers BS 2876
         BM April p32. 300w. 4

4503 GRAHAM Central Station. Mirror.   Warner Bros BS 2937
         BM Sept. p44. 175w. 5

4504 GRAY, Dobie. Best of.   MCA MCF 2736 (E) (Reissue)
         CMR April p42. 300w. $4\frac{1}{2}$
         RR Feb. p66. 25w. 3

4505 GRAY, Dobie. New Ray of Sunshine.   Capricorn CP-0163.
      Cart. M8-0163.   Cass. M5-0163
         BM May p39. 150w. 2
         CAC March p488. 125w. 3
         GR April p1670. 50w. $2\frac{1}{2}$
         HF May p104. 200w. 3
         MG April p39. 50w. 3
         PRM March p47. 400w. 4
         RS March 25 p64. 150w. $3\frac{1}{2}$
         RR April p77. 75w. 3
         SR May p83. 50w. 3

4506 GRAY, Owen. Bongo Natty.   Third World 4 (E)
         BM Nov. p30. 150w. 3

4507 GREEN, Al. Full of Fire.   HI SHL 32097
         CAC July p148. 100w. 2
         CRE July p12. 25w. $4\frac{1}{2}$
         MG June p52. 50w. 2
         MM April 17 p41. 450w. $3\frac{1}{2}$
         RS June 3 p70. 225w. $2\frac{1}{2}$

4508 GREEN, Al. Greatest Hits. HI 32089 (Reissue)
      BM May p59. 100w. 4

4509 GREEN, Al. Is Love. HI SHL-32092. Cass. 0-532092
      BM Nov. p30-1. 200w. 4
      CIR March 2 p20. 200w. 4
      CRE Jan. p12. 50w. $4\frac{1}{2}$
      LP Jan. p24. 75w. $2\frac{1}{2}$

4510 GUITAR Red. Hard Times. Mod-Art 1976
      LB July-Aug. p36-7. 275w. 3

4511 HAMMOND, Johnny. Gambler's Life. Salvation SAL 702 S1.
      Cart. SA8 702. Cass. SAC 702
      SR June p76, 79. 150w. 3

4512 HARRIOTT, Derrick. Greatest Hits. Trojan (E) (Reissue)
      BM Nov. p32. 150w. 4

4513 HAYES, Isaac. Best of. Stax STX 1041 (Reissue)
      BM Jan. p26. 50w. 4
      BM Dec. p20. 200w. 4
      CAC Feb. p448. 50w. 3

4514 HAYES, Isaac. Black Moses. Stax STDX 4003/4 (2 discs)
      BM Oct. p28. 150w. 3

4515 HAYES, Isaac. Chocolate Chip. ABC ABCD 874. Cart.
      8022-874. Cass. 5022-874H
      SR Oct. p78. 150w. $2\frac{1}{2}$

4516 HAYES, Isaac. Golden Hour Presents. Golden Hour GH 844
      (E) (Reissue)
      MM March 13 p23. 25w. $3\frac{1}{2}$

4517 HAYES, Isaac. Groove-a-thon. ABC 925
      BM June p34. 225w. 4
      MM March 6 p35. 500w. 3

4518 HAYES, Isaac. Juicy Fruit. ABC 953
      BM Nov. p45. 150w. 3

4519 HAYWOOD, Leon. Come and Get Yourself Some. 20th Cen-
      tury T 476
      BM Oct. p27. 75w. 3

4520 HEADHUNTERS. Survival of the Fittest. Arista 4038
      BM April p32. 300w. 4

4521 HEATWAVE. Too Hot to Handle. GTO 013 (E)
      BM Dec. p53. 100w. 2
      MM Dec. 4 p24. 50w. 3

4522 HELLO. Keep Us Off the Street. Bell (E)
          MM June 12 p25. 175w. 1½

4523 HELMS, Jimmy. Gonna Make You an Offer. Cube Hifly 21
      (E)
          BM April p51. 100w. 3

4524 HEMPHILL, Julius. 'coon Bid'ness. Arista AL 1012
          SOU Jan. p39. 100w. 2½

4525 HENDERSON, Michael. Solid. Buddah BDS 5662
          CRA Dec. p74. 225w. 3

4526 HENDRICKS, Jon. Tell Me the Truth. Arista 4043
          CRA Jan. p71. 400w. 4½

4527 HEPTONES. Island ILPS 9381
          MG Oct. p65. 50w. 2

4528 HEPTONES. Cool Rasta. Trojan 128 (E)
          BM Nov. p49. 150w. 3

4529 HEPTONES. Night Food. Island ILPS 9381
          AU Oct. p130. 400w. 3
          BM May p38. 250w. 4
          CRA July p69. 50w. 3
          CRE Dec. p14. 50w. 3½
          RS Sept. 9 p56. 175w. 5

4530 HI Rhythm. On the Loose. HI SHL 32099
          CRE Dec. p14. 125w. 4½

4531 HIDDEN Strength. United Artists UALA 555G
          BM Aug. p43. 50w. 3

4532 HIGGS, Joe. Life of Contradiction. Grounation 508 (E)
          BM June p34. 175w. 5

4533 HINES, Justin. Jezebel. Island ILPS 9416
          BM Nov. p49. 225w. 4

4534 HOLDER, Mark. Cameo. Vulcan 003
          BM Oct. p45. 100w. 2

4535 HOLMES, Nick. Soulful Crooner. Just Sunshine JSS3
          HF June p105. 25w. 2½

4536 HOLMES, Rupert. Epic KE 33443
          MM Jan. 24 p26. 250w. 3½

4537 HOLMES, Rupert. Singles. Epic PE 34288
          PRM Nov. p35. 450w. 1

4538   HOLT, John. Time Is the Master. Cactus 109 (E)
          BM   Oct.   p34.   175w.   3

4539   HONEYBOY. Lovers. Third World 108 (E)
          BM   Sept.   p48.   100w.   2

4540   HOPKINS, Linda. Me and Bessie. Columbia PC-34032.
       Cart. PCA-34032
          SR   Aug.   p76.   425w.   0

4541   HOT Chocolate. Big Tree 89512
          AU   May   p78-9.   450w.   4
          CRE   June   p12.   25w. $3\frac{1}{2}$
          MG   Jan.   p34.   50w.   3

4542   HOT Chocolate. Man to Man. Big Tree BT 89519
          AU   Dec.   p83-4.   550w.   1
          PRM   Oct.   p22.   50w. $2\frac{1}{2}$

4543   HOUSTON, Thelma. I've Got the Music in Me. Sheffield
       Lab 2
          BS   Aug.   p61.   200w. $4\frac{1}{2}$

4544   HUDSON, Keith. Too Expensive. Virgin V 2056 (E)
          BM   Oct.   p45.   150w.   3
          MM   Sept.   11   p26.   225w.   2

4545   HUDSON, Keith. Torch of Freedom. Atra 1001 (E)
          BM   Jan.   p25.   250w.   4

4546   HUES Corporation. Love Corporation. RCA APL1-0938
          CAC   March   p493.   50w. $3\frac{1}{2}$

4547   HUES Corporation. Rockin' Soul. RCA APL1-0775. Cart.
       APT1-0775. Cass. APK1-0775
          SR   March   p76.   75w.   4

4548-9 HUNT, Tommy. Live at Wigan Casino. Spark SRLP 117
       (E)
          BM   June   p36.   100w.   3

4550   HUTCH, Willie. Concert in Blues. Motown M6-854
          BM   Aug.   p45.   75w.   3
          MG   June   p52.   25w.   0
          MM   June   12   p21.   325w.   2
          RS   May 6   p74.   250w.   3

4551   HUTCH, Willie. The Mark of the Beast. Motown M6-815S1
          LP   July   p13.   100w.   4
          MM   June   19   p28.   50w.   3

4552   HUTCH, Willie. Ode to My Lady. Motown M6-838
          BM   March   p20.   200w.   5

MM Feb. 14 p29. 125w. 3

4553 HUTSON, Leroy. Curtom 5002
      BM Aug. p62. 150w. 3

4554 HUTSON, Leroy. Feel the Spirit. Curtom 5010
      BM May p38. 100w. 3
      MM April 17 p41. 275w. $1\frac{1}{2}$

4555 IMPACT. Atco SD 36-135
      BM Sept. p45. 125w. 4

4556 IMPRESSIONS. First Impressions. Curtom 5003
      BS March p65. 75w. 2

4557 IMPRESSIONS. For Your Precious Love. DJM (E) (Reissue)
      MM Dec. 25 p17. 150w. 1

4558 IMPRESSIONS. Loving Power. Curtom 5009
      BM May p37-8. 150w. 3
      CAC July p140. 150w. $3\frac{1}{2}$

4559 IMPRESSIONS. Originals. ABC
      MM Nov. 20 p29. 100w. 4

4560 ISLEY Brothers. Harvest for the World. T-Neck PZ 33809.
      Cart. PZA 33809. Cass. PZT 33809
      BM Sept. p44. 200w. 3
      GR Aug. p351. 50w. 3
      MM June 19 p28. 300w. 3
      RS July 29 p52. 275w. 3
      SR Sept. p94. 225w. 4

4561 The ISLEY Brothers. The Heat Is On. T-Neck PZ 33536.
      Cart. PZA 33536. Cass. PZT 33536
      SR Oct. p78. 200w. $3\frac{1}{2}$

4562 ISLEY Brothers. Live It Up. T-Neck PZ 33070. Cart.
      PZA 33070. Cass. PZT 33070
      SR Jan. p86, 87. 500w. $4\frac{1}{2}$

4563 ISLEY Brothers. Super Hits. Tamla Motown STMA 8024 (E)
      (Reissue)
      MM Feb. 21 p30. 100w. 3

4564 ISLEY Brothers. Twist and Shout. DJM 22028 (E) (Reissue)
      MM March 6 p27. 100w. 3

4565 JACKSON, Jermaine. My Name Is.... Motown M6-842
      BM Oct. p43. 125w. 3

4566 JACKSON, Millie. Spring SP-1-6709. Cart. 8T-1-6709.
      Cass. CT-1-6709

        SR   Sept.   p95.   125w.   4

4567 JACKSON, Millie.   Free and in Love.   Spring 6709
        BM   July   p53.   250w.   4
        CAC   Aug.   p181.   150w.   5
        CRE   Aug.   p14.   25w. $3\frac{1}{2}$
        MM   June 19   p28.   500w.   4

4568 JACKSON, Millie.   Still Caught Up.   Spring 6708
        BM   Oct.   p27.   150w.   4

4569 JACKSON, Shawne.   RCA APL1-1320
        CRA   April   p74.   250w. $2\frac{1}{2}$

4570 JACKSON, Walter.   Feeling Good.   United Artists UALA
        656-G
        PRM   Oct.   p45.   350w. $2\frac{1}{2}$

4571 JADE Warrior.   Waves.   Island ILPS 9318
        DB   April 8   p26-7.   275w.   4
        LP   March   p8.   100w. $4\frac{1}{2}$

4572 JAH Lion.   Columbia Colly.   Mango 9386
        BM   Sept.   p48.   125w.   3
        RR   July   p80.   25w.   2

4573 JAH Woosh.   Dreadlock Affair.   Trojan 133 (E)
        BM   Dec.   p57.   125w.   2

4574 JAMES, Jimmy and the Vagabonds.   Now.   Pye NSPL 18495
        (E)
        BM   Sept.   p47.   125w.   3

4575 JARREAU, Al.   Glow.   Reprise M5 2248
        BM   Sept.   p47.   250w.   3
        MM   Aug. 28   p21.   350w.   3

4576 JARREAU, Al.   We Got By.   Reprise MS 2224
        BM   Dec.   p30.   200w.   5
        LP   April   p23.   100w. $1\frac{1}{2}$

4577 JBs.   Giving up Food for Funk.   Polydor 2392 204 (E)
        BM   May   p39.   200w.   4
        CAC   July   p140.   175w.   3

4578 JBs.   Hustle with Speed.   People 6606
        MM   Feb. 7   p23.   300w. $2\frac{1}{2}$

4579 JOHNSON Brothers.   Look Out for No. 1.   A&M SP 4567
        BM   July   p50.   225w.   4
        BS   June   p36.   50w.   3
        DB   Sept. 9   p22, 24.   225w. $1\frac{1}{2}$
        MM   May 22   p30.   150w. $2\frac{1}{2}$

RR Aug. p78. 75w. 3

4580 JOHNSON, Syl. Total Explosion. Hi 32096
      CRE July p12. 50w. 4

4581 JORDAN, Louis. MCA MCFM 2715 (E) (Reissue)
      ST June-July p194-5. 275w. $4\frac{1}{2}$

4582 JORDAN, Louis. Choo Choo Ch'boogie. Philips Int'l 6336
      246 (E) (Reissue)
      MM March 13 p26. 300w. $3\frac{1}{2}$

4583 JORDAN, Louis. Great Rhythm and Blues Oldies, Volume 1.
      Blues Spectrum 101
      CO May p16, 17. 225w. 4
      LB March/April p46. 225w. $4\frac{1}{2}$

4584 JORDAN, Louis. Swings! Black Lion BLP 30175 (E)
      RR Aug. p80. 25w. $2\frac{1}{2}$

4585 JOSEPH, Margie. Margie. Atlantic SD 18126
      BM Nov. 1975 p30. 200w. 3

4586 JOSEPH, Margie. Hear the Words, Feel the Feeling. Co-
      tillion SD 9906
      RS Nov. 4 p79. 100w. 2

4587 JOSEPH, Margie. Makes a New Impression. STX 1050 (Re-
      issue)
      BM Aug. p44. 50w. 3
      MM July 10 p22. 100w. $2\frac{1}{2}$

4588 KAY Gees. Hustle with Every Muscle. Polydor 2310 407
      (E)
      BM Oct. p41. 150w. 4
      MM Sept. 4 p22. 275w. $2\frac{1}{2}$

4589 KC and the Sunshine Band. Jay Boy JSL 9 (E)
      BM Oct. p28. 125w. 4

4590 KC and the Sunshine Band. Part 3. TK 605
      CRE Jan. p80, 82. 50w. $1\frac{1}{2}$
      RM Dec. p34. 150w. $2\frac{1}{2}$
      RS Dec. 16 p86, 88. 100w. 3

4591 KC and the Sunshine Band. Sound of.... Jay Boy JSL 8 (E)
      BM April p32. 225w. 2

4592 KENDRICKS, Eddie. Goin' up in Smoke. Tamla T6-346
      MM Nov. 27 p31. 325w. 2

4593 KENDRICKS, Eddie. He's a Friend. Tamla T6-343
      BM April p31. 150w. 3

RR Feb. p31. 125w. 3

4594 KENDRICKS, Eddie. The Hit Man. Tamla T6-338
        BM Nov. p32. 200w. 3

4595 KING, Ben E. I Had a Love. Atlantic SD 18169. Cart.
      TP-18169. Cass. CS-1869
        BM July p50. 175w. 5
        MM June 12 p25. 325w. 2
        RR Aug. p78. 25w. 3
        SR Aug. p76. 175w. 2

4596 KING, Ben E. Story of.... Atlantic K 50139 (E) (Reissue)
        BM Oct. p33. 125w. 2

4597 KING, Ben E. Supernatural. Atlantic SD-18132. Cass.
      CS-18132
        LP Aug. p17. 50w. 4
        SR Aug. p78. 200w. $4\frac{1}{2}$

4598 KING Tubby. Meets the Upsetters. Fay (E)
        MM March 13 p25. 100w. $2\frac{1}{2}$

4599 KING Tubby. Shalom Dub. Klik 9002 (E)
        BM Oct. p33. 100w. 3

4600 KISSOON, Mac and Katie Kissoon. Two of Us. State 2192
        BM Nov. p47-8. 125w. 2

4601-2 KNIGHT, Frederick. I've Been Lonely for So Long. Stax
      STX 1006 (Reissue)
        BM Aug. p44. 50w. 3
        MM July 10 p22. 100w. $3\frac{1}{2}$

4603 KNIGHT, Gladys and the Pips. Best of. Buddah BDS 5653
      (Reissue)
        BM May p34. 125w. 5
        BM Dec. p21. 300w. $4\frac{1}{2}$
        BS April p67. 100w. 4
        CAC April p16. 150w. $4\frac{1}{2}$

4604 KNIGHT, Gladys and the Pips. Bless This House. Buddah
      BDS 5651
        RS Dec. 30 p63. 50w. $2\frac{1}{2}$

4605 KNIGHT, Gladys and the Pips. A Little Knight Music. Soul
      S6-744
        BM April p31. 150w. 2
        GK March p1518. 50w. $2\frac{1}{2}$
        MM March 27 p28. 75w. $1\frac{1}{2}$

4606 KNIGHT, Gladys and the Pips. Pipe Dreams. Buddah (E)
        MM Nov. 27 p31. 475w. $2\frac{1}{2}$

4607 KNIGHT, Gladys and the Pips. Second Anniversary. Buddah
      BDS 5639
            BM   Dec. 1975. p30. 200w. 3
            CRE Feb. p12. 50w. 3
            SR   Feb. p83. 50w. 5

4608 KNIGHT, Gladys and the Pips. Super Hits. Tamla Motown
      STMA 8026 (E) (Reissue)
            BM   Nov. p40. 100w. 5
            CAC Nov. p296. 175w. $3\frac{1}{2}$
            GR   Oct. p666. 50w. 2
            MM   Oct. 16 p22. 75w. $2\frac{1}{2}$

4609 KNIGHT, Jean. Mr. Big Stuff. Stax STX 1044 (E)
            BM   April p32. 250w. 3
            MM   Jan. 24 p26. 150w. 3

4610 KOOL and the Gang. Greatest Hits. De-Lite 2015 (Reissue)
            BM   Oct. p28. 100w. 4

4611 KOOL and the Gang. Light of Worlds. De-Lite Dep-2014.
      Cart. 8088-2014. Cass. 5088-2014
            SR   March p76. 200w. 4

4612 KOOL and the Gang. Live at the "Sex Machine". Polydor
      2343 083 (E)
            MM   March 6 p34. 200w. 2

4613 KOOL and the Gang. Love and Understanding. De-Lite 2018
            BM   July p53. 175w. 4
            MM   July 3 p23. 200w. 3
            RR   Aug. p78. 25w. $2\frac{1}{3}$

4614 KOOL and the Gang. Spirit of the Boogie. De-Lite 2016
            CAC April p20. 75w. 4
            RR   Feb. p66. 25w. 2

4615 LABELLE. Nightbirds. Epic KE 33075. Cart. EA 33075.
      Cass. ET 33075
            SR   Feb. p93-4. 425w. 5

4616 LABELLE. Phoenix. Epic PE-33579. Cass. PET-33579.
      Cart. PEA-33579
            BM   Oct. p27. 150w. 5
            CIR Jan. 20 p21. 275w. $2\frac{1}{2}$
            CRE Feb. p12, 72. 25w. $2\frac{1}{2}$
            GR   Jan. p1258. 75w. $3\frac{1}{2}$
            HF   Jan. p102. 150w. $3\frac{1}{2}$
            LP   Jan. p24. 150w. 3
            SR   Jan. p83. 225w. 3

4617 LABELLE. Chameleon. Epic PE 34189
            CAC Dec. p341. 250w. 5

CIR   Nov. 10   p12-3.   425w.   3½
MM   Oct. 16   p26.   350w.   3
RR   Dec.   p99.   25w.   2½
RS   Oct. 7   p70.   250w.   3½

4618   LAFAYETTE Afro Rock Band.   Voodounon.   Editions Makossa
EM 23 04 (West Africa)
BM   Aug.   p40.   50w.   4

4619   LEE, Byron.   Disco Reggae.   Mercury SRM 1-1063
SOU   April   p45-6.   350w.   2½

4620   LEWIS, Linda.   Not a Little Girl Anymore.   Arista AL4047.
Cart. 8301-4047H
SR   Jan.   p84.   175w.   4

4621   LEWIS, Ramsey.   Salongo.   Columbia PC34273.   Cart. PCA
34173.   Cass. PCT 34173
BM   Nov.   p47.   125w.   4
SR   Nov.   p122-3.   100w.   3½

4622   LIGGINS, Joe.   Great Rhythm and Blues Oldies, Volume 6.
Blues Spectrum 106
CO   May   p16, 17.   225w.   4

4623   LIVINGSTONE, R. D.   Home from Home.   Charisma CAC
1119 (E)
BM   Oct.   p42.   175w.   4

4624   LOMAX, Jackie.   Livin for Lovin.   Capitol ST 11558
MG   Nov.   p56.   75w.   3
PRM   Sept.   p36.   325w.   2

4625   LOVE, Preston.   Omaha Bar-b-q.   United 7757 (Reissue)
LB   May-June   p38.   100w.   4

4626   LOVE Unlimited.   Music Maestro, Please.   20th Century
T 489
BM   March   p19-20.   200w.   3
MM   Feb. 7   p24.   75w.   2½

4627   LOVEQUAKE.   Power Exchange (E)
MM   Nov. 20   p26.   50w.   0

4628   LTD.   Love to the World.   A&M SP 4589
BM   Nov.   p47.   150w.   3

4629   LYNNE, Gloria.   I'm So in Love.   DJM (E) (Reissue)
MM   March 13   p24.   175w.   2½

4630   MFSB.   Philadelphia Freedom.   Philadelphia Int'l PZ 33845
CRA   April   p78.   100w.   1
HF   March   p106.   25w.   2

MM   Feb. 14 p30.   300w.   2
SOU Feb.   p46.   200w.   3

4631 MFSB. Summertime. Philadelphia International PZ 34238
BM   Oct. p41. 250w.   4

4632 McCOOK, Tommy. Horse 706 (E)
BM   Dec. p30. 150w.   2

4633 McCOOK, Tommy and the Agrovators. King Tubby Meets the
Agrovators at Dub Station. Live and Love 02 (E)
BM   April p34. 150w.   3

4634 McCOY, Van. Disco Kid. Avco AV 69009
LP   March p27. 100w.   2

4635 McCOY, Van. From Disco to Love. Buddah BDS 5648
SR   Nov. p98. 150w. $2\frac{1}{2}$

4636 McCRAE, George. Jay Boy JSL 10 (E)
BM   Oct. p8. 150w.   4

4637 McNEIR, Ronnie. Motown M6-870
BM   Oct. p43. 125w.   3

4638 MAGIC Disco Machine. Discotech. Motown M6-821
BM   Nov. p32. 100w.   3

4639 MAIN Ingredient. Euphrates River. RCA APL1-0335
AU   March p77. 300w.   1

4640 MAIN Ingredient. Super Hits. RCA APL1-1858 (Reissue)
BM   Nov. p45-6. 100w.   4
MM   Oct. 2 p30.   75w. $2\frac{1}{2}$

4641 MAJOR Harris. Jealousy. Atlantic SD 18160
BM   April p31. 250w.   3
MM   Feb. 28 p25. 200w. $2\frac{1}{2}$

4642 MANDRILL. Beast from the East. United Artists UALA
577G
BM   June p34. 125w.   2
MM   April 24 p35. 250w. $3\frac{1}{2}$

4643 MANDRILL. Best of.... Polydor PD1-6047 (Reissue)
BM   Oct. 1975 p28. 125w.   3

4644 MANHATTANS. Columbia PC 33820
BM   Nov. p45. 100w.   3
MM   Aug. 7 p18. 225w.   3

4645 MANHATTANS. I Want to Be Your Everything. DJM (E)
(Reissue)

MM Dec. 25 p17. 150w. 2

4646 MARLEY, Bob and the Wailers. The Birth of a Legend.
ATV Calla 2-CAS-1240 (2 discs) (Reissue)
    CRA Nov. p76. 175w. 4

4647 MARLEY, Bob and the Wailers. Catch a Fire. Island ILPS
9241
    MG Feb. p38. 50w. 3

4648 MARLEY, Bob and the Wailers. Live. Island ILPS 9376
    AU May p78. 250w. $3\frac{1}{2}$
    AU May p78-9. 450w. 4
    BM Jan. p24. 250w. 5
    DB Sept. 9 p24. 250w. 4
    GR March p1518. 25w. $2\frac{1}{2}$
    RM Dec. p31. 100w. $3\frac{1}{2}$
    RR Jan. p62. 50w. $1\frac{1}{2}$
    RS April 8 p76. 150w. 4

4649 MARLEY, Bob and the Wailers. Natty Dread. Island ILPS
9281. Cart. Y819281
    SR July p81. 275w. 1

4650 MARLEY, Bob and the Wailers. Rastaman Vibrations. Island
ILPS 9383. Cart. Y81-9383. Cass. ZCI-9383
    AU Sept. p73, 75. 550w. $3\frac{1}{2}$
    BM Sept. p44. 125w. 5
    CR Aug. 10 p11-2. 375w. $3\frac{1}{2}$
    CRA July p65-6, 69. 1900w. 4
    CRE Aug. p65. 225w. 1
    CRE Sept. p14. 75w. $3\frac{1}{2}$
    CRE Sept. p65. 50w. 3
    CRE Dec. p63. 50w. 1
    DB Sept. 7 p24. 250w. 4
    MM May 1 p31. 800w. $4\frac{1}{2}$
    PRM May p45. 800w. 4
    RR Aug. p78. 75w. 3
    RS June 17 p49. 1250w. $3\frac{1}{2}$
    SR Aug. p78. 275w. 2

4651 MASEKELA, Hugh. The Boy's Doin' It. Casablanca 7017
    BM Dec. p30. 100w. 4

4652 MASQUERADERS. Everybody Wanna Live On. ABC Hot But-
tered Soul ABCD 921
    LP Jan. p24. 100w. 3

4653 MAYFIELD, Curtis. Give, Get, Take and Have. Curtom 5007
    BM Oct. p43. 200w. 4
    BM Dec. p20. 300w. 4
    CRE Sept. p14. 50w. 4
    MM July 24 p24. 225w. $3\frac{1}{2}$

RS   Aug. 12   p58.   600w.   5

4654   MAYFIELD, Curtis.   Got to Find a Way.   Curtom CRS 8604
       SR   May   p82.   175w.   2

4655   MAYTALS.   Monkey Man.   Trojan Records TBL 107 (E)
       SO   May/June   p43.   125w. $2\frac{1}{2}$

4656   MELVIN, Harold and the Blue Notes.   Philadelphia Interna-
       tional PZ 33808.   Cart. PZA 33808.   Cass. PZT 33808
       HF   March   p106.   25w.   2

4657   MELVIN, Harold and the Blue Notes.   Greatest Hits.   Phila-
       delphia International PIR 81431 (E) (Reissue)
       BM   Sept.   p44.   150w.   5
       CAC   Oct.   p258.   50w. $4\frac{1}{2}$
       MM   July 31   p37.   75w. $2\frac{1}{2}$

4658   MELVIN, Harold and the Blue Notes.   Wake Up Everybody.
       Philadelphia International PZ 33808
       BM   March   p20.   200w.   4
       CAC   April   p18.   150w. $2\frac{1}{2}$
       CRA   April   p78.   100w.   1
       MM   March 6   p34.   600w.   3
       RR   April   p77.   200w.   4
       RS   Feb. 26   p74, 76.   325w. $3\frac{1}{2}$

4659   MEMPHIS Horns.   High on Music.   RCA APL 1-1355
       BM   Aug.   p46.   75w.   3

4660   METERS.   Best of....   Reprise (E) (Reissue)
       MM   July 31   p37.   75w. $2\frac{1}{2}$

4661   METERS.   Fire on the Bayou.   Reprise MS 2228
       BM   Dec.   p27.   250w.   4
       CRE   Jan.   p12.   25w. $3\frac{1}{2}$

4662   METERS.   Trick Bag.   Reprise MS 2252
       CRA   Oct.   p72.   250w.   4
       MG   Nov.   p56.   50w.   2
       MM   Aug. 14   p27.   275w.   2
       RR   Nov.   p106.   25w. $2\frac{1}{2}$
       RS   Oct. 7   p73, 75.   250w. $2\frac{1}{2}$

4663   MIGHTY Clouds of Joy.   Kickin'.   ABC ABCD 899
       CRA   May   p79.   250w.   2
       CRE   March   p12.   50w.   3
       SR   April   p86.   125w.   1

4664   MIGHTY Diamonds.   Right Time.   Virgin PZ 34235
       AU   Oct.   p130.   400w. $2\frac{1}{2}$
       BM   July   p50.   250w.   4
       MM   May 29   p26.   700w. $4\frac{1}{2}$

       RR July p80.   50w.   3
       RS Aug. 26 p60, 62.   200w. $3\frac{1}{2}$

4665 MILLINDER, Lucky. Lucky Days (1941-1945).   MCA 510.065
      (France) (Reissue)
       BU Jan. -Feb. p26-7.   350w.   4

4666 MILLS, Stephanie. For the First Time.   Motown M6-859
       BM July p51-2.   175w.   4
       SR March p86.   175w.   2

4667 MIRACLES. City of Angels.   Tamla T6-33951
       CRE April p72.   75w. $3\frac{1}{2}$
       LP March p27.   125w.   1

4668 MIRACLES. Love Machine.   Tamla Motown STML 12020 (E)
       BM May p35-6.   200w.   3

4669 MIRACLES. The Power of Music.   Tamla T6-344
       BM Dec. p53.   200w.   3

4670 MOMENTS. Sharp.   All Platinum 9109 302 (E)
       BM Oct. p27.   100w.   3

4671 MOON. Too Close for Comfort.   CBS 81456 (E)
       BM Oct. p43.   175w.   3

4672 MOORE, Dorothy. Misty Blue.   Contempo 535 (E)
       BM Oct. p41.   200w.   3

4673 MOORE, G. T. and the Reggae Guitars. Reggae Blue.
      Charisma (E)
       CAC Jan. p403.   100w. $2\frac{1}{2}$

4674 MOORE, Jackie. Make Me Feel Like a Woman.   Kayvette 801
       BM May p36.   125w.   3
       MM March 13 p24.   175w. $3\frac{1}{2}$

4675 MOORE, Melba. This Is It.   Buddah BDS 5657
       BM Aug. p42.   150w.   3
       MM June 19 p28.   225w.   2

4676 MUSCLE Shoals. Cream of.   Atlantic K 50283 (E) (Reissue)
       BM Sept. p47.   125w.   4
       MM Aug. 28 p20.   275w.   3

4677 NASH, Johnny. Tears on My Pillow.   Epic
       BM Oct. p34.   200w.   4

4678 NATURAL Four. Heaven Right Here on Earth.   Curtom 5004
       BM Oct. 1975. p27.   75w.   3

4679 NATURAL Four. Night Chaser.   Curtom 5008

BM   Aug.   p45.   125w.   3
MM   June 5 p19.   200w. $2\frac{1}{2}$

4680   NEGRIL.   Klik 9005 (E)
BM   April   p51.   325w.   4

4681   NELSON, Tracy.   Sweet Soul Music.   MCA MCA494.   Cart.
MCAT-494.   Cass.   MCAC-494
LP   Jan.   p11.   200w.   3
MG   Jan.   p33.   50w. $3\frac{1}{2}$
SR   Jan.   p88.   250w.   4

4682   NEW Birth.   Blind Baby.   Buddah BDS-5636.   Cass.   5320-
5636(H)
BM   Nov. 1975.   p32.   200w.   4
BM   Dec.   p19-20.   300w.   4
LP   Aug.   p17.   50w.   3

4683   NEW Edition.   Sunshine Saturday.   CBS 81432 (E)
MM   July 24 p25.   50w.   1

4684   NIGHTINGALE, Maxine.   Right Back Where We Started From.
United Artists UALA 626G
BS   Aug.   p61.   125w.   2

4685   NKENGAS.   Destruction.   Orbitone OT 005 (E)
BM   Aug. 1975 p40.   50w. $3\frac{1}{2}$

4686   NKENGAS.   In London.   Orbitone OT 006 (E)
BM   Aug. 1975 p40.   50w.   4

4687   NOTATIONS.   Gemingo 5501
BM   July   p52.   175w.   5

4688   OHIO Players.   Mercury SRM1-1122
BM   Aug.   p44.   150w.   5

4689   OHIO Players.   Contradictions.   Mercury SRM1-1088
MM   June 19 p28.   375w. $1\frac{1}{2}$

4690   OHIO Players.   First Impressions.   DJM DJ SLM 2015 (E)
(Reissue)
JJ   Jan.   p40.   50w.   1

4691   OHIO Players.   Honey.   Mercury SRM1-1038
BM   Nov. 1975 p30.   250w.   5
CRE   Jan.   p12.   50w.   4

4692   O'JAYS.   Family Reunion.   Philadelphia International PZ
33807.   Cart. PCA 33807.   Cass. PCT 33807
BM   March   p19.   200w.   5
CAC   May   p60, 62.   225w. $3\frac{1}{2}$
CRA   April   p78.   100w.   1

       CRE April p72, 74. 50w. 2
       HF March p106. 25w. 2
       MM Jan. 17 p39. 425w. $3\frac{1}{2}$
       RS Feb. 26 p73. 500w. 4

4693 O'JAYS. Message in the Music. Philadelphia International
      PZ 34245
       BM Nov. p46. 200w. 3
       MM Nov. 27 p31. 525w. $2\frac{1}{2}$
       RS Dec. 16 p88. 200w. $3\frac{1}{2}$

4694 ORIGINALS. California Sunset. Motown M6-826S1
       LP July p18. 75w. 2

4695 ORLEANS. Waking and Dreaming. Asylum 7E-1070. Cart.
      ET-1070. Cass. TC-1070
       AU Dec. p83-4. 550w. 1
       CIR Nov. 10 p16. 350w. $2\frac{1}{2}$
       GP Dec. p105. 25w. 3
       MM Sept. 20 p24. 400w. 4
       PRM Oct. p22. 100w. 3
       SR Nov. p108. 100w. 3

4696 OSIBISA. Ojah Awake. Island ILPS 9411
       MM Nov. 20 p28. 350w. 3

4697 OSIBISA. Welcome Home. Island ILPS 9355
       BM March p19. 200w. 5
       BM March p19. 200w. 5
       CRA July p78. 150w. 2
       GR March p1518. 50w. 2
       MM March 27 p28. 350w. $3\frac{1}{2}$
       RR Feb. p66-7. 50w. 4

4698 OTIS, Johnny. Great Rhythm and Blues Oldies, Volume 3.
      Blues Spectrum 103
       CO May p16, 17. 225w. 4

4699 OTIS, Shuggie. Inspiration Information. Epic KE-33059
       LP Aug. p11. 125w. 5

4700 OZO. Listen to the Buddah. DJM 4
       MM Nov. 27 p28. 75w. $1\frac{1}{2}$

4701 PAGE, Gene. Lovelock. Atlantic SD 18161
       CRA May p79. 200w. 3
       MM Feb. 28 p25. 200w. $2\frac{1}{2}$

4702 PARKS, Lloyd. Loving You. Trojan 126 (E)
       BM July p50. 300w. 2

4703 PARLIAMENT. Mothership Connection. Casablanca 7022
       BM Aug. p42. 225w. 5

RS   March 25 p66.   200w.   3

4704 PAUL, Billy. When Love Is New.   Philadelphia International
      PZ 33843
          BM   March p20.   300w.   4

4705 PEEBLES, Ann. Tellin' It.   Hi SHL 32091
          BM   March p19.   200w.   3
          CRE March p13.   50w.   3
          MM   Feb. 14 p30.   250w. $2\frac{1}{2}$
          RS   Jan. 29 p48.   200w. $2\frac{1}{2}$
          SR   March p90-1.   100w.   0

4706 PEOPLE's Choice. We Got the Rhythm.   Philadelphia Inter-
      national PZ 34124
          BM   Sept. p44.   150w.   4

4707 PERSUASIONS. I Just Want to Sing with My Friends.   A&M
      SP-3656
          LP   July p19.   125w. $3\frac{1}{2}$

4708 PHILLIPS, Esther. Confessin' the Blues.   Atlantic SD 1680.
      Cart. TP 1680
          BS   April p67.   125w.   3
          CAD April p31-2.   150w.   5
          DB   May 6 p24.   325w. $3\frac{1}{2}$
          SOU July p40-1.   75w.   3
          SR   June p94-5.   75w.   3

4709 PHILLIPS, Esther. For All We Know.   Kudu KU28.   Cart.
      KU828. Cass. KUC28
          CAC Aug. p181.   25w. $4\frac{1}{2}$
          HF   June p104.   125w.   2
          MG   June p52.   50w.   2

4710 PHILLIPS, Esther. Performance.   Kudu KU-18
          SR   Jan. p90.   350w.   5

4711 PHILLIPS, Esther, With Joe Beck. What a Difference a Day
      Makes.   Kudu KU-23
          BM   Dec. p30.   200w.   2
          CRE Feb. p72.   25w. $3\frac{1}{2}$

4712 PICKETT, Wilson. Chocolate Mountain.   Wicked 9001
          RS   Oct. 12 p68.   200w.   2

4713 PICKETT, Wilson. Peace Breaker.   DJM DJSL 064 (E)
          BM   Jan. p25.   250w.   2

4714 POLNAREFF, Michael. Atlantic K52081 (E)
          BM   Sept. p45.   100w.   3

4715 PRESTON, Billy. Billy's Bag.   DJM DJB 26082 (E) (partial

Reissue)
    BM   Dec. p55.   100w.   3
    MM   Nov. 20 p25.   200w.   3

4716 PRICE, Lloyd. Misty. DJM DJLS 074 (E) (Reissue)
    BM   Aug. p45.   125w.   3
    CAC Oct. p260.   325w.   2
    MM   June 26 p22.   50w. $2\frac{1}{2}$

4717 PRINCE Jazzbo. Kick Boy Face. Third World 109 (E)
    BM   Dec. p57.   225w.   4

4718 RADICE, Mark. Ain't Nothin But a Party. United Artists
LA 629G
    BM   Sept. p47.   200w.   3

4719 RANSOME-KUTI, Fela. Shakara. Creole CRLP 501 (E)
    BM   Aug. p40.   50w.   4
    MM   Aug. 21 p19.   225w.   4

4720 RARE Earth. Midnight Lady. Rare Earth R6-550
    BM   Aug. p44.   75w.   3

4721 RAS Michael and the Sons of Negus. Rastafari. Grounation
505 (E)
    BM   March p21.   350w.   4

4722 RAS Michael and the Sons of Negus. Tribute to the Emperor.
Trojan 132 (E)
    BM   Aug. p46.   150w.   4
    CRA Nov. p80.   100w. $3\frac{1}{2}$
    MM   June 26 p22.   225w.   3

4723 RAWLS, Lou. All Things in Time. Philadelphia International
PZ33957
    BM   Sept. p45.   125w.   5
    DB   Oct. 21 p23.   250w.   3
    MM   Aug. 28 p21.   350w. $3\frac{1}{2}$
    RS   Oct. 7 p81.   100w.   3

4724 REAL Thing. Pye NSPL 18507. United Artists UALA 676G
    BM   Dec. p51.   175w.   3

4725 REDDING, Otis. Live in Europe. Atco SD 33-286
    CRA March p77-8.   175w. $4\frac{1}{2}$

4726 REFLECTION. Love on Delivery. Capitol ST 11460
    BM   May p35.   150w.   4

4727 REVELATION. RSO 2394 161 (E)
    BM   April p32.   200w.   3
    MM   Feb. 7 p24.   200w. $2\frac{1}{2}$

4728   RHYTHM Heritage. Disco-Fied.   ABC 934
       BM   Aug.   p42.   100w.   3

4729   RIDGLEY, Tommy.   The New King of the Stroll.   Flyright
       LP519 (E) (Reissue)
       BM   Sept.   p45.   100w.   3
       BU   May-June p31-2.   250w. $2\frac{1}{2}$

4730   RIPERTON, Minnie.   Adventures in Paradise.   Epic PE 33454.
       Cart. PEA 33454.   Cass. PET 33454
       SR   Oct.   p85.   100w.   3

4731   ROBINSON, Smokey.   A Quiet Storm.   Tamla T6-337S1.
       Cart. T-337T.   Cass. T-337T
       LP   July   p19.   175w.   4
       SR   Aug.   p80.   100w.   5

4732   ROBINSON, Smokey.   Smokey's Family Robinson.   Tamla
       T6-341
       BM   June   p34.   225w.   4
       MM   April 24   p22.   550w.   3
       RS   May 6   p60, 62.   550w. $3\frac{1}{2}$

4733   ROBINSON, Smokey and the Miracles.   The Season for Mira-
       cles.   Tamla Motown T6-307
       RS   Dec. 30   p63.   100w.   3

4734   ROGERS, D. J.   It's Good to Be Alive.   RCA APL1-1099
       BS   April   p67.   100w.   3

4735   ROMEO, Max.   Revelation Time.   Sound Tracs 1000 (E)
       BM   March   p22.   400w.   4

4736   ROMEO, Max.   War in a Babylon.   Island ILPS 9392
       BM   Nov.   p49.   150w.   4

4737   RONETTES.   Greatest Hits.   Philadelphia International 2307
       003 (E) (Reissue)
       BM   Nov.   p31.   200w.   4

4738   ROSS, Diana.   Motown M6-861
       MM   April 17   p21.   100w.   2
       RS   May 6   p65.   225w.   3

4739   ROSS, Diana.   Greatest Hits, v. 2.   Motown M6-869 (Re-
       issue)
       BM   Oct.   p40.   125w.   2
       CAC   Nov.   p296.   175w. $3\frac{1}{2}$
       MM   Sept. 11   p26.   25w.   3

4740   ROY, C.   Mice.   Mercury SRM1-1056
       BM   Jan.   p25.   250w.   4

4741 ROY, I. Crisus Time. Virgin V2011 (E)
          BM Nov. p48-9. 200w. 3
          MM Sept. 18 p21. 400w. 1

4742 ROY, I. Truths and Rights. Grounation 504 (E)
          BM April p32, 34. 225w. 4

4743 RUFFIN, David. Everything's Coming Up Love. Motown
      M6-866
          BM Aug. p46. 125w. 3
          MM Aug. 28 p21. 350w. 3
          RS July 29 p50. 175w. 2½

4744 RUFFIN, David. Love Is All We Need. Polydor 2383 337
      (E)
          BM Oct. p28. 100w. 3

4745 RUFFIN, David. Who Am I? Motown M6-849-S1. Cass.
      M75-849-H
          BM March p29. 200w. 3
          LP March p28. 150w. 2
          MM Jan. 24 p27. 375w. 2½
          RS Jan. 1 p56. 225w. 3

4746 RUFUS, Featuring Chaka Khan. ABC ABCD-909. Cass.
      5022-909H. Cart. 8022 909H
          GR March p1518. 25w. 4
          HF April p129. 100w. 3
          LD March p28. 100w. 1½
          SR April p90. 150w. 4

4747 SAIN, Oliver. Blue Max. A-Bet 407
          LB May-June p38. 100w. 4

4748 SAIN, Oliver. Bus Stop. A-Bet 406
          LB May-June p38. 100w. 4

4749 SAIN, Oliver. Main Man. A-Bet 404
          LB May-June p38. 100w. 4

4750 SALSOUL Orchestra. Christmas Jollies. Sal-Soul SZS 5507
          MM Dec. 11 p22. 25w. 1
          RS Dec. 30 p64. 125w. 4

4751 SALSOUL Orchestra. Nice 'n' Nasty. Sal-Soul 5502
          MM Dec. 11 p22. 25w. 1½

4752 SALSOUL Orchestra. Salsoul Hustlers. Sal-Soul SZS 5501
          BM March p21. 300w. 4
          HF April p129. 200w. 1

4753 SAM and Dave. Back at 'Cha. United Artists UA-LA524-G
          LP April p24. 75w. 3

SR   Feb.   p85.   225w.   5

4754 SANBORN, David. Taking Off.   Warner BS 2873
      DB   Jan. 15   p26-7.   250w.   3

4755 SANTOS, Larry. You Are Everything I Need.   Casablanca
      7030
      BM   Nov.   p47.   50w.   2

4756 SATTERFIELD, Esther. The Need to Be.   A&M SP 3411
      CAD   Aug.   p25.   75w.   5
      SR   Nov.   p126.   125w.   3

4757 SATTERFIELD, Esther. Once I Loved.   A&M SP 3408
      DB   April 22   p33.   200w.   3
      LP   March   p18.   125w.   2

4758 SCORPIONS. Fly to the Rainbow.   RCA PPL1-4025
      CRE   June   p57-8.   100w.   2

4759 SCOTT, Bunny. To Love Somebody.   Klik 9004 (E)
      BM   March   p21.   250w.   3

4760 SCOTT-HERON, Gil. From South Africa to South Carolina.
      Arista 4044
      BM   May   p34-5.   350w.   4
      CRE   Feb.   p61-2.   475w.   1
      CRE   March   p13.   50w.   4
      RS   Jan. 15   p55.   225w.   3

4761 SCOTT-HERON, Gil. It's Your World.   Arista AL 5001 (2
      discs)
      MM   Nov. 13   p24.   600w.   3

4762 SEARCHERS. ATV/Pye
      CIR   Feb. 10   p48.   150w. $3\frac{1}{2}$

4763 SENSATIONAL Soul Orchestra. Tonight's the Night.   Gull
      (E)
      MM   May 15   p24.   50w.   1

4764 SHAKERS. Yankee Reggae.   Asylum 7E-1057
      CRA   July   p69.   50w.   3
      CRE   Sept.   p69.   25w.   1

4765 SHARP, Dee Dee. Happy Bout the Whole Thing.   Philadelphia
      International PZ 33839
      RS   March 3   p76.   225w. $2\frac{1}{2}$

4766 SHAW, Marlena. Just a Matter of Time.   Blue Note BN LA
      606-G
      BM   Oct.   p41-2.   200w.   3
      CAC   Oct.   p261.   125w.   2

CAD   Aug.   p25.   75w.   4

4767   SHAW, Marlena.   Who Is This Bitch, Anyway?   Blue Note
       BN-LA397-G.   Cart.   EA397-H
           SR   July   p82.   150w.   3

4768   SHEER Elegance.   ABC 963
           BM   Sept.   p46.   100w.   2

4769   SIGLER, Bunny.   My Music.   Philadelphia International PZ
       34267
           RS   Dec. 2   p99.   250w.   3

4770   SILVER Convention.   Midland International BKL1-1369
           CRA   April   p74.   250w.   2
           CRE   July   p82.   50w.   3
           RR   Feb.   p66.   25w. $2\frac{1}{2}$

4771   SILVER Convention.   Discotheque, v. 2.   Magnet MAG 5011
       (E)
           BM   June   p36.   200w.   1
           MM   May 22   p25.   75w. $2\frac{1}{2}$

4772   SILVER Convention.   Great Disco Soul.   Magnet (E)
           CAC   June   p98.   150w.   3

4773   SILVER Convention.   Save Me.   Midland International BKL
       1-1129
           CRE   Jan.   p80.   50w.   3

4774   SILVERSPOON, Dooley.   Selville SEL 1 (E)
           BM   Nov.   p31.   200w.   4

4775   SIMON, Joe.   The Chokin' Kind/Better Than Ever.   Monu-
       ment BZ 33879 (2 discs) (Reissue)
           BM   Sept.   p46.   150w.   4
           MM   June 19   p28.   50w.   3

4776   SIMON, Joe.   Drowning in the Sea of Love.   Polydor 2482
       278 (E) (Reissue)
           BM   May   p38.   175w.   4
           CAC   July   p143, 146.   225w. $3\frac{1}{2}$
           MM   March 6   p34.   200w. $2\frac{1}{2}$

4777   SIMON, Joe.   Get Down.   Spring 6706
           BM   Nov.   p31.   175w.   3

4778   SIMON, Joe.   Today.   Spring 6710
           BM   Dec.   p53.   150w.   2
           MM   Oct. 16   p26.   375w.   4
           RS   Sept. 9   p58.   150w.   4

4779   SIMONE, Nina.   Fine and Mellow.   Golden Hour GH 607 (E)

(Reissue)
   BM   Nov.   p31.   150w.   3

4780   SIMONE, Nina.   The Finest of....   Bethlehem BCP 6003 (Re-
       issue)
       CRA   April   p78.   150w. $4\frac{1}{2}$

4781   SIMONE, Nina.   I Love You Porgy.   Bethlehem BCP 6003
       (Reissue)
       CAD   Feb.   p27.   75w. $2\frac{1}{2}$
       SR   Feb.   p91-2.   100w.   4

4782   SIMONE, Nina.   In Concert.   Contempo 531 (E)
       BM   Jan.   p26.   50w.   3

4783   SIMONE, Nina.   Live at Berkeley.   Contempo 530 (E)
       BM   April   p51.   125w.   3

4784   SIMONE, Nina.   Sings Billie Holiday.   Contempo 529 (E) (Re-
       issue)
       BM   Jan.   p26.   50w.   4

4785   SIMONE, Nina.   Songs of the Poets.   RCA APL1-1788
       SR   Nov.   p126.   325w.   3

4786   SIR COXSON Sound.   King of the Dub Rock.   Safari 100 (E)
       BM   Oct.   p33.   150w.   4

4787   SLEDGE, Percy.   Golden Voice of Soul.   Atlantic K 50169 (E)
       (Reissue)
       BM   Oct.   p34.   250w.   3

4788   SLEDGE, Percy.   I'll Be Your Everything.   Capricorn
       CP-0147.   Cass. M5-0147
       LP   July   p19.   125w. $3\frac{1}{2}$

4789   SMALL, Millie.   Free and in Love.   Spring
       BS   Aug.   p61.   50w.   3

4790   SNAFU.   All Funked Out.   Capitol ST 11473
       RR   Feb.   p67.   25w. $2\frac{1}{2}$

4791   SONS of Negus.   Freedom Sounds.   Dynamic 3004 (E)
       BM   Sept.   p45.   100w.   4

4792   SOUL Affair Orchestra.   Creole CRLP 506 (E)
       BM   July   p51.   125w.   1

4793   SOUL Children.   Finders Keepers.   Epic PE 33902
       MG   June   p52.   250w.   3
       RS   June 3   p79.   175w.   4

4794   SOUL Children.   Friction.   Stax STX 1005

BM Dec. p20-1. 300w. 5

4795 SPENCE, Barrington. Speak Softly. Trojan 117 (E)
      BM Dec. p28. 200w. 4

4796 SPENCE, Barrington. Tears on My Pillow. Klik 9014 (E)
      BM Dec. p57. 225w. 3

4797 SPINNERS. Happiness Is Being with the Spinners. Atlantic
      SD 18181
      BM Oct. p40. 250w. 4
      DB Dec. 2 p21. 225w. 4
      MM Sept. 4 p22. 425w. $3\frac{1}{2}$

4798 SPINNERS. Atlantic SD2-910. Cart. TP2-910
      LP April p24. 225w. $2\frac{1}{2}$
      MM Jan. 17 p39. 400w. $1\frac{1}{2}$
      SR April p92. 150w. 2

4799 SPINNERS. Pick of the Litter. Atlantic SD 18141. Cart.
      TP 18141. Cass. CS 18141
      BM Oct. 1975 p28. 100w. 4
      CRE April p74. 50w. $3\frac{1}{2}$
      SR Jan. p93-4. 125w. 2

4800 SSO. Tonight's the Night. Shadybrook 33001
      BM July p52. 25w. 1

4801 STAIRSTEPS. Second Resurrection. Dark Horse 2004
      BM May p26. 175w. 4
      HF July p104-5. 325w. $3\frac{1}{2}$
      RS April 8 p77. 300w. $3\frac{1}{2}$

4802 STAPLE Singers. Let's Do It Again. Warner Brothers
      BM Jan. p24-5. 250w. 4
      BS March p64. 50w. $2\frac{1}{2}$

4803 STAPLE Singers. Pass It On. Warner Brothers BS 2945
      RS Nov. 4 p70, 72. 200w. $2\frac{1}{2}$

4804 STATON, Candi. Young Hearts Run Free. Warner Brothers
      BS 2948
      BM Aug. p42. 100w. 3
      RS Aug. 26 p55. 175w. $2\frac{1}{2}$

4805 STEWART, Al. Year of the Cat. Janus JXS 7022
      AU Dec. p87. 100w. $4\frac{1}{2}$

4806 STONE, R. & J. We Do It. RCA RS 1052 (E)
      BM Aug. p45. 75w. 3

4807 STONE, Sly. Heard Ya Missed Me, Well I'm Back. Epic
      PE 34348

MM Dec. 11 p22. 475w. 1

4808 STONE, Sly. High on You. Epic PE 33835
      BM March p19. 200w. 4
      CRE April p74. 25w. 3
      DB March 25 p30-1. 250w. 4
      LP March p28. 75w. $3\frac{1}{2}$
      MG Jan. p34. 50w. 3
      RR March p72. 150w. $4\frac{1}{2}$
      SR March p92. 200w. 3

4809 STONEHAM, Harry. This Is. DJM 22045 (E)
      MM Nov. 20 p26. 100w. 1

4810 STREETWALKERS. Mercury SRM-1-1060
      SR March p94. 175w. 0

4811 STRONG, Barrett. Stronghold. Capitol ST 11376
      BM Oct. p27. 200w. 4

4812 STYLISTICS. Fabulous. H & L 69013
      BM July p52-3. 125w. 2
      CAC July p146. 150w. 1
      MM June 19 p28. 300w. $1\frac{1}{2}$

4813 STYLISTICS. You Are Beautiful. H & L 69010
      BS March p65-6. 150w. 4
      HF March p113. 50w. $3\frac{1}{2}$
      RR Feb. p166. 50w. 1

4814 SUMMER, Donna. Love to Love You Baby. Oasis OCLP
      5003
      HF March p107. 250w. $2\frac{1}{2}$
      SR July p95. 200w. 4

4815 SUMMER, Donna. A Love Trilogy. Oasis OCLP 5004. Cart.
      5004. Cass. 5004
      BM July p51. 225w. 4
      CRE Sept. p70. 50w. $3\frac{1}{2}$
      SR Sept. p104, 107. 150w. 2

4816 SUN. Love On, Dream On. Capitol ST 11461
      BM July p50. 100w. 2

4817 SUPREMES. High Energy. Motown M6-863
      BM July p52. 200w. 3
      CAC Aug. p183. 150w. 2
      MM June 19 p28. 325w. $1\frac{1}{2}$

4818 SWAMP Dogg. Greatest Hits. Swamp Dogg 3002
      CRA Oct. p81. 225w. 4
      RS June 17 p58. 350w. $3\frac{1}{2}$

4819 SWAMP Dogg.   You Ain't Never Too Old to Boogie.   DJM
      DJF 20476 (E)
          BM   Sept.   p47-8.   125w.   5
          CAC Oct.   p260.   200w. $2\frac{1}{2}$
          MM   Aug. 21 p18.   25w.   3

4820 SWEET Honey in the Rock.   Flying Fish FF 022
          CAD Dec.   p31-2.   200w. $2\frac{1}{2}$

4821 SWEET Sensation.   Sad Sweet Dreamer.   Pye 12110
          LP   July   p19.   75w.   2

4822 TAVARES.   In the City.   Capitol ST 11396
          BM   Dec.   p30.   200w.   4
          CRE Jan.   p80.   50w.   4

4823 TAVARES.   Sky High.   Capitol ST 11533
          BM   Nov.   p45.   150w.   3
          CAC Nov.   p298.   150w. $3\frac{1}{2}$
          CRE Dec.   p70.   75w.   3
          MM   Aug. 7 p18.   225w.   3

4824 TAYLOR, Johnnie.   Best of....   Stax STX 1049 (Reissue)
          BM   Sept.   p45.   100w.   5
          MM   July 10 p22.   100w. $3\frac{1}{2}$

4825 TAYLOR, Johnnie.   Eargasm.   Columbia PC 33951
          BM   June   p34.   200w.   4
          MG   June   p52.   200w. $4\frac{1}{2}$
          MM   April 24 p35.   550w. $3\frac{1}{2}$
          RS   June 3 p79.   250w.   3

4826 TEMPREES.   Three.   Stax STX 1040
          BM   Oct.   p33.   75w.   3

4827 TEMPTATIONS.   Do the Temptations.   Gordy G6-975
          BM   Oct.   p43.   300w.   4
          RS   Nov. 18 p75.   250w.   3

4828 TEMPTATIONS.   House Party.   Gordy G6-973 S1
          CAC March p493.   150w. $2\frac{1}{2}$
          LP   April p24.   50w. $2\frac{1}{2}$

4829 TEMPTATIONS.   A Song for You.   Gordy G6-969S 1.
      Cart. G969T.   Cass. G969T
          SR   July   p82.   175w.   4

4830 TEMPTATIONS.   Wings of Love.   Gordy G6-971
          BM   June   p34.   250w.   4
          MM   April 24 p22.   550w.   3

4831 THIRD World.   Island ILPS 9369
          AU   July   p70.   250w.   3

     BM   Sept. p45. 150w. 4
     CRE July p68. 25w. 3
     MM July 3 p22. 200w. 3
     RR July p80. 75w. $3\frac{1}{2}$
     RS May 20 p69, 71. 150w. $2\frac{1}{2}$

4832 THOMAS, Rufus. Best of....   Stax STX 1046 (Reissue)
     BM June p37. 100w. 3
     MM March 13 p23. 75w. $1\frac{1}{2}$

4833 THOMPSON, Lenval. Don't Cut Off Your Dreadlocks. Third
    World 010 (E)
     BM Oct. p45. 125w. 4

4834 The THREE Degrees. International. Philadelphia Interna-
    tional KZ 33162. Cart. ZA 33162. Cass. ZT 33162
     SR Nov. p106. 100w. 2

4835 THREE Degrees. Live. Philadelphia International PZ 33840
     RR Feb. p66. 25w. 3

4836 THREE Pieces. Vibes of Truth. Fantasy F 9476
     AU Feb. p87, 93. 500w. $4\frac{1}{2}$

4837 TIPPETTS, Julie. Sunset Glow. Utopia BUL1-1248
     DB May 6 p29-30. 275w. 5

4838 TOOTS and the Maytals. Funky Kingston. Island ILPS 9330
     CRA Jan. p73. 225w. 3
     CRE Jan. p65. 175w. $4\frac{1}{2}$
     CRE Jan. p84. 50w. 5
     DB Jan. 15 p27-8. 150w. 3
     SO May/June p42-3. 50w. $3\frac{1}{2}$
     SR Feb. p89. 100w. 5

4839 TOOTS and the Maytals. In the Dark. Dragon DRLS 5004
     DB Jan. 15 p27-8. 150w. 3
     SO May/June p43. 25w. $2\frac{1}{2}$

4840 TOOTS and the Maytals. Reggae Got Soul. Island ILPS 9377
     AU Oct. p130. 400w. 4
     BM May p38. 300w. 4
     CIR Oct. 12 p15-6. 575w. 3
     CRA July p65-6, 69. 1900w. $3\frac{1}{2}$
     RR Aug. p78. 25w. $3\frac{1}{2}$
     RS July 29 p49. 275w. $3\frac{1}{2}$
     SR Nov. p112. 100w. 3

4841-6 [No entries.]

4847 TOSH, Peter. Legalize It. Columbia PC 34253
     AU Oct. p130. 400w. 4
     BM Nov. p49. 350w. 4

CRA Oct. p72, 74. 300w. $4\frac{1}{2}$
MM Aug. 7 p18. 475w. 3
RM Nov. p29. 175w. 3
RR Nov. p106. 50w. $2\frac{1}{2}$
RS Aug. 26 p60, 62. 200w. 3
SR Nov. p112. 250w. 2

4848 TOUSSAINT, Allen. Southern Nights. Reprise MS 2186.
Cart. M 82186. Cass. M 52186
SR July p73. 450w. $4\frac{1}{2}$

4849 TOWER of Power. Ain't Nothin Stoppin' Us Now. Columbia
PC 34302
MM Nov. 20 p26. 75w. $1\frac{1}{2}$
RS Nov. 4 p62, 65. 500w. 4

4850 TOWER of Power. In the Slot. Warner BS 2880. Cass.
M5 2880
BM April p51. 125w. 2
CRA Feb. p74. 150w. $3\frac{1}{2}$
LP March p28. 50w. $3\frac{1}{2}$
RR Feb. p66. 25w. $1\frac{1}{2}$

4851 TOWER of Power. Live and in Living Colour. Warner
Brothers BS 2834
BM Aug. p42. 150w. 4
MM May 8 p22. 175w. 3

4852 TOWNSEND, Ed. Now. Curtom 5006
BM May p36. 200w. 4
MM April 17 p41. 275w. $1\frac{1}{2}$

4853 TRAMMPS. Philadelphia International KZ33163
BM May p38. 100w. 2

4854 TRAMMPS. The Legendary "Zing" Album. Buddah BDS
5641 (Reissue)
BM Dec. p21. 300w. 4

4855 TRAMMPS. Where the Happy People Go. Atlantic SD 18172
BM July p50. 200w. 3
RS July 1 p75-6. 300w. 3

4856 TREMELOES. Shiner. DJM DJLPA 2A
MG Sept. p58. 25w. $3\frac{1}{2}$

4857 TRUE, Andrea. More, More, More. Buddah BDS 5670
BM Aug. p46. 75w. 3
CRE Dec. p70. 50w. $3\frac{1}{2}$

4858 TURNER, Ike. Funky Mule. DJM DJSLM 2010 (E) (Reissue)
BM Nov. 1975 p32. 150w. 3
BU Jan.-Feb. p29-30. 300w. $2\frac{1}{2}$

4859 TURNER, Ike and Tina. Her Man ... His Woman. Capitol
      SM 571 (Reissue)
            MM May 15 p24. 50w. $2\frac{1}{2}$

4860 TURNER, Ike and Tina Turner. Souled from the Vaults.
      DJM 8006 (E) (Reissue)
            BM Dec. p28, 30. 250w. 3

4861 TURNER, Ike and Tina Turner. The Very Best of. United
      United Artists UALA 592G (Reissue)
            CAC July p146. 200w. $3\frac{1}{2}$
            MM May 22 p25. 100w. $1\frac{1}{2}$

4862 TURNER, Tina. Acid Queen. United Artists UALA 495G.
      Cart. EA 495-H. Cass. CA 495-H
            BM Dec. p30. 125w. 4
            CAC Jan. p403. 225w. $4\frac{1}{2}$
            GR Jan. p1258. 50w. 3
            LP March p28. 100w. 2
            SR Jan. p76-7. 325w. 5

4863 TURNER, Tina. Tina Turns the Country On. United Artists
      UA-LA200 G. Cart. EA200-G
            SR Jan. p95, 96. 300w. 4

4864 TWENTIETH Century Steel Band. "Yellow Bird" Is Dead.
      United Artists 29980 (E)
            BM Nov. p45. 150w. 4
            MM Oct. 16 p22. 175w. 3

4865 TWINKLE Brothers. Rasta Pon Top. Grounation 506 (E)
            BM May p39. 300w. 4

4866 TYMES. Up. RCA APL 1-1072
            BM May p35. 200w. 4

4867 U Brown. Satta Dread. Klik 9018 (E)
            BM Dec. p57. 125w. 3

4868 U Roy. Best of. Live and Love 008 (E) (Reissue)
            BM Dec. p57. 225w. 3

4869 U Roy. Dread in Babylon. Virgin PZ 34234
            BM May p35. 200w. 4
            CRA July p69. 75w. 3
            RS Aug. 26 p60, 62. 200w. $3\frac{1}{2}$

4870 U Roy. Natty Rebel. Virgin V 2059 (E)
            BM Oct. p45. 125w. 3

4871 UNDISPUTED Truth. Higher Than High. Gordy G6-972
            CRE March p72. 450w. 3
            GR Feb. p1389. 125w. 3

4872 UPSETTERS. Superape. Island ILPS 9417
        BM Oct. p45. 150w. 5

4873 VELEZ, Martha. Escape from Babylon. Sire SASD-7515.
      Cart. 8147-7515-H
        CRA July p76. 175w. 3
        MM Sept. 11 p29. 200w. 3
        RS May 20 p71, 73. 300w. 3
        SR Sept. p107. 100w. 0

4874 The VOICES of East Harlem. Can You Feel It? Just Sun-
      shine JSS-3504. Cart. 8156-3504 H. Cass. 5156-3504 H
        SR Jan. p96. 200w. 4

4875 WAILER, Bunny. Blackheart Man. Island ILPS 9415
        BM Nov. p49. 200w. 5
        CRA Nov. p76. 100w. 3½
        MM Aug. 28 p20. 800w. 3
        MM Dec. 25 p19. 250w. 4½
        RS Dec. 2 p104, 107. 225w. 3

4876 WAILERS. African Herbsman. Trojan TRLS 62 (E)
        SO May/June p43. 50w. 4½

4877 WAILERS. Catch a Fire. Island SW-9239
        SO May/June p43. 75w. 2½

4878 WAILERS. Rasta Revolution. Trojan TRLS 89 (E)
        SO May/June p43. 75w. 3½

4879 WAKELIN, Johnny. Reggae Soul and Rock 'n' Roll. Pye
      NSPL 18487 (E)
        MM Sept. 25 p24. 50w. 2½

4880 WALKER, Junior. Sax Appeal. Soul S6-747
        BM Oct. p41. 150w. 2
        GR Sept. p493. 25w. 2

4881 WALKER, Junior. Whooper Bopper. Soul S6-748
        PRM Nov. p44. 350w. 3

4882 WALKER, Junior and the All-Stars. Hot Shot. Soul S6-745
        BM May p34. 150w. 3
        MM April 3 p29. 275w. 3½
        RS March 25 p64. 175w. 3

4883 WAR. Greatest Hits. United Artists UALA 648G. Cart.
      EA648H. Cass. CA648H (Reissue)
        BM Dec. p53, 55. 150w. 4
        CRE Dec. p63. 125w. 3
        MM Oct. 23 p27. 225w. 2½
        SR Dec. p116. 100w. 4½

4884   WAR.   Why Can't We Be Friends?   United Artists UA-LA441-
       G.   Cart. UA-EA441-H.   Cass. UA-CA441-H
           BM   April p31.   225w.   4
           MM   Feb. 21 p29.   425w.   2
           RR   May p74.   50w.   2
           SR   Nov.   p110.   100w. $4\frac{1}{2}$

4885   WASHINGTON, Delroy.   I-sus.   Virgin V 2060 (E)
           BM   Oct.   p45.   150w.   4

4886   WASHINGTON, Dinah.   Philips SON 026 BS (E) (Reissue)
           MM   Oct. 16 p30.   350w.   3

4887   WASHINGTON, Geno.   Geno's Back.   DJM 457 (E)
           BM   April p51.   100w.   1
           MM   April 17 p23.   150w.   4

4888   [No entry.]

4889   WASHINGTON, Grover Jr.   All the King's Horses.   Kudu 07
           BM   Dec.   p28.   125w.   4

4890   WASHINGTON, Grover Jr.   Feels So Good.   Kudu 24
           BM   May p34.   225w.   4
           CRA   Feb.   p76.   150w. $2\frac{1}{2}$
           DB   March 11 p22-3.   300w. $2\frac{1}{2}$

4891   WASHINGTON, Grover Jr.   Mister Magic.   Kudu KU-20.
       Cart. KU8-20.   Cass. KUC-20
           BM   Dec. 1975 p28.   125w.   4
           CAC   March p488.   50w. $3\frac{1}{2}$
           SR   Aug.   p89.   100w.   4

4892   WASHINGTON, Grover Jr.   Soul Box Vol. 1, 2.   Kudu KUX
       1213 (2 discs) (Reissue)
           HF   May p103.   250w.   2

4893   WATSON, Johnny "Guitar".   Ain't That a Bitch.   DJM 3
           BM   Nov.   p46.   300w.   4
           CAC   Nov.   p298.   125w.   3
           MM   Sept. 25 p24.   250w.   3

4894   WATSON, Johnny "Guitar".   The Gangster Is Back.   Red
       Lightnin' 0013 (E) (Reissue)
           BM   April p35.   275w.   3
           CZM   June p40.   125w.   4
           LB   May/June p43.   425w. $4\frac{1}{2}$
           MM   May 15 p27.   300w.   2

4895   WATSON, Johnny "Guitar".   I Don't Want to Be a Lone
       Ranger.   Fantasy 9484
           LB   May-June p43-4.   150w.   4

4896 WATSON, Johnny "Guitar". Listen. Fantasy 9437
     LB May-June p43-4. 150w. 4

4897 WATSON, Wah Wah. Elementary. Columbia PC 34328
     CRA Dec. p74. 225w. $2\frac{1}{2}$
     MM Oct. 16 p26. 450w. 3
     RS Dec. 16 p97-8. 250w. 4

4898 WEST Wing. 20th Century T 488
     LP April p24. 50w. 1

4899 WHITE, Barry. Greatest Hits. 20th Century T 493 (Re-
     issue)
     BM Dec. p27. 200w. 5
     BM Dec. p20. 300w. 4

4900 WHITE, Barry. Just Another Way to Say I Love You. 20th
     Century T-466. Cart. 8466. Cass. C466
     SR Oct. p88. 75w. 4

4901 WHITE, Barry. Let the Music Play. 20th Century BT 502
     BM March p21. 300w. 4
     MG June p52. 50w. 1
     MM Feb. 28 p25. 200w. $2\frac{1}{2}$

4902 WILD Cherry. Epic PE 34195
     BM Dec. p55. 250w. 4

4903 WILD Tchoupitoulas. Island ILPS 9360
     AU Oct. p136-7. 200w. $2\frac{1}{2}$
     CRA Sept. p80-1. 175w. 3
     RS Aug. 26 p58. 275w. 3

4904 WILLIAMS, Danny. To Know You Is to Love You. Philips
     6382 116 (E)
     BM April p51. 100w. 3

4905 WILLIAMS, Deniece. This Is Niecy. Columbia PC 34242
     CRA Nov. p80. 150w. 3

4906 WILSON, Jackie. Very Best. Brunswick BRLS 3016 (E)
     (Reissue)
     BM Oct. p34. 150w. 4

4907 WITHERS, Bill. The Best of Bill Withers. Sussex SRA-8037.
     Cass. F-58037
     LP Aug. p18. 50w. 4

4908 WITHERS, Bill. Making Music. Columbia PC 33704. Cart.
     PCA 33704. Cass. PCT 33704
     BS March p65. 200w. $3\frac{1}{2}$
     LP March p28. 100w. $2\frac{1}{2}$
     MHF June-July p69-70. 150w. $2\frac{1}{2}$

RR   Feb.   p66.   50w.   3
RS   Jan. 1   p62.   200w. $3\frac{1}{2}$
SR   March   p94-5.   50w.   4

4909   WOMACK, Bobby.   B W Goes C & W.   United Artists UALA 638G
BM   Oct.   p42.   200w.   4
CMP   Nov.   p41.   200w.   3
CMR   Oct.   p34.   150w.   3
CS   Nov.   p41.   125w. $2\frac{1}{2}$
MM   Sept. 4   p22.   300w.   3

4910   WOMACK, Bobby.   I Don't Know What the World Is Coming To.   United Artists UA-LA353-G.   Cart. EA353-H.   Cass. CA353-H
SR   Aug.   p85.   200w.   4

4911   WOMACK, Bobby.   Safety Zone.   United Artists UALA 544G.   Cass. UACA 544H
BM   June   p37.   200w.   5
CIR   Feb. 10   p48.   200w. $3\frac{1}{2}$
LP   April   p24.   100w.   3
RS   Jan. 15   p55.   225w. $2\frac{1}{2}$

4912   WONDER, Stevie.   Songs in the Key of Life.   Tamla T13-340 (2 discs)
BM   Dec.   p50-1.   1400w.   5
CAC   Nov.   p298, 300.   300w. $4\frac{1}{2}$
CIR   Dec. 30   p12.   675w.   3
CK   Dec.   p48.   400w. $4\frac{1}{2}$
CRA   Dec.   p65-6.   2100w. $4\frac{1}{2}$
GRA   Dec.   p1076.   100w.   2
ME   Nov.   p55.   55w. $4\frac{1}{2}$
MM   Oct. 9   p32.   1000w.   4
MM   Dec. 25   p19.   350w. $4\frac{1}{2}$
RS   Dec. 16   p74, 77-8.   2300w.   5

4913   WRIGHT, Betty.   Explosion.   Alston 4402
RS   July 1   p67.   325w.   4
RR   Dec.   p105.   25w.   3

4914   WRIGHT, O. V.   Memphis Unlimited.   Back Beat 72
LB   May-June   p37.   475w. $2\frac{1}{2}$

4915   ZAP Pow.   Now.   Vulcan 004 (E)
BM   Oct.   p44.   250w.   4

4916   ZAP Pow.   Revelation.   Trojan 103 (E)
BM   Nov.   p48.   125w.   3

POPULAR RELIGIOUS MUSIC

Without regard to genre, this section comprises all religious items except for classically based church music such as cantatas, masses, "authorized" hymns, and soundtracks. Here will be found those items expressed in another genre: the country and western hymn, the old timey call, the spiritual and gospel elements, the jazz masses, the "Jesus Rock," and so forth. In other words, "secular" or "vulgar" religious music.

There is no one review medium for this music as there is for classical church music reviewed under "Classical" sections in magazines. Secular items are reviewed when they appear in a genre format. Jazz Journal seems to be the best for jazz, and both Blues Unlimited and Jazz Journal are the best for gospel. The latter, plus country and western hymns, are still underdeveloped areas in the recording field. Most blues and country albums have a smattering of religious music, but seldom are the tracks ever compiled into one specific disc. This is still a big singles market. There are, though, two distinct markets of appeal, based on the dichotomy between the styles of the happy black gospel and the solemn white country hymn. Bluegrass magazines usually give much information on sacred music, as well as the British Country Music People.

4917   ALEXANDER Brothers.   One Way Up Above.   Pine Tree 536
       BGU   Nov.   p36.   75w.   1½

4918   ALLEN, Rance.   Sanctified.   Stax STX 1036
       BM   Dec.   p21.   300w.   4

4919   ANDREWS, Inez.   War on Sin.   ABC SBLP 266
       CRA   Oct.   p70.   75w.   2½

4920   AUSTIN, Harold.   Kentucky Bluegrass Preacher Man.   Atteiram APL1 1519A
       BGU   Feb.   p23.   125w.   2½
       MN   V7/#1   p24.   250w.   2½

4921   BAILEY, Charles.   Everlasting Joy: Early Bluegrass Gospel.
       Old Homestead OHCS 102 (Reissue)
       BGU   Dec.   p26-7.   550w.   3
       MN   V7/#6   p17-8.   400w.   2½
       OTM   Autumn   p22.   75w.   2½

4922 BALL, E. C. and Orna Ball. Fathers Haven Home Sweet
      Home. Rounder 0072
          OTM Autumn p23. 150w. 4

4923 BLUEGRASS Meditations. Remember the Cross. NRP 6596
          BGU June p46. 150w. $2\frac{1}{2}$

4924 BOONE, Pat. S-A-V-E-D. Lamb & Lion LL 2011
          CMP Jan. p26. 250w. 5

4925 BRYSON, Wally. Follow His Footsteps. Davis Unlimited
      33019
          BGU Jan. p16. 150w. 3
          OTM Winter p28. 300w. $2\frac{1}{2}$
          PIC April p68. 100w. 2

4926 BYRD Family. A Million Years in Glory. Grand DB
      3006
          BGU Aug. p37. 75w. $2\frac{1}{2}$

4927 CAMPBELL, Ethna. The Old Rugged Cross & Other Favou-
      rites. Phillips 6382 115 (E)
          CMP Aug. p31. 300w. 3

4928 CASH, Johnny. Precious Memories. Columbia PC 33087
      (Reissue)
          CMR April p37. 125w. 1

4929 CEASER, Shirley. Be Careful of the Stones You Throw.
      HOB HBX 2181
          CRA Oct. p70. 50w. $2\frac{1}{2}$

4930 CEASER, Shirley. No Change. HOB HBX 2176
          BM Oct. 1975 p38. 75w. 4

4931 CHUCK Wagon Gang. The Sweetest Songs We Know. Colum-
      bia KC 34033
          CMR Sept. p33. 100w. $2\frac{1}{2}$

4932 CLEVELAND, James. Give It to Me. Savoy 14412
          CRA Oct. p70. 100w. $3\frac{1}{2}$

4933 CLEVELAND, James. To the Glory of God. Savoy 14360
          BM Oct. 1975 p38. 150w. 4

4934 COLYER, Ken. Spirituals. Joys 235/6 (2 discs) (E)
          CO June p15. 450w. 4

4935 CRANK, Tommy. Best Bluegrass Gospel. Pine Tree PTS 350
          BGU Nov. p27. 150w. 2

4936 CRANK, Tommy. Sings Revival Songs. Pine Tree PTSLP
          BGU Nov. p27. 150w. $3\frac{1}{2}$

4937 CROWE, J. D.   The Model Church.   Lemco 611
      CMR   April   p37.   250w.   3

4938 DAVIS, Jimmie.   Lord, Let Me Be There.   Canaan CGS
      8506
      CMP   March   p22.   250w.   5

4939 DIXIE Hummingbirds.   Wonderful to Be Alive.   ABC PLP
      59266
      CRA   Oct.   p70.   50w.   3

4940 DIXON, Prince.   It's a Sad Situation.   Joliet Records CA
      90067
      CK   March   p48.   50w.   3

4941 DOUGHERT, Tommy.   Touch My Soul.   Emerald GES 1139 (E)
      MM   Feb. 21   p30.   50w. $1\frac{1}{2}$

4942 DRANES, Arizona.   Barrell House Pianos with Sanctified
      Singing, 1926-28.   Herwin 210 (Reissue)
      ST   Oct./Nov.   p34.   100w. $3\frac{1}{2}$

4943 ELLINGTON, Duke.   Second Sacred Concert.   Prestige P-
      24045 (2 discs) (Reissue)
      SR   Feb.   p98-9.   237w. $4\frac{1}{2}$

4944 FARRIS, Rev. Lonnie.   East Vernon Blues.   Southern Sound
      200 (E)
      LB   May-June   p36-7.   75w.   4

4945 FLATT Lester & The Nashville Grass.   Flatt Gospel.   Canaan
      CGS 8508
      CMP   May   p17.   300w.   5
      CMR   April   p36.   250w.   3
      MN   V6/#11   p28.   250w. $3\frac{1}{2}$
      PIC   Jan.   p47.   350w.   4

4946 GOSPEL Ramblers.   Most of All.   King Bluegrass 546
      PIC   Nov.   p54, 56.   100w.   3

4947 GRANT, Bill and Delia Bell.   There Is a Fountain.   Kiamichi
      SO   V25/#1   p68.   50w. $3\frac{1}{2}$

4948 HACKETT, Bobby.   The Spirit Swings.   Jazz Club N4104/02
      (2 discs)
      JF   May   p41-2.   500w. $2\frac{1}{2}$

4949 HARPER, Redd.   Gospel--Country Style.   Emerald Gem GES
      1138 (E)
      CMP   Oct.   p22.   300w.   2
      CMR   Sept.   p32.   175w. $1\frac{1}{2}$

4950 HEWITT, Garth.   Love Songs from the Earth.   Myrhh

MM   Nov. 13 p28.   50w.   1

4951 ISAACS, Joe and Lily Isaacs.   The Family Circle.   Pine
      Tree PTSLP 526
            BGU   Jan.   p20.   250w. $2\frac{1}{2}$

4952 JACKSON, Mahalia.   How I Got Over.   Columbia KC 34073
            CRA   Oct.   p70.   100w. $2\frac{1}{2}$
            SR   Sept.   p94.   250w.   4

4953 JACKSON, Wanda.   Make Me Like a Child Again.   Myrhh
      MYR 1043
            CMR   Dec.   p25.   300w. $4\frac{1}{2}$

4954 JACKSON Five.   Christmas Album.   Tamla Motown MS 713
            RS   Dec. 30   p63.   100w.   3

4955 JETER, Rev. Claude.   The Little Wooden Church on the Hill.
      Savoy 14374
            BM   Oct.   p38.   100w.   4

4956 JOHNNY and Jack.   Collectors Classics 11-01 (Reissue)
            SO   V25/#1   p67.   25w.   3

4957 KING's Countrymen.   A Better Way.   Hope 1035
            BGU   Feb.   p22.   75w. $2\frac{1}{2}$
            PIC   Aug.-Sept.   p83-4.   75w. $4\frac{1}{2}$

4958 LAMBETH, David.   Standing in the Shadows.   King Bluegrass
      541
            BGU   May   p33.   150w. $1\frac{1}{2}$

4959 LAST, James.   Christmas.   Polydor (E)
            MM   Dec. 25   p17.   100w. $2\frac{1}{2}$

4960 LEWIS Family.   Lewis Family-Style Gospel.   Canaan CAS
      9782
            BGU   Aug.   p34.   150w. $2\frac{1}{2}$
            MN   V7/#2   p17.   375w. $2\frac{1}{2}$
            PIC   Aug.-Sept.   p82.   50w. $3\frac{1}{2}$

4961 LEWIS Family.   We'll Keep Praising His Name.   Canaan
      CAS 9795
            MN   V7/#7   p16.   400w. $2\frac{1}{2}$

4962 LILLIMAE and the Dixie Gospelaires.   Hymn Time.   Glory-
      land GSP 1164
            BGU   Oct.   p23.   75w.   2

4963 LILLIMAE and the Dixie Gospelaires.   There's a Big Wheel.
      Gloryland GSP 1149
            BGU   April   p28.   125w.   2

4964 McGEE, Sam. God Be with You Until We Meet Again.
      Davis Unlimited DU 33021 (Reissue)
            BGU   March p18.   175w.   3
            PIC   May p62-3.   150w.   4

4965 MARSHALL, David. King Bluegrass KB 555
            BGU   Nov. p32.   75w. $2\frac{1}{2}$

4966 MONTGOMERY, Melba. The Greatest Gift of All.   Elektra
      CM 6
            CMR   Sept.   p32.   1000w.   1

4967 NELSON, Willie. Troublemaker.   Columbia PC 34112
            CS Dec.   p42.   200w.   3
            MG Oct.   p70.   100w.   5

4968 O'DAY, Molly. A Sacred Collection.   Old Homestead 101
      (Reissue)
            BGU   Dec.   p30.   225w. $2\frac{1}{2}$
            OTM   Autumn p21-2.   150w. $3\frac{1}{2}$
            PIC   June p70.   200w.   4
            SO   V25/#1   p67.   75w.   3

4969 PACK Duet. When I've Climbed the Last Hill.   Vetco 3033
            BGU   May p35.   150w. $1\frac{1}{2}$

4970 PADMASAMBAVA Chopa. Lyric Chord LLST 7270
            ARG Dec.   p46.   100w.   3

4971 PHIPPS Family. In the Sweet Bye and Bye.   Pine Mountain
      PMR 130
            BGU   Aug.   p32.   100w. $2\frac{1}{2}$

4972 PHIPPS Family. Just a Few More Days.   Pine Mountain
      PMR 134
            BGU   Aug.   p32.   100w. $2\frac{1}{2}$

4973 PHIPPS Family. Only Through Grace: Early American Sing-
      ing.   Pine Mountain PMR 127
            BGU   July p33. 100w.   4

4974 PHIPPS Family. Sings 'em Mountain Style.   Pine Mountain
      PMR 131
            BGU   July p33. 100w.   4

4975 PRESLEY, Elvis. Sings the Wonderful World of Christmas.
      RCA LSP 4579
            RS Dec. 30 p61, 63.   75w.   4

4976 PRIDE, Charley. Sunday Morning with....   RCA APL1 1359.
      Cart. RCA APS1 1359
            CM Sept.   p56.   100w.   3
            CMP Oct.   p21.   225w.   5

MG July p58. 50w. $2\frac{1}{2}$

4977 RICH, Charlie. Silver Linings. Epic KE 33545
      MG June p55. 25w. 3
      RS May-June p62. 350w. $3\frac{1}{2}$

4978 RICHARDSON, Larry. Walking and Talking with My Lord
      MN V7/#4 p17. 225w. 3

4979 SAMUELSONS. From Sweden with Love. Impact R 3323
      (Sweden)
      CMR Nov. p30. 50w. 0

4980 SHENANDOAH Cutups. A Tribute to the Louvin Brothers.
      Revonah RS 919
      BGU Dec. p26. 250w. $3\frac{1}{2}$

4981 SHENANDOAH Cutups. Sing Gospel. Revonah 908
      PIC June p66. 125w. 4

4982 SHUPING, Garland. Take My Hand Precious Lord. Old
      Homestead OHS 90047
      BGU March p17. 125w. $1\frac{1}{2}$
      PIC July p57. 100w. $2\frac{1}{2}$

4983 STANLEY, Ralph. Let Me Rest on a Peaceful Mountain.
      Rebel 1544
      BGU Jan. p15. 250w. 3
      MN V7/#1 p21. 250w. 4
      SO V25/#1 p68. 25w. $3\frac{1}{2}$

4984 STANLEY Brothers. V. 4. County 754 (Reissue)
      OTM Autumn p26. 125w. 4

4985 The STANLEY Brothers. An Empty Mansion. Rimrock
      RLP153
      OTM Summer p27. 125w. $3\frac{1}{2}$

4986 STAPLE Singers. The Best of.... Stax STX 1042
      CAC April p20. 75w. 2

4987 STAPLE Singers. Great Day. Milestone M-47028 (2 discs)
      (Reissue)
      BU Jan.-Feb. p30-1. 375w. 4

4988 STAPLE Singers. Let's Do It Again. Curtom
      CRE March p13, 72. 100w. 1

4989 The STARS of Faith. Living to Live Again. Nashboro 7143
      SR June p86. 275w. 4

4990 The STATLER Brothers. Songs of the New Testament. Mer-
      cury SRM-1052

CM   March p58.   325w. $2\frac{1}{2}$
PIC   Oct.   p55-6. 175w. $1\frac{1}{2}$
SR   Feb.   p87, 89. 175w.   4

4991 STORY, Carl. The Bluegrass Gospel Collection.   CMH 9005
      (2 discs)
         OTM Summer p24-5. 125w.   3
         PIC Oct.   p55-6.   175w. $1\frac{1}{2}$

4992 STORY, Carl. Mother's Last Word and Other Bluegrass
      Gospel Favorites.   Atteiram AP1L-1520 A
         BGU March p17.   150w. $2\frac{1}{2}$
         MN   V7/#1 p24.   250w. $2\frac{1}{2}$

4993 SUPREMES. Merry Christmas.   Tamla Motown 638
         RS Dec. 30 p63.   125w.   4

4994 SWAN Silvertones. Try Me Master.   HOB HBX 2182
         CRA Oct.   p70.   50w. $2\frac{1}{2}$

4995 TOGETHER. Don't You Want to Go.   Peacock PLP 59207
         BM Oct.   p38.   50w.   3

4996 TOWNSLEY, Nat Jr. And the Lighthouse Ensemble.   ABC
      ABCD 881 (Reissue)
         BM Oct.   p38.   50w.   4

4997 TUNSTAN Trio. On the Sunny Banks With. [No label specified]
         MN V7/#7 p17.   125w. $1\frac{1}{2}$

4998 21st Century Singers. The Storm Is Passing.   Creed 3060
         BM Oct.   p38.   125w. $3\frac{1}{2}$

4999 WALKER, Albertina. God Is Love.   Polydor PD 5201
         BM Oct.   p38.   100w.   0

5000 WHITEWATER Gospel Singers. Harvest Time for Mama.
      Pine Tree PTSLP 537
         BGU Dec.   p31.   50w.   2

5001 WILKIN, Marijohn. I Have Returned.   Myrrh MYR 1020
         CMP June 6 p13.   150w.   4

5002 WILKIN, Marijohn. Where I'm Going.   Word WST 9545
         CMP Aug.   p31.   250w.   3

5003 WILLIAMS, Jimmy. O Yes Lord.   Gospel Grass
         PIC Oct.   p52.   50w.   3

5004 WILLIAMS, Mary Lou. Mary Lou's Mass.   Mary M 102
         SR Oct.   p96.   50w.   4

5005 WILSON Brothers. Sacred Songs in the Stanley Tradition.

Old Homestead 90028
    BGU Dec. p29. 200w. $3\frac{1}{2}$
    OTM Autumn p26. 125w. 3
    PIC Nov. p52-3. 125w. 4

5006 WONDER, Stevie. Someday at Christmas. Tamla Motown
281
    RS Dec. 30 p63. 100w. $3\frac{1}{2}$

5007 ZION Harmonizers. You Don't Have to Get in Trouble.
Flying Fish 002
    SR March p87. 175w. 4

SHOW and HUMOR

Included here are soundtracks from films, radio and television; original cast stage productions; studio recordings of the original item; and reissues of original soundtracks. The chief criterion is music, but those soundtracks which have little or no music will be found here. Additional albums are conveniently located here when the performers have associations with the media.

There is no proper review medium for soundtracks. Reviews are scattered, often depending on content for inclusion among regular records. Consistently good, well-thought-out reviews appear in the Gramophone, with Stereo Review and High Fidelity not far behind. Stage shows are reviewed most often, followed by film soundtracks. Television and radio music is virtually non-existent. Reviews of any kind are usually harsh and the lack of an audience usually precludes tape release. At best, most soundtracks serve as mementoes, except for the outstanding stage musicals and classically-derived film soundtracks.

According to the reviews for 1976, there were no outstanding or best-selling discs in this category for this year.

5008   ADVENTURES of Robin Hood (Korngold).   Delos F25409
          AU   Feb.   p103.   350w.   1
          HF   April   p136.   100w. $2\frac{1}{2}$

5009   AT Long Last Love.   RCA ABL2-0967 (2 discs) (Original film soundtrack)
          SR   Sept.   p90.   375w. $2\frac{1}{2}$

5010   L'AVENTURE du Jazz (various).   Jazz Odyssey 005 (France) (2 discs) (Original film soundtrack)
          JJ   Feb.   p32.   250w. $1\frac{1}{2}$

5011   Ben BAGLEY'S Ballet on Broadway.   Painted Smiles PS-1364
          SR   Nov.   p122, 123.   250w.   4

5012   Ben BAGLEY'S Jerome Kern Revisited.   Painted Smiles PS-1363

466

   LP March p35. 100w. $1\frac{1}{2}$
   SR Oct. p98. 325w. $3\frac{1}{2}$

5013 BARKER, Ronnie and Ronnie Corbett. The Best of the Two
   Ronnies. Transatlantic TRA 328 (E)
   GR Dec. p1079. 100w. $3\frac{1}{2}$

5014 BATES, Blaster (Derek). The Explosive Exploits, v 1/6.
   Polydor Big Ben BBMC 6/11 (6 discs) (E)
   CAC Aug. p196. 300w. 3

5015 BEYOND the Fringe. EMI One-Up OUM 2151 (E) (Reissue)
   (Original London cast)
   GR Dec. p1079. 125w. 5

5016 The BINGO Long Traveling All-Stars & Motor Kings (Gold-
   stein) MCA 2094 (Original film soundtrack)
   CA Aug. p25. 75w. 3
   MM Nov. 20 p29. 75w. 1
   RR Dec. p98. 75w. 3

5017 The BLACK Mikado. (Gilbert & Sullivan). Transatlantic TRA
   300 (E) (Original London cast)
   GR Jan. p1253. 400w. 4

5018 BLAKEY, Art. Selections from 'My Fair Lady,' 'Brigadoon,'
   'Paint Your Wagon.' RCA FXM 1-7196 (France) (Reissue)
   JJ May p26-7. 450w. 4

5019 BORGE, Victor. Borgering on Genius. Polydor MGM 2354
   029 (E)
   CAC Jan. p416. 175w. $3\frac{1}{2}$
   GR Feb. p1389. 100w. 3

5020 BROOKE-TAYLOR, Tim, Barry Cryer and John Junkin. The
   Least Worst of "Hello Cheeky." BBC REH 189 (E)
   (Reissue)
   GR Feb. p1386-7. 125w. 3

5021 BROOKS, Albert. A Star Is Bought. Asylum 7E-1035. Cart.
   ET8 1035
   CRE March p12. 50w. 4
   SR Feb. p90. 75w. 1

5022 BUGSY Malone (Parker). RSO 3501 (film soundtrack)
   CAC Oct. p276. 100w. $2\frac{1}{2}$
   RR Oct. p101. 100w. 1

5023 CAPTAIN from Castille (Newman). Delos DEL/F 25411
   HF April p136. 250w. $3\frac{1}{2}$

5024 CARLIN, George. An Evening with Wally Lando, Featuring

Bill Slaszlo.   Little David 1008
   MG   Jan.   p34.   50w.   3
   MM   Dec.   11   p22.   200w. $2\frac{1}{2}$

5025   CARROTT, Jasper.   Rabbitts On and On.   DJM DJF 20462
(E)
       CAC   Jan.   p416.   75w. $3\frac{1}{2}$

5026   CHEECH and Chong.   Sleeping Beauty.   Ode
       MM   Oct.   16   p22.   75w. $2\frac{1}{2}$

5027   CHICAGO (John Kander-Fred Ebb).   Arista AL 9005 (Original
Broadway cast recording)
       SR   Oct.   p100, 101.   1800w.   4

5028   A CHORUS Line (Marvin Hamlish-Edward Klehan).   Columbia
PS 33581 (Original Broadway cast recording)
       AU   Feb.   p103.   350w. $4\frac{1}{2}$
       GR   Sept.   p484.   300w. $4\frac{1}{2}$
       MM   July 24   p25.   25w. $2\frac{1}{2}$
       SR   Oct.   p100-1.   1800w.   4

5029   CITIZEN Kane (Herrmann).   United Artists UALA 372 G
(Original film soundtrack)
       LP   March   p34.   100w.   4
       SR   Jan.   p95.   250w.   4

5030   COLE, Nat King.   Sings Songs from the Movies.   Capitol
VMP 1006 (E) (Reissue)
       RR   Feb.   p65.   50w.   3

5031   COLE (Porter).   RCA CRL2-5054 (2 discs) (Original cast
recording)
       SR   Sept.   p90.   375w.   2

5032   COOK, Peter and Dudley Moore.   Derek and Clive.   Island (E)
       MM   Dec.   11   p22.   200w. $2\frac{1}{2}$

5033   CO-OPTIMISTS.   World Records SHB25 (2 discs) (Highlights
from the film)
       GR   Oct.   p22.   200w. $2\frac{1}{2}$

5034   COPLAND Film Scores.   CBS 61672 (E)
       RR   April   p76.   650w.   5

5035   COSBY, Bill.   Bill Cosby Is Not Himself These Days, Rat
Own, Rat Own, Rat Own.   Capitol ST-11530.   Cart. 8xT-11530
       AU   Sept.   p75-6.   200w.   4
       CIR   Dec.   30   p18-9.   575w.   3
       CRE   Dec.   p63.   50w.   2
       SR   Oct.   p92.   325w.   2

5036   DEATH Wish (Hancock).   Columbia PC 33199 (Original film

soundtrack)
 CO March p22. 225w. $2\frac{1}{2}$
 DB April 10 p18-9. 300w. 5

5037 DIAMOND Mercenaries (Garvarentz). Pye NSPL 28219 (E)
 (Original film soundtrack)
  MM March 20 p22. 25w. 3

5038 DR. No (Norman). United Artists Sunset SLS 50395 (E) (Reissue) (Original film soundtrack)
  RR Dec. p98. 50w. $2\frac{1}{2}$

5039 The EDDY Duchin Story. MCA CDL 8040 (E) (Reissue)
  RR April p81-2. 75w. 3

5040 EMMANUELLE 2. Warner Brothers (Original film soundtrack)
  MM Dec. 4 p24. 50w. 2

5041 ERWIN, Lee. America. Angel DS-36092
  SR June p90-1. 450w. 4

5042 FAREWELL My Lovely (Shire). United Artists UALA 556 G
 (Original film soundtrack)
  GR Sept. p484. 250w. $3\frac{1}{2}$
  RR Dec. p98. 100w. $2\frac{1}{2}$

5043 FIELDS, W. C. The Best of.... Columbia CG 34144 (2
 discs) (Reissue)
  AU Oct. p139. 200w. $3\frac{1}{2}$

5044 FIRESIGN Theatre. Don't Crush That Dwarf, Hand Me the
 Pliers. Columbia C 30102
  CRA March p80-1. 200w. 4

5045 FIRESIGN Theatre. In the Next World, You're on Your Own.
 Columbia
  CRE Jan. p68. 300w. 3

5046 FITZGERALD, Ella and Louis Armstrong. Porgy and Bess.
 Verve VE-2-2507 (2 discs) (Reissue)
  CAD Sept. p27. 150w. 3
  DB Nov. 18 p30. 275w. $3\frac{1}{2}$

5047 FITZGERALD, Ella. Sings the Harold Arlen Songbook. Verve
 2683 064 (2 discs) (Reissue)
  JJ April p30. 300w. $4\frac{1}{2}$

5048 FITZGERALD, Ella. Sings the Jerome Kern/Johnny Mercer
 Songbooks. Verve 2610 025 (E) (2 discs) (Reissue)
  GR Dec. p1076. 75w. 5

5049 FOUR Horsemen of the Apocalypse (Previn). Polydor 2353125
 (E) (Reissue) (Original film soundtrack)

RR   Oct.   p100-1.   200w.   3

5050   FOXX, Redd.   You Gotta Wash Your Ass.   Atlantic SD 18157
       PRM   March   p47.   450w.   4

5051   FRANCIS, Connie.   Sings the Great Movie Hits.   MGM 2353-
       121 (E)
       MM   April 24   p23.   75w. $2\frac{1}{2}$

5052   FROM Russia with Love (Barry).   United Artists UAS 5114
       (Original film soundtrack)
       CAC   Feb.   p459.   75w. $2\frac{1}{2}$

5053   FUNNY Lady (John Kander-Fred Ebb-Billy Rose).   Arista Al
       9004.   Cart. 8301-9004N.   Cass. 5301-9004N (Original sound-
       track recording)
       LP   Aug.   p15.   225w.   5
       SR   July   p70-1.   550w.   4

5054   GABLE and Lombard (Legrand).   MCA 2091.   Cart. T2091
       (Original film soundtrack)
       HF   Sept.   p113.   75w.   0
       RR   Oct.   p101.   100w.   1

5055   The GHOST and Mrs. Muir.   FMC 4 (E) (Original film sound-
       track)
       RR   Feb.   p65.   325w.   4

5056   GIVE 'em Hell, Harry.   United Artists UALA540-H2 (2 discs)
       (Original soundtrack) with James Whitmore
       LP   March   p34-5.   250w. $3\frac{1}{2}$

5057   GOLDEN Age of Hollywood: Laurel and Hardy (Warner
       United Artists 29676 (E) (Film soundtrack)
       CAC   Feb.   p459.   200w.   4

5058   The GOLDEN Voyage of Sinbad (Miklos Rozsa).   United Ar-
       tists UA-LA308-G (Original soundtrack recording)
       SR   Feb.   p100, 103.   325w.   4

5059   GOODTIME Charley (Grossman; Hackady).   RCA ARL 1-1011
       (Original Broadway cast recording)
       SR   Sept.   p94.   350w.   1

5060   GOON Show Classics.   Pye 12118 (Reissue)
       GR   Feb.   p1386-7.   125w.   4
       SR   Feb.   p90.   200w.   4

5061   GREAT Expectations.   (Jarre) (Film soundtrack)
       CAC   Jan.   p415-6.   175w.   3

5062   GROCE, Larry.   Junkfood Junkie.   Warner Brothers BS 2933
       MG   June   p44.   50w.   1

5063　The HARDER They Come.　Mango MLPS 9202 (Reissue)
　　　　SO　May/June　p43.　175w.　3½

5064　HARRY and Tonto.　Casablanca NBLP-7010.　Cass.　F-7010
　　　　(Original motion picture soundtrack)
　　　　LP　Aug.　p25.　225w.　4

5065　HATCH, Tony.　Mr. Nice Guy.　Pye Golden Hour GHX 628 (E)
　　　　GR　Dec.　p1076.　25w.　2½

5066　HERRMANN, Bernard.　Concert Suites: the Devil and Daniel
　　　　Webster; Welles Raises Kane.　Unicorn UNS 237
　　　　SR　Jan.　p95.　250w.　4

5067　HERRMANN, Bernard.　Great British Film Scores: Music
　　　　from Oliver Twist, Anna Karenina, an Ideal Husband, Things
　　　　to Come, the Invaders.　London Phase 4 SPC 21149
　　　　CR　Sept.　p539.　325w.　4
　　　　HF　June　p108.　400w.　4
　　　　RR　June　p81.　500w.　3½

5068　HERRMANN, Bernard.　Music from Great Shakespearian
　　　　Films.　London SPC 21132
　　　　SR　Sept.　p100.　200w.　5

5069　HERRMANN, Bernard.　Mysterious Film World of....　Lon-
　　　　don SPC 21137.　Cass. 521137
　　　　LP　March　p35.　200w.　3
　　　　SR　Jan.　p95.　250w.　4

5070　The HINDENBURG.　MCA 2090 (Film soundtrack [excerpts])
　　　　MG　March　p43.　50w.　1

5071　HINGE and Bracket.　V. 1.　Emi One-Up OU2125 (E)
　　　　GR　July　p225.　175w.　3½

5072　HORNE, Kenneth.　The Best of "Round the Horne."　BBC
　　　　REH 193 (E) (Reissue)
　　　　GR　Feb.　p1386-7.　125w.　4

5073　HORNE, Kenneth.　"Round the Horne," v. 2.　BBC (E)
　　　　MM　Dec. 18　p16.　500w.　2

5074　HOWARD, Frank.　Please Yourselves.　BBC REH 230 (E)
　　　　GR　July　p226.　75w.　4

5075　HUMPHRIES, Barry.　Housewife--Superstar.　Charisma (E)
　　　　MM　Dec. 11　p22.　200w.　2½

5076　IRENE.　EMI EMC 3139 (E) (Original London cast recording)
　　　　CAC　Oct.　p276.　125w.　4
　　　　GR　Sept.　p484.　175w.　3

5077 JAWS (Williams).   MCA 2087 (Original film soundtrack)
          RR   April   p76.   375w.   4

5078 The KANGEROO.   Pepita SLPX 17460 (Hungary) (Original
      film soundtrack)
          RR   Dec.   p98.   50w.   2½

5079 KEEPING, Charles.   Cockney Ding Dong.   Line L2032 (E)
          GR   Feb.   p1389.   125w.   3

5080 KING, Davis and John Junkin.   The Seedy Sounds of "Hello
      Cheeky."   EMI EMC 3112 (E)
          CAC   April   p30.   200w.   3½
          GR   July   p226.   150w.   2½

5081 KING Kong (Steiner).   United Artists UALA 373 G (Original
      film soundtrack)
          LP   March   p35.   225w.   3

5082 LAINE, Cleo and Ray Charles.   Porgy and Bess.   RCA
      CPL2-1831 (2 discs).   Cart. CPS2-1831.   Cass. CPK2 1831
          SR   Dec.   p130.   600w.   4

5083 LEADBELLY.   ABC 939 (Original film soundtrack)
          CAD   Oct.   p18.   150w.   4
          LB   July-Aug.   p37-8.   775w.   4

5084 LENNY.   United Artists UALA 359H (Original film soundtrack)
          RR   Feb.   p65.   100w.   3½

5085 LET's Do It Again (Mayfield).   Curtom CU 5005 (Original)
      film soundtrack, with the Staple Singers)
          RR   Feb.   p65.   50w.   2
          RS   Feb. 12   p92.   275w.   3

5086 LIPSTICK (Polnareff).   Atlantic SP 18178 (Original film sound-
      track)
          MM   July 24   p25.   50w.   2

5087 LISZTOMANIA (Wakeman).   A&M SP 4546.   Cart. 4546.
      Cass. 4546 (Original film soundtrack)
          CAC   Feb.   p459.   100w.   1
          HF   April   p138.   150w.   0
          LP   March   p35.   200w.   2
          MG   Jan.   p34.   50w.   4
          SR   April   p97.   200w.   5

5088 The LITTLE Prince (Lerner & Loewe).   Anchor ABCL 5143
      (E) (Original film soundtrack)
          GR   Sept.   p487.   175w.   4½

5089 LOGAN's Run (Goldsmith).   MGM 5302 (Original film sound-
      track)

MM Nov. 13 p28. 50w. $1\frac{1}{2}$
RR Dec. p98. 200w. $3\frac{1}{2}$

5090 LUCKY Lady (Kander; Ebb). Arista AL 4069 (Original film soundtrack)
HF July p107. 175w. $1\frac{1}{2}$
SR April p98. 400w. 3

5091 McRAE, Carmen. Mad About the Man: The Songs of Noel Coward. Stanyan SR 10115
SR Feb. p94-5. 175w. $4\frac{1}{2}$

5092 The MAGIC Show (Stephen Schwartz-Doug Henning). Bell 9003 (Original Broadway cast recording)
SR Feb. p103. 225w. $4\frac{1}{2}$

5092a MAHOGANY (Holdridge). Motown M6-858 (Original film soundtrack)
BM April p51. 100w. 2
LP March p35. 125w. 3

5093 The MAN Who Would Be King (Jarre). Capitol SW 11474 (Original film soundtrack)
HF July p107. 225w. 1

5094 MANCINI, Henry. Conducts the London Symphony Orchestra in a Concert of Film Music. RCA RS1058 (E)
GR Oct. p666. 75w. $4\frac{1}{2}$

5095 "ME and Bessie." Columbia PC 34032 (Original Broadway stage soundtrack)
ST Aug. -Sept. p230-2. 500w. 5

5096 MEROPA. Philips (E) (Original stagecast recording)
MM Sept. 11 p26. 50w. $3\frac{1}{2}$

5097-8 MISSOURI Breaks (Williams). United Artists UALA 623 G (Original film soundtrack)
CMR Sept. p30. 75w. $1\frac{1}{2}$
RR Dec. p98. 50w. $2\frac{1}{2}$

5099 MONTY Python. Live! At City Center. Arista AL 4073
HF Sept. p107-8. 250w. $4\frac{1}{2}$
SR Oct. p110, 111. 275w. 4

5100 MORECAMBE, Eric and Ernie Wise. What Do You Think of the Show So Far? Polydor/BBC (E)
CAC Jan. p416. 25w. $2\frac{1}{2}$

5101 MORRIS, Joan. Vaudeville: Songs of the Great Ladies of the Musical Stage. Nonesuch H 71330
SR Nov. p87-8. 550w. 5

5102 MOSES, the Lawgiver (Nicolai). RCA TBL 1-1106 (Original
      television soundtrack)
            HF Jan. p105-6. 350w. 4

5103 MOTHER, Jugs and Speed (Yates). A&M SP 4590 (Original
      film soundtrack)
            BM Nov. p45. 125w. 3
            RR Dec. p98. 50w. 2½

5104 MURDER on the Orient Express. Capitol ST-11361 (Original
      motion picture soundtrack)
            LP Aug. p25. 125w. 3

5105 MY Fair Lady (Alan Jay Lerner-Frederick Loewe). Columbia
      PS 34197. Cart. KSA 34197. Cass. KST 34197 (Original
      1976 Broadway cast recording)
            MM Nov. 13 p29. 100w. 2
            SR Oct. p111-2. 375w. 3

5106 NASHVILLE. ABC ABCD-893. Cart. 8022-893 H (Original
      film soundtrack recording)
            GR Sept. p487. 150w. 4
            SR Oct. p55-6. 1800w. 2

5107 NATIONAL Lampoon. Goodbye Pop. Epic PE 33956
            RS March 25 p62, 64. 250w. 4

5108 The NUN's Story (Waxman). Stanyan SR 4022 (Original film
      soundtrack)
            LP March p35-6. 150w. 4

5109 OBA Koso (The King Did Not Hang). Kaleidophone KS 2201
      (2 discs) (Original film soundtrack)
            SR Dec. p120. 300w. 4½

5110 OBSESSION (Hermann). London SPC 21160. Cart. SPC8
      21160. Cass. SPC5 21160 (Original film soundtrack)
            CIR Dec. 14 p16. 100w. 4½
            SR Dec. p120, 122. 275w. 4

5111 ODE to Billy Joe (Legrand). Warner Brothers BS 2947 (Ori-
      ginal film soundtrack)
            MM Oct. 16 p25. 125w. 2
            RR Dec. p98. 75w. 2

5112 The OMEN (Goldsmith). RCA Tattoo BJL1-1888
            RR Dec. p98. 250w. 3½

5113 ON a Clear Day You Can See Forever. Columbia Special
      Products AS-30086 (Original soundtrack recording)
            LP Aug. p25-6. 100w. 3

5114 ONE Flew Over the Cuckoo's Nest (Nitzche). Fantasy F 9500

(Original film soundtrack)
CRE   April   p62.   475w. $2\frac{1}{2}$
HF   April   p136, 138.   300w. $3\frac{1}{2}$
MG   March   p43.   50w.   2

5115   The OUTLAW Josey Wales (Fielding).   Warner Brothers BS
2956 (Original film soundtrack)
MM   Sept.   18   p21.   25w. $2\frac{1}{2}$
RR   Dec.   p98.   125w.   2

5116   PACIFIC Overtures (Sondheim).   RCA ARL1-1357.   Cart.
ARS1 1369.   Cass. ARK1 1367 (Original Broadway cast)
AU   Nov.   p103-4.   500w. $3\frac{1}{2}$
GR   Sept.   p487.   325w. $2\frac{1}{2}$
SR   May   p89.   425w.   3

5117   PAL Joey (Rodgers & Hart).   Capitol VMP 1005 (E) (Reissue)
RR   Feb.   p65.   75w. $2\frac{1}{2}$

5118   PAPER Moon.   Paramount PAS 1012 (Original motion picture
soundtrack recording)
LP   Aug.   p26.   100w.   3

5119   PAPER Tiger (Budd).   Capitol SW 11475 (Original film soundtrack)
HF   April   p138.   250w.   4

5120   PARAMOUR, Norrie.   40 Years of BBC TV Themes.   BBC
REB 238 (E)
GR   Dec.   p1079.   50w.   3

5121   PERREY & Kingsley.   The Essential Perrey & Kingsley.
Vanguard VSD 71/72 (2 discs)
CK   March   p48.   150w.   4

5122   PORGY and Bess (Gershwin).   Bethlehem 3BP 1 (3 discs)
(Reissue)
CAD   Jan.   p26-7.   50w.   3
MJ   Feb.   p47.   50w.   3
SR   Feb.   p91-2.   350w.   3

5123   The PRISONER of Zenda (Newman).   United Artists UALA
374-G (Original film soundtrack)
LP   March   p36.   125w. $2\frac{1}{2}$

5124   PROCTOR and Bergman.   What the Country Needs.   Columbia
CRE   Jan.   p68.   300w.   3

5125   PRYOR, Richard.   Is It Something I Said?   Warner BS 2227
AU   March   p80.   150w. $4\frac{1}{2}$
BM   April   p51.   125w.   4

5126   PRYOR, Richard.   That Nigger's Crazy.   Reprise MS 2241

MG   Feb.   p36.   50w. $2\frac{1}{2}$

5127   PSYCHO (Herrmann).   Unicorn RHS 336 (Original film sound-
track)
GR   Feb.   p1382.   300w. $2\frac{1}{2}$
RR   Feb.   p65.   350w. $3\frac{1}{2}$

5128   RAINTREE Country (Green).   Entr'acte Recordings Society
ERS 6503 ST (2 discs) (Reissue) (Original film soundtrack
recording)
HF   Jan.   p109.   450w.   5

5129   RANCHO Deluxe (Jimmy Buffett).   United Artists UA-LA466-G.
Cart. UA-EA466-H (Original soundtrack recording)
SR   Nov.   p123.   150w.   2

5130   REALLY Rosie (Maurice Sendak; Carole King).   Ode SP 77027
(Original TV soundtrack)
SR   June   p89.   175w.   2

5131   REQUIEM for a Cavalier (Thomas).   Delos DEL/F 25409 (Reissue)
HF   April   p136.   100w. $2\frac{1}{2}$

5132   RICH Man, Poor Man (North).   MCA 2095 (Original television
soundtrack)
RR   Dec.   p98.   75w. $3\frac{1}{2}$

5133   The ROCKY Horror Show (Richard O'Brien).   Ode SP-77026.
Cart. 8T-77026.   Cass. CS-77026
CAC   Feb.   p459.   100w.   3
SR   June   p89.   275w.   2

5134   ROLLERBALL (Previn).   United Artists UALA 470G (Original
film soundtrack)
GR   Jan.   p1254.   250w. $\frac{1}{2}$

5135   ROSKIN, David.   Conducts the Great Film Scores: Laura, Forever Amber, The Good, the Bad and the Ugly.   RCA ARL 1-1490
AU   Nov.   p105.   100w. $1\frac{1}{2}$

5136   ROZSA, Miklos.   Conducts His Great Film Music.   Polydor
2383 327 (E)
GR   Sept.   p484.   250w. $3\frac{1}{2}$
HF   Jan.   p106.   300w. $3\frac{1}{2}$
RR   Oct.   p100.   800w.   4

5137   RUDOLPH Friml in London.   World Records SHB 37 (2 discs)
(Original London cast)
GR   Oct.   p665.   350w. $2\frac{1}{2}$

5138   RUSSELL, Anna.   Columbia MG 31199 (2 discs) (Reissue)
OLR   Sept.   p187.   50w.   4

5139 SCHWARTZ, Arthur. From the Pen of ... Arthur Schwartz. RCA LPL1-5121
    SR Oct. p112. 250w. 0

5140 SEVILLE, David and the Chipmonks. Alvin for President. London (Reissue)
    CRE July p68. 125w. $2\frac{1}{2}$

5141 SHENANDOAH (Geld; Udell). RCA ARL1-1019. Cart. ARS1-1019. Cass. ARK1-1019 (Original Broadway cast recording)
    SR Sept. p100. 250w. 5

5142 A SHINE on Your Shoes. Polydor MGM 2353 112 (E)
    GR Jan. p1254. 300w. 4

5143 SHOW Boat (Kern; Hammerstein). RCA AVM1-1741
    SR Dec. p122. 300w. $3\frac{1}{2}$

5144 SIDE by Side. RCA CBL 2 1851 (2 discs) (E) (Original London cast)
    GR Aug. p347. 375w. 4

5145 STARDUST. Arista AL-5000 (2 discs). Cass. 5301-5000(T)
    LP Aug. p8. 200w. 4

5146 STAVISKY (Stephen Sondheim). RCA ARL1-0952. Cart. ARS1-0952 (Original soundtrack recording)
    SR July p300. 200w. $4\frac{1}{2}$

5147 SUNSET Boulevard (Waxman). RCA ARL1-0708 (E)
    CAC Sept. p228, 230. 450w. $3\frac{1}{2}$

5148 TAXI Driver (Herrmann). Arista AL 4079 (Original film soundtrack)
    HF July p107. 225w. $1\frac{1}{2}$
    MM Oct. 2 p30. 75w. 4
    RR Dec. p98. 125w. $2\frac{1}{2}$

5149 THACKRAY, Jake. Very Best of. EMI (E)
    CAC March p499. 150w. 4

5150 THAT's Entertainment, Part II. MGM G 5301 (Film soundtrack excerpts)
    GR Oct. p665. 350w. $2\frac{1}{2}$

5151 The THOMAS Crown Affair (Legrand). United Artists UALA 295G (Original film soundtrack)
    CAC Feb. p459. 75w. $2\frac{1}{2}$
    RR Feb. p65. 50w. 3

5152 THUNDERBALL (Barry). United Artists U3012 (Original film soundtrack)
    RR Dec. p98. 50w. 3

5153 TOMLIN, Lily. Modern Scream. Polydor PD 6051. Cart.
      8F-6051
            CIR Feb. 10 p12. 450w. 4
            CRA Jan. p76. 150w. $2\frac{1}{2}$
            CRE Jan. p82. 50w. $3\frac{1}{2}$
            SR Feb. p79. 275w. 3

5154 TOMMY (The Who). Polydor PD2-9502 (2 discs). Cart. 8F2
      9502. Cass. CF2 9502 (Original film soundtrack recording)
            SR June p80, 81. 950w. 2

5155 TURNABOUT (Forman Brown). Pelican LP 142 (Original cast
      recording)
            SR Sept. p110. 250w. 3

5156 TUSCALOOSA'S Calling Me (Heyer; Beeke). Vanguard VSD
      79376 (Original cast recording)
            SR Sept. p110. 400w. 3

5157 UTAH Symphony Orchestra. Porgy and Bess. Vanguard
      Everyman Classics SRV 345
            AU Nov. p104-5. 500w. 5

5158 W. C. FIELDS and Me (Mancini). MCA 2092 (Original film
      soundtrack, music and dialogs)
            HF Sept. p112-3. 200w. 1
            RR Dec. p98. 125w. $3\frac{1}{2}$

5159 A WINDOW to the Sky (Peerce). MCA MCF 2712 (E)
            RR April p76. 50w. $2\frac{1}{2}$

5160 The WIZ (Smalls). Atlantic SD 18137 (Original Broadway cast
      recording)
            SR Sept. p95. 350w. 1

5161 YANKEE Doodle Flops. Electric Lemon PLP 1919 (Original
      film soundtrack)
            SR Dec. p122, 124. 125w. 2

5162 YOUNG Frankenstein. ABC ABCD-870 (Original motion picture
      soundtrack)
            LP July p21. 125w. 4

ANTHOLOGIES and CONCERTS

"Anthology" is derived from Greek words meaning "flower gathering." Presumably, this means either the best that is available or a mixed bag, with some parts showing off the rest by means of contrast. Certainly the display should be stunning, for why else anthologize?

In the music world, anthologies serve as samplers or introductions to a company's products. These collections of popular performers sell to a captured audience that is used to having preselected and convenience items before their eyes. At the same time they are invaluable for rapidly building up a music record library, or for fleshing out an area of popular music not already covered in the library. There will be little duplication among the collections if the library does not already have the originals.

Within the past three years, aided by the soaring costs of studio time and performers' fees plus the recognized fad for nostalgia of the past, more anthologies and collections than ever before have been released. From a manufacturer's point of view, they are cheap to produce: the material has virtually paid for itself already; the liner notes are few, if any, or standardized; there is uniform packaging and design; there is a ready market which the rackers and jobbers love, and hence little advertising is necessary; and anthologies act as a sampler of the performer or to the catalogue, hence promoting future sales. Selection of the program depends on the co-operation of music publishers in granting reduced rates.

Personally, we are quite partial to anthologized performances. For a pure musical experience there has been nothing quite like, say, on a hot and humid night, throwing on a pile of 45 RPM singles and sitting back guzzling beer while tapping to the rhythms. At this point, our attention span is about three minutes; thus a new record with a new voice comes on just as our minds start to wander. With older records the effect is familiarity and fond, past memories. For the sake of convenience and better musical reproduction, it is easier to do all this with a stack of anthologized long play records. Most new records today can be quite boring between the highlights, and it is not uncommon for a group to have an album with a hit single, fleshed out with 9 duds. You really wouldn't want to hear it all again. While most people might all like or remember one or two particular numbers, they also like other tracks individually. An anthology or "best" album attempts to take those

479

most popular selections which we all enjoy and market them so that
most people might like the whole reissue album.   One man's meat
is not another man's poison in the case of the anthology.

There are many reservations about compilations.   In many
instances, there are only 10 tracks to a disc.   These may have
fewer tracks than the original albums, and certainly it makes each
number more expensive at a per selection cost.   Yet there are distinct advantages for a certain market that has low-fidelity equipment:
the wider grooves give a full range of sound and increase the bass
proportionately, thus making this particular disc virtually ideal for
home stereo consoles and for older "heavier" cartridges.   As the
wider grooves don't wear out as quickly as compressed ones, the
records may be played over and over again with less wear than an
"original" disc.   In other instances, some "best" collections (especially multi-volume sets) almost equal the catalogue material from
which they are drawn, and hence cost more in the long run.

A number of gimmicks such as "electronic enhancement"
for stereo has a vast echoing sound being reminiscent of a train
station lobby.   These types are dying out as it costs money to re-
channel, some of the public are demanding original monophonic
sound, and--the biggest marketing blow of all--these discs have been
relegated to the semi-annual Schwann-2 Catalog with the mono discs.
Sometimes the informative print was very small, or it was printed
as, say, yellow on orange, and the consumer virtually couldn't read
the notice "enhanced for stereo."

Another problem with the vinyl product is that anthologies
are mostly regional pressings.   Duplicate masters are used in fac-
tories not as careful as the home plant.   Then they are shipped
directly to the regional distributor.   Of course, a careless pressing
sounds worse than a skillfully crafted product, and the polyvinyl
chloride content can drop to below 85%.   This is important, for the
extender in a disc can be exposed to the stylus riding on the other-
wise soft plastic, and great harm can occur.   Classical records are
generally 95 - 99% vinyl, with pop recordings being around 90%.
Anything lower than 90% can be detrimental to sound reproduction.

The material is usually selected by the producer or company, so that it may have no relation to what the performers themselves think is their best material.   Many such groups are anthologized after they leave the company for greener pastures, and the
manufacturer can keep churning out the reissues year after year,
relying on the groups' future success to advertise the old reissued
product.   Some anthologies are passed off as shoddy memorials after
death.   This keeps the name in front of the record buying public, but
too often the album is at full list price and the cover only mentions
that it is a reissue in passing.

With the new packaging gatefold, it is likely that all notes
will be inside the shrink-wrapped cellophane parcel, and the consumer will not know what he is supposed to buy until he reads a

review, ad, or opens the package (thus forfeiting a "return" if he already has the item). As these records rarely get reviewed or advertised, there is no certain way of knowing what is on them. Schwann does not often give track listings for them. England is the best place to go for inexpensive reissues in all fields, and more so if the reissue is not available on the North American market.

Mail order houses are a direct development from the recording companies, and some of the latter have gone into the business themselves. By leasing the material for a one-shot appearance, the selected items are pure gravy for the companies. Thus, with groove compression of $2\frac{1}{2}$ minute songs, 18 - 24 titles can appear on some of these albums. Usually these discs are only promoted by television commercials or direct mail. Other reissue companies (mostly prevalent in England) lease material from the original companies and repackage it as they see fit. Pickwick International is most successful at this, drawing on the large Capitol and Mercury catalogues (which is one reason why these two companies do not do much disc reissuing).

The records listed below consist of reissued material, either in the form of anthologies, or "live" versions of studio tracks which enjoy reasonably good sound. Concerts in this same context refers to issued (or reissued) recordings of several artists or groups that performed as part of a show or benefit. They are anthologies in the sense that no one artist predominates; most of these recordings come from music festivals. All are listed by title entry, and exhaustive artist indexing is beyond the time available to the compilers. Recent examples have included the various Newport Folk Festivals, Newport in New York, 1972, Concert for Bangladesh, Woodstock, Wattstax, and so forth.

5164   ALAN Freeman's First Lesson. Decca SKLR 5229 (E)
         CAC   July p146. 200w. 3

5164a ALL Platinum Gold. All Platinum 3016 (Reissue)
         BM April p31. 125w. 4
         RR April p77. 75w. $3\frac{1}{2}$

5165   ALL Them Blues. DJM DJMD 8005 (E) (Reissue)
         DB June p36. 200w. 3

5166   ALL This and World War II. Riva RVIP2 (2 discs) (E) (Reissue)
         MM Nov. 6 p22. 800w. $2\frac{1}{2}$

5167   ALLA Blues. Muskadine 103 (Reissue)
         LB July-Aug. p46. 275w. $4\frac{1}{2}$

5168   ALTO Artistry. Trip Jazz TLP-5543 (Reissue)
         CO June p14. 425w. 4

5169 ALTO Masters, v. 2. Swing Treasury 109
      JJ   Jan. p31, 32. 300w. 4

5170 AMERICA Sings: The Founding Years, Vol. 1 (1620-1800)
      (Anthology). Vox SVBX 5350 (3 discs)
      SR   Sept. p117. 200w. 4

5171 The AMERICAN Blues Legends '74 (Anthology). Munich
      Records BM 150-202 (E)
      BO   May p19. 350w. 3

5172 AMERICAN Dream: The London-American Legend. London
      Dream R 1/2 (E) (2 discs) (Reissue)
      BM   Jan. p26. 50w. 4

5173 AMERICAN Dream: Cameo-Parkway Story, 1957-62. London
      Dream U 3/4 (E) (2 discs) (Reissue)
      BM   Jan. p26. 75w. 2
      RR   Feb. p67. 50w. 4

5174 AMERICAN Graffiti, Vol. 3. MCA 8008 (2 discs) (Reissue)
      GR   April p1669-70. 150w. 3
      MM   March 27 p28.   75w. $3\frac{1}{2}$

5175 AMERICAN Revolution in Song and Ballad. Folkways FH 5277
      LP   March p29. 175w. 3

5176 AMERICAN Sampler. Personal Touch 88WL
      SR   Aug. p93. 300w. 3

5177 AMERICANS in Europe 1933/38 (Anthology). Tax m-8008
      (Sweden) (Reissue)
      JJ   April p28. 575w. $4\frac{1}{2}$

5178 ARCHIVES of Jazz, vol. 6/7. Archives of Jazz AJ 507/8
      (2 discs) (Reissue)
      DB   Feb. 12 p29-31. 200w. 1

5179 AT the Hop. ABC 5175 (E) (Reissue)
      MM   Oct. 2 p30. 50w. 3

5180 ATLANTIC Black Gold, v. 2. Atlantic K 50164 (E) (Reissue)
      BM   Dec. p27. 50w. 3
      MM   Jan. 17 p32. 125w. 3

5181 The AWAKENING, Hear, Sense and Feel. Black Jazz BJQD 9
      CO   May p18, 19. 225w. 3

5182 BACK in the Country. DJM DJD 28025 (E) (2 discs) (Reissue)
      CMP Dec. p20. 350w. 5
      MM   Nov. 20 p26. 150w. $3\frac{1}{2}$

5183 BACK in the Streets. DJM (E) (Reissue)

MM   Dec. 25 p17. 150w. 3

5184 A BAG of Sleepers, v. 1/2.   Arcadia 2003/4 (2 discs) (Re-
      issue)
         JJ   Feb.   p34.   300w.   4

5185 A BAG of Sleepers. Vol. 3.   Arcadia 2005 (Reissue)
         JJ   May p40.   150w. $4\frac{1}{2}$

5186 BANDS on Film. World Records SH197 (E) (Reissue)
         RR   April p82.   75w.   3

5187 BARRELHOUSE Blues and Stomp, v. 4/5.   Euphonic 120415
      (2 discs) (Reissue)
         LB   Nov.-Dec.   p36-7.   450w. $2\frac{1}{2}$

5188 The BASS. Impulse ASY-9284-3 (3 discs) (Reissue)
         DB   March 27 p22-4.   1200w. $2\frac{1}{2}$
         LP   July p11.   200w.   4
         SR   March p92.   225w. $4\frac{1}{2}$

5189 BBC TV's Best of the Top of the Pops.   Super Beeb (E)
      (Reissue)
         MM   Dec. 18 p16.   175w. $3\frac{1}{2}$
         MM   Feb. 7 p24.   50w. $2\frac{1}{2}$

5190 BEALE Street Mess-Around.   Rounder 2006 (Reissue)
         BU   May-June p27.   450w.   4
         LB   March/April p35-6.   250w.   4

5191 BESERKLEY Chartbusters, v. 1.   Beserkley
         CRE   April p12.   50w. $4\frac{1}{2}$

5192 The BEST of the British Invasion.   Pye 506 (Reissue)
         HF   April p130.   150w.   1

5193 BEST of Country Music America, v. 2.   MCA MCF 2742 (E)
      (Reissue)
         CMR   June p30-1.   200w. $3\frac{1}{2}$
         MM   May 15 p26.   75w.   4

5194 BEST of Okeh, v. 1.   Epic MEPC 81224 (E) (Reissue)
         BM   June p35.   175w.   4
         MM   March 20 p23.   800w.   3

5195 BEST of Okeh, v. 2.   Epic EPC 81532 (E) (Reissue)
         BM   Nov. p45.   125w.   4

5196 BEST of the 60s.   Embassy EMB 31253 (E) (Reissue)
         CMR   Aug. p30.   75w.   2

5197 BIG Band Spectacular.   Verve 2352099 (E)
         CAC   Jan. p414.   225w. $3\frac{1}{2}$

RR   Feb.   p68.   75w. $2\frac{1}{2}$

5198 BIG Bands in Hi-Fi Stereo.   Polydor 2482-289 (E) (Reissue)
      CAC   July   p146.   25w. $2\frac{1}{2}$

5199 BIG Little Bands.   Onyx ORI220 (Reissue)
      SR   March   p92-3.   500w.   1

5200 BIG Terror Movie Themes.   Music for Pleasure MFP 50248
      (E)
      RR   April   p76.   100w.   3

5201 BLACK Cat Trail.   Mamlish 3800 (Reissue)
      CAD   Aug.   p32, 33.   175w.   4

5202 BLACK Giants.   Columbia PG 33432 (2 discs) (Reissue)
      MJ   Jan.   p20.   100w. $2\frac{1}{2}$

5203 BLACK Magic Treats.   Black Magic BML 1000 (E)
      BM   July   p52.   100w.   1

5204 BLUE Bay.   Messaround Records MRS 011
      GP   Sept.   p87.   275w.   4
      LB   Nov./Dec.   p31.   400w.   3

5205 BLUE Ridge Barndance.   County 746
      PIC   May   p62.   100w. $4\frac{1}{2}$

5206 BLUE Ridge Mountain Field Trip.   Leader LEA 4012 (E)
      ETH   Sept.   p623-5.   500w.   4

5207 The BLUES.... "A Real Summit Meeting."   Buddah BDS
      5144-2 (2 discs)
      LB   May/June   p49-50.   550w. $2\frac{1}{2}$

5208 BLUES Avalanche.   Chess 2CH-60015 (2 discs)
      LB   March/April   p48-50.   350w.   2

5209 BLUES and Boogie, 1928-36.   Whoopee 103 (E) (Reissue)
      ST   Oct.-Nov.   p31-2.   375w. $2\frac{1}{2}$

5210 BLUES Box 1: 64 Rare Blues Recorded 1934-40 (Anthology).
      MCA Coral PCOX7526/1-4 (West Germany) (4 discs) (Reissue)
      BU   May-June   p27-9.   1775w.   5

5211 BOOGIE Woogie Kings.   Euphonic Sounds ESR 1209 (Reissue)
      CAD   Jan.   p26.   250w.   3
      MJ   March   p23.   50w.   3

5212 The BRAVE Ploughboy.   Xtra XTRA1150 (E)
      MM   Jan. 24   p30.   175w. $2\frac{1}{2}$
      TM   No. 4   p24, 25.   675w.   4

5213 BRITISH Film Music. Decca Phase Four PFS 4363 (E)
         GR   June   p95-6.   375w.   3

5214 BROTHERS and Other Mothers. Savoy SJL 2210 (2 discs)
         (Reissue)
         CAD   Sept.   p26.   175w.   4
         DB   Dec. 2   p25.   200w.   4½

5215 BRUM Folk '76: Souvenir Album. Brum 1096 (E)
         MM   Oct. 16   p29.   150w.   3½

5216 BRUNSWICK: The Strongest Sound Around. Brunswick BRLS
         3019 (E) (Reissue)
         BM   Aug.   p44-5.   125w.   3

5217 BULL City Blues. Flyright 106 (E) (Reissue)
         LB   July-Aug.   p47.   275w.   4

5217a C.J.'s Roots of Chicago Blues, Vol. 2 (Anthology). Blue
         Flame 102
         CAD   Feb.   p30.   75w.   3
         LB   Jan./Feb.   p45.   250w.   3

5218 CAFE Society. Onyx ORI 210 (Reissue)
         CO   April   p15.   250w.   4

5219 CALIFORNIA Sunshine. ABC 302 (E) (2 discs) (Reissue)
         MM   Aug. 21   p18.   55w.   3

5220 CANTOS Costeños: Folksongs of the Atlantic Coastal Region
         of Colombia. Ethno Sound EST 8003
         ETH   May   p393.   500w.   4

5221 CARNEGIE Hall Concert, Xmas 1949 (Anthology). IAJRC 20
         JJ   Feb.   p38.   200w.   5

5222 CELEBRATION. Island ILPS ST002 (Reissue)
         CAD   Jan.   p17.   250w.   2½

5223 CHANGING Face of Harlem. Savoy 2208 (2 discs) (Reissue)
         JA   Summer   p41-2.   100w.   4
         PRM   May   p63.   125w.   3
         SR   Nov.   p133.   100w.   2½

5224 CHELSEA Chartbusters. Chelsea 2306-111 (E) (Reissue)
         CAC   July   p146.   100w.   3

5225 CHICAGO Jazz, 1923-1929. Biograph BLP-12005 (Reissue)
         LP   July   p11.   150w.   2½

5226 CHICAGO Jazz, 1925-1929. Herwin 109 (Reissue)
         JJ   Sept.   p30.   600w.   4

5227 CHICAGO of the 30s. Tax 8007 (Sweden) (Reissue)
        CO Sept. p25. 1100w. 5

5228 CHICAGO Slickers. Nighthawk 102 (Reissue)
        BU May-June p29. 600w. 4½

5229 CLASSIC Rags and Ragtime Songs. The Smithsonian Collection
        N 001
          CAD April p40. 75w.   3½
          MJ April p28. 125w. 3
          SR April p107. 250w. 4½

5230 COLE--A Musical Tribute to Cole Porter. Stanyan SR 10136
        SR Sept. p109-10. 225w. 0

5231 COLORADO Album. KBPI 106-FM
        GP Sept. p87. 25w. 3

5232 The COMEDIANS Sing. BBC REB 251 (E)
        GRA Dec. p1079. 25w. 1

5233 COMEDY Spectacular. BBC REB 249 (E)
        GR Dec. p1079. 50w. 3

5234 COMMODORE Jazz, v. 1. London HMC 5015 (E) (Reissue)
        GR Jan. p1263. 225w. 2½
        JJ Oct. p31. 100w. 3

5235 COMPOSERS Do Their Own Thing. Pelican LP-120
        LP July p20-1. 300w. 3½

5236 CONCERT at Carnegie Hall. DJM DJD 28023 (2 discs) (E)
        (Reissue)
          MM Nov. 13 p31. 425w. 4
          RR Dec. p102. 50w. 3

5237 CONTEMPORARY Ragtime Guitar. Kicking Mule KM 107
        RT May-June p6. 100w. 1½

5238 COOL Blues. DJM DJSLM 3032 (E) (Reissue)
        RR June p84. 50w. 2½

5239 COPULATIN' Blues. Stash ST-101 (Reissue)
        BU Jan.-Feb. p30. 850w. 5
        CAO June p23, 26. 100w. 3½
        CZM June p31. 300w. 3
        JJ Jan. p29. 250w. 4
        MM Feb. 7 p32. 50w. 4

5240 COUNTRY Capitol, v. 2. Ember (E) (Reissue)
        CAC Jan. p415. 125w. 3

5241 COUNTRY Classics. DJM DJH 44306 (E) (Reissue)

CAC Oct. p276. 50w. 3

5242 COUNTRY Comfort. K-Tel (E) (Reissue)
MM Nov. 20 p26. 125w. 2½

5243 COUNTRY Giants. RCA Camden PDA 019 (E) (2 discs) (Reissue)
CMP Dec. p13. 100w. 4

5244 COUNTRY Giants, vol. 6. RCA Camden CDS 1153 (E) (Reissue)
CMR June p30. 175w. 3

5245 COUNTRY Gold. Music for Pleasure MFP 50247 (E) (Reissue)
CMR Oct. p32. 50w. 1½

5246 COUNTRY Music Hall of Fame. London 628314 (2 discs) (West Germany) (Reissue)
CMR April p39-40. 300w. 4

5247 COUNTRY Music's Golden Hit Parade. Readers' Digest GMUS 6A (6 discs) (E) (Reissue)
CMP Oct. p23. 350w. 5

5248 COUNTRY Round Up. MGM 2354 112 (E) (Reissue)
CMP Oct. p21. 225w. 3
MM Sept. 11 p26. 25w. 3½

5249 COUNTRY Special. Bulldog BDL 1006 (E) (Reissue)
CMR Sept. p29-30. 50w. 1½

5250 COUNTRY & Western-Shannon Style. London ZGD 138 (E)
CMP May p18-9. 425w. 4

5251 COWBOY Songs. National Geographic 07786
SR Sept. p109. 350w. 5

5252 CUT and Dry Dolly. Topic 12TS278 (E)
EDS Winter p111. 225w. 3½

5253 CYPRUS: A Collection of Best-Loved Greek Songs. Vanguard Everyman Nomad SRV 73012
AU June p104-6. 800w. 3

5254 DANCE Bands: The Cardboard Dance Hall. Sunbeam MFC-9 (Reissue)
JJ Jan. p40. 75w. 2½

5255 DANCE, Dance, Dance. Contempo (E) (Reissue)
MM Jan. 17 p32. 125w. 3

5256 DANCE to the Big Hits. Polydor 2482-276 (E) (Reissue)
CAC June p112. 25w. 2½

5257 DARK Muddy Bottom. London HAU 8459 (E) (Reissue)
          LB Nov.-Dec. p34, 36. 100w. $2\frac{1}{2}$

5258 DEE Jay Round Up. Trojan 135 (E) (Reissue)
          BM Oct. p57. 200w. 3

5259 DETROIT after Hours. Trix 3311
          CK Dec. p49. 25w. $2\frac{1}{2}$
          LB Nov.-Dec. p31. 300w. $4\frac{1}{2}$

5260 DETROIT Blues (Anthology). United US 7783 (Reissue)
          JJ Feb. p38. 325w. $3\frac{1}{2}$

5261 DINGLE's Regatta. DIN 301 (E)
          EDS Winter p113. 100w. $3\frac{1}{2}$

5262 DISCO Bumpers. Music for Pleasure MFP 50239 (E) (Re-
      issue)
          BM April p51. 75w. 2

5263 DISCO Dancers. CBS 81430 (E) (Reissue)
          BM Sept. p47. 50w. 3

5264 DISCO Express. RCA APL1-1401 (Reissue)
          CAC Feb. p448. 125w. $2\frac{1}{2}$

5265 DISCO Hits of the 60s. International Artists (E) (Reissue)
          CAC May p62. 25w. $2\frac{1}{2}$

5266 DISCO Machine, v. 2. Tamla Motown STML 12028 (E) (Re-
      issue)
          BM Aug. p43. 75w. 1

5267 DISCO-Tech. Motown M6-824 (Reissue)
          BM Nov. p31. 100w. 3

5268 DISCO Trek. Atlantic SD 18158 (Reissue)
          CRE June p12. 75w. $3\frac{1}{2}$

5269 DR. Demento's Delights. Warner Brothers BS 2855
          CRE Feb. p63. 325w. 2
          LP March p29. 150w. 4
          MM May 22 p23. 175w. 0

5270 DOOWOP Doowop. DJM 22026 (E) (Reissue)
          BM May p39. 225w. 4
          MM Sept. 25 p24. 200w. $2\frac{1}{2}$

5271 DREAD in Session. Summertime BUS10 (E) (Reissue)
          BM Nov. p30. 225w. 3

5272 A DREAM Deferred. Flying Dutchman CYL2-1449 (2 discs)
          MJ Oct. p23. 25w. 3

5273 DREAM Soul.   DJM (E) (Reissue)
      MM   May 22 p25. 125w. 3

5274 The DRUMS.   Jazz Odyssey BX2 (E)
      RR   Feb. p68. 25w. 3

5275 DRUMS Odyssey.   Jazz Odyssey 010
      CO   Feb. p24. 200w. 4
      RR   Feb. p68. 50w. 1

5276 EARLY Bones.   Prestige P-24067 (2 discs) (Reissue)
      CAD Oct. p26, 27. 750w. 3

5277 EARLY Cante Flamenco, v. 1.   Folklyric 9001
      ETH May p389-393. 250w. 4

5278 The EARLY Days of Bluegrass, v. 1, 2, 5.   Rounder
      1013/14/17 (3 discs) (Reissue)
      JEMF Spring p51-2. 175w. 3
      PIC Feb. p55-6. 775w. $3\frac{1}{2}$

5279 The ELECTRIC Muse.   Island/Transatlantic (E) (4 discs) (Re-
      issue)
      MM   Jan. 3 p23. 50w. $3\frac{1}{2}$

5280 ELLINGTONIA!   Onyx OR1 216 (Reissue)
      CO   April p15. 250w. 4

5281 ELLINGTONIANS.   Jazz Trip TLP-5549 (Reissue)
      CO   March p17. 400w. 3
      DB   Jan. 29 p25. 50w. $4\frac{1}{2}$
      JJ   Nov. p26. 350w. 2
      RR   Dec. p102. 100w. 3
      SR   July p87. 400w. 4

5282 ENCYCLOPEDIA of Jazz on Records Volume 1-2.   The Twen-
      ties, the Thirties (Anthology).   MCA 2-4061 (2 discs) (Re-
      issue)
      CO   May p16. 300w. 3

5283 ENGLISH Country Music.   Topic 12T296 (E)
      TM   No. 4 p11, 12. 1275w. 4

5284 The ENTERTAINER: Rags of Scott Joplin Arranged for the
      6-String Guitar.   Kicking Mule 122
      CAD Sept. p28, 29. 150w. 4
      GP   Nov. p104. 25w. $2\frac{1}{2}$

5285 ETHIOPIA: The Falasha and the Adjuram Tribe.   Folkways
      FE 4355
      ETH May p398-9. 500w. 3

5286 FATELAKA and Baegu Music.   Philips 6586 018 (France)

ETH   Sept.   p615-6.   750w.   4

5287   FESTIVAL of the Championship Brass.   Decca STBC 7/9 (3
       discs) (E) (Reissue)
           GRA   Dec.   p1075.   200w. $4\frac{1}{2}$

5288   FESTIVAL Jazz (Anthology).   J.T.P. 106/7 (2 discs)
           CAD   Oct.   p34.   300w.   5

5289   FIDDLE/Banjo.   Union Grove 10
           BGU   April   p27.   100w.   2

5290   52nd Street, Volume 2.   Onyx OR1 217 (Reissue)
           CO   April   p15.   250w.   4

5291   The FIFTY-Year History of Country Music.   MCA 3013/7 (5
       discs) (Japan) (Reissue)
           JEMF   Summer   p107-8.   300w.   3

5292   FILM Themes for the Road.   Polydor Tape Only (E)
           CAC   Aug.   p182.   50w.   3

5293   The FINEST of Folk Bluesmen.   Bethlehem BCP-6017 (Re-
       issue)
           ARG   Nov.   p57.   150w.   4
           CAD   Aug.   p26.   75w.   4
           MJ   Dec.   p26.   75w.   4

5294   FIRST Annual Brandywine Mountain Music Convention.   Heri-
       tage VI
           OTM   Winter   p30.   250w. $2\frac{1}{2}$
           PIC   Aug.-Sept.   p80.   175w.   4

5295   FLASHBACK to the 20s/30s/40s/50s.   International Artists
       (E) (4 discs)
           CAC   May   p62.   100w. $2\frac{1}{2}$

5296   FOLK Ballads from Donegal and Derry.   Leader LEA 4055 (E)
           ETH   Jan.   p155-60.   300w.   4

5297   FOLK Music in America, v. 1/2.   Library of Congress LBC
       1/2 (2 discs) (Reissue)
           BGU   July   p31.   400w. $3\frac{1}{2}$
           HF   July   p109.   400w.   3

5298   FOLKSONGS of Louisiana Acadians.   Arhoolie 5015
           OLR   Sept.   p189-90.   25w.   3
           OTM   Summer   p20.   250w. $4\frac{1}{2}$

5299   FOR the First Time, Vol. 2.   IAJRC 21
           JJ   July   p28.   450w.   4
           ST   Oct./Nov.   p36-7.   425w. $3\frac{1}{2}$

5300 FORT Valley Blues.   Flyright-Matchbox SDM 2502 (E)
      LB July-Aug. p39-40. 470w. 4

5301 FREE and Easy.   Arista AFSO-1
      CO Feb. p18. 275w. 3

5302 The FRONT Line.   Virgin V503 (E) (Reissue)
      BM Oct. p45. 50w. 4

5303 FULL Strength Disco.   Decca (E) (Reissue)
      MM Dec. 4 p24. 75w. 1

5304 FUNKY Christmas.   Cotillion SD 9911 (Reissue)
      RS Dec. 30 p64. 50w. 3

5305 FUNKY Party 2.   Contempo CLP 534 (E) (Reissue)
      BM April p51. 100w. 1

5306 GAELIC Psalms from Lewis.   Tangent TNGM 120 (E)
      ETH Jan. p156-60. 300w. 4

5307 GALA Performance.   Polydor 2489-103 (E) (Reissue)
      CAC Feb. p447. 25w. 3

5308 GEORGIA Blues.   Rounder 2008
      LB Sept./Oct. p40. 250w. 5

5309 GET Down With Spring Records.   Polydor 2482 271 (E) (Re-
      issue)
      BM Jan. p26. 50w. 3
      CAC April p19. 75w. 3

5310 GIRLS of the 30's.   Pelican LP-122
      LP Aug. p24-5. 100w. 4

5311 GIVE Me Another Jug: Jug Bands 1924-1931, Vol. 1.   Whoopee
      102 (E) (Reissue)
      BU Jan.-Feb. p27-8. 925w. $4\frac{1}{2}$
      ST Feb.-March p114. 575w. $4\frac{1}{2}$

5312 Lud GLUSKIN et Son Jazz.   Wolverine 1
      ST Oct.-Nov. p31. 275w. $3\frac{1}{2}$

5313 [No entry.]

5314 GOING Back to Tifton.   Flyright LP 509 (E)
      LB Sept./Oct. p38, 39. 325w. $4\frac{1}{2}$

5315 GOING Down Slow.   Mainstream MSL 1037 (E) (Reissue)
      BU Jan.-Feb. p29. 350w. $3\frac{1}{2}$

5316 GOLDEN Hour of Stax Hits.   Golden Hour GH 841 (E) (Re-
      issue)

> BM   Nov.   p31.   125w.   2

5317 GOLDEN Instrumentals in Hi-Fi Stereo.   Polydor 2482-291
      (E) (Reissue)
          CAC   July   p146.   25w. $2\frac{1}{2}$

5318 GOLDEN Summer.   United Artists UALA627H (Reissue)
          CRA   Sept.   p76.   550w. $2\frac{1}{2}$

5319 GONNA Head for Home.   Flyright LP 517 (E) (Reissue)
          BM   June   p36.   250w.   4
          CZM June   p39-40.   200w.   4
          JJ   Sept.   p33-4.   800w. $2\frac{1}{2}$

5320 GOOD Rock Music, No Schlock Music.   Phil Spector Int'l
      (E) (Reissue) (5 discs)
          MM   Aug. 7   p18.   425w.   4

5321 GOOD Time Blues: St. Louis, 1926-34.   Manlish S3805 (Re-
      issue)
          LB   Nov.-Dec.   p31-2.   300w.   4

5322 GOOD Time Music: National Folk Festival.   Philo 1028
          BGU   June   p45.   150w.   3
          OTM   Summer   p21.   125w.   3
          PIC   June   p70.   175w.   3

5323 GRAND Ole Opry Road Show.   Xtra 1156 (E)
          PIC   July   p60.   100w. $1\frac{1}{2}$

5324 The GREAT Blues Men.   Vanguard VSD-25/26 (2 discs) (Re-
      issue)
          LP   Aug.   p10.   100w.   4

5325 GREAT Bluesmen--Newport (Anthology).   Vanguard VSD-77/78
      (2 discs) (Reissue)
          CAD   Sept.   p19.   250w.   5
          GP   Oct.   p97.   200w.   5

5326 GREAT Country Hits, v. 1.   Emerald Gem GES 1147 (E) (Re-
      issue)
          CMR   Aug.   p29.   150w. $2\frac{1}{2}$
          MM   June 26   p22.   50w. $1\frac{1}{2}$

5327 GREAT Duets from MGM Musicals.   Polydor 2353116 (E)
      (Reissue)
          RR   April   p81.   100w.   3

5328 The GREATEST of the Big Bands (Anthology).   Volume 8.
      RCA FXM 1-7228 (France) (Reissue)
          JJ   Sept.   p28-9.   575w. $4\frac{1}{2}$

5329 The GREATEST Jazz Concert in the World.   Pablo 2625 704

(3 discs)
    CAC Feb. p450. 475w. $3\frac{1}{2}$
    SR Nov. p114, 116. 250w. 5

5330 GUITAR Solos. Caroline C1518 (E)
    MM July 31 p22. 375w. 3

5331 GUITAR Workshop, v. 2. Transatlantic (E)
    MM May 8 p24. 225w. $3\frac{1}{2}$

5332 GUSSIE Presents the Right Tracks. Cactus 115
    BM May p38. 125w. 3

5333 HAMMOND for the Road. Polydor Tape Only (E)
    CAC Aug. p182. 50w. $2\frac{1}{2}$

5334 HAPPY South America. Polydor 2482-292 (E)
    CAC July p146. 25w. 2

5335 HARD Time Blues: St. Louis, 1933-40. Mamlish S3806 (Reissue)
    LB Nov.-Dec. p31-2. 300w. 4

5336 HARD Times. Rounder 4007
    JEMF Summer p108. 200w. 3
    LB Sept./Oct. p39. 200w. 5

5337 HARLEM Odyssey. Xanadu 112 (Reissue)
    DB June 3 p32. 75w. 3

5338 HARMONICA Blues. Yazoo 1059 (Reissue)
    JJ Aug. p34. 500w. 5

5339 HAVE Moicy! Rounder 3010
    BGU Aug. p37. 50w. $2\frac{1}{2}$
    CM Aug. p56. 400w. $3\frac{1}{2}$
    CRA July p79-80. 100w. 3
    OTM Summer p30. 25w. 3

5340 HAWAIIAN Guitar Hot Shots. Yazoo, L-1055 (Reissue)
    GP Aug. p80. 50w. $3\frac{1}{2}$

5341 HAWAIIAN Steel Guitar 1920's to 1950's. Folklyric Records 9009 (Reissue)
    AU Nov. p121-2. 300w. $3\frac{1}{2}$
    GP Aug. 10 p80. 100w. $3\frac{1}{2}$
    JEMFQ Winter p235. 175w. 4

5342 HERE'S Johnny: Magic Moments from the Tonight Show. Casablanca SPNB 1296 (2 discs)
    SR April p76. 400w. $2\frac{1}{2}$

5343 HI-Fi Stereo Festival. Polydor 2482-293 (E)

CAC July p146.   25w.   2½

5344   HIGH Atmosphere.   Rounder 0028
       SO   V25/#1   p68-9.   450w.   3½

5345   HIGHLIGHTS of Montreux, 1975.   Pablo 2683061 (2 discs)
       MM   Feb. 7   p26.   575w.   4

5346   HILLBILLY Jazz.   Flying Fish
       CAD   Jan.   p22-3.   500w.   2½

5347   HISTORY of British Rock, vol. 3.   Sire SASH-3712/2 (2
       discs).   Cass. 5147-3712N (Reissue)
       LP   April   p8.   175w.   3
       MG   Feb.   p36.   50w.   4

5348   HIT Explosion, v. 4.   EMI 4054 25406X (Belgium) (Reissue)
       CMR   April   p40-1.   300w.   3

5349   HITS for the Road.   Polydor Tape Only (E) (Reissue)
       CAC   Aug.   p182.   50w.   2½

5350   HOLLOW Poplar, 1974.   Log Cabin 8003
       OTM   Summer   p21.   125w.   3½

5351   HONG Kong: Instrumental Music.   EMI Odeon C064 17968
       (France)
       ETH   May   p399-400.   600w.   4

5352   HONKY Tonk Train (Anthology).   Pierre Cardin 93509 (France)
       (Reissue)
       JJ   Feb.   p38.   150w.   3

5353   HOORAY for Hollywood (Anthology).   United Artists.   Cart.
       UA-LA 361-H-1.   Cass. EA361-H (Original soundtrack re-
       cordings)
       LP   Jan.   p27.   150w.   4
       SR   Oct.   p98.   400w.   3½

5354   HOT Sweet Home.   Fay 3090 (E)
       BM   May   p39.   250w.   3

5355   HULA Blues.   Rounder 1012 (Reissue)
       BGU   April   p32.   75w.   2½
       JEMF   Winter 1975   p211.   100w.   3
       OTM   Spring   p47-8.   325w.   1½
       PIC   Nov.   p54.   75w.   4

5356   HUNGARIAN Folk Music.   Pepita SPLX 17482
       SR   Oct.   p112.   225w.   4

5357   I'M Sorry; I'll Read That Again.   One-Up OUM2119 (E) (Re-
       issue)

      GR July p225.   225w. $3\frac{1}{2}$

5358 INFINITE Sound. Arch 1755
      CAD Feb. p27. 125w.   2

5359 INSTANT Disco.   Pye 28216 (E) (Reissue)
      BM Jan. p26. 100w.   3

5360 INTERNATIONAL Jam Sessions.   Xanadu 122
      CAD Dec. p24. 200w.   3

5361 JACK o' Diamonds.   Flyright Matchbox SDM 265
      ST Oct.-Nov. p37-8. 200w. $2\frac{1}{2}$

5362 JAM Session.   Charly (E)
      MM Feb. 21 p29. 550w.   4

5363 JAM Session in Swingville.   Prestige PR 24051 (2 discs) (Re-
      issue)
      JJ July p32. 425w.   4

5364 JAPAN: Semi-Classics and Folk Music.   EMI Odeon CO64
      17967 (France)
      ETH Jan. p169-70. 1000w. $2\frac{1}{2}$

5365 JAZZ: The Connecticut Traditional Jazz Club.   CTJC SLP 11
      ST Oct.-Nov. p33. 350w.   2

5366 JAZZ Giants.   Sackville 3002 (Canada)
      CAD Aug. p21. 150w.   5

5367 The JAZZ Guitar Album.   Verve 2683065 (E) (2 discs) (Re-
      issue)
      GP April p79. 200w.   4
      GR July p229. 300w.   4
      JJ April p32. 300w. $2\frac{1}{2}$

5368 JAZZ Odyssey.   Jazz Odyssey 005 (2 discs) (E)
      RR Feb. p68. 100w. $2\frac{1}{2}$

5369 JAZZ from Ohio, Volume 3 (Anthology).   Ohio Theater Con-
      cert.   Blackbird C6002
      SR Nov. p116. 250w. $4\frac{1}{2}$

5370 JAZZ at the Philharmonic: At the Montreux Jazz Festival,
      1975.   Pablo 2310 748
      CAC Jan. p412, 414. 100w. $3\frac{1}{2}$
      CAD Jan. p18-9. 200w. $4\frac{1}{2}$
      DB April 8 p22-4. 100w.   5
      RR Feb. p68. 50w.   3

5371 JAZZ at the Philharmonic: The Historic Recordings, 1944-46.
      Verve VE2-2504 (2 discs) (Reissue)

CAC Aug. p195. 1050w. 3
DB Oct. 7 p33. 150w. 4
JA Summer p40-1. 175w. 3
JJ July p32. 500w. 3
MJ Oct. p52. 75w. 3
MM July 10 p24. 300w. 4

5372 JAZZ at the Philharmonic, vol. 2 (1946). Verve 2610 024
(2 discs) (E) (Reissue)
JJ Dec. p29-30. 400w. $3\frac{1}{2}$
MM Nov. 20 p30. 800w. $3\frac{1}{2}$

5373 JAZZ at the Philharmonic: Live at Nichigek Theatre, 1953.
Verve (3 discs) (E)
GR Feb. p1390. 325w. $3\frac{1}{2}$

5374 JAZZ Showcase. Black Lion SAM 20130 (E) (Reissue)
JJ June p40. 75w. 3

5375 JAZZ in the 30s. World Records SHB 39 (2 discs) (E) (Reissue)
RR Dec. p102. 50w. $3\frac{1}{2}$

5376 JAZZ Tribute. RCA FXM2-7217 (2 discs) (France) (Reissue)
JJ July p32, 34. 500w. 4
RR Aug. p80. 225w. 3

5377 The JITTERBUG Ball. Coral CDLM 8047 (E) (Reissue)
MM May 29 p30. 425w. 3

5378 JUG Washboard Bands, 1924-32. Pierre Cardin 93522 (France)
(Reissue)
BM Aug. p43. 100w. 3

5379 JUMPIN at the Go Go. RCA 1066 (E) (Reissue)
BM Nov. p46. 200w. 3
MM Oct. 2 p30. 50w. 2

5380 JUMPING on the Hill: Memphis Blues & Hokum 1928-1941.
Policy Wheel PW459-1 (E) (Reissue)
BU May-June p31. 325w. 0

5381 KING of Country Collection. Pickwick PDA 013 (E) (Reissue)
CMP Sept. p21. 325w. 2

5382 KINGS of Swing. Volume 2. Verve 2683 067 (E) (2 discs)
(Reissue)
JJ July p35. 825w. 5
MM Aug. 14 p30. 800w. 3

5383 KLIKERS. Klik 9006 (E) (Reissue)
BM March p21-2. 175w. 4

5384 KOREAN Music. Philips 6586 011 (France)
      ETH   May p394-6. 1500w. 5

5385 LADIES on the Flatboat, 1975. Log Cabin 8004
      OTM Summer p21. 125w. $3\frac{1}{2}$

5386 LARGER Than Life. Warner K56283 (E) (Reissue)
      MM Oct. 23 p27. 150w. $3\frac{1}{2}$

5387 LATIN Delights. Verve 2352-139 (E)
      CAC April p30. 100w. $3\frac{1}{2}$

5388 LEGENDS of Jazz. Crescent Jazz Productions CJP-1
      CO Sept. p17, 18. 325w. 4

5389 LET's All Sing. Hallmark (E) (Reissue)
      CAC Feb. p447. 25w. 2

5390 LIVE at CBGB's. Atlantic SD2-508 (2 discs)
      CIR Dec. 14 p15-6. 700w. $3\frac{1}{2}$
      CRA Dec. p67. 550w. 2
      MG Dec. p63. 50w. $4\frac{1}{2}$
      MM Aug. 21 p19. 850w. 1
      RS Dec. 16 p85. 175w. 3
      SR Nov. p62. 600w. 4

5391 LJUBLJANA '74, 15th International Jazz Festival. Jugoton
      LSY 65007/8 (2 discs) (Yugoslavia)
      JF No. 41 p28. 75w. 4

5392 LONESOME Harmonica. London HAU 8455 (E) (Reissue)
      LB Nov./Dec. p34, 36. 100w. 2

5393 LOVE Songs in Hi-Fi Stereo. Polydor 2482-294 (E) (Reissue)
      CAC July p140. 25w. $2\frac{1}{2}$

5394 MAROC-MUSIQUE berbère. Vogue LDY 28-029 (France)
      ETH Jan. p167-8. 750w. 4

5395 The MASTER Musicians of Jajouka. Adelphi AD 3000
      AU Dec. p100-2. 500w. 4

5396 MERSEY Beat 62-64. United Artists (2 discs) (E) (Reissue)
      MM May 22 p25. 75w. $2\frac{1}{2}$

5397 MISSISSIPPI Bottom Blues: 1926-35. Mamlish 3802 (Reissue)
      CAD Aug. p32, 33. 175w. 4

5398 MISSISSIPPI River Blues. Flyright-Matchbox. SDM 230 (E)
      LB July-Aug. p39-40. 475w. 4

5399 MODERN Maya, Mexico. Folkways FE 4377
      ETH Sept. p616-7. 700w. $3\frac{1}{2}$

5400   MONSTER Soul.   DJM (2 discs) (E) (Reissue)
       MM   Nov. 20   p29.   50w.   3

5401   The MONTREUX Collection.   Pablo 2683 061 (2 discs)
       CAC   Jan.   p412, 414.   100w. $3\frac{1}{2}$
       DB   April 8   p22-8.   100w.   4
       JJ   Jan.   p34, 36.   275w.   4
       LP   April   p16.   200w. $4\frac{1}{2}$

5401a MORPETH Rant: Northumbrian Country Music.   Topic
       12TS267 (E)
       EDS   Summer   p73.   50w.   3

5402   MOTOWN Disco, 2.   Tamla Motown 12019 (E) (Reissue)
       BM   May   p39.   50w.   4

5403   MOTOWN Gold.   Tamla Motown STML 12003 (E) (Reissue)
       BM   Jan.   p25-6.   200w.   4

5404   MOTOWN Songbook--Original Artists.   Tamla Motown STML
       12026 (E) (Reissue)
       MM   July 31   p37.   100w.   3

5405   MURDERERS' Home.   Vogue VJD 515 (France) (Reissue)
       MM   Feb. 28   p23.   750w. $3\frac{1}{2}$
       RR   April   p78.   325w. $3\frac{1}{2}$

5406   MUSIC of the Algonkians.   Folkways FE 4253
       ETH   Jan.   p165-6.   500w. $1\frac{1}{2}$

5407   MUSIC City Soul.   Charly (E)
       MM   April 17   p21.   50w. $3\frac{1}{2}$

5408   MUSIC of Dawn and Day: Music and Dance Associations of the
       Igeda of Nigeria.   Love Records LXLP 513/4 (2 discs) (Fin-
       land)
       ETH   May   p397-8.   500w. $4\frac{1}{2}$

5409   The MUSIC Festival Show.   Westwood WRS 072 (E)
       CMP   March   p27.   200w.   4
       CMR   Jan.   p32.   125w.   3

5410   MUSIC Industry Arts, 1975.   MIA 1976 (Canada)
       CC   Nov.   p34.   50w. $2\frac{1}{2}$

5411   MUSIC of Morocco.   Library of Congress LC 3 L64
       AU   Dec.   p100-2.   500w. $3\frac{1}{2}$

5412   MUSIC in Sirkim.   ABC Command COMS 9002
       AU   May   p83-4.   850w.   4

5413   MUSIC of the Venezuelan Yekuana Indians.   Folkways FE 4104
       ETH   Jan.   p162-4.   1200w.   5

5414 MUSIC in the World of Islam. Tangent TBX 601 (E) (6 discs)
CAC Sept. p228. 850w. 3½

5415 MUSIC for Xaba. Sonet SNTF 642 (E)
CO June p18. 400w. 2½

5416 MUSICAL Heritage of America, v. 1. CMS 650/4L (4 discs)
JEMF Summer p108. 100w. 3

5417 NEGRO Songs of Protest. Rounder 4004
SO V24/#6 p46. 175w. 3½

5418 NEW American Music, v. 1. Folkways FTS 33901
DB April 8 p30-2. 100w. 5

5419 NEW Beehive Songsters, v. 1. Okehdokeh OK 75003
BGU Aug. p37. 75w. 3
OTM Summer p20. 600w. 3½

5420 NEW Deal Blues: 1933-1939. Mamlish 3801 (Reissue)
CAD Aug. p32, 33. 75w. 4

5421 The NEW Goodies. Precision Bradleys (E)
CAC Jan. p416. 25w. 2½

5422 NEW Orleans, Volume 4. RCA B&W FXM 1-7227 (France)
(Reissue)
JJ Sept. p36-7. 475w. 4

5423 NEW Orleans Sounds in New York 1924-1926 (Anthology).
Herwin 107 (Reissue)
ST Dec. 1975-Jan. 1976 p72. 250w. 5

5424 NEWPORT All Stars. Black Lion BL 303
CAD June p28-9. 150w. 2

5425 The 1930's--Vol. 1/2. Aircheck #1/2 (Canada) (2 discs)
CAD Sept. p23. 300w. 5
ST Dec. '75-Jan. '76 p77-8. 200w. 2

5426 NON-Stop Rock 'n' Roll. MCA CDLM 8049 (E) (Reissue)
MM Nov. 27 p24. 175w. 2

5427 NORTH Country. Look LK 2020 (E)
CMP Feb. p30. 75w. 3

5428 NORTH Florida Fives. Flyright LP 510
LB Sept./Oct. p38, 39. 325w. 4½

5429 OLD Time Fiddlers' Repertory. University of Missouri (no
serial no.) (2 discs)
JEMF Summer p104-5. 250w. 3½

5430 OLD Time String Band Classics. County 531 (Reissue)

MN   V7/#6   p17.   250w. $2\frac{1}{2}$

5431   OLD Time Tunes from Cool Creek.   Heritage V
      OTM   Winter   p30.   350w. $2\frac{1}{2}$
      PIC   Aug.-Sept.   p84, 85.   150w.   3

5432   The ORIGINAL American Folk Blues Festival.   Excello 8029
    (Reissue)
      LB   March/April   p48.   150w.   0

5433   ORIGINAL Boogie Woogie Giants.   Columbia KC 32708 (Re-
    issue)
      SR   May   p91.   275w.   4

5434   ORIGINAL RCA Swing Sounds.   Starcall RCA DHY 0012X (E)
    (2 discs) (Reissue)
      RR   Aug.   p80.   125w.   3

5435   OUT on the Streets Again.   ABC (E) (Reissue)
      MN   Nov. 20   p29.   75w.   3

5436   The OUTLAWS.   RCA APL1-1321.   Cart. APS1-1321.   Cass.
    APK1-1321
      AU   Sept.   p82.   550w.   4
      CAC   July   p153.   325w.   3
      CM   May   p56.   475w.   2
      CMP   April   p20.   400w.   5
      GR   July   p226.   50w.   3
      MM   April 17   p21.   450w.   3
      RS   March 11   p64.   300w. $3\frac{1}{2}$
      SOU   May   p37-8.   375w. $2\frac{1}{2}$
      SR   Oct.   p104-6.   2200w.   4

5437   PACKIN up My Blues: Blues of the Deep South, 1950-61.
    Muscadine 102 (Reissue)
      LP   March   p18.   100w.   3

5438   PARIS Session Banjo, v. 1.   Musigrass Diffusion (France)
      BGU   Jan.   p19.   275w.   2
      PIC   Aug.-Sept.   p79.   50w. $4\frac{1}{2}$

5439   PARTY Sing Along.   Hallmark 198 (E)
      CAC   Feb.   p447.   25w.   2

5439a   PHIL Spector's Christmas Album.   Warner Brothers SP
    9103 (Reissue)
      BM   Jan.   p26.   50w.   3
      RS   Dec. 30   p63.   175w.   5

5439b   PHIL Spector's Wall of Sound, v. 4.   Phil Spector Interna-
    tional 2307 007 (E) (Reissue)
      BM   July   p52.   125w. $2\frac{1}{2}$

5439c PHIL Spector's Wall of Sound, v. 6.   Phil Spector International (E) (Reissue)
MM Nov. 27 p24. 175w. 3

5440   PHILLYBUSTERS, v. 3.   Philadelphia International 81011 (E)
(Reissue)
BM Jan. p24. 200w. 3

5441   PIANO Blues 1927-1937: 'Stomp 'em Down'.   Oldie Blues OL
2808 (Holland) (Reissue)
JJ Jan. p36, 37. 225w. 4$\frac{1}{2}$

5442   PIANO Power, v. 2.   MPS/BASF BAB 9013 (E) (Reissue)
GR Aug. p352. 200w. 3$\frac{1}{2}$
JJ June p36. 325w. 4
MM July 10 p24. 125w. 3

5443   PIANO Ragtime of the 40s.   Herwin 403 (Reissue)
RT Jan./Feb. p6-7. 125w. 4
ST Feb.-March p118. 375w. 4$\frac{1}{2}$

5444   PIANO Ragtime of the 50s.   Herwin 404 (Reissue)
FT June/July p19. 200w. 2$\frac{1}{2}$
JJ Oct. p36. 325w. 4$\frac{1}{2}$
ST Aug.-Sept. p236-7. 325w. 2

5445   PIANO Summit.   77 Records 775 58 (E)
JJ Nov. p34-5. 350w. 3
MM Dec. 4 p30. 250w. 3
RR Dec. p102. 50w. 3

5446   PICKING Around the Cookstove.   Rounder 0040
OTM Winter p28. 300w. 2$\frac{1}{2}$

5447   PIPE, Spoon, Pot and Jug.   Stash 102 (Reissue)
CAD June p26. 100w. 3

5448   PORTUGAL.   EMI Odeon CO64 17843 (France)
ETH May p389-93. 250w. 4

5449   PRIMITIVE Piano.   Sirens Records 101 (Reissue)
CAD Jan. p14. 100w. 2$\frac{1}{2}$
CK Jan. p48. 200w. 3
MJ April p29. 75w. 3

5450   PROJECT One (Anthology).   National Association of Jazz
Educators NAJE 1
CAD Oct. p12, 13. 200w. 5

5451   PUT the Hammer Down.   Realistic SL 8017.   Cass. SL 8017
SR Nov. p116-7. 750w. 3

5452   RAGTIME Entertainer.   Folkways RBF 22 (Reissue)

RT   March/April   p5-6.   50w.   3

5453 RALPH Stanley Festival.   Live at McClure, Virginia.   Rebel
      SLP 1554/55 (2 discs)
          MN   V7/#2   p18.   400w.   3

5454 RARE Tracks.   Polydor 2482 274 (E)
          CAC June   p100.   225w. $3\frac{1}{2}$

5455 RASS Claat Dub.   Grounation 509
          BM   July   p51.   200w.   3

5456 The RED Bird Era.   Charly CR 30108/9 (2 discs) (Reissue)
          MM   Sept. 18   p22.   450w.   3

5457 REEFER Songs.   Stash ST 100 (Reissue)
          JJ   Jan.   p37.   175w. $3\frac{1}{2}$
          ST   Aug.-Sept.   p234, 236.   525w.   4

5458 REGGAE, Reggae, Reggae.   Trojan TBL 130 (E) (Reissue)
          SO   May/June   p43.   25w. $2\frac{1}{2}$

5459 REGGAE Chartbusters.   Trojan TBLS 105 (E) (Reissue)
          SO   May/June   p43.   50w. $2\frac{1}{2}$

5460 REGGAE Confusion.   Third World 3 (E) (Reissue)
          BM   May   p38.   100w.   2

5461 REGGAE Spectacular.   A&M SP 3529 (2 discs) (Reissue)
          BS   Aug.   p61.   150w.   3
          CIR   Aug. 24   p14-5.   250w. $3\frac{1}{2}$

5462 RHYTHM and Blues Christmas.   United Artists UALA 654 R
      (Reissue)
          RS   Dec. 30   p64.   100w.   4

5463 RHYTHM and Blues Party.   Philips 6436 023 (E) (Reissue)
          MM   Nov. 27   p27.   350w.   2

5464 The RICH-R-Tone Story.   Rounder 1017 (Reissue)
          SO   V25/#1   p67.   75w. $2\frac{1}{2}$

5465 RIVERSIDE Blues.   Whoopee 103 (E) (Reissue)
          BM   Oct.   p44.   200w.   4

5466 The ROAD That Jesus Walked.   Lamb & Lion LL 2014 (Re-
      issue)
          CMP   July   p28.   300w.   2

5467 The ROARING Twenties.   Capitol VMP 1022 (E) (Reissue)
          JJ   Sept.   p41.   75w. $2\frac{1}{2}$

5468 ROCK Express.   Bulldog (E)

MM July 24 p25. 50w. 3

5469 ROCK for the Road. Polydor Tape Only (E)
CAC Aug. p182. 50w. 3

5470 ROCK and Roll at the Capitol Tower. Capitol (2 discs) (E)
(Reissue)
MM Aug. 21 p18. 425w. 4

5471 ROLLIN' Along. Tishomingo TSHO 2220 (Reissue)
CM Dec. p63. 600w. 4

5472 ROLLIN' the Rock. Rollin' Rock LP 009 (Reissue)
CM Dec. p67. 350w. 3

5473 ROOSTER Crowed for Day. Flyright LP 518 (E) (Reissue)
JJ Sept. p33-4. 800w. $2\frac{1}{2}$

5474 ROOTS of British Rock. Sire SASH-3711-2 (2 discs) (Reissue)
LP April p11. 150w. $2\frac{1}{2}$

5475 ROSKO Road Show, v. 3. Atlantic K50119 (E) (Reissue)
BM May p59. 50w. 3

5476 RUSSELL Peewee Memorial Stomp. Jersey Jazz 1001
JJ May p46. 75w. 4

5477 SAN Diego Blues Jam. Advent 2804
SR Oct. p89. 175w. $3\frac{1}{2}$

5478 The SAN Francisco Traditional Jazz Jamboree. NOJC NOJ
102
JJ Sept. p37. 325w. $2\frac{1}{2}$

5479 SHETLAND Fiddle Music. Tangent TNGM117 (E)
ETH June p150-5. 300w. 4
TM No. 5 piv-vi. 600w. 4

5480 SHETLAND Fiddlers. Leader LEA 2052 (E)
ETH Jan. p156-66. 300w. 4
TM No. 5. piv-vi. 600w. 3

5481 The SILVER Bow: Shetland Folk Fiddling, v. 1. Topic
12TS289 (E)
EDS Winter p112. 100w. 3
TM No. 5 piv-vi. 600w. $4\frac{1}{2}$

5482 SINGIN' the Blues. MCA 2-4064 (2 discs) (Reissue)
CO May p16. 350w. 5

5483 SIX-Five Special. BBC REB 252 (E)
GR Dec. p1079. 25w. 3

5484   SIXTEEN Big Band Greats, v. 2.   MCA CDLM 8046 (E) (Re-
        issue)
            MM July 3 p24. 375w. $3\frac{1}{2}$

5484a   SIXTEEN Country Greats, v. 2.   MCA CDL 8039 (E) (Reissue)
            CMR Feb. p33. 150w. $2\frac{1}{2}$
            CMR Dec. p26. 100w. $3\frac{1}{2}$
            MM Nov. 20 p26. 125w. $2\frac{1}{2}$

5485   SODA Pop Jive.   DJM 22038 (E) (Reissue)
            MM Aug. 21 p18. 25w. 3

5486   SOME People Play Guitar ... Like a Lotta People Don't !
        Kicking Mule Record CoSNKF102
            CMP Jan. p23. 50w. 3
            LP July p14. 250w. 4

5487   SONGS of the Open Road.   Topic 12T253 (E)
            EDS Summer p73. 75w. 5
            TM No. 3 p14, 15. 1150w. 5

5488   SONGS of Rebels and Redcoats.   National Geographic Society
        07788
            SR Nov. p115, 118. 225w. $4\frac{1}{2}$

5489   SORROW Come Pass Me Around.   Advent 2805
            SR Aug. p85. 300w. 2

5490   SOUL Christmas.   Atco SD 33-269 (Reissue)
            RS Dec. 30 p64. 100w. 4

5491   SOUL Deep, v. 1.   Contempo CLPJ2 (E) (Reissue)
            BM Oct. 1975. p33. 100w. 5

5492   SOUL Factory.   Polydor 2482 339 (E)
            BM Sept. p46-7. 100w. 3
            CAC Oct. p258. 50w. 3

5493   SOUL Food.   ABC 5179 (E) (Reissue)
            MM Aug. 21 p18. 25w. $3\frac{1}{2}$

5494   SOUL Motion.   K-Tel (E) (Reissue)
            MM Nov. 20 p29. 50w. 3

5495   SOUL Peepers.   Phonogram SON 003 (E) (Reissue)
            CAC Oct. p256. 50w. 3

5496   SOUL of the Road.   Polydor Tape Only (E) (Reissue)
            CAC Aug. p182. 50w. 3

5497   SOUL Train Gang.   Soul Train BVL1-1287
            BM July p53. 225w. 3
            LP April p22. 125w. $4\frac{1}{2}$

5498 The SOUND of the Nickelodeon and Dance Organ.   Pye (E)
         MM   Aug. 14   p28.   200w.   3

5499 SOUNDS of Bluegrass.   Evny
         BGU   Feb.   p25.   50w.   2

5500 SOUTH Mississippi Blues.   Rounder 2009
         LP   March   p19.   75w.   3

5501 SOUTHERN Cornet Blues.   Flyright LP 2100 (E) (Reissue)
         ST   June-July   p192, 194.   575w.   2

5502 SPIVEY's Blues Cavalcade.   Spivey LP 1015
         LB   May/June   p48.   175w. $2\frac{1}{2}$

5503 SPRINGTIME in the Mountains.   County 749 (Reissue)
         JEMF   Spring   p52.   50w. $4\frac{1}{2}$
         MN   V7/#2   p17.   400w. $4\frac{1}{2}$
         OTM   Summer   p23.   225w.   5
         SO   V25/#1   p67.   50w.   4

5504 STAR Artist.   Third World 202 (E)
         BM   Dec.   p57.   125w.   2

5505 The STARBOARD List.   Adelphi.
         SO   Sept./Oct.   p51.   75w.   4

5506 STAX Northern Disco Sounds.   Stax STX 3002 (Reissue)
         BM   Jan.   p26.   50w.   3

5507 STAX Southern Disco Sound.   Stax STX 3003 (Reissue)
         BM   Jan.   p26.   50w.   4

5508 STAX Story.   Stax STX 5004 (2 discs) (Reissue)
         BM   May   p59.   100w.   5

5509 STEEL Guitar Classics.   Old Timey LP 113 (Reissue)
         CMR   March   p30.   550w.   4
         ETH   Sept.   p618-9.   500w.   5

5510 STEP Forward Youth.   Third World 03 (E) (Reissue)
         BM   Dec. 1975   p30.   175w.   3

5511 STRETCHIN' Out.   London HAU 8456 (E) (Reissue)
         LB   Nov./Dec.   p34, 36.   100w.   4

5512 STRING Ragtime: To Do This You Got to Know How.   Yazoo
         L-1045 (Reissue)
         CO   May   p21, 22.   250w.   2
         OTM   Summer   p19.   175w.   4

5513 STUFF.   Just Sunshine BS 2698
         CRA   Dec.   p74.   225w.   1

5514   SUMMIT Meeting.   Charisma (E)
          MM   June 5   p19.   400w. $1\frac{1}{2}$

5515   SUN: The Roots of Rock V. 1/6.   Charly CR 30101/06 (E)
          (2 discs) (Reissue)
          CMR   Aug.   p33-4.   350w.   3

5516   SUN: The Roots of Rock, v. 2/5.   Charly CR 30102/03 (E)
          (2 discs) (Reissue)
          BM   April   p35.   600w.   3

5517   SUN: The Roots of Rock, v. 8/10.   Charly CR 30108/10 (E)
          (2 discs) (Reissue)

5518   SUNSHINE Special.   VJM VLP 39 (E) (Reissue)
          JEMF   Spring   p52.   25w.   3
          JF   No. 41   p66.   400w.   4

5519   SUPER Hits of the Seventies, Part One.   Polydor 2482-323
          (E)
          MM   July 24   p25.   25w. $2\frac{1}{2}$

5520   SUPER Jazz.   Monument MNT 22009 (2 discs) (E)
          RR   Aug.   p80.   75w.   1

5521   SUPER Kickers.   ABC C 05696502 (West Germany) (Reissue)
          CMR   Sept.   p30.   125w.   4
          MM   June 26   p22.   50w. $2\frac{1}{2}$

5522   SUPPER Club Singers.   Stanyan SR 10112 (Reissue)
          SR   Feb.   p97.   325w.   3

5523   SUSSEX Harvest.   Topic 21T258 (E)
          EDS   Winter/Spring   p33.   75w.   2
          TM   No. 3   p14, 16.   650w.   4

5524   SWING Sounds.   RCA Starcall DHY 0001 (2 discs) (E) (Re-
          issue)
          CAC   Oct.   p274.   175w.   3
          JJ   Aug.   p39.   100w. $3\frac{1}{2}$

5525   SWING Street, v. 1.   Tax M 8026 (E) (Reissue)
          JJ   Dec.   p36.   300w.   3

5526   TAG Along: The Legendary Jay Miller Sessions, v. 1.   Fly-
          right LP516 (E) (Reissue)
          CZM   June   p39-40.   200w.   4

5527   TAQASIM and Layal: Cairo Tradition.   Philips 6586 010
          (France)
          ETH   Sept.   p611-2.   750w. $2\frac{1}{2}$

5528   TEA Pad Songs.   Volume 2.   Stash ST 104 (Reissue)

CAD June p26. 100w. 3
JJ Sept. p38-9. 575w. $2\frac{1}{2}$

5529 TEN chansons finalises du concours de la chanson d'adieu.
Solo SO 21101 (Canada)
CC Nov. p33. 50w. 3

5530 TENINO Old Time Music Festival, 1973-74. Voyager VRLP
313S
BGU Jan. p17. 150w. $2\frac{1}{2}$

5531 The TERRITORY Bands. Vol. 1/2. Arcadia 2006/7 (2 discs)
JJ June p39. 75w. 5
ST Aug.-Sept. p23-4. 550w. 4

5532 The TERRITORY Bands. Tax m-8009 (Sweden) (Reissue)
JJ June p39. 75w. 2
ST Aug.-Sept. p229. 450w. 4

5533 TEXAS Country. United Artists UALA574-H2 (2 discs) (Re-
issue)
MG June p55. 50w. 3
MM Junc 26 p21. 125w. $2\frac{1}{2}$

5534 TEXAS-Mexican Border Music, volume 2. Corridos, Part 1,
1930-34. Folklyric 9004 (Reissue)
AU June p102-4. 2500w. 4
JEMF Autumn p171-2. 400w. 5
SR April p94. 250w. 4

5535 THAT's TV Entertainment. BBC REB 250 (E)
GR Dec. p1079. 25w. $2\frac{1}{2}$

5536 THIRD Annual Battleground Fiddlers Gathering, 1975. Log
Cabin 5004
BGU Oct. p24. 100w. $2\frac{1}{2}$

5537 THIS Is Jazz, v. 1/2. Rarities 33/34 (E) (2 discs) (partial
reissue)
JJ Dec. p30. 225w. 3

5538 THIS Is Reggae Music, v. 1/2. Island ILPS 9251 and 9327
(2 discs) (Reissue)
BM May p34. 100w. 5
CIR July 22 p18. 475w. 4
MM March 13 p39. 50w. 3
RS May 20 p69. 200w. $2\frac{1}{2}$
SO May/June p43. 50w. $2\frac{1}{2}$

5539 THOSE Glorious MGM Musicals. MGM
AU Feb. p103-5. 1250w. 4

5540 THREADS of Glory. London 6SP 14000 (6 discs)

LP Jan. p26-7. 175w. 3

5541 TIBETAN Buddhism. Nonesuch H72071
      ARG Dec. p46. 275w. 4

5542 TONGAN Festival Contingent, v. 1/2. Hibiscus HLS 30/40
      (2 discs) (New Zealand)
      ETH Sept. p612-4. 700w. 3½

5543 TOOTIN' Through the Roof, Volume 1. Onyx ORI 209 (Re-
      issue)
      CO April p15. 250w. 4

5544 A TOUCH of Country. Topaz (E) (Reissue)
      MM May 15 p26. 75w. 2½

5545 TRAD Jazz v. 2. Pye Golden Hour GH 602 (E) (Reissue)
      DB April 8 p30-2. 50w. 3
      JJ Jan. p38, 40. 225w. 2½

5546 TRADITIONAL Music of Chile. ABC Command COMS 9003
      AU June p106-7. 900w. 3

5547 TRADITIONAL Music of Mississippi, v. 1/2. County 528/9
      (2 discs) (Reissue)
      JEMF Spring p50. 150w. 4

5548 TRADITIONAL Music of Tonga. Hibiscus HLS 65 (New Zea-
      land)
      ETH Sept. p612-4. 700w. 3½

5549 TRADITIONAL Music of West Virginia. Heritage XII
      OTM Summer p21. 125w. 2½

5550 TRADITIONAL Songs and Dances from the Soko Banja Area.
      Selo LP1
      ETH Sept. p627-8. 500w. 5

5551 TRAVELING Through the Jungle. Testament T 2223
      LP March p31. 75w. 3½

5552 TRIBUTE to Louis Armstrong. RCA FXL1-7159 (France)
      JA Summer p38. 350w. 4½

5553 The TROJAN Story. Trojan TALL-1 (E) (3 discs) (Reissue)
      SO May/June p43. 75w. 2½

5554 TURKEY--A Musical Journey. Nonesuch H-7206
      SR April p94. 225w. 4

5555 TURN on a Party. Phonogram Tape Only (E)
      CAC July p146. 100w. 2½

5556 TV Big Bands and Orchestras. BBC REB 245 (E)
GR Dec. p1079. 25w. $2\frac{1}{2}$

5557 TV Themes. BBP USR 8153
LP April p31. 200w. 0

5557a 12 Hits of Christmas. United Artists UALA 669 (Reissue)
RS Dec. 30 p63-4. 50w. $3\frac{1}{2}$

5558 20 Fantastic Soul Hits. Contempo CLP 527 (E) (Reissue)
BM Oct. p33. 50w. 3

5559 25 Years of Prestige (Anthology). Prestige P-24046 (2 discs)
(Reissue)
CO May p15, 16. 1000w. 4

5560 25 Years of Top Ten Country Hits. RCA LSA 3263/64 (E)
(2 discs) (Reissue)
CAC July p153. 200w. 3
CMP Aug. p30. 450w. 5
CMR Aug. p29-30. 200w. 4

5561 TWO's Company, vol. 2. BBC REC 211 (E)
CAC June p98. 75w. 4

5562 200 Years of American Heritage in Song. CMH 1776. Cart.
CMH 8-1776
CM Sept. p58. 50w. 2
JEMFQ Winter '75 p211. 100w. 3

5563 200 Years of Fiddlin'. American Heritage AH 401 521 (Re-
issue)
BGU July p33. 250w. 1
PIC Nov. p50. 175w. 3

5564 200 Years of Traditional American Music. Heritage Productions 751120
OTM Summer p29. 100w. $2\frac{1}{2}$

5565 TWO White Horses Standing in Line. Flyright SDM 264 (E)
(Reissue)
BM Nov. p48. 325w. 4
ST Oct.-Nov. p37-8. 200w. $3\frac{1}{2}$

5566 UGANDA: Musik der Bavuma. Klang dokumente Musikwissen-
schaft KM 0004 (West Germany)
ETH Jan. p161-2. 1200w. 4

5567 The UNEXPLAINED: Electronic Musical Impressions of the
Occult. RCA APL1-1217
LP April p27. 100w. 3

510   Record Reviews, 1976

5568 USA Jazz Live. MPS/BASF BAP 5068 (E) (2 discs)
      JJ July p38. 350w. 3½
      RR Aug. p80. 125w. 2½

5569 VICTORY Parade of Spotlight Bands. Aircheck 6 (Canada)
      HF Feb. p109-10. 375w. 3

5570 The VOCAL Touch. Verve 2352 171 (E) (Reissue)
      CAC Oct. p261. 175w. 3½

5571 The VOICE of the Blues. Yazoo L-1046 (Reissue)
      CAD May p25-6. 100w. 3½
      CO May p17, 18. 250w. 4
      LB Sept./Oct. p41. 300w. 5

5572 VOICES from Hollywood's Past. Delos DEL/F 25412
      LP March p36. 250w. 4½

5573 VOLUNTEER Jam. Capricorn CP 0172
      CM Dec. p65, 67. 450w. 3
      CS Nov. p41. 200w. 3½
      GP Sept. p87. 50w. 3½
      MM Oct. 2 p30. 75w. 2½

5574 WASHO: Peyote Songs. Folkways FE 4384
      ETH Jan. p165. 250w. 4

5575 WEST Coast Jazz. Trip TLP-5537 (Reissue)
      CO May p19, 20, 21. 525w. 3

5576 WEST Coast Jazz, v. 1/2. (Anthology). Arcadia 2001/2 (2
      discs) (Reissue)
      JJ Feb. p43. 150w. 3

5577 WESTERN Swing, v. 1/3. Old Timey 105/116/117 (3 discs)
      (Reissue)
      CM Feb. p48, 50-1. 1050w. 3½

5578 WESTERN Swing, vol. 2. Old Timey LP 116
      SR Oct. p107. 250w. 3

5579 WESTERN Swing, v. 2/3. Old Timey 116/117 (2 discs) (Re-
      issue)
      AU May p82-3. 700w. 4
      PMS V4/#3 p191. 50w. 4

5580 WHAT Now, People. Paredon
      SO V24/#6 p47. 225w. 3

5581 WHEN Women Sang the Blues. Blues Classics 26 (Reissue)
      JJ Sept. p39-40. 700w. 2½
      MM Oct. 16 p29. 375w. 4

5582   WHEN Sheepshearing's Done.   Topic 12T254 (E)
           TM   No. 3   p14, 16.   200w.   4

5583   WILDFLOWER Roots.   Opal PL 1001 (E)
           MM   March 13   p39.   50w. $2\frac{1}{2}$

5584   WINNERS!   The American Song Festival.   Buddah BDS 5624
           SR   July   p84, 85.   1800w.   3

5585   WITCHCRAFT and Ritual Music.   Nonesuch H 72066
           LP   March   p36.   150w.   4

5586   YESTERDAY's Hits Today.   Phil Spector International 2307-007
           (E) (Reissue)
           MM   April 17   p21.   50w. $3\frac{1}{2}$

DIRECTORY OF RECORD LABELS

This address directory is divided by three countries--the United States, England, and Canada. "See" references will direct the searcher to the appropriate distributor for a manufacturer that does not distribute for itself. Each distributor listing also contains the names of the labels that it distributes. Certain names which are not labels but series lines (such as "Explorer") were added to these lists for purposes of clarification; the "See" references will direct the searcher to the manufacturer (in this case, for example, "Elektra," which distributes "Nonesuch," the producer of the "Explorer" series). Ownership of the labels has not been determined. The name of the manufacturer has not been repeated in the listing address.

These lists are given in terms of the following restrictions: (a) only record labels which were indexed for 1976 are included; (b) only English and Canadian labels and records which were not also released in the United States are listed; and (c) no addresses are provided for labels manufactured outside the three countries. It is suggested that a record store or record importer could deal with the foreign pressings, perhaps better than a library or an individual could. There were many addresses that proved virtually impossible to find; try the specialty stores for these two. Most of these latter records are bootleg issues and they would rather not be found.

United States

A & M   1416 North LaBrea Ave., Hollywood, Cal.   90028   Distributes: Ode

ABC   8255 Berverly Blvd., Los Angeles, Cal.   90048   Distributes: Blue Thumb, Dot, Duke, Dunhill, Impulse, Peacock, Shelter, Sire

ABKCO   1700 Broadway, New York, N.Y.   10019

ADELPHI   P.O. Box 288, Silver Spring, Md.   20907   Distributes: Hope, Piedmont, Skyline

ADITI   2266 Cambridge St., Los Angeles, Cal.   90006

ADVENT PRODUCTIONS   P.O. Box 635, La Habra, Cal.   90631   Distributes: Muskadine

ADVENT RECORDS (JAZZ) 23366 Commerce Park Rd., Cleveland, Ohio 44122

ALADDIN 101 North Columbus St., Alexandria, Va. 22314

ALL PLATINUM 96 West St., Englewood, N.J. 07631 Distributes: Cadet, Checker, Chess, Custom, Janus, Kent

ALLEN-MARTIN 9701 Taylorsville Rd., Louisville, Ky. 40299 Distributes: Bridges

ALLIGATOR P.O. Box 11741, Fort Dearborn Sta., Chicago, Ill. 60611

ALSHIRE INTERNATIONAL P.O. Box 7107, Burbank, Cal. 91505

AMERICAN HERITAGE 912 N. 8th St., Boise, Idaho 87307

AMERICAN MUSE 130 W. 57th St., New York, N.Y. 10019

AMPEX 555 Madison Ave., New York, N.Y. 10022

AMSTERDAM see RCA

ANGEL see CAPITOL

ANITA O'DAY Box 442, Hesperia, Cal. 92345

APPLE see CAPITOL

ARBOR P.O. Box 946, Evanston, Ill. 60204

ARCANE Maple Leaf Club, 5560 W. 62nd St., Los Angeles, Cal. 90056

ARCHIVE OF FOLK AND JAZZ MUSIC see EVEREST

ARHOOLIE 10341 San Pablo Ave., El Cervito, Cal. 94530 Distributes: Blues Classics, Folklyric, Old Timey

ARISTA 6 W. 57th St., New York, N.Y. 10019 Distributes: Haven, Savoy

ASCH see FOLKWAYS

ASYLUM see ELEKTRA/ASYLUM/NONESUCH

ATCO see ATLANTIC

ATLANTIC 75 Rockefeller Plaza, New York, N.Y. 10019 Distributes: Atco, Big Tree, Cotillion, Embryo, Little David, Nemperor, Rolling Stone

ATTEIRAM   P.O. Box 606, Marietta, Ga.   30061

AUDIOFIDELITY   221 W. 57th St., New York, N.Y.   10019   Distributes: BASF, Black Lion, Chiaroscuro, World Jazz

AUDIOPHILE   see   HAPPY JAZZ

AVCO EMBASSY   1301 Ave. of the Americas, New York, N.Y.   10019

BASF   see   AUDIOFIDELITY

BANANA   see   STACY-LEE

BANG/BULLET   2107 Fawkner Rd. N.E., Atlanta, Ga.   30324   Distributes: Bang

BANON   11 Dogwood Lane, Larchmount, N.Y.   10538

BARNABY   816 N. La Cienga Blvd., Los Angeles, Cal.   90064

BATTERY   1860 Broadway, New York, N.Y.   10023   Distributes: Painted Smiles

BAY   5801 Margarido Dr., Oakland, Cal.   94618

BEARSVILLE   see   WARNER BROTHERS

BENSON, JOHN T.   see   JOHN T. BENSON

BERKELEY RHYTHM   3040 Benevenue, Berkeley, Cal.   94705

BERSERKLEY RECORDS   see   PLAYBOY

BEVERLY HILLS   P.O. Box 4009, Hollywood, Cal.   90028

BIG STAR   4228 Joy Rd., Detroit, Mich.   48204

BIG TREE   see   ATLANTIC

BIOGRAPH   16 River St., Chatham, N.Y.   12037   Distributes: Center, Historical, Melodeon

BIRCH   Box 92, Wilmette, Ill.   60091

BIZARRE   see   WARNER BROTHERS

BLACK EAGLE   128 Front St., Marblehead, Mass.   01945

BLACK JAZZ   see   OVATION

BLACK LION   see   AUDIOFIDELITY

BLACKBIRD   Lakco Record Co., 3902 N. Ashland Ave., Chicago, Ill.   60613

BLINET RECORDS   Box 11366, Denver, Col.   80211

BLUE CANYON   1037 7th St., Las Vegas, Nev.   87701

BLUE GOOSE   245 Waverly Place, New York, N.Y.   10014

BLUE GRASS REVUE   3608 Ann Arbor Place, Oklahoma City, Okla.
   73122

BLUE HORIZON   see   ABC

BLUE NOTE   see   UNITED ARTISTS

BLUE SKY   see   COLUMBIA

BLUEGRASS EXPRESS   6808 Robin Dr., Chattanooga, Tenn.   37421

BLUEGRASS SOUTHLAND   2704 Haley Ave., Fort Worth, Tex.
   76117

BLUES CLASSICS   see   ARHOOLIE

BLUGRAS   Rt. 2, Box 397, Princeton, W. Va.   24740

BOB THIELE MUSIC   see   RCA

BOUNTIFUL   12311 Gratiot Ave., Detroit, Mich.   48205

BRIAR   P.O. Box 5853, Pasadena, Cal.   91107

BRIDGES   see   ALLEN-MARTIN

BRIKO   P.O. Box 15075, Phoenix, Ariz.   85060

BRUNSWICK   888 Seventh Ave., New York, N.Y.   10019

BRUT   1345 Avenue of the Americas, New York, N.Y.   10019

BUCKSHOT RECORDS   Box DH, Panorama City, Cal.   91402

BUDDAH/KAMA SUTRA   810 Seventh Ave., New York, N.Y.   10019
   Distributes: Celebration, Kama Sutra

BURCHETTE BROTHERS   P.O. Box 1363, Spring Valley, Cal.
   92077

CBGB/OMFUG   315 Bowery, New York, N.Y.   10003

CK RECORDS   1000 S. 7th St., Ann Arbor, Mich.   48203

CMH RECORDS   P.O. Box 39439, Los Angeles, Cal.   90039

CMS   14 Warren St., New York, N.Y.   10007

CTI   see   MOTOWN

CADET   see   ALL PLATINUM

CAMBRIDGE   125 Irving St., Framingham, Mass.   01701

CAMDEN   see   RCA

CANAAN   see   WORD

CAPITOL   1750 N. Vine St., Hollywood, Cal.   90028   Distributes:
Angel, Apple, Harvest, Melodiya/Angel

CAPRICE   907 Main St., Nashville, Tenn.   37206

CAPRICORN   see   WARNER BROTHERS

CAROUSEL $1273\frac{1}{2}$ N. Crescent Heights Blvd., Los Angeles, Cal.
90046

CASABLANCA   8255 Sunset Blvd., Los Angeles, Cal.   90046   Distributes: Douglas

CASSANDRA   2027 Parker St., Berkeley, Cal.   94704

CELEBRATION   see   BUDDAH/KAMA SUTRA

CENTER   see   BIOGRAPH

CENTURY PRODUCTIONS   171 Washington Rd., Sayreville, N.J.
08872

CHAIRMAN   Box 4413, Sunnyside Station, New York, N.Y.   11104

CHECKER   see   ALL PLATINUM

CHESS/JANUS   see   ALL PLATINUM

CHIAROSCURO   see   AUDIOFIDELITY

CHOICE   245 Tilley Place, Sea Cliff, N.Y.   11579

CHRYSALIS   9255 Sunset Blvd., Suite 212, Los Angeles, Cal.
90069

CHYTOWNS   1410 E. 72nd St., Chicago, Ill.   60619

CINNAMON   1805 Hayes St., Nashville, Tenn.   37203

CLASSIC JAZZ   see   MUSIC MINUS ONE

CLUB OF SPADE   Box 1771, Studio City, Cal.   91604

COLLEGIUM 35-41 72nd St., Jackson Heights, N.Y. 11372 Distributes: Minstrel

COLUMBIA 51 W. 52nd St., New York, N.Y. 10019 Distributes: Blue Sky, Daffodil, Epic, Harmony, Kirshner, Monument, Philadelphia International, Portrait, Spindizzy, T-Neck, Virgin

CONCERT 3318 Platt Ave., Lynwood, Cal. 90262

CONCORD JAZZ P.O. Box 845, Concord, Cal. 94522

CONNOISSEUR 390 B West End Ave., New York, N.Y. 10024

CONTEMPORARY 8481 Melrose Place, Los Angeles, Cal. 90069 Distributes: Good Time Jazz

COPLIX 152 W. 42nd St., Suite 536, New York, N.Y. 10036

CORAL see MCA

COTILLION see ATLANTIC

COUNTRY LIFE C. P. O. 1322, Berea, Ky. 40403

COUNTRY MUSIC HISTORY Box 39439, Los Angeles Cal. 90039

COUNTRY Box 191, Floyd, Va. 24091

CREATIVE WORLD 1012 S. Robertson Blvd., Los Angeles, Cal. 90035

CREED see NASHBORO

CREED TAYLOR INC. see MOTOWN

CRESCENDO 3725 Crescent St., Long Island City, N.Y. 11101

CURTOM 5915 N. Lincoln Ave., Chicago, Ill. 60645

CUSTOM see ALL PLATINUM

D RECORDS c/o H. W. Daily Inc., 314 11th Ave. E., Houston, Tex. 77088

DAFFODIL see COLUMBIA

DAKAR see BRUNSWICK

DAVIS UNLIMITED Route 11, 16 Bond St., Clarkesville, Tenn. 37040

DAWN P.O. Box 544, Annapolis, Md. 21404

DAYBREAK   6725 Sunset Blvd., Suite 504, Hollywood, Cal.   90028

DECCA   see   MCA

DELITE   200 W. 57th St., New York, N.Y.   10019

DELMARK   4243 N. Lincoln, Chicago, Ill.   60618

DELUXE   see   GUSTO

DEMO RECORDS   Trails End, 1893 San Luis, Mountain View, Cal.
   94040

DERAM   see   LONDON

DEUTSCHE GRAMMOPHON   see   POLYDOR

DEVI   see   TAKOMA

DIAL   P.O. Box 1273, Nashville, Tenn.   37202

DIRTY SHAME   4552 Shenandoah, St. Louis, Mo.   63110

DISCREET   see   WARNER BROTHERS

DOMINION   P.O. Box 993, Salem, Va.   24153

DOT   see   ABC

DOUGLAS   see   CASABLANCA

DOVE   see   SOLID SOUL

DOWN HOME   J. D. Jarvis, Box 3113, Hamilton, Ohio   45013

DRIFTWOOD   P.O. Box 579, Mineral Wells, Tex.

DUKE   see   ABC

DUNHILL   see   ABC

DUTCHLAND   1860 W. Main St., Ephrata, Pa.   17522

EBM   see   EUBIE BLAKE MUSIC

EGM   Lothlovien Co.   2111 Vanderbilt Lane, Austin, Tex.   78723

EPI RECORDS   G. P.O. Box 2301, New York, N.Y.   10001

ESP   5 Riverside Drive, Krumville, N.Y.   12447

ELEKTRA/ASYLUM/NONESUCH   962 N. LaCienega, Los Angeles,
   Cal.   90069 Distributes: Asylum, Nonesuch

EMANEN   P.O. Box 46, Shady, N.Y.   12479

EMBASSY   see   AVCO EMBASSY

EMBRYO   see   ATLANTIC

ENVY   c/o Norm Vincent Sound Recording Studios, 4541 Brown Ave.,
   Jacksonville, Fla.   32207

EPIC   see   COLUMBIA

ETHELYN   13240 Fidler Ave., Downey, Cal.   90242

EUBIE BLAKE MUSIC   284A Stuyvesant Ave., Brooklyn, N.Y.   11221

EUPHONIC   P.O. Box 476, Ventura, Cal.   93001

EVEREST   10920 Wilshire Blvd. W., Los Angeles, Cal.   90024
   Distributes: Archive of Folk and Jazz Music, Olympic

EVERYMAN   see   VANGUARD

EXCELLO   see   NASHBORO

EXPLORER (NONESUCH)   see   ELEKTRA/ASYLUM/NONESUCH

EXTREME RARITIES   Ken Crawford, 215 Steuben Ave., Pittsburgh,
   Pa.   15205

F & W   Box 12, Plymouth, Vt.   05056

FAMILY   see   REQUEST

FAMOUS DOOR   40-08 155th St., Flushing, N.Y.   11354

FANIA   888 Seventh Ave., New York, N.Y.   10019   Distributes:
   Vaya

FANTASY   10th and Parker Sts., Berkeley, Cal.   94710   Distributes:
   Milestone, Prestige

FARGO   1419 Fargo Ave., Chicago, Ill.   60626

FAT CAT'S JAZZ   Box 458, Manassas, Va.   22110

FIDDLER'S GROVE   P.O. Box 38, Union Grove, N.C.   28689
   Distributes: Union Grove

FIRST TIME   P.O. Box 03202-R, Portland, Ore.   97203

FLAT TOWN   P.O. Drawer 10, Ville Platte, La.   70586   Distributes: Swallow

FLYING DUTCHMAN see RCA

FLYING FISH 3320 N. Halstead, Chicago, Ill. 60657

FOLK HERITAGE University of West Virginia, Morgantown, W.
    Va. 26505

FOLK LEGACY Sharon Mt. Rd., Sharon, Conn. 06069

FOLKLYRIC see ARHOOLIE

FOLKWAYS 43 W. 61st St., New York, N.Y. 10023 Distributes:
    Asch, Mankind (Asch), RBF

FOREFRONT 1945 Wilmette Ave., Wilmette, Ill. 60091

400 11 Dogwood Lane, Larchmount, N.Y. 10588

FOX HOLLOW RD 1, Petersburg, N.Y. 12138

FOX-ON-THE-RUN P.O. Box 40553, Washington, D.C. 20016

FREEDOM P.O. Box 888, Easley, S.C. 29640

FRETLESS see PHILO

GHB see JAZZOLOGY

GNP CRESCENDO 9165 Sunset Blvd., Hollywood, Cal. 90069

GRC Greater Recording Co., 164 Manhattan Ave., Brooklyn, N.Y.
    11206

GRC GENERAL 174 Mills St., Atlanta, Ga. 30313

GALAX MOOSE LODGE Box 665, Galax, Va. 24333

GITFIDDLE 114 W. Montclair Ave., Greenville, S.C. 29609

GLORYLAND 1414 E. Broad St., Columbus, Ohio

GOINS W. Prestonburg, Ky. 41668

GOLDBAND P.O. Box 1485, Lake Charles, La. 70601

GOLDEN CREST 220 Broadway, Huntington Station, N.Y. 11746

GOOD TIME JAZZ see CONTEMPORARY

GORDY see MOTOWN

GOSPEL GRASS Box 534, Elba, Ala. 36323

GRANITE   6255 Sunset Blvd., Los Angeles, Cal.   90028

GRATEFUL DEAD   see   UNITED ARTISTS

GROOVE MERCHANT   Suite 3701, 515 Madison Ave., New York,
   N.Y.   10022

GRUNT   see   RCA

GUITAR WORLD   43 W. 61st St., New York, N.Y.   10023

GUSTO   220 Boscobel St., Nashville, Tenn.   37213   Distributes:
   Deluxe, King, Starday

HALCYON   302 Clinton St., Bellmore, N.Y.   11710

HALO   Township Group, Box 7084, 10 Michael Dr., Greenville,
   S.C.   29610

HAPPY JAZZ   P.O. Box 66, San Antonio, Tex.   78291   Distributes:
   Audiofidelity, Paseo Stereo

HARMONY   see   COLUMBIA

HARVEST   see   CAPITOL

HAVEN   see   ARISTA

HERITAGE PRODUCTIONS   P.O. Box 2284, West Lafayette, Ind.
   47906

HERWIN   45 First St., Glen Cove, N.Y.   11542

HI   see   LONDON

HICKORY   2510 Franklin Rd., Nashville, Tenn.   37204

HILLTOP   see   PICKWICK INTERNATIONAL

HISTORICAL   see   BIOGRAPH

HOPE   see   ADELPHI

HYANNISPORT   Box 337, Hyannisport, Mass.   02647

I.A.J.R.C.   c/o Eugene Miller, 40 Prince George Dr., Islington,
   Ont., Canada M9B 2X8

I.P.S. RECORDS   P.O. Box 329, Lincolnton Station, New York,
   N.Y.   10037

IMPROVISING ARTISTS   26 Jane St., New York, N.Y.   10014

IMPULSE see ABC

INDIA NAVIGATION P.O. Box 559, Nyack, N.Y. 10960

INTERNATIONAL P.O. Box 593, Radio City Station, New York,
N.Y. 10019

INTERNATIONAL ASSOCIATION OF JAZZ RECORD COLLECTORS
see I.A.J.R.C.

IRMA see MELODY

ISLAND 7720 Sunset Blvd., Los Angeles, Cal. 90046

JALYN 1806 Brown St., Dayton, Ohio 45409

JANUS see ALL PLATINUM

JAZUM 5808 Northcumberland St., Pittsburgh, Pa. 15217

JAZZ ARCHIVES P.O. Box 194, Plainview, N.Y. 11805

JAZZ COMPOSERS' ORCHESTRA ASSOCIATION 6 W. 95th St.,
New York, N.Y. 10025

JAZZOLOGY 3008 Wadsworth Mill Pl., Decatur, Ga. 30032
Distributes: GHB, Paramount, Southland

JESSUP 3150 Francis St., Jackson, Mich. 49203 Distributes:
Michigan Bluegrass

JEWEL 728 Texas St., Shreveport, La. 71163 Distributes:
Paula, Ronn

JEWEL 1594 Kinney Ave., Cincinnati, Ohio 45231

JEZEBEL 1233 Greenleaf St., Allentown, Pa. 18102

JIM TAYLOR PRESENTS 12311 Gratiot Ave., Detroit, Mich.
48205

JOHN EDWARDS MEMORIAL FOUNDATION c/o Center for Study of
Folklore & Mythology, U.C.L.A., Los Angeles, Cal.

JOHN T. BENSON 1625 Broadway, Nashville, Tenn. 37202 Dis.
tributes: Heart, Vista

JOLICT Box 67201, Los Angeles, Cal. 90067

JUNE APPAL RECORDS Box 743, Whitesburg, Ky. 41858

KPL c/o Lin Michael, Rt. 2, Killen, Ala. 35645

KAMA SUTRA   see   BUDDAH/KAMA SUTRA

KANAWHA   P.O. Box 267, Dayton, Ohio   45420

KENT   see   ALL PLATINUM

KICKING MULE   P.O. Box 3233, Berkeley, Cal.   94703

KILMARNOCK   300 W. 57th St., New York, N.Y.   10019

KIM-PAT   P.O. Box 654, Fayetteville, Tenn.   37344

KING   see   GUSTO

KING BLUEGRASS   6609 Main St., Cincinnati, Ohio   45244   Distributes: Lemco

KINGFISH   P.O. Box 427, Oak Lawn, Ill.   60454

KIRSHNER   see   COLUMBIA

KLAVIER   10515 Burbank Blvd., N. Hollywood, Cal.   91601

KO-KO   888 Seventh Ave., New York, N.Y.   10019

KUDU   see   MOTOWN

LAB   Box 5038, North Texas Sta., Denton, Tex.   76203

LAND O' JAZZ   P.O. Box 26393, New Orleans, La.   70126

LANDERS ROBERTS   9255 Sunset Blvd., Los Angeles, Cal.   90048
    Distributes: Mums

LAVAL   266 N. Burdick St., Kalamazoo, Mich.   49006

LAWRENCE, RAY   see   RAY LAWRENCE

LEGACY   see   OWL

LEGEND   see   MCA

LEMCO   see   KING BLUEGRASS

LIBRARY OF CONGRESS   Washington, D.C.

LIGHT   see   WORD

LITTLE DAVID   see   ATLANTIC

LIVING FOLK RECORDS   65 Mt. Auburn St., Cambridge, Mass.
    02128

LONDON 539 W. 25th St., New York, N.Y. 10001 Distributes:
Deram, Hi, Parrot, Threshold

LOTUS Box 450, Miami, Fla. 37145

LYRICHORD 141 Perry St., New York, N.Y. 10014

MBA 8914 Georgian Dr., Austin, Tex. 78753

MCA 100 Universal City Plaza, Universal City, Cal. 91608 Distributes: Decca, Legend, Rocket, Uni

MGM see POLYDOR

MAINSTREAM 1700 Broadway, New York, N.Y. 10019

MAJOR 151 W. 46th St., New York, N.Y. 10036

MAMLISH Cathedral Sta., Box 417, New York, N.Y. 10025

MANKIND (ASCH) see FOLKWAYS

MANMADE 812 N.W. 57th St., Miami, Fla.

MASTER JAZZ RECORDINGS 955 Lexington Ave., New York, N.Y.
10024

MEADOWLANDS 3135 Sedgwick Ave., Bronx, N.Y. 10463

MEGA 1605 Hawkins St., Nashville, Tenn. 37203 Distributes:
Caprice

MELODEON see BIOGRAPH

MELODIYA/ANGEL see CAPITOL

MELODY 1912 St. Clair St., Hamilton, Ohio 45011 Distributes:
Irma, Pine Tree

MERCURY see PHONOGRAM

MESSAROUND Box 1392, Burlingame, Cal. 94010

METROMEDIA 1700 Broadway, New York, N.Y. 10019

MICHIGAN BLUEGRASS see JESSUP

MILESTONE see FANTASY

MINSTREL see COLLEGIUM

MISSION RECORDS General Delivery, Floyd, Va. 24091

MONMOUTH/EVERGREEN 1697 Broadway, Suite 1201, New York, N.Y. 10019

MONUMENT see COLUMBIA

MOON P.O. Box 4001, Kansas City, Kan. 66104

MORNINGSTAR see SPRINGBOARD

MOTOWN 6255 Sunset Blvd., Hollywood, Cal. 90028 Distributes: CTI, Gordy, Kudu, Mowest, Rare Earth, Soul, Tamla

MOUNTAIN Box 231A, Rt. 3, Galax, W. Va. 24333

MOUNTAIN RAILROAD 728 1st Ave., Rockford, Ill. 61108

MOWEST see MOTOWN

MUMS see LANDERS ROBERTS

MUSE Blanchris Inc., 160 W. 71st St., New York, N.Y. 10023

MUSIC CITY WORKSHOP 38 Music Sq. E., Suite 115, Nashville, Tenn. 37203

MUSIC MINUS ONE 43 W. 61st St., New York, N.Y. 10023 Distributes: Classic Jazz

MUSICORE see SPRINGBOARD

MUSKADINE see ADVENT

MYRRH see WORD

NASHBORO 1011 Woodland St., Nashville, Tenn. 37206 Distributes: Creed, Excello

NASHVILLE INTERNATIONAL 20 Music Sq. W., Nashville, Tenn. 37203

NATIONAL GEOGRAPHIC SOCIETY Dept. 100, Wash., D.C. 20036

NEMPEROR see ATLANTIC

NEW MUSIC DISTRIBUTION SERVICE 6 W. 96th St., New York, N.Y. 10024 Distributes: Shih Shih Wa As, Upstairs

NEW ORLEANS 1918 Burgundy, New Orleans, La. 70116

NONESUCH see ELEKTRA/ASYLUM/NONESUCH

NORTH TEXAS LAB BAND see LAB

ODE   see   A & M

OKEHDOKEE   370 West 1st St. South, Salt Lake City, Utah   84101

OLD DOMINION   P.O. Box 27, Gallatin, Tenn.   37066

OLD HOMESTEAD   P.O. Box 100, Brighton, Mich.   48116   Distributes: Pretzel Bell

OLD TIMEY   see   ARHOOLIE

OLYMPIC   200 W. 57th St., New York, N.Y.   10019

OMNISOUND   Delaware Water Gap, Pa.   18327

ORIGIN JAZZ LIBRARY   Box 863, Berkeley, Cal.   94701

ORIGINAL SOUND   7120 Sunset Blvd., Los Angeles, Cal.   90046

OVATION   1249 Waukegan, Glenview, Ill.   60025   Distributes: Black Jazz

OWL   P.O. Box 557, Lithia Springs, Ga.   30057   Distributes: Legacy

OWL   P.O. Box 711, Sebastopol, Cal.   95472

P.M. RECORDS   20 Martha St., Woodcliff Lake, N.J.   07675

PA DA   27 Washington Sq. N., Suite 4D, New York, N.Y.   10011

PABLO   see   RCA

PAINTED SMILES   see   BATTERY

PALOMINO   Box 6, Fairlawn, N.J.   07410

PANINI   Box 15808, Honolulu, Hawaii   96813

PARAGON   1265 Broadway, New York, N.Y.   10001

PARAMOUNT   see   JAZZOLOGY

PAREDON   P.O. Box 889, Brooklyn, N.Y.   11202

PARROT   see   LONDON

PAULA   see   JEWEL

PEACABLE   Box 77038, Los Angeles, Cal.   90007

PEACOCK   see   ABC

PEERLESS Record Distributors of America, 780 W. 27th St.,
    Hialeah, Fla. 33010

PELICAN P.O. Box 34732, Los Angeles, Cal. 90034

PEOPLE see POLYDOR

PERCEPTION 165 W. 46th St., New York, N.Y. 10036

PETER PAN 145 Kormon St., Newark, N.J. 07105 Distributes:
    Power

PHILADELPHIA INTERNATIONAL see COLUMBIA

PHILIPS see PHONOGRAM

PHILO c/o The Barn, North Ferrisburg, Vt. 05473 Distributes:
    Fretless

PHOENIX JAZZ 7808 Bergenline Ave., Bergenfield, N.J. 07047

PHONOGRAM 1 IBM Plaza, Chicago, Ill. 60611 Distributes:
    Mercury, Philips, Smash, UK, Vertigo

PICKWICK INTERNATIONAL 135 Crossways Park Dr., Woodbury,
    Long Island, N.Y. 11797 Distributes: Hilltop

PIEDMONT see ADELPHI

PINE MOUNTAIN Box 584, Barbourville, Ky.

PINE TREE see MELODY

PLAYBOY Playboy Music Inc., 8560 Sunset Blvd., Los Angeles,
    Cal. 90169 Distributes: Berserkley

POLYDOR 810 Seventh Ave., New York, N.Y. 10019 Distributes:
    Deutsche Grammophon, MGM, People, RSO, Spring, Verve

POPPY see UNITED ARTISTS

PORTRAIT see COLUMBIA

POWER see PETER PAN

PRESTIGE see FANTASY

PRETZEL BELL see OLD HOMESTEAD

PRINCESS 8127 Elrita Dr., Los Angeles, Cal. 90046

PRIORITY 2300 Lincoln Ave., Fort Worth, Tex. 76106

PRIZE   JEM Entertainment, 707 18th Ave. S., Nashville, Tenn.
    37203

PROJECT THREE   Total Sound Inc., 1133 Ave. of the Americas,
    New York, N.Y.   10036

PURITAN   P.O. Box 946, Evanston, Ill.   60204

PYRAMID   5930 Genoa, Oakland, Cal.   94608

RBF   see   FOLKWAYS

RCA   1133 Ave. of the Americas, New York, N.Y.   10036   Distrib-
    utes: Amsterdam, Bob Thiele Music, Camden, Chelsea, Day-
    break, Flying Dutchman, Grunt, Pablo, Signature

RCS   P.O. Box 362, Tacoma, Washington 98409

RSO   see   POLYDOR

RACCOON   see   WARNER BROTHERS

RAM   397 Saundersville Rd., Old Hickory, Tenn.   37138

RANWOOD   9034 Sunset Blvd., Los Angeles, Cal.   90069

RARE EARTH   see   MOTOWN

RAY LAWRENCE   P.O. Box 1987, Studio City, Cal.   91604   Dis-
    tributes: Sheba

REAL EARTH   6207 Brooke Jane Dr., Clinton, Md.   20735

REBEL   Rt. 12, Asbury, W. Va.   24916 Distributes: Zap

REFLECTION SOUND   1018 Central Ave., Charlotte, N.C.   28204
    Distributes: Revelation

REM   3805 White Creek Pike, Nashville, Tenn.   37207

REPRISE   see   WARNER BROTHERS

REQUEST   3800 S. Ocean Dr., 2nd Floor, Hollywood, Fla.   33019
    Distributes: Family

REVELATION   see   REFLECTION SOUND

REVONAH   Box 217, Ferndale, N.Y.   12734

RICO   748 10th Ave., New York, N.Y.   10019 Distributes: Solo

RIDGE RUNNER   3035 Townsend Dr., Fort Worth, Tex.   76110

RIM ROCK   Concord, Ark.   72523

RISING STAR   see   TREEHOUSE

ROCK ISLAND   P.O. Box 1333, Camden, N.J.   08105

ROCKET   see   MCA

ROLLIN' ROCK   1722 Whitley Ave., Hollywood, Cal.   90028

ROLLING STONES   see   ATLANTIC

ROME   1414 E. Broad St., Columbus, Ohio   43205

RONN   see   JEWEL

ROULETTE   17 W. 60th St., New York, N.Y.   10023

ROUND   see   UNITED ARTISTS

ROUNDER   186 Willow Ave., Somerville, Mass.   02143

ROYAL RECORDS   397 S. Walter Ave., Newbury Park, Cal.   91320

RURAL RHYTHM   Box A, Arcadia, Cal.   91006

SAVOY   see   ARISTA

SCEPTER   254 W. 54th St., New York, N.Y.   10019

SEQUATCHIE   Star St., Box 432, Dunlap, Tenn.   37327

1750 ARCH RECORDS   1750 Arch St., Berkeley, Cal.   94709

SHANNON   P.O. Drawer 1, Madison, Tenn.   37115

SHEBA   see   RAY LAWRENCE

SHEEPWATER   Box 505, Hailey, Idaho   8333

SHEFFIELD LAB   P.O. Box 5332, Santa Barbara, Cal.

SHELBY SINGELTON CORPORATION   3106 Belmont Blvd., Nashville, Tenn.   37212   Distributes: Sun

SHELTER   see   ABC

SHIH SHIH WA AS   see   NEW MUSIC DISTRIBUTION SERVICE

SIGNATURE   see   RCA

SIRE   see   ABC

SIRENS   616 N. Rush St., Chicago, Ill.   60611

SKYLINE   see   ADELPHI

SKYLITE-SING   1008 17th Ave. S., Nashville, Tenn.   37212

SMASH   see   PHONOGRAM

SMITHSONIAN CLASSIC JAZZ   P.O. Box 14196, Washington, D.C. 20044

SMITHSONIAN COLLECTION   P.O. Box 23345, Washington, D.C. 20024

SOLID SOUL   7341 Mack Ave., Detroit, Mich.   48214   Distributes: Dove

SOLO   see   RICO

SOUL   see   MOTOWN

SOUTHLAND   see   JAZZOLOGY

SPANISH MUSIC CENTER, Belvedere Hotel, 319 W. 48th St., New York, N.Y.   10036

SPARK Peer-Southern Prods.,   1740 Broadway, N.Y., N.Y.   10019

SPECIALTY   8300 Santa Monica Blvd., Hollywood, Cal.   90069

SPINDIZZY   see   COLUMBIA

SPITBALL   Box 680, Gratigny, Miami, Fla.   33168

SPIVEY   65 Grand Ave., Brooklyn, N.Y.   11205

SPRING   see   POLYDOR

SPRINGBOARD   947 U.S. Highway 1, Rahway, N.J.   07065   Distributes: Morningstar, Musicore, Trip, Viva

STACY-LEE   425 Park St., Hackensack, N.J.   07601   Distributes: Banana

STANYAN   8440 Santa Monica Blvd., Hollywood, Cal.   90069

STARDAY KING   see   GUSTO

STARR   1414 E. Broad St., Columbus, Ohio   43205

STASH   c/o Record People, 66 Greene St., New York, N.Y.

STINGER PRODUCTIONS   Box 66, Dayton View Sta., Dayton,

Ohio   45406

STONEWAY   2817 Laura Koppe, Houston, Tex.   77016

STRATA EAST   156 Fifth Ave., Suite 612, New York, N.Y.   10010

SUN   see   SHELBY SINGLETON CORPORATION

SUNBEAM   13821 Calvert St., Van Nuys, Cal.   91401

SUNNY MT.   P.O. Box 14592, Gainesville, Fla.   32604

SUPER   Box 92, Wilmette, Ill.   60091

SURVIVAL   P.O. Box 1171, New York, N.Y.   10080

SUSSEX   6255 Sunset Blvd., Suite 1902, Hollywood, Cal.   90028

SWALLOW   see   FLAT TOWN

SYMPOSIUM   204 Fifth Ave. S.E., Minneapolis, Minn.   55414

T-NECK   see   COLUMBIA

TAKOMA   P.O. Box 5369, Santa Monica, Cal.   90405   Distributes:
Devi, Thistle

TAMLA   see   MOTOWN

TENNVALE   P.O. Box 1624, Huntsville, Ala.   35807

TESTAMENT   577 Lavering Ave., Los Angeles, Cal.   90024

THISTLE   see   TAKOMA

360 RECORDS   269 W. 72nd St., New York, N.Y.   10023

THRESHOLD   see   LONDON

TITANIC   43 Rice St., Cambridge, Mass.   02140

TOM CAT   450 N. Roxbury Dr., Beverly Hills, Cal.   90210

TORCHE   P.O. Box 96, El Cevrito, Cal.   94530

TORO   7027 Twin Hills Ave., Dallas, Tex.   75231

TOWA   Box 161E, Rt. 1, Beckley, W. Va.   25801

TRADEWINDS   Box 8294, Honolulu, Hawaii   96815

TRADITIONAL   P.O. Box 8, Cosby, Tenn.   37722

TREEHOUSE   4413 South River, Independence, Mo.   64055   Distributes: Rising Star

TRIBE   81 Chandler, Detroit, Mich.   48202

TRIP   see   SPRINGBOARD

TRI-STATE   Rt. 1, Box 15, Hope Mills, N.C.   28348

TRIX   Drawer AB, Rosendall, N.Y.   12472

TRUTONE   428 Briarwood Lane, Northvale, N.J.   07647

TULIP   Box 3155, San Rafael, Cal.   94902

TUMBLEWEED   1368 Gilpin St., Denver, Col.   80218

TUNE   2211 Woodward Ave., Muscle Shoals, Ala.   35660

20th CENTURY   8255 Sunset Blvd., Los Angeles, Cal.   90046

UK   see   PHONOGRAM

UNANIMOUS ANONYMOUS   see   NEW MUSIC DISTRIBUTION SERVICE

UNI   see   MCA

UNION GROVE   see   FIDDLER'S GROVE

UNIT CORE   P.O. Box 3041, New York, N.Y.   10001

UNITED ARTISTS   6920 Sunset Blvd., Hollywood, Cal.   90028
    Distributes: Blue Note, Brown Bag, Douglas, Grateful Dead,
    Poppy, Round

UPSTAIRS   see   NEW MUSIC DISTRIBUTION SERVICE

VANGUARD   71 W. 23rd St., New York, N.Y.   10010

VAYA   see   FANIA

VERTIGO   see   PHONOGRAM

VERVE   see   POLYDOR

VETCO   5828 Vine St., Cincinnati, Ohio   45216

VIRGIN   see   COLUMBIA

VISTA   800 Sonora Ave., Glendale, Cal.   91201

VIVA   see   SPRINGBOARD

VOX 211 E. 43rd St., New York, N.Y. 10017

VOYAGER 424 35th Ave., Seattle, Wash. 98122

WANGO 4802 Harford Rd., Baltimore, Md. 21214

WARNER BROTHERS 3300 Warner Blvd., Burbank, Cal. 91505
Distributes: Bearsville, Bizarre, Capricorn, Dis-Creet, Raccoon,
Reprise

WARPED RECORDS 8924 S. Austin, Oak Lawn, Ill. 60453

WARREN COUNTY P.O. Box 433, Indianola, Iowa 50125

WATT Watt Works, 6 W. 95th St., New York, N.Y. 10025

WES FARRELL 9200 Sunset Blvd., Suite 620, Los Angeles, Cal.
90069

WESTWOOD 541 Fulmer Ave., Akron, Ohio 44312

WINDFALL 1790 Broadway, New York, N.Y. 10019

WINKLE c/o Bob Emberton, 1301 Lee St., Carthage, Tex. 75633

WISHBONE 4014 Kingman Blvd., Des Moines, Iowa 50311

WOODEN NICKEL 6521 Homewood Ave., Los Angeles, Cal. 90028

WORD 4800 W. Waco Dr., Waco, Tex. 76703 Distributes:
Canaan, Lights, Myrrh

WORLD JAZZ see AUDIOFIDELITY

XANADU 3242 Irwin Ave., Kingsbridge, N.Y. 10463

YAZOO 245 Waverly Pl., New York, N.Y. 10014

ZAP see REBEL

ZEBRA BREATH 320 Ohio River Blvd., Sewickly, Pa. 15143

ZIM P.O. Box 158, Jericho, L.I., N.Y. 11753

England (Britain)

A & M see CBS

A RECORDS Flat 4, 14 Blakesley, Ealing, London W5

ABBEY Abbey St., Eynsham, Oxford

ACE OF CLUBS   see DECCA

ACTION   see   B & C

AD-RHYTHM   14a The Broadwalk, Pinner Rd., North Harrow, Middlesex

APPLE   see   EMI

ARGO   115 Fulham Rd., London SW3

ARISTA   49 Upper Brook St., London W1Y 2BT

ATLANTIC   17 Berners St., London W1

B & C TROJAN   326 Kensal Rd., London W10   Distributes: Action,
Charisma, Mooncrest

BASF   see   DECCA

BBC RECORDS   see   POLYDOR

BALLAD   16 Cradley Park Rd., Dudley

BARCLAY   see   RCA

BELL   49 Upper Brook St., London W1Y 2BT

BELTONA   see   DECCA

BIG BEAR   see   TRANSATLANTIC

BIG BEN   52 Shaftesbury Ave., London W1V 7DE

BLACK LION   see   TRANSATLANTIC

BRADLEYS   12 Bruton St., Mayfair, London

BROWN LABEL   30 Madden Ave., Chatham, Kent

CBS   17/18 Soho Square, London W1V 6HE   Distributes: A & M,
Blue Horizon, Embassy, 7-60,000 series, York

CAMDEN   see   PICKWICK INTERNATIONAL

CAPITOL   see   EMI

CARNIVAL   see   POLYDOR

CAROLINE   2-4 Vernon Yard, 119 Portobello Rd., London W11

CHAPTER ONE   see   DECCA

CHARISMA   see   B & C

CHECKER   see   PHONOGRAM

CHELSEA   see   RCA

CHESS   see   PHONOGRAM

CHRYSALIS   388/396 Oxford St., London W1N 9HE

CLADDAGH   c/o CRD, Lyon Way, Rockware Ave., Greenford,
   Middlesex UB6 OBN

COLUMBIA   see   EMI

COLUMBIA STUDIO 2   see   EMI

CONTOUR   see   PICKWICK INTERNATIONAL

CORAL   see   DECCA

CUBE RECORDS   Essex House, 19-20 Poland St., London W1V 3DD
   Distributes: Hi Fly

DJM   71 New Oxford St., London   WC1

DANDELION   see   WEA

DAWN   see   PYE

DECCA   9 Albert Embankment, London SE1 7SW   Distributes: Ace
   of Clubs, BASF, Beltona, Chapter One, Coral, Deram, Eclipse,
   Emerald, Gem, Gull, London, Rex, Teldec, Telefunken, Threshold, Uni

DERAM   see   DECCA

DOUBLE-UP   see   EMI

DOVETAIL   10 Seaford Ave., New Malden, Surrey

EMI   20 Manchester Square, London W1A 1ES   Distributes: Apple,
   Capitol, Columbia, Columbia Studio 2, Double-Up, Elektra, HMV,
   Harvest, Hi Fly, Invictus, MCA, One-Up, Parlophone, Probe,
   Purple, Rak, Regal Starline, Regal Zonophone, Rhino, Stateside,
   Talisman, Vine, Wave, Waverley

ECLIPSE   see   DECCA

ELEKTRA   see   EMI

EMBASSY   see   CBS

EMBER   Suite 4, Carlton Tower Place, Sloane St., London SW1

EMERALD   c/o Vogue Records, 113-115 Fulham Rd., London SW3

ENGLISH FOLK, DANCE, AND SONG SOCIETY   2 Regent's Park
   Rd., London NW1 7AY

ENTERPRISE   1367 High Rd., Whetstone, London N20

FLYRIGHT   21 Wickham Ave., Bexhill-on-Sea, Sussex

FONTANA   see   PHONOGRAM

FOUNTAIN   see   RETRIEVAL RECORDINGS

GTO   17 Barlow Pl., Broton St., London W1X 7AE

GALLIARD   c/o Stainer & Bell Ltd., 82 High Rd., London N2 9PW

GEM   see   DECCA

GOLDEN GUINEA   see   PYE

GOLDEN HOUR   see PYE

GROSVENOR   16 Grosvenor Rd., Handsworth Wood, Birmingham
   B20 3NP

GULL   see   DECCA

HMV   see   EMI

HALCYON   see   VINTAGE JAZZ MUSIC SOCIETY

HALLMARK   see   PICKWICK INTERNATIONAL

HARVEST   see   EMI

HY FLY   see   EMI

IMPACT   see   TOPIC

INCUS   87 Third Cross Rd., Twickenham, Middlesex

INVICTA   c/o Sydney Thompson, 513 Uxbridge Rd., Hatch End,
   Middlesex

INVICTUS   see   EMI

ISLAND   8-11 Basing St., London W11

JOY   see   PRESIDENT

LEADER   see   TRANSATLANTIC

LIBERTY   see   UNITED ARTISTS

LONDON   see   DECCA

MCA   see   EMI

MFP   see   MUSIC FOR PLEASURE

MGM   see   POLYDOR

MARBLE ARCH   see   PICKWICK INTERNATIONAL

MATCHBOX   see   SAYDISC MATCHBOX

MERCURY   see   PHONOGRAM

METRO   see   POLYDOR

MIDDLE EARTH   see   PYE

MOONCREST   see   B & C

MOSAIC   c/o Graham Collier Music, 51 Nevern Sq., London SW5
   9PF

MUSIC FOR PLEASURE   8 Blyth Rd., Hayes, Middlesex Distributes:
   Classics for Pleasure, Sounds Superb

NEPENTHA   see   PHONOGRAM

OGUN   4 Chequers Parade, Eltham, London SE9

ONE-UP   see   EMI

OUTLET   63-67 Smithfield Square, Belfast BT1 1JD, Northern Ireland

PAMA   see   PYE

PAN   see   SAGA

PARLOPHONE   see   EMI

PEARL   Pavillon Records, 48 High Street, Pembury, Tunbridge
   Wells, Kent

PENNY FARTHING   see   PYE

PHILIPS   see   PHONOGRAM

PHONOGRAM   Stanhope House, Stanhope Place, London W2 2HH

Distributes: Checker, Chess, Fontana, Mercury, Nepentha, Philips, SSS International, Vertigo

PICKWICK INTERNATIONAL   The Hyde Ind. Estate, The Hyde, London NW9 6JU Distributes: Camden, Contour, Hallmark, Marble Arch, Sun

POLYDOR   17-19 Stratford Place, London W1N OB1 Distributes: BBC Records, Carnival, MGM, Metro, Select, Track, Verve

PRESIDENT RECORDS   Kassner House, 1 Westbourne Gardens, Porchester Rd., London W2 5NR Distributes: Joy, Rhapsody

PROBE   see   EMI

PURPLE   see   EMI

PYE   17 Great Cumberland Place, London W1H 8AA Distributes: A & M, Dawn, Golden Guinea, Golden Hour, Middle Earth, Pama, Penny Farthing, Sonet, Spark, Specialty, Spiral, Stax, Vanguard

QUALITON   c/o Selecta, 125/127 Lee High Rd., Lewisham, London SE13 5NX

R & O   48 Smithfield Square, Belfast BT1 1JO, Northern Ireland

RAK   see   EMI

RCA   50-52 Curzon St., London W1Y 8EU Distributes: Barclay, Chelsea, RCA International

RCA INTERNATIONAL   see   RCA

RAFT   see   WEA

READERS' DIGEST   7-10 Old Bailey, London EC99 1AA

RED LIGHTNIN'   35 Cantley Gardens, Gants Hill, Ilford, Essex

REDIFFUSION   9 Dean St., London W1

REGAL STARLINE   see   EMI

REGAL ZONOPHONE   see   EMI

REPRISE   see   WEA

RETRIEVAL RECORDINGS   48 Eversley Ave., Barnehurst, Kent DA7 6RB Distributes: Fountain

REVELATION   287 Camden High St., London NW1 7BX

REX   see   DECCA

RHAPSODY   see   PRESIDENT

RHINO   see   EMI

RISTIC   c/o John R. T. Davies, 53 Britwell Rd., Burnham, Bucks

S. C. A. M.   P. O. Box 202, Leith D. O., Edinburgh EH6 5RD

SRT   17 Royal Terrace, Glasgow

SSS INTERNATIONAL   see   PHONOGRAM

SAGA   326 Kensal Rd., London W10   Distributes: Pan

SAYDISC MATCHBOX   Saydisc Specialized Recordings, The Barton,
Inglestone Common, Badminton, Gloucestershire, GL9 1BX

SELECT   see   POLYDOR

77 RECORDS   Dobells Jazz Record Shop, 77 Charing Cross Rd.,
London WC2   Distributes: Swift

SONET   see   PYE

SOUNDS SUPERB   see   MUSIC FOR PLEASURE

SOUTHERN SOUND   Chris Wellard Records, 4 Chequers Parade,
Off Passey Place, London SE9

SPARK   see   PYE

SPECIALTY   see   PYE

SPIRAL   see   PYE

SPOTLITE   Tony Williams, 300 Brocklesmead, Harlow, Essex

STAGFOLK   Shackleford Social Centre, Nr. Godalming, Surrey

STARLINE   see   EMI

STATESIDE   see   EMI

STAX   see   PYE

STEM   11 Mount Ephraim Rd., London SW16 1NQ

STRING   33 Brunswick Gardens, London W8 4AW

SUN   see   PICKWICK INTERNATIONAL

SUNSET   see   UNITED ARTISTS

SWEET FOLK ALL   74 Shrewsbury Lane, Shooters Hill, London
    SE 18

SWIFT   see   77 RECORDS

TBB   3 The Quillett, Neston, Wirral, Cheshire

TALISMAN   see   EMI

TAMALA MOTOWN   6 Lygon Pl., Belgravia, London 5W1

TANGENT   176a Holland Rd., London W14

TANGERINE   570 Kingsland Rd., London EC8

TELDEC   see   DECCA

TELEFUNKEN   see   DECCA

THERAPY   21 Pinewood Court, Broad St., Sale

THRESHOLD   see   DECCA

TOPIC   27 Nassington Rd., London NW3 2TX   Distributes: Impact

TRACK   see   POLYDOR

TRAILER   see   TRANSATLANTIC

TRANSATLANTIC   86 Marylebone High St., London W1M 4AY   Dis-
    tributes: Big Bear, Black Lion, Leader, Trailer, Village Thing,
    Xtra

TROJAN   see   B & C TROJAN

TURTLE   33-37 Wardour St., London W1

UNI   see   DECCA

UNITED ARTISTS   37-41 Mortimer St., London W1   Distributes:
    Liberty, Sunset

VJM   see   VINTAGE JAZZ MUSIC SOCIETY

VANGUARD   see   PYE

VERTIGO   see   PHONOGRAM

VERVE   see   POLYDOR

VILLAGE THING   see   TRANSATLANTIC

VINE   see   EMI

VINTAGE JAZZ MUSIC SOCIETY   12 Slough Lane, Kingsbury, London NW 9   Distributes: Halcyon, VJM

VIRTUOSI RECORDINGS   18 Chancer Cres., Donnington, Newbury, Beaks, RG13

WEA   54 Greek St., London W1   Distributes: Atlantic, Dandelion, Elektra, Raft, Reprise, Warner Brothers

WARNER BROTHERS   see   WEA

WAVE   see   EMI

WAVERLEY   see   EMI

WESTWOOD   Camp Farm, Montgomery, Mid-Wales SY15 6LU

WORLD RECORD CLUB   Box 11, Parkbridge House, Richmond, Surrey

XTRA   see   TRANSATLANTIC

YORK   see   CBS

ZONOPHONE   see   EMI

Canada

A & M   939 Warden Ave., Scarborough, Ont. M1L 4CS   Distributes: Casino, Haida, Penny Farthing

AQUARIUS   see   LONDON

ARPEGGIO   see   RCA

ATTIC   see   LONDON

AXE   see   GRT

BANFF   see   LONDON

BIG WHEEL   3933 30th Ave. S.E., Calgary, Alta. T2B 2C7

BIRCHMOUNT   see   QUALITY

BOOT   see   LONDON

BROADLAND   see   QUALITY

CBC   see   RADIO CANADA INTERNATIONAL TRANSCRIPTION

CBS   see   COLUMBIA

CANADIAN TALENT LIBRARY   2 St. Clair Ave., W., Toronto,
Ont.

CAPITOL   3109 American Dr., Mississauga, Ont. L4V 1B2

CAPRICE   see   LONDON

CASINO   see   A & M

CELEBRATION   see   QUALITY

CODA   Box 87, Sta. J, Toronto, Ont. Distributes: Dogwood,
Sackville

COLUMBIA   1121 Leslie St., Don Mills, Ont.   M3E 2J9 Distributes:
CBS, Harmony, True North

CORNER STORE   see   QUALITY

CYNDA   see   LONDON

DAFFODIL   see   GRT

DISQUES ZODIAQUE   see   TRANS WORLD

DOGWOOD   see   CODA

DOMINION   Canadian Music Sales, 44 Advance Rd., Toronto, Ont.

FRANCO DISQUE   see   TRANS-CANADA

FUNKEBEC   see   LONDON

GRT   3816 Victoria Park Ave., Willowdale, Ont. M2H 3H7 Distributes: Axe, Daffodil, Smile

GOLDFISH   see   LONDON

HAIDA   see   A & M

HARMONY   see   COLUMBIA

IXTLAN   271 Davisville Ave., Toronto M4S 1H1

JS   186 Old Orchard Road, Burlington, Ont.

KANATA   see   QUALITY

LONDON   1630 Midland Ave., Scarborough, Ont. M1P 3C2 Distributes: Aquarius, Attic, Banff, Boot, Caprice, Cynda, Funkebec,
Goldfish, Rodeo, Spark

MCA 2450 Victoria Park Ave., Willowdale, Ont. M2J 4A2

MWC see QUALITY

MARCHE see TRANS WORLD

MUSHROOM 1234 W. 6th Ave., Vancouver, B. C. V6H 1A5

NIMBUS 9 see RCA

OLD ROAD 5207 Cavendish Blvd., Montreal

PENNY FARTHING see A & M

POLYDOR 600 Cote de Liesse, Montreal, Que. H4T 1E3

QUALITY 380 Birchmount Rd., Scarborough, Ont. M1K 1M7 Distributes: Birchmount, Broadland, Celebration, Corner Store,
Kanata, MWC

RCA 101 Duncan Mills Rd., Suite 300, Don Mills, Ont. M3B 1Z3
Distributes: Arpeggio, Nimbus 9

RADIO CANADA INTERNATIONAL TRANSCRIPTION C. B. C. International Service, Box 6000, Montreal, Quebec Distributes: CBC

RODEO see LONDON

RUMOUR Box 173, Stratford, Ont.

SPPS see TRANS-CANADA

SACKVILLE see CODA

SMILE see GRT

SPARK see LONDON

SPRINGWATER 56 Clinton St., Guelph, Ont. N1H 5G5

TRANS-CANADA 7033 Route Trans Canadienne, St. Laurent, Que.
H4T 1S2 Distributes: Franco Disque, SPPS

TRANS WORLD 1230 Monte de Liesse Rd., Montreal, Que. Distributes: Marche, Disques Zodiaque

TRUE NORTH see COLUMBIA

UNITED ARTISTS 6 Lansing Sq., Suite 208, Willowdale, Ont. M2J
1T5

WEA 1810 Birchmount Rd., Scarborough, Ont. M1P 2S1

WOODSHED R. R. 1, Emsdale, Ont.

SPECIALTY RECORD STORES

The following record stores handle specialized orders for rare or difficult to acquire material (mainly in the fields of jazz, blues, folk, country, and ethnic). With many labels, record stores are the only source of distribution. Superior service for the smaller, independent labels makes the following stores highly recommended. Write for catalogues. While these stores are not mainly library suppliers, they may offer discounts.

UNITED STATES

County Sales
Box 191
Floyd, Va.   24091

Rare Record Distributing Co.
417 East Broadway
P.O. Box 10518
Glendale, Cal.   91205

Roundhouse Record Sales
P.O. Box 474
Somerville, Mass.   02144

Southern Record Sales
5001 Reynard
La Crescenta, Cal.   91214

CANADA

Coda Jazz and Blues Record
  Centre
893 Yonge Street
Toronto M4W 2H2

Round Records
46 Bloor Street West
Toronto

ENGLAND (handles Europe as
  well)

Dave Carey--The Swing Shop
18 Mitcham Lane
Streatham, London SW16

Collet's Record Centre
180 Shaftesbury Ave.
London WC2H 8JS

Dobell's Record Shop
75 Charing Cross Road
London WC 2

Flyright Records
18 Endwell Rd.
Bexhill-on-Sea
East Sussex

Peter Russell Record Store
24 Market Avenue
Plymouth PL1 1PJ

ARTIST INDEX

An alphabetical index of artists and groups with variant names. Records with several artists are not analyzed (unless displayed prominently on the album titles), nor are individuals' names indexed from the groups they comprise.

Jazz Crusaders 3280
Jazz Messengers 2620-20a
JBs 4577-8
Jefferson, Blind Lemon 4156
Jefferson, Eddie 3282-3
Jefferson, Ron 3284
Jefferson Starship 459-61
Jelly Roll Jazz Band 3807
Jenkins, Bobo 4157
Jenkins, LeRoy 3285
Jenkins, Snuffy 2136h
Jenkins, Cockerham and Jarrell
  2137
Jennings, Frank 1721
Jennings, Waylon 1722-34
Jensen, John 3286
Jet 462
Jeter, Rev. Claude 4955
Jethro Tull 463-6
Jigsaw 467
Jiva 468
Jobim, Antonio Carlos 3287
Jodoin, Alain 1498
Johansson, Sven-Ake 3796
John, Elton 469-72
Johnny and Jack 4956
Johnson, Alphonso 3288
Johnson, Buddy 3289
Johnson, Bunk 3290
Johnson, Earl and His Clodhop-
  pers 2138
Johnson, Henry "Rufe" 4158
Johnson, Herman E. 4159
Johnson, J. J. 3022, 4038
Johnson, James P. 3291-2
Johnson, Kenny 1735
Johnson, Lois 1736
Johnson, Lonnie 4160
Johnson, Luther 4161
Johnson, Mike 2139
Johnson, Pete 3293
Johnson, Syl 1252, 4580
Johnson, Vera 2392
Johnson Brothers 4579
Jolson, Al 1253-4
Jones, Al 2140
Jones, Bill 2141
Jones, David 2393
Jones, Eddie Lee 4162
Jones, Elvin 3294-8
Jones, George 1737-42
Jones, Grandpa 1743-5
Jones, Isham 1255

Jones, Jack 1256
Jones, Jo 2697, 3299, 3847-8
Jones, Jonah 3300
Jones, Philly Joe 3301
Jones, Quincy 1164a, 3301a-01b
Jones, Salena 1257
Jones, Thad 3302-7
Jones, Tom 1258-60
Jones Brothers 2142
Jonic, Bettina 1261
Joplin, Scott 3308-9
Jordan, Clifford 3310-2
Jordan, Duke 3313-5
Jordan, Louis 3316-7, 4581
Jordan, Sheila 3318
Joseph, Margie 4585-7
Journey 473
Joy, Jimmy 3853
Joy, Mabel 2394
Judas Priest 474
Juice Newton 1746
Juju 3319
Julien, Pauline 1262
Junkin, John 5020, 5080

Kaempfert, Bert 1263-6
Kafka, Bernard 3951
Kamahl 1267
Kamuca, Richard 3320
Kane, Ray 475, 3321
Kansas 476
Karmen, Steve 1268
Karolak, Wojciech 3322
Kasai, Kimiko 3323
Katzman, Nick 4163-4
Kay Gees 4588
Kayak 477
Kaye, Milton 3324-5
KC and the Sunshine Band 4589-91
Kearney, Chris 478
Keeping, Charles 5079
Keith, Bill 2143
Keller, Greta 1269
Kelly, John 2395
Kendricks, Eddie 4592-4
Kennebec Valley Boys 2225
Kennedy, Clive 479
Kenton, Stan 3326-35
Kentucky Colonels 2144-5
Kentucky Gentlemen 2146-7
Kentucky Grass 2158-9
Kentucky Mountain Boys 2077

Sullivan, Joe 3876
Sullivan Family 2282
Sumlin, Hubert 4262
Summer, Donna 4814-5
Summerfield, Saffron 900
Sun 1477, 4816
Sundance 2015
Sundown Valley Boys 2281
Sunnyland Slim 4263-4
Sunshine, Monty 3877-8
Supercharge 901
Supertramp 902
Supremes 4817, 4993
Surfaris 903
Surman, John 3485
Surprise Sisters 1478
Sutherland Brothers and Quiver
    904-6
Sutton, Ralph 3879
Svenson, Lalle 3880
Swallow, Steve 2712
Swamp Dogg 4818-9
Swan, Billy 907-8, 1936-7
Swan Silvertones 4994
Swansen, Chris 3881
Swedish Radio Jazz Group 3307
Sweet 909-10
Sweet, Gene 2283
Sweet Blindness 911
Sweet Honey in the Rock 4820
Sweet Sensation 4821
Sweet Spirit 912
Swingle II 1479
Sykes, Roosevelt 4265-6
Sylvers 1480
Sylvester, Terry 1481
Symphonic Slam 913
Syms, Sylvia 1482
Synergy 914-5
Szabados, Gyorgy 3882
Szobel, Herman 3883

T. Rex 916
Tabackin, Lew 2493-4
Tabor, June 2426
Taj Mahal 4267-9
Talley, James 916a-17
Talton, Stewart, and Sand-
    lin 918
Tamblyn, Ian 919
Tampa Red 4270-2
Tangerine Dream 920-3

Tanner, Gid 2284
Tansey, Seamus 2452-4
Tarlton, Jimmy 2083
Taste 924
Tate, Buddy 3884-5
Tattoo 925
Tatum, Art 3886-95
Tavares 4822-3
Taylor, Carmol 926, 1938
Taylor, Cecil 3896-3900
Taylor, Chip 1939
Taylor, Eddie 4155, 4273
Taylor, Geoff 1483
Taylor, Hound Dog 4274-6
Taylor, James 927-9
Taylor, Johnnie 930, 4824-5
Taylor, Koko 4277-8
Taylor, Tim Brook see Brook-
    Taylor, Tim
Taylor, Tut 2285-6
Teagarden, Jack 3901-4
Temprees 4826
Le Temps 931
Temptations 4827-30
10 CC 932-3
Tennessee Singers 1940
Tennessee Stud 1941
Terry, Clarke 3680, 3905-8
Terry, Sonny 4279-80
Thackray, Jake 5149
Thee Image 934
Thelin, Eje 3909a
Them 935
Theoret, Sandy 1742
Thibeault, Fabienne 2455
Thiele, Bob 3909b
Thielemans, Toots 3909c
Thin Lizzy 936-7
Third World 4831
Thomas, B. J. 1484-5
Thomas, Buddy 2287
Thomas, Henry 4281
Thomas, Ian 938
Thomas, Joe 3909d
Thomas, Ray 1486
Thomas, Rene 3909e
Thomas, Rufus 4832
Thomason, Ron 2288
Thompson, Don 3909f
Thompson, Eddie 1360
Thompson, Hank 1943-4
Thompson, Lenval 4833
Thompson, Linda 2457